Jim W. Corder

Texas Christian University

CONTEMPORARY WRITING

Process & Practice

Scott, Foresman and Company

Glenview, Illinois   Dallas, Tex.   Oakland, N.J.
Palo Alto, Cal.   Tucker, Ga.   London, England

Library of Congress Cataloging in Publication Data

Corder, Jimmie Wayne.
    Contemporary writing.

    Includes index.
    1. English language—Rhetoric.   I. Title.
PE1408.C5945   808'.042   78-20848
ISBN 0-673-15100-X
    2345678910-KPH-85848382818079

Acknowledgments

Entries: *carnivore* and *subject.* Copyright © 1969, 1970, 1971, 1973, 1975, 1976, 1978 by Houghton Mifflin Company. Reprinted by permission of *The American Heritage Dictionary of the English Language.*
From "Foreign Financing Is Sought By City to Produce Jobs" by Michael Stern. *New York Times,* February 9, 1975. Copyright © 1975 The New York Times Company. Reprinted by permission.
From "Face in the Mirror," an editorial. *New York Times,* February 9, 1975. Copyright © 1975 The New York Times Company. Reprinted by permission.
From "America At Sea," an editorial. *New York Times,* February 9, 1975. Copyright © 1975 The New York Times Company. Reprinted by permission.
From *The Poetry of Robert Frost* edited by Edward Connery Lathem. Copyright 1923, 1930, 1939, © 1969 by Holt, Rinehart & Winston. Copyright 1951, © 1958 by Robert Frost. © 1967 by Lesley Frost Ballantine. Reprinted by permission of Holt, Rinehart & Winston, Publishers.
Excerpted from the book *The Fire Next Time* by James Baldwin. Copyright © 1963, 1962 by James Baldwin. Reprinted by permission The Dial Press.
From "A Shropshire Lad"–Authorized Edition–from *The Collected Poems of A. E. Housman.* Copyright 1939, 1940, © 1965 by Holt, Rinehart & Winston. © 1967, 1968 by Robert E. Symons. Reprinted by permission of Holt, Rinehart & Winston, Publishers and The Society of Authors as the literary representative of the Estate of A. E. Housman; and Jonathan Cape Ltd., publishers of A. E. Housman's *Collected Poems.*
From "The Way To Rainy Mountain" by N. Scott Momaday. Copyright © 1969 by The University of New Mexico Press. Reprinted by permission of The University of New Mexico Press.
From "The Limitations of Language," *Time,* March 8, 1971. Reprinted by permission from TIME, The Weekly Newsmagazine; Copyright Time Inc. 1971.
From *The Collected Poems of A. E. Housman.* Copyright 1936 by Barclays Bank Limited. Copyright © 1964 by Robert E. Symons. Reprinted by permission of Holt, Rinehart & Winston, Publishers and The Society of Authors as the literary representative of the Estate of A. E. Housman; and Jonathan Cape Ltd., publishers of A. E. Housman's *Collected Poems.*
A selection from *The Painted Word* by Tom Wolfe. Copyright © 1975 by Tom Wolfe. Reprinted with the permission of Farrar, Straus & Giroux, Inc.
From "Let's Spoil the Wilderness" by Robert Wernick from *The Saturday Evening Post.* Copyright © 1965 The Curtis Publishing Co. Reprinted by permission of the author.
From a Kenwood advertisement. Reprinted by permission of Kenwood Electronics, Inc.
From a J & B Rare Scotch Whisky advertisement. Reprinted by permission of The Paddington Corporation.
From a Business Committee for the Arts, Inc. advertisement. Reprinted by permission.

Acknowledgments continue on pages 499–500, which constitute an extension of the copyright page.

Preface

What is good in writing seldom grows old: what was well done two hundred years ago we can usually still recognize as good today. Yet today's writer may find a way of saying things that was not possible formerly, and who knows what marvels tomorrow may bring? A writing text, then, needs to borrow from both the old and the new, prizing such rules, principles, and traditions as have come down to us for the guidance of writers. Yet we know that there is scarcely a text (including some that are dear to us) that doesn't in some way at one place or another set aside or even violate those same rules, principles, and traditions.

A writing text needs to treasure the observance of the rules, principles, and traditions and to allow the departure from them when that is justified. A writing text can't say everything that might or should be said about the arts of writing, but it can describe the processes of good writing according to the author's judgment while not ignoring the variations and contrary views of others. Writers must, after all, be responsible for their own work and serve as their own judges and critics. A writing text, then, ought to display the surest guidance available, yet do so with the knowledge that humans in general and free citizens in particular are at liberty to use the best guidance however they will.

Given all that a writing text must do and ought to do, I should explain, before going any further, what *Contemporary Writing: Process and Practice* actually does do.

The organization of the book. The text, as you will see, is in three parts. The first part describes the process of writing from the time before a writer even has a subject until the time a writer's formed ideas manifest themselves on paper as words, sentences, and paragraphs. This first part is quite traditional in its form, though it is not always traditional in particular sections. More specifically,

> the first five chapters explore what students of rhetoric might call *invention* and what others might call *pre-writing;*
> Chapters 6 and 7 examine *organization, structure,* and *development;*
> the last four chapters of Part One (Chapters 8–11) discuss the diverse features of *style.*

Part Two is an exploration of particular occasions for writing and of particular kinds of writing. Chapter 12 studies the relationships between occasions and the kinds of writing they need or make possible. The remaining chapters of Part Two discuss the possible character and form of letters, reports, arguments, and critical essays.

The two chapters of Part Three are intended both for assigned study and for continuous reference: Chapter 17 presents some guides, recommended procedures, and standard forms for use in research writing; Chapter 18 is a brief handbook of grammar, punctuation, and usage.

Considerations when using the text. Three points, especially, should be called to your attention.

First, this text does not have a separate chapter or section that details all of the possible steps and techniques involved in the writing of a research paper. I have tried, instead, to suggest that research is always a possibility and sometimes a necessity in any kind of writing. The first five chapters suggest more than once that research is not limited to a particular kind of writing, but may be necessary at any time, depending upon the nature of the subject, the knowledge of the author, and the requirements of the occasion. Chapters 12, 14, 15, and 16 recommend and discuss research as occasions and particular forms of writing require it. Chapter 17, then, provides a brief account of resources for research, evaluation of resources, note-taking, compilation of bibliographies, and forms for notes and bibliographies.

Second, an early notice about Part Three is in order. Neither Chapter 17, on procedures and forms for research writing, nor Chapter 18, a brief guide to grammar, punctuation, and usage, pretends to be complete. Each is intended simply to help at specific and troublesome points.

Third, exercises occur throughout Parts One and Two of the text. They most often occur within the chapters immediately adjacent to the discussion they relate to; they also appear at the ends of chapters. Wherever possible, the exercises are such as to invite thinking and writing from the students, rather than short responses.

What is different about this book? Perhaps the best way for me to indicate what features I believe are new, particularly significant, or especially different from other writing texts is simply to list them.

1. I believe the first five chapters of the book provide an uncommonly thorough account of the meditative, exploratory, and investigative processes that precede and accompany the actual process of writing.

2. I believe that Chapter 6, Designing Your Work, provides more real alternatives for organizing a piece of writing than most texts do, and the chapter does more than is common to *show* how an organizational structure takes form.

3. I believe that Chapter 8, Saying the Words, gives a fuller account than usual of the significance and consequence of words and of writers' responsibilities in using words.

4. I believe that Chapter 9, Making Sentences, defines and illustrates more techniques for sentence formation and variation than is customary.

5. I believe that Chapter 12, Occasions and Choices, is a novel feature which attempts to show the relationships between occasions and the kinds of writing they call for or make possible.

6. I believe that the chapters on special kinds of writing (letters, reports, arguments, and critical essays) provide useful guidelines for these special forms while taking account of the nearly endless variations that are possible.

7. I believe that the text is particularly rich with examples, short, long, and medium, at every point where examples are useful.

8. I believe that the text interruptions—Insights—that occur are especially useful. These Insights—printed in a second color—are used to provide asides, warnings, examples, corollary information, or views contrary to my own.

9. Finally, I believe that the text presents and confronts—squarely and usefully, I hope—both the moral responsibilities and the exciting possibilities of language and writing. Whether it does or not, in the long run, is for others to judge.

Acknowledgments.   I owe a host of debts to many people for their help with this book, and if I could, I would pay them in better coin than this brief acknowledgment.

I am particularly grateful to Professor Linda Woodson for preparing many of the exercises and for helping to locate many of the examples.

I thank friends at Scott, Foresman and Company for their interest, trust, and companionship. Richard Welna has been a good friend and kind advisor. I want to thank Amanda Clark especially: she has been uncommonly helpful in the preparation of this book, responsive to the needs of readers, faithful to the possibilities of the text, and thoughtful of me. Lynn Reickert was cheerful and competent in performing the final editing.

I am indebted to a crowd of scholars and colleagues. I want to name some, though I know that in doing so I omit many: Robert Bain, Dennis Baron, Monroe C. Beardsley, Wayne Booth, Haig A. Bosmajian, George Bramer, Virginia Burke, Seymour Chatman, E. P. J. Corbett, Harry Crosby, Paul F. Cummins, George Estes, Richard Gambino, Walker Gibson, Wallace Graves, Hans Guth, Maxine Hairston, Dennis R. Hall, Richard Harp, E. M. Jennings, William Jovanovich, James Kinneavy, Richard L. Larson, San-Su C. Lin, James Moffett, Richard Ohmann, Mario Pei, Kenneth Pike, Dolores Polomo, Paul Rodgers, Muriel R. Schulz, Charles I. Schuster, James Sledd, Geneva Smitherman, Wilson Snipes, Arthur A. Stern, Donald C. Stewart, Marinus Swets, Gary Tate, Winston Weathers, Richard Weaver, Otis Winchester, Ross Winterowd, and Richard Young.

Finally, I want to thank Patsy Corder for all that she is and does.

Jim W. Corder

Contents

1

THE PROCESS OF WRITING

OCCASIONS FOR WRITING

Looking for Subjects

Exploring Subjects

Claiming a Subject

Sharing a Subject with an Audience

Connecting Author, Subject, and Audience

Designing Your Work

Developing Your Material

Saying the Words

Making Sentences

Shaping Paragraphs

An Interlude on Style

Part One

The Process of Writing

*It takes little talent
to see clearly what lies under one's nose,
a good deal of it to know
in which direction to point that organ.*

W. H. Auden, *The Dyer's Hand*

1

Looking for Subjects

How do you find a subject to write about? This chapter will try to answer that question and make some suggestions, by discussing different ways of looking at

1. found subjects, those you come upon yourself, and given subjects, those you are required to write about (p. 4);

2. broad areas that you can look to for subjects, and ways you can see your mind working toward subjects, such as keeping a journal (p. 9), trying Charlie Brown sentences and word associations (pp. 10 and 11), examining questions, problems, and conflicts (pp. 14, 18, 20), and exploring new ways of looking at common things (p. 21).

Where do you start? When you must write something—a report, a book review, an English theme, a committee report, a term paper, a letter of application, an essay examination—how do you begin? What do you do first?

On rare, lucky occasions we already know where to start, what to do first. Some inner necessity moves us, perhaps—a sudden conviction, some insight that quickly overwhelms us, perhaps even some vanity. Or we are pushed into writing by external need: some injustice outrages us, some public stupidity demands that we put it right, we see some public or private good in action that we can describe, we see some possibility of gain, even if only in getting something done. Someone sees a serious lack of support for the public schools in his community and writes a letter to the local newspaper urging voter backing for new school board members. Someone else finds a major flaw in the sequence of communication among the offices in her company and prepares a report proposing correction. Sometimes, in such circumstances, we are ready to write and have no trouble getting started.

Most of us, however, do not write habitually now; most of us never have, and most of us never will. But we can write if we must. Samuel Johnson remarked one time that a person may write at any time "if he set himself doggedly to it." Of course we have different ways of setting ourselves to work. Given an assignment to write an essay, one student may go promptly to work, trying ten lines in one direction, sixteen in another, three in another, to settle at last on some tolerable topic, and then write in trim discipline a little each day until it's done. Another may enter into paralysis, convinced that he has nothing to say and that the assignment is hopeless anyway, and then at the last hour give up paralysis in favor of feverish activity. Another may work in quick short spurts.

We have different tempos and different temperaments, and so we work in different ways. However we work, except on those rare occasions when we may be moved to write something, we all raise similar questions: Where do I start? What is my subject? What am I supposed to do?

There are some easy answers to questions like these, and other answers not so easy. Though it may not seem so when it is late in the night before an essay is due, it is relatively easy to answer these questions and to write. If you accept the first ideas and thoughts that come into your mind, or if you accept the notions and attitudes that you hear or see expressed about you, or if you write down some generalized, proper, and entirely expectable statements (*generalized* because you have not made them your own, *proper* because they're likely to be acceptable commonplace notions, *expectable* because they are common and unsurprising)—then you really can get an essay written in little time. We've all taken this way at one time or another; sometimes, when it's late and our brains have been dislocated, there seems no other choice than to write what occurs to us most easily or to put down statements that no one will find objectionable.

The trouble is, writing done in this way will almost always suffer from two major ailments. First, writing that develops from easy, conventional thoughts has little chance of being any better than barely adequate. Readers may say, "Well, yes, I guess that's all right," but be otherwise unmoved, uninformed, unpersuaded. Second, writing that starts in this way is limited because the writer is a prisoner. If we simply accept and use the first quick ideas that pop up, or take over the commonplace attitudes and trite responses that are all around us, we are in slavery to our own ideas that we haven't taken time to examine, or in slavery to the ideas of other people.

If we value ourselves enough to know that we can write something to be read for pleasure or for utility, and if we wish to use the language according to our own sense of decent responsibility, then we may have to dig out the harder answers to the questions I have mentioned (Where do I start? What is my subject? What am I supposed to do?). The rest of this chapter and Chapters Two and Three will discuss some ways to answer these questions. Nothing in any one of these chapters will tell you all you need to know, but you can often find guidance or comfort in the efforts other writers have made in finding their subject and their starting place.

Exercise

Margaret Mead begins *Blackberry Winter.* "When I was sixteen years old, I read a text set like a flowered valentine on the office wall of an old country doctor: 'All things work together for good to them that love God.' I interpreted this to mean that if you set a course and bend your sails to every wind to further the journey, always trusting that the course is right, it will, in fact, be right even though the ship itself may go down at any time during the voyage."²

Write a few sentences about your early life as if you were beginning an autobiography. Read those sentences, asking yourself what sort of person is talking. Does that person satisfy you? Rewrite those sentences once, changing the content little, but working toward a "voice" you like.

FOUND SUBJECTS AND GIVEN SUBJECTS

sub·ject (sŭb' jikt) n. 2.a. A person or thing concerning which something is said or done; topic.
b. That which is treated or indicated in a work of art. 3. A course or area of study. 4. A basis for action; cause. . . . [Middle English su(b)get, subject, from Old French su(b)get, from Latin subicere (past participle subjectus), to bring under : sub−, under + jacere, to throw. . . .]—American Heritage Dictionary

More often than not, most of us write on given subjects. A teacher gives students a set of questions, and they write answers. Some local issue is not being handled well, so we write to the city council or to the board of education. We wish to make our opinions known in some national controversy and so write to our congressional representatives. A teacher requires a term paper and sets before the students a proposed set of topics from which they must choose. A committee has to make a recommendation for action on an issue; before it can do so someone must collect and report information to the other participants. A customer's records do not agree with the bill sent by a department store, and the customer must reconcile the difference.

In each of these instances—and every week in any life could provide more—the subject is given. Either someone has specifically established a subject (such as the teacher with test questions), or the circumstances have determined the subject (as in the case of the department store bill). If a particular subject isn't given, we're often assigned to a particular territory, where the subject is within certain specified boundaries. For a history term paper an instructor might suggest that a student examine what's known about American Indian drugs and medications and see if there is something there worth looking into closely. Indian drugs and medications may not turn out to be the student's actual subject (which might be, for example, "Early American Addicts," or "Native American Fever Medications") but only the territory in which the students finds a subject.

Or suppose the students on a particular college campus or the citizens of some community wish to establish a useful, functioning station for paper recycling. Their goal outlines a territory in which particular subjects must be explored—someone has to determine what is already being done in the vicinity; someone has to investigate what specific chore needs to be done to promote the community's participation in recycling. Someone has to learn necessary techniques. Someone has to scout out effective ways of giving public notice to the project. Someone has to explore financial, legal, and other practical problems and limitations. The goal gives a territory in which subjects are found.

Of course we do have occasions in which we're left entirely on our own to find the subject we're to write about. Outside of personal letters, however, such opportunities (or obligations, if you please) are scarce enough for most of us. In some English composition classes teachers leave determination of both subjects and types of writing up to the student writers. Term paper or research paper topics in college are often chosen by the writers, though in some classes teachers will suggest a range of topics for consideration and in others teachers will direct students to particular areas of interest that deserve exploration. And of course people in professions that require or encourage research and publication (papers in professional journals, for example, or papers delivered before groups of professionals) may have the freedom to determine the subject of their work. Even there, however, the nature of the work undertaken by a professional group, a company, a research team, may narrow the range of possibilities. Much of the writing that many people do is on subjects given by the needs of their work, or by the social, political, economic circumstances and issues of the days they live through.

But even when a subject is given, you still have to find it. You still have to scout out its size and shape, and see what parts it has and which of them needs attention.

A CASE TO CONSIDER

Problems in searching out a subject

The short essay that follows was written in a freshman composition course. The particular title was not assigned, but a generally related subject was given. The class fell to talking briefly one day about the different modes of speaking people practice in different circumstances. Two or three subjects of general interest seemed to emerge from the short discussion and were listed for the student writers to choose from. One was "Pretense, Affectation, and Behavior Change." The essay below was one student's way of considering this general topic.

Masks: A Crutch We All Use

Coming to any new environment with new people to meet, new experiences to experience, new anxieties to conquer, and the desire to be known and understood is a difficult situation for anyone. People, therefore, create masks to appear self-sufficient in front of a newly found peer group. It is hard for anyone to perceive someone as he truly is on first meeting because of each person's mask.

The title and the first paragraph indicate that the author has a special view of masks—they are crutches (by implication then masks are not needed by those who are healthy); they are put on for purposes of appearing self-sufficient; and they are false. The reader will probably expect these aspects of masks to be developed in the essay.

Masks can be displayed in many forms, depending on the person. There is the person who plays the role of total independence, a haughty, arrogant individual who inside is just as nervous and eager as everyone to make new friends. Another mask portrayed is found more often in adolescents, the silly, giggly type who bubbles continuously in front of his newfound friends. Finally, there is the wall-flower

The second paragraph appears to be comprehensive but isn't. Three types of masks are given, and the last is introduced with finally, indicating that there are no other examples of masks,

who makes no real effort to meet new people because of a fear of rejection.

though there probably are a large number. Two of the instances cited contradict the opening paragraph, which seems to say that all masks are in aid of self-sufficiency.

In the Bible, there is the story of Jesus, on the third day after He died, and two men whom He met on the road to Emmaus. Because of their masks they did not recognize Him, but when they ate together they realized who He was. Just as the two men recognized Jesus when they ate with Him, so it is true today that much is learned about a person at a dinner table. Eating with people and associating with them daily are ways in which we begin to see behind their masks.

The illustration given in the third paragraph is not entirely clear and does not appear to illustrate the use of masks for self-sufficiency. It seems likely at this point that the author knows other uses for masks, but hasn't brought this knowledge before his or her reader.

A mask is a crutch used to make a person feel at ease with himself and others. The role-playing is only dropped when a person does not fear rejection. A new environment creates a new community for each person in this situation. It is only stabilized when masks that were created are no longer used and each member is at ease in his new society.

The author is free to view masks in any way. Mask-using is probably more intricate than it is shown to be here, however, though the author has given no sign that he or she has taken a single view out of many that are possible. As a result, the essay appears to be thorough, though it isn't. It's as if the author had mistaken a single view of masks for the whole truth about masks.

Questions

1. What would you do before trying to revise this essay?
2. How many essays could be made from this?

What I have suggested in these last few pages is that whether the subject is found or given, assigned or selected, some exploration and investigation is still necessary and useful before you write. You must still fall back on your own experience, your reading, your reflection in order to find a way of taking possession of a subject. For investigative uses you can also rely on some ways of thinking that will usually lead to good, productive questions about both general and particular subjects.

Exercises

1.   Formulate a sentence that states a problem about the following broad subjects. As you do, ask yourself: What do I already know about the subject? What can I find out about it?
   a. Grading practices in Freshman English
   b. Coping with laundry
   c. Buying a stereo system
   d. Computer dating
   e. Biorhythm charts

2.   Devise some questions for the problems you have stated in exercise one that could form the basis for the organization of a paper.

SOME WAYS OF LOOKING FOR SUBJECTS

This exploratory and investigative stage was called *invention* in early rhetoric texts. It comes from a Latin verb, *invenire*, which usually means (1) to come upon, or find; or (2) to fabricate mentally, to create or devise in the mind—two activities that are likely to occur before you write. You come upon your own experiences, the things you know, and the things other people know, and then you make something out of them in your mind by finding what they mean to you and how they fit together.

No one can tell you exactly how to do this, but you can find help in exploratory methods other writers have used. In this section I'll suggest seven ways of thinking about subjects. Any one of them may be useful in different ways. They may help you locate a subject when none is given, and then may help you think out ways of handling a subject once you've found it, or of handling a subject that has been assigned. And they may be helpful after you've written a draft and have returned to the paper for revision. You may need to try several or all of these suggestions, and there is still the possibility that none of them will give you your subject.

INSIGHT

Getting started

For some help in (a) finding a subject where none is given, (b) thinking through a subject that has been assigned, or (c) checking and revising a paper that you have already written, try one of these:

1. Keep a journal.
2. Try some Charlie Brown sentences.
3. Try some word associations.
4. Ask a sequence of prepared questions.
5. Search out a problem that has to be solved.
6. Look for conflicts and unknowns.
7. Try looking at the things around you in different ways.

Keep a journal

It's too late to start keeping a journal if you wait until after an essay or some other piece of writing has already been assigned. What I am recommending, as many others have recommended, is that you begin keeping a daily journal—even if you're not in a writing class. Some thoughts are too interesting to let slip away. If a journal is to be any help to you in your writing, however, you'll have to meet some conditions.

First, put something in the journal *every* day. Don't wait until Sunday night and try to catch up for the week. Part of the purpose of a journal is to provide some record of how you feel about experiences during or near the time they occur. If you're in a certain mood on Wednesday evening, you may not be able to understand it very well or to write a specific account of it if you wait until some day later in the month. The point is to get into the habit of putting something in the journal regularly.

Second, don't worry too much about what you put in the journal. Enter whatever interests or puzzles or excites or angers or pleases you. Include passages from essays, stories, newspaper articles, lines from songs, headlines, TV commercials, puzzling or perceptive remarks you hear. Write down the questions that enter your mind. Let your entries be long or short, complete or fragmented, original or copied.

The more faithfully you do this, the more the journal will make you acquainted with your own world. Some subjects may occur frequently in your entries, or you may find yourself collecting passages from the work of other people that will indicate what subjects catch your mind. If you make full and regular entries, you may begin to see what there is in your world that you can present to a reader. And besides, the daily practice in writing—even copying from the writing of others—may enable you to feel more at ease with writing.

Keeping a journal isn't just an arbitrary and unnatural practice useless except in an English composition class. Evidence shows that journals, letters, and other private forms of writing have been useful ways for men and women to track down their own thoughts and try out their own abilities. Surviving private papers of the English poet Alexander Pope show him practicing various techniques: similes, metaphors, synecdoches, and other forms of figurative language recur as he sets himself particular tasks and practices. And approximately two years before John Keats was to complete the "Ode on a Grecian Urn," with its famous closing lines,

> *"Beauty is truth, truth beauty," —that is all*
> *Ye know on earth, and all ye need to know,*

he was thinking out and discussing, in a letter to Benjamin Bailey, his belief that "What the imagination seizes as Beauty must be truth."

Try some Charlie Brown sentences

Some will see right away that the term "Charlie Brown sentences" is a highly technical designation borrowed from a recently influential psychological treatise entitled "Peanuts." A Charlie Brown sentence usually looks like this:

> *An abstract noun + the verb* is *+ specific terms to identify or*
> *characterize the abstract noun*

Examples similar to statements that appear in "Peanuts" may clarify what I mean:

> *Happiness is a warm blanket.*

> *A friend is someone to talk to.*

> *Love is a new puppy.*

When you write a Charlie Brown sentence, it is as if you were establishing an equation: you are saying that as your mind comprehends an abstraction (like *honor* or *fame* or *security*), it is equal to the specific terms you assign to it at a given time, as in the following examples:

> *Security is not having to identify yourself when you want to cash a check at your local grocery store.*

> *Relaxation is knowing that you can afford to wait a day or so before you start writing the paper that's due the week after next.*

> *Anxiety is hearing an ambulance in a rainstorm when part of your family is overdue on a car trip.*

The point in making a Charlie Brown sentence is to give the abstraction a particular and concrete identity.

If you try writing Charlie Brown sentences—they could be a regular part of your journal entries—the sentences may let you see which way your mind is running. If you write such sentences regularly for a while and then look back over them, you may see that certain kinds of subjects are more likely to attract you than others are.

Writing Charlie Brown sentences is good practice in another way, too. Any subject you are assigned, or any subject you find on your own, is an abstraction until the paper you write gives it particular meaning. A Charlie Brown sentence is a miniature essay. Being specific in a Charlie Brown sentence may help you remember to be specific in an essay.

Exercises

Try some Charlie Brown sentences.

1. Complete the following:
    a. Excitement is. . . .
    b. Frustration is. . . .
    c. Panic is. . . .
    d. Contentment is. . . .
    e. Hypocrisy is. . . .
2. Write five Charlie Brown sentences of your own.

Try some word associations

If you are given a subject to develop in your own way, or if you are left to find your own subject, some practice in deliberately tracking down word associations may help you see the range of possibilities a given subject holds, or to see the possibilities in your own mind. Word association may encourage you to break away from customary subjects and to see connections among possible subjects that you had not seen before.

Word association of this kind is not new to most people. Perhaps you can recall an occasion when you interrupted your own thought or conversation, wondering how you came to the subject of the moment. Tracking backward from where you are at that moment to where you had come from may lead you over an interesting and surprising path. Associations usually are erratic and wandering. When you're hunting a subject, however, it may be useful if you set out to track associations deliberately.

Any word may belong in several contexts. The word *grade*, for example, may first suggest marks in schoolwork, but it will also lead you elsewhere: to a year or level in school, to the possibility of making the grade (that is, succeeding, or measuring up in some enterprise), to inspecting eggs (which are graded), to grading roads, or to the degree of inclination (or slope) that is desirable as a highway or a railroad track goes up through a mountainous landscape. In the series above, *grading* or inspecting *eggs* seemed to be a dead end; I returned to the notion of *making the grade* and went from there to *grading roads*. The example at the bottom of the page illustrates one way that *grading* could become a subject for a paper.

Remember, too, that each context you are led to may have a set of words that are linked with it. You may discover that if you follow a sequence of associations, one of them may be in a context that opens up possibilities for you to write about. A word such as *driving* may lead you to *traffic*, or to *golf*, or to *music* (as in "a driving rhythm"), or to *ambition*. Each of these words provides a context, and in each context the line of association may veer off to the new set of words associated with that context. For example, *driving* might lead through several contexts to *ambition*; that word, then, might set you off on a train of associations in that particular context—*ambition*, *aggression*, *intensity*, *energy*.

There is nothing in word associations that will guarantee you a good subject, but they may reveal to you more possibilities for writing than you were aware of. The various directions in which you are led by word association may seem like a three-dimensional crossword puzzle. Your line of thought may move horizontally, staying pretty well within one context. If you start with the word *street*, for example, your mind may move on to *road*, *freeway*, *boulevard*, *sidewalk*, *intersection*, and so on. But it's possible that when you get to the word *sidewalk*, your mind veers off vertically into another context—*sidewalk*, *pedestrian*, *shoppers*, *office workers*, *mall*, *stores*, and so on. Or when you get to *mall*, your mind may be pulled into a set of words associated only with *mall*. The number and direction of associations will depend upon how much you sense in a word, upon how you connect words, and upon your own experience and point of view.

INSIGHT

Tracing word associations

1. Suppose that you have been assigned an essay on one of five general subjects that you may develop in any way you wish. Suppose further that none of the possible subjects makes you very enthusiastic and that the only one of them that seems to be anywhere near your neighborhood is "The Grading System." Actually, that one doesn't interest you very much, but it's the best thing available. So you start with the word *grading* to initiate a series of associations. It leads you to letter or number *grades* in school, to levels or *grades* (as in tenth grade), to making the *grade*. So far, nothing has happened to get you started writing. You try again, and this time *grading* leads you to *road grading*. Nothing yet. Then you remember hearing and using the expression *going up a steep grade*.

That starts another line of associations, words and phrases associated with *steep grade*, including *slope*, *hill*, *ramp*. When you get to *ramp*, you remember a friend who goes about the campus in a wheelchair, and you recall his difficulties with curbs and building entrances, because there are no ramps in the curbs or alongside steps into buildings. And there's your paper, entitled "The University Needs a New Grading System," which argues the need for a system of ramps everywhere on campus for wheelchairs. The association of *grades* with *ramps* (by an indirect route) seems to justify the paper, and the subject itself is worth time and attention.

2. Suppose, instead, that no topics have been assigned or suggested. You're on your own, with not an idea in sight. You start out deliberately, taking the nearest object as the beginning place—*desk* leads to *chair*, to *furniture*, to *bed*, to *chest of drawers*. All but one of the terms refer to specific items in your room, and none of them leads you nearer a subject for your paper. You go back to the odd term, *furniture*, and start over from there, though it doesn't seem very promising. The word leads you to *furniture store*, to *home furniture*, and then you're off, recalling particular pieces of furniture at home. Suppose then you go back to *home furniture* and start again, trying to locate other furniture categories. That gives you *office furniture* and *church furniture* and *school furniture*. With that, you seem to be back where you started, with *desk*. But suppose that when you get to school furniture, you find yourself wondering where school furniture (for classrooms and dormitories) comes from. How often is it replaced? Who on campus is responsible for ordering, replacing, and repairing? Who designs it? Is it designed and made only with economy in mind, or is there some principle for designing school furniture? If a train of associations leads you finally to some questions, then you've begun to locate a subject. Answers to some of the questions above may belong together in a single paper. One or two of the questions alone may be enough for a paper. Responding to these questions, of course, will require some interviews and perhaps some reading, but you will have a useful starting point.

Exercise

Take an adjective like *blind* or a noun like *power* or an even more concrete noun like *lightbulb* and play with it for awhile. Enjoy yourself and move from word to word freely. When you arrive at a word that interests you, try to move to a phrase or sentence. From there move to questions. Stop when you have arrived at one or two questions that genuinely interest you.

Ask a sequence of prepared questions

If you must write a paper and you have only some general areas of interest or a set of general topics provided by your instructor, then you may learn what your particular subject is if you will systematically and deliberately work your way through the sequence of questions shown below. The purpose of such deliberate questioning is to understand your own experiences more thoroughly, to remember the details of your experiences, to see the connections among the details and the implications of your experiences. The questions are grouped so that you can select a series that is most appropriate to the idea you are considering or the general topic that you have before you.

Questions to ask about concrete items.   If you are planning to write about a single item that presently exists, such as your home, or your car, or the building you work in, or the program of study you're taking and its requirements:

What are its precise physical characteristics?

How does it differ from things that resemble it?

What is its range of variation (how much can it be changed and still be the thing you started with)?

Does it remind you of other objects you have observed earlier in your life? Why? How?

From what points of view can it be examined?

What sort of structure does it have?

How do its parts work together?

How are the parts put together?

How are the parts proportioned in relation to each other?

To what class or sequence of things does it belong?

Who or what produced it in this form? Why?

Who needs it?

Who uses it? For what?

What purposes can it serve?

If you are planning to write about a single completed event, or part of a process such as a major event in your life or a meeting you attended (these questions can also apply to scenes and pictures and to works of fiction and drama):

Exactly what happened? (Tell the precise sequence: who? what? when? how? why? Who did what to whom? Why?)

What were the circumstances in which the event occurred?

How was the event like or unlike other similar events?

What were its causes?

What were its consequences?

What does its occurrence imply? What action (if any) is called for?

What was affected by it?

To what group or class might it be assigned?

Is it good or bad? By what standard?

How do we know about it? What is the authority for our information? How reliable is the authority? How do we know it to be reliable, or unreliable?

How might the event have been changed or avoided?

To what other events was it connected?

If you are planning to write about an abstract concept, such as love or sportsmanship:

To what specific items or events does the word or words connect in your imagination?

What characteristics must an item or event have before the name of the concept will apply to it?

How do the things you associate with the concept differ from things you associate with similar concepts?

How has the term been used by writers whom you have read?

Does the word have persuasive value? Does its use in connection with another concept seem to praise or condemn the other concept?

Are you favorably disposed to all things included in the concept? Why or why not?

If you are planning to write about collections of items, such as your personal book collection, or record and tape collection, or television programs that you watch:

What, exactly, do the items have in common?

If they have features in common, how do they differ?

How are the items related to each other?

How may the group be divided?

Into what class can the group as a whole be put?

If you are planning to write about groups of completed events such as past political campaigns (these questions also apply to literary works, such as a collection of short stories):

What have the events in common?

How do they differ?

How are the events related to each other (if they are not part of a chronological sequence)?

What is revealed by the events when taken as a group?

How can the group be divided? On what bases?

Into what class, if any, can the events taken as a group fit?

Does the group belong to any structures other than simply a larger group of similar events?

To what antecedents does the group of events look back? Where can they be found?

What implications, if any, does the group of events have? Does the group point to a need for some sort of action?

Asking and answering these questions cannot, of course, guarantee you a good paper. But any one of them may lead you to something to write about. Several of them taken together may give you material for a paper. You may discover that the subject you are working on can be compared in some way to another subject or to an experience you remember well; that comparison may lead you to an interesting generalization about the two that could in turn lead to an insight that forms the basis of a paper. These questions are useful if they help you arrive at a fruitful generalization—an assertion or an observation about relationships that can be developed in your writing. Remember that while a good piece of writing ought to rest on specific details, information, and observations, much good writing starts when the writer discovers something to claim, an assertion to make.

For example, suppose you were using the last set of questions as a way of looking at a group of short stories that you have read. Suppose a little further that when you set out to answer the first question (What have the events or stories in common?), you discover that several or perhaps all of the stories are not told in strict chronological order. Perhaps the authors use several different narrators, who mix up the time sequence; perhaps they depend on flashbacks, in which characters recall something in the past. When you've done that much, you have discovered a quality that the stories have in common.

But the sequence of your thought may not end there. If you keep your mind open and stay alive to thought associations and memories, the discovery that the stories have mixed time sequences may cause you to remember how you finally learned the truth about the scandal in the life of your great-uncle George, who drinks a little every day. Chances are you learned about it piece by piece, overhearing a little here, catching a little gossip there, surprising the older members of your family in a deep conversation when you walked in unannounced. When you couple that family recollection with what you have observed about the stories, you may come to a general observation, an assertion that you can develop in your writing—the assertion that in the lives of most people and in the design of much fiction, chronological time is much less important than other kinds of time.

These sequences of questions may lead you to discover some conflict or contradiction or inconsistency in a subject you are thinking about. Any discoveries of this kind—an interesting comparison, reasons for making a judgment, an unresolved problem—can set you on your way to the informative exploration of a subject.

Questions to ask about abstract items.   The questions above are intended for inquiries about things, persons, or events. Some of the time you may face judgments or propositions or questions as possible subjects. Another set of questions may be useful in that case.

If you are planning to write about statements that are to be proved or disproved:

What must be established for the reader before he will believe it?

What smaller assertions does the statement contain?

What are the meanings of key words in the statement?

Can you trace back to the line of reasoning that led to this conclusion?

How can we contrast the statement with other propositions?

To what class of propositions does it belong?

How inclusive is the statement?

How can the statement be illustrated?

What kinds of evidence will support the statement?

What can be said in opposition to it?

Is it true or false? How do you know—from observation, authority, statistics, other sources?

Why might someone not believe it?

Does the statement take anything for granted?

Must some action be taken as a result of the statement?

Can the action be taken? Will the action called for work?

If you are planning to write in response to a question:

Does the question refer to the present, the past, or the future?

What does the question take for granted?

Where might answers be sought?

Why does the question come up?

What exactly is in doubt?

What propositions might be advanced in answer to the question?

Don't expect these questions to be appropriate all of the time, or even to work all the time when they are appropriate. They may be more effective in leading you to the most interesting features of a good subject after you have used them awhile. They may also be more effective if you work with two or three other students as you are asking and answering, testing each other's potential subjects.

Exercise

For each of the sets of questions in the preceding pages, list *three* topics that would seem to be appropriate to those questions. Then, take one set of questions and one of your topics for that set and answer the questions as well as you can with the information you have at hand. Did the topic, in fact, prove to be appropriate for the questions?

Look for a problem that has to be solved

If in your browsing and reading and talking about possible subjects for writing you come across a problem, seize the problem and any possible solution as the material for your writing. Having a problem to solve will usually give you a purpose in studying your subject so that you will begin to know what information or experience to use, what to discard.

A problem may show up in any number of ways. If you discover conflicting views about the material you are considering, or if you realize that some action is called for, or if you see that something doesn't fit in the material you are considering, then you may look for ways to resolve the conflict or take appropriate action to solve the problem. For example, suppose you are a member of a student committee that hopes to sponsor the publication of student evaluations of their instructors. Your membership in this group and your support of its work means that you already have a problem: some action is called for (evaluation and publication), and you must help find the most suitable way of carrying the action out. But other problems may arise. Presumably your group has agreed on the need for evaluation and publication, but conflicting views may be expressed before you have acted. For example, suppose a small group of popular and thoughtful teachers comes to discuss the evaluation with your group and expresses the view that publication of the results may have no effect except to enable some students to select teachers that seem easy. If you respect their view, you have another kind of problem that must be resolved. Or suppose another student raises the thorny question that publication of the evaluation may be construed as a violation of privacy. Problems that arise in your thinking—often because some action must be taken, or because some conflict has developed, or because some element doesn't fit—give some purpose to your thinking and some direction to your explorations.

When you do encounter a problem, you may find it useful to think through the steps shown below. Your response to any one of these steps may determine the content of your paper. You may, however, find that you need to work out in writing several or all of these steps.

1. *Definition of the problem*.   It is always helpful to articulate a clear statement of what is to be decided (for example, which of two or more possible courses of action is to be chosen, or what undesirable condition needs to be corrected).

2. *Determination of why the problem is a problem*.   If the problem is to choose among several courses of action, you need to determine why the value of each is in doubt; if the problem is to get rid of an undesirable condition, you need to know exactly why it is undesirable.

3. *Determination of the goals that must be served by whatever action is taken*.   Before you can determine exactly what to do, you will need to know what you are trying to achieve and what you are trying to avoid.

4. *Determination of the goals that have the highest priority*.   Some of the things you may be trying to achieve may be more important than others; some of the things you are trying to avoid may be more critical than others.

5. *Development of procedures that might attain the desired goals*.   If your problem is to choose among several possible courses of action, this step may not be necessary, since the courses of action themselves may include ways of attaining the desired goals; often, however, you may need to combine possible procedures or check courses of action to determine if they are really feasible.

6. *Prediction of the results that will follow from taking each possible action*.   Here, of course, you can only deal with what will *probably* occur as the evidence and the circumstances you are in enable you to predict; predictions of the consequences that will follow from a course of action may enable you to see whether the course of action will indeed bring you close to your goal.

7.   *Weighing the predictions*.   Comparing the consequences of the possible courses of action gives you another opportunity to decide which course of action will bring you nearest your goal.

8.   *Evaluation of the choice that seems best*.   Does the decision you've made really eliminate the undesirable condition? Does it really lead to the best course of action: does it avoid, where possible, disagreeable results?

This sequence of steps represents the kinds of thinking and action that often occur whenever anyone has a decision to make or a problem to solve. Working your way through these steps, remember, will not guarantee that you have a finished paper, but any one of the steps, or several of them together, or the whole sequence may help you focus on a meaningful subject, see what needs to be said about it, and even in what order it needs to be said. Finding a problem or focusing on one of the steps above also gives you a purpose in weighing your experience and information and consequently a way to choose what is usable.

Look for conflicts and unknowns

A conflict can occur when some element in your experience or knowledge doesn't fit in the whole range of your experience or knowledge, or when some element of your world turns out to be inconsistent with the rest of your world. You learn throughout your life, for example, that your government stands for certain principles, but then you discover that it can act in ways to violate those principles. You see a company's advertisements over a period of two years, let us say, and note that the company professes its concern for our resources, but when you go to the local drugstore you find that the same company markets disposable plastic razors. Often trying to resolve such conflicts will give you ample material for a paper; since most of us usually want our world to hold together and make some sort of sense, we set out to determine the unknown (temporarily, at least) reasons for the conflict in order to eliminate it or at least to bring it under the control of our understanding.

There is no sure way to organize your thinking to handle conflicts. One beginning place is to identify the conflicting elements precisely—a politician's public statements, on the one hand, and his private behavior, on the other. The same conflict may occur if someone you know well and talk with often suddenly seems distant; your normal ease and familiarity conflict with this new aloofness. Identifying these conflicting elements is a first step in using conflict to provide the materials for writing.

But a second step is also necessary. In some ways our minds are like ecological systems, each seeking to maintain its own balance and stability. When a conflict occurs, the balance and stability are disrupted, and the system seeks to right itself, to recover its balance and stability, by eliminating the conflict. A second step, then, after the conflicting elements have been identified, is to determine the *unknown*, whatever it is that will eliminate the conflict, or if not that, at least ease the puzzlement and pressure it may create. When you can name the warring elements in a conflict and then specify what may ease or end the conflict, you may have the whole outline for a paper. If not, you may have at least a new set of ideas to explore on your way to writing a paper.

Exercise

Find something in your adjustments to college life that conflicts with your image of yourself. Perhaps the drinking habits of your new friends are causing you to question your definite opinions about drinking, or the demands of your new social life are making you do your studying at the last minute, whereas before now you have always been well organized.

Write an explanation of the conflict. Then in writing explore how you can change the situation, or if it cannot be changed, how you can resolve it without sacrificing your self-image. It may be that the situation cannot be resolved, but at least explore your possibilities.

Try looking at the things around you in different ways

If you will deliberately shift your perspective when you look around yourself, almost anything may become an interesting subject as you learn more about it from seeing it in different ways. If you already have a subject in mind, learning to see it from different perspectives may help you find a good way of writing about it. Richard Young, Alton Becker, and Kenneth Pike have suggested three ways of looking at parts of your experience that may be particularly useful.

Suppose that you have no subject in mind, though it's time to write a paper for your composition class. Let's suppose that you are alongside your desk—not really *at* your desk, but draped alongside it, wondering. Stretched out in front of you is your leg. At the end of it is a foot. Upon the foot there is a *shoe*. What happens if you look at the shoe as if it were *static*, a thing complete in itself, of interest to you only in its present form? When you look at a shoe as a static thing, you must consider its shape, size, design, color, marks created as part of a design, marks created by use and wear, the materials of which it is made.

But then suppose you look at the shoe as part of a *dynamic* process. You are no longer particularly interested in the same features, but must see the shoe as part of a process that changes in time or space or in your way of perceiving it. Looking at the shoe in this way may lead you to notice carefully the signs it shows of wearing; when you see the shoe in this way, the shoe as it is in the present is simply an instant in a process of aging. Or you might see the shoe as part of a process of crafting or manufacturing. Or you might see the shoe as the present moment's example out of a history of shoe styles that you have tried and discarded—and that may even show you a way of writing about yourself.

Finally, try looking at the shoe as part of a *field* of similar or related experiences. The shoe then becomes an example in the field of shoes, which would include different types of footwear for different purposes and occasions and different styles of design. Or you might see the shoe in a larger field, as an example of a certain kind of fashion, which could lead you to observations about, for example, a whole fashion with its preferences in color, shape, design, texture, and composition.

A shoe is a pretty simple object, yet seen in different ways even a shoe can begin to yield interesting possibilities for writing. These variations in perspective can also be useful to you in examining more complex subjects. Close observation of five of your classes as static instances (for example, what kind of exams are given in each?), as moments in a process (is the type of exam part of a process of teaching, each of whose stages reveals similarities to the others?), and as specimens from larger fields (for example, is the process of teaching in one class linked to certain views of education?) may lead you to explorations of educational methodology and philosophy. And these explorations are likely to be more useful than they otherwise would be to the extent that they are based on your observation of five particular classes.

Exercises

1.   Take any common object from your writing desk—a stapler, a paper clip, a calculator—and write a few short sentences describing first how it looks as a static thing, then as a part of a changing, dynamic process, and finally as a part of a field of similar objects.

2.   *Concepts* can be examined from the same three perspectives. Take *nuclear disarmament, capitalism, space colonization, violence on television, welfare reform, reverse discrimination,* or a similar concept, and examine it from the same perspectives used in the first part of this exercise. You may use your dictionary, encyclopedia, or other sources if you need them.

Sometimes, when you have to write, it simply seems that there is nothing to say on any imaginable subject. Sometimes, the problem lies at the other extreme: there are so many subjects floating around that it is not reasonable or possible to choose among them. But even when the circumstances seem desperate and your pencil or typewriter just won't go, you can find a subject that is worth your time. The methods of searching for subjects suggested in this chapter may help you. Three final suggestions may also help. First, learn to trust your own experience: what you are counts for something, and what you think counts for something. Second, remember that nothing is trivial; *anything* can become an interesting subject if you think about it, poke at it, and turn it this way and that. Third, remember that there is some help available to you in exploring subjects; that, indeed, is the concern of the following chapter.

Exercises

1. Listed below is an odd assortment of objects, events, and people. They are not meant to be taken as titles for essays or as subjects for essays, but only as random things that any one of us might see or think of if we were hunting around for a subject when none has been given. Try any of the methods of exploration suggested above with each item on the list and see if you are led to a subject and a possible set of materials for an essay that you would be willing to give your time to.

    a. CB radios   d. UFO's
    b. Computers   e. Chairman Mao
    c. Indianapolis "500"   f. "Bay of Pigs"

2. Listed below are five general topics, such as might be suggested by a composition teacher. Try any of the methods suggested above with each item on the list and see if you are able to find some useful and interesting and *particular ways of writing* about these *general* topics.

    a. Sports violence
    b. High school preparation for college
    c. Television commercials
    d. Censorship of college and university events
    e. Victimless crimes

3. Given below is a short essay written in a freshman composition class. Read it carefully and then see whether any of the methods suggested above will help you determine how the essay might be usefully revised.

Technology: Is It Really Our Enemy?

I am very disturbed by the view of some people that, since modern technology has created such problems as pollution of the environment and depletion of our natural resources, we should turn away from science. They feel we should return to a more simple era of minimum technology and maximum emphasis on "human" values. While this dream of a simple life may seem reasonable on the surface, it actually contains several weaknesses.

First, it would be virtually impossible to feed, clothe, or house our present large population without a certain amount of technology. The land simply could not produce enough food without modern farming methods. Neither could we provide adequate clothing or housing without modern manufacturing technology.

By freeing people from the necessities of struggling for their survival, technology also provides them with the leisure they need to pursue human goals. A person is unlikely to take much interest in social reform when he is preoccupied with producing his next meal. He must have leisure to be able to devote time to higher pursuits.

Technology benefits the pursuit of humanitarian goals in more concrete ways, as well. Where, for example, would our health services be without modern technology?

The problem then is not a basic one in the nature of technology itself, but rather one of the proper application of technology. It can be used as a tool to eliminate pollution and to find ways of using resources more effectively. Technology can be applied to solve the problems that it may create.

a. What word associations can you make with *technology*? Do any of these seem more fruitful than the ideas the author included?

b. Notice that the author has three developmental paragraphs, although none of them is entirely satisfactory. Look at *technology* first as a *static* thing and write a few sentences about it. Next, write a few sentences about *technology* as a *dynamic* process. Finally, view *technology* as a part of a *field*, and write a few sentences.

c. Reread the essay, and as you do make a list of questions that come into your mind that are left unanswered by the author.

d. Jot down some tentative answers about *technology* to the questions on page 17 concerning an *abstract concept*.

*Though thy beginning was small, yet thy latter end
should greatly increase.*

Job 8:7

2

Exploring Subjects

Just having a subject in mind doesn't necessarily help you know all
that can or should be said about it. This chapter suggests some ways
of examining possible subjects so that you can begin to know what
to say. It proposes four methods to use for exploring subjects and
finding additional information:

1. ask the journalist's questions (p. 26);

2. use the topics as ways of thinking about your subject (p. 31);

3. try some simple linkages (p. 45); and

4. use available resources (p. 47).

Fortunately, there are times when finding a subject is easy. Sometimes, too, when a subject comes readily to mind, we can easily see all that must be said if we are to treat the subject well and fairly.

But it is not always that way. Sometimes, even when you know what you want to write about, you will still not be able to see immediately all that can or should be said. Indeed, one of the most common failures in writing is the failure to see and to record all that ought to be put down on paper. Whatever subject you settle on can be valuable. It's worth something to a reader to see something in a new way, your way. An honest record of your thinking about a subject can merit a reader's time. Everything matters in some way. No subject is trivial unless it's treated in a trivial, careless, thoughtless way—as, for example, much of what passes for commentary about television programming has been repetitious and superficial. Any subject has various features and parts. Any subject can be seen in various ways. A subject comes from somewhere; it has some kind of origin. A subject goes somewhere; it has some kind of consequence. When you take on a particular subject, then, you take on particular responsibilities—at the very least to explore it fully and to try to find what there is in it that has worth.

EXPLORING A SUBJECT'S POSSIBILITIES

The various methods of exploration suggested in the preceding chapter may help you not just look for subjects, but also to investigate a subject once you've found it and to see its parts and possibilities. This chapter offers some additional suggestions, particularly intended for exploration of subjects that you already have in mind.

Ask the journalist's questions

Student journalists are taught to ask *Who? What? Where? When? Why?* and *How?* And they are taught early to get the answers to these questions into the opening paragraphs of news stories. The questions are also useful ways of learning about any subject for other kinds of writing.

It's usually easy enough to see how the questions are answered in the opening of a typical news story. The passage below includes the first two paragraphs of a front-page story by Michael Stern, "Foreign Financing Is Sought by City to Produce Jobs" (*New York Times*):

who —————— Mayor Beame disclosed yesterday ——— when

where ———————— that the city was actively seeking foreign ——————— what

why ——————— capital to create new industries and new

jobs here and asserted that New York "is

becoming increasingly attractive to over-

seas investors."

As a first step in that effort, Alfred Eisenpreis, the city's Economic Development Administrator, made a tour of Britain, France and West Germany three months ——— how ago in which he discussed the benefits and opportunities New York could offer foreign investors. . . .

What we sometimes don't notice, however, is that other kinds of writing also seek out and offer answers to the same questions. The paragraphs below are the openings to two editorials:

The request of a bipartisan group of ——— who 22 Senators that Secretary of State Kis- ——— what singer be placed in personal charge of United States negotiations at the resumed Law of the Sea Conference in Geneva next ——— when ———where month merits urgent attention at the White House. — "America at Sea," *New York Times*, February 9, 1975, p. 14E

when ——— Throughout most of history, men ——— who have acted as if life were cheap. In the an-
what ——— cient era, there were brief, sunlit interludes in Athens and in Rome when life was highly valued but even then only in the governing classes. In most Western history, men have ——— where routinely squandered lives—their own and those of others—in the waste of war, they have fatalistically accepted high death rates
how ——— from disease and accident, and have casually engaged in cruel and life-endangering customs. — "Face in the Mirror," *New York Times*, February 9, 1975, p. 14E

And consider the opening of Tennyson's poem "Ulysses":

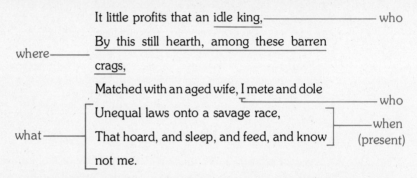

You can begin to see in these examples—particularly if you read the rest of "Ulysses"—that the journalist's questions (Who? What? When? Where? Why? How?) are usually answered more than once. The openings of the two editorials above and of "Ulysses" provide *initial*, brief answers to some or all of the questions. One way of understanding the remainder of the two editorials and of the poem is to see that *full* answers are given to the same questions. The rest of "Ulysses" identifies and characterizes the speaker, Ulysses (*who*); explains both what he has been doing and what he proposes to do (*what*); allows him to say why he is setting out on another voyage (*why*) and what he hopes to accomplish (*how*); and clarifies the setting in time and place (*when* and *where*).

Look at one more example:

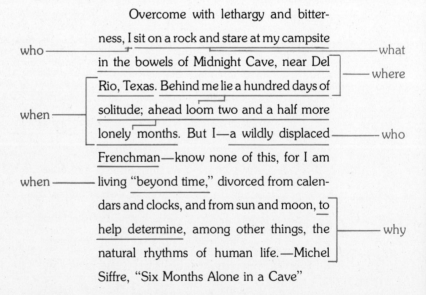

This is the opening paragraph of a narrative of over two thousand words. It does much the same thing that the opening of a news story does, explaining who, what, when, where, and why. But how does answering these questions help you learn what is in a subject, or explore a subject that you already have in mind? Look again at the opening paragraph above: The *initial answers* in this example are the subjects for *full answers* in the essay that follows. The writer discusses himself and how he came to be where he was (the cave), why he was there, and what happened during the time he spent there. In other words, one way to conceive of an essay and to see what needs to be in it is to see the opening as answering the journalist's questions and the body of the essay as amplifying the answers already given. Each thing introduced in the opening paragraph above is represented fully in the body of the essay that follows this opening.

Exercise

Answer the journalist's questions (Who? What? When? Where? Why? How?) for the following student paragraphs:

a. Would you ever think that a big pile of dirt could be impressive? When I was a tad our neighborhood had a vacant lot with a big pile of dirt that took many days to mold the lives of so many kids. Hour upon hour was spent building "miles" of roads and tunnels for our toy cars, airports for our toy planes, and for landscaping the forests of weeds. Our bridge construction was not too sturdy—fact is, we had more than a few collapse—but at the time, bridge safety was of little consequence.

b. Parents who protect, love, give, and care—this is what I knew as I was growing up, and I couldn't have asked for anything more. They provided a nice home, a good education, a car, travel opportunities, and many other luxuries. Having experienced this, I naturally want my children to have the same; but since my parents didn't have it while growing up, I'm puzzled as to what motivated them.

Were there any of the journalist's questions left unanswered that would have generated more interest?

INSIGHT

Trying out the journalist's questions

Suppose you have learned of a rumored change in the general curriculum requirements at your college; also suppose that you are a very careful planner and wish to have all of the details of your degree program clearly worked out well in advance. Since you have to write a paper anyway, and since the rumored curriculum change is immediately interesting to you, you settle on that as your subject. But in this instance, a subject is about all you have. You don't have the information necessary to talk about the proposed change or to make any judgment of it.

Let's suppose, then, that you set out to learn what you can about the rumored change. You go to the office of the department in which you are majoring. The departmental secretary there knows that some kind of planning is under way, but cannot offer any particular details. The chairman of the department is not in his office—he's no help. The secretary suggests that you see the dean's secretary. You go by, and sure enough the dean's secretary gives you some early information. "Why yes," she says, "a review of the general requirements is under way. The committee just had its first meeting day before yesterday. They'll be having regular meetings, and I heard the dean say that the work will probably take a year." "What got the committee started?" you ask. "Well," she says, "there was apparently a lot of feeling on campus that the requirements were too rigid—but if you want to know more about what they're doing, why don't you go see Professor Taliaferro in the History Department— he's committee chairman."

When she has said that much, you have the *initial answers* to the journalist's questions:

Who?   A review committee chaired by Professor Taliaferro of the History Department.

What?   A review of the college's general requirements is under way.

When?   The first meeting was the day before yesterday, and there will be regular meetings.

Where? All you know here is that the study will be conducted in regular meetings.

Why?   The review is apparently under way because of some belief that the requirements are too rigid.

How?   All you know is that the study may go on for a year.

That's a start, but it is not enough either to still your curiosity and concern or to enable you to write a paper. The same questions can lead you to fuller information, but you will have to carry the questions a bit further. A next step is to multiply the questions by each other, as shown below.

You have an *initial answer* to the question Who? A review committee chaired by Professor Taliaferro. You may be able to amplify this answer then by asking these questions:

What who?   This should at least enable you to learn who the other members of the committee are.

When who?   An answer to this question should begin to tell you such things as when the committee was chosen and when the regular meetings will be held.

Where who? Here you should learn where the committee will meet, and you may learn other things, such as whether or not the meetings will be open.

Why who?   Pursuing this question may let you learn why particular committee members were chosen.

How who?   An answer here may tell you more about how the committee will proceed with its work.

If you take each of the journalist's questions and compound it by affixing to it each of the other questions, and if you then seek out answers to all of these questions, you ought to have more information than you can handle.

Exercises

1.   See for yourself how much actual information can be produced by asking the journalist's questions. Choose one of the following events that almost everyone has experienced, and recall the incident using as many of the questions and compound questions as are applicable. Follow a list: Who? What? When? Where? Why? How? What who? When who? Where who? Why who? How who? Who what? When what? Where what?

    a. The First Birthday Party I Remember
    b. My First Day on Campus
    c. The Day We Moved
    d. Learning to Drive
    e. A Trip Away from Home
    f. Flunking an Exam
    g. Getting Caught in a Lie

2.   Choose an event that made national news, and write a paper illustrating how it affected you personally. Use the journalist's questions to collect your information and then to organize the paper.

Use the topics as ways of thinking about your subject

Topics in the sense used here is from the Greek *topoi*, which literally means "places." It was used by Aristotle and other classical rhetoricians to signify the "places" from which a speaker or writer derived his argument or material.

The "places" designated topics are ways of thinking common to us all—comparing, defining, looking for causes and effects. These ways of thinking about subjects are particularly useful as aids to begin thinking out a subject. There is no one established list of topics; those below are the most common and useful. You may see, too, that the topics are not only useful in thinking about a subject that you already have in mind, but also in thinking toward a subject when you have none in mind. When you use the topics to think about parts of your own experience, what you learn may help you see a subject.

Definition.   We often try to explain ourselves and to clarify what we are saying by defining key words or words that are subject to misinterpretation. One way, then, to search out the information, insights, and ideas that are important to your subject is to define important words, state the meanings of key phrases, or focus attention on one meaning where several meanings are possible. In a particular sense, everything you write is a definition: an essay, for example, exhibits what a subject *is* as the writer understands it and excludes what is not relevant to the subject.

But there is a pattern you can use in definition. Starting with a *term to be defined*, the first step is to determine the *class* of things that the term to be defined belongs to. The second step, then, is to make clear how the term to be defined can be *differentiated* from other things in the same class.

INSIGHT

Some definitions

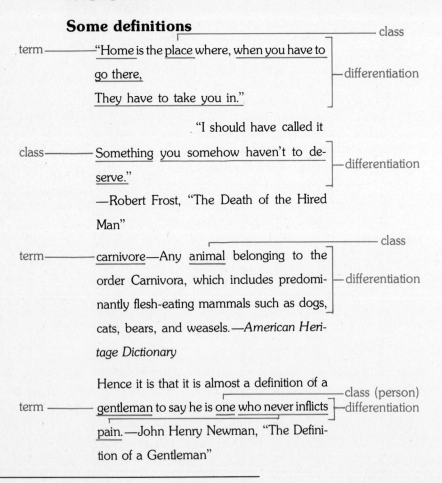

Many terms, of course, can be put into more than one class. A *chair* may be a *piece of furniture*, for example, or an *office* or *position*. One of the ways to learn about your subject is to explore the various ways of classifying it. You may begin to learn more about the subject as you determine which class seems most useful or appropriate to your definition. You can easily see that the second step, differentiating the term from other members of the class, may require more attention.

Defining can be useful to you in several ways. More than anything else, perhaps, defining key words and stipulating your meanings may help you see what there is about your subject that requires explanation and illustration. Suppose, for example, that an interest in architecture has led you to a more particular interest in church architecture, and that this interest, in turn, has led you to explore in a paper the origins of the *cruciform* design in church architecture. Even a cursory examination of your subject matter will lead you to see that some definitions will be useful: *cruciform* requires definition, and so do *nave*, *transept*, *altar*, *lectern*, *clerestory*, and other terms that are likely to occur in your discussion.

Defining can also give you a plan for your work. An entire essay may be a definition, or a section of a longer paper may be a definition. Perhaps an interest in energy resources has led you to read widely in newspapers and magazines about the oil supply in this country; this interest has turned up a number of subjects and terms that you want to know more about, including the *oil depletion allowance*. You don't feel that you can write about energy resources in a short paper, but you do see that the *oil depletion allowance*, important since it is associated with fuel use and fuel resources, could be presented, explained, and judged briefly in a paper. Definition might give you a pattern for your paper: your first task is to show what kind of thing—a tax deduction—the depletion allowance is (put it into a class); your second step is to show the distinguishing feature of the depletion allowance (having shown how it is in the class of tax deductions, show how it is distinct from most tax deductions). This two-step sequence may give you a plan for portions of papers as well.

The second step in definition provides a useful way of organizing a piece of writing. Suppose I start with this definition:

> A *western* is a novel limited to a particular geography for its setting, to a particular history for its place in time, and to a particular sociology for its conflicts and themes, though its total effect may transcend these limitations.

This is a definition: the term to be defined is "western"; it has been assigned to a class, *novel*, and the rest of the sentence seeks to distinguish the western from other kinds of novels. The distinguishing features of the western in the definition above could easily, then, serve as the subjects for sections of the paper:

1. *the western defined*

2. *its limitation to a particular geography*

3. *its limitation to a particular history*

4. *its limitation to a particular sociology*

5. *its capacity to transcend limitations*

With that, we have the beginning of a plan for a paper of five parts—five paragraphs, five sections, five chapters. *Definition*, like the other topics, is useful both in *thinking* about your material and in *writing* about your material.

Exercises

1.   Give some short *personal* definitions of the following terms, using the pattern *term, class, differentiation.*

a.	School advisor	g.	Pet peeve
b.	Put-down	h.	Prejudice
c.	Jogging	i.	Growing pains
d.	Confusion	j.	Busy work
e.	Old age	k.	Sports fan
f.	Dishonesty	l.	Privacy

2.   Choose a broad subject that interests you, such as sexism, science-fiction novels, welfare reform, hockey, and so on, and write a paper on that subject organized in the following manner:

a. A definition: term, class, differentiation

b. Paragraphs suggested by the parts of the definition

Comparison. Comparisons of various kinds show up frequently in your reading; they may be useful in any number of ways as you write or think about writing.

Comparison may help you see a number of things about your subject. It may be useful to explain what your subject is like by showing what it resembles. It may be important to know how your subject fits into analogous relationships. An analogous relationship (an analogy) is a comparison between two different kinds of things that nevertheless have something in common, as in the example from Keats on page 00, where the wonder of the first explorers as they looked out upon the Pacific Ocean is used to suggest Keats' own wonder as he first read Chapman's translation of Homer. It may be necessary to learn how your subject differs from similar things. It may be important to show how your subject differs only in degree from similar things.

Suppose, for example, I decide to write about the western, which I defined above, believing that the western has some cultural importance, but knowing that not everyone reads westerns or sees any importance in them. It might be useful to my account to show the western's similarities (if there are any) to detective stories and to science-fiction stories. I might be able to show some of the importance I see in westerns if I can show that the typical good western is analogous to stories of universal interest in many cultures—journey stories, quest stories, stories of the proving of a hero, and the like. If there are similarities between the western and the detective story, for example, I should also take care to note any differences detected. Or if I find that there are marked similarities between the western and the science-fiction story, I should look to see whether there are differences in degree. One student of westerns remarks that what they all have in common is a frontier. Frontiers are often important to science-fiction stories as well, but the western frontier and the space frontier may differ in degree—both may be alien territory, both may be inhabited by strange new people, but the space frontier may seem all the stranger for its odd vegetation, odd food, odd air.

SOME COMPARISONS

1. A comparison that focuses on similarities between like things:

Dear James:

I have begun this letter five times and torn it up five times. I keep seeing your face, which is also the face of your father and my brother. Like him, you are tough, dark, vulnerable, moody—with a very definite tendency to sound truculent because you want no one to think you are soft. You may be like your grandfather in this, I don't know, but certainly both you and your father resemble him very much physically. Well, he is dead, he never saw you, and he had a terrible life; he was defeated long before he died because, at the bottom of his heart, he really believed what white people said about him. This is one of the reasons that he became so holy. I am sure that your father has told you something about all that. Neither you nor your father exhibit any tendency toward holiness: you really *are* of another era, part of what happened when the Negro left the land and came into what the late E. Franklin Frazier called "the cities of destruction." You can only be destroyed by believing that you really are what the white world calls a *nigger.* I tell you this because I love you, and please don't you ever forget it.—James Baldwin, *The Fire Next Time*

2.   A comparison that focuses on similarities in different kinds of things (analogy):

Much have I traveled in the realms of gold,
And many goodly states and kingdoms seen;
Round many western islands have I been
Which bards in fealty to Apollo hold.
Oft of one wide expanse had I been told
That deep-browed Homer ruled as his demesne;
Yet did I never breathe its pure serene
Till I heard Chapman speak out loud and bold:
Then felt I like some watcher of the skies
When a new planet swims into his ken;
Or like stout Cortez when with eagle eyes
He stared at the Pacific—and all his men
Looked at each other with a wild surmise—
Silent, upon a peak in Darien.
—John Keats, "On First Looking into Chapman's Homer"

3.   A comparison that detects differences:

Oh, when I was in love with you,
    Then I was clean and brave,
And miles around the wonder grew
    How well did I behave.

And now the fancy passes by,
    And nothing will remain,
And miles around they'll say that I
    Am quite myself again.
—A. E. Housman, *A Shropshire Lad*

4.   A comparison that reveals differences in degree among similar things:

Once there was a lot of sound in my grandmother's house, a lot of coming and going, feasting and talk. The summers there were full of excitement and reunion. The Kiowas are a summer people; they abide the cold and keep to themselves, but when the season turns and the land becomes warm and vital they cannot hold still; an old love of going returns upon them. . . . There were frequent prayer meetings, and great nocturnal feasts. When I was a child I played with my cousins outside, where the lamplight fell upon the ground and the singing of the old people rose up around us and carried away into the darkness. There were a lot of good things to eat, a lot of laughter and surprise. And afterwards, when the quiet returned, I lay down with my grandmother and could hear the frogs away by the river and feel the motion of the air.

    Now there is a funeral silence in the rooms, the endless wake of some final word. The walls have closed in upon my grandmother's house. When I returned to it in mourning, I saw for the first time in my life how small it was. . . . —N. Scott Momaday, *The Way to Rainy Mountain*

Exercises

Think about the students on your campus. Have some fun for a while listing the types of students—"the playboy," "the fashion expert," "the dude," "the study freak," "the champion chug-a-lugger." Choose two types that interest you most. Write paragraphs that do each of the following:

1. Compare the similarities of the two types as students.

2. Compare several variations on the dominant characteristics of each type.

3. Compare the two types of students to other kinds of things (vegetables, animals, types of landscapes, etc.).

4. Explain how the two types of students differ.

Cause and effect. If you already have a subject in mind, you may be able to learn more of what can be said about it by exploring cause-effect relationships. The questions below indicate some possible lines of thought:

1. Is the subject interesting or important as the *cause* of some effect?

2. Does seeing the subject as a cause enable you to concentrate on some features of the subject and to minimize others?

3. Are there other causes for the same effect?

4. If the subject is interesting as a cause, can you learn more about it by examining the effect it produces?

5. Is the subject more interesting or more important when considered as an *effect*?

6. If so, what can you learn about the subject by reasoning back to the causes?

7. Is it possible to think of the subject as both a cause and an effect?

Cause and effect relationships, like definition and comparison, are ways of thinking that come to us early and stay with us. We want to know what things are and what they are like, and once we see that something exists, we want to know why and what becomes of it.

But there are some precautions we need to remember when we are trying to think out relationships between causes and effects. It can be tempting to make things too simple, to find a single cause to match each single effect. That would be tidy, but it might not be realistic. A given effect *might* have a number of possible causes. If a particular class has for weeks in a row a high number of absences, I might be tempted to blame all the absences on simple student laziness, but in all likelihood a number of possible causes could be at work—my ineptitude as a teacher, exorbitant demands being made by some other teacher, simple laziness, the hour at which the class is held, and so on. To be fair and honest I should try to find the cause or causes at work in each student's case. Even then, some care and deliberation would be necessary. If I am going to say that A caused B, I should first take care to accumulate enough evidence and experience to know that A *can* produce B. A malfunctioning alarm clock *can* be a cause of continued absences from a class. So can simple laziness, but laziness is probably not an adequate cause for *continued* absences.

If I am going to assign a cause for a particular effect, I also should keep clearly in mind the possibility that there are other adequate causes. And I should consider whether the conditions are right for the cause I have singled out to produce the effect in question. The butler may be capable of killing the strange visitor at the country estate, and he may have sufficient motive, but the circumstances have to be such as to give him the opportunity to do murder.

SOME EXAMPLES OF CAUSE AND EFFECT

effect————————Semantic aphasia is that numbness of
ear, mind and heart—that tone deafness to
the very meaning of language—which re-
sults from the habitual and prolonged abuse ————cause
of words. As an isolated phenomenon, it can
be amusing if not downright irritating. But
when it becomes epidemic, it signals a disas-
cause————————trous decline in the skills of communication,
to that mumbling low point where language ———— effect
does almost the opposite of what it was
created for. With frightening perversity—the

evidence mounts daily—words now seem to cut off and isolate, to cause more misunderstanding than they prevent.—Melvin Maddocks, "The Limitations of Language"

effect —— Here dead lie we because we did not choose
To live and shame the land from which we ├———cause
sprung.
Life, to be sure, isn't much to lose,
But young men think it is, and we were young.

—A. E. Housman, *More Poems*

Today there is a peculiarly modern reward that the avant-garde artist can give his benefactor: namely, the feeling that he, like his mate the artist, is separate from and aloof from the bourgeoisie, the middle classes . . . the feeling that he may be *from* the middle class but he is no longer *in* it . . . the feeling ├——— effect that he is a fellow soldier, or at least an aide-de-camp or an honorary cong guerrilla in the vanguard march through the land of the philistines. This is a peculiarly modern need and a peculiarly modern kind of salvation
cause —— (from the sin of Too Much Money) and something quite common among the well-to-do all over the West, in Rome and Milan as well as New York. That is why collecting contemporary art, the leading edge, the latest thing, warm and wet from the Loft, appeals specifically to those who feel most

effect —

uneasy about their own commercial wealth
. . . See? I'm not like *them*—those Jaycees,
those United Fund chairmen, those Young
Presidents, those mindless New York A.C.
goyisheh hog-jowled, stripe-tied goddamn-
good-to-see-you-you-old-bastard-you oys-
ter-bar trenchermen . . . Avant-garde art,
more than any other, takes the Mammon
and the Moloch out of money, puts Levi's,
turtlenecks, muttonchops, and other mantles
and laurels of bohemian grace upon it.

effect —

That is why collectors today not only
seek out the company of, but also want to
hang out amidst, lollygag around with, and
enter into the milieu of . . . the artists they
patronize. They *want* to climb those vertigin-
ous loft building stairs on Howard Street that
go up five flights without a single turn or
bend—*straight up!* like something out of a
casebook dream—to wind up with their
hearts ricocheting around in their rib cages
with tachycardia from the exertion mainly
but also from the anticipation that just beyond this door at the top . . . in this loft . . . lie
the real goods . . . paintings, sculptures that
are indisputably part of the new movement,
the new *école*, the new wave . . . something
unshrinkable, chipsy, pure cong, bour-
geois-proof. —Tom Wolfe, *The Painted Word*

Exercise

Choose a situation that a college student might experience—failing an exam, running out of money, fighting with a roommate over responsibilities, disillusionment with the college—and make a list of the possible causes of that situation. Write four paragraphs from four letters in which you pretend to be the student and explain the cause of the situation to the following: your parents, your best high-school friend who attends another college, your campus advisor, your diary. Try to change your tone each time to fit the receiver of the letter.

Antecedent and consequence.   Remember that the aim in using the topics is to learn all that can be said about your subject. One way to explore all that your subject contains is to inquire *what went before* and *what follows*. This is a kind of inquiry and thinking (closely related to cause and effect study) that we often practice. "What's going to happen if we submit this petition?" we ask ourselves. "What will he do if we don't go to class?" "Why did he get so mad?—we weren't doing anything." The topic of antecedent and consequence asks that you do deliberately what you often do naturally—ask where something came from, and ask where it is going. If, for example, you want to explore what advertising does, one way to learn about your subject is to ask, "What will happen if someone takes the advertisements in this magazine seriously?" Another way would be to ask, "What led an advertiser to produce this kind of advertisement?"

SOME EXAMPLES OF ANTECEDENT AND CONSEQUENCE

In the first example below, Commager alludes to the consequence when a government or society silences certain ideas.

If we are to have the kind of society where thought and expression are free, we must take our chances on some thoughts being, in the words of Justice Holmes, "loathsome and fraught with death." Nor is the danger really a desperate one. Those who disagree with the loathsome thoughts are equally free to express thoughts that are beautiful.

Let us not suppose that all this is but a matter of theory. We have ample evidence, in our own history, and in the history of other nations, of what happens when government or society silences, by whatever means, dangerous or loathsome ideas. And we know, too, that ideas which one generation thinks dangerous are regarded by the next as salutary; ideas which one society thinks loathsome are accepted by another as noble.—Henry Steele Commager, "The Nature of Academic Freedom"

Old Man Warner, one of the characters who speaks in the passage below, predicts dire consequences that follow upon certain antecedents: If people give up the lottery, he says (antecedent), then society will regress (consequence).

"They do say," Mr. Adams said to Old Man Warner, who stood next to him, "that over in the north village they're talking of giving up the lottery."

Old Man Warner snorted. "Pack of crazy fools," he said. "Listening to the young folks, nothing's good enough for *them.* Next thing you know, they'll be wanting to go back to living in caves, nobody work any more, live *that* way for a while. Used to be a saying about 'Lottery in June, corn be heavy soon.' First thing you know, we'd all be eating stewed chickweed and acorns. There's *always* been a lottery," he added petulantly. "Bad enough to see young Joe Summers up there joking with everybody."

"Some places have already quit lotteries," Mrs. Adams said.

"Nothing but trouble in *that*," Old Man Warner said stoutly. "Pack of young fools."—Shirley Jackson, "The Lottery"

What antecedents and their consequences are predicted in the following example?

Certainly what we need most is deglomeration of people. Excessive pollution of air as well as of water can deglomerate, even decimate, cities unhealthily crowded with men and cars. But there must be more pleasant ways.

One way less unpleasant than mass biocide by gas asphyxiation would be to lean a trifle harder on that phase of research seeking to produce a combustion engine that completely combusts its fuel and emits a minimum of poisons. Our present combustion engines waste oceans of fuel every year. Can the gas turbine engine be perfected? Chrysler's directional turbine nozzle is a smart advance in fuel efficiency and is hopeful. But why, ask the automobile industry's Members of the Board behind closed doors, throw in a wrench when you've got such a good thing going? No reason at all.

But the White House has given out a hint that a reason may be made. The President's Science Advisory Committee, newly alarmed about the leads and additives that have pushed air pollution to critically high levels, has been mumbling (not too indistinctly) about tighter federal controls under a sort of Food and Drug Administration type setup. They are going so far as to suggest that the time is coming "when it will be necessary to get rid of the present engine and fuels altogether." They have asked automakers seriously to "mull the idea of scrapping present engines and powering cars with non-toxic fuel cells instead."

This is no small request. Fuel cells, while they would completely do away with auto smog and all its train of miseries, are rather far from perfection; indeed, they are far from any practical application. The fact is, the condition of our cities' air is so bad we cannot afford to wait for them. What, then?

Since most families have two cars already it is suggested that one of them be a small electric cart for city driving and the other a high-powered machine for the road. No, the electric cart will not leap forward like a rocket at the green light, but consider this: No more poisonous vapors, odors, smoke clouds, corrosion, gluey oils, inflammatory gasoline; accidents cut to a tenth, less noise, easier parking, the innovation of a relaxed kind of driving (not to mention the cut in incidence of lung cancer, bronchitis, heart conditions, and smarting eyes).—Robert Rienow and Leona Train Rienow, *Moment in the Sun*

Exercise

Explore the antecedents and consequences (both positive and negative) of the following propositions:

a. A student committee should have the final say in censorship of student publications.
b. Smoking should be banned in public places.
c. Advertising that is aimed solely at children should be removed from television.
d. If people want to work, the government should provide jobs for them.

Contraries and contradictions.   With some kinds of subjects, particularly those that are controversial, you may find it useful to explore contrary propositions or contradictory propositions. You may get interested in some subjects because they exist side by side with contraries or contradictions and because you've been involved in the arguments that resulted.

Contrary propositions involve incompatible things of the same kind. If you argue that it is good for journalists to be free to protect their sources of information, while a friend says that it is bad for them to do so, the two of you have made contrary propositions. If you argue that it is fitting for dormitories to be open, with no restrictive hours or rules, while the dean of students says that it is harmful for dormitories to be open, the two of you have made contrary propositions.

Contradictory propositions are reversals of each other, as when, for example, you argue that excessive dieting is harmful while a friend argues that excessive dieting is *not* harmful. At issue in contradictions is the principle that a thing cannot simultaneously both be and not be.

SOME CONTRARIES AND CONTRADICTIONS

The trumpeting voice of the wilderness lover is heard at great distances these days. He is apt to be a perfectly decent person, if hysterical. And the causes which excite him so are generally worthy. Who can really find a harsh word for him as he strives to save Lake Erie from the sewers of Cleveland, save the redwoods from the California highway engineers, save the giant rhinoceros from the Somali tribesmen who kill those noble beasts to powder their horns into what they fondly imagine is a wonder-working aphrodisiac?

Worthy causes, indeed, but why do those who espouse them have to be so shrill and intolerant and sanctimonious? What right do they have to insinuate that anyone who does not share their passion for the whooping crane is a Philistine and a slob? From the gibberish they talk, you would think the only way to save the bald eagle is to dethrone human reason.

I would like to ask what seems to me an eminently reasonable question: *Why shouldn't we spoil the wilderness?*—Robert Wernick, "Let's Spoil the Wilderness"

The contradictory proposition is, of course, "Why should we spoil the universe?"

The lack of visual training in the sciences and technology on the one hand and the artist's neglect of, or even contempt for, the beautiful and vital task of making the world of facts visible to the enquiring mind, strikes me, by the way, as a much more serious ailment of our civilization than the "cultural divide" to which C. P. Snow drew so much public attention some time ago. He complained that scientists do not read good literature and writers know nothing about science. Perhaps this is so, but the complaint is superficial. It would seem that a person is "well rounded" not simply when he has a bit of everything but when he applies to everything he does the integrated whole of all his mental powers. Snow's suggestion that "the clashing point" of science and art "ought to produce creative chances" seems to ignore the fundamental kinship of the two. A scientist may well be a connoisseur of Wallace Stevens or Samuel Beckett, but his training may have failed nevertheless to let him use, in his own best professional thinking, the perceptual imagination on which those writers rely. And a painter may read books on biology or physics with profit and yet not use his intelligence in his painting. The estrangement is of a much more fundamental nature.—Rudolf Arnheim, *Visual Thinking*

The author of this passage assumes that the ways of thinking of the artist and the scientist represent contrary natures.

While contraries and contradictions may come ready-made from arguments and controversies you have been involved in, you may learn more about your subject if you set out deliberately to locate contrary propositions and contradictory propositions. Knowing what can be *opposed* to your subject, in other words, may help you know your subject.

And if you write a paper about a controversial subject, you will have to acknowledge and answer contraries and contradictions (see Chapter 15, Arguments).

Exercise

Write a dialogue between yourself and a friend about one of the following subjects, or one of your own choosing, in which you illustrate the contrary or contradictory propositions through your friend's conversation.

    a. Marijuana laws
    b. Cohabitation before marriage
    c. The value of television
    d. School spirit
    e. Living off campus
    f. The value of grades

Testimony.   Another way of thinking about your subject is to seek out usable evidence about it—the testimony of authorities, available factual and statistical information, laws, precedents, and the like. For further discussion of this avenue of thought, see "Using Available Resources" (p. 47).

Try some simple linkages

Almost any subject has more in it, more relationships, implications, and connections, than we could ever write about, but we don't always know that from the first. Oftener than not, we have to sit and doodle and scratch out trial notes, trying to see what can be said, waiting for some kind of inspiration. Instead of waiting around and hoping that you'll think of something to say, try connecting your subject with other things in the relationships below suggested by W. Ross Winterowd. As you do, you may begin to see the context your subject fits into more clearly and to learn some of the useful directions you can go with it.

Ask what can be linked to your subject by **and.**   If you try to answer this question, you should find out more about your subject by learning what other things are similar to it, what other things exist alongside it, what other things are coordinate with it. ("Many shopping centers have new kinds of small craft shops *and* . . . ." "The extracurricular programs at this university are inadequate and . . . .") These relationships may also be expressed by linking your subject with something else through words such as *furthermore, in addition, too, also, again.*

Ask what can be linked to your subject by but.   Answers to this question should lead you to things that occur as exceptions to your subject and to particular observations about your subject, especially observations that take notice of unusual or contrasting features ("Laura is a good roommate, *but* . . . ." "The lakeside was placid in approaching twilight, *but* . . . ."). Similar relationships can be expressed with words like *yet, however, on the other hand,* and others.

Ask what can be linked to your subject by for.   When you can connect your subject to something else by *for,* you are ordinarily naming some kind of causal relationship where the thing you have linked to your subject is seen as a cause leading to your subject ("Catherine will be a good dormitory counselor, *for* . . . ," where what follows *for* is a list of qualities she has that make her suitable for the work).

Ask what can be linked to your subject by so.   In an uncomplicated statement such as, "I am hungry, so I am going to go ahead and eat right now," the part of the sentence that follows *so* may be seen as a conclusion or as a result of what goes before *so.* If you can link other things to your subject by *so,* it should help you to see what kinds of consequences attach to your subject. Similar relationships can be expressed in words like *therefore, thus, for this reason,* and others.

Ask what can be linked to your subject by or.   This question should lead you to see alternatives that can be set alongside your subject. It may be that you will be able to write an entire paper consisting of *or* linkages, where your paper is an exploration of the alternatives available in a particular situation. ("If I move off campus, I'll have to find someone to share apartment costs, *or* . . . .") Or, having named two or three likely alternatives, you may want to give the rest of the paper over to full exploration of each one of them so that you can arrive at a reasonable choice.

Ask what can be linked to your subject by a colon.   In a sentence such as this one, "It's just a dormitory room: mostly clutter, some plain trash, twenty-five posters, piles of books and papers, a coffee pot, two beds almost hidden, and yesterday's clothes," the part of the sentence that follows the colon is a listing of things that are included in what goes before the colon. Stating your subject simply and putting a colon after it gives you a reason to name all the things your subject includes. Your whole paper might consist of such a listing. You might make such a list in order to explore each element more fully. You might make a list in order to isolate one or two important elements for discussion.

Exercise

Five statements are given below. Assume that each statement identifies a subject you might work with. Then use the linkages shown above to see what might be said about each of the subjects. Wherever possible, use the linkages not only to determine what might be said, but also to predict the organization of your paper.

1. Science fiction is an important form of literature.

2. My form of humor is slightly bizarre.

3. I am still unsettled as to what my career goals will be.

4. Differences between generations are inevitable.

5. High-school courses of study do not always prepare students for the challenges ahead.

Write a paper using one of the subjects and its linkages.

USING AVAILABLE RESOURCES

If you are going to write well, you must take pleasure in yourself as a source of information, ideas, and insights for other people. Enjoy yourself as someone who can say things to others that will be useful, informative, entertaining, even corrective. You have a bank of *internal resources* available—your own ways of thinking, your own experiences, your own feelings, your own thoughts that run quietly through your mind, your own accumulated information. The purpose of this chapter has been to suggest ways for you to use your own internal resources. The various suggestions for finding subjects and the various suggestions for making the most of subjects once you have found them—the journalist's questions, the topics, the linkages—are not ways in which you *must* think. They are suggested ways of thinking that you can rely on if you need to, all of them meant to remind you of what you already know.

But you're not limited to what you already know. You have access to a wide variety of *external resources*—books, magazines, newspapers, radio, television, cinema, conversation, interviews, laws, precedents, the testimony and advice of people who have experienced what you are interested in learning about. Sometimes your exploration of a subject will show you that there are things you don't know about it. In that case, go find out. Treat every paper you write as if it might have to become a research paper. Accept as a normal part of the writing process the necessity of learning something about your subject that you don't already know. Chapter 17, on documentation, will show you, if you don't already know, how to give credit to external resources that you use, how to incorporate things other people have said into the text of your own paper, how and when to use notes, and how to prepare a bibliography, should that be necessary.

Exercises

1.   Read the student essay below and determine how it might be revised. Use the journalist's questions, the topics, and the linkages suggested above to see how the essay might be amplified or otherwise altered. Show what possible uses might be made, too, of external resources.

But I Don't Want Any Wild Hickory Nuts

Every time I go to the grocery store I am amazed by the myriads of goods which flaunt their closeness to nature. Their labels explode with bright block letters informing me that the product has 100% natural grains with no artificial preservatives added. But what if I don't like natural foods? I may be one of those rare oddballs who like food with plenty of artificial flavor, artificial color, and artificial preservatives. How many products have you seen advertising artificial preservatives? Sometimes I feel as though Madison Avenue has added an eleventh commandment— "Thou shall desire none other than natural foods."

My life is intimately associated with nonnatural foods. For example, I prefer instant orange juice to real orange juice any day. When I get up in the morning, I don't feel like slicing an orange, grating it up, and putting it in a blender. It is a lot easier to dissolve a spoonful of Tang in a glass of water. I even think Tang tastes better. Another example is that of oatmeal. Natural oatmeal tastes terrible. The oatmeal I eat has enough maple and brown sugar flavoring to cover nature's naturally repulsive taste. There are many cases in my diet where I believe man has improved on nature.

My point is simply that artificial foods are not inherently evil. I have nothing against natural foods. I simply represent a large part of the population who dislike the taste of wild hickory nuts and who wonder why the advertising industry represents only the back-to-nature movement.

a. Identify the location of the answers to the journalist's questions.
b. Which of the topics are at work in the paragraph?
c. Can you restate the author's thesis as a linkage sentence?

2.   Examine the following advertisements and determine how each uses one or more of the topics. Then use any of the methods of thinking about subjects suggested here and determine what kind of response might be made to each advertisement.

If a singer sounds nasal on these, she probably has a cold. Every three-way speaker tries to give you the most accurate reproduction of sound.

But most can't do it, for a very simple reason: their mid-range speakers are remarkably inefficient. And since 90% of the sound you hear is in the mid-range, those inefficient speakers make singers sound slightly nasal and applause sound like a rainfall.—An ad for stereo speakers

Uncomfortable thought: Your concert ticket pays for less than half a seat. Admission charges to any form of the visual or performing arts usually pays for less than half the operating costs.

The difference between admission charges and operating costs is an income gap—bridged by contributions.

Without such contributions, many of us couldn't afford to attend. It would mean a less stimulating, less entertaining, narrower world for many people.

Please support the arts financially if you can. But there are other ways you can help. In fund-raising activities. In urging support by governments. By sponsoring local art groups. By underwriting scholarships for talented young people. Do more than be part of the audience. Please be a patron, too.

Support the arts.—Business Committee for the Arts, Inc.

Many try, but none succeed. You just can't copy a true original. Because it's rare.—A scotch ad

*Arts and sciences are not cast in a mould, but are found
and perfected by degrees, by often handling and polishing,
as bears lick their cubs into shape.*

Michel Montaigne

How do I know what I mean till I see what I say?

E. M. Forster

3

Claiming a Subject

The first two chapters suggested some ways of searching for subjects and exploring their possibilities. This chapter is about a further stage in the process of writing:

1. determining what you believe should be said, what your purpose is, and understanding your point of view (p. 51), and

2. helping your readers see your purpose and point of view (p. 58).

You've probably seen western movies or television programs in which a hopeful gold miner *stakes a claim*, or *claims* a promising piece of land to prospect for ore. When that happened, the gold miner was giving public notice that the land in question was his or hers to keep and dig and grow rich on. In the earlier part of the twentieth century in some parts of the United States, young people used the word *claim* to indicate romantic relationships of more than momentary duration. A young man or boy *claimed* a young woman or girl; a young woman or girl *claimed* a young man or boy. That was supposed to signify that the two belonged to each other, at least romantically. To *claim* a young person of the other sex was to give public notice of at least temporary fidelity and availability.

It's not enough just to find and explore a subject. You have to *claim* it, make it yours, and give public notice that you have made it yours. It is possible to know a large number of things about a subject and still not know what you are going to write. You might, for example, with a mild, general interest in the political beliefs and activities of college students, already know some things to say on the topic, and you might find other things to say by using some of the searching strategies and possibilities suggested in the first two chapters. But knowing a number of things that might be said about a given subject is not the same thing as being ready to write about it.

You are closing in on a subject when you are able to begin *composing* what you know, putting things together, sorting, arranging, discarding some things, saving others for special attention. On any topic there are a number of things that *might* be said; as you begin to compose your thoughts, you begin to see which of them *must* be said. Writing does set some obligations upon us: to treat the subject fairly, to deal fairly with an audience, and to deal fairly with ourselves. The hope of meeting these expectations may help you begin to see which of the things that can be said, should be said.

In other words, it is usually not enough simply to have a topic in mind and a pile of things that can be said about it. Most of us have probably written with no more preparation than that; when we do, we usually sound disorganized or uncertain or uninvolved. A subject starts taking shape for us when we can begin to see what it *means* to us, when we can begin to see what writing about the subject is *for*, and when we can begin to understand the relationships that exist among a writer, a subject, and an audience.

DISCOVERING A PURPOSE AND A POINT OF VIEW

After a while, if you put your mind to it, you can learn where to put commas and how to make subjects and their verbs agree. And once you learn, those chores usually don't have to be done again. But you may have to wrestle with yourself for a subject every time you write anything, in school or later. Locating your subject is not a simple process, and it cannot be done once and then put away. Since the circumstances in which you write will never be the same twice, you're likely to have to think your way through to a subject every time you write—though there are times, fortunately, when you will be ready to write about a particular subject, and you will already know what needs to be said.

Getting a subject clearly in mind isn't just a matter of selecting one item out of a list of twenty-three, or of finding most of the things that could possibly be said about that one item. If you have only an item in mind, together with a list of things to say about it, you don't have a direction, a reason for writing, a point to make.

Read the student essay below; the writer hasn't yet found a purpose or direction. Compare that essay with the opening paragraphs on page 54, where each writer makes clear at the outset the purpose of the essay.

[Untitled]

Perhaps the central and foremost feature which distinguishes man as being unique in the animal kingdom is his inherent ability to *reason*. He does not acquire *this ability* at some point during his lifetime, nor does he gradually develop *it* as he grows older, although he unconsciously sharpens his *reasoning* as he daily encounters new experiences and situations which may teach him how to use *the ability*. The *sense* is inborn, a gift of nature's mysterious evolutionary process.

It is clear in the first paragraph that the author wants to talk about reason, described as an inborn gift that can be sharpened with use. The italicized words show that the author keeps reason at the center of attention. It is not yet clear why the author wants to talk about reason; nothing predicts a point to be made.

One of the prime *characteristics* of this *gift* is man's *tendency* to question. In our *society*, most people reach a *period* in their lives when they begin to seek their own *identity*. They question their *function*, *purpose*, and the very *meaning* of their *existence*. The *process* also includes an *examination* of their *beliefs*, the *beliefs* of their parents, friends, and all those people who have contributed in

A tendency to question, the author says, is associated with reason. If a questioning attitude is to be the primary subject, as the length of the second paragraph indicates, then the questioning attitude deserves a fuller explanation, and its connection with reason needs clearer discussion (other things can give rise to questioning—impulse, emotional response, stubbornness, for example). Attention in this

some way to shaping their lives and their *personalities*. The *individual* must then decide if he will blindly accept those *ideals* and moral *standards* or if he will follow his *sense* of questioning in a *search* for true and meaningful *identity*. For those who choose the latter *option*, the *quest* for *enlightenment* is a tedious and frustrating *process*. In contrast, however, those who never question and who never seek a higher *level* of *awareness* are perhaps the saddest *failures* of our *society*. Each believes that he has the answer. His religious *sect* or *group* is right, and he refuses to listen to the rest of *society*. This *type* of *attitude* only serves to confuse the questioner, often making him feel guilty, but at the same time resulting in still more *uncertainties*. The *process* creates a *cycle*, a never-ending *cycle*. Eventually, the *cycle* does break. After collecting and formulating a considerable *amount* of *data*, the *individual* must employ his *reason*. Usually he will reach a satisfying *conclusion*. Some, however, never do. Their *life* is a continuous *series* of *questions*, *answers*, and more *questions*. We have come to recognize these people as the great philosophers of our *society*.

paragraph is divided—six sentences are about the questioner, three are about those who don't question, four are about the cycle of questioning, and the last three are about philosophers, who have not previously been mentioned.

We can sense a process of development in what the author says. Presumably reason, as a base for living, gives rise to a process of questioning; in the process of questioning there is a cycle of growth, best illustrated by philosophers. However, the author doesn't say that there is a process of development. Instead, the process splinters into separate parts. Reason attracts attention because it's mentioned first. Philosophers attract attention because they're mentioned last. The questioning process attracts attention because it gets most of the space. We do not learn what is at stake here. We do not see what has made reason, or questioning, or philosophers an issue to write about.

The italicized words in the second paragraph give us a signal of what has happened in this short essay. The frequency of these abstract words suggests that the author has not yet discovered his specific, individualized way of thinking about the subject, or of treating the subject. As a consequence, there is no sign of a clear, personal meaning or of a particular purpose in the essay. Anyone could have written this; it has no marks of identity on it.

SOME SIGNS OF PURPOSE AND DIRECTION

Given below are the openings of six pieces of writing. Notice the various ways in which the authors indicate their purpose and direction.

1.   Our principal enemies of the True Word are two: the Idle Word and the Black Magician.—W. S. Auden, "The Real World"

This is the first sentence of Auden's essay. He has already decided what is at stake. As the essay shows, Auden is convinced that our language is in danger of being corrupted, especially by those who use it trivially (the Idle Word) and by those who use it to deceive and dominate (the Black Magician). We know from this first sentence that he is not going to discuss these two casually and generally: they are "enemies of the True Word" and cannot be let off so easily.

2.   The house in which I live is what some people would call "shut in." It is on a not much traveled road near the top of a hill, but there are higher hills round about and there is not much "view."

That is the way I like it, and this, I suppose, is one of the signs that I belong to that class called introverts, of whom the wake-up-and-live psychologists so sharply disapprove. Many of us, however, are not particularly sorry for ourselves, and some of these psychologists would be surprised at how much satisfaction we take in things which would not suit them at all. We do not mind being shut in if we can choose the people and the things we are shut in with.

Too long a view in either time or space makes people miss a great deal that is close at hand, and it is my experience that those who are quickly bored in the country are usually those who lack "the microscopic eye," those to whom "nature" means "scenery," and "scenery" means only "views." . . . —Joseph Wood Krutch, "The Microscopic Eye"

In two and a half paragraphs Krutch sets a scene (his "shut in" house and its environs), shows us that he has particular views and values, and indicates a direction he is going to take: he disapproves of "Too long a view," and seems intent on celebrating "the microscopic eye" and what it reveals.

3.   "Someday, maybe," Erik Erikson has written, "there will exist a well-informed, well-considered and yet fervent public conviction that the most deadly of all possible sins is the mutilation of a child's spirit."

If that day ever comes, American educators may be able to reflect with some horror upon the attitudes and procedures that have been allowed to flourish within a great many urban public schools.—Jonathan Kozol, *Death at an Early Age*

No commentary seems necessary. There is little doubt that Kozol plans to attack "attitudes and procedures" in some public schools that he thinks mutilate a child's spirit.

4. Since dawn I had climbed up and down the steep mountain slopes and pushed my way through the dense valley forests. Again and again I had stopped to listen, or to gaze through binoculars at the surrounding countryside. Yet I had neither heard nor seen a single chimpanzee, and now it was already five o'clock. In two hours darkness would fall over the rugged terrain of the Gombe Stream Chimpanzee Reserve. I settled down at my favorite vantage point, the Peak, hoping that at least I might see a chimpanzee make his nest for the night before I had to stop work for the day.—Jane Van Lawick-Goodall, *In the Shadow of Man*

A real person doing particular things in particular places is speaking to us here, and we know that the writer is recording a particular vigil that had a particular purpose.

5. Into each life, it is said, some rain must fall. Some people have bad horoscopes, others take tips on the stock market. McNamara created the TFX and the Edsel. Churches possess the real world. But Indians have been cursed above all other people in history. Indians have anthropologists.—Vine Deloria, Jr., *Custer Died for Your Sins*

It's pretty plain that the author here has something particular in mind, and it looks as if the anthropologists will not escape.

6. The domestic farm industry is one of the most price-competitive industries as exemplified by the incredible lack of return on the invested dollar. It is a sorrowful state when the sale price of agricultural production does not even meet the farmer's variable costs, far from meeting his fixed costs. The American farm industry feeds over 220 million domestically and many more abroad. Notably, food plays a comparatively small part in the total family expenditure in the United States—only 14%—a deceptively high percentage when contrasted to total farm revenue. There seems to be a great imbalance somewhere. Farmers are not even recovering their variable costs and, yet, the average family spends about 14% of their income to be fed. Where is all the profit going? All the profit, now, goes to the middleman. Unionized labor is starving farmers!—A student paragraph

The author of this paragraph leaves no doubt as to where he stands, and it looks as if he intends to use factual background information to support his argument.

Exercises

1. Write out answers to the following questions about the student essay on page 52:
    a. What sort of person is the author?
    b. What is your impression of the purpose of the piece?
    c. What is your overall impression of the essay?

2.   Reread the student essay on page 52 and make a list of the questions raised in your mind but left unanswered by the essay.

3.   Indicate the purpose and direction suggested to you by the following pieces of writing:

> Two widely divergent but interrelated experiences, psychoanalysis and work as an anthropologist, have led me to the belief that in his strivings for order, Western man has created chaos by denying that part of his self that integrates while enshrining the parts that fragment experience. These examinations of man's psyche have also convinced me that: the natural act of thinking is greatly modified by culture; Western man uses only a small fraction of his mental capabilities; there are many different and legitimate ways of thinking; we in the West value one of these ways above all others—the one we call "logic," a linear system that has been with us since Socrates.—Edward T. Hall, *Beyond Culture*

> There are millions of people who groan when they hear a pun. It is a standard response, and my impression is that they are simply envious or bent on denying themselves one of the delights that language offers.—Edwin Newman, *Strictly Speaking*

> For the last few years I've noticed two trends in literature about the future. Journals like *Audubon Magazine*, *Sierra Club Bulletin*, and *Cry California* are generally concerned about imminent ecological disaster—the death of canyons and valleys, the end of whales, big cats, eagles, falcons, pelicans, and even man. The magazines popularizing science, such as *Popular Science* and *Popular Mechanics*, speak of the technological Utopia of the future—a television screen attached to every telephone, a helicopter on every rooftop, and sleek supersonic transports for the fortunate few within them who cannot hear their sonic boom. The two kinds of journal seem oblivious of each other and mutually exclusive. Yet there is a connection: The more we strive to reach the popular science future, the more likely we are to achieve the ecological disaster.—Garrett De Bell, *The Environmental Handbook*

You shouldn't expect *every* writer to tell you precisely what his or her purpose is in the first two paragraphs. You shouldn't feel obliged yourself to make a clear statement of purpose in your opening sentences. You certainly shouldn't conclude that it is necessary to raise a flag next to any statement of purpose, or to say, "My purpose is to. . . ." When the subject and the situation make it possible and desirable for you to declare your purpose clearly and quickly, do so. But don't be afraid to work your way slowly toward a clear grasp of your purpose. Sometimes a purpose emerges in the process of writing, and is to be pursued rather than stated.

In the essay opening shown below the author moves slowly into the discussion of his subject, an account of his visit to and meditations upon the 1939 World's Fair. Later in the essay the author remarks that "I made a few notes at the Fair, a few hints of what you may expect of Tomorrow, its appointments, its characteristics," and we learn that he is both entertained and a little doubtful as he sees the Fair's glimpses of a promised future. But as the essay opens, the author does not assert a purpose or a thesis; instead he moves toward his subject and purpose and we are able to see him as a thoughtful, observant spectator:

> I wasn't really prepared for the World's Fair last week, and it certainly wasn't prepared for me. Between the two of us there was considerable of a mixup.
>
> The truth is that my ethmoid sinuses broke down on the eve of Fair Day, and this meant I had to visit the Fair carrying a box of Kleenex concealed in a copy of the *Herald Tribune*. When you can't breathe through your nose, Tomorrow seems strangely like the day before yesterday. The Fair, on its part, was having trouble too. It couldn't find its collar button. Our mutual discomfort established a rich bond of friendship between us, and I realize that the World's Fair and myself actually both need the same thing—a nice warm day.
>
> The road to Tomorrow leads through the chimney pots of Queens. It is a long, familiar journey, through Mulsified Shampoo and Mobilgas, through Bliss Street, Kix, Astring-O-Sol, and the Majestic Auto Seat Covers. It winds through Textene, Blue Jay Corn Plasters; through Musterole and the delicate pink blossoms on the fruit trees in the ever-hopeful back yards of a populous borough, past Zemo, Alka-Seltzer, Baby Ruth, past Iodent and the Fidelity National Bank, by trusses, belts, and the clothes that fly bravely on the line under the trees with the new little green leaves in Queens' incomparable springtime. Suddenly you see the first intimation of the future. . . .—E. B. White, "The World of Tomorrow"

Sometimes when you are writing—in an essay examination, for example, or a laboratory report, or a set of instructions, or a letter of complaint—you may want to announce your purpose as quickly and as forthrightly as possible. In such kinds of writing, you are usually trying to represent something outside yourself, to describe, to report, or to map out something "out there," not "in here." When that is your intention, whatever your specific purpose is, then directness, brevity, and exactness are appropriate qualities. The selections from Auden, Kozol, and the others quoted above illustrate this kind of writing. They have made an accounting of some part of experience and have charted it out plainly to show to us.

But in other kinds of writing—the essay by E. B. White is an example—you will be more interested in thinking out a subject in the company of an audience, working your way toward a point and a purpose. E. B. White is not trying to represent the World's Fair accurately; he is thinking about what he saw and did. In this kind of writing, directness, brevity, and exactness are not necessarily primary virtues—more appropriate qualities may be adventurousness and a willingness to meditate and even to appear to ramble.

Exercise

Below are some openers of paragraphs. Analyze the commitment each makes to the reader; that is, based upon the one sentence, what course could a reader legitimately expect the writer to pursue?

1.   There was once a time in my life when a special friend completely dominated me, causing me to mimic her speech, walk, slang words, and even clothes.

2.   I have always been the kind of person who is patient in situations when other persons would explode.

3.   Many things happen in a week of one's life.

4.   Crossing the street may be a routine event for adults, but to a small child it can be an intoxicating experience.

5.   Many girls are talked into abortion as an alternative to having a baby.

6.   Of all the packages to be opened at Christmas, the largest one is always the most intriguing.

7.   The work of Jasper Johns receives highly favorable critical comment.

8.   Helen Keller seemed to sense that her brain had a latent capacity for language.

HELPING READERS SEE YOUR PURPOSE

However you proceed, remember that when you give what you have written to some reader, the written words are all that the reader will have. The words on the page are your only testimony to the reader. They must reveal the subject and the way you think about it to a reader who can't see or hear you. A reader may find it easier to read and to believe what you have written if you give him some tracks to follow. A purpose announced early and followed diligently gives a clear set of tracks.

Remember that you are not a conduit, but a human being. A *conduit* is a natural or artificial channel (a pipe, for example) through which something (water or gas, for example) is conveyed. If you are a conduit, it's probably all right just to let information, ideas, and observations flow through you onto the page from somewhere else, untouched, unchanged, unassimilated. But you're not a conduit. You think about things, or if you don't, you can. You arrange things in your mind, though sometimes you aren't fully aware that you have arranged things. You decide and choose. You'd probably not be hesitant about claiming your bicycle or your car or your home if somebody else proposed to declare ownership. Claim what's in your own mind. Announce your decisions and judgments. Don't be afraid of your own point of view.

No one can tell you precisely how to do these things; you can learn, however, by watching what other writers do. Browse through this book—not just this chapter—and look at all the examples. See how other writers reveal their purposes and notice whether or not they stick to their purpose. Study the examples to see how other writers reveal the direction they're moving in, with or without a plainly stated purpose. Find out how other writers let readers know how they look at things. How do other writers reveal or declare where they are standing, what point of view they have taken toward their experience? Notice the many ways the author of this example reveals his purpose and claims his subject:

> I have understood the population explosion intellectually for a long time. I came to understand it emotionally one stinking hot night in Delhi a couple of years ago. My wife and daughter and I were returning to our hotel in an ancient taxi. The seats were hopping with fleas. The only functional gear was third. As we crawled through the city, we entered a crowded slum area. The temperature was well over 100, and the air was a haze of dust and smoke. The streets seemed alive with people. People eating, people washing, people sleeping. People visiting, arguing, and screaming. People thrusting their hands through the taxi window, begging. People defecating and urinating. People clinging to buses. People herding animals. People, people, people, people. As we moved slowly through the mob, hand horn squawking, the dust, noise, heat, and cooking fires gave the scene a hellish aspect. Would we ever get to our hotel? All three of us were, frankly, frightened. It seemed that anything could happen—but, of course, nothing did. Old India hands still laugh at our reaction. We were just overprivileged tourists, unaccustomed to the sights and sounds of India. Perhaps, but since that night I've known the *feel* of overpopulation.—Paul R. Ehrlich, *The Population Bomb*

Given the title of the book from which this passage is taken, and given the opening and closing sentences in the selection, it is fairly easy to begin to understand the author's purpose. The author wishes to make the population explosion known to us both intellectually and emotionally, and we can reasonably guess that he will sooner or later urge us all to action. But notice, too, how each part of the passage contributes to a sense of purpose. The author uses narrative purposefully, to take us through a scene of clustered, dirty, apparently hopeless life. As the narrative begins, the author and his family "were returning to our hotel." Then the narrative proceeds with "we crawled" and "we entered," and comes to an end with "Old India hands still laugh at our reaction." Description serves the central purpose: "The seats were hopping with fleas"; "cooking fires gave the scene a hellish aspect." Asyndetonic sentences (sentences in which customary connecting words or punctuation have been omitted) serve the purpose of awakening consciousness to the peril of the population bomb: the middle passage that begins with "People eating" and ends with "People, people, people, people," relentlessly piles up the raw data of an overcrowded existence. Ehrlich uses narration and description to serve his purpose, to tell us and show us what he knows and experiences, to awaken us to what he is declaring. He tells us some things, he shows us some things, he explains some things to us in order to make it possible for us to see and feel and think and believe as he does. At the very least, it is clear that the author does not view this scene as quaint, picturesque, and exotic. It is dirty, clamorous, squalid; it is too dense and crowded for life; it is dangerous.

When it comes to putting the words down on the page, you'll have to decide what your purpose is and how you'll reveal it to others, and you'll have to decide how you'll reveal your own point of view to any possible readers. As you work at that, you'll face an interesting and crucial question: How can I be myself and write to serve my own purposes and still get an audience to listen to what I am saying?

There isn't an easy answer. You may have to wrestle with that question every time you write anything. You may find yourself pulled in different directions. On the one hand, for example, is the need to satisfy yourself by saying things just as you want them to be said. Not long ago, in one of a series of British Broadcasting Company lectures, Richard Hoggart asked,

> . . . are we thinking of others when we are actually writing, when we are drawing on personal experience and trying to make sense of it? And if we do think we are writing for others, why are we doing so? To persuade them? To be admired? I expect most of us would give a carefully qualified yes to both those questions. But if we take one more step, and ask ourselves whether we want to persuade our readers to our point of view, or want their admiration, *at the expense of* what we think is the truth of what we are saying, then I think most of us would answer no.
>
> So finally we are not, in any of the obvious senses, writing for others. We hope they will listen, but we are prepared to lose them in the last resort.

But notice, on the other hand, that Hoggart does say, "We hope they will listen." And it's worth remembering that Samuel

Johnson said long ago: "That book is good in vain if a reader throws it away."

The question of how to be true to yourself, true to your purpose, and also get an audience to listen to what you are saying is a good one, and can never easily be dismissed. The following chapters explore some of the relationships that can exist between an author and audience.

Exercise

Discuss the purpose of each of the following paragraphs. How do the authors reveal their purpose? What can you discover in their writing that contributes to their claim on their subject?

Time talks. It speaks more plainly than words. The message it conveys comes through loud and clear. Because it is manipulated less consciously, it is subject to less distortion than the spoken language. It can shout the truth where words lie. —Edward T. Hall, *The Silent Language*

The choice of qualities of a nation's heroes is a reliable index to that nation's health. This is particularly true of political heroes rather than poets or actors or even the first men on the moon. For it is the statesmen who have made an impact on the nation's political and emotional life, men who have been followed with passionate idolatry and attacked with consuming hatred—heroes of the quality of Washington, Jefferson, Lincoln, and Franklin Roosevelt, and men of potential heroic stature like John and Robert Kennedy—who have a continuing vitality in the fantasies of large segments of the American people.

It is commonplace that one man's hero is often another man's tyrant, and it is becoming increasingly apparent that the very concept of the hero throughout this troubled and violent century has been so abused and downgraded that in some countries the very idea is suspect. . . . —Fawn M. Brodie, "The Political Hero in America: His Fate and His Future"

The *Florence Daily News* carried the story on the first page of its February 16, 1618, edition: "Senator Proxmire gives Golden Fleece Award to Galileo." The article went on to detail how government research funds were being squandered on silly experiments, such as dropping objects of different weights off a tower, and how Galileo was spending hours looking at stars to prove that the earth moves around the sun. *Che ridicolo!* Imagine, taxpayers' lire being wasted on such foolishness. The Istituto per Studi Astrofisici was duly admonished for having funded the studies, and told that if supervision of grants didn't improve, its annual budget request would not be treated kindly. The Istituto responded that it had funded only the development of the telescope, not the observation of the stars, and that Galileo's trips to the towers had not been included in the original research proposal.

Some 350 years later, the same issues are with us: "At U.S. Expense, Sociologists Study a Brothel in the Andes," proclaimed the headline of a story in the *Washington Post* describing a project funded by the National Institute of Mental Health. Another Golden Fleece Award, more laughter in the Senate hearing room, more threats of cutting the funding institute's annual budget, more disclaimers by the institute that the original research grant—for the study of ethnic and class relationships in the mountains of Peru— said nothing about visiting brothels.—E. Fuller Torrey, "Proxmirism from Pisa to Peru"

. . . the only relevant standard by which to judge any straightforward piece of prose is the ease with which it conveys its full intended sense to the readers to whom it is addressed, rather than its correctness by the laws of formal English grammar.

Robert Graves and Alan Hodge,
The Reader Over Your Shoulder

4

Sharing a Subject With an Audience

Once a subject is yours, then a major goal of writing is to give it away, to share it in some way with others. This chapter and the next are about some of the possibilities of reaching an audience. This chapter provides

1. a general account of how writers and readers come to seem real to each other (p. 64); and

2. some recommendations about the use of particular details and evidence and of specific language (p. 71).

Most of the writing that most people do is clearly intended for some audience. A laboratory report is intended to convey information to those who will use the results. A book review is for potential book readers. A social-work case history is intended to keep information and insights available on some social or personal problem, for anyone working on the case in question. A term paper is for a teacher, if not for the class. All school assignments have at least one person as an audience.

APPROACHING AN AUDIENCE

It may be, though we might at first think otherwise, that *all* writing is for an audience. That probably even includes some forms of writing that we might think of as private and not intended for any audience—diaries, for example, or personal reminders, or private meditations. In a *New York Times* review (June 15, 1975) of Edmund Wilson's book *The Twenties: From Notebooks and Diaries of the Period*, Joseph Epstein writes, "The first question to be asked about a writer's diaries and notebooks is for whom were they written—who is the intended audience? Diaries and notebooks can function in any number of ways—as an attempt to freeze time, as a poor man's psychoanalysis, as a conscious work of literature. Wilson's function in all these ways. Even though he intended to publish them, the intended audience for the entries in *The Twenties* seems largely to have been Wilson himself, for one of the things that the book makes clear is Wilson's absolute dependence on writing. He appears to have been a man for whom nothing was quite real till he had written it down."

The principal character in *Olivia*, a mystery by Gwendoline Butler, meditates: "I've always been a compulsive diary-keeper. One day I will re-read what I have written. I write in code, of course, not *en clair*, only a fool or an exhibitionist who wants the world to read does that. But I can read my own code. How strange it would be if I could not. Imagine writing down words for ever after lost to you, like the day you have recorded." So even writing that seems private may be for an audience—if not someone else, then the author as a reader in another time or place.

When you are talking to someone, you can usually tell when the person you are talking to hears and understands what you are saying. If the listener doesn't understand, or is not able to follow you, you can back up and try again. You can't do that with a piece of writing, which is likely to be read out of your presence. When you are writing for someone, any aid you can give a reader in understanding your writing comes to an end when the sheets of paper leave your hand. You're not likely to have further chances to revise, modify, or otherwise help your reader, and you certainly can't be around to punch a possible reader on the shoulder and say, "Be sure to pay close attention to the last paragraph!" Ordinarily, your care can only be exercised before you surrender what you have written.

That doesn't mean that you have to become a servant to any possible reader. Of course, you can try to write just what you think some reader (an English teacher, for example) will want to read, if that's what you want to do—but you'll probably get pretty tired of yourself. Your writing is yours first; someone who writes just to please a particular audience or to seek favor seems to be denying his or her own views and values in order to please another.

But if you shouldn't forget yourself, neither should you forget your possible audience. Readers matter too. When you're deeply involved in an intricate subject, it's sometimes difficult to keep a reader in mind, but usually it is possible, even when you've written yourself into a tough place, to look up and notice your reader. Remember that your reader will encounter that tough place too, and it's your responsibility to give the directions for the way out.

Don't forget yourself. Don't forget your audience. That's not much help to a writer wanting to write honestly and to engage an audience. But common sense and normal respect suggest some other guides.

Some beginning propositions

First among these guides are some primary assumptions, some basic propositions upon which relationships between authors and their audiences ought to be based. These are not instructions or guidelines that are to be amplified and illustrated, with a set of steps given to show how each is fulfilled. These basic propositions are part of the hard, sure base of trust that can be created between authors and audiences. They are articles of faith that we want writers to abide by when they approach us; as a consequence, they should also be articles of faith that we abide by when we approach others:

Proposition 1:   *Good writing is based on honesty.* Writers should be honest with themselves, honest about their subject, and honest to their audience.

Proposition 2:   *In good writing, evidence is treated faithfully.* The trust that sometimes develops between audience and writer is legitimate when information is presented without falsification or manipulation.

Proposition 3:   *Good writing reveals the motives from which it springs.* A writer may be successful if he or she works from base motives, or uses good causes to mask self-serving motivation, but the work itself is likely to be intolerable, later if not sooner.

Proposition 4: *Good writing rests upon a suitable history.* Writing offers a kind of promise to the audience that the author has had the experience, acquired the evidence, and done the thinking implied in what he or she has written.

Proposition 5: *Good writing functions as nearly as possible without coercion or manipulation.* The reader is as real as the writer and is not to be treated as a slave or as a thing.

Perhaps such things can go without saying. Some forms of public behavior, including public writing, however, indicate that we cannot take such propositions for granted. Skill in writing can be used to serve an uncountable number of purposes, some virtuous by some measures, some base by some measures, some monstrous, some exalting. If you add fervor to skill, there's scarcely any telling what might be done for what purpose. In the face of all the possibilities, we need to be able to count on each other for at least as much as these propositions suggest.

When we go on from these given propositions, we have to acknowledge that there are some specific and effective ways of reaching an audience and eliciting agreement. Propagandists, advertisers, and other manipulators of public opinion have at times, after all, been entirely successful in securing the audience reaction that best suited them. That something is *possible*, however, doesn't necessarily mean that it is *desirable*. In fact, it's easy enough most of the time to realize that some coercive and manipulatory strategies aren't desirable: if you find yourself yearning to control others by careful strategic moves, remember how much you would dislike being managed and manipulated yourself.

But some guides to shaping public opinion and winning audiences will set out procedures for reaching and persuading readers ("Seven steps to self-assertion," "Five keys to winning through persuasion," and the like). You should, of course, be willing to learn from any source that is fruitful. At the same time, you should probably be cautious of anyone who proposes to tell you exactly how to reach an audience. If you accept unquestioningly another person's way of approaching an audience, you risk being dishonest both with yourself and with any possible reader. *Instructions* about reaching an audience are not in order, then. *Suggestions* are possible.

How does a writer reach an audience, involve an audience in what he or she is writing, bring an audience into some agreement? How can a writer and an audience enter a mutual transaction, in which the writer offers honesty, fair evidence, and understandable thinking while the audience offers at least a willingness to believe?

It helps, at the outset, if your subject matter is compelling, or informative, or dramatic, or amusing, or interesting, or satisfying to readers by fulfilling some need they have. If you have a story to tell about a saturnine gentleman of unorthodox habits, who lives in a remote castle in the Carpathian Mountains where visitors have been known to turn gray within a few days, and who, when he travels, carries with him coffin-shaped boxes filled with soil from his home, then you may have a head start on capturing the attention of an audience. Or if you argue the proposition that unlimited population growth is as explosive and deadly as a bomb, do so with copious and significant evidence, and present your argument before the proposition has become a common topic for discussion, then you may have a head start on capturing the attention of an audience. You may win an audience, too, if you come to them at just the right moment with the solution to all their health problems in a down-home-purely-ecological-mountain-or-prairie-style natural remedy made of collard greens and dandelion wine, or if you announce a new diet to solve all fat problems—collard greens and dandelion wine three times a day.

Sometimes, in other words, a subject is just right. It's intriguing, or you catch readers with it at just the right moment. Most of the time, however, a subject has to be *made* interesting, and there are no guaranteed methods for doing so. You may have a fascinating subject, and you may write it out fully, wisely, and well—and no one will notice.

But there is some hope. Readers do sometimes find themselves drawn into what they are reading. It can happen, I think, if you don't cramp your readers and if you don't hide from them.

Readers, remember, are as real as writers are. They are themselves, and they probably want to continue being themselves. They may not want to be what you want them to be, or to think precisely the way you want them to think. If your writing is full of dogmatic assertions, if you insist that the truth is what you say it is, if you *tell* them something is true and don't try to *show* them that it is true, then they may not find your world spacious enough for them to be in. At best they may think you're silly. At worst, they may be threatened—emotionally, intellectually, physically—by your views.

If, for example, you join in the recent discussions about property taxes and other taxes (the so-called tax revolt of 1978, which led voters in some areas of the country to repudiate tax increases and deny tax revenues to some public services such as schools), and argue dogmatically that property tax evaluations must not go up in any circumstances, then the people who are eager to change and improve public schools may be shut out by your argument and threatened by it. On the other hand, if you argue dogmatically that more tax revenues must come in, then, for example, retired people and others on fixed incomes may be shut out by your argument and threatened by it.

One of the problems with writing is that it wants to make possible a sharing among people who are different. The hope of sharing experience in writing should not be used as justification for destroying differences; the fact that we are different from each other should not be used as an argument against the possibility of sharing.

INSIGHT

An exception

Sometimes, of course, you *want* to change people's minds with what you write, and that may seem to threaten their beliefs. Sometimes it *does* threaten their beliefs. If the cause you advocate is significant and just and well-supported by careful thinking and by evidence, the time may come when you may have to set your views plainly against those of others with the hope of enabling them to accept your views. Apparently some changes cannot occur without a disruption of conventional or customary thinking. See Chapter 15 in Part Two, Arguments, for more discussion of this.

Leaving tracks for an audience

Sharing between a writer and readers is likely to be more nearly possible if readers can follow in the writer's tracks, trace the thinking process that ends in the writing, accompany the writer through his or her experience. If you are writing directions for the installation of a new electric light fixture, the main thing is to be clear and to get the steps in the right order. If, however, you want to share a more complex experience—to show a reader a way of looking at a poignant scene, or to persuade a reader to a new way of thinking—readers have to see enough of your thought processes to be able to recognize and respect them as thought processes. It's nice, though not mandatory, for readers to like you and for you to like readers. It's better if your writing enables them to know that you are responsible in what you say, reasonably confident, ready for change, and if your writing recognizes that they are genuine people, not things to be moved around solely at your will. No one can sensibly promise you that all of this can be accomplished easily. It helps if you are as specific as you can be in talking about yourself or your subject, pointing to particular examples here, dramatizing or picturing pertinent illustrations there, itemizing your experience throughout.

SOME EXAMPLES TO CONSIDER

Examine the pieces given below to see what you can determine about how the author is approaching an audience.

1. When I was teaching English at the Colorado Rocky Mountain School, I used to ask my students the kinds of questions that English

teachers usually ask about reading assignments—questions designed to bring out the points that *I* had decided *they* should know. They, on their part, would try to get me to give them hints and clues as to what I wanted. It was a game of wits. I never gave my students an opportunity to say what they really thought about a book.

I gave vocabulary drills and quizzes too. I told my students that every time they came upon a word in their book they did not understand, they were to look it up in the dictionary. I even devised special kinds of vocabulary tests, allowing them to use their books to see how the words were used. But looking back, I realize that these tests, along with many of my methods, were foolish.

My sister was the first person who made me question my conventional ideas about teaching English. She had a son in the seventh grade in a fairly good public school. His teacher had asked the class to read Cooper's *The Deerslayer*. The choice was bad enough in itself; whether looking at man or nature, Cooper was superficial, inaccurate, and sentimental, and his writing is ponderous and ornate. But to make matters worse, this teacher had decided to give the book the microscope and X-ray treatment. He made the students look up and memorize not only the definitions but the derivations of every big word that came along— and there were plenty. Every chapter was followed by close questioning and testing to make sure the students "understood" everything.

Being then, as I said, conventional, I began to defend the teacher, who was a good friend of mine, against my sister's criticisms. The argument soon grew hot. What was wrong with making sure that children understood everything they read? My sister answered that until this class her boy had always loved reading, and had read a lot on his own; now he had stopped.—John Holt, "How Teachers Make Children Hate Reading"

2. For three thousand years, poets have been enchanted and moved and perplexed by the power of their own imagination. In a short and summary essay I can hope at most to lift one small corner of that mystery; and yet it is a critical corner. I shall ask, What goes on in the mind when we imagine? You will hear from me that one answer to this question is fairly specific: which is to say, that we can describe the working of the imagination. And when we describe it as I shall do, it becomes plain that imagination is a specifically *human* gift. To imagine is the characteristic act, not of the poet's mind, or the painter's, or the scientist's, but of the mind of man.

My stress here on the word *human* implies that there is a clear difference in this between the actions of men and those of other animals. Let me then start with a classical experiment with animals and children which Walter Hunter thought out in Chicago about 1910. That was the time when scientists were agog with the success of Ivan Pavlov in forming and changing the reflex actions of dogs, which Pavlov had first announced in 1903. Pavlov had been given a Nobel Prize the next year, in 1904; although in fairness I should say that the award did not cite his work on the conditioned reflex, but on the digestive gland. —Jacob Bronowski, "The Reach of Imagination"

3. In the search for the Holy Grail of complete harmony, liberation, and integrity, which it is the duty of all true Americans to conduct, adventurers have stumbled upon a road sign which appears promising. It says, in bold letters, "All problems arise through lack of communication." Under it, in smaller print, it says: "Say what is on your mind. Express your feelings honestly. This way lies the answer." A dangerous road, it seems to me. It is just as true to say, This way lies disaster.

I would not go so far as Oliver Goldsmith, who observed that the principal function of language is to *conceal* our thoughts. But I do think that concealment is one of the important functions of language, and on no account should it be dismissed categorically. . . . Semantic environments have legitimate and necessary purposes of their own which do not always coincide with the particular and pressing needs of every individual within them. One of the main purposes of many of our semantic environments, for example, is to help us maintain a minimum level of civility in conducting our affairs. Civility requires not that we deny our feelings, only that we keep them to ourselves when they are not relevant to the situation at hand. Contrary to what many people believe, Freud does not teach us that we are "better off" when we express our deepest feelings. He teaches exactly the opposite: that civilization is impossible without inhibition. Silence, reticence, restraint, and, yes, even dishonesty can be great virtues, in certain circumstances. They are, for example, frequently necessary in order for people to work together harmoniously. To learn how to say no is important in achieving personal goals, but to learn how to say yes when you want to say no is at the core of civilized behavior. There is no dishonesty in a baboon cage, and yet, for all that, it holds only baboons. —Neil Postman, *Crazy Talk, Stupid Talk*

Exercises

1. Describe as accurately as you can your *initial* impression of the writer in each of the three passages, pages 68 to 70.

2. Write a paper describing a favorite relative. Since the subject matter should present itself readily, concentrate as you write not only on making the relative known to the reader, but also on making the "written voice" someone you are pleased with as well.

LANGUAGE TO FOLLOW, EXAMPLES TO SHOW THE WAY

We walked down the path to the well-house, attracted by the fragrance of the honeysuckle with which it was covered. Some one was drawing water and my teacher placed my hand under the spout. As the cool stream gushed over one hand she spelled into the other the word water, first slowly, then rapidly. I stood still, my whole attention fixed upon the motions of her fingers. Suddenly I felt a misty consciousness as of something forgotten—a thrill of returning thought; and somehow the mystery of language was revealed to me. I knew then that "w-a-t-e-r" meant the wonderful cool some-thing that was flowing over my hand. That living word awakened my soul, gave it light, hope, joy, set it free! There were barriers still, it is true, but barriers that could in time be swept away. —Helen Keller, **The Story of My Life**

A good tracker, it's often been said, can follow a person or an animal to its destination. And knowing the destination of a person or animal, a good tracker can also track backward to where it has been. Specific, accurate language and significant illustrations may enable readers to follow you on your way to your destination, or once they've learned your destination—your conclusion, your argument—to backtrack along the path you took, learning what you saw and heard and thought and felt that led you to think and speak as you do.

The trouble is, words aren't the same as things; they won't take the place of your experience. The water flowing over Helen Keller's one hand was not the same thing as the letters being formed in her other. What came to her was the knowledge that there was a correspondence be-tween them. The letters were related to the water; they signified water, but they were not water. One of the problems that you have as a writer is that your readers will not always see the correspondence between words and things in the same way that you do.

For example, if some evening you're visiting a friend, and your friend says, "The books you wanted to see are on the table," you will probably know which table to go to. The word *table* and the thing across the room with books on it correspond pretty closely to each other. But change the time, and change the place, and remember that even a relatively simple word like *table* has a number of other meanings (the multiplication table, setting a good table, putting a motion on the table, and so on, not to mention thousands of different kinds of furniture pieces). Then, *even table* may not mean the same thing to both sayer and hearer. And if you use a word that stands for a more complex thing (*honor*, say, or *sincerity*), the variations in meaning are likely to be greater still.

If you want words and things to correspond for your readers in the same way they do for you, then it may be necessary to point to the things that you want your words to signify. One of the ways to do that is to use language that is as specific and concrete as possible, language that makes clear reference to particular things in your experience. Another way to do that is to show your readers what you are talking about by giving them detailed examples and illustrations. Concrete language and careful illustrations won't prove anything; they won't guarantee that an audience will listen to you, or agree with you. But they will let an audience track you. If an audience knows what you've seen or heard or felt, if they know what has happened to you, if they know what you have experienced, they will be better able to hear your words as you mean them, and they will be better able to understand how you think and why you arrive at certain conclusions (see also Chapter 8 on words).

When your language is general rather than specific, abstract rather than concrete, and when you provide no references, no illustrations of your meaning, you rapidly narrow the possible responses an audience can make to what you write. If they already think or feel about your subject pretty much as you do, they may think your writing is fine and appropriate. But if they dislike what you have generalized about, or disagree with your argument, they will more than likely either condemn or ignore what you've said since you have not given them reason to respect it. And if your subject is not particularly controversial, if they are not already interested one way or another, they will more than likely be unmoved. There are not too many ways in which readers can respond to a piece of writing that has no hint in it of actual people or actual things or actual occurrences.

If you *care* about what you are writing, if it means something to you, then for your own sake and for the sake of the subject—as well as for a potential audience—give it your full attention, present it in full or significant detail, and let an audience follow you through your experiences in the writing.

SPECIFIC LANGUAGE AND POINTED EXAMPLES: SOME PASSAGES TO STUDY

1.   A single knoll rises out of the plain in Oklahoma, north and west of the Wichita Range. For my people, the Kiowas, it is an old landmark, and they gave it the name Rainy Mountain. The hardest weather in the world is there. Winter brings blizzards, hot tornadic winds

arise in the spring, and in summer the prairie is an anvil's edge. The grass turns brittle and brown, and it cracks beneath your feet. There are green belts along the rivers and creeks, linear groves of hickory and pecan, willow and witch hazel. At a distance in July or August the steaming foliage seems almost to writhe in fire. Great green and yellow grasshoppers are everywhere in the tall grass, popping up like corn to sting the flesh, and tortoises crawl about on the red earth, going nowhere in the plenty of time. Loneliness is an aspect of the land. All things in the plain are isolate; there is no confusion of objects in the eye, but *one* hill or *one* tree or *one* man. To look upon that landscape in the early morning, with the sun at your back, is to lose the sense of proportion. Your imagination comes to life, and this, you think, is where Creation was begun. —N. Scott Momaday, *The Way to Rainy Mountain*

Notice how the first two sentences specify the location. First, it is just a "single knoll." It is then more clearly identified by its relation to the Wichita Range in Oklahoma. Then it is given its specific name, Rainy Mountain. Notice, too, how Momaday spells out what he means by the world's "hardest weather": it means blizzards in winter, tornadic winds in the spring, and fierce heat (on the "anvil's edge") and dry, crackling grass in the summer. The generalized term, "green belts," is made more specific with "linear groves of hickory and pecan, willow and witch hazel." The grasshoppers are pictures specifically for us: they are green and yellow, and they pop up "like corn to sting the flesh." When Momaday says near the end that "To look upon that landscape . . . is to lose the sense of proportion," we can understand what he means, though we might not have experienced it in the same way ourselves. We can understand because of the details he provides: the landscape is huge, spacious, uncrowded, filled with fierce weather, dwarfing the mere isolated human observer.

2.   Cooper's gift in the way of invention was not a rich endowment, but such as it was he liked to work it, he was pleased with the effects, and indeed he did some quite sweet things with it. In his little box of stage properties he kept six or eight cunning devices, tricks, artifices for his savages and woodsmen to deceive and circumvent each other with, and he was never so happy as when he was working these innocent things and seeing them go. A favorite one was to make a moccasined person tread in the tracks of the moccasined enemy, and thus hide his own trail. Cooper wore out barrels and barrels of moccasins in working that trick. Another stage-property that he pulled out of his box pretty frequently was his broken twig. He prized his broken twig above all the rest of his effects, and worked it the hardest. It is a restful chapter in any book of his when somebody doesn't step on a dry twig and alarm all the reds and whites for two hundred yards around. Every time a Cooper person is in peril and absolute silence is worth four dollars a minute, he is sure to step on a dry twig. There may be a hundred handier things to step on but that wouldn't

satisfy Cooper. Cooper requires him to turn out and find a dry twig, and if he can't do it, go and borrow one. In fact, the Leatherstocking Series ought to have been called the Broken Twig Series.—Mark Twain, "Fenimore Cooper's Literary Offenses"

Twain refers to Cooper's "little box of stage-properties" and then uses the moccasin trick and the broken twig trick to illustrate what he means. The essay from which this passage is taken is a model of the pointed use of specific illustrations, usually quotations from Cooper's work. The next two examples also use specific details to make their points. Angelou's use of details is ironic; Eiseley uses a microscopic view of a puddle to show the macroscopic miracle of water.

3.   Mrs. Bertha Flowers was the aristocrat of Black Stamps. She had the grace of control to appear warm in the coldest weather, and on the Arkansas summer days it seemed she had a private breeze which swirled around cooling her. She was thin without the taut look of wiry people, and her printed voile dresses and flowered hats were as right for her as denim overalls for a farmer. She was our side's answer to the richest white woman in town.—Maya Angelou, "A Lesson in Living"

4.   If there is magic on this planet, it is contained in water. Its least stir even, as now in a rain pond on a flat roof opposite my office, is enough to bring me searching to the window. A wind ripple may be translating itself into life. I have a constant feeling that some time I may witness that momentous miracle on a city roof, see life veritably and suddenly boiling out of a heap of rusted pipes and old television aerials. I marvel at how suddenly a water beetle has come and is submarining there in a spatter of green algae. Thin vapors, rust, wet tar and sun are an alembic remarkably like the mind; they throw off odorous shadows that threaten to take real shape when no one is looking.—Loren Eiseley, *The Immense Journey*

Exercises

1.   Write a description of a room and its significance in your life. Be sure to include specific details.

2.   Pretend that you arrive on Earth from another planet. You end up in a room with only a TV set. You watch it for a while and decide that this must be a "window on the Earth." Write an imaginary letter back to your planet describing Earth life as you know it. Use illustrations and examples.

3.   Find a piece of writing that has a "written voice" you like. Analyze specifically what the writer does to achieve that voice.

4.   Do a piece of writing that could be included in your autobiography, concentrating on the particular sights, sounds, and smells of a short period in your childhood.

And they said, Go to, let us build us a city and a tower, whose top may reach unto heaven; and let us make us a name, lest we be scattered abroad upon the face of the whole earth.

And the Lord came down to see the city and the tower, which the children of men builded.

And the Lord said, Behold, the people is one, and they have all one language; and this they begin to do: and now nothing will be restrained from them, which they have imagined to do.

Go to, let us go down, and there confound their language, that they may not understand one another's speech.

Genesis 11

5

Connecting Author, Subject, and Audience

The preceding chapter discussed some first steps in approaching an audience, exploring the possibilities of trust between an author and a reader, and recommending specific language and specific examples as means of showing an audience what an author means. This chapter discusses

1. some ways an author, a subject, and an audience may stand in relation to each other (p. 76);

2. what can be assumed about an audience (p. 82);

3. referential, active, and personal relationships (p. 84); and

4. some other ways of describing relationships (p. 90).

The first three chapters of this book are given over to thinking about a subject. That seems to be an appropriate *beginning* point in a book about writing. The fourth chapter and this one are about finding an audience. That may seem to you an *ending* point—an audience being the person or persons who may or may not read what you have written *after* you are through with it. But if there is to be an audience for your work—if you think of your writing as something other than pure revery, self-expression, or private meditation—then the audience probably needs to be in your mind from the start. Knowing your relation to your subject and your audience will help you determine the purpose of your writing, what resources can or should be used, and what ways of seeing and thinking and writing are possible.

AUTHOR, SUBJECT, AND AUDIENCE

Every possible subject for writing deserves fair and accurate treatment. Every possible subject deserves your full and honest attention. When you write about a subject, your writing is testimony that you have experienced the subject in some way, learned it in some way, thought about it in some way. If you expect to have a reader, then it is only fair to remember that the reader can have some expectations of you, that you are writing about the subject because it has some kind of meaning and value that you believe can be conveyed to another.

There is no "right" way to address an audience—except, perhaps, to remember that any reader is as real as you are. That means that he or she is not to be lied to, tricked, or manipulated. Language can create community, a bond between writer and reader, speaker and hearer. And while a subject awaits honest scrutiny and an audience awaits an honest transaction, you still have your own needs and expectations to deal with. Few of us would want to give up our own expectations of ourselves *just* to meet the expectations of someone else.

These three primary constituents of the writing process—a writer, a subject, a potential audience—require some balancing, and knowing something about the relationships among them from the start may help you to see what you can do or what you want to do in your writing.

Imagine yourself as a writer fixed at one of the points of a triangle. At the other two points are a subject and a possible audience. Different kinds of writing result from and sometimes create different relationships within this triangle.

In some kinds of writing you may be pretty much unconcerned with either a subject or an audience, focusing instead on yourself. In a diary, for example, or a journal, you may be your own subject and audience. In some essays you may be chiefly intent upon exploring your own thoughts or attitudes or working out some problem for your own satisfaction.

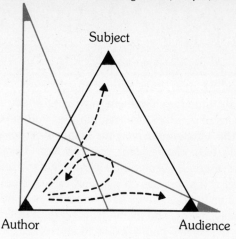

At other times, however, the subject may be the point of focus. In some forms of writing, your own feelings and attitudes and opinions may not be important because some subject outside yourself requires or deserves attention for its own sake. An audience may be present, but speaking to an audience is not the primary goal of such writing. Laboratory reports are usually focused on a subject, for example, as are case histories, some kinds of reports, most newspaper writing, some textbooks, and most encyclopedia articles. Note how, if the author is closer to the subject, the audience seems to become farther away.

But on some occasions the audience comes first. People who write advertisements, for example, want to have some kind of influence on the people who see or read the advertisement. A minister in a pulpit presumably wants the congregation to be influenced by the sermon. A lawyer in a courtroom may urge a judge and a jury to think in a particular way by his or her presentation of the evidence. Editorial writers sometimes express opinions about a current issue in order to solicit agreement from their readers. You may have many occasions to write or speak with the intention of changing a particular audience. And as you can see, the closer the audience is to the author, the more remote the subject.

The relationships shown in the triangle suggest some different kinds of writing. In the rest of this chapter and from time to time through the rest of the book, this triangular scheme will recur as a basis for some terms that are useful. Writing that focuses on the author seems to rest chiefly upon *personal relationships* and can be called *personal writing*. Writing that concentrates principally on a subject, where the author is referring to something other than himself or herself, seems to rest chiefly upon *referential relationships* and can usefully be called *referential writing*. Writing that intends to have an effect on an audience seems to rest chiefly upon *active relationships*, since the author wishes to do something with, to, or for an audience, and can be called *active writing*.

INSIGHT

What you focus on governs what you can fairly say

You're always standing somewhere when you say something. The circumstances of your life, the assumptions you make, the attitudes you have, the information at your disposal—these and countless other factors help shape what you can say. These factors, if we could name them all, constitute your identity, and your identity disposes you to see certain things and to see them in given ways. And most of us look at things in different ways at different times, as circumstances, needs, and interests indicate. If as a writer you focus intently on a subject, you are not likely to see or respond to an audience. If as a writer you turn toward an audience, you'll not be able to see a subject as clearly. Try a simple experiment: hold a rock at arm's length in front of your eyes and between yourself and a group of people, focusing on the rock. How clearly do you see the people? When you focus on the group of people, can you see the rock clearly?

If your view is out of focus, you'll probably say the wrong thing

How many times have you heard a politician talk about his or her record (look at himself or herself) when you were waiting for him or her to talk about the facts in some case (look at the subject)? How many times has a teacher hurried on to the next topic (looked at the subject) when you desperately needed him or her to slow down and clarify an assignment (to look at you)? The situation in which you and a subject and an audience come together often gives rise to certain needs. In a laboratory report, for example, the primary need is to explore the subject thoroughly; the writer and the audience are less important. If you are trying to get others to sign a petition, your appeal to the audience serves the primary need, though in some petitions the cause itself (the subject) is sufficiently compelling to be persuasive. Of course you have needs, too, and in the long run they must also be met when you write.

Here are some examples of how distances vary between subject, author, and audience, and how those relationships affect the writing. The speaker in the first passage below is close to his subject. He has observed it closely himself ("I found a deep tank of clear, cool water almost over my head. . . ."), and he stays close enough to see and record details—he knows where the water holes are, and he records by name the animals that come for the water.

After the storm has passed and the flash floods dump their loads of silt into the Colorado River, leaving the streambeds as dry as they were a few hours before, water still remains in certain places on rimrock, canyon bench, and mesa top. These are the pools which fill, for a time, the natural tanks and cisterns and potholes carved by wind and weather out of the sandstone. Some of these holes in the rock may contain water for days or weeks after rain, depending upon their depth, exposure to the sun, and consequent rate of evaporation. Often far from any spring or stream, these temporary pools attract doves, ravens, and other birds for so long as they last, provide the deer and the wandering coyotes with a short-lived water supply; you too, if you know where to look or find one by luck, may slake your thirst there, and fill your canteens. Such pools may be found in what seem like improbable places: at Toroweap in Grand Canyon I found a deep tank of clear, cool water almost over my head, countersunk in the top of a sandstone bluff which overhung my campsite by a hundred feet. . . .—Edward Abbey, *Desert Solitaire*

In this next passage, Churchill focuses on his audience, to stir patriotism and fighting spirit during a dark time for England in World War II:

I have, myself, full confidence that if all do their duty, if nothing is neglected, and if the best arrangements are made, as they are being made, we shall prove ourselves once again able to defend our Island home, to ride out the storm of war, and to outlive the menace of tyranny, if necessary for years, if necessary alone. At any rate, that is what we are going to try to do. That is the resolve of His Majesty's Government—every man of them. That is the will of Parliament and the nation. The British Empire and the French Republic, linked together in their cause and in their need, will defend to the death their native soil, aiding each other like good comrades to the utmost of their strength. Even though large tracts of Europe and many old and famous States have fallen or may fall into the grip of the Gestapo and all the odious apparatus of Nazi rule, we shall not flag or fail. We shall go on to the end, we shall fight in France, we shall fight on the seas and oceans, we shall fight with growing confidence and growing strength in the air, we shall defend our Island, whatever the cost may be, we shall fight on the beaches, we shall fight on the landing grounds, we shall fight in the fields and in the streets, we shall fight in the hills; we shall never surrender, and even if, which I do not for a moment believe, this Island or a large part of it were subjugated and starving, then our Empire beyond the seas, armed and guarded by the British Fleet, would carry on the struggle, until, in God's time, the New World, with all its power and might, steps forth to the rescue and the liberation of the old.—Winston Churchill, Speech following the evacuation of Dunkirk, 1940

And in this passage a poet focuses on himself in his diary. Notice that he doesn't bother to locate or explain the places and people he writes about. Nor can a reader easily track his thoughts; his concern is to write them down only as they come into his mind:

September 11th.
Last night a dream which I dream several times a year—a great house which I recognise as partly Coole and partly Sandymount Castle—though not by any exact physical resemblance. In all these dreams Sandymount gives the tragic element—in one which I remember vividly the house was built around a ruin and Sandymount was the ruin. This time all the house was castellated and about to pass into other hands, its pictures auctioned. I remember looking at a picture and thinking that it would now lose its value, for its value was that it had always hung in a particular place and had been put there by some past member of the family. Coole as a Gregory house is near its end, it will be before long an office and residence for foresters, a little cheap furniture in the great rooms a few religious oleographs its only pictures, and yet when in my dream I had some such thought I stood in a Gothic door which I now recognise as the door at Sandymount. I never think of Sandymount Castle and would not have seen it except from the road had I not been shown over it by the headmaster of the school that had what remained, the garden disappeared long ago. The impression on my subconscious was made in childhood, when my uncle Corbet's death and bankruptcy was a recent tragedy, the book with Sandymount Castle printed on the cover open upon my knees. I vividly recall those photographs of ornamental waters, of a little rustic bridge, of the oak room where celebrated men had sat down to breakfast, of garden paths, of a great door suggesting not Abbotsford but Strawberry Hill—the door that my dream recalled. Yet do I speak the truth when I say I never think of it? The other day at my uncle Isaac's funeral I thought how little I had seen of him and that fear had kept me away. He was so much better bred than I—he had about him the sweetness of those gardens, so too have my old aunts who spent their childhood there. I have intellect, scornful, impatient, dissatisfied and always a little ashamed.—William Butler Yeats, *Pages from a Diary Written in Nineteen Hundred and Thirty*

Sometimes, perhaps most of the time, when you write you may not be thinking about the distance between yourself and a subject or between yourself and an audience. But you will have to think about these distances sometime—if not when you are writing a first draft, then perhaps later, when you are checking what you have written, or when you are revising it. Asking what distance exists between writer and subject or writer and audience gives you a good way of checking on your own work. You may be failing yourself, mistreating an audience, and violating a subject if you have the distances wrong. If accurate observation of details is your goal, you must be close enough to see them, whether you are writing about a spider, a tree, or a moment in history (you get closer to a tree by moving; you get closer to a moment in history by research). If reaching an audience matters to you, then you must find a way of being with an audience.

Exercises

1.   Do a piece of writing in which you try to write down whatever comes into your mind without worrying about audience. Let your writing wander, disregarding consideration of coherence, unity, or transitions.

2.   Take a common object and look at it from the three perspectives of the writer's triangle:
   a.   First write a few sentences in which you concentrate on the subject. Describe the object as deliberately and objectively as possible.
   b.   Write a few sentences in which you focus on your relationship to the object. Do you see it in ways others might not?
   c.   Write a few sentences intended to persuade an audience to a new way of looking at the object.

3.   Describe the writer-subject-audience relationship in each of the following examples:

> The land division lists also give information on the relative standing of the men elected to govern and represent the town but here again one cannot find any true aristocracy or oligarchy. In the first place, it must be remembered that selectmen were elected annually, not appointed, and as shall be seen, many different men were chosen. —B. Katherine Brown, "Puritan Democracy: A Case Study"

> Love and knowledge, so far as they were possible, led upward toward the heavens. But always pity brought me back to earth. Echoes of cries of pain reverberate in my heart. Children in famine, victims tortured by oppressors, helpless old people a hated burden to their sons, and the whole world of loneliness, poverty, and pain make a mockery of what human life should be. I long to alleviate the evil, but I cannot, and I too suffer. —Bertrand Russell, *The Autobiography of Bertrand Russell, 1872–1914*

But let's be fair: Is your faculty, by and large, any more uninspired, boring and dull than, say, your classmates? (Don't mistake adolescent agitations for sublime inspiration.) Does not youth always think most adults uninspired and unimaginative? And are there enough competent, intriguing teachers to go around? (Where are they hiding?) And does not your most "uninspired, boring, dull" teacher know more about the course he is teaching than you do? I think it fair to say: "Few persons invent algebra on their own."—Leo Rosten, "To an Angry Young Man"

What can be assumed about an audience?

Making any assumptions about an audience may seem foolhardy—the whole enterprise a misguided attempt to predict what people are going to be like and how they are going to react in a particular situation. Probably the best answer to the question of what can be assumed is, "Not a whole lot."

Still, there are some things worth remembering about the other people who make up audiences.

First, remember what has already been noted frequently: audiences are real people, not nonentities who have no existence except when they read your writing. They each have a history, and it's not the same as yours. Each of them has come to think in particular ways, and their ways may not be your ways. If you and a given audience walked together across a landscape, each of you might notice different things. What looks like evidence to you may not look like evidence to them.

You may, of course, for some writing have a select audience made up of people much like yourself, already willing to trust you, perhaps even already interested in what you're saying. You may be fortunate enough to find an audience not necessarily like yourself, but made up of people who need to know what you are saying and know they need to know it.

But generally, outside these special circumstances, you probably should assume that audiences are mostly different from you and from each other. Any single audience may include people wildly different from you and from each other. Audiences for different pieces of writing may be extraordinarily different from each other. The same piece of writing may reach an astonishing variety of audiences. Perhaps the range of possibilities in a single audience or from audience to audience suggested below may help you remember qualities in your audience. (It would probably be useful, too, if you tried your own hand at depicting the variations in audiences.) Notice, in this diagram, that possible audiences may be increasingly remote from you:

Yourself (author)

People very much like yourself, with similar backgrounds and similar interests

People who share a similar background, but whose interests are different

People who have different backgrounds, but who for one reason or another have some of the same interests you have

Aliens, people of markedly different backgrounds, different generations, different cultures, different value systems, who may be entirely uninterested in what you're saying

Hostiles, people who are antagonistic to what you are saying (and perhaps to you) and who may feel either threatened or repelled by your writing.

Probably most writers and most kinds of writing don't go much past the third remove shown above in trying to reach an audience. How far you go depends at last upon you and how much missionary zeal you have for spreading to others what you have to say.

Is there anything else you can assume about an audience? Perhaps one or two things. You can assume that they read, either voluntarily or necessarily. You can assume that if there were such a thing as a literacy scale, they would be pretty close to where you are on the scale, some a little less skilled with language, some perhaps a little more skilled in some ways. You can assume that each member of a possible audience probably believes in his or her own identity, just as you do, and probably believes in his or her own capacity to judge and to decide, just as you do.

You can probably assume that some audiences are *waiting*, some *can be arrested*, and some *have to be created*. Some audiences are already prepared to listen; they are *waiting*. Some audiences will be interested enough and perhaps receptive if you can gain their attention; they *can be arrested*. But sometimes you have to *create* an audience.

That means that, for example, you have to see something new that others haven't dreamed of, announce it, show its significance, and keep doing so until an audience has been generated.

You can assume that the people in a possible audience have full, busy lives. They're doing things. Other things besides your writing impinge on their lives. You're asking for their time, their patience, and their willingness to listen and perhaps to see things as you see them for a moment.

WRITER-AUDIENCE RELATIONSHIPS

An audience won't be changed, enlarged, or given new understanding by your writing if they ignore it or if they resist it. If readers find your work trite, stale, trivial, vague, or lacking in energy, they're likely to discard it. If readers feel threatened by your work, if they think it is destructive to their beliefs, if they think you are too dogmatic, too insistent, they're not likely to respond warmly to your work. If a fruitful response from readers is essential or desirable to you, you have to find a way of being with them and of making it possible for them to be with you. If you want to speak to others, you may find yourself walking a narrow, chancy path between extremes. At one extreme, if you write just like everybody else writes, you risk denying your own personality by not expressing yourself, and you risk becoming a fake in order to sound like others. At the other extreme, if you write only as you wish to write and completely express yourself in your own particular way, you take the chance that nobody will listen because you are incomprehensible. It's a chancy path, but it can lead to exciting places, where you and an audience come together.

At any rate, no one can predict, describe, or legislate the way for you to approach an audience. You must do your writing, and that includes determining how important it is for readers to respond to you and how you are going to speak to them. It isn't possible to prescribe how you can manage this. Each writer speaks in his or her own way to readers who respond in their own ways. There are, however, some writer-audience relationships that can be usefully named and discussed. Writers may be entirely individual in their way, yet share some attitudes or procedures with other writers. It is possible, then, to speak of some general kinds of writer-audience relationships.

Referential relationships

I want to use this term to designate kinds of writing that, however different they may be from each other in other respects, seem to have in common the desire to point to and discuss some subject separate from both the author and any possible audience. It's as if both the author and the audience were set aside for the time being so that the focus of attention may be on a subject apart from them both. The writer *refers* to a subject for the reader. The subject is central in this kind of writing, not the writer's way of thinking, not any action the reader may take after reading. The subject is central, and the writer's mission seems to be to accumulate evidence about the subject and transmit to readers a clear and orderly representation of the subject. The goal is an authentic rendering of the subject, as in the following passage:

> Thirsty Americans drained beer and soft drinks from 80 billion bottles and cans last year and threw away three-quarters of these containers—enough to build more than ten stacks to the moon. Virtually omnipresent in the landscape, bottles and cans may comprise more than two-thirds of the nation's litter by volume. Moreover, the number of beverage containers continues to grow faster than the beverages themselves. Between 1959 and 1969, the amount of beer and soft drinks consumed in the United States rose 29 percent while, under the slogan "no deposit, no return," the number of containers used rose 164 percent.
>
> The primary issue that has emerged from such statistics goes beyond the problem of litter. . . . The issue is the *use* of resources. . . .
>
> It is the economics of large-scale recycling—not the technology—that is most troublesome. To break even, a resource recovery plant should have a capacity of about 500 tons of trash a day—an amount equivalent to that produced by a city of 250,000 people. This exceeds the plant size of most units planned.
>
> Finding markets is also a headache. The aluminum industry is eager to buy back clean, shredded aluminum, since it is not only interchangeable with primary alloy for most purposes, but is also cheaper.
>
> The economics are totally different for steel and glass. Glass cullet [waste glass]—cleaned and sorted by color—costs at least $30 a ton, while raw materials cost only $16 to $20 a ton. Aside from its use in the factory, there is not much demand for recycled glass. . . .
>
> The economics of recycled steel are also shaky. At the resource recovery operation in New Castle, Delaware, for example, it currently costs about $60 to isolate one ton of steel cans; their market value is only between $10 and $14.—Jane Stein, "The Bottle and Can Problem"

Elsewhere in this essay the author may have different intentions—she may want to express her own convictions or to stir an audience to some kind of action—but in the passage shown above, she seems chiefly concerned to provide information about the scope and complexity of a subject. She is looking closely at a subject, not at herself or at an audience. For further discussions of some kinds of referential writing, for example, see the chapters on letters, reports, and critical writing.

Active relationships

I want to use this term to designate writing or segments of writing in which the author seems to want to act upon the audience in some way—for example, to change their thinking, or to spur them to some kind of action. In *referential relationships* the message itself is central; in *active relationships* the *effect* of the message is central. The writer's mission is to convey a message that is sufficiently relevant to an audience and immediate in their interest to win a commitment from them, a commitment to change behavior or thinking. The goal of such writing is to have an impact on an audience, to energize them, as in the following passage.

You know you have to read "between the lines" to get the most out of anything. I want to persuade you to do something equally important in the course of your reading. I want to persuade you to "write between the lines." Unless you do, you are not likely to do the most efficient kind of reading.

I contend, quite bluntly, that marking up a book is not an act of mutilation, but of love.

You shouldn't mark up a book which isn't yours. Librarians (or your friends) who lend you books expect you to keep them clean, and you should. If you decide that I am right about the usefulness of marking books, you will have to buy them. Most of the world's great books are available today [1940], in reprint editions, at less than a dollar.

There are two ways in which one can own a book. The first is the property right you establish by paying for it, just as you pay for clothes and furniture. But this act of purchase is only the prelude to possession. Full ownership comes only when you have made it a part of yourself, and the best way to make yourself a part of it is by writing in it. An illustration may make the point clear. You buy a beefsteak and transfer it from the butcher's ice-box to your own. But you do not own the beefsteak in the most important sense until you consume it and get it into your bloodstream. I am arguing that books, too, must be absorbed in your bloodstream to do you any good.

Confusion about what it means to *own* a book leads people to a false reverence for paper, binding, and type—a respect for the physical thing—the craft of the printer rather than the genius of the author. They forget that it is possible for a man to acquire the idea, to possess the beauty, which a great book contains, without staking his claim by pasting his bookplate inside the cover. Having a fine library doesn't prove that its owner has a mind enriched by books; it proves nothing more than he, his father, or his wife, was rich enough to buy them. —Mortimer J. Adler, "How to Mark a Book"

The title of the essay from which this selection was taken, "How to Mark a Book," indicates that the author wants to explain something. But in the passage above, he wants to influence readers, to have an effect upon them. He is expressing his own views, to be sure, and he is talking about a subject, marking books, but changing his audience is his chief goal.

Personal relationships

But after all, if you want an audience to hear you and believe you, or if you want them to believe in the validity of your views (even while they may not be accepting them as their own), then you have to be believable. The writer is central in all forms of writing, and all relationships in writing are personal. Your character is in what you write, and your character is at stake in what you write.

INSIGHT

A note on character in writing

In his *Rhetoric* Aristotle says that a speaker's character is the most potent of all the means to persuasion. He is talking specifically about how character is revealed in what a person says. Sometimes we respond to and believe in a speaker or writer for not very noble reasons. We may respond only because the speaker or writer is saying what we already believe and advocate. Sometimes we respond because the speaker or writer seems to be able to satisfy some need we have—he or she will feed us when we're hungry, or lead us out of political corruption if elected next November, or banish our social, racial, or educational frustrations by imposing our kind of order.

To offer easy kinship to your audience is one way to bring them into relationship with you. To offer them gratification of their wishes, fulfillment of their needs, is another. Sometimes it is important to do just this: if people are hungry, they should be fed; if they seek learning, they should be taught. But sometimes the effort to gratify an audience only means that you lose your own identity and submerge your own character.

We hear much these days about the *credibility* of public officials and about the public's loss of confidence in its institutions and in the representatives of those institutions. There is no particular value in *seeming* to be credible and trustworthy, though many speakers do succeed because they *seem* credible (it's a popular pastime among politicians and advertisers). Value lies in *being* credible. That means allowing an audience to see you in what you write, somebody real writing for others who are real. That means making it possible for an audience to follow your thought processes and to see what you regard as evidence. That means that it is probably better if you can manage to be flexible, rather than rigid, tentative and seeking, rather than dogmatic and authoritative. That means it is probably better *to show* your audience what you think the truth is, rather than simply *to assert* what you think the truth is.

Of course you can't always be flexible and unthreatening. On some occasions—they're probably rare—you'll decide that you cannot bend or yield. When they wrote the Declaration of Independence, its authors could no longer expect to reconcile themselves with the English. Some audiences won't like you or what you say; sometimes you may not like your audience. But you can be honest with them. You can be patient and hope for patience. You can be willing to risk revealing yourself to them so that they may know you and perhaps for a while live in the same world.

No one can tell you ahead of time how to write so as to reveal your character. If someone offered you five infallible steps for character revelation in writing, and if you followed these steps carefully, the chances are your enterprise would fail. You'd be following steps that some one else devised, accepting that person's way of writing. The kind of character revelation I'm talking about is likely to be different in each piece of writing; it occurs when your involvement in what you are writing becomes apparent in the writing itself.

Notice that I have been talking about the writer's character as it is *revealed* in the writing. Of course it is also possible for a writer to *create* a character for readers to respond to. Novelists and dramatists obviously create characters. Essayists sometimes present themselves in their work as a particular kind of character. Public speakers sometimes reveal their character, and sometimes they create character for themselves, as when, for example, a politician represents himself or herself as "good ole country folks" to a rural constituency, even though the politician is at other times far removed from the country. Much of the work of public relations and of image-building is in the creation of character, not in the revelation of character. The two passages below—quite unlike each other—may illustrate some ways that character emerges in writing. The first is from an individual, the second from an institution.

> Tell General Howard I know his heart. What he told me before, I have it in my heart. I am tired of fighting. Our chiefs are killed. Looking Glass is dead. Toohoolhoolzote is dead. The old men are all dead. It is the young men who say "yes" or "no." He who led the young men is dead. It is cold, and we have no blankets. The little children are freezing to death. My people, some of them, have run away to the hills, and have no blankets, no food. No one

knows where they are—perhaps freezing to death. I want to have time to look for my children, and see how many of them I can find. Maybe I shall find them among the dead. Hear me, my chiefs! I am tired. My heart is sick and sad. From where the sun now stands I will fight no more forever.—Chief Joseph, on his surrender to General Howard

We read with interest recently that President Carter has signed an executive order requiring federal regulations to be written in understandable English. Mr. Carter said even he sometimes couldn't understand the government's pronouncements, and once he had to send back a staff order three times before getting a revision he could comprehend.

It's quite a problem, as William Zinsser remarks in *On Writing Well* (Harper & Row, $7.95):

"Clutter is the disease of American writing. We are a society strangling in unnecessary words, circular constructions, pompous frills and meaningless jargon."

George Orwell once illustrated the malady with this deliberately bloodless passage:

"Objective consideration of contemporary phenomena compels the conclusion that success or failure in competitive activities exhibits no tendency to be commensurate with innate capacity, but that a considerable element of the unpredictable must inevitably be taken into account."

The source of Orwell's translation? Ecclesiastes: "I returned, and saw under the sun, that the race is not to the swift, nor the battle to the strong. . . ."

Lacking divine inspiration, governments at several levels are turning to more prosaic remedies. In California's San Mateo County, a bureaucrat who calls himself a "language ombudsman" is assigned to eliminate puffed-up doubletalk (gobbledygook, to its opponents) from government reports. In New York State, the Senate and Assembly passed a bill requiring amendments and other matters submitted to voters to be written in understandable language. A ban on legalese in some consumer contracts was enacted earlier and is to take effect this fall.

In Washington, source of so much linguistic clutter, a number of consultants are reported to have been hired to restore English to various departments and agencies. The Federal Trade Commission, for example, has hired Rudolf Flesch, an expert on readable writing.

Such government efforts are nothing new. Mr. Zinsser recalls that Franklin D. Roosevelt tried to convert into English his own government's memos, such as a 1942 blackout order:

"Such preparations shall be made as will completely obscure all Federal buildings and non-Federal buildings occupied by the

Federal government during an air raid for any period of time from visibility by reason of internal or external illumination."

The President's response: "Tell them that in buildings where they have to keep the work going to put something across the windows."

Three centuries ago Samuel Butler observed: "Some writers have the unhappiness, or rather Prodigious Vanity to affect an obscurity in their Stiles, in devouring by all meanes not to be understood. . . ."

All of which suggests a remark by Tom Lehrer, a former Harvard mathematician and songwriter of some past note, who observed that we hear much in these troubled times of problems in communication—wives and husbands who cannot communicate, children who cannot communicate with their parents. His conclusion might also be applied to bureaucrats and their regulations—that if a person cannot communicate, the very least he can do is to shut up.— © 1978 Mobil Corporation, "Gobbledygook and Other Grotesqueries"

There's no particularly good reason for you to expect that a writer must *always* do the same kind of thing, or *always* generate the same kind of relationship. Within a single, relatively short piece of writing an author may need to gather information, or reveal his or her way of thinking, or goad some audience into action. But you may want to ask of yourself (and of other writers) whether you are doing the best kind of thing at the best time. Politicians, for example, have a habit of turning the attention on themselves just when you want them to provide honest, useful information about some issue at hand. In some kinds of writing, of course, a single intention and a single relationship may be maintained throughout. For example, the author of a laboratory report should probably aim throughout at what I've called *referential writing*.

Other ways of describing author-audience relationships

In the pages just past I have used the terms *referential*, *active*, and *personal* to label certain kinds of relationships that may exist between a writer and an audience; there are other ways of identifying such relationships, too. One way that has been suggested is to classify different kinds of writing according to the writer's attitude toward his or her subject and audience, because a major part of a writer's message is the attitude that becomes apparent in what he or she says. The writer's attitude influences what kind of things get said and how they get said. With this in mind, Winston Weathers and Otis Winchester differentiated nine kinds of discourse, each determined by the writer's attitude: *confident, judicious, quiet, imperative, compassionate, impassioned, critical, angry,* and *absurd.*

Another way of seeing writer-audience relationships, proposed by

James Moffett, depends upon the time and space relationships between a writer and an audience. A first kind of discourse, which might be called *reflection*, engages a writer in communication with himself or herself, as in a journal or a private meditation. A second kind, *conversation*, engages a speaker in communication with a second person who is within speaking range. A third, *correspondence*, engages a writer in communication with individuals remote from him or her in space. A fourth, *publication*, engages a writer in communication with readers who may be remote from him or her in space or time or both.

Two points are important to remember. First, the kinds of relationships that can develop between writers and readers are so many and so diverse that they can't all be listed. They probably can't even be satisfactorily sorted and classified. What is offered in the preceding pages is some suggested ways for looking at these relationships. Second, some kind of relationship always exists between a writer and his or her audience. It may be favorable, warm, close, and trusting. It may be distant and distrustful. Even the reader who tears up and spits upon what you have written has entered a relationship with you: such a reader has decided from your writing that you are a person of little worth and low value. Knowing that a relationship between you and a reader does occur gives you another choice to make when you write. You can leave the relationship to chance and let your reader, yourself, or the devil take the hindmost. Or you can take pains to know what you are doing and seek to enter thoughtfully into some kind of bonding with your reader.

Knowing what to call certain kinds of writer-audience relationships is not the same thing as knowing how to create them. Each relationship may require different things of a writer. Each may need a certain language, a certain tone, a certain kind of sentence structure. No one can tell you precisely and authoritatively how to achieve a particular kind of positioning with your audience. But being aware that there always is some kind of relationship is the first step toward being able to establish the kind of relationship you want.

Exercises

1.   Find a set of statistics about something that interests you (solar energy, population growth, deaf education, etc.) and using them, write a referential essay. Then, use the same statistics to write a persuasive essay in which you allow yourself to reveal your character.

2.   Find a piece of writing that is informative. See if you can identify phrases or sentences that actually reveal the writer's own attitudes or assumptions about the subject or about the world.

3.   Find a factual front-page article from a newspaper that gives the information about an event and rewrite the article in such a way that a real writer emerges.

Prose is architecture. . . .

Ernest Hemingway, *Death in the Afternoon*

*Once the plan is made and the material parcelled
out, then the dry skeleton of this structure
should be hidden beneath a surface which is all
variety and interest.*

Herbert Read, *English Prose Style*

6

Designing Your Work

This chapter suggests some ways of organizing information, ideas,
attitudes, opinions, and emotional responses into useful designs for
your writing. It includes

1. a general account of the relation between subjects and structures (p. 93);

2. some suggestions about forming a thesis statement and using the thesis to determine organization (p. 93);

3. some patterns of organization, formal and informal (p. 101);

4. some suggestions about maintaining continuity (p. 118);

5. an account of some options in organization and some new patterns (p. 122);

6. some recommendations about using structures that other writers use (p. 125).

Somewhere along the way, as you're thinking about what you want to say, your ideas and opinions and information begin to get sorted out. This sometimes happens without your quite knowing about it—things fall into place, one idea suggests another, one set of information gets associated with another, a hunch leads you to some evidence, the evidence leads you to a conclusion, and the first thing you know, you've arranged or organized your writing. Sometimes your familiarity with your subject, the time you spend on it, and the trial runs you make trying to write it out in your mind enable you to know, even if only half-consciously, what ought to go first, what ought to go last, and what ought to go in between. Sometimes this all turns out very well. Sometimes it doesn't.

This chapter offers some suggestions about ways to organize what you have to say. The suggestions are likely to be most useful on those occasions when you don't know where to begin, or don't quite see how to shape what you know.

Everything has a structure, although we may be unaware of it. Even an apparently unstructured experience, such as an "unstructured class discussion," has a structure—sometimes it is present from the outset as the instructor sets the topic or controls the order in which students speak; sometimes a structure is created as someone takes control of the discussion, setting its tempo and determining what gets emphasized.

In your writing, the structure contains and governs the meaning of what you say. The structure determines what your readers will focus on, the tempo of their reading, and the points that will get notice and emphasis as they read. The structure, in other words, may determine how readers take your meaning. On almost any subject in human experience, a number of things could be said. The structure of your work defines the limits of what you choose to say on the subject. It is your arrangement of what you can say about the subject.

The structures you create or use and the subjects you write about usually serve each other best if they are suited to each other. Most of the writing you will do for college courses and for career uses calls for relatively plain and straightforward plans displayed in a clear sequence that a reader can follow. Some personal writing and some writing intended for a public may need more intricate and less conventional plans. Most of this chapter offers suggestions about conventional planning and orderly sequences that can be surveyed with relative ease. The section on options in organization and on some new patterns for planning has some suggestions about less typical designs.

THESIS AND ORGANIZATION

One of the clearest, surest, and most useful ways of establishing a direction and determining a sequence for your work is to form and display a *thesis sentence*. A thesis sentence is your declaration of the

INSIGHT

Testing the relationship of structure and meaning

You can get a sense of the relationship of structure and meaning for yourself by checking your own experiences. Most of us can recall leaving a committee meeting or a discussion, muttering to ourselves, frustrated, perhaps angry, saying something like, "When he said [supply your own completion], I should have said [finish it yourself]," or "When she brought up [   ], I should have told her [   ]," or "I should have told them right at the start about the [   ]." When such things happen, our frustration oftener than not results from our failure to influence the structure (the plan, including the timing and emphasis) of the discussion. We don't get the right thing said at the right time, we don't introduce evidence at the appropriate moment, or we don't offer rebuttal of opposing views at just the right spot. It's a simple test, but such an experience seems to show how structure determines and governs meaning; if your words don't get into the structure so as to fit in some telling way, then your thoughts don't influence the meaning. And you get frustrated.

---

central point in your paper. It is your major proposition, a one-sentence summary of your entire paper.

The thesis sentence is not just an announcement of what your subject is; it is an announcement of the chief thing you have to say *about* your subject. A thesis sentence requires a *subject* and a *predication*. When you predicate something about a subject, you declare or affirm something about it. If you say, "My subject is making bread," that is not a thesis sentence. It only names your subject. But if you go on to say, "Making bread is good for your stomach, your emotions, and your mind," that is a thesis sentence. Look at it in this way:

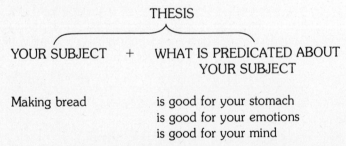

THESIS

YOUR SUBJECT   +   WHAT IS PREDICATED ABOUT YOUR SUBJECT

Making bread   is good for your stomach
                             is good for your emotions
                             is good for your mind

Some features of the thesis sentence can be described. First of all, of course, a thesis sentence is a single sentence, not two, or a paragraph full of sentences. Two sentences are likely to make two points, or two predications. The purpose of a thesis sentence is to propose a single point for discussion. Second, a thesis sentence should probably be either a simple sentence or a complex sentence. Compound sentences and compound-complex sentences, by virtue of their grammatical structure, contain at least two main ideas (two independent clauses). An essay built on a compound sentence as a thesis may go off in at least two directions, but a thesis sentence should advance one presiding claim. That doesn't mean that a thesis sentence has to be short and plain. The simple sentence used as a thesis may have as many modifiers as necessary, and the complex sentence used as a thesis may have a series of modifiers and dependent clauses, as in the following examples:

Making bread is good for your stomach, your emotions, and your mind.	*Simple sentence of 12 words.*
Making bread, *a pleasant anachronism in a world full of packaged foods*, is good for your stomach, *providing cheap, filling, good food*, for your emotions, *providing a good way to work off stress and frustration*, and for your mind, *providing a quiet time for reflection*.	*Simple sentence of 45 words. The italicized additions are contributions to the primary thesis, not new predications in themselves.*
While making bread is a pleasant anachronism in a world full of packaged foods, the process is good for your stomach, *since it results in good, cheap food*, good for your emotions, *since kneading the dough works off stress and frustration*, and good for your mind, *since the process offers a quiet time for reflection*.	*Complex sentence of 55 words. The italicized additions are four dependent clauses that are minor predications amplifying the one major predication.*

A thesis sentence serves several purposes. As I've noted above, it is an announcement of your major predication, the chief thing you have to say. It is also a commitment on your part: when you write a thesis sentence, you are committing yourself to deal with that one key point that you have announced. The thesis sentence, then, serves as a kind of measuring stick for your writing; anything that is not clearly related to the thesis sentence should probably be omitted from your work. A thesis sentence is a bond between you and a reader. It says, "This—and only this—is what I am going to write about."

Developing a thesis sentence

Most of the time, writing a thesis sentence comes late in the process of thinking about your work. A lot of thinking, some poking about, some trial notes, some false starts—in other words, much of the kind of thing described in the first chapters of this book—probably must take place before you can put things together in a thesis sentence. Sometimes, of course, you may know what to say right away, particularly if you are writing in response to a particular question or assignment. You may spend considerable time working out a thesis, however, but remember that once you've done so, much of your planning is over. The illustration below may suggest to you some of what happens in the search for a thesis sentence.

Assignment *500 words — recent local controversy*

3 possible topics—last chosen because of assigned length (other two would take longer)

gas rate increase— what's the real % increase over last 3 years?

Reduction in language programs

Parking on campus — new landscape plan

Subtopics, ideas that have to be dealt with—listed in no special order

① - new landscape in front of student Center
⑤ - removes 2 small parking lots < faculty ✗ / staff ✗
1 large parking lot < staff / students
⑧ - plans already drawn
② - grass, shrubbery, trees
③ - eliminates traffic from main quadrangle area
⑦ - sponsors ?
④
⑥
opposed — but adequate parking elsewhere

Tentative judgments

for the new plan
opponents make sense
don't like the way it's been proposed

Two thesis sentences—the last selected

Though I understand the objections of those who will lose parking spaces, I think the new campus landscape plan will improve the campus, removing traffic and adding green space.

On the basis of the thesis, items above are numbered in the order to be discussed

While I like the new campus landscape plan and believe opponents will soon get used to it, I think the sponsors were wrong in the way they proposed it to the university community.

Notice two things about this sample of the development of a thesis. First, the whole project is relatively simple. The assignment calls for 500 words, so the subject and the thesis cannot be too complicated—500 words is scarcely more than two pages of typewritten text. Second, notice that when the author settles on the thesis sentence, then it's possible for him or her to arrange the material to be discussed. A thesis sentence is a decision; once it is reached, the planning is just about over with.

Your thesis sentence should usually appear in your essay, but where it occurs depends on the thesis sentence, the kind of essay you're writing, and your own mood and attitude. Usually, the thesis sentence will occur early in your essay; it's your main point, after all, and saying it at the first is a good way to get started. The thesis sentence worked out above, for example, could stand by itself as a short opening paragraph for a short essay:

> *While I like the new campus landscape plan and believe that opponents will soon get used to it, I think the sponsors were wrong in the way they proposed it to the university community.*

That opening, however, presupposes that all your readers are familiar with the local controversy. Sometimes, you may need to delay the appearance of your thesis sentence so that you can establish a context for it or show the occasion that led you to this thesis, as in this example:

> *We haven't had much to complain about on campus recently. No one has censored anything. No one has changed the grading system without telling anybody. No one has tried to bring a controversial speaker to campus. Perhaps that's the reason that the new proposal for removing three parking lots and replacing them with green space has created such a furore here. Some were delighted when they read of the plan in the campus newspaper and saw the landscape architect's drawing; others were enraged when they saw what happened to the parking lots. For myself, while I like the new campus landscape plan and believe that opponents will soon get used to it, I think the sponsors were wrong in the way they proposed it to the university community.*

Or consider the bread sentence proposed a little earlier:

> *Making bread is good for your stomach, your emotions, and your mind.*

This sentence could be used in a number of different places, depending upon what kind of essay an author wished to compose. Moving the thesis sentence about may change the tone and character of what you are writing. If the bread sentence were the *first* sentence in a short essay, its positioning would predict a simple, straightforward, three-part discussion. But sometimes you may need to create a paragraph that gives a kind of setting for your thesis sentence so that readers will understand at the beginning the context you are working in. Since you would create a whole paragraph in order to conclude with the thesis sentence, it's likely that you would have the beginning for a different kind of essay, as in this sample opening paragraph:

> *When I was poor, before old-fashioned methods were in, I used to make my own bread because it tasted good and was filling and was pretty cheap. But I didn't want everyone to know I was poor, and I did want everyone to think of me as a thoughtful, deliberative type, not the sort who would do something without a good reason. So I worked out a good explanation to account for making all that bread. Making bread, I told everyone, is good for your stomach, your emotions, and your mind.*

INSIGHT

A warning about thesis sentences

Don't expect to find a neat thesis sentence somewhere near the first of every essay you read, every magazine article, or every chapter in every book. A clear, early statement of a thesis is characteristic of writing that is generally direct and straightforward. Some writers work in more indirect ways, working their way slowly toward a thesis at the end, for example, or leaving their readers to decide for themselves the chief meaning of what they read. Remember that in this section the main concern is with the thesis sentence as a useful tool in planning *usual* writing jobs for college courses and career needs.

Using the thesis sentence to organize an essay

The effects of moving the bread sentence around suggest another advantage in using the thesis sentence. *A thesis sentence can organize your entire essay.* As a consequence, the parts of a thesis sentence can serve as an outline, as in this excerpt from a speech by Abraham Lincoln:

> I have stated upon former occasions, and I may as well state again, what I understand to be the real issue in this controversy between Judge Douglas and myself. On the point of my wanting to make war between the Free and Slave States, there has been no issue between us. So, too, when he assumes that I am in favor of introducing a perfect social and political equality between the white and black races. These are false issues upon which Judge Douglas has tried to force the controversy. There is no foundation in truth for

the charge that I maintain either of these propositions. The real issue in this controversy—the one pressing upon every mind—is the sentiment on the part of one class that does look upon slavery as a wrong, and of another class that does not look upon it as a wrong.—Abraham Lincoln, Alton Speech, 1858

The last sentence in this passage, naming the real issue, serves as a thesis sentence and as an outline for the rest of the speech. Immediately following this passage Lincoln takes up discussion of those who look upon slavery as wrong. Then, as the sentence predicts, he turns to those who do not look upon it as wrong.

The bread sentence, as I have already suggested, outlines a three-part essay. The thesis sentence on the campus landscape also outlines a three-part essay:

> While I like the new campus landscape plan

> > *First section, explaining the author's attraction to the plan—a minor section of the paper, as indicated by its appearance here in a minor grammatical construction.*

> and believe that opponents will soon get used to it,

> > *Second section, also minor, explaining opposition and author's account of why opposition will wane.*

> I think the sponsors were wrong in the way they proposed it to the university community.

> > *The main clause of the sentence and the chief point of the thesis—the third section of the essay.*

If you regard the first version of your thesis sentence as tentative, then you can, by manipulating the form of the thesis sentence, test your organization and be sure that you have settled on the best plan. The version of the landscape sentence, for example, cites three points but puts the stress on the author's objection to the way the proposal was presented. That portion of the sentence gets the emphasis because it is in the main clause and because it comes last (usually the portion of a sentence that has the greatest impact on a reader). But suppose the sentence were rewritten:

> *While I think the sponsors were wrong in the way they proposed it to the university community, I like the new campus landscape plan and believe that opponents will soon get used to it.*

This revised sentence provides an outline for a different essay. It reduces the author's objection to the manner of presentation to a minor point and emphasizes the author's pleasure in the plan and his conviction that opponents will soon get used to it. Or it might be rearranged in this way:

> *I like the new campus landscape plan and believe that opponents will soon get used to it, though I think the sponsors were wrong in the way they proposed it to the university community.*

In this version, the author is presenting his major emphasis first, leaving his minor objection to trail along at the end.

You can gain some particular advantages by using the thesis sentence as a way of organizing your essay. First, a sentence is easier to organize and manipulate and shift around than a whole essay is. Second, getting all of your points into your thesis sentence in the right order decides the content and plan of your essay before you start writing and so leaves you free to concentrate on the way you are writing. Finally, getting all your points into your thesis sentence in the right order helps guarantee continuity in your essay. If your points fit together in a sentence, then their connection with each other is probably clear in your mind, making it easier for you to maintain the continuity in your essay.

Exercises

1. Describe the arrangements for papers suggested by the following student and professional thesis sentences:

   a. Being able to live all over the world really has its advantages as well as its disadvantages, and I have experienced many of them.—A student essay

   b. Travel, in the younger sort, is a part of education; in the elder, a part of experience.—Francis Bacon, "Of Travel"

   c. I feel that one of the hardest and most important lessons I learned through cheerleading was loyalty.—A student essay

   d. There is another kind of ghetto that is not restricted to social or racial classes of people but concerns the mind and where we put our values.—A student essay

   e. If I had ten minutes to talk to the president of the university, the first thing I would discuss would be the need for more courses in black history.—A student essay

   f. Bureaucracy, as Max Weber pointed out, did not become the dominant mode of human organization in the West until the arrival of industrialism.—Alvin Toffler, *Future Shock*

   g. I guess the man I admired, respected, and loved the most was my dad.—A student essay

   h. A young boy must somehow learn to be a man, and no one could have been more instructive to me than James West.—A student essay

    i. The closed earth of the future requires economic principles which are somewhat different from those of the open earth of the past.—Kenneth E. Boulding, "The Economics of the Coming Spaceship Earth"

    j. By analyzing the funnies of certain time periods, it becomes apparent that one can judge the time by the comics, and vice versa.—A student essay

    k. Barbara Jordan's knowledge of her duties as a congresswoman, the strong, smooth articulate voice that grasps her listener's ear, and the determination to strive for what she believes is right, all serve as ingredients to the recipe of a dynamic and confident woman.—A student essay

2. For each of the following general topics, work in the way suggested by the example about campus landscaping to a thesis sentence that could be handled in 500 words:

    a. Freshman writing
    b. Campus politics
    c. Off-campus housing
    d. Terrorism
    e. Prison reform
    f. Skiing

3. Choose one of the thesis sentences that you wrote in exercise two and expand it by adding modifiers and dependent clauses to extend the commitment that it makes.

4. Take the thesis sentence that you wrote in exercise three and move the parts around, each time describing the change the shifting of the parts would make in the emphasis of the resulting paper.

5. After you have shifted the parts of the sentence in exercise four, choose the sentence that seems best and write a paper using it as the thesis.

SOME PATTERNS OF ORGANIZATION

When you know what steps you must take in order to say all that you want or need to say, your work is already organized. But it's not always easy to know these steps. A subject may be clear in your own mind, but a reader may need a slow, careful accounting of your thought processes, your evidence, and your way of connecting things. For this reason, it's useful to examine how other writers arrange their material and to note ways of designing that others have used. These patterns of organization are meant only as a convenience, but they may help if you are having trouble organizing your work.

Formal patterns of organization

Schemes of organization that have been widely and thoughtfully used have the merit that allowed them to survive trial and error. Any writer can often learn how much to tell readers or what steps to take by following the practice of good writers of former times and other places. Two traditional ways of organizing your work are described in the following pages.

A traditional plan based on public speaking.   One useful plan for organizing your work is based on common practices and patterns in public speaking. First devised by ancient rhetoricians who used their own observation and study of public speeches as a basis for the plan, this scheme proposes from five to eight particular steps to take in designing a piece of work. I'll use the traditional Latin names for these steps since they have been used more commonly than any English version.

Step 1:   *Exordium.* This is a conventional opening. Traditional instructions for the opening suggested that the writer or speaker accomplish three things: attract the audience's attention, establish the author's reliability, and create a sense of the author's good intentions. Often, in popular writing, an anecdote or illustration of the subject being discussed is used to accomplish these purposes. These traditional expectations of the opening also account in part for the habit of so many public speakers beginning with a joke.

Step 2:   *Narratio.* This is the occasion for providing background for the discussion at hand—information and circumstances important to the points the author wishes to make.

Step 3:   *Propositio.* This is a statement of the major proposition, or thesis (see discussion above).

Step 4:   *Partitio.* This is a "partitioning" of the work, a forecast of the steps that will follow in support or illustration of the proposition. It is what is happening when you hear a speaker say something like, "I want to tell you three reasons why you should vote for Christopher Smythe for president."

Step 5:   *Confirmatio.* This is typically the largest part of the discourse, the "proof" or support or evidence or collection of illustrations in support of the chief point you are making.

Step 6:   *Confutatio.* This step will usually appear only in discourses dealing with controversial matter. It is the occasion for refuting opposing views.

Step 7:   *Digressio.* This is a digression, but not in the sense that the word is most often used. We typically use the term to signify an element introduced into a discourse that does not belong there. In the sense intended here, a *digressio* is the introduction of an illustration, a parallel, a useful point from some other area of interest to support your discussion.

Step 8: *Peroratio.* This is the conclusion, frequently used to summarize key points, to stress a single major point, to recommend appropriate action, or to speculate on the future of your subject.

If you are having trouble organizing your work, it is possible to make an essay by going through these steps. The plan is especially useful if you are in a hurry, or if you have a close time limit, as when you're writing an essay examination. However, the plan hasn't been used exclusively in such cramped circumstances. John Milton's long and eloquent essay *Areopagitica* is organized along these lines; so are Jonathan Swift's "A Modest Proposal," the Declaration of Independence, Wordsworth's Preface to *Lyrical Ballads*, and countless political speeches.

One of the qualities that makes this plan useful is its flexibility: the order of the steps can be changed, and the number of the steps can be decreased.

For example, the *propositio*, or thesis, may be so startling or important or innovative that it should be moved to the first to accomplish part of what the *exordium* is supposed to do—attract the audience's attention. Or, in an argumentative piece, the *confutatio* or rebuttal might come first, if, for instance, people who hold contrary views have said something that seems blatantly wrong. In an argument, too, it might be useful at times to move the *confirmatio* to the end of your essay so that the major part of your argument can be the last thing a reader sees. In other words, you can arrange these eight things in the order that best suits you.

And you don't have to include all eight. In a short essay, for example, a *partitio* may not be necessary, and your *propositio* might be a part of your *exordium*. In an essay on a noncontroversial topic, there might well be no need for a *confutatio*. You may have no need for the *digressio*. You can make a good, straightforward essay, for example, with five steps: *exordium, narratio, propositio, confirmatio,* and *peroratio*. The example below may help you see how the plan appears in popular use.

A new dust-bowl threat

Little by little the sky was darkened by the mixing dust, and the wind felt over the earth, loosened the dust, and carried it away . . . The finest dust did not settle back to earth now, but disappeared into the darkening sky . . . The corn fought the wind with its weakened leaves until the roots were freed by the prying wind and then each stalk settled wearily sideways toward the earth.
—*The Grapes of Wrath,* 1939

EXORDIUM—The headline and the italic print alone attract attention. The drama and accuracy of Steinbeck's description pull readers into the article.

For many farmers, John Steinbeck's description of the Dust Bowl is as tragically apt today as it was in the 1930s. The drought and winds that four decades ago turned large parts of the U.S. into an agricultural disaster area have returned to some areas of the Great Plains, parching crops and whipping topsoil into sun-darkening clouds. In the 1930s the victims of the drought—the impoverished Okies memorialized in Steinbeck's novel—were lured westward by California's verdant fruit groves. But this time California is suffering from its most severe drought since 1921 and is in the midst of an agricultural crisis.

NARRATIO—This section, by recalling the 1930s Dust Bowl, establishes a context and a comparison and a history of concern.

Some experts attribute the lack of rain to an absence of sunspots, others to recurring drought cycles. In any event, parts of the Great Plains have received so little rain that they are actually drier than at the onset of the great drought of '34. Starved for moisture, the rich topsoil in hard-hit areas of the Great Plains is turning into a fine brown silt. Winds hurl the dust particles against the still-growing sprouts, until they lose their color and die.

PROPOSITIO—This is not clearly a thesis, for this article is describing an area of concern rather than making a single major point.

Green Bugs. Colorado expects to lose 70% of its winter wheat crop, and parts of Oklahoma anticipate a two-thirds decline in this year's harvest. Other sections are also suffering. In parts of the once lush wheat-growing belt that extends from New Mexico and Texas into Kansas and Iowa, the wheat shoots are stunted. Many farmers are choosing to sacrifice their crops in an effort to save the topsoil. By plowing their fields to turn the silt beneath less fragile clods and by planting soil-gripping crops, the farmers hope to conserve their valuable topsoil that otherwise may be swept away. Complicating the problem, unseasonably warm weather in some areas has produced an early infestation of cutworms and green bugs that attack the weakened plants.

CONFIRMATIO—The section headed "Green Bugs" and the section headed "Fresh Sprouts" make up the body of the discussion.

Despite the impending harvest failures, wheat prices so far have moved upward only slightly. A big crop in other parts of the U.S. could offset the expected losses. Nonetheless, many individual farmers stand to be wiped out by this year's losses. Says Minnesota Agricultural Expert John Wefald: "Some farmers are going to kiss rural America goodbye and good night."

Fresh Sprouts. Much of California was drenched by rain last week, but after almost six months of unrelieved drought, the downpours were too late to be of much help to farmers. As Gordon Snow, an official in the state Department of Food and Agriculture, put it: "It is going to have to rain for 40 days and 40 nights to make any difference." Because of the lack of rain, California's usually green fields are burned brown. Wildlife, starved for fresh sprouts, is migrating to the few irrigated areas. Fruits and vegetables have been withering for lack of moisture. Many cattlemen faced with skyrocketing hay prices are selling their stock for slaughter now at below break-even prices. So far, California growers and cattlemen estimate their losses at $410 million—and the cost is rising daily. Governor Jerry Brown has declared 29 agricultural counties disaster areas, which will allow the hard-pressed farmers to apply for emergency state and federal aid.

At first, farm experts and weather forecasters had feared that the present drought might be only the start of a cycle. In 1933, the parched earth spread northward from Kansas and Oklahoma until by 1935 most of the Middle West was afflicted. Mercifully, an onset of rain in Iowa and other parts of the Midwest has alleviated that worry. Still, in areas already seriously stricken by drought, it will take several years of normal rainfall and intensive soil husbandry before Dust Bowl conditions are overcome.

PERORATIO—The article ends with a final comparison and a projection into the future.

Exercise

Choose a subject about which you feel strongly and write tentative summary sentences for the parts of the traditional plan presented: *exordium, narratio, propositio, partitio, confirmatio, confutatio, digressio, peroratio.*

Organizing by outlining.   Probably the best-known system of organizing written work is outlining. Various meanings of the word *outline* are useful, even though some are connected to other fields and interests. An outline, in one sense, is the bordering line that defines a figure; an outline for a piece of writing is the bordering line that determines what is to be included and what is to be excluded. An outline tells how far you are to go with your subject, and as a "border" keeps out all that is not necessary to your subject. In another sense, an outline is a preliminary sketch, a general plan, that tells you what to do in the actual writing. In still another sense, an outline is *a thorough, systematic account of the structure or content of a piece of writing.*

Used seriously, an outline can help insure that all points get covered in your work: you may be able to assure yourself that you are saying enough, and you should be able to see that you have not included material that is irrelevant or inconsequential. The outline is also a way of determining the design of your work. Careful work in the outline will determine which parts of your writing will get primary emphasis, which parts will need the most space, which parts will need the least.

Outlines may be made in many ways. One writer may write down every thought, every piece of information, every example that he has collected on a given subject, then, on the same scrawly page, go back and number the items in a sequence that will help him write his essay. Another may write down everything she has collected on the subject, then return and enclose key points in a square, minor points in a circle, and then draw arrows from the circles to the squares they belong with. In other words, writers often develop their own private codes in outlining. If they work, they're fine.

One form of outlining does, however, have some advantages, particularly in planning long papers such as term research papers. A formal outline (described below) is generally understandable to more people than a private code would be. For that reason, a formal outline is submissible to another reader—as when a teacher requires that an outline be submitted with papers, or when the necessities of a job to be done require that co-workers have access to a quick survey of the work you have been doing. A formal outline also has the advantage of being easily expandable, so it is particularly well suited to longer writing projects.

Formal outlines often seem bothersome and even a little mysterious to students. The Roman numerals, capital letters, Arabic numerals, lower-case letters, bracketed numbers, and so on sometimes seem to be a tedious formality. If you'll think of the practices in formal outlining as a public code, they may seem less tiresome to you. These practices provide a set of mutually recognizable signals that can indicate to any user such things as which elements in a piece of writing are to be taken as major, which are to be taken as minor, which elements stand alone, which elements contribute to the making of other elements, and which elements are to be taken as near-equivalents in function and value.

But there is no point at all in trafficking with a formal outline unless you are willing to make two commitments.

First, you have to be willing to work thoroughly with the outline *before* you write anything. If you have been in classes where instructors required that outlines be submitted with your papers, you probably know (from hearsay, not from personal practice, to be sure) that it is easier to make an outline if you first write the paper, then outline what you have already written, since this method very nearly guarantees that the outline and the essay will agree with each other. Anyone who does this may temporarily satisfy some teacher, but that's all that can be gained. Otherwise, it's a futile and wasteful—not to mention deceitful—practice. An outline is useful only if it outlines for you, if it puts down the design that you will follow in your writing.

Second, you have to be willing to make the outline *thorough*. Jotting down two or three or four key ideas by themselves won't do you much good. Unless the outline itemizes all that is going to be in the piece of writing, it is mostly useless work.

WORKING THROUGH AN OUTLINE

Suppose we start with a subject already in mind. The subject, let us say, is the typical school schedule, or more properly, flaws in the typical school schedule. Or, perhaps, the subject is really the possibility of a new kind of school schedule. The subject, in other words, is not really yet settled; it may not be settled until the outline begins to take shape so that we can see what is to be said. Perhaps all that is really in mind at this point is a general discontent with the present kind of school schedule. We might start with this kind of outline:

School Schedules

I. The present schedule
II. Flaws in the present schedule
III. A new kind of schedule

That may look pretty silly. It *is* pretty silly. It doesn't tell anything; it doesn't show clearly what is to be included and what is to be excluded. It doesn't provide a systematic look at the structure and content of the essay to follow. If we tried to use this outline, it would do us no good, because it would still be necessary to think of what to say about each of those divisions. One of the things an outline can accomplish, if it is thorough, is to list all that is going to be said in the order it is going to be said before the writing begins. The little outline may look silly, but it is just the kind of outline that inexperienced writers sometimes try to work from. Nothing in the outline tells us whether each Roman numeral item will be a paragraph, or a page, or a chapter.

So it's necessary to start again. This time, we list—without worrying about the order—the ideas and information we have in mind about school schedules.

> —clocks control class time
> —all classes are the same length
> —most classes last for a term, 4–4½ months
> —subjects get chopped up
> —present system is convenient
> —just when you get interested in something, you have to go to another class
> —the system is inflexible
> —would a new system be possible?
> —can we let the subject determine the time spent?
> —we're in a 50-minute prison
> —do all classes need to last the same length of time?
> —could it be possible to spend a lot of time in one class for a while, then go away and study for several weeks without class?
> —different kinds of classes need different kinds of time

That may or may not be enough, but we'll begin to find out as we start to make a design out of it.

Looking at the random items listed above, it's possible to see connections among some of them.

> —clocks control class time
> —all classes are the same length
> —most classes last for a term, 4–4½ months
> —subjects get chopped up
> —just when you get interested in something, you have to go to another class
> —we're in a 50-minute prison
> —the system is inflexible
>
> —present system is convenient
>
> —would a new system be possible?
> —can we let the subject determine the time spent?
> —do all classes need to last the same length of time?
> —could it be possible to spend a lot of time in one class for a while, then go away and study for several weeks without class?
> —different kinds of classes need different kinds of time

When that is done, it is possible to go back through the grouped items and begin to put them in some kind of order. First, it's possible to give a general heading to each group. Then it's possible to number the items in each group to show the order in which they might be used. As this is done, it may be possible to see places in the list where there are gaps or inconsistencies.

All items in the first group suggest flaws in the present system of school schedules *and calendars (added to show that whole terms as well as days are controlled)*

① —clocks control class time *← first as dramatic opening*
② —all classes are the same length
④ —most classes last for a term, 4–4½ months
⑤ —subjects get chopped up
⑥ —just when you get interested in something, you have to go to another class
③ —we're in a 50-minute prison
⑦ —the system is inflexible

items ①②③ and ④ describe the system items ⑤ & ⑥ are consequences of the system – item ⑦ is a summation

item ⑦ could go 1st as a general topic for the group, but moved to last so as to connect with next group

The second group so far contains only a single item about the present system

① —present system is convenient
②- *useful systems have been abandoned before when better systems have been devised*

the one item in this group is not enough; it doesn't provide a way to connect with the 3rd group

the new item will require some research – may need to find out when the present type of schedule was introduced and what kind of schedule was common before that

The third group of items all suggest hopes for a new system

1st because it can be connected to item ② of the previous group

① —would a new system be possible?
4 ② —can we let the subject determine the time spent?
3 ② —do all classes need to last the same length of time?
⑤—could it be possible to spend a lot of time in one class for a while, then go away and study for several weeks without class?
2 ④—different kinds of classes need different kinds of time

If the hope for a new system ① is the central idea in this group, then item ② could be taken as one way of realizing this hope, and items ③,④,⑤ are different ways of talking about the idea in ② – item ③ can be eliminated as repetitious of ②

By this time, we're getting close to an outline. Grouping the items and marking them in order, as shown above, is one way of discovering where more is needed, where repetitions occur, and where connections are not possible, as the added notes indicate. It's now possible to make a fairly workable outline.

Rewind the Clock and Get a New Calendar

I.   Flaws in the present system of school schedules

   A. The restrictive nature of the system
      1. Clocks and calendars as determiners of class time
      2. Uniform length of class meetings
      3. Fifty-minute prison
      4. Uniform duration of courses (term)

   B. Consequences of the restrictive system
      1. Subject chopped up
      2. Interest interrupted by time limit

   C. An inflexible system

II. Convenience and change

   A. Convenience of an inflexible system

   B. Convenience or improvement

III. Hope for a new system

   A. Possibility of a new system

   B. Subject and need as determiners of schedule
      1. Different subjects, different times
      2. Subject as determiner of schedule
      3. Student need as determiner of schedule

SOME NOTES ON THE OUTLINE

1.   The title is taken from the first item listed; it seems the most noticeable or dramatic of the items.

2.   The amount of detail that goes into your outline depends in large part upon how much of your written work you think is represented by each unit of the outline. In the outline above, for example, if I.A., I.B., and I.C. each represent one paragraph, then this outline has nearly enough in it to use as a basis for the writing. On the other hand, if each of the Arabic numeral sections under I.A., for example, is to become a paragraph, then further details would be useful in the outline, as shown below:

   I.   Flaws in the present system of school schedules

      A. The restrictive nature of the system
         1. Clocks and calendars as determiners of class time
            a. The typical high-school schedule
            b. The typical college schedule

         2. Uniform length of class meetings
            a. The history class on Monday

   b. The physical education class on Tuesday
   c. The writing class on Wednesday

3.   If the outline above is followed, the paragraph represented by I.C. will be shorter than the paragraphs represented by I.A. and I.B.

4.   The middle of the essay to be written from this outline is relatively less important than the beginning and the end. The middle, represented by II, is chiefly a way of getting from the criticism in I to the hope in III.

   No one can determine for you exactly what kind of outline you may need to make for any particular purpose. There are, however, some general patterns of usage that may be useful to you. First, note the conventional form of the outline:

   I.   Primary idea, division, or topic

   A. Idea, information, judgment necessary to discussion of I
      1. Idea, information, judgment necessary to discussion of A
      2. Idea, information, judgment necessary to discussion of A
      3. Idea, information, judgment necessary to discussion of A
         a. Idea, information, judgment necessary to discussion of 3
            (1). Idea, information, judgment necessary to discussion of a
            (2). Idea, information, judgment necessary to discussion of a
         b. Idea, information, judgment necessary to discussion of 3

   B. Idea, information, judgment necessary to discussion of I
       [Subdivisions as above as far as needed]

   II. Second primary idea, division, or topic
       [Subdivisions as above as far as needed]

   [Roman numeral main divisions as far as needed]

Items occurring at the same level in the outline are roughly equivalent in value and in their contribution to the piece of writing. For example, items I.A. and I.B. are at the same level in the outline and both are contributions to the discussion of I. Items 3.a. and 3.b. are at the same level, and both are contributions to the discussion of 3. Notice, too, that when a unit is divided, usually two or more subdivisions result. For example, I is divided, and subdivisions A and B result. A is divided, and subdivisions 1,

2, and 3 result. The usual assumption is that when you divide something, at least two subdivisions must occur.

It is not possible to say how detailed an outline should be, or how many divisions, subdivisions, and subsubdivisions there should be. That depends largely on how long and how complex a piece of writing you are working on. A five-hundred-word theme doesn't need the same kind of outline that a forty-page chapter in a book might need. Usually, your outline should be sufficiently thorough to account for every paragraph in your writing. A good rule-of-thumb suggests that you carry your outline far enough to include specific examples and illustrations. For example, consider one section of the sample outline above:

> 3. Idea, information, judgment necessary to discussion of A
>   a. Idea, information, judgment necessary to discussion of 3
>   (1). Idea, information, judgment necessary to discussion of a
>   (2). Idea, information, judgment necessary to discussion of a
>   b. Idea, information, judgment necessary to discussion of 3

According to the rule-of-thumb suggested above, the section above would represent *at least* two paragraphs. One paragraph would be represented by item a. Items (1) and (2) would be illustrations, examples, pieces of information contained in that paragraph. The second paragraph would be represented by item b. The whole unit 3 would be, then, a two-paragraph unit.

INSIGHT

A warning about formal outlines

Because of their appearance, formal outlines sometimes may tempt you to focus your attention on separate units of thought, one at a time. That's all right, of course, unless you get so preoccupied with working out the shape and content of separate units that you forget to connect them. An outline tends to keep divisions and subdivisions apart, but a reader needs to be able to see their connection. This potential problem can be partially eliminated if you use whole sentences at every level in your outline. Writing whole sentences will usually keep you conscious of how one idea connects with another. (See the section below on continuity.)

Exercises

1. Describe what is wrong with the following outline for an essay:

Thesis: Since science fiction, like science, is concerned mainly with extrapolation and the "what if" proposition, the reader of science fiction is well prepared for the advances of science.

    I. Rate of change of our world

        A. Relation of man to progress
            1. Changes must come at the same rate to both the physical and the mental worlds
            2. Future shock

    II. Definitions of science fiction

    III. Past successes at prediction by science fiction

        A. Television
        B. Robots
        C. Communications satellites
        D. Help for preventing future shock
            1. Science fiction shows readers that change is inevitable

    IV. Science fiction is entertaining

2. Using the same ideas, rework the above outline into a successful topic or sentence outline.

3. Jot down some notes on one of the following subjects or one of your choosing. Compose a thesis sentence from your notes, and make a topic or sentence outline.
    a. Institutional food
    b. On-campus parking
    c. Registration procedures at this college or university
    d. Unrealistic faculty expectations
    e. Advertisers' image of America

4. Write the paper suggested by the outline you made in exercise 3.

Informal patterns of organization

Some far less formal plans may help you in certain kinds of writing. Almost anything that gives you an idea, that tells you what to put first, or that provides a sequence for you to follow in your work may be used as a basis for planning what you are to write. The standard to use is whether or not your plan justifies itself by being appropriate to what you are trying to write and the context in which you are writing. A private, meditative essay may not need a long, logically developed plan. A breezy, chatty, casual plan based on the train of associations in a private revery will not be the right kind of plan for an official report on a technical process.

Organizing with sentence predictors.   The discussion of thesis sentences above showed that single sentences can be used as organizers of your work. If you are willing to take the time to formulate a good thesis sentence or a good summary sentence, especially if you try rearranging it in a number of ways, you may be able to outline your work with a single sentence. A sentence predictor will almost always serve as a useful outline for *short* pieces of writing. Otherwise, its uses are limited.

Make no mistake—writing one good single sentence that will predict the content and shape of a short essay will take time. If you're not used to doing so, writing this kind of sentence may seem to take almost as much time as it does to write the essay itself. With a little practice, however, you can become familiar with the technique and be able to form a predicting sentence in four or five minutes. It's worth doing, for two good reasons. First, an essay written from a predicting sentence has a kind of unity and continuity built into it. If the chief elements that you plan to talk about in your essay will fit nicely into a single sentence, then you can be reasonably sure that they will fit together well when they are amplified into a short essay. Second, the predicting sentence—if you are used to it and can form one quickly—is an excellent technique to use when you are writing an essay examination. A moment's thought on the subject matter of the question, a listing of available information and ideas, then a quick formulation of a predicting sentence, and you're almost guaranteed a neat, cohesive essay answer.

You will probably have to find your own best way of developing predicting sentences. One way to start, especially if the method is new to you, is to go through a gradual process of amplification and combination. Suppose that you have to produce a short essay on an unspecified subject. Because of a general interest in horticulture, gardening, and landscape design, you decide to write something about trees. A few minutes' reflection enables you to see that in a short essay you can't say much about trees, so you decide to focus on choosing trees for home planting. When you've come that far, you can begin to jot down notes on what you think will go into the essay—perhaps just key words, phrases, or ideas, in any order:

> *shade*
> *fruit-bearing*
> *ornamental*
> *size and growth rate*
> *right ground*
> *color*

A little reflection and a little work will let you amplify the terms in this list into simple complete sentences:

Our family wanted trees mostly for shade and ornament, not for fruit.
We wanted fast-growing trees to reach 20–30 feet.
Our rocky ground wouldn't be right for some trees.
Leaf and bark color didn't matter much to us.

And then you remember that your family, being a bit on the daft side, wanted to plant trees that had interesting names. Just for the sound of the names they preferred linden and laurel and bois d'arc and silver maple and sequoia over elm and beech and ash. So you add another sentence:

The family also wanted trees with romantic-sounding names.

Now these five simple sentences can be combined into a single sentence that will predict the whole content of your essay:

When the family set out to choose trees for planting in the front yard, where the soil is rocky and won't accommodate some trees, we were looking not so much for particular colors but for fast-growing trees to reach 20–30 feet and provide shade and orna-ment, not fruit, with the condition that they had to have romantic-sounding names.

This sentence can also predict the design of your essay. You could, for example, make a five-paragraph essay out of the sentence:

Paragraph 1: In a pinch, the sentence above could stand as an introductory first paragraph.

Paragraph 2: This paragraph, then, would expand the opening clause, "When the family set out to choose trees for planting in the front yard," and tell when this happened, why only the front yard was at issue, where and how long you looked for trees.

Paragraph 3: This paragraph would explain more fully the re-strictions set by the soil, perhaps including some anecdotes about the rockiness (such as how you broke the pickax trying to dig a hole).

Paragraph 4: This paragraph would be the key part of the essay; it would expand the one main clause in the sentence, "we were looking not so much for particular colors but for fast-growing trees to reach 20–30 feet and provide shade and ornament, not fruit." The sentence above predicts that this paragraph will probably be the fullest and most important. All the other portions of the sen-tence are dependent constructions; the part amplified in this para-graph is the one independent grammatical construction.

Paragraph 5:   The last paragraph would expand the last dependent portion of the sentence, "with the condition that they had to have romantic-sounding names."

That wouldn't be bad. But suppose, as you're still planning and thinking about the essay, you decide that you want to show how the family finally gave up its insistence that the trees have interesting names and decided to choose on a more conventional, somewhat more logical basis. The predicting sentence could be revised to suggest a different organization:

Paragraph 1 {
Although the family had really wanted trees

with romantic-sounding names and some

members had poked through tree books,

rolling lovely names about for each other,
}

Paragraph 2   when the time came to choose, we chose | Paragraph 3

trees for their accommodation to rocky soil

and for shade, height, and rapid growth.   Paragraph 4

That sentence would let you explore the family's pleasure in names and sounds, but it puts the stress on the family's decision to follow arboreal logic instead of their own fancies. But, finally, suppose you cherish the family's whimsicality about tree names and want to stress it in your essay. The predicting sentence could be modified again so as to outline a different kind of essay:

While the family finally decided, when the time came to choose, that they would be sensible and choose trees for their suitability to the soil, their shade, height, and rapid growth, they still cherished trees with lovely names and, after poking through tree books, called the chosen trees by their plain names or, for good sound, by their scientific names.

Predicting sentences don't have to be long. A simple version of one of the sentences above, with a series to predict the paragraphs of your paper, would work well, too:

Almost against our wishes, we chose mulberry and sweet gum for soil suitability, shade, height, and rapid growth.

It may take a bit of practice to get used to writing sentences that forecast the content and organization of essays. But the practice is worthwhile because the technique is useful in emergency circumstances, such as essay examinations or those days when you have to write a short paper in class, as well as being a good guide to and test for organization.

Exercises

1.   "Despite my mother's eternal vigil over costs and the insistence of my father, the incurable teacher, that vacations be educational, my family managed somehow to have two relaxing, joyful weeks together every summer touring places that will remain a part of my memories."
    a. The emphasis of this sentence predictor is on the pleasure of the family vacations. Rewrite the predictor so the emphasis could be on the "quirkiness" of the mother and father.
    b. Rewrite the predictor so the emphasis could be on the places visited.

2.   Write sentence predictors for essays on the following subjects:
    a. Organizing time
    b. Grades as motivators
    c. Homecomings
    d. Rising tuition costs
    e. How I make decisions

Other informal organizing methods.   The first chapters of this book, you may recall, discuss some ways of hunting and thinking about subjects. Some of those methods will also serve as schemes for organizing your work.

1.   The method of *word association* described on pages 11 – 13 can sometimes be used as the basis for a design, though probably only for certain kinds of writing. If what you are writing is meditative, personal, exploratory, and informal, then you can probably organize your essay by following the track of your own associations. This is not a method you'd want to use all of the time, or even frequently. It ought to be saved for personal writing in which you're trying to think something through or track down a feeling. The diary entry written by William Butler Yeats (page 80) traces associations.

2.   The sequence of *prepared questions* given on pages 14 – 18, though intended first to lead you toward discovery of a good subject, can also be used to organize an essay. There might be rare occasions when you could use the entire sequence of questions as a plan for a long, explanatory essay, where your essay is, in effect, the answers to the given questions. More often, one part of the sequence—a few connected questions—would provide a useful outline for an essay.

3.   The eight-step *problem-solving sequence* suggested on pages 19-20 was first meant as a series of questions to lead you toward a subject, or toward the key issue in a subject already decided upon. But the eight-step series can also serve very well as an outline, particularly for an essay discussing a controversy, a conflict, or a problem of some kind.

4.   Any one of the six simple *linkages* shown on pages 45 – 47 may give you a way of organizing what you have to say. Each of these linkages is intended to help you determine what can be connected with the subject you are thinking about. Since a plan of organization is in a way one means of saying how things are connected with each other, any one of these linkages may provide a scheme or plan. For example, one of the linkages is contrast: What can be linked to your subject with *but?* That simple linkage is a basis for a short essay developing a contrast.

5.   The next chapter is an account of some ways to develop or amplify your material, a discussion of what you can do to put flesh on the bare bones of an outline. As you will see, some of the methods discussed there (comparison, contrast, illustration, for example) may also give you some ideas about how to plan what you are writing.

CONTINUITY AND TRANSITION

As you plan your work, try to look ahead and think about how the various things you will say are going to fit together. Most of the time, both for your own sake as a writer and for the sake of your reader, the parts of your writing should be clearly connected to each other, with each shift of direction (from one paragraph to another, for example, or from one subtopic to another) clearly marked, with each stage of your thinking clearly designated, and with each transition clearly notifying your reader of stages in your writing and of shifts in your thinking.

Continuity in writing is the quality that enables the parts of the writing to hang together and make one uninterrupted progression from beginning to end. *Transition* is the process of crossing over from one place to another, from one idea to another, from one episode to another. A transitional word, phrase, sentence, or paragraph allows you to get from one place in your writing to another and to take your reader with you. Continuous, uninterrupted progressions with clear transitions make it possible for a reader to track along with you, but continuity and transition are not just for the reader's sake. They give value to the writer, too. When you're writing, the need for clear continuity and easy transition sharpens your focus on your subject. Knowing that you want your reader to see how the various parts of your essay fit together is likely to keep you alert to detect irrelevancies and breaks in your writing.

There is no single sure way to guarantee continuous progression. Looking consistently at your subject will always help. Tying everything you say to a stated thesis will always help. Sometimes there is a natural logic and order that you can follow in handling your subject—as when you describe a landscape starting with the near view and proceeding to the far view, or when you explain something by starting with the least important feature and proceeding to the most important, or when you tell about an event chronologically.

Certain signals will show your readers the connections you want to make:

—Connect two sentences or two paragraphs by repeating key words or phrases.

—Connect elements in your writing by using a pronoun in the second element that refers to an antecedent in the first element.

—Use synonyms in later sentences or paragraphs for key words in earlier sentences or paragraphs.

—Link connected ideas by expressing them in identical grammatical constructions.

—Connect two elements by establishing their logical relationship; for example, if the first element states a cause, then the second can state a result, or if the first gives one term in a comparison, the second can give the other.

And you can use connectives, words, and phrases such as those shown below that have specific transitional functions:

and, in addition, also, moreover, furthermore, first, second, third	—used to introduce statements similar to or parallel with preceding statements
for example, for instance, to illustrate	—used to introduce examples
however, but, on the other hand, nevertheless, still, yet	—used to introduce contrasts
consequently, as a result, therefore, accordingly, in conclusion	—used to introduce conclusions

The best way to learn about continuity and transition is to read habitually and notice how interesting writers handle connections in books and articles. The examples below show how these various connecting signals are used throughout even short pieces of writing.

STUDYING CONTINUITY

After considering the connections marked in the first example below, examine the other two passages to see how continuity is managed. Analyze the passages in the same way the first example has been done.

key phrase repeated

similar openings

key word repeated

similar phrases

pronoun refers to Trident

signals contrast

pronoun reference

Next to Gerald Ford and Leonid Brezhnev, the *most powerful man in the world* is not Mao Tse-tung or the head of any other government. The third *most powerful man in the world* is a commander of a Trident submarine.

A single Trident submarine today carries *more destructive force* than all the military establishments of Great Britain, Italy, Spain, Brazil, Argentina, West Germany, Japan, the Philippines, India, and Pakistan put together.

A Trident has built into it an undersea launching platform for thermonuclear bombs, some of which contain *more explosive force* than a thousand atomic bombs of the kind that destroyed Hiroshima in 1945.

Theoretically, the American people ought to feel completely secure in the fact of such power being deployed in their behalf. The Trident has almost unlimited mobility; it can launch an attack on any country of its choosing, yet it is practically immune to counterattack by being able to hide in the sea.

But there are problems. A Trident has both the advantages and the disadvantages of being an autonomous war machine. The men who operate it . . . —Norman Cousins, "The Third Most Powerful Man in the World"

1   By the rivers of Babylon, there we sat down, yea, we wept, when we remembered Zion.

2   We hanged our harps upon the willows in the midst thereof.

3   For there they that carried us away captive required of us a song; and they that wasted us required of us mirth, saying, Sing us one of the songs of Zion.

4   How shall we sing the Lord's song in a strange land?

5   If I forget thee, O Jerusalem, let my right hand forget her cunning.

6   If I do not remember thee, let my tongue cleave to the roof of my mouth; if I prefer not Jerusalem above my chief joy.—Psalm 137

In those days it was either live with music or die with noise, and we chose rather desperately to live. In the process our apartment—what with its booby-trappings of audio equipment, wires, discs and tapes—came to resemble the Collier mansion,* but that was later. First there was the neighborhood, assorted drunks and a singer.

We were living at the time in a tiny ground-floor-rear apartment in which I was also trying to write. I say "trying" advisedly. To our right, separated by a thin wall, was a small restaurant with a juke box the size of the Roxy. To our left, a night-employed swing enthusiast who took his lullaby music so loud that every morning promptly at nine Basie's brasses started blasting my typewriter off its stand. Our living room looked out across a small back yard to a rough stone wall to an apartment building which, towering above, caught every passing sound and rifled it straight down to me. There were also howling cats and barking dogs, none capable of music worth living with, so we'll pass them by.

But the court behind the wall, which on the far side came knee high to a short Iroquois, was a forum for various singing and/or preaching drunks who wandered back from the corner bar. From these you some-times heard a fair barbershop style "Bill Bailey," free-wheeling versions of "The Bastard King of England," the saga of Uncle Bud, or a deeply felt rendition of Leroy Carr's "How Long Blues." The preaching drunks took on any topic that came to mind: current events, the fate of the long-sunk *Titanic* or the relative merits of the Giants and the Dodgers. Naturally there was great argument and occasional fighting—none of it fatal but all of it loud.

I shouldn't complain, however, for these were rather entertaining drunks. . . .—Ralph Ellison, "Living with Music"

*The home of two brothers who lived as hermits, filling their house with junk and bales of newspapers.

Exercises

1.   The following is a rewrite of a paragraph from a student essay. The paragraph has been altered to remove many of the transitional devices and much of the subordination. Rewrite the paragraph so that the prose

once again flows smoothly. Ask your teacher to read the original paragraph to the class to see how close to the original your rewrite came.

> We grew tired of controlling the world. We would play circus. The circus was small. It was better than any other. My big brother wore my dad's hat. He cracked his bullwhip at my frightened little brother, the lion. He always had to be the growling lion. He was too small to do anything else. Right next to our bunk beds was the net, my father's bed. We would all jump off the bunk beds onto his bed. I was the only one who could do a flip. I got to be the trapeze artist. It did not matter how neat the room looked when my dad left for work. It was always in shambles when he returned. Then came the day when he never returned.

2.   Rewrite a paragraph that you have written earlier in this course and remove the transitional devices. Give the paragraph to a classmate and ask him or her to reconstruct the original. When the student returns your paragraph, check it for accuracy. If the student had too much trouble reconstructing your paragraph, the paragraph itself may have lacked coherence.

ALTERNATIVES IN DESIGNING YOUR WORK

Most of this chapter has been about conventional forms of planning, orderly sequences appropriate to most college or career writing assignments. Regularity, orderly progressions, and neat connections are suitable to most of our writing. These qualities promote thoroughness in the treatment of a subject, and they make it easier for readers to follow a writer's line of development.

But not all writing is regular, orderly, and neat. Some of the alternatives to conventional planning or progression—violations of chronology, fragmentation, deliberate jumpiness, unorthodox construction, irregular typography—are associated most often with fiction. Some of them—those listed above and others—can also be used in other kinds of writing, and they have become more familiar to readers of the last ten years or so through their increasing use by such writers as John Cage, John Barth, Donald Barthelme, Norman Mailer, and Tom Wolfe:

> If you happen to attend a conference at which whole contingents of the O'Hare philosophers assemble, you can get the message in all its varieties in a short time. Picture, if you will, a university on the Great Plains . . . a new Student Activities Center the color of butter-almond ice cream . . . a huge interior space with tracks in the floor, along which janitors in green twill pull Expando-Flex accordion walls to create meeting rooms of any size. The conference is about to begin. The students come surging in like hormones.

You've heard of rosy cheeks? They *have* them! Here they come, rosy-cheeked, laughing, with Shasta and 7-Up pumping through their veins, talking chipsy, flashing weatherproof smiles, bursting out of their down-filled Squaw Valley jackets and their blue jeans—looking, all of them, boys and girls, Jocks & Buds & Freaks, as if they spent the day hang-gliding and then made a Miller commercial at dusk and are now going to taper off with a little Culture before returning to the co-ed dorm. They grow quiet. The conference begins. The keynote speaker, a historian wearing a calfskin jacket and hair like Felix Mendelssohn's, informs them that the United States is "a leaden, life-denying society." —Tom Wolfe, "The Frisbee Ion"

Some of the irregular forms that have become more popular recently are not necessarily new inventions. *Tristram Shandy*, a novel by the eighteenth-century writer Laurence Sterne, is a catalogue of unusual forms—wildly mixed chronological sequences, chapters a half page long, blank pages, marbled pages, diagrams of the novel's progress.

This departure from conventional forms is important to us, for several reasons. First, unconventional and irregular forms are often refreshing; different from customary forms, they attract attention by their novelty and may stimulate interest just by looking different. Second, irregular or unorthodox forms of organization may offer a realistic way of handling your subject. If you want to try to suggest the disparate activities that go on simultaneously at a hectic hour in a busy giant supermarket, for example, it may be helpful to use a form that will let you jump from place to place, item to item, person to person without apparent continuity, that will let you list items and pile up details, that will let you suggest by impression the swirl of color and movement in the scene. Unorthodox forms of organization are important, too, for a third reason. They represent a liberty we have: there is no set of "official" or "proper" forms that we must all observe. In the end, such a liberty is to be guarded and cherished.

It may seem overreacting to say that such a liberty is to be guarded and cherished, yet all writers haven't been able to exercise their liberty of form and maintain their liberty of life. In some times and places, unusual or unconventional or avant-garde forms are considered to represent unusual, unconventional, and therefore dangerous thoughts that must be silenced for the good of the state.

The very nature of unorthodox forms of organization makes it difficult to describe them, but two fairly common characteristics may be noted. First, openings and closings are not likely to be as clear-cut and definite as they are, for example, in an essay using a thesis sentence and an outline. A piece of writing may seem to begin in the middle of things, without background or explanation, and its conclusion may be indefinite and open-ended. Second, many instances of alternative organization are discontinuous and jumpy. While clear transitions and easy continuity are prized in most conventional writing, unconventional forms may be fragmented and broken with no effort being made to achieve orthodox continuity. The sample on this page is a mild example. It is a page from a recent textbook on various forms of language used for propaganda and commercial purposes. Instead of the usual straight text that one might expect in such a book, the sample uses a headline, different type styles, and quotations by three different writers (as well as a fourth by Harry Walker Hepner that begins at the bottom of the page).

Great men speak of advertising . . .

Advertising nourishes the consuming power of men. It sets up before a man the goal of a better home, better clothing, better food for himself and his family. It spurs individual exertion and greater production.

Sir Winston Churchill

If I were starting life over again, I am inclined to think that I would go into the advertising business in preference to almost any other. . . . The general raising of the standards of modern civilization among all groups of people during the past half century would have been impossible without the spreading of the knowledge of higher standards by means of advertising.

Franklin D. Roosevelt

ADVERTISING

Advertising, no less than art, is founded on eternal verities.

The latter responds to our aspiration to be something more than human: the former to a perverse insistence on remaining something less, manipulable objects in the service of notions like "success" or "happiness."

Thomas Albright

Every alert person must recognize that advertising has been a stimulating influence in our modern civilization. It often has stimulated people to want the new and desirable. As such, advertising may be considered an "accelerator of civilization." We now have more facilities for comfort than the preceding generations, which had no automobiles, airplanes, or television sets. We believe that such devices contribute to better living. . . .

Advertising helps to bridge the gap between undeveloped resources and informs people of the good things available to them. One reason why advertising has been more potent here than in some other countries is that we have the kind of people who differ from those of other countries: our people assume that anything that is satisfactory today can be made even better tomorrow.

Advertising contributes toward the greater availability of goods. Purchasing power is not a static quantity, like water in a bucket or the number of seats in a theater. Actually, the quantity of goods

88

Most writing jobs you'll face in your college work or in your career can be done with the more conventional forms of organization. A drastically different form may attract one reader by its novelty, to be sure, but it may repel another because it is unfamiliar and unexpected. It's probably a good idea not to try some unusual plan simply to satisfy some whim.

Any organizational form you use ought to justify itself: you ought to know why you are using it, and it ought to be appropriate to the subject you are dealing with.

Exercise

Try an unusual plan of organization for a paper on "How I Get Ready to Write," "Images of a Summer," or a topic of your own choosing.

USING FORMS THAT OTHER WRITERS USE

Samuel Johnson once remarked that "it is far easier to learn than to invent." Remember that you don't have to create a brand-new system of organization every time you write something. It is often possible and usually appropriate to use a design or form that other writers have used. There is nothing dishonest about such a practice. Every one of us belongs to some community, and we depend upon others in that community for various kinds of services. The same thing is true in the community of writers. Every novel owes something to the novels that defined the art of the novel, to the innovative novels of the past. Every tragedy owes something to other tragedies. Use other writers. Adapt their schemes of organization to suit your own purposes, or use them as they are. Lecturing young painters, Sir Joshua Reynolds told them, "Study therefore the great works of the great masters, for ever. . . . consider them as models which you are to imitate, and at the same time as rivals with whom you are to contend." Read as much as you can, and don't hesitate to borrow as your own the structure another writer has developed.

Borrowing a plan of organization from another writer doesn't mean that you have to give up your own ideas or your own original notions. In the examples that follow, a well-known writer adapts a child's verse for his own purposes; and two students use an essay by an artist as a model of form:

> However, at this point I hit upon a kind of *Ersatz* promise for an ending. As you will see, it is concerned with perfection on a grand scale. And it has in its favor the further fact that it involves the modernizing, or perfecting, of a traditional vision, one even so primal as to be expressed in a nursery jingle. I shall give the traditional jingle first, and then my proposed modernized perfecting of it. The older form ran thus:
>
>> If all the trees were one tree
>> What a great tree that would be.
>>
>> If all the axes were one axe
>> What a great axe that would be.

If all the men were one man
What a great man he would be.

And if all the seas were one sea
What a great sea that would be.

And if the great man
Took the great axe
And chopped down the great tree
And let it fall into the great sea

What a Splish-Splash that would be!

Modernized, perfected, the form runs thus:

If all the thermo-nuclear warheads
Were one thermo-nuclear warhead
What a great thermo-nuclear warhead that would be.

If all the intercontinental ballistic missiles
Were one intercontinental ballistic missile
What a great intercontinental ballistic missile that would be.

If all the military men
Were one military man
What a great military man he would be.

And if all the land masses
Were one land mass
What a great land mass that would be.

And if the great military man
Took the great thermo-nuclear warhead
And put it into the great intercontinental ballistic missile
And dropped it on the great land mass,

What great PROGRESS that would be!

—Kenneth Burke, "Language as Symbolic Action"

My capsule recommendation for a course of education is as follows:
Attend a university if you possibly can. There is no content of knowledge that is not pertinent to the work you will want to do. But before you attend a university work at something for a while. Do anything. Get a job in a potato field; or work as a grease-monkey in an auto repair shop. But if you do work in a field do not fail to observe the look and the feel of earth and of all things that you handle—yes, even potatoes! Or, in the auto shop, the smell of oil and grease and burning rubber. Paint of course, but if you have to

lay aside painting for a time, continue to draw. Listen well to all conversations and be instructed by them and take all seriousness seriously. Never look down upon anything or anyone as not worthy of notice. In college or out of college, read. And form opinions! Read Sophocles and Euripides and Dante and Proust. Read everything that you can find about art except the reviews. Read the Bible; read Hume; read Pogo. Read all kinds of poetry and know many poets and many artists. Go to an art school, or two, or three, or take art courses at night if necessary. And paint and paint and draw and draw. Know all that you can, both curricular and noncurricular—mathematics and physics and economics, logic, and particularly history. Know at least two languages besides your own, but anyway, know French. Look at pictures and more pictures. Look at every kind of visual symbol, every kind of emblem; do not spurn signboards or furniture drawings or this style of art or that style of art. Do not be afraid to like paintings honestly or to dislike them honestly, but if you do dislike them retain an open mind. Do not dismiss any school of art, not the Pre-Raphaelites nor the Hudson River School nor the German Genre painters. Talk and talk and sit at cafés, and listen to everything, to Brahms, to Brubeck, to the Italian hour on the radio. Listen to preachers in small town churches and in big city churches. Listen to politicians in New England town meetings and to rabble-rousers in Alabama. Even draw them. And remember that you are trying to learn to think what you want to think, that you are trying to co-ordinate mind and hand and eye. Go to all sorts of museums and galleries and to the studios of artists. Go to Paris and Madrid and Rome and Ravenna and Padua. Stand alone in Sainte Chapelle, in the Sistine Chapel, in the Church of the Carmine in Florence. Draw and draw and paint and learn to work in many media; try lithography and aquatint and silk-screen. Know all that you can about art, and by all means have opinions. Never be afraid to become embroiled in art or life or politics; never be afraid to learn to draw or paint better than you already do; and never be afraid to undertake any kind of art at all, however exalted or however common, but do it with distinction.—Ben Shahn, *The Shape of Content*

Education of the Writer

My little old Jewish grandmother-in-law had only two questions for me when she was informed that I was going back to school at the age of twenty-five. She was told at my wedding, and when she had been told, she stopped for a minute and then looked up from the plate of chopped liver she had been picking at to say, "Why you got to go now? Why you didn't go before?" For me, those two questions said more about her view of life than any amount of explanation she could give. She doesn't view life as a learning experience; she views life as something you survive in. You go to school to *become* something in order that you may find a job and survive in the world. My advice to the would-be writer is to ignore people like my grandmother-in-law. Don't be misled into thinking that life is a job, or that life is a task to be completed. Life is an experience and it is the writer's task to organize and clarify the experience; in order to do this the writer must live the experience.

"Attend a university if you possibly can. There is no content of knowledge that is not pertinent to the work you will want to do. But before you attend a university work at something for a while." Be a cab driver. Get out into the hustle and bustle of the work-a-day world. Watch people in the act of surviving. Jot down on scraps of paper your reactions to the people you see. Talk to people; while driving a business man to the airport try to find out what experiences he is a part of. Observe the reactions of people on the sidewalks as they move to and fro. Compare and contrast all the facets of human existence that flow about you. Be all the things you can as you experience the give and take of humanity that surrounds you. Pass nothing off as insignificant. Let no thought go by unexamined. Write as much as possible, and when you can't put words on paper organize them in your head.

Read! Read anything and everything you can. Pay attention to how an author puts his thoughts on paper. Read Melville and notice how he creates his images. Read Twain and see how his humor and insight combine to produce a new perspective on life. Read and read and read, and when you're not reading, write. Write as much and as often as you can. Write down feelings, thoughts, and experiences; and after you have written—rewrite, for rewriting is rethinking, and only by rethinking can you start to create order from the chaos that is life.

Do all these things and more, but most of all "remember that you are trying to learn to think what you want to think, that you are trying to coordinate mind and hand and experience." Experience all that you can: from the sleazy to the sophisticated, from the bowery to the East Side, from the deep South to the far North, from Los Angeles to Singapore, and from all corners of the globe and back again. Never be afraid to grab life by the belt loops, hitch it up over your waist, and wade on in. Let life surround you, and examine its parts while trying to create a whole by writing. And finally, never be afraid to write "however exalted or however common, but do it with distinction."—A student essay

(All quotations are from Ben Shahn's statement to artists.)

Toward the Education of a Writer

Anything, anywhere, anytime, but write.
One, two, learn about you,
Three, four, learn about lore,
Five, six, pick up Styx,
and Odysseus, and Caesar, and Christ, and all the other writings of
ancient times for similes, for metaphors, for you.
Seven, eight, sate, sate, sate,
Nine, ten, then do it again.
After you've learned all you can about ancient times, go back and
find the essentials of the character. Attend a university if you wish,
but don't let it retard your education. Learn all you can about all
there is, then learn a little more. Everything, everywhere,
everytime, but write. All the world's a scene, and you must give it
life by writing of it. Learn to sense all that is around you as totally as
possible, then make it better and write it down. Create a universe
with phrases, and clauses, and sentences, and paragraphs, and
chapters, and . . . but do start with words. Before you can see the
world, you must first see out of your crib. Travel, and voyage, and
perambulate. To catch the little quirks and mannerisms of your own
sub-category, you must first experience others. Write about everything, everyone, everyplace, then narrow it down. Something,
somewhere, sometime, and write. Have you learned about yourself and about everything else you can? Have you written about it
all? Then recombine it and write it again, but add a little, embroider
a little, imagine a lot. Look at language as a tool.
Eleven, twelve, find the helve,
Thirteen, fourteen, create the in-between.
Create a world that is not quite like real life, nor yet totally fabri-
cated, but incorporate the best of both. Perfect it, polish it, make it
yours, then make it everybody's. Never write for the chest. You are
a creator, and your creation must be read, and enjoyed, and
criticized, and defenestrated if necessary. But after it's been thrown
through a window, pick it up, dust it off, and take it home to let it
sleep it off. Only then will you be a writer.—A student essay

Exercise

Choose a piece of writing such as Jonathan Swift's "A Modest
Proposal," or one of Samuel Johnson's *Rambler* essays, or one of Mark
Twain's *Letters from the Earth*, or one of the Platonic dialogues, or
Thoreau's "Where I Lived and What I Lived For," or a Woody Allen
essay, or any short piece of writing that you like, and consciously imitate
its form in a piece of writing of your own.

Suppose you sat writing at your desk
Between days, long before dawn,
The only one up in town,
And suddenly saw out the window
A great star float by,
Or heard on the radio sweet voices
From wandering Venus or Neptune,
A little hello from the voids.
Who would believe you in the morning
Unless you'd practiced for years
A convincing style?
So you must learn to labor each day.
Finally a reader may write he's certain
Whatever you've written or will write is true.
Then all you need is the patience to wait
For stars or voices.

Carl Dennis, "Useful Advice"

7

Developing
Your Material

This chapter suggests some ways of amplifying and developing your ideas and materials. It includes discussion of development by

Sometimes, even when you have good ideas and some good material to work with, your writing may seem bare and hurried. Sometimes, even when you have a good working outline and you get an essay written, the essay doesn't seem to have any more to it than the outline does. In some circumstances, such as when you are giving directions or providing simple information, a short, bare essay is what you want. But other times a short, bare essay won't do. For some subjects a plain, short essay may not give readers the flavor of your subject, may not give them a sharp, vivid sense of the thing.

Even a good outline may not let you see how to show the full body and character of your subject. You may have to poke and pull and stretch your work until you begin to see all there is to your subject and to find out where it leads and to discover how it gets connected with other subjects. This chapter suggests some ways of developing your material, of amplifying and clarifying what you have said, of giving texture and immediacy to your subject. You'll find some similarities between this set of methods of development and the "topics" discussed in Chapter Two. In the first chapter some methods were suggested for learning what your subject is. Here, some similar methods are suggested as ways not only of learning about your subject, but also as ways of presenting your subject most appropriately and effectively. Some of the methods discussed in this chapter will also show up again in a later chapter when they will be suggested as ways of constructing paragraphs. Again, the purposes are similar. The way you construct a paragraph helps to determine what you can tell about the subject you are working on.

Twelve methods are described and illustrated below. Some of them might be combined. Some of them are close kin to each other. Others might be added. There is no magic either in the number twelve or in the methods suggested. They are useful, sometimes, for getting yourself started, for setting yourself in motion, for getting your mind in gear. They may give you a way of seeing and handling your subject, of exploring all of its potential content, so that readers may see and know it well.

DEFINITION

In a sense, because anything you write is a way of telling readers what you mean, anything you write may be taken as a definition. But definition also takes a particular form that is useful in exploring or developing a subject. A two-step procedure usually serves to make a definition. Given a term to define, you can first put the person, thing, or idea you are talking about into *an appropriate class*, as in the following examples:

A *pipe* (term to be defined) is a *device* (class of things it belongs to).

A *pipe* (term to be defined) is a *prized possession* (class of things it belongs to).

Patriotism (term to be defined) is an *attitude* (class of things it belongs to).

Patriotism (term to be defined) is a *principle* (class of things it belongs to).

Patriotism (term to be defined) is a *characteristic* (class of things it belongs to).

Putting a term to be defined into a class, the first step in definition, puts limits to the term's meaning. When a pipe is put in a class with other devices, we at least know that it is not a toy, or food, or clothing.

The second step in a definition is to differentiate the term to be defined from other members of the class you have put it in. Thus, for example, "a pipe is a device used in smoking tobacco." Here the words "used in smoking tobacco" serve to show how a pipe differs from other devices. The first step of a definition, putting the term in a class, limits the term's possible meaning; the second step *specifies* its meaning. Definitions that occur in writing are often extended; they may use a sentence, a paragraph, several paragraphs, a whole essay, sometimes a whole book. In such extended definitions, usually the greater amount of time, attention, and space is given to the second step.

Most terms to be defined can be put in more than one class. In the examples above, *pipe* is put in two classes; it is a *device*, or it is a *prized possession*. The class you choose to put a term in and the details you choose to distinguish it from other members of the class must depend upon what you are trying to do with your subject. If you are on your way toward working out an essay that will oppose smoking in all forms, for example, your account of the pollution caused by pipe-smokers might define the pipe as "a device used for smoking tobacco and for dirtying the air that others breathe." If you wish to go further in the vilification of smokers, you might define the pipe by putting it in another class: "A pipe is a weapon used by the oblivious few against the suffering many."

Definition is a crucial function of any writing. It is a primary way of setting limits to your discussion, of clarifying your meaning. Definition is important any time you are dealing with terms that are ambiguous, controversial, or unfamiliar. The first step in a definition, putting the term to be defined in a class, provides a good opportunity for amplification of your material by focusing on its connections with similar things. The second step, differentiation from other members of the same class, provides a good opportunity to specify your meaning by focusing on the unique traits of your subject, the features that make your subject unlike any other in its class.

Some of the ways that definition appears in extended form in writing are shown in the passages that follow.

term to be defined	Terrorism is yet another of the <u>new and bitter</u> <u>truths</u> we must learn to face, constantly. Like
class the term belongs to	political corruption and high-priced oil, it is here to stay, day in, day out, in your life and
similarity to other members of the class	mine. Nobody in public life is ready to admit this fact. Terrorist incidents like the explosion at La Guardia Airport in 1975 that killed eleven
beginning of attempt to differentiate term from other members of class	and the recurrent attempts to kill or kidnap politicians are being blamed on the "sick," the "irresponsible," "extremists of right and left," or "madmen," plain and simple. But these are not explanations. They are either lies or tragic mistakes, and we should be ready now—after being misled so often by official analyses in the past—to unravel the truth for ourselves. It doesn't require expensive teams of psychologists or reams of statistical tables. All it takes is indignant common sense, freed from the
term used here requires definition here	<u>myths</u> and illusions with which we have collectively been supplied throughout this century.

The grandest myth of all is that we live in an advanced state of civilization, in which the brute passions of men and women have been exorcised by education and material well-being. . . —Douglas Davie, "Living with Terrorism"

All written language is a kind of code for the transmission of messages over space and time; messages that might be conveyed in a face-to-face encounter through sign language, but ordinarily are transmitted by means of the spoken word. For communication to take place, both sender and receiver must know the code—must know what each symbol stands for and in what order the symbols are arranged. The code for the written form of most present-day languages is an alphabetic code in which letter symbols are used to represent the units of sound that make up the spoken word.

A *phoneme* is the smallest practical unit of speech sound that can serve in a particular language to distinguish one utterance from another. The first sound, represented by the letter *p*, in the word *pan* is a phoneme because substituting for it the sound that the letter *t* usually represents would create a different word with a different meaning. Similarly, the letter *a* in *pan* represents a middle phoneme. . . .—Paul R. Hanna and Jean S. Hanna, "Regularity in English Spelling"

Man is an organism that seeks and demands explanations. He has sought to understand the mysteries of his environment. He has asked questions, and searched for answers, about his origin and the meaning of his existence. He has been profoundly concerned and anxious about his ability to survive in the face of his comparative physical weaknesses and the multiple dangers of his environment. Man asks these questions and seeks their answers because he is an intelligent being who is not limited to mere behavioral reactions with his environment. He is a conscious, reflective, evaluative being who is required to be as responsive to the realities of his ideational and created environments as to his physical and biological environments. The fact of human intelligence demands this. Human intelligence also provides the key to the answers to the questions it is capable of raising. Man believes that he has survived as a species and will continue to survive in spite of his skeletal weakness because he has the intelligence necessary to probe, to seek to understand and to control the environmental forces that threaten him.—Kenneth B. Clark, "Intelligence, the University, and Society"

INSIGHT

Methods in combination

This chapter discusses twelve different methods of developing material. You'll notice, however, that they aren't always separate from each other. Sometimes two or more methods will combine to form a single method, as the schematic representations below may suggest.

A *definition* may be formed by putting the term to be defined in a class and then by providing an *illustration* of what you mean by the term; the illustration serves to differentiate your term from others in its class.

A *comparison* may be formed by using two *definitions*.

A *definition* may be formed by using a well-developed account of *contrast* to differentiate your term from others in the same class.

A series of *illustrations* arranged in a *chronological* sequence may be a way of showing a *cause-effect* relationship.

Don't feel that the methods discussed here have to be kept isolated from each other.

Exercises

1. Discuss whether or not the following meet the requirements of a definition:
   a. A photograph is a portrait painted by the sun.—Dupin
   b. What is art? Nature concentrated.—Balzac
   c. *Expletive*: An interjection to lend emphasis to a sentence or, in *verse* especially, the use of a superfluous word (some form of the verb "to do" for example) to make for *rhythm*. Profanity is, of course, another form of *expletive* use. Careless speech is full of superfluous words which are *expletive* in nature. A common colloquial *expletive* is "you know" added frequently to a statement, as "I went home, you know, at ten o'clock."—Thrall, Hibbard, and Holman, *A Handbook to Literature*
   d. Our knowledge is the amassed thought and experience of innumerable minds.—Emerson, *Letters and Social Aims*
   e. Good luck is a lazy man's estimate of a worker's success.—Anonymous

2. Use one of the above definitions as a starting place for an extended definition.

3. Do a personal extended definition of a subject of your own following the form of class and differentiation.

ILLUSTRATION

The value of specific illustrations has already appeared as a subject more than once here (see especially pp. 71–74). It may occur again, for nothing is more important to your writing than clear, particularized illustrations and examples. Illustrations clarify your meaning; they fulfill the intentions and possibilities of what you are saying; they give texture and color to your writing. Illustrations are vital whether your subject is simple or complex. They show your reader the material you use to make meaning, just as a graph can help illustrate certain statistics. They are the data that you put together in order to make some kind of sense or some kind of judgment. When you show your readers detailed illustrations, you give them some of the same basis you had for your observations and judgments. When you show your readers detailed illustrations, you tell them, "See, that's what I mean."

Sometimes you may need to use a number of short, quick, vivid illustrations. At other times, a few extended illustrations will serve. In either case, make the examples as specific as you can. The world is full of meanings; try to point your readers toward the particular meaning that is yours. Some ways of using illustrations are shown in the passages below.

Most of the manipulating of personnel in industry, I should stress, was done to achieve the constructive purpose of making employees happier and more effective at their jobs. Very often this simply involved giving them recognition and individual attention or recognizing that status symbols can become enormously important to a person caught in a highly stratified company, as with the case of a man who had all the seeming status and privileges of his peers but still felt grossly unhappy. Investigation turned up the root cause: his desk had only three drawers while the desks of associates in comparable jobs had four drawers. As soon as he was given a four-drawer desk his grousing ended. Some of the advice given management by psychologists, I should also add, has been in the direction of urging the companies to give employees more freedom and individual responsibility as a means of increasing efficiency. Few of us would argue with that.—Vance Packard, *The Hidden Persuaders*

Bad grammar is never good.

But what one generation holds to be bad grammar is occasionally adjudged by the next generation to be good: and the new generation loses no time in wondering why on earth the formerly condemned practice was ever condemned at all. Nor is the feeling confined to young and vigorous countries such as Australia or the United States, New Zealand and South Africa. Oddly enough, it is usually the young countries which cling longest to certain grammatical conventions, partly for the same reason that causes them to cling to and retain words that, in Britain, have long passed into disuse. This retention, however, has occurred more frequently in the United States than in the British Dominions.

There are two quite remarkable instances of bad grammar becoming good. When I was at school, or might have been, in the first decade of this century, I should have been reprimanded—if not worse—if I had ended a sentence with a preposition. As one of my reprimanders said, all unconscious of the irony, "*With* is a bad word to end a sentence *with*." In *The King's English*, 1906, the brothers Fowler of sainted memory spoke of "the modern superstition against putting a preposition at the end" and most appositely cited the Authorized Version's "I will not leave thee, until I have done that which I have spoken to thee of." When, twenty years later, the surviving brother H. W. Fowler's classic, *A Dictionary of Modern English Usage*, appeared, the brothers' campaign had succeeded.

The other remarkable instance is that of the former prejudice against splitting an infinitive: you could split your opponent's skull and merely incur a hanging and all was over; but no editor dared to split even an enemy's infinitive and would have committed suicide if he had found himself doing so. . . .—Eric Partridge, *A Charm of Words*

Exercise

Give a definition of one of the following and then illustrate it from your own experience:

a. Obstinacy
b. Team effort
c. Prejudice
d. Selfishness
e. Flattery

f. Envy
g. Common sense
h. Carelessness
i. Audacity
j. Class

CIRCUMSTANCES AND DETAILS

Developing a subject by exploring the circumstances and details of its appearance or character is a technique similar to both the preceding methods. It is like development by illustration in the sense that the method calls for you to be as specific as possible in citing and showing the particular characteristics of your subject. It is like development by definition, especially like the second stage of definition, in which the identifying marks that distinguish a subject from all others are given. No particular pattern can be given for this kind of development. What is required is that you see and know particular things about your subject and show them to your readers. Sometimes it may be useful simply to pile up details one after another in order to show as much of the texture and flavor and feel of a subject as possible; in other instances it may be better to present the details of your subject in some kind of order. The examples below may help to show what development by exploring circumstances and details can be like.

In this first passage notice how many particular details are shown to create the dominant sense of neatness:

Mr. Massy's stateroom—a narrow, one-berth cabin—smelt strongly of soap, and presented to view a swept, dusted, unadorned neatness, not so much bare as barren, not so much severe as starved and lacking in humanity, like the ward of a public hospital, or rather (owing to the size) like the clean retreat of a desperately poor but exemplary person. Not a single photograph frame ornamented the bulkheads; not a single article of clothing, not so much as a spare cap, hung from the brass hooks. All the inside was painted in a plain tint of pale blue; two big sea-chests in sailcloth covers and with iron padlocks fitted exactly the space under the bunk. One glance was enough to embrace all the strip of scrubbed planks within the unconcealed corners. The absence of the usual settee was striking; the teakwood top of the washing-stand seemed hermetically closed, and so was the lid of the writing-desk, which protruded from the partition at the foot of the bed-place, containing a mattress as thin as a pancake under a threadbare blanket with a faded red stripe, and a folded mosquito-net against the nights spent in the harbor. There was not a scrap of paper anywhere in sight, no boots on the floor, no litter of any sort, not a speck of dust anywhere; no traces of pipe-ash even, which, in a heavy smoker, was morally revolting, like a manifestation of extreme hypocrisy; and the bottom of the old wooden chair (the only seat there), polished with much use, shone as if its shabbiness had been waxed. The screen of leaves on the bank, passing as if unrolled endlessly in the round opening of the port, sent a wavering network of light and shade into the place. —Joseph Conrad, *Youth*

In the following passage the opening paragraph announces that whales have become less terrifying and more intriguing. The next eight paragraphs then cite particular details of their nature and circumstances of their behavior to show that they are intriguing, but not terrifying. And each is further amplified by an illustration.

The more experiences the *Calypso* has had with whales, however, the less terrifying—and the more intriguing—these leviathans have become.

Diving is perhaps one of their more stupendous feats. The sperm whale is the undoubted master, the only whale that can dive 4,000 feet down—or more. As he prepares to penetrate the depths, he jackknifes with an utter grace—especially in his tail movements, which seem desultory and almost casual. His grace, however, is deceptive; the power in that tail is the estimated equivalent of that of a 500-horsepower engine.

A more flashy display of a whale's abilities is a stunt called breaching, or skyhopping. The whale leaps completely from the water, at a take-off speed of about 30 knots. He does a half roll in midair and falls back, hitting the water with the thunderous clap of massive flesh against water. The reasons that whales perform this showy trick remain unknown. It could be a sexual rite. One oceanographer I know believes that breaching aids digestion— that whales jump to help the food go down.

Perhaps the most mystifying of the habits peculiar to whales is their "singing." Humpback whales are the most renowned for a wide range of tones, and whole herds often join together in "songs" composed of complete sequences, which, repeated, can last for hours. Some evenings, we listened to the humpbacks starting to make a few sounds, like musicians tuning their instruments. Then, one by one, they began to sing. Underwater canyons made the sounds echo, and it seemed as though we were in a cathedral listening to the faithful alternating verses of a psalm.

One of the most "human" qualities of the whale is its intense devotion to other whales, which is best displayed by the relation-ship between a mother whale and her calf.

The mother's first task is to lift her baby to the surface for its first breath. She continues this careful attention to his breathing when she nurses him, all the while cradling the baby in her flippers to keep his head above the surface.

Mothers punish their offspring as well. Once, a crew member on board our ship saw a calf rub against the hull. The mother went after the calf, pushed it far away from the ship, and then struck it several times with her flippers. Never again, that baby was taught, should it confuse a ship with its mother's stomach.

This sort of concern is typical not only of the relationship between mother and calf but also of the relations between members of the whole herd. When a huge sperm whale rammed into our hull one day, the chirping of the herd suddenly became frantic. Whales emerged from everywhere, rushing to the side of the stricken whale to support it at the surface.

Whales are affectionate as well as protective—they love to nuzzle one another, especially as a prelude to mating. Humpbacks actually embrace with their flippers. More than once, flirtatious female whales have rubbed even against our divers. The most touching of our experiences came one day as we were filming. A mother whale and her calf were swimming directly toward Bernard Delemotte, chief diver on our ship. Bernard passed between them with his camera—and the mother gently pulled back a flipper so as not to harm him.

I am touched by a certain sadness, then, when I leaf through volumes of ancient folklore. Rising from the pages are images of monsters from the deep, overturning ships and attacking men. I know that it has been the other way around in real life.—Jacques-Yves Cousteau, "Jonah's Complaint"

COMPARISON OR CONTRAST

This method of development is based on the simple assumption that a subject can sometimes be explained or shown clearly to an audience by comparing or contrasting it to something else. Comparison and contrast are old techniques used by parents talking to children ("No, honey, this one's a cat—say it, CAT—it does look like a dog with four feet and hair and all, but this one makes a different noise"), by students talking to teachers ("But if the past tense of *sin* is *sinned*, how come the past tense of *win* isn't *winned*—they're alike"), by teachers talking to students ("While there were some superficial similarities in the movements that led to the American revolution and to the French revolution, the two movements were in most important ways entirely dissimilar"), by people talking to people ("I mean, that party was like nothing you *ever* saw").

A comparison or a contrast does more than just single out and clarify comparable or contrasting features. When you set a subject in comparison or in contrast with another, you are providing a setting or a context for the subject you are trying to explain or show. The second term, the thing you are comparing or contrasting your subject to, provides a backdrop or scene for your subject. Your reader no longer has to see your subject in isolation; it has some connection with the world.

Comparisons and contrasts shouldn't be used unquestioningly, and you probably shouldn't try to carry either of them too far. Most things that can be compared are probably different in more ways than they are alike. Many things that can be contrasted probably share some common features. You'll have to *select* features that are worth comparing or contrasting: if a comparison seems useful, focus on the comparable features; if a contrast seems useful, focus on the points of contrast.

No special design will work for all comparisons and all contrasts. Sometimes a block design will work—that is, a design in which a writer first presents *all* that he is going to say about one term of the comparison or contrast and follows that with all of the second term's points of comparison or contrast. Put simply, an essay developed in this way might be outlined as (1) introduction, (2) first term described and explained, (3) second term described and explained, and (4) conclusion.

This block design may not work, however, if the terms being compared or contrasted are complex. If to present the first term requires pages and pages of writing, then you are probably asking your readers to remember too much as you move into a long account of your second term. Where your subject is complex, it may be more useful to work with a pattern of alternating design in which you move back and forth comparing or contrasting your two terms on each point of likeness or dissimilarity. This kind of design may work better with any subject that requires extended discussion.

The examples below may help you see how comparisons and contrasts are used. In the first, dog food is set beside hamburger meat for both comparison and contrast. Buyers cannot be expected to know what a dog food is like; they can be expected to know what hamburger meat is like, and the familiar is used as a way of telling about the unfamiliar. In the second selection, by Samuel Johnson, the alternating design mentioned above is illustrated. In the third selection only points of similarity between the Bermuda Triangle and the Devil's Sea are raised; the author is not concerned with possible differences.

[The passage below is accompanied by a picture of a terrier wearing a Sherlock Holmes hat and studying two containers through a hand magnifying-glass; the contents of both containers appear to be hamburger meat.]

It's elementary!

Gaines Top Choice Chopped Burger for Dogs looks almost identical to hamburger.

And there's no mystery why. Top Choice is made with beef by-products and real beef, so it's moist and meaty. It even holds together just like hamburger.

But it's better for your dog than hamburger, because it also contains vegetables, vitamins and minerals for a fully balanced diet.

Which brings us to Country Style Top Choice. The only chopped burger for dogs with real cheese flavor and protein-rich egg, the equivalent of a quarter of an egg in every serving.

Original Top Choice and Country Style Top Choice. You don't need an investigation to prove they're both great for your dog.—Gaines® print ad

In acquired knowledge the superiority must be allowed to Dryden, whose education was more scholastic and who before he became an author had been allowed more time for study with better means of information. His mind has a larger range, and he collects his images and illustrations from a more extensive circumference of science. Dryden knew more of man in his general nature, and Pope in his local manners. The notions of Dryden were formed by comprehensive speculation, and those of Pope by minute attention. There is more dignity in the knowledge of Dryden, and more certainty in that of Pope.

Poetry was not the sole praise of either, for both excelled likewise in prose; but Pope did not borrow his prose from his predecessor. The style of Dryden is capricious and varied, that of Pope is cautious and uniform; Dryden obeys the motions of his own mind, Pope constrains his mind to his own rules of composition. Dryden is sometimes vehement and rapid; Pope is always smooth, uniform, and gentle. Dryden's page is a natural field, rising into inequalities and diversified by the varied exuberance of abundant vegetation; Pope's is a velvet lawn, shaven by the scythe and levelled by the roller.

Of genius, that power which constitutes a poet; that quality without which judgment is cold and knowledge is inert; that energy which collects, combines, amplifies, and animates, the superiority must with some hesitation be allowed to Dryden. It is not to be inferred that of this poetical vigor Pope had only a little because Dryden had more, for every other writer since Milton must give place to Pope; and even of Dryden it must be said that if he has brighter paragraphs, he has not better poems. Dryden's performances were always hasty, either excited by some external occasion or extorted by domestic necessity; he composed without consideration and published without correction. What his mind could supply at call, or gather in one excursion, was all that he sought and all that he gave. The dilatory caution of Pope enabled him to condense his sentiments, to multiply his images, and to accumulate all that study might produce or chance might supply. If the flights of Dryden therefore are higher, Pope continues longer on the wing. If of Dryden's fire the blaze is brighter, of Pope's the heat is more regular and constant. Dryden often surpasses expectation, and Pope never falls below it. Dryden is read with frequent astonishment, and Pope with perpetual delight.—Samuel Johnson, *The Life of Pope*

Investigators of the Bermuda Triangle have long noted the existence of another mystery area in the world's oceans, southeast of Japan, between Japan and the Bonin Islands, specifically between Iwo Jima and Marcus Island, with a record and reputation indicative of special danger to ships and planes. Whether the ships have been lost from underwater volcanoes or sudden tidal waves, this area, often called the Devil's Sea, enjoys at least officially an even more sinister reputation than the Bermuda Triangle in that the Japanese authorities have proclaimed it a danger zone. This action came about after an investigation carried out by Japanese surface craft in 1955.

The Devil's Sea had long been dreaded by fishermen, who believed it was inhabited by devils, demons, and monsters which seized the ships of the unwary. Aircraft and boats had disappeared in the area over a period of many years, but during the time when Japan was at peace, nine modern ships disappeared in the period of 1950 to 1954, with crews totaling several hundred persons, in circumstances characteristic (extensive air-sea searchers, lack of wreckage or oil slicks) of the happenings in the Bermuda Triangle.

The Bermuda Triangle and the Devil's Sea share a striking coincidence. The Bermuda Triangle includes, almost at its western terminus, longitude 80° west, a line where true north and magnetic north become aligned with no compass variation to be calculated. And this same 80° W changes its designation when it passes the poles, becoming 150° E. From the North Pole south, it continues on, passing east of Japan, and crosses the middle of the Devil's Sea. At this point in the center of the Devil's Sea, a compass needle will also point to true north and magnetic north at the same time, just as it does at the western border of the Bermuda Triangle on the other side of the world.

The unexplained losses in this Japanese equivalent of the Bermuda Triangle were instrumental in inspiring a government-sponsored investigation of the area, which took place in 1955. This expedition, with scientists taking data as their ship, the *Kaiyo Maru* No. 5, cruised the Devil's Sea, ended on a rather spectacular note—the survey ship suddenly vanished with its crew and the investigating scientists!—Charles Berlitz, *The Bermuda Triangle*

Exercises

1. Take two everyday objects or experiences and make a list of the ways in which they are alike (for example, taking a final and a tennis match), but extend your list until the comparison is no longer valid.

2. Find and bring to class examples of essays that compare two things by discussion of each separately and essays that make point-by-point comparisons.

3. Bring to class examples of advertisements that make use of comparison.

4. Find a "Letter to the Editor" that seems to you to be ineffective. Extend its effectiveness by the use of a comparison.

5. Write a comparison of two things which seem to you to be logically associated though that association is rarely noticed.

ANALOGY

The word *analogy* might be defined as agreement or resemblance in certain respects between otherwise dissimilar things. Sometimes, in our casual conversations, the word is used to mean any similarity or agreement. A student of logic might define *analogy* as a form of reasoning in which resemblances are inferred from others that are known—that is, one reasons that if two things are alike in some respects, they must be alike in others.

We see analogies of this last kind in print and hear them in conversation more frequently, in all likelihood, than we encounter analogies as mere resemblances. Analogies between marijuana and alcohol, or between marijuana and tobacco, are used as arguments for the legalization of marijuana. Other people note political corruption in fourth-century Rome and an occasional orgy, and then note the Watergate experience and the appearance of a good many movies featuring undressed ladies, gentlemen, kangaroos, together with unlikely congresses amongst them, and then they argue that the United States will fall (soon) just as Rome fell, in decay and corruption. Every day in advertisements we are invited to become participants in analogies: if, for instance, the men among us will only use Rye Whiskey, the new deodorant, as Joe Wonderful, the swinging quarterback, does, then we will also be like him in other interesting ways.

Analogies, in other words, sometimes get overused, or used badly. If there is fault, however, it probably lies among the users, not among the analogies. Development by analogy is a useful and dramatic way of presenting a subject. In the analogy that follows, the analogy between cancer and war makes the point that war is destructive of all society more effectively than a straightforward statement would.

> We say that the aim of life is self-preservation, if not for the individual, at least for the species. Granted that every organism seeks this end, does every organism know what is best for its self-preservation?
>
> Consider cancer cells and non-cancer cells in the human body. The normal cells are aimed at reproducing and functioning in a way that is beneficial to the body. Cancer cells, on the other hand, spread in a way that threatens and ultimately destroys the whole body.
>
> Normal cells work harmoniously, because they "know," in a sense, that their preservation depends upon the health of the body they inhabit. While they are organisms in themselves, they also act as part of a substructure, directed at the good of the whole body.
>
> We might say, metaphorically, that cancer cells do not know enough about self-preservation; they are, biologically, more ignorant than normal cells. The aim of cancer cells is to spread throughout the body, to conquer all the normal cells—and when they reach their aim, the body is dead. *And so are the cancer cells.*
>
> For cancer cells destroy not only all rival cells, in their ruthless biological warfare, but also destroy the larger organization—the body itself—signing their own suicide warrant.
>
> The same is true of war, especially in the modern world. War is the *social cancer* of mankind. It is a pernicious form of ignorance, for it destroys not only its "enemies," but also the whole superstructure of which it is a part—and thus eventually it defeats itself.
>
> Nations live in a state of anarchy, not in a state of law. And, like cancer cells, nations do not know that their ultimate self-interest lies in preserving the health and harmony of the whole body (that is, the community of man), for if that body is mortally wounded, then no nation can survive and flourish.
>
> If the aim of life is self-preservation—for the species as well as for the individual—we must tame or eradicate the cancer cells of war in the social organism. And this can be done only when nations begin to recognize that what may seem to be "in the national interest" cannot be opposed to the common interest of mankind, or both the nation and mankind will die in this "conquest."

The life of every organism depends upon the viability of the system of which it is a member. The cancer cells cannot exist without the body to inhabit, and they must be exterminated if they cannot be re-educated to behave like normal cells. At present, their very success dooms them to failure—just as a victorious war in the atomic age would be an unqualified disaster for the dying winner.—Sydney J. Harris, "War Is Cancer of Mankind"

Exercises

1.   Bring to class some examples of advertisements that imply, rather than state, certain analogies between the users of the product and the person featured in the ad.

2.   Choose an activity in which you have participated (writing an essay, trying to make a good impression, etc.), and write a description of it, making use of analogy.

CLASSIFICATION AND DIVISION

In the standard system of biological arrangement, the domestic or house cat belongs to a larger group, the family *felidae*. This family includes several *genera*—the genus *panthera*, which includes the large cats, the genus *lynx*, which includes the Canada lynx and bobcat, the genus *acinonyx*, which includes only the cheetah, and the genus *felis*, which includes the mountain lion, several kinds of smaller cats, and the domestic cats. Not all domestic cats are alike, however; two principal subgroups are the *long-hair cats* (Persian) and the *short-hair cats* (Siamese, Abyssinian, Burmese, Russian Blue, Manx, Rex, and domestic short-hair).

Thus, a writer who wished to study and write about the domestic cat might go in two directions. The writer might *classify* the domestic cat and present an account of how the domestic cat shares features with other members of the genus *felis* and beyond that with other members of the family *felidae*. Or the writer might *divide* the group known as domestic cats and give an account of long-hair cats and short-hair cats.

It is in something like this way that developing a subject in a piece of writing by classification and division works out. Almost any subject may be approached in this way since almost any subject belongs to a larger group and is capable of being divided into smaller segments. If, for example, you decided to write about Phantom, a very particular and local female cat of unspecified ancestry and uncertain temperament, you could, by classifying her as a domestic short-hair, one of several kinds of short-hair cats, a member of the genus *felis* and family *felidae*, begin to present her general appearance, anatomy, and physiology, and some features of her behavior, sometimes pantherish, sometimes leonine, sometimes kittenish. But if she is really a very particular and local female cat, there's more to be said about her. She can be divided into parts: perhaps she is a peculiar combination of animal behavior on the one hand and human behavior on the other; or perhaps she is a strange mixture of queen, hunter, harlot, and clown.

The examples below may show you some of the ways in which classification and division are used in writing. The first selection uses division; the subject is the naming of streets, and four different versions (divisions) of street-naming are discussed. The second selection uses both classification and division: an attempt is made to differentiate between two members of the pepper family.

No one passed any laws about naming streets, or even wrote a book of advice. As often in democracy, however, the result of complete freedom was not complete chaos. The town-planners tended to repeat traditionally, with slight variation, what was already familiar. So arose the four basic patterns of American street-names, more or less associated with different great cities, which served as models.

First of all, there was the pattern which might be said by paradox to be no pattern. The streets running in both directions bore names, and these followed no system. Boston furnished the model in the farther north. Most of the New England towns copied the Boston names, so that the typical pattern included State Street, Federal Street, and Congress Street, and probably Summer, Winter, Spring, Pleasant, and Commercial.

The older South also named its streets in both directions, taking its chief model perhaps from Baltimore. . . .

The most truly American pattern, however, remained that of Philadelphia—to have streets designated by numbers in one direction and by names in the other. The Philadelphia pattern spread west into Ohio and Kentucky and beyond. It followed down the Mississippi through Memphis, and took over many of the American-founded towns of Louisiana. It had outposts in New England—Bangor, New Bedford, Pittsfield, and others. It encroached strongly upon Virginia and Tennessee. Even in the farther South it furnished the pattern for many towns, such as Charlotte and Macon.

Like all systems of naming, it offered some problems. Where, for instance, should First Street lie? . . .

The planning and naming of the national capital offered a third model for new towns. The whole city was split by two main axes into four sections, designated by the half-points of the compass. East and west of one axis the streets began with First, and so continued. North and south of the other axis the streets began with A Street and continued through the alphabet. Broad diagonal thoroughfares, called avenues, bore the names of the states. The avenues and the alphabetically designated streets were the important innovations. . . .

In 1807 a Commission was appointed to lay out a plan for the as yet unbuilt parts of Manhattan Island—"The leading streets and great avenues." On April 1, 1811, the map was finished and filed. It presented the basic plan and name pattern of midtown and uptown New York which by the prestige of the city have become familiar to the whole world. The cross-town streets were numbered, after the Philadelphia fashion. The broad north-south thoroughfares were called Avenues after the Washington fashion; but, again after the Philadelphia fashion, they were numbered successively from First along the East River. . . .—George R. Stewart, *Names on the Land*

One discussion concerning *jalapeños* and *cuaresmeños* all but boiled over in a market in Querétaro. I was determined to sort out these two middle-sized, hot, smooth, green, tapering peppers, very alike, but to my eye, and to my palate, not identical. I had found botanists who said they were the same species. I'd found others who said they were different. My friends in the market confirmed my view that they were not identical, though almost, they said, *gemelos* (twins), each with its own character, the *cuaresmeños* much hotter and not quite so elegantly shaped. They can, of course, be used interchangeably; the cookpot does not niggle over very minor differences the way I am apt to when stalking the pepper family.—Elisabeth Lambert Ortiz, "Picking a Peck of Peppy Peppers"

Exercises

1. Classify the courses you are taking in as many ways as you can (by type, by difficulty, etc.).

2. Record your experiences for a day (or you may want to extend the assignment to a week). Classify your experiences into kinds of activities (busywork, self-initiated activities, and so on). Then write a paper in which you classify your day's or week's activities, give some examples of those activities, and finally reflect on some generalizations about what these activities say about you and your life.

ANALYSIS

Development by analysis is a method of determining or describing the nature of a subject by separating it into its parts. While it scarcely seems different from division (above), since both depend upon examination of parts, analysis goes a step further. Ordinarily, when you're working with division, you are chiefly interested in division for its own sake— that is, you examine a subject just to see what its parts are. Analysis, ordinarily, looks to see what the parts are, but does so for a specific purpose. When you study the cat mentioned above and divide her into various features, you are usually just interested in knowing what the separate features are. When you analyze a poem, on the other hand, you may look at its parts, but you usually do so in order to make some other point or to serve some rationale—for example, to show how characteristics of each part indicate despair, or to show an inconsistency that you have detected.

Remember that most subjects can be separated into their parts in a number of different ways. You can analyze a poem stanza by stanza— that is, determine what goes on in each stanza—and that is a separation into parts. But you can also divide a poem in another way and explore its metrical patterns, its rhyming patterns, and its stanza forms, or explore its figurative language and its sensory images, or explore its images of darkness and images of light, or explore the contrasting views of characters within the poem. Each of these sets results from a separation of a poem into its parts.

Analysis is a useful method. Since most subjects can be separated into parts in a variety of ways, analysis will give you justification for continuing to scrutinize a subject, turning it this way and that, sorting it into parts differently, until you find your way of talking interestingly and usefully about the subject.

But don't divide a subject into its parts just for the sake of division. A reader deserves to know, since a subject is divisible in more than one way, why you have chosen the particular scheme of division that you are using. Your way of dividing a subject into its parts should somehow support and fulfill your purpose in writing. Say, for example, you want to explore some of the reasons for a recent high dropout rate among second-semester freshmen at your school; if you set out to interview a large number of them, trying to include several in each category you've created, it hardly seems promising to divide the dropouts into three classes, the right-handed, the left-handed, the ambidextrous. But if you sort the dropouts into two groups, the highly motivated and the minimally motivated, and then interview representatives, you may begin to acquire some useful information. No one gains much from knowing why left-handers drop out, but your school might learn a great deal from knowing why highly motivated students have dropped out.

In the sample that follows, various kinds of partitioning occur. In the opening paragraphs, quick, sometimes implied divisions separate the young and the old, the fair-skinned and the darker-skinned, the curable cancers and the incurable cancers, and American taxi drivers and English taxi drivers. Then a specific and more extended division occurs which shows us the types of skin cancers.

Sunshine is one of the most wonderful things in our world. It floods all of our lives with glowing warmth, light and general feelings of well-being. We bask in it happily, sometimes thoughtlessly, and often dangerously because too much sunshine can be very harmful.

Skin cancer is significantly on the rise in the United States, and our sports-oriented, sun-worshipping, lightly clothed life-style is almost entirely to blame. For fair-skinned people especially, overexposure to the sun can be a long-term time bomb. What we must realize is that each sunburn or overexposure—even for little children—will only add to our skin problems later in life. According to Dr. Eugene M. Farber, chief of dermatology at Stanford University Medical School, this year's sunburn can be starting 1999's cancer.

Today, doctors are finding many more skin disorders in young people than ever before. In the past, wrinkles and skin cancer usually appeared in people over 40 and most often in those over 50 years old. Now, dermatologists say, it is not uncommon to find wrinkles, precancerous conditions and even skin cancer itself in people in their twenties.

It is estimated that as many as 500,000 new cases of skin cancer will occur in the U.S. this year. But these malignancies are not considered a major health problem because, if caught early, they are 99 percent curable. Nevertheless, skin cancer can be painful, disfiguring and expensive to treat. Untreated, the cancer can eat into deeper tissues and, if the spread is unchecked, it can even kill.

Although not all skin cancers are caused by sunshine (the use of certain chemicals as well as radiation treatments can also trigger it), most cases can be traced to the sun's rays. And more than 90 percent of these cancers occur on those areas of the body most often exposed—face, neck and backs of hands. For example, "The lower lip is more likely to get cancer than the naturally shielded upper lip," explains Dr. Perry Robbins of New York University Medical School's Skin and Cancer Unit. "So is the rim of the ear rather than the lobe; the lower eyelid rather than the upper."

To use a dramatic illustration of this, doctors report that United States' cab drivers get more cancers on the left sides of their faces where the sun is constantly hitting them. In England, where the steering wheel is on the right, the reverse is true.

The kind of constant exposure which cab drivers experience

is the most harmful, according to Dr. Farber. "It is a straight-line process as direct as A to B to C," he says. "Repeated sunburning leads to premature aging and wrinkling of the skin and *actinic keratoses* (horny growths), which are the forerunners of cancer." An occasional sunburn will not cause the damage.

The most common type of skin cancer—and the simplest to cure—is called *basal cell carcinoma.* This cancer may invade surrounding tissues, but it rarely spreads to internal organs. Caught early, it is 100 percent curable. A less common type, *squamous cell carcinoma,* can also start as a sun-related cancer, and its danger is that it does spread to internal organs. An even more uncommon type is *melanoma,* which develops in the pigmented cells of the skin, such as black moles. It occurs more often in sunnier sections of the country, but it is not certain that the sun actually causes this cancer or merely stimulates an existing condition. Melanoma is very serious and spreads readily; 3,500 victims die of it each year.—Barbara Yuncker, "Warning: Sunshine Can Be Harmful to Your Health"

CAUSE AND EFFECT

Many subjects can be usefully explored, their nature amplified and clarified, through examination of cause-and-effect relationships. Your subject may be interesting and important as an effect, and it may often be necessary to show readers how it came into being. They may not be able otherwise to understand or appreciate what you are saying. Your subject may be interesting and important as a cause for something else, and it's always vital to know what consequence things have, or how they matter hereafter.

As you think about cause-and-effect relationships and try to reason your way toward some understanding of them, remember that it's sometimes perfectly all right to be tentative. A good, sane skepticism is healthy and wise when you're studying causes and effects. Most things arise from more than one source, have more than one cause. It's seldom, indeed, that you can safely point to a single cause for a given effect. And most causes result in more than one effect. A force or an idea or a thing or a person that you have singled out as a cause for a given effect may indeed have generated the result you are talking about, but it probably also filters and trickles out elsewhere, to generate other effects as well. It may be dramatic to focus on a single cause for a particular phenomenon, or on a single effect that ensues from a particular phenomenon, but it's usually also a little simplistic. Consider all the evidence, handle the evidence tentatively, and look for all the possibilities.

Considering causes and effects can be extremely important in your writing. Readers may understand what you are saying without this kind of exploration, but one of the ways of showing the full significance of a subject is to show that it matters—it comes from somewhere (it arises from a cause or causes), and it goes somewhere (it has some effect, it carries some weight of meaning).

The examples that follow show some of the ways that reasoning about causes and effects appears in writing. The first passage comes from the same discussion about naming streets that was quoted above in illustration of classification and division; the author is now discussing the effect of some American attitudes on street-naming. In the second passage de Beauvoir explores the causes for both the increase in urban population during the nineteenth century and the increase in poverty.

In naming their streets, the Americans were obviously torn between two basic emotions. First, they were a practical people, and vastly admired themselves for being so. Numbered and lettered streets thus attracted them greatly. One writer declared that a good street plan was incomplete:

> *unless there exists an orderly and methodical system of suitable names, so arranged as to enable the resident and the stranger within its gates to ascertain for themselves and without needless trouble or delay the relative positions of the different highways through which they may be called to pass.*

Boston and Baltimore failed entirely to meet this requirement, and were rejected. Washington raised undue complications, and tended to defeat its own object. New York was the ideal of practicality, with the result that of all great cities it remains (with the exception of its downtown district) the easiest for anyone, resident or stranger, to find his way around in. Philadelphia was a compromise.

Its strength lay in that very fact. For, besides being practical, the Americans were like all people in having a strong tinge of sentiment in association with names. Names may be poetry; they readily become symbols of patriotism, achievement, or love of home. Numbers and letters sometimes attain symbolic value, but less easily and often.

The Philadelphia pattern allowed sentiment along with practicality, and its success fell little short of overwhelming triumph. More than half of all our towns, perhaps three-quarters of them, have a system of numbered streets. The numbered avenues, after the model of New York, fail to appear in more than about one in six. About one town in ten shows the Washington pattern of lettered streets.—George R. Stewart, *Names on the Land*

Three closely linked phenomena accompanied the growth of population in all countries: industrial revolution; a movement away from the countryside and a consequent urban increase; and the appearance and development of the new class, the proletariat.

In England the depopulation of the countryside had begun with the enclosures, which reduced a great number of peasants to destitution. At the beginning of the nineteenth century one side-effect of the poor-laws was a lowering of the incomes of the farmers and the agricultural workers, a lowering that forced them off the land. The coming of free trade in 1846 meant that industrial and commercial England had finally triumphed over agricultural England.

In France there had been an important flight from the land at the end of the eighteenth century, raising the urban population from a tenth of the total to a fifth, or about five and a half million people. The peasants' sons moved chiefly into the small towns, where they became shopkeepers, employees or civil servants, thus rising socially. At the beginning of the nineteenth century, on the other hand, this movement came to a halt: between 1800 and 1851 the urban population did rise by three and a half million, but because of the total increase in numbers, only twenty-five percent of the French lived in towns. Thanks to a decrease in taxes the total amount of money at the peasants' disposal grew larger, but this increase was offset by the simultaneous growth of the population. Between 1840 and 1850 the countryside could no longer feed those who lived upon it, and more and more people left the land between 1850 and 1865. During the years that followed, the concentration of urban industry caused the withering away of rural industry, an important source of supplementary income for the peasants. Technical progress made it harder for the poor to work the land; they could not stand up against the competition of the capitalist methods introduced by the middle-class owners. What is more, after 1880 the improvement in communications allowed America to export wheat to France; in the resulting serious economic crisis the flight from the land continued. By 1881 a third of the population was concentrated in the towns. As the century drew to its end it was industry that offered openings for the peasants' sons: they came to swell the ranks of the proletariat.

These changes were disastrous for the old. Neither in France nor in England had their condition been so cruelly hard as it was in the second half of the nineteenth century. Labour was not protected: men, women and children were pitilessly exploited. As they grew old, the workers were unable to keep up with the rhythm. The industrial revolution was carried through at the cost of an unbelievable wastage of human material. Between 1880 and 1900 Taylorism wrought havoc in the United States: all the workers died before their time. In every country, those who managed to survive were reduced to extreme poverty when their age deprived them of their jobs. After the Bourbon restoration mutual insurance societies were tolerated in France, and in 1835 they were officially recognized: in 1850 and 1852 they were once more placed under strict supervision. The Third Republic gave them complete freedom by the law of 1 April 1898. But even in the best of conditions their means were always insufficient when it was a question of guaranteeing a risk as heavy as old age. This also applied to the friendly societies in England. 'Produce savings rather than children,' said J. B. Say. This advice, addressed to workers, was a mockery. England and France saw an immense increase in the number of aged tramps and beggars, destitute old people.—Simone de Beauvoir, *The Coming of Age*

Exercises

1. In your campus or local newspaper, find an article that describes a situation that exists on your campus or in your local community. Probe the situation for all its possible causes, including those that do not seem obvious.

2. Think back to a disagreement you have had with someone. Write a paper about that disagreement in which you explore all of its possible causes. What immediate and long-range effects did the disagreement have on you?

3. Remember a situation in which someone you knew seemed to act irrationally. What were some of the possible causes for their behavior? What were the effects of their behavior on those around them?

4. "Trend is not destiny." With these words René Dubos concludes *A God Within*. Statements such as that often have remarkable effects; in other words, persuasive statements sometimes produce the intended result. In that sense, words are sometimes magic. Make a personal list of statements that have had an effect on you or on others. Choose one of the statements and write a paper about the effects it had.

PROCESS

If your subject is something that creates or is created, if it is something that manufactures or is manufactured, if it is something that changes or grows, then an account at the appropriate place of how it grows, changes, creates, was created, manufactures, or was manufactured, will help readers see the nature of your subject. Even if you are interested in what your subject is like in the present, or how it behaves in the present, a representation of how it came to be, how it grew or developed, may help your readers understand better why the subject is what it is. For example, if you are exploring failures in the workings of your local county government, it may be necessary to show how county governments derived their powers (as opposed to city governments and state governments). The process in this instance is not your subject, which is failures in county government, but a way of showing something about your subject. It may turn out, for instance, that your county government does not have certain powers and so cannot be held accountable for some failures.

Sometimes, of course, a process *is* your subject, rather than a way of showing something about your subject. In an essay on the development of a new breed of broccoli, or a study of how industrial smoke pollution has increased in your community, or an extensive analysis of how James Thomson revised his poem *The Seasons* over a period of twenty years, a process is your subject.

Developing an essay or a part of an essay by exploring a process essentially means presenting a chronological sequence. In a process, the first step comes before any other. But while a process is a chronological sequence, you don't have to treat all time alike. In some processes, each step or stage of development may be as important as each of the others, but often it will be possible to pace your work so that you may use most of your writing space on key steps or developments, reducing less important steps to smaller space.

In the example below, a process is the subject. The passage is from a section of White's book that deals specifically with methods of open-water canoeing, and White's purpose is to tell how something is done.

A light canoe will stand almost anything in the way of a sea, although you may find it impossible sometimes to force it in the direction you wish to go. A loaded canoe will weather a great deal more than you might think. However, only experience in balance and in the nature of waves will bring you safely across a stretch of whitecaps.

With the sea dead ahead you must not go too fast; otherwise you will dip water over the bow. You must trim the craft absolutely on an even keel. Otherwise the comb of the wave, too light to lift you, will slop in over one gunwale or the other. You must be perpetually watching your chance to gain a foot or so between the heavier seas.

With the sea over one bow you must paddle on the leeward side. When the canoe mounts a wave, you must allow the crest to throw the bow off a trifle, but the moment it starts down the other slope you must twist your paddle sharply to regain the direction of your course. The careening tendency of this you must counteract by a corresponding twist of your body in the other direction. Then the hollow will allow you two or three strokes wherewith to assure a little progress. The double twist at the very crest of the wave must be very delicately performed, or you will ship water the whole length of your craft.

With the sea abeam you must simply paddle straight ahead.

The adjustment is to be accomplished entirely by the poise of the body. You must prevent the capsize of your canoe when clinging to the angle of a wave by leaning to one side. The crucial moment, of course, is that during which the peak of the wave slips under you. In case of a breaking comber, thrust the flat of your paddle deep in the water to prevent an upset, and lean well to leeward, thus presenting the side and half the bottom of the canoe to the shock of water. Your recovery must be instant, however. If you lean a second too long, over you go. . . .—Stewart Edward White, *The Forest*

In the example below, which describes a process, the process is not the subject, but a revealing contribution to the subject. In the essay from which this passage is taken, the author is talking about changes in American habits, especially as revealed in the way they cook outdoors. The process presented below is an example of the pleasant simplicity the author feels has been lost.

. . . let this same man begin to believe himself a chef, acquire, in his pride, an outdoor cooking machine, and attempt dishes having to do with delicate sauces or, worse, flaming swords, and we would all be better off staying indoors. Indoors, Daddy disdains to help with the cooking. It is not cooking he loves; it is his machine.

There is still some good outdoor cooking going on in this country, but none of it needs machinery, and none of it comes from Escoffier.

The first meal that comes to mind as I ruminate happily through my own recent memories of outdoor eating is a clambake last summer in Maine. Here is the authentic recipe for a clambake: dig a hole in a beach. If you have a Maine beach to dig your hole in, so much the better, but any beach will do. Line the hole with rocks. Build a big fire on the rocks, and take a swim. When the fire is all gone, cover the hot rocks with seaweed. Add some potatoes just as they came from the ground; some corn just as it came from the stalk; then lobsters, clams, then another layer of seaweed. Cover the whole thing with a tarp and go for another swim. Dinner will be ready in an hour. It will make you very happy. No machine can make a clambake.—Charles Kuralt, "The Summer Life, Outdoor Cookery from Barbe to Queue"

Exercises

1.   Explain how to do something that perhaps no one else but you knows how to do in quite that way, for example, how to make the best spaghetti sauce ever, how to wash your dog without getting wet, how to make mismatched socks seem appropriate.

2.   Incorporate an explanation of a process into a narrative in an informal way.

3.   Describe the process you generally use in writing your papers. Be honest!

CLARIFICATION AND RESTATEMENT

When you say something to someone, it's not clear just because you've said it. When you write something, it's not clear just because you've written it.

Sometimes, you have to keep saying what you've said, keep writing what you've written. Sometimes you have to keep learning how to say or write what you mean to say. Instead of developing a thought or a passage by some specific method such as those suggested above, you may need to rephrase what you've said, or to modulate it in some way, or to put its focus in a slightly different way. Clarification and restatement are not the same as repetition. Repetition has very limited uses in writing. Clarification and restatement, in the sense intended here, are *incremental*, or *redirecting*, or, less often, *diminishing*. An *incremental* restatement says again what was said before, but adds a little to it, a new sense, a new dimension, as when you say to a fellow student, for example, "My major program is nice and steady and solid, but it doesn't have any pizzazz— you know, it doesn't have any zip or zing to it. It's not known for any one thing in particular. It has no special flair. It has no drama to it." A *redirecting* clarification shifts the focus of what was said before, as, for example, when one of us rises tardily from our sluggard's bed and mourns, "I just don't have any discipline," only to remark ten minutes later, over coffee, "No, that's not true. What I've got probably looks like an undisciplined character, but what it really is is that I'm not motivated. I haven't found my thing. The world hasn't yet discovered my talent. I haven't either." A *diminishing* restatement rules out some of the meanings that are possible in what was originally said, as when the author of a textbook says that restatement does not mean simple repetition, but a new statement with some amplification or alteration of the old.

In the passage that follows, notice how the author keeps working with the problem of changing agricultural habits, exploring the problem, restating it, clarifying the need for change.

The new environment demanded a change in agricultural habits. The change from living in a forested area to the exposed, treeless Plains made the lack of trees so striking that the settler wanted to recreate the environment he had left in the East. It is doubtful that most farmers believed that "rain followed the plow" or that climatic conditions were subject to human control, but they did not regard treelessness as a permanent condition of nature. The pioneer farmer had seen his father and grandfather transform a prairie environment in Iowa, Illinois, Minnesota, or possibly Ohio, into a cozy homestead surrounded by trees where only few trees had been growing before their arrival, and he sought the benefits attributed to windbreaks and shelterbelts in previously settled regions. The prairie-plains farmer, who may have possessed even more optimism than the average nineteenth-century American, believed that he could convert his quarter section in Kansas or Nebraska or, later, North or South Dakota into a successful farming operation enhanced by woodlots, orchards, and tree-lined fields. He could not change the climate, but he could reduce the wind velocity and provide a measure of protection for his home, livestock, and crops. Trees had done these things in Ohio and Iowa, why not in Kansas or Nebraska? As the pioneer moved westward, his plants and trees, both seeds and seedlings, moved with him. Even the Norwegian, Dane, or German-Russian brought seeds from the homeland; but, with the exception of the Russian mulberry, introduced to Kansas by Russian Mennonites in 1874, these invaders seldom thrived. The farmer faced two alternatives: he could try native species gathered from the stream banks, or he could obtain exotic or imported varieties from nurseries in the states to the east. The immigrant farmers who had seeds sent from their former homes were among the most successful in establishing windbreaks and shelterbelts on the Plains. Success eluded those who chose to secure planting stock from nurseries in the East or from unscrupulous tree agents.—Wilmon H. Droze, *Trees, Prairies, and People*

Exercises

1.   Make a comment that seems to be worth making; then restate it, or clarify it, in as many ways as you can.

2.   Add a second sentence to each of the following sentences that restates or clarifies the first sentence:
   a. It is better that a judge should lean on the side of compassion than severity.—Cervantes
   b. Fear always springs from ignorance.—Emerson, *The American Scholar*
   c. Man would not be man if his dreams did not exceed his grasp.—Loren Eiseley, *The Invisible Pyramid*
   d. The starting point of change is discontent.—Herbert R. Kohl, *The Open Classroom*
   e. If an individual is able to love productively, he loves himself too; if he can love *only* others, he cannot love at all.—Erich Fromm, *The Art of Loving*

SPATIAL ORDER

Any subject that exists in space can sometimes be usefully explored according to the *way* it occupies space. People, places, things may be shown as they arrange themselves in space; even abstract ideas (such as patriotism, for example) may be arranged spatially since their nature may be different in different spaces.

More often than not, presenting a subject in a spatial arrangement means *describing* it. Description can be valuable in its own right, of course, but more often you'll probably use description to serve some other purpose, such as describing something in order to explain it to someone, or describing something in order to persuade an audience to see and believe as you do.

There is no particularly right pattern for a spatial development. Some patterns of arrangement suggest themselves quickly—you can present a subject as it exists from right to left in space, or from left to right, or from near to far, or from far to near, or from low to high, or from high to low. What matters is that the way you present your subject in space should be useful to what you are trying to say about your subject. For example, if you should be writing about chemical pollution of a river in your community, presentation of the river from upstream to downstream as it passes various sources of pollution might be a forceful way of showing the urgency of the problem. A presentation of the river from a single point of view on the bank showing first what is near and then moving toward what is far, on the other hand, may not be useful at all. Such an arrangement would limit you to one view of the river and would commit you to presenting a far view (the other side of the river), where the distance might prevent your giving any specific details of pollution.

In the account that follows, consider whether the configuration of the landscape and the disposition of the people across the landscape helps to explain what happens. Notice, too, the order in which the author shows us how the people are arranged:

> They got very little sleep, for it was not long before Charlton and two of the Tonkawas reported that they had relocated the trail, which had led them to a large concentration of Indians in Palo Duro Canyon, four miles to the north-northwest. As the first faint streaks of day appeared in the east, the command came to the precipice of Palo Duro Canyon just below its junction with Blanca Cita Canyon, about five miles below the present limits of the state park.
>
> Peering over the rim of the chasm, which had a vertical drop of seven hundred to nine hundred feet, MacKenzie and his men were overawed by what they beheld. Ninety million years of erosion had created in the depths below an ideal haven for the Indians. Palo Duro (hard wood) Canyon, at this point approximately six miles from rim to rim, and Blanca Cita, more than a half mile in width, had a good supply of cottonwood, cedar, wild cherry,

mesquite, and hackberry trees from which the Indians could obtain firewood, lodge poles, and arrows. At the bottom of the gorge meandered a stream of good water, fed by springs along the canyon walls. Extending for two or three miles along the banks of the stream stood an estimated two hundred tipis, roughly grouped into five villages, and hundreds of horses grazed nearby. Deceived by the distance, one of the Seminoles [cavalry scouts] exclaimed: "Lor' men, look at de sheep and de goats down dar."

The encampment on the floor of the canyon consisted of a Kiowa band led by Mamanti, a large band of Comanches under O-ha-ma-tai, and a small band of Cheyenne led by Iron Shirt. . . .

Mamanti, the Kiowa medicine man, was in general charge. After "making medicine," he assured the people that no blue-coated soldiers would ever disturb them in the canyon. Thus assured, the women erected their tipis, began preparing new lodge poles from the cedars in the canyon and getting ready for winter, and at daylight on the morning of September 18 the unsuspecting villagers slept without fear while from the rim of the canyon high above them the tenacious and daring MacKenzie, bent upon their complete destruction, decided to take the most daring risk he had yet encountered and led his hardened cavalrymen into what one of them later called the "jaws of death." A mistake in stratagem could turn the canyon into literal "jaws of death"; perhaps the Indians, reputedly well-armed, were prepared to man advantageous barricades and pick off each intruder as he scrambled almost helplessly down the narrow trail!

The command had to march along the canyon rim about a mile before finding a trail, directly above the Comanche tipis, leading down the canyon wall. Meanwhile, the chance of an early dawn attack had gone. The sun had changed the eastern sky from rose to ochre, and finally rose above the opposite rim of the canyon as the men moved down the tortuous trail. When he found the narrow, zig-zag path, MacKenzie quietly turned to Lieutenant Thompson, in command of the scouts, and said: "Mr. Thompson, take your men down and open the fight."—Ernest Wallace, *Ranald S. MacKenzie on the Texas Frontier*

Exercises

1.   Find a quiet corner in a busy area of your campus (library, dorm lobby, snack bar) and describe that area to a friend or relative back home. In your description try to accomplish the following:

   a. Show by the perspective and spatial arrangement that you choose something of your feelings about yourself in relation to the area.

   b. Capture in your description some of the mood of the area.

2.   Go to a nearby art museum or gallery and annotate your visit there; that is, attempt to describe both what you see, where it is located, and your reaction to it. Feel free to be selective so that the reader gets an impression of you, as well as the exhibit.

3.   Look at several paintings or drawings and describe their spatial arrangements.

4.   Describe the same setting first spatially, then at random as objects catch your eye. Make a list of times when the second arrangement would be more effective than the first.

CHRONOLOGICAL ORDER

Everything exists in time. People are born, they grow and change and die in time. Things alter, enlarge, diminish, mutate, and wither in time. Places wash and erode, mountains rise up, and boulders shift in time. Ideas shift and change, they emerge and disappear, they are subverted and elevated in time. A chronological development can always be used to present and explore a subject.

Most of the time the pattern of a chronological development is inevitable: it is governed by the clock and the calendar, and the first thing that happens is the first thing presented. Sometimes, of course, it is possible and useful to rearrange time. You can, for example, always justify focusing on key moments in a chronological sequence, even if it means skipping chunks of time. You can start late in a chronological sequence and return to earlier moments in flashbacks. Other mixtures of time are possible. You can start in the present with your subject and move back to key moments in the past that will reveal something of how your subject came to be. Remember, too, from the discussion above on process, that you are not required to treat all time alike. Sometimes a brief instant is powerful and dramatic in its effect and may require three pages, while a week or a month may be passed over quickly. The moments that are crucial to your subject deserve the fullest attention and space in your writing.

The first passage below shows a quick history—two or three key moments in the subject's history. The second passage tells how sparrows are hatched and develop over a period of a few weeks.

Let us sing the praises of the humble ball-point pen. The gadget that scribblers the world over love to use—and now, love to throw away—is a technological marvel. The 1-millimeter tungsten carbide ball in the typical pen rolls around freely in its socket—but not freely enough to fall out. As the ball inks the paper, it pulls more ink from its tubular reservoir by a principle of physics known as capillary action.

Although ball points were widely used in the 1940's and triumphed during the 50's, the pioneer concept was patented in America back in 1888 by John J. Loud of Weymouth, Mass. He described his invention as "an improved reservoir or fountain pen, especially useful, among other purposes, for working on rough surfaces—such as wood, coarse wrapping paper and other articles." Not trusting his ink to the mysterious phenomenon of capillary action, Loud designed his pen so that a sturdy spring held the ball in place; when the ball was rolled against a surface, it moved back against the pressure of the spring, and the ink flowed around it.

Alas, Loud's pioneer ball point was commercially impractical, and Americans had to wait more than another half century before they were offered a chance to write upside down, under water. The modern ball-point pen went on sale Oct. 29, 1945—for $12.50.—Stacy V. Jones, "More Major Minor Inventions"

Although the male house sparrow covers the eggs about a third of the time, true incubation is performed only by the female. The male has no brood patch—the featherless area on the breast against which a bird's eggs are nestled. As is true of most of the smaller birds, the house sparrow's incubation period is no more than a fortnight, varying from ten to fourteen days. For the first several days after the chicks emerge, the adults feed them on delicate flies and on regurgitated food, largely animal. To satisfy a brood of four, each parent must make about twenty trips to the nest every hour. The nestlings stay in the nest for between fifteen and seventeen days. By the sixth or seventh day, the parents have stopped offering regurgitated food. They bring large, soft-bodied fare, like caterpillars, instead. By the fifteenth day, the young are usually ready to fly.

Departure time is normally in the morning—sometimes quite early. The fledglings are strong on the wing, and once they are out it is next to impossible for a human pursuer to catch one. They are fed for about two weeks more by the adults, but within a week after quitting their cradle they can feed themselves. . . .—Eugene Kinkead, "In Numbers Too Great to Count"

Exercises

1. Use the *Oxford English Dictionary* to write the history of a word that you are interested in.

2. Do some research on an object in present existence and write its history.

3. Look at several history books and see if you can tell, by the events that the author focuses on, something about his philosophy of history.

4.   Set a beginning point and an ending point on a period of time in your past and describe that period chronologically, focusing on the events in that period that seem to have had some influence on who you are today.

5.   Describe an incident step-by-step on a series of 3-by-5 cards. Move the cards around so that you achieve a different sequence. Use the cards to describe the incident by flashbacks or linking the events with the thoughts of the various participants or by some other mixture of time.

A LAST NOTE

All of these methods can be used both as a general organizational design for an essay or to fill out, to develop, or amplify an essay that you have already written. If, when you've finished a draft of a paper, it looks bare, sparse, or unsubstantial, you may discover that you can go back through it and put a little meat on its bare bones by developing a definition here, by adding an illustration there, or by using any of the other methods suggested here.

You may discover, incidentally, that some of these methods of development may be more useful in one kind of writing than in another. A definition and a classification, for example, may be particularly helpful if you are trying to explain a subject to an audience, while a comparison and a spatial development may be especially useful if you are trying to describe a subject to an audience. Each of the methods can be used in any kind of writing, but some of them may be uniquely adaptable to certain kinds of writing.

Exercises

1.   Identify in a professional essay the places where the author uses any of the methods of development described in this chapter.

2.   Choose one of the following subjects or one of your own and write about it, incorporating several of the methods of development presented here in this chapter.
   a.   My Direct Experience with a Social Issue
   b.   The Sources of One of My Prejudices
   c.   A Word That Ought to Be in the Dictionary
   d.   A Problem That I Have Solved

3.   Find a newspaper article that gives just the essentials of a story. Enlarge it by adding your own illustrations, definitions, analogies, examples, and other methods of development.

You see, for her words were medicine;
they were magic and invisible.
They came from nothing into sound and meaning.
They were beyond price; they could neither be bought or sold.
And she never threw words away.

N. Scott Momaday, *House Made of Dawn*

8

Saying the Words

After some introductory pages on the relationship of words, writing, and experience, this chapter gives some suggestions about the following:

1. restless words, changing words (p. 164), an account of changes in language;

2. which words, which language? (p. 169), a brief account of language choices, dialects, and other versions of language;

3. your own language, growing (p. 175), with some suggestions about accuracy, specificity, denotation, connotation, and figurative language;

4. languages that tyrannize (p. 193), an account of common errors in the use of language, including clichés, euphemisms, jargon, and various kinds of crooked words.

Everything depends on words—speaking, even thinking. We cannot conceive of a sentence unless we have the word *sentence* or some set of words to describe the thing. A subject doesn't become a subject that we can write about until we have the words that will name and hold it in our minds. Everything depends on the words.

The question is: Which words? Or for that matter: Which language?

Most of the time, when we talk or write, we do so without giving the language or the words we're using very much thought. Indeed, if we stopped and waited all the while to figure out a language and to select our words, we'd probably stumble into silence. If we're talking, we sometimes pause, to be sure, and search for a word, or start over to put things another way. If we're writing, we more often stop and think our way to the words we want to use. Most of the time, however, we use language without too much thought and say words without too much choice being exercised. We automatically speak and write the language we already own.

That may be our loss, for the world is full of languages to speak and words to say. Each one of us already has a variety of languages—all English—that we might use: a public language, perhaps, and a private language, a language for parents and a language for peers, a more formal language and a less formal language, regional or folk or cult dialects, languages borrowed from sports, computers, and elsewhere. And then there are all of the other languages that we don't yet know and can't yet speak or write.

Writers have to search for their language, their words, a little more thoroughly and deliberately than speakers do. Speakers can get rapid response from their hearers and quickly clarify or rephrase what they are saying. Writers usually can't do this, for writing is a long-distance art, and they can only imagine or expect what the effect on any possible audience may be. If they have chosen the wrong language, or used a good language poorly, if they misjudge an audience's response, or if they have been careless with either the words or the expected audience, then what they write can make no connection between them and their readers.

Words deserve and need great care, more perhaps in writing than in speaking. Written words will let us speak out our own minds and make our identity intelligible to others in other times and other places. Written words give a name and character to our experiences and allow us to preserve them. Written words are our only connection to the past and to the future. Great care with words, then, is only proper: it is a debt we owe to others and to ourselves, a debt we owe for the magic we can make with words.

RESTLESS WORDS, CHANGING WORDS

Our word *okra* comes from *nkrumah*, the vegetable's name in the Tshi language of Africa. A *ladybird* is not a bird. *Weather* and *wither* come from a common source. A *catapult* doesn't throw things the way you may think it does. Alexander Graham Bell did not call the telephone a telephone, but a *harmonic telegraph*, and the early standard greeting on the instrument was not *hello*, but *ahoy*. The *currant* gets its name from Corinth. If you take words literally, you can't properly say that an old, falling-down wooden house is *dilapidated*. *Falsies*, an interesting modern accessory, were in an earlier form called *palpitators*. A *Jerusalem artichoke* doesn't come from Jerusalem and is a member of the sunflower family; the first word is a corruption of the Italian *girasole*, which indicates that the plant turns to follow the sun.

The words we speak come to us from interesting places, and they have interesting histories. The English language is dynamic, shifting, growing, as it has been from its beginnings. Students of the language estimate that about one-fifth of our vocabulary comes from the original Anglo-Saxon stock, with Scandinavian additions brought to England by the Danes, and that about three-fifths of our vocabulary comes from Latin, Greek, and French. The remaining fifth comes from everywhere. Celtic, with Irish, Scottish, and Welsh words, gives us *plaid*, *blarney*, *slogan*, *flannel*, *shillelagh*, and others. We have from the Italian such words as *malaria*, *manifesto*, *trombone*, and *broccoli*, and from Spanish and Portuguese we have *bonanza*, *cockroach*, *cargo*, *cork*, *mosquito*, *tornado*, and *molasses*. From the Dutch-Flemish, we have borrowed, among many others, *yacht*, *schooner*, *drawl*, *deck*, *nap*, *gin*, and *landscape*. We have borrowed frequently from modern German and modern Slavic languages. From Arabic and Persian come such words as *algebra*, *alcohol*, *divan*, *magazine*, *caravan*, *crimson*, *jungle*, and *shawl*. We have borrowed from Hebrew (*camel*, *sapphire*, *ebony*), from various tongues of India (*punch*, *bandanna*, *bungalow*, *calico*, *veranda*, and *seersucker*), from Chinese (*tea*, *tycoon*), and from African languages (*gorilla*, *voodoo*, *jazz*). From the Indian tongues of North America, Mexico, the West Indies, and South America we have many words, including *moccasin*, *terrapin*, *hominy*, *mackinaw*, *chocolate*, *tomato*, *coyote*, *barbecue*, *hurricane*, *cannibal*, *maize*, *potato*, *tobacco*, *quinine*, and *jaguar*. The list might go on and on. The history of our words is mixed, curious, and often uncertain. We cannot always tell which language gave us a word: the Greek word *pepon* (ripe), for example, became the Latin word *pepo*, and the French turned it into *pepon* and *pompon*. From that the English made *pompion*, then *pumpion*, and finally *pumpkin*. Some words won't give up their history, and some words are made up. The whole world conspires to give us a vocabulary. The vocabulary is wide, cosmopolitan, funny and commonplace, strange and familiar. The dictionary is full of extraordinary histories.

The hoard of words available to us has grown and changed throughout history. Some vocabulary changes are not to be explained—words simply appear in use—but many vocabulary developments occur in persisting patterns. Obviously, one continuing pattern of growth comes from our habit of borrowing, as noted above. But we also make words by combining words with words, or words with prefixes or suffixes. One form of combination is called *derivation*, making new words by adding suffixes or prefixes to words already in use, as in *useful*, *undress*, *unfold*, and *devilish*. Another form of combination is called *compounding*, often seen in new words made by joining two nouns, or a noun and an adjective, as in *weekend*, *downfall*, and *airtight*. And sometimes we combine by shoving words together (a process known as *blending*): thus we acquired the word *twirl* by putting *twist* and *whirl* together, the word *smog* by putting *smoke* and *fog* together.

We also acquire new vocabulary by shifting the function or form of words already in use over to new purposes. A common form of shifting occurs as we change the grammatical function of a word: *eye* and *elbow* were available to us as nouns long before we got new use from them by making them serve also as verbs; *show* and *hit* and *smoke* were used as verbs before we converted them into nouns. Another form of shifting is called *clipping*. This occurs when we make a new word by shortening one we already had, as we made *fan* from *fanatic*, *curio* from *curiosity*. A curious process called *back formation*, another form of shifting, also gives us new words. Sometimes we take away from a word what appears to be a suffix in order to use the basic word, but in many instances by doing that we have created new words. Thus, for example, we had the word *beggar*, then took away the last three letters as if they were a suffix, and got the word *beg*. Students of language history indicate, however, that there never was before such a root word, so *beg* is a new word. In much the same way we got *gloom* from *gloomy*, *diagnose* from *diagnosis*, *peddle* from *peddler*, *enthuse* from *enthusiasm*.

And, to be sure, another common pattern of vocabulary change is invention. We make new words from little or nothing. By analogy with existing words we make new words: we already had *cavalcade*, and by analogy we invented *motorcade* and *aquacade*; from the existing *marathon* come *talkathon* and *telethon*. We take over trade names and make them common words, as with *zipper* and *cellophane*. We make up words to echo sounds, as in *fizz*, *hiss*, *sizzle*, *titter*. We convert acronyms into words: *Situation Normal, All Fouled Up* (sometimes put more colorfully) gave us *snafu*; the *Committee for American Relief in Europe* gave us CARE, now sometimes appearing in expressions such as *care package*. *Nonce words* are another kind of invention; these are words formed for use on some particular occasion, but some survive and enter the standard vocabulary. For example, *forceful*, *racial*, and *intellectual* were once considered nonce words.

Other patterns of change are discernible. Over the centuries or generations the meaning of many words has been extended. Through a process known as *generalization*, a word that once had a specific, limited use acquires a much more extensive range of meanings. *Saucer*, for example, once meant specifically a dish that holds sauce, but now names a dish used for various purposes. The word *butcher* once referred only to the person who killed and dressed goats. *Quarantine* once meant a forty-day period of isolation. More common, probably, than *generalization* is *specialization*, a pattern of change in which a word loses its broader meaning and narrows to a specific meaning. *Dirt* once signified a number of things that could stain, soil, or otherwise mess up, including excrement, mud, and dust. *Starve* once meant *die*, but now means *die* in a particular way. *Meat* once meant any kind of food. By a process of *amelioration* some words have lost meanings suggesting the low, base, or unexalted: *marshal* once signified a tender of horses, and *governor* once meant *pilot*. By a contrary process, called *pejoration*, some words have lost "respectable" meanings and acquired meaning that suggests baseness: *hussy* once meant *housewife*; *lewd* once meant *ignorant*; *notorious* meant *well-known*.

And of course some words disappear from use. Many are still registered in unabridged dictionaries, but they are marked *archaic* or *obsolete*. We don't use *mizzle* any more, and seldom use *beau*. We don't use *runabout*, but often refer to *station wagons*. The word *demit*, which means *dismiss*, has just about disappeared, though it is still used in some formal circumstances. Even when we have a system of military drafting, we don't refer to those who are called into service as *conscripts*.

But new words and phrases keep entering the language. New experiences summon up new words to give them names. When English-speaking people entered the American Southwest, they took existing Spanish words for topographical features that were new to them, and our language acquired such words as *canyon*, *mesa*, *sierra*. They also took over words for architectural features new to them, including *patio*, *plaza*, and *adobe*. And they borrowed from Spanish, sometimes mispronounced, a number of words associated with ranching and the cowboy culture: *chaps* (from *chaparrejos*), *lariat* (from *la reata*), *desperado*, *bronco*, *buckaroo* (mispronounced *vaquero*), *vamoose* (mispronounced *vamos*), *calaboose* (mispronounced *calabazo*), *hoosegow* (mispronounced *juzgado*), *burro*, *pinto*, and *corral*.

New experiences call for new words. Old and continuing experiences require sometimes to be named and described in new ways, as insight, information, prejudice, perspective, and other factors cause us to begin to know them in new ways. We find new ways of saying things by appropriating words from our own street talk, from our current slang forms, from our television sets. Sometimes we must make new words. New words from such sources, and from others, are around us: *additive*, *ecocide*, *doublespeak*, *workaholic*, *jawbone*, *monokini*, *happy hour*, *Saturday night special*, *back-burner*, *designated hitter*, *headshop*, *exobiology*.

The size and variety of the English vocabulary and its capacity for growth give us copious blessings. If we learn to say the words, we can be efficient. We can say what our own nature is and name the things about us in the places where we live. We can make communities. Learning to say the words just right may make magic. But it isn't easy to say the words. The same size and variety and growth that confer blessings on us also confuse us. The language shifts, changes, grows, extending and sometimes complicating the choices we have to make among words. A rich hoard of words is available to us. How do we know which words to use?

INSIGHT

Some reading about language

The growth and development of the English language is a history of interesting, curious, funny stories and whims, and strange appearances and sad disappearances. The history of the language also reveals a great deal about our various English-speaking cultures, about our beliefs and prejudices. If you want to explore this curious language further, read some of the following books:

J. Donald Adams, *The Magic and Mystery of Words* (New York: Holt, Rinehart and Winston, 1963)

Lincoln Barnett, *The Treasury of Our Tongue* (New York: Alfred A. Knopf, 1964)

Albert C. Baugh, *History of the English Language* (New York: Appleton-Century-Crofts, 1957)

Stuart Chase, *The Tyranny of Words* (New York: Harcourt Brace Jovanovich, 1953)

Peter Farb, *Word Play* (New York: Alfred A. Knopf, 1974)

H. L. Mencken, *The American Language* (New York: Alfred A. Knopf, 1946)

Casey Miller and Kate Smith, *Words and Women* (New York: Doubleday, 1976)

Mario Pei, *The Story of the English Language* (New York: Simon and Schuster, 1967)

Exercises

1.   Make a list of ten words that particularly interest you and investigate their origins and changes in meaning in the *Oxford English Dictionary*.

2.   Make up your own word, define it, and illustrate its use.

3.   Supply two or three examples of your own for the following:
   a. Derivation
   b. Compounding
   c. Blending
   d. Change in grammatical function
   e. Clipping
   f. Back formation

g. Analogy
h. Trade names
i. Sound words
j. Acronyms
k. Nonce words

l. Generalization
m. Specialization
n. Amelioration
o. Pejoration

4. Make a list of as many words as you can that have been added to our language in the past ten years or so.

5. What are the current slang words among your friends? Speculate about their chances for survival.

6. Choose some words like *bucket*, *creek*, etc., and do some investigating among your friends to see if friends from different parts of the country vary in the word they use for the same object.

WHICH WORDS, WHICH LANGUAGE?

Each of us knows many languages, and more languages ring out around us. Any one of us can speak many and can understand more. Any given student, for example, may be able to speak "classroom English," and at another time speak the near-inarticulate language shared with one or two close friends (often single words or short phrases, where the friendship supplies the rest of the meaning), then at another time speak sports lingo and understand fully what "pick one out" or "hitting the seams" means, at still another time speak the cool, near-wit of the "Tonight Show," then at another time speak gently to a grandmother. And more: at times each of these languages may be flavored by a regional dialect; at times none of them will be. Each one of us knows many languages. All of us together know far more.

These languages have been classified in any number of ways. One starting place is to distinguish between language characteristic of speaking and language characteristic of writing, though there is a great area of overlap. If someone asks you whether or not you'd be willing to make a parachute jump, you might, for example, say "No way!" But if you used that expression in a college essay, your instructor might mark it "Colloquial" (meaning that the expression is all right for speaking, but not for writing), or ask you to rewrite the passage. Remember that when you are talking to some one in person and say, "No way," the rapidity or slowness of your answer, the tone of your voice, its relative loudness or quietness, and the expression on your face can tell your hearer whether your "No way" means normal caution, reluctance to perform without instruction, fear of heights, intelligent cowardice, or sheer, bloodcurdling, sweat-starting fear. But if you write "No way," and the reader is five hundred miles away, all he or she has to provide meaning is the two words. There is some reason, in other words, for a distinction to be made between spoken and written language, and the reason has nothing to do with whether one is superior to the other. Spoken language is different in some real ways from written language: for example, a writer almost always uses a slightly larger vocabulary in writing than he or she does in speaking, and a speaker almost always depends more on elliptical statements (single words or phrases that stand in place of grammatically complete sentences) than a writer does.

Dialects

At any rate, one place to start in sorting out our various languages is with the distinction between spoken and written languages. Each includes a variety of language forms. Spoken English may be said to include everything from unusual regional dialects to the general English that a great majority of native speakers speak and hear. *Regional dialects* occur wherever a community of speakers develops and preserves a vocabulary and usage not common to other communities. Regional dialects occur for various reasons; a local language may take on special character because the pattern of migration into the region makes one cultural and ethnic tradition and language usage dominant over others, because differences in geography, work, and social habits generate vocabulary differences, because of a hundred other factors. A northern hearer might not easily understand the beauties of grits and red-eye gravy, but a southern hearer might understand right away. A Texas speaker may say, "I'm going to meet her *at noon* for lunch," while an Iowa speaker may say "I'm going to meet her *this noon* for lunch." Regional dialects are not simple, and they are not always clear-cut. What some students refer to as Black English offers interesting examples. While some white speakers of English have mistakenly thought of Black English as *one* dialect, it is many. In one east Texas community, for instance, students of dialect have identified upwards of twenty different dialects among black speakers within a radius of twenty miles.

Occupational dialects may develop anywhere a job, a hobby, or a pastime creates a special vocabulary. Football fans, surfers, carpenters, plumbers, high-steel workers, English teachers, and other groups may build occupational dialects. Such dialects may occur sometimes in isolated pockets; at other times they may be shared by people of similar interests all over the country. Words and phrases from such dialects often slip into general usage: many have taken over from sports dialect such expressions as "He's some kind of ball player" and "The kid's got all the moves."

Public dialects grow out of our general exposure to television, radio, motion pictures, political discourse, newspapers, and advertising. We listen to a particular disk jockey on the radio and borrow his way of talking. We watch "M.A.S.H." or "Happy Days" and take over words, phrases, or stylistic manners. Sometimes we learn to speak the fantasy language of advertising. The language that matters most in magazine or television advertisements occurs in the headline, and we occasionally speak the short-form language of catchy words, dramatic phrasings, and incomplete grammatical constructions.

Slang, localisms, and *fad words,* all common in spoken English, modify and sometimes feed the language with new words and phrases. Slang, usually newly made words such as *groupie* or *teenybopper* or old words used in a new way, such as *heavy* or *cool,* almost continually feeds words into the language, some to survive, as *mob* did long ago, most to disappear. Who knows what will happen to *nerd, turkey, roper, dog,* and *jock?* Localisms are words and phrases common to one area, though they are different from regional dialects, which usually grow through a long history of folk movements. In almost any high school in the country the students have special words they use that might well mystify students from another high school in the same city. *Fad words* are current clichés, words such as *viable* that come into widespread use and overuse.

General English

All of these forms of language are a part of what can be called General English. The majority of spoken language that most of us hear on a given day is a spoken language that doesn't have the distinctive traits given by various dialects and slangs. The language we hear on television, for example, or in classrooms, or among friends is so common that it appears not to have any distinctive character. Even so, spoken General English is different in some ways from written English. Most speakers speak shorter sentences than those used by writers, many use partial sentences, and almost all depend on repetition and restatement to make their meaning clear rather than pausing while they speak to hunt for the precise word for a particular meaning and context. Even in the college classroom, the spoken lectures of many professors may be characterized in this way, though they may write a complex and elegant form of English. Try counting the pauses in a lecture, note the interruptions for rephrasing, and follow the sentences to see if all are completed.

It is in this common spoken General English that the overlapping between spoken and written English occurs. What we read in most newspapers and magazines and popular books is an *edited* form of the common spoken language—the language is edited so as to make punctuation consistent, sentences complete, grammar orthodox, and vocabulary more precise. Written English, of course, is capable of extensive variety, too, from highly informal usage, with short, ordinary sentences and a vocabulary much like that used in routine conversation, to highly formal usage, usually associated with technical, academic, scientific, and scholarly writing in which sentences are often longer, the vocabulary is often much more specialized, and the tone is sometimes more impersonal.

DIFFERENT LANGUAGES

The passages below came from a single issue of *The New York Times Magazine* (July 25, 1976). When you've examined them, try characterizing the language in each.

1. You meet more and more people who are worried that they will never become grandparents. It's a side effect of the falling birthrate, and in the next few years, I suppose, if unbirth continues to increase, it will escalate into one of those national "problems"—the grandparent shortage, grandchild frustration anxiety—so dear to special Presidential commissions, sociologists and magazine editors.

I know grizzled men with hairy ears who have already given up hope of ever making their gruff-but-lovable old grandfather ratings, as they watch their children having beach houses, divorces and new cars every three years, but never a grandchild. . . . —Russell Baker, "Grandchildless"

2. Carlyle's Crate. The packing crate you can sleep in! The look is foreign, the comfort is Carlyle. Squooshy loose cushions wrapped in dacron on the seat and 100% dacron back cushions wrapped in muslin conceal the firmest convertible mattress available anywhere, giving you a truly individual sofa-bed. —Advertisement for Carlyle Custom Convertibles

3. Washington. Like a jet transport accelerating down the runway, a new strategic bomber is about to take off on potentially the most expensive weapons program ever undertaken by the Defense Department. The bomber is the B-1, the Air Force's supersonic successor to the B-52, which for 20 years has been the airborne symbol of America's nuclear might. With a needlelike nose and a bulbously streamlined body that give it the look of a wasp coming in for the attack, the B-1 is a remarkable airplane, a tribute to the technological prowess of the United States. The only thing is, the executive branch and Congress are backing the multibillion-dollar investment without a clear, logical examination of whether a sophisticated new strategic bomber is needed—whether the plane is off on a Strangelovian flight of Air Force pride and fancy or on a mission essential to the nation's security. —John W. Finney, "Who Needs the B-1?"

4. Other tests that have high diagnostic efficiency among the ill seem to offer an unacceptably low yield among the healthy. Proctoscopy (sigmoidoscopy) is of proven value in the detection of rectal cancer in the patient who has already developed symptoms of that disease. The test involves the insertion of a rigid tube approximately 10 inches long and one inch in diameter through the anus and into the rectum, permitting the physician to see into the lower bowel. The technique has been advocated as a means of detecting early rectal cancer where no symptoms exist. Dr. Charles Moertel, of the Mayo Clinic, has reviewed several studies of proctoscopies performed on patients free of any symptoms. A total of

42,207 patients were examined, and only 55 cancers were found. The conclusion was that "the truly routine proctoscopic evaluation does not seem to be a practical screening test."—Richard Spark, "The Case Against Regular Physicals"

5. Sometimes enough New York's enough.

It really is The Big Apple.

There really are a hundred places to find Szechwan oysters, kinesiology classes, maritime lawyers or a Spode gravy boat like the kids broke.

But sometimes New York can get to be too much of a good thing.

Unless you know somewhere to hide.

Welcome to The Barclay.

The Barclay is a small east side hotel. (The lobby is about fifty steps across. The Big Conference Room holds twenty people.)

The Barclay is elegant without being stuffy, expensive without being ridiculous.

Next time you need to get in out of New York, remember The Barclay.—Advertisement for The Barclay Hotel

---

Levels of usage

The diversity offered by the variety of languages creates a problem for writers, determining what is sometimes called "the right level of usage." That way of referring to the problem is not good, but it is common among editors, teachers, and manuals on writing. To talk about "levels of usage" seems to imply that all of the various ways of talking and writing are ranked from low to high in virtue and quality, which is not so. Often we have no real difficulty in shifting from one kind of language to another (though it is much more difficult to do in speaking and writing than it is in listening and reading). We do often have difficulty, however, in choosing which language to shift to.

Though many English languages, or versions of the English language, are available, recommendations on which language to use in writing are limited. No one can declare what the "right" language is for another. No one with ordinary generosity should want to. The usual advice on choosing a language, or on what some call choosing a "level" of language, comes down to this: (1) *find the language that is right for yourself, your subject, and your audience*, and (2) *avoid mixing different languages unless you are mixing them deliberately as in conversation.* Both of these suggestions are good advice. A formal language is not needed in an informal essay, and a regional dialect probably wouldn't work too well in a speech on a scholarly topic to a mixed audience. In general, it is only sensible to find a language that will say what needs to be said about your subject, that will be understandable to your audience, and that will be tolerable for you. And in general, it's usually better not to mix languages or levels of diction within the same piece of writing, as, for example, when breezy colloquial language interrupts a formal letter of application for a job. To be sure, mixtures are sometimes used for particular effect. A black comedian once entertained an audience by concluding his imitation of the opening of the old radio show, "The Shadow," with the sonorous, proper, "Who knows what evil lurks in the hearts of men," only to answer himself with "De Shadow do!" And consider the passage below. The author mixes languages in order to drive home the point she is making, that the differences between White English (WE in the passage) and Black Idiom (BI in the passage) are not fundamental:

> One searches in vain for any discussion of surface vs. deep structure in the so-called "scholarly" literature on BI. I'm talkin bout deep structure in the Chomskian sense of the term. What, after all, is the underlying semantic differentiation between *He work all the time* and *He works all the time*? Or even between *My mother's name is Mary* and *My mother name Mary*? But this is logical, because if BI were really deep structurally different from WE, then there would be a situation of mutual unintelligibility. Oh, yeah, white folks understand BI speakers, it ain't a question of communication. Whites might not like what they hear, but they bees hearin and comprehendin every bit of it. Just as white speakers from one region of the country understand whites from another region. As a matter of fact, though I doubt if many white folks would admit it, they have far greater difficulty with British English than with BI. . . .—Geneva Smitherman, "God Don't Never Change: Black English from a Black Perspective"

The thing is, you see, all languages are natural. They grow and change among the people who speak them, and they prosper or decline. Edited American English is not a holy language, and it is not a permanent language. It is not the same as it was 150 years ago, or even thirty years ago. It is a practical language, widely used in commerce, industry, technology, politics, education, and cultural exchanges. It is not *the* ideal language, which everyone must learn to speak and write. Any language may let us get something valuable said, and we may need the diverse riches of all languages to get good things said:

> If it is really true—and of course it would take a good deal more argument to establish the thesis—that thought cannot be understood except as an operation carried out in a language (or other symbol-system), it seems to follow that the effectiveness of our thinking—its range, energy, depth, subtlety, refinement, and so on—must partly depend on the capacities of the languages (or other symbol-systems) we have at our disposal to think with or *in*.—Monroe C. Beardsley, "Putting Down Words: Some Vicissitudes of Language"

If there are "bad" languages, they are not regional dialects, folk dialects, the lively slang forms of the young, or other languages mentioned above. "Bad" languages are languages that repress and frustrate and perpetuate poverty and incite unthinking violence and persuade us to try to be like the foolish pretenders in advertisements. "Bad" languages are languages that tyrannize.

Exercise

One position on language that some people take is to recommend what has been called "bidialectalism," a requirement that some students master two languages, their own dialect and a standard "right" English. In an essay, "Soul 'N Style," Geneva Smitherman points out that in addition to the bidialectalist position, there also exists the "eradicationist" position, that all nonstandard dialects should be eliminated from school, and the "legitimizer" position, that all dialects should be considered standard. Which of these three terms best characterizes your own position?

YOUR OWN LANGUAGE, GROWING

I walked along an unfamiliar road
And all around, the birds twittered and danced
Through the hedgerows blowing in a flat-land wind.
I wished I knew their names and then instead
Of saying "small, brown, with a spearing beak,
Taking a little run then going back,
Twittering a note that rose to a whistle then sank,
You know, those birds you see in hedgerows
Somewhere along the roads from Hertfordshire"
I could say "thirp" or whatever bird it was,
And you would know in an instant what they were
How looked, what doing. I'd have caught the birds
In that one word, its name, and all the knowledge
You might have had that I'm not master of
Would straight away be there to help me out.
Naming is power, but now
The birds twitter and dance, change and so escape me.
  —Jenny Joseph, from "Language Teaching: Naming"

No single language is sufficient, but recommendations about the languages you use are limited. There is no language that someone else can declare is exactly right for you. Your language should let you speak clearly about the topics you wish to speak of. Your language should let you enjoy community with other people. And in the end your language should let you go your own way. But there's the catch. You can't go your own way unless you are free to. If your language won't let you talk about everything you want to talk about, you are not free. If your language won't let you speak to everyone you want to speak to, you are not free. If your language won't let you identify yourself in the way you want to be identified, you are not free. If you can only speak or write a language that someone else has defined for you, you are not free. If you can only use the language that you absorb through living or listening to the television, you are not free.

Of course, no one is fully "free" in this sense. No one can say everything he or she might want to, or reach every audience he or she might want to reach. Most of us fail to define ourselves as we might wish. Our language sets limits to us, and we cannot say all that there is to be said. Yet if none of us is fully free in this sense, we can be moving toward freedom. That may require that we know how to use various languages, many languages. None of us can be freed simply by clinging to a single language or dialect, even if it is one that has been labeled "standard." We move toward freedom to the extent that our language is large enough and varied enough to let us be precise and clear in what we choose to talk about. None of us can justifiably claim that the language we already know is enough. That would be vain confidence. Unassisted, the language we already have will seldom serve all our purposes. Any dialect or language that we grow up with is a good and useful one, but no dialect or language is enough unless its range grows to make precision and clarity possible. And there are some things we can do to extend the dimensions of our language and to improve our control of it.

We can learn more.   Learning something means that you come to know its name, or how to talk about it, or what to do with it. Learning something means that you come to know new words, or new niches for old words. Reading and studying and doing extend both the vocabulary you recognize and the vocabulary you use. Reading—reading books, magazines, newspapers, even billboards—gives you more words to use, shows you the languages of many writers being used, and keeps you in the habit of watching what other people do with words. Listening accomplishes many of the same things. Read. Listen. Watch.

We can work for precision.   The world, it often seems, wants words to be produced quickly. We want tomorrow morning's newspaper to have in it words that were not in this afternoon's paper, even if nothing of note occurs to be reported. We don't want a TV comedian to tell the same joke twice—he must find new words before the next program—and we'd rather every commercial, if there must be commercials, were new and not a repetition of the same old words. We tire quickly of politicians because they're guilty of the "same old political oratory." In a given term at school large numbers of students may have to produce three to five term research papers, even though many professional writers would never dream of attempting so much in so little time. Many students are asked regularly to write 300- to 500-word essays in a fifty-minute freshman English class, and more are expected to produce new words in well-organized sequence in every final examination. The world seems to want words and uses them up quickly.

But you can pause. You can wait. You can stay a while to search. You can stop and study and hunt for the word that says what you wish to say, and when you find it, you can pause again to be sure you put it in the right place. No one can predict ahead of time what your right word will be, and no one can set out a group of infallible rules for finding the accurate word. Consistent use of a good dictionary will help, and watching the choice and significance of words in the writing of other people will help. Some examples may be useful.

The passage below, from a book that is both a personal meditation on the author's home country and a cultural study, occurs when the author has moved back in time from his exploration of his present culture and terrain to a portion of its nineteenth-century history. "The People" alluded to early in the passage are the Comanches. Two short passages have been italicized for later reference.

> It seems clear that The People were good haters. So were the whites, though, and that was a year before a war unconnected with Indians was to draw away many of the tough young ones. *The Brazos frontier stewed*; citizens and Rangers and soldiers joined into a pursuit to follow the party and its big herd of horses (500 or 600 by the time they left the settlements) to the Comanche winter villages in the northwest. Charles Goodnight was along, and Sul Ross, and Captain Jack Cureton, and nearly everybody else, and most of them left accounts of it which flatly conflict. What is sure is that they found Comanches on the Pease, and *smote them hip and thigh*, man and woman and child, and took back Mrs. Sherman's Bible and a blue-eyed, sullen squaw who turned out to be Cynthia Ann Parker, kidnapped twenty-four years previously on the Navasota. Her Uncle Isaac Parker (Parker County is named for him, and he died there) journeyed up to Camp Cooper to identify her when the expedition returned. She lived for four captive years among relatives, scarcely ever breaking silence except to beg brokenly that they let her go back to her husband and her children and the free, dirty, shifting life of the plains. Since of course they wouldn't, she died in the damp windless forests of East Texas. But Peta Nocona had sired a son on her, Quanah, who was to be one of the great chiefs in the last years of the fighting. . . .—John Graves, *Goodbye to a River*

Notice the two passages italicized, and how pointedly accurate the words are. The frontier, we're told, *stewed*. *Stewed* is in the first place a colloquial usage, common in southern and southwestern speech and therefore fitting to the subject, the time, and the place the author is dealing with. Taken literally, it denotes boiling, seething, and suggests a picture of a surface broken by bubbles, stirred by heat-driven surges, active with steam. Taken figuratively, it suggests nervous agitation, sudden blow-ups of energy, agonies of worry and frustration. One word, then, can conjure up the exact picture the author intends us to see.

The other designated passage echoes the Old Testament book Judges, in which we're told that Samson rose up against the Philistines and "smote them hip and thigh with a great slaughter." The author's use of this language from the King James Version of the Bible serves at least two purposes: it echoes the idea of the "great slaughter," and it reveals some of the character of the whites as they attack the Indians, suggesting their biblical orientation and their sense of Anglo-Saxon godliness in their mission against a people presumed to be wicked heathens.

The passage below occurs in the opening pages of the first chapter of a book in which the author explores the devastating effects of pesticides and other manufactured blights upon the landscape and the general ecological order. As the book opens, the author presents a fable dramatizing a new stillness and death in nature.

> . . . The few birds seen anywhere were moribund; they trembled violently and could not fly. It was a spring without voices. On the mornings that had once throbbed with the dawn chorus of robins, catbirds, doves, jays, wrens, and scores of other bird voices there was now no sound; only silence lay over the fields and woods and marshes.
>
> On the farms the hens brooded, but no chicks hatched. The farmers complained that they were unable to raise any pigs—the litters were small and the young survived only a few days. The apple trees were coming into bloom but no bees droned among the blossoms, so there was no pollination and there would be no fruit.—Rachel Carson, *Silent Spring*

Notice a couple of examples from this passage. Note first that the author presents a specific, not a general, view; the devastation is seen among specific animals and plants: robins, catbirds, doves, jays, wrens, other birds, hens, chicks, pigs, and apple trees. Note, too, that the language seems to belong to rural animal husbandry—"the hens brooded, but no chicks hatched"—so as to create a sense of serene natural order to contrast with the ominous threat of human intrusion through pesticides and other killers.

One last example: when Abraham Lincoln opened his speech with

"Four score and seven years ago our fathers brought forth on this continent a new nation . . . ," the word *score* turned out to be uniquely accurate for the context. The entire address at Gettysburg moves us at least partly because it so strikingly looks both back to our beginnings and ahead to our future. The word *score*, already out of common use in Lincoln's time, by its archaic sound succeeds in helping to bring the past into the President's speech.

We can work for accuracy. "Respect for the word," Dag Hammarskjöld wrote, "is essential if there is to be any growth in society or in the human race. To misuse the word is to show contempt for man. It undermines the bridges and poisons the wells." Respect for the word, he continued, means using it "with scrupulous care and incorruptible heartfelt love of truth."

Exercises

1.   Examine a famous speech such as an inaugural address of a President for evidence of the use of words with biblical or historical significance and describe the effect you think the author was trying to achieve.

2.   Look for a piece of prose in which one word that seems inappropriate destroys the whole intended effect of the passage, or try writing one yourself.

3.   By capturing just the right words, the student writer of the following passage said more than he could have in a five-hundred word theme:

> Bartender.
> My father is a bartender.
> He never finished grade school.
> Has been working since the age of six.
> He has five sons and one daughter by my momma.
> He would work for weeks without time off.
> "I don't owe you anything, son, you are grown now."
> He had a finger cut off at the age of ten, while working at a mill.
> He worked so much that he never had time to get with his boys and
>   talk or go fishing.
> He's a genuine hustler.
> His complexion is very bright for a black man and he has green
>   eyes. His body is slender and neat.
> He left Momma for another woman.

Try the same kind of compact, specific description for one of your relatives.

***We can choose the word of specific meaning over the word of general
meaning.***   Since writers and their readers are apart from each other,
the space between them makes the work that words must do more
difficult. The words that a writer puts down on a page, though clear
enough to him and precise in their meaning, may not mean the same
thing or have the same precision to a reader.

If a writer, then, can point specifically to the things he or she is
talking about, then a reader may find it easier to know the writer's
meaning. The surest meanings of all, perhaps, rest in *proper nouns*, the
names of particular people, particular places, particular things (Henry
David Thoreau; Laura Kidd; Muleshoe, Texas; the Jefferson Memorial;
the Gulf of Mexico). If a writer mentions Muleshoe, Texas, a reader can
hardly be confused about which town is meant; it can be located on a
map, and a good almanac will provide information about the town. It is a
specific place, not duplicated anywhere else. If a writer mentions "the
town that has a statue of a mule," a reader may, on the other hand, have
some difficulty in realizing the specific meaning intended.

No one, however, can write an essay or a book or a newspaper
article or a technical report using only proper nouns. Often, indeed, they
appear only infrequently. What we can do, however, is rely as much as
possible on concrete nouns, accurate verbs, and significant modifiers. A
concrete noun is a noun (naming a person, place, thing, quality, or
condition) that makes a specific reference more or less agreed upon by
the people who use the word. *Typewriter* is a concrete noun, but *imple-
ment* isn't. *Sidewalk* is a concrete noun, but *route* isn't. *Desk* is a concrete
noun, but *furniture* isn't. An accurate verb is the verb that gets as close as
possible to naming the action or state that is in question. *Run* may be an
accurate verb, but in some contexts *gallop, lope, stride,* or *jog* may be
more accurate. *Cry* may be an accurate verb, but in some contexts *wail,
sob,* or *blubber* may be more accurate. A significant modifier is an
adjective or adverb that tells readers something specific about the word it
modifies. *Green, fluorescent, dilapidated, lazily, stealthily,* and *gangre-
nous* signify qualities or manners that most readers will understand right
away; but *truly, really, genuine, genuinely, awfully,* and *very* don't tell
readers very much.

Less specific words, including abstract nouns (such as *honor, glory,
fear,* and *patriotism*), and functional words (such as prepositions and
conjunctions and articles) whose work is to connect other words are, of
course, essential to talking and writing. But it is the specific meaning,
clearly designated, that usually gives color and character to writing. What
claims our attention and our interest, sometimes even our belief, is the
particular thing caught in words. When you can embody your meaning in
particular things, showing readers what you intend, those particulars can
serve as a bond to bring you and readers together. (See "Language to
follow, examples to show the way," p. 71.)

CHECKING THE LANGUAGE
OF OTHER WRITERS

Most of the words in the following passage have been categorized on a chart. Try categorizing the words in the next two passages yourself; you may be able to get some idea of the value of specific words in this way, and it may give you one small way of discriminating among different writers.

The choice of qualities of a nation's heroes is a reliable index to that nation's health. This is particularly true of political heroes rather than poets or actors or even the first men on the moon. For it is the statesmen who have made an impact on the nation's political and emotional life, men who have been followed with passionate idolatry and attacked with consuming hatred—heroes of the quality of Washington, Jefferson, Lincoln, and Franklin Roosevelt, and men of potential heroic stature like John and Robert Kennedy—who have a continuing vitality in the fantasies of large segments of the American people.—Fawn M. Brodie, "The Political Hero in America: His Fate and His Future"

Proper Nouns
> Washington, Jefferson, Lincoln, Franklin Roosevelt, John and Robert Kennedy

Concrete Nouns
> heroes, poets, actors, first men on the moon, statesmen, American people

Specific Verbs
> (none appear in this selection)

Significant Modifiers
> *political* heroes, *political* and *emotional* life, *passionate* idolatry, *consuming* hatred

General and Abstract Words and Phrases
> choice of qualities, reliable index, nation's health, impact, idolatry, hatred, potential, heroic stature, continuing vitality, fantasies, large segments

Function Words
> the, of, of a, a, to, that, this, of, rather than, or, or, the, for, the, an, on (and so on)

Yesterday I set out to catch the new season, and instead I found an old snakeskin. I was in the sunny February woods by the quarry; the snakeskin was lying in a heap of leaves right next to an aquarium someone had thrown away. I don't know why that someone hauled the aquarium deep into the woods to get rid of it; it had only one broken glass side. The snake found it handy, I imagine; snakes like to rub against something rigid to help them out of their skins, and the broken aquarium looked like the nearest likely object. Together the snakeskin and the aquarium made an interesting scene on the forest floor. It looked like an exhibit at a trial—circumstantial evidence—of a wild scene, as though a snake had burst through the broken side of the aquarium, burst through his ugly old skin, and disappeared, perhaps straight up in the air, in a rush of freedom and beauty.—Annie Dillard, *Pilgrim at Tinker Creek*

The face of the water, in time, became a wonderful book—a book that was a dead language to the uneducated passenger, but which told its mind to me without reserve, delivering its most cherished secrets as clearly as if it uttered them with a voice. And it was not a book to be read once and thrown aside, for it had a new story to tell every day. Throughout the long twelve hundred miles there was never a page that was void of interest, never one that you could leave unread without loss, never one that you would want to skip, thinking you could find higher enjoyment in some other thing. There never was so wonderful a book written by man; never one whose interest was so absorbing, so unflagging, so sparklingly renewed with every reperusal. The passenger who could not read it was charmed with a peculiar sort of faint dimple on its surface (on the rare occasions when he did not overlook it altogether); but to the pilot that was an *italicized* passage; indeed, it was more than that, it was a legend of the largest capitals, with a string of shouting exclamation-points at the end of it, for it meant that a wreck or a rock was buried there that could tear the life out of the strongest vessel that ever floated. It is the faintest and simplest expression the water ever makes, and the most hideous to a pilot's eye. In truth, the passenger who could not read this book saw nothing but all manner of pretty pictures in it, painted by the sun and shaded by the clouds, whereas to the trained eye these were not pictures at all, but the grimmest and most dead-earnest of reading-matter.—Mark Twain, *Life on the Mississippi*

We can become aware of all of the meanings that words collect.   Sometimes an orchestra sounds a chord, or a guitarist strums one, and we are able to know each separate note for what it is, and yet hear the loveliness the notes make together as a chord. If we're lucky thereafter, and if our ears are tuned to hear, whenever we hear one of the single notes, it sets off reverberations in our ears of the whole sweet chord. The note has that power for us; its use in the chord associates it with the chord, and it echoes the chord even when it is struck alone.

Words work in much the same way. Some words, in addition to their own relatively straightforward meanings, acquire through usage the power to suggest other meanings. Writers should be able to understand and use both kinds of meanings. The first kind is called *denotation*. The second is called *connotation*. One standard college dictionary defines *denotation* as "the specific meaning of, or the object or objects designated by, a word as distinct from that which it suggests." The same dictionary defines *connotation* as "the suggestive or associative significance of an expression, additional to the explicit literal meaning." The word *home*, for example, denotes the place where one lives; it connotes far more, suggesting privacy, rest, security, comfort, and intimacy. The word *wall* denotes one of the vertical surfaces that surrounds and gives shape to a room or a building, but it may connote a defensive position, the structure separating East from West Berlin, or the thing that many of us climb several times a day.

Some words and expressions may not suggest much to you or to anyone. *Nitric acid* may not set off any associations for you, and *hot-water faucet* may leave you cold. But many words do have connotative power. These associated meanings and suggested values come from many sources. A word may gather suggested meanings simply because it is associated in your mind with some particular person, or because you heard it in a particular place, or because the people among whom you normally move use it in a given way. Meanings accumulate in many ways, and they do not necessarily stay fixed. Just before, during, and after World War II, the word *appeasement* acquired unpleasant meanings suggesting obsequiousness, subservience, even cowardice because of its association with British efforts to forestall Germany's military excursions. The word has just about lost that association now, and is probably used chiefly for its denotative value of *conciliation* or *satisfaction*. The expression *at this point in time* came to seem silly jargon through its frequent repetition during the Watergate hearings, but judging from its common use now, the expression has lost its unfavorable association—and that's a pity, for it's not nearly so useful and economical as the single word *now*.

If you use words in your writing without knowing all the meanings they contain, your writing, quite simply, will get away from you. It will have meanings that you don't want it to have. If you use the word *pedagogue* believing that it will only mean *teacher* to your readers, unaware that to many of them it will mean *a narrow-minded teacher*, then your writing is out of your control, and your words are getting away from you. Words are not the private property of any single user of words; they belong to all who speak the language, and they often accumulate far more meaning than might appear in a literal, denotative definition.

The thing to do, then, is to use these accumulated meanings. Through reading and studying and listening, learn to hear all the meanings a word may have, and then use the connotative values in words to say just what you want to say. *Walk*, *stride*, and *stroll* may share pretty much the same denotative meaning, but each suggests a different kind of movement. One of them may come much nearer than the others to creating the image you want. Both denotation and connotation provide means for being accurate. Connotation has the additional power of suggesting sensory images and calling up memories. To refer to a *harvest moon* may be an accurate way of describing a moon that has a particular appearance. But beyond that accuracy, the phrase summons up other images and reverberates with recollections for many readers.

This connotative power, of course, has often been used for trivial or even mischievous purposes. Connotative values in words inevitably have an emotional effect upon many readers. Advertisers, propagandists, and politicians know this, and some are skilled in loading a speech or a piece of writing with words whose connotative associations are all either favorable to their own views or unfavorable to opposing views. A good advertising writer can charm us into buying by linking his or her product to attitudes or qualities we prize through the connotative power of the words selected to describe the product, such as describing expensive neckties as "understated and tastefully elegant" to appeal to a man who hopes to project such an image.

STUDYING DENOTATION AND CONNOTATION

The first passage below is from a newspaper column (later part of a book), in which the author plays with connotations. He shows how we shift words, often using the word with the most favorable connotation to refer to ourselves, those with a less favorable connotation to refer to others, the connotation becoming less favorable as the distance between us and the people we refer to increases. The other passages illustrate various uses of denotation and connotation. Examine them, try to determine about what proportion of the words in each is connotative, separate favorable from unfavorable associations, and see what you can conclude about the general effect or tone of the passage.

1.   My senator is making a "probe"; your senator is on a "fishing expedition"; his senator is starting a "witch-hunt."

I am "cautious"; you are "timid"; he is "cowardly."

I believe something to be a fact because "I saw it in black and white"; but you mustn't believe something to be a fact "just because you happened to see it in print somewhere."

Our country is engaged in "security measures"; your country is engaged in an "arms race"; his country is engaged in "stockpiling weapons."

My church denomination lives by a "creed," but yours subscribes to a "dogma."

The ceremony I approve of had "dignity and grandeur"; the ceremony I disapprove of had "pomp and ostentation."

I believe in "authority"; you believe in "force"; he believes in "violence."

I am a "man of few words"; you are "taciturn"; he is "unresponsive."

My outburst was "indignation"; yours was "anger"; his was "petulance."

My crude friend is "a diamond in the rough"; yours is "a touch on the common side"; his is "a loudmouthed boor."

If she picks up men in bars, she is a "floozie"; if she picks up men at a Hollywood shindig, she is a "swinger"; if she picks up men at a fashionable garden party, she is a "femme fatale."

I am a great champion of "tolerance"—as long as you let me define the precise point at which it becomes intolerable.

My cutting remark is an "epigram"; yours is a "wisecrack"; his is a "cheap jeer."

I am a "realist" when I am doing to you that which, if you were doing it to me, I would call "ruthless."

If it was your fault, we had a "collision," but if it was my fault, we just "banged the bumpers up a little."

There are really no "juvenile gang leaders" because, according to the parents, each of the boys "just happened to get in with the wrong crowd."

I am opposed to your newfangled ideas because I believe in "the value of tradition," but you are opposed to my sensible reforms because you are "blindly clinging to the past."

Why is the female of the species called a "songstress," when the male isn't called a "songster"?—Sydney J. Harris, "Antics with Semantics: 5"

2.   With precious few exceptions, all the books on style in English are by writers quite unable to write. The subject, indeed, seems to exercise a special and dreadful fascination over schoolma'ms, bucolic college professors, and other such pseudo-literates. One never hears of treatises on it by George Moore or James Branch Cabell, but the pedagogues, male and female, are at it all the time. In a thousand texts they set forth their depressing ideas about it, and millions of suffering high-school pupils have to study what they say. Their central aim, of course, is to reduce the whole thing to a series of simple rules—the overmastering passion of their melancholy order, at all times and everywhere. They aspire to teach it as bridge whist, the American Legion flag-drill and double-entry bookkeeping are taught. They fail as ignominiously as that Athenian of legend who essayed to training a regiment of grasshoppers in the goose-step.

For the essence of a sound style is that it cannot be reduced to rules—that it is a living and breathing thing, with something of the devilish in it—that it fits its proprietor tightly and yet ever so loosely, as his skin fits him. . . . —H. L. Mencken, "Literature and the Schoolma'm"

3. [This advertisement appears as a two-page spread. The left-hand page is a picture of a soaring eagle. The right-hand page is text. At the top in large letters are two questions: What have we done? Where are we going? These are the first four paragraphs:]

One hundred years ago the American eagle filled the skies. A glorious winged symbol of our highest standards: Pride. Honor. Honesty.

Today a pathetic handful linger desperately on the brink of extinction. And what of the standards? Are they endangered, too?

At Whirlpool we believe these standards, and what they mean to all of us, are too important to forget.

We start with pride. Over the years we've found there are no short cuts. Making an appliance the right way requires only the best: In workmanship, materials and design. We couldn't put our name on anything less. —Whirlpool advertisement

---

Loading a speech or a piece of writing with words whose connotative values are all either favorable to one's own views or unfavorable to any opposing views is often called *slanting*, and the product is often called *slanted writing*. Political writing is often slanted, and advertising is often slanted. The writers want to slant things so they lean in the direction they want. *Slanted writing* has designs on us, and we learn pretty early to watch out for propagandizers and others who do the slanting.

But notice a curious thing. *Slanted writing* has some of the qualities we expect of good writing. Consider this example:

> If you want to capture someone's attention, whisper.
> Nuance.
> An exquisitely delicate new fragrance that lasts and lasts.
> And like a whisper is impossible to resist.
> Introducing NUANCE by COTY. —Advertisement for Coty

Notice that everything in this passage contributes to the message. All the connotative values are of the same kind: the passage is unified by the consistent suggestions of delicacy. The title of the product, *Nuance*, suggests a delicate hint; *whisper* suggests the quiet and subtle; *fragrance* suggests the daintiest kind of odor. The sound of the passage, filled with sibilants (exquisitely, fragrance, lasts, impossible, resist), suggests a whisper. All the parts of the ad, especially the connotative powers present, clearly enough suggest the delicacy of the product. In this respect, at least, what we sometimes condemn as *slanted writing* has superficial similarities to writing that we expect to find in anthologies of fine literature. Notice this short poem, from A. E. Housman's *A Shropshire Lad*:

Into my heart an air that kills
From yon far country blows.
What are those blue remembered hills,
What spires, what farms are those?

That is the land of lost content,
I see it shining plain;
Those happy highways where I went
And cannot come again.

Everything in the first stanza foreshadows the sadness, the "lost content" of the second stanza. The air is a killing air, blowing melancholy, and it blows from a "far country," distant, remote, and as we learn later, unrecoverable. The hills, too, are distant (they are "blue remembered hills," the blue suggesting distance), and the speaker is clearly removed from the spires and the farms. The poet, like the advertiser, packs his lines with the words that will suggest the meaning, tone, and attitude that he wants to create.

In this sense, then, both the advertisement and the poem are *slanted*. Each is packed with unified connotations. But the two pieces are not comparable in other ways. The author of the advertisement is in a different relationship with the subject and the audience from that enjoyed by the speaker in the poem. The speaker in the poem meditates at a distance on his subject and leaves readers free to respond as they will. The speaker in the poem seems to have no visible cause except to speak, to meditate. The speaker in the advertisement keeps the subject close before us and seeks to bring us into the world he or she speaks of. We hear and observe what transpires in the poem, but the speaker has no designs on us. The speaker in the advertisement has a cause, to sell the product, and so enlists our participation in the world presented by the advertisement. The speaker in the poem is generous with us; we receive, but we do not pay. We gain by finding another human who will share with us and whose words may awaken in us an understanding of our own remembered losses. The speaker in the advertisement does not have generosity in mind; we pay, but we do not receive.

But remember that there are at least superficial similarities. *Slanted writing* is not by definition *bad writing*. Our lives might be pleasanter if it were; we could spot the propagandizer or the writer who wants to tell us how to think and act by the grossness of his or her writing. But most slanters are skilled, and we are therefore obliged to be vigilant, asking of each writer, "Will you share with me, or only take from me?"

Exercises

1. Find three examples of advertisements in which the advertiser seems particularly to be relying on the connotative meanings of the words used.

2.   Try to find and list some concrete and proper nouns that suggest each of the following abstract ideas:

a. Hate   e. Benevolence
b. Treachery   f. Despair
c. Innocence   g. Style
d. Aggression   h. Patriotism

We can learn to hear and use the figurative power of words.   Both the denotative and the connotative values of words are vital as you work for accuracy and precision in saying what you wish to say. But words have another kind of potency that can also contribute to the precision of your meaning. Words can be used *figuratively*.

Figurative language is language that uses words or expressions for something other than their literal meaning. *Figurative language* is language that occurs in figures of speech. A *figure of speech*, in turn, is an expression that deliberately abandons the literal meaning of the words in order to create some meaning or effect not possible through the literal meaning. *Figurative language* departs from the denotative value of words in order to make new meaning from their connotative values. Most figures of speech develop from the connotative suggestions and associations that surround words, but figurative language is not precisely the same thing as connotative language.

Words acquire connotative value chiefly because people fall into the habit of using them in particular ways, because they get heard in special contexts. From such sources and others words accumulate meanings. But most, perhaps all, of the figurative uses of words occur intentionally, originating when some writer or speaker deliberately deviates from literal meaning. Connotations arise generally from custom and habit; figures are generally created deliberately.

Words have different kinds of figurative uses. Early texts sometimes identified as many as forty or fifty different kinds of figures. That means that the list of figures of speech that follows is probably not to be taken as comprehensive or final. It does include the more common and familiar figures of speech.

1.   A metaphor is a comparison between two things that are not alike. In a metaphor, the comparison is not specifically stated but implied. The writer says, "A *is* B," implying that "in these particular ways, A is *like* B." *Example*: "No man is an island, entire of itself; every man is a piece of the continent, a part of the main. If a clod be washed away by the sea, Europe is the less, as well as if a promontory were, as well as if a manor of thy friend's or of thine own were: any man's death diminishes me, because I am involved in mankind, and therefore never send to know for whom the bell tolls; it tolls for thee." —John Donne, Meditation XVII

2. *A simile* is a stated comparison (using "like" or "as") between two things that are not alike, and yet, as with metaphor, are found to have some similarities. *Example*:

> Alone, as if enduring to the end
> A valiant armor of scarred hopes outworn,
> He stood there in the middle of the road
> Like Roland's ghost winding a silent horn.
> —E. A. Robinson, "Mr. Flood's Party"

3. *A synecdoche* uses a part to stand for the whole, or less often, a whole to stand for a part. *Examples*: Senator Phaug is skilled at *twisting arms* (He's good at persuading people). Notre Dame met Southern California in the Rose Bowl.

4. *Metonymy* is the substitution of some associated word for what is really meant, as when *the crown* is used to mean *the king*, or when *brass* is used to signify *military officers*.

5. *A pun* is a general name for different kinds of figures that make a play on words. One form of pun uses words alike in sound but different in meaning, as in "He's a forthright man—he's right about a fourth of the time." Braniff International recently advertised "the end of the plain plane." Another form of pun repeats words in different senses, as when a political opponent remarked of the 1976 election, "If Ford and Dole win, I'll lose my Ford and have to go on the dole."

6. *Syllepsis* is the use of a word understood differently in its relation to two or more other words that it modifies or governs. *Example*: Our shortstop made five errors in tonight's game. He missed three grounders, second base, and the Hall of Fame.

7. *Oxymoron* occurs when two normally contradictory terms are brought together. *Example*: I have committed myself to lethargy and propose to enjoy a busy idleness.

8. *Periphrasis* most often occurs, probably, as the substitution of a descriptive word or phrase for a proper noun. *Example*: Sportswriters often refer to the Pittsburgh Steelers' front four as the *Steel Curtain*.

9. *Personification* occurs when a writer gives abstractions or inanimate objects some human qualities or abilities. *Example*: A blue norther howled the news of winter down our chimney.

10. *Hyperbole* is deliberate exaggeration for emphasis. *Example*: "Contemplate me through leather—*don't* use the naked eye! I'm the man with a petrified heart and biler-iron bowels! The massacre of isolated communities is the pastime of my idle moments, the destruction of nationalities the serious business of my life!"—Mark Twain, from *Huckleberry Finn*

11. *Litotes* is deliberate understatement, intended to make what is being said all the more notable by contrast. *Example*: "Last week I saw a woman flayed, and you will hardly believe how much it altered her appearance for the worse."—Jonathan Swift, from *A Tale of a Tub*

12. *Irony* is the use of words so as to give the reader a meaning opposite to the literal meaning of the words. *Example*: He was not a notorious criminal, having been put in jail only twice and fined only four times for trifling oversights.

Occasionally figures of speech such as these and others get used for the sake of adornment, almost as if the writer wrote what he or she had to say and then went back through the work adding embroidery. Such "flowery writing," as some people call it, is hardly a proper use for figurative language. Useful, lively, and significant figures are probably more likely to occur, not as a result of going back through a piece of writing and adding decorations, but as a natural consequence of the writer's way of looking at the world. Many of the figures, for example, are made up out of contrary impulses, out of contrary kinds of experience. Oxymoron, simile, and metaphor put unlike things together, and irony says one thing but means another. Happy and useful occurrences of these figures seem to indicate that their author is able to see contraries, and is able to see likenesses, sometimes startling, in things that are unlike. Writing that has such figures in it is *thick*: behind it there are at least two versions of experience, two ways of seeing things that come together.

But, more simply, figures of speech are important because they are often lively and highly descriptive, and they provide variety from literal meanings. When Andrew Marvell personifies time in "To His Coy Mistress," the figure makes the passing of time more immediate and more ominous:

> But at my back I always hear
> Time's winged chariot hurrying near.

In one of his *Spectator* papers, Joseph Addison uses a simile to show what wit is. If a writer says, "My mistress' bosom is as white as the snow," Addison suggests, that is merely a trite simile. But if the writer completes the simile, "My mistress' bosom is as white as the snow, and as cold," that, Addison says, is wit. It is also a sharp, funny encapsulation of the relationship between the speaker and his would-be love.

The two figures just cited also help to show that figurative language at its best, far from being added decoration, is a precise and economical instrument. Most of us would use far more words to convey so bitingly the relationship presented with quick self-mockery in Addison's figure. In "Mr. Flood's Party," quoted above to illustrate the simile, the poet represents Mr. Flood, who is returning home alone after going to town to get his jug filled. On the road he stops to take a drink or two, and the poet says he stands there "like Roland's ghost winding a silent horn." That single line, a simile, compresses into a small space a great deal of information. We know from the simile that Mr. Flood has lifted the jug to his lips (as Roland lifted the horn), and we learn that he tilts the jug for the reason that Roland lifts the horn, to call back his friends, who have died and left him alone. We can't read the simile and then dismiss Mr. Flood as just an old drunk.

More important in many ways than short, identifiable figures such as those illustrated above is another kind of figurative usage. *Extended figures*, often unacknowledged, sometimes run through a long passage of writing. How often have you heard political speakers talk about their campaigns or practices of their offices in terms associated with sports? The specific figure of speech may not be stated, but when a political speaker refers to his or her *game plan*, or when party leaders cite the need of getting a new *quarterback*, or when a business executive refers to employees who are *loyal game players*, who *have the good moves*, then the speaker is depending upon a figure that likens politics or business to football. Political and military leaders sometimes use the game figure when they talk about war, and sportscasters, reversing the circumstances, frequently talk about football as if it were war. Teams go on the *defense* or the *offense*, their game plan calls for them to go *on the attack* at the outset, their quarterbacks *bring the troops up to the line,* pro-ball players can face *sudden death* in overtime.

Speakers and writers in business, politics, various kinds of management, even in education and in close personal relations, often speak from an underlying, extended, but unstated figurative comparison between the human being and the computer: when they talk, they want to get audience *feedback*; when they confer, they want to get lots of *input*; when action is needed, they want to get everyone *programmed*; when a decision is required, they want to get *a good data base*.

What is particularly important and revealing about extended figures is that since they often show up throughout a piece of writing, they may reveal a great deal about the author's thinking. Since they are often unstated, such extended figures may show what a writer is assuming, what he or she is taking for granted. Most writers who use terms like *input*, *feedback, programming*, and *data base* may not believe that they are comparing human actions to computer actions, but their language reveals that in fact they are. To be sure, not all extended figures are unstated, and not all are unfortunate. In the passage about the Mississippi River quoted on page 182, Mark Twain uses the figurative comparison of the river and a book effectively and plainly.

SOME SAMPLES OF FIGURATIVE LANGUAGE TO WORK WITH

In the passages below, determine what kind of figurative language—if any—is used and what effect it has.

1.   Wild Meadow is violets and jasmine from the hidden valleys in the South of France. Rare geranium and chamomile from special gardens in North Africa. And roses, unforgettable Bulgarian roses blended together to make a fragrance that's like no other. So every girl can have her own Wild Meadow of the mind.—Advertisement for Wild Meadow

2.   All her Kamikaze friends admired my aunt,
     their leader, charmed in vinegar,
     a woman who could blaze with such white blasts
     as Lawrence's that lit Arabia.
     Her mean opinions bent her hatpins.

     We'd take a ride in her old car
     that ripped like Sherman through society:
     Main Street's oases sheltered no one
     when she pulled up at Thirty-first
     and whirled that Ford for another charge.

     We swept headlines from under rugs, names
     all over town, which I learned her way, by heart,
     and blazed with love that burns because it's real.
     With a turn that's our family's own,
     she'd say, "Our town is not the same"—

     Pause—"And it's never been."
               —William Stafford, "A Family Turn"

3.   Nothing communicates like a Parker.
     Parker. We are writing.—Advertisement for Parker Pens

Near the beginning of this section ("Your own language, growing," p. 175) I imply that there is a connection between our personal freedom and our use of language. We approach that freedom, as William Jovanovich suggests, "when there is expression that is plain in intent, consonant in tone, and explicit in meaning. Everyman's innate competence to learn language is perhaps warranted to him with life, but his very own, his particular use of language is neither promised nor foretold. His command of language is enlarged and freed by desire, by practice, and by reward."

Many languages are available to you. From the resources they offer and from your own experience, learning, and wit, you must make your own language. Don't settle for a language that is fixed and finished, its limits determined by someone else's standards or by your own unwillingness to change. Your own worth, the power and potential of the human mind, and the rich diversity of the language deserve better than that. Make a language that grows, that lets you speak freely, that lets you ask your questions, explore the answers, and understand your own decisions.

LANGUAGES THAT TYRANNIZE

Many languages are available to you, but, whether by design or by accident, some uses of language are full of peril. Languages can be abused and corrupted.

One source of abuse and corruption is carelessness, or disregard for the meanings and uses of words. Perhaps some people are careless just because they are careless. Others seem to disregard the possibilities of plain, sure meaning in words out of a conviction that language is simply not adequate to express the complexities of human nature. To be sure, saying words may not be as sweet as watching a gentle child reach out, longing to help a robin fly. But words will let us savor that scene in our memory and call it back again and again, and words will let us tell someone else, either now or later. Besides, words and word-combinations usually have the power to say more complex things than we are ready to cope with at any given moment.

At any rate, the language you use may well be corrupted by carelessness or by distrust. Such threats as these, however, may not be the most perilous sources of abuse.

We risk corrupting the language and imprisoning ourselves when, however thoughtlessly or accidentally, we simply accept and use the language that is in the air around us, when we take over the words, phrases, and expressions that have currency and use them as our own. When we do that, we give up our own voice, and when we give up our own voice, we give up our own way of thinking. When we accept someone else's phrasing, we accept his or her thoughts, and by doing so make ourselves the willing victims of tyranny. We're no longer free if the language we use is not our language. The language suffers, too. Continued use of popular phrasings, especially when we begin to use the catch words and phrases indiscriminately in different contexts, robs the language of some possibilities for precision and dulls its flavor by repetition.

This form of corruption and self-imprisonment probably occurs most frequently in our use of *clichés*, *euphemisms*, and some forms of *jargon*. A *cliché* is a trite, worn-out expression, made stale by repetition, as when twenty-five television sports announcers say "He's some kind of ball player" eleven hundred times in a single football season, or when an executive declares for the forty-seventh time that "Competition is the name of the game," or when a teacher informs a class that they will study a novel "in depth."

A *euphemism* is a mild or pleasant expression substituted for one thought to be too blunt, coarse, or unpleasant, as, for example, in the substitution of *the culturally deprived* for *the poor and ignorant*, or in the use of the expression *a meaningful relationship* to refer to what might otherwise be called *an affair. Jargon* in its most literal sense means *confused, unintelligible speech*, and there are many kinds of jargon, from the specialized speech of a profession that is unintelligible only to outsiders to the pompous, formulaic speech that sometimes simply fills up space and sometimes hides real meaning. George Orwell called attention to the latter kind of jargon in his essay "Politics and the English Language": "Defenseless villages are bombarded from the air, the inhabitants driven out into the countryside, the cattle machine-gunned, the huts set on fire with incendiary bullets: this is called *pacification*. Millions of peasants are robbed of their farms and set trudging along the roads with no more than they can carry: this is called *transfer of population*." Recently, we have heard expressions such as *At that point in time*, which just means *then*, but might seem to give the impression of greater objectivity and precision, and we are familiar with speakers who announce that they are *trying to make an appropriate value judgment*, which, though it sounds philosophically disposed, probably just means that the speakers are trying *to decide*. (Further examples of clichés, euphemisms, and jargon appear below.) When we unthinkingly accept and use such language, we accept tyranny.

Some abuses and corruptions of language are more ominous still. Sometimes language is used in such a way as to obscure meaning, or to cover the truth with words that favor the speaker or writer, and sometimes we have to conclude that the practice is deliberate, that the speaker or writer seeks to impose his or her will upon those who hear or read. On some occasions we accept tyranny voluntarily; on other occasions tyranny wants to control or delude us.

It may well be that language is always under threat, always in danger of losing to carelessness, passivity, or calculation the precision and honesty it is capable of. Since words are printed, shown, and spoken more abundantly than we can manage, it is often easy for us to be careless, easy for us to be passive, easy for us to be uncritical. Language is rather commonly abused. As a consequence, it is worth considering more fully some of the corrupted and corrupting forms that language can take.

Some forms of language are nonhuman.　When speakers and writers, for whatever reason, use language that treats human beings as objects or machines or animals, then the language is no longer appropriate for human beings. When an educator, for example, speaks of "conditioning" students to meet new objectives in class, he or she has reduced students to white mice. When John Dean, testifying before the Senate's Watergate committee, remarked that he "dealt with people telephonically," he was no longer talking about human beings, but about objects. When men refer to women by terms such as "skirt," "piece," or various terms for various parts of the anatomy, they are treating the women as objects, whether or not that is their immediate and conscious intention. Some language, of course, is clearly intended to dehumanize: "pig," "bitch," and other terms designate animals, not human beings. Other forms of language convert us into machines. "Input," "output," "feedback," "programming," and other terms are, as noted above in the discussion of figurative language, part of an extended figurative treatment of human actions as machine actions. The trouble with such language is that if we speak of human beings long enough as animals, or as objects, or as machines, then eventually we think of them as animals, objects, or machines.

Considerable evidence can be found around us to show human beings translating their language to make it seem systematic, or to try to create a scientific-sounding style in a context not otherwise very scientific. Monroe C. Beardsley (in "Putting Down Words: Some Vicissitudes of Language") cites two interesting examples of this process. The first is from *Executive Decisions and Operations Research*, by David W. Miller and Martin K. Starr, and it shows how language gets translated for the computer: "The Golden Rule is another codification of consideration which should govern our choice of actions lest we end by sub-optimizing in terms of our interpersonal objectives." The second is from *The Pentagon Papers*; it is a chilling specimen of language that has left out all that is human. The passage is part of a memorandum drafted by Assistant Secretary of Defense Robert McNaughton on November 6, 1964, describing some of the options available to President Johnson in Vietnam:

> *Option B. Fast full squeeze. Present policies plus a systematic program of military pressures against the north, meshing at some point with negotiation, but with pressure actions to be continued at a fairly rapid pace and without interruption until we achieve our central present objectives.*
> *Option C. Progressive squeeze-and-talk. Present policies plus an orchestration of communications with Hanoi and a crescendo of additional military moves against infiltration targets. . . .*

This is chilling language. Human lives are obliterated in favor of "central present objectives." Games theory takes over, and human movements become "pressure actions" or a "crescendo of additional military moves." There are no human enemies, only "infiltration targets."

Some forms of language are mean-spirited.   Professor San-Su C. Lin (in "'Standard Dialects' and Substandard Worlds") suggests that, while dialects are not inherently either good or bad, there are some "wrong" languages—specifically, ways of talking or writing that repudiate or even destroy the generosity, the openness, and the mutuality that human beings are capable of. Among these can be listed a language of poverty, frustration, and repression: "Shut up!" "Be quiet!" "Do like I told you!" "Get out of here!"—the language of rejection and defeat. Another "wrong" language is the language of exclusion, the language that constructs walls, the language that says, "Keep out!" As Professor Lin suggests, this kind of language is oftener than not recognizable by its preoccupation with *we* and *they*: "Why don't *they* stay in *their* schools and let *ours* alone?" "Why do *they* want to move into *our* neighborhood where they'll be strangers?" "What do *they* want from *us?*" A third "wrong" language is the "dialect of make-believe":

> *Glamorous cars, gleaming appliances, glorious life of luxury and leisure, anything one can wish for, anything one can dream of, can be had for just so much, or next to nothing. Buy now, pay later. Money is never a problem, for here is a world of inexhaustible riches. Here youth and beauty and happiness are synonymous with a brand of cigarette, or beverage, or cosmetics. Heroism means to shoot and be shot at, all for fun. To be a good mother means to give your children a certain cereal; to be a good wife means to serve a certain coffee, and to be a wonderful lover, use a certain mouth wash. Life is so easy, so carefree. No problems to solve. No decisions to make. This, certainly, is the "standard dialect" of fantasy created by undisciplined affluence and power. With this dialect, the American merchant and his agents, sex and violence, rule the world.*

And fourth, Professor Lin proposes, is the "wrong" language of authoritarianism, often associated with schools: "Because it is wrong," "Because the textbook says so," "Because I say so," "That isn't the correct answer."

And there are other kinds of mean-spirited languages, languages in which the speaker or writer brutalizes others or denies their humanity or claims power and virtue for himself or asserts superiority. Ours has been a male-dominated society, and our language reveals the domination. We have used words such as *congressman*, *statesman*, and *businessman*, never letting the language reveal that any one or all might be female. The language has granted superiority to males: a man can be a *poet*, but a woman is often only a *poetess*; a man can be a *judge*, but a woman is only a *lady judge*. In places where sex appears to be irrelevant, our language has assumed that men belong naturally, but women have to be especially identified. We expect truckdrivers and doctors and writers to be male, and so label women as *lady truckdrivers*, *lady doctors*, and *woman writers*. Generations of students have been taught to use male pronouns to refer to singular noun antecedents where the gender is not known, as in "If a *student* forgets *his* homework, *he* will have to stay and complete the work after the class is over." (In this case, it would be easy, and much fairer, to convert to plurals: "If *students* forget *their* homework, *they* will have to complete the work after the class is over.") Many of the words associated with human intercourse ("bang," for example, or "screw") are brutal and violent words suggesting total masculine domination, and many words that men use to refer to women ("chick," "broad," "skirt," "piece") transform women into objects, presumably existing for men's pleasure and convenience. We have used a male-dominated language that is mean-spirited in its treatment of women.

And our language has frequently been mean-spirited in its racist attitudes. In some of our discussions of problems between races, we have used "whites" as the standard, thus making "non-whites" inferior at the outset. In some public language, white people have been patronizing, even though they intended to be allies, by referring to "our colored troops in Vietnam," or "our colored friends in the South." White people have often kept the races apart by identifying people as Negro when the designation is irrelevant: public discourse reveals references to "black poets," "black school superintendents," "black athletes," and others.

Some forms of language violate their users.   When you use some forms of language, you do yourself in. Old, beat-up expressions that were dull when they were new use up the space that might have gone to convey your own way of thinking and speaking. If you write clichés into your work, it means that your mind has gone out of gear and the clichés are controlling your thoughts. Clichés are handy. We can't talk without them. They are in some ways like the "ers" and "uhs" and "wells" that mark our speaking: we use the clichés to fill up space in the air or on the paper, to hold our sentences together, while we're thinking. They appear, often frequently, in the work of good writers. But handy as they are, clichés are someone else's language, not yours; they are substitutes for your own thoughts.

Words and expressions often become clichés because, initially, they seem to be magic; they seem to name things or qualities of great value to us, and so we use them over and over again. *Creative* is such a word, and so are *meaningful, dialogue, charismatic, ambience,* and *dichotomy.* Words and expressions become clichés, too, because at one time they seemed to be catchy, or highly descriptive, or picturesque. The samples in the passage below will surely remind you of others.

> I should like to read or hear, just once, about tacks that aren't brass, questions that aren't moot, coasts that aren't clear, fates that aren't worse than death, and a mean that isn't golden.
> And, just once, a null without a void, a might without a main, a far without a wide, a six of one without a half-dozen of the other, tooth without a nail, and ways without means.
> And, just once, an unfit fiddle, a warm cucumber, a young hill,

a stupid owl, a hard impeachment, a black elephant, a sage's paradise, feet of gold, the pepper of the earth, an unbloated plutocrat, and a sad Lothario.

And, just once, a social caterpillar, Father Nature, the orange of one's eye, an uncracked dawn, a picture of illness, ignorance after the event, a tower of weakness, an unsure slowness, a low dryness, and a lively earnestness.

And, just once, a fair without a square, a safe without a sound, a sackcloth without ashes, a wear without a tear, a fast without a loose, a rack without a ruin, a kill without a cure, a long without a short, and a storm without a port.

And, just once, a merciless errand, an ungrieved error, an unpsychological moment, a light horse, a live certainty, an indecisive effect, an embarrassment of poverty, an eternal quadrangle, an emaciated calf, and someone who has been frightened into his wits.

And, just once, a nail that isn't hit on the head, a feather that can't knock you down, a gift that doesn't come from the gods, a bad Samaritan, a delicate exaggeration, and a pin that doesn't drop.

And, just once, an ungilded lily, good dirty fun, tepid congratulations, a wagon hitched to a meteorite, something that costs an ugly penny, someone who is gone and forgotten, and someone who would go through fire but not through water.

And, just once, a hue without a cry, a hem without a haw, a hit without a miss, a hither without a yon, a head without a shoulders, a spick without a span, a hammer without a tongs, fish on a string or a net or a pan but not in a kettle, a prophet with honor, and purely without simply.

And, just once, sweet grapes, soft facts, an unpicked bone, a tempest in a coffeepot, a ducksong or a goosesong but not a swansong, a bull that is taken by the tail, and a rhinestone in the rough.—Sydney J. Harris, "A Pretty Kettle of Clichés"

Surely, if you will just put your shoulder to the wheel and get heavy into clichés, you'll get it all together and remember to avoid clichés like the plague, though they are thick as flies in all languages.

But clichés aren't the only kind of language that turns back upon the user to limit what he or she can say or to subvert meaning. In the past few years we've all seen curious specimens of language in which, apparently, the speakers and writers have made some attempt to strip away the moral qualities of the matter under discussion. Almost invariably, the effort to cleanse language of moral terms serves not to purify the users, or to rescue them from blame, but to reveal their foolishness, their search for what someone has called a language of nonresponsibility. If a company seeks to influence a sale by giving a prospective buyer "increments in the form of currency," that may seem to be a cleaner, more ethically neutral act than bribing a buyer, but the language sooner or later reveals the act for what it is. This kind of language became commonplace during the various investigations and hearings associated with the Watergate break-in and its aftermath. One witness, for example, reported that his superiors did not approve projects and tactics, but "signed off on them," which seems at once more casual and less calculating than a deliberate decision. Other samples of this language of nonresponsibility, as reported by Richard Gambino, show speakers trying to hide their own questionable behavior by ridding the language of words that carry moral value:

> *illegal activity* becomes *games*
> *criminal conspiracy* becomes a *game plan*
> *conspirators* become *team players*
> *burglary* becomes *surreptitious entry*
> *spying* becomes *visual surveillance*
> *lying and covering up* become *containing the situation*

Finally, the *absence* of language violates the user of language. When speakers assume that a minimal vocabulary can be used to cover everything, they are in effect admitting that they cannot make careful distinctions. "Groovy" and "gross" and "the pits" are used in hundreds of different situations, but the expressions will not discriminate among the different circumstances. When a speaker uses "gross" to describe twenty-five different things that he or she disapproves of, the language turns back on the user and reveals that he or she is "gross"—that is, unable to make sure distinctions among different things. When a speaker says that he or she is "heavy into folk crafts," or "heavy into ecology," or "heavy into" something else, we do not know whether the speaker is (a) deeply committed, (b) a professionally committed expert, (c) an intensely interested amateur, (d) merely curious, or (e) something else. For a while we may assume that it is our fault that we do not know what the meaning is, but sooner or later we are going to remember that the speaker didn't tell us. A limited, infantile style of speech won't say much.

In this connection, it is important to notice what has been happening to taboos in our vocabulary. Many words—especially those associated with sexual apparatus and function and with animal and human alimentary systems—have been banned from discussion and analysis even though they are common enough in use to be vividly present in our awareness. They are, as John H. Bens (in "Taboo or Not Taboo") describes them, "awful words—awful because they are disagreeable, objectionable, and unpleasant and awful in that they inspire profound and reverential fear." In recent years, of course, many of the taboo words have appeared in public forms of discourse where they would never have appeared before—the milder ones on television, the rest on stage and in motion pictures. When they are faced and examined, they are revealed for what they are, limited and stultifying forms that do more to reveal the narrowness of the speaker than they do to characterize whatever the speaker is talking about. The phrase *piece of meat*, for example, when used to refer to a woman as an object of sexual pleasure, does not characterize the woman so much as it characterizes the speaker, who by using the phrase in such a way reveals himself to be self-serving in attitude and brutalizing in speech.

Some forms of language are used for lying.   We like to think that no one gets up in the morning and plans to be mean, evil, wicked, and nasty during the coming day. We mostly prefer to think that mischief and evil arise from good gone astray, that they occur when someone, for self-serving purposes, repudiates the humanity of others and treats them as objects. If this is so, evil may be said to rise out of good.

In much the same way, some forms of language that are often used for mischievous and immoral purposes originated out of an effort to do good. *Euphemisms*, remember, may originate in an effort to do good. If a speaker asks a widow, "How long has your husband been gone?" it is probably not to obscure the truth of death, but to keep from sharpening her grief, if possible. Even pompous *jargon* may sometimes occur out of an honorable wish to help people see themselves in a better way, as when a term such as *sanitation engineer* is used to replace *janitor*.

But when people start using language in such ways, perhaps for good enough motives, their usage makes the language available for misdirection and lying. If language can be used to make the truth more palatable, then it can also be used to hide the truth and to govern minds by revealing only what is useful. That makes it all too easy for a few to seize the language, make it say only what they want said, and allow the rest of us to hear things only in particular ways. Then "slums" become "inner cities," and "prisons" become "correctional facilities," and "aggressive raids" become "incursions." Then the speaker does no wrong, though he or she "may act inappropriately in a particular time frame." Then a "program of concentrated airborne defoliation missions" becomes "routine improvement of visibility in jungle areas." Then speakers cease planning; instead they "construct scenarios programmed toward terminal objectives in an effort to maximize output." And after a while, the language loses touch with our reality and is connected only to some private reality belonging to some speaker, as in the following passage, a notice sent to customers by a department store: "Any holder of this consumer credit contract is subject to all claims and defenses which the debtor could assert against the seller of goods or services obtained pursuant hereto or with the proceeds hereof. Recovery hereunder by the debtor shall not exceed amounts paid by the debtor hereunder." A handsome reward (one used pipe and a half-pouch of tobacco) awaits anyone who translates that into a usable language.

INSIGHT

A writer of bad prose, to become a writer of good prose, must alter his character. He does not have to become good in terms of conventional morality, but he must become honest in the expression of himself, which means that he must know himself. There must be no gap between expression and meaning, between real and declared aims. For some people, some of the time, this simply means *not* telling deliberate lies. For most people, it means learning when they are lying and when they are not. It means learning the real names of their feelings. It means not saying or thinking, "I didn't *mean* to hurt your feelings," when there really existed a desire to hurt. It means not saying "luncheon" or "home" for the purpose of appearing upper-class or well-educated. It means not using the passive mood to attribute to no one in particular opinions that one is unwilling to call one's own. It means not disguising banal thinking by polysyllabic writing or the lack of feeling by clichés that purport to display feeling. — Donald Hall, *The Modern Stylists*

Exercises

1. Find a spot on campus and describe the scene before you using as many clichés as you can. Then use the same content, but replace each cliché with a fresh phrase.

2. How many metaphors can you find?

Nora galloped into the room, plopped into a chair in the corner, and scoured the room for sight of an easy target. Spying poor old, plodding George in the corner, Nora slithered over to him and perched on the edge of the table. Bumming a cigarette, she launched a tirade about how mulish Professor Brown had been that day when she had tried to weasel out of the paper that was due Friday. Wallowing in self-pity that he was Nora's victim, George had to listen as Nora droned on and on about the kind of princely tyrant that the old goat must think he is!

Try to write your own version of a metaphor-filled paragraph.

3. Bring to class some examples of writing that are nonhuman, sexist, or mean-spirited. Choose one example and rewrite it in human terms.

4. Choose some clichés and think back to the time when they might have been highly descriptive or picturesque. You might even want to do some research on one of them and write the history of its first use. Or, write an imaginative paper in which you speculate on the circumstances in which a cliché might have been used.

. . . let us think of literature as sentences.

Richard Ohmann

9

Making Sentences

In this chapter, following some opening observations about sentences, you'll find

1. an account showing some ways of writing and rewriting sentences for different purposes and different effects (p. 203);

2. some notions about the uses of sentences in different kinds of writing (p. 237);

3. some suggestions about how to get from one sentence to another (p. 242); and

4. some recommendations about revising sentences for economy and variety, with notes about sentence openings, sentence lengths, and sentence types (p. 245).

Most of us are usually willing to accept and abide by the conventional expectation that a sentence begin with a capital letter and end with a period. Fortunately, no one has successfully dictated what shall go in between. To be sure, most English sentences do contain a subject and a verb, and most make some kind of statement that can be read and understood by itself. But all kinds of things get punctuated as sentences—whole sentences, whether simple, compound, complex, compound-complex, whether short, long, or middling; fragments and pieces of sentences, single words, grunts spelled out and standing alone, single exclamations. What that means is that both the content of your sentences and the form of your sentences are yours to determine. Readers probably have the right to expect that most of your sentences will be grammatically conventional, but in the long run you determine what gets said and how it gets said. (For a short review of sentence grammar and punctuation, see pp. 461–493.)

WRITING AND SHAPING SENTENCES

A good part of the time when we are writing, most of us simply write the sentences as we think of them. The form they first take in our heads is the form we're likely to give them when we put them on paper. There's nothing necessarily wrong with that—it's close to the way we talk, and it's a natural way to write. But if we write that way all the time—simply accepting the first available form for our sentences—we're overlooking perhaps the most interesting and most potent feature of the English sentence: *many of its parts are movable.*

That means that a sentence can be written and then rearranged. Portions of a sentence can be moved around. What was first can be put last; what was last can be moved elsewhere in the sentence. If the tone or emphasis or meaning of a sentence seems wrong, the sentence can be kneaded into another shape. Words, phrases, and clauses can be moved around within a single sentence, and things can sometimes be moved from one sentence to another, parts of Sentence A being taken out to combine with Sentence B, parts of both Sentence A and Sentence B being combined with parts of Sentence C to form a new Sentence D, the parts of Sentence X being separated to form new sentences Y and Z. Parts can be added, parts can be taken away, parts can be carried off and used elsewhere.

Writing a sentence, then, is an exercise of choice, and the range of choices is astonishing. Consider this example:

He thought the truth was sometimes dull and artistically unpleasing, so he occasionally lied, or exaggerated, or told tall tales.

The sentence is all right and presumably a forthright account of the person in question, but the matter can be put in other ways:

> *He occasionally lied, or exaggerated, or told tall tales because he thought the truth was sometimes dull and artistically unpleasing.*

That's a relatively minor rearrangement, but the sentence may read a little better because it makes a clear cause-and-effect statement rearranged in this way. A further rearrangement may help, by giving the sentence a little hook at the end:

> *The truth being sometimes dull, as he saw it, he occasionally exaggerated or told tall tales, and sometimes lied, for artistic effect.*

The shape of a sentence also helps determine its meaning. If you rewrite a sentence by moving some of its parts, or by putting them into a different relationship with each other, you change the quality and effect of the sentence. As I discussed in Chapter 8, words alone can mean something other than their speaker or writer intends. A sentence is a structure of meaning, a context, that predicates the speaker's or writer's meaning. A word alone may mean different things to different people; but when a word is put into a sentence, the context has the effect of whittling off part of the word's meaning—the context of the sentence puts some limits to what the word can mean.

At any rate, the sentence is a primary unit of understanding, and you can begin to control the kind of understanding your sentence achieves with an audience by shaping the sentence so as to show its parts to readers in the order you want with the emphasis you want. Writing a sentence is a pretty bold undertaking: a sentence organizes a piece of the world in a particular way, and when you write a sentence for others to read, you're asking them to accept things for a moment at least in the order you have determined—all the more reason for you to practice ways of making your sentences say what you want them to say.

The pages that follow suggest some techniques you can try. These methods of sentence organization—all generally practiced by other writers—may help you see some things you can do with your own sentences. And they may help you remember that you don't have to settle for sentences in the form they first take in your mind. You're a sentence-maker, and you can move and sort and shape and reshape until your sentences say exactly what you want them to say.

You can put short sentences together to make longer ones

These sentences

> *I remember riding that road in 1941 with my aunt.*
> *The road was rougher then.*
> *My aunt was young then.*
> *She was pretty frisky.*
> *She's old now.*

It was an early summer night.
The moon was big.
Its light was bright and clean and lovely.
The world was clear with moonlight.
She decided she could drive without headlights.
So she did.
We drove for miles enthralled.

combine to make this sentence:

I remember riding that road, much rougher then, in 1941 with my
aunt –she was young and frisky then, though she's not now: it was
an early summer night, the moon was big, and its light was bright
and clean and lovely, so she decided that the world was so clear
with moonlight that she could drive without the headlights, and she
did, and we drove for miles enthralled.

The sentences are correct in their first short version, and there is no reason to tamper with them by combining them unless there is something to be gained. There is no point in making long sentences just for the sake of making long sentences. In this case, there does appear to be something to gain. Oddly enough, though the sentence is long, the memory is given shorter treatment—it's compressed into one sentence without all the full stops created by twelve periods in the short-sentence version—and the memory becomes more clearly a single, unified recollection since it is not broken up into twelve distinct parts. Notice, too, that the series of short statements following the colon present the episode as one rushing memory, all of a piece. When the writer chose to link most statements to each other with the conjunction *and*, he or she was able to show that the memory is an accumulation of quick, continuous impressions.

Obviously, there are other ways of combining short sentences to make long sentences; some of these other methods will be suggested later. The point to remember is that you *can* make longer sentences if you need to in order to change a rhythm in your writing, or in order to show your reader that certain things belong close together, or in order to get some other effect that you want.

You can break up long sentences into shorter ones

This sentence

While I used to take pleasure in mowing the lawn, sensing the
abundance of life twined in the grass and remembering that cut
grass would spring to a fuller new growth, it is harder to do so now
that the lawn mower is heavier, the yard wider, the slope higher,
now that real and imaginary weights encumber my hands and
arms.

can be broken up to make these sentences:

> *I used to take pleasure in mowing the lawn, sensing the abundance of life twined in the grass and remembering the cut grass would spring to a fuller growth. It is harder to do so now. The lawn mower is heavier. The yard is wider. The slope is higher. Real and imaginary weights encumber my hands and arms.*

Unless there is something at stake, there is no particular reason to break a long sentence up into shorter sentences. It is a useful technique, however, if for example you have written a series of long sentences that you decide should be interrupted for the sake of variety, or if some single part of a long sentence needs to be isolated from the rest of the sentence for the sake of emphasis. In the revision above, the first half of the sentence has been converted into a separate complete sentence, and the second part of the original sentence has been rewritten as five separate short sentences. The effect of doing so is to stress what each of the five separate short sentences says and to slow the reading to make the pace of the five sentences reflect the weariness that the sentences talk about.

Exercises

1.   Discover some subjects that seem to require long sentences, and write two or three long sentences about them.

2.   Discover some subjects that seem to be better served by shorter sentences. Write several passages about these subjects using short sentences.

You can put your main idea first and let minor or contributing ideas follow

Probably the favorite sentence form in modern American writing is the *loose* sentence. In a loose sentence the principal elements of the sentence (the subject, the verb, and the complement) occur at or near the first of the sentence, with modifiers, supporting phrases, and supporting dependent clauses filling out and closing the sentence. It is a common form, characteristic of one of our standard ways of talking—we often make our point, and then tack on additional details and supporting information. (The preceding two sentences are loose.) The loose sentence is a convenient, flexible form. It does require that you choose what is primary and put it first, as in the following sample.

These ideas and observations

> —*how I got to know the canyons*
> —*geologist's soil survey*
> —*lost canyon*

> —map of trail to lost canyon
> —spent time alone there
> —hunting around and looking
> —dry water course just as wide as foot
> —named a dry waterfall

combine to make this loose sentence:

> I knew my corner of the canyons in a way not told by the geologist's
> soil survey, from days and hours alone, poking here and there,
> naming a dry waterfall in one place, marking the way to a special
> "lost canyon" in another, marveling at a dry water course just the
> width of my foot from some rivulet an eon ago.

In this sentence, *I* is the subject, *knew* is the verb, and *corner* is the direct object; all of the major grammatical elements of the sentence occur early. Everything after the word *corner* amplifies the meaning: it all works to tell how the speaker knew the territory he or she is talking about. But the key point of the sentence is that the speaker *knew* his or her country. As you may be able to tell from the sample above, the loose sentence fits easily into the colloquial, tale-telling style of much conversation: the speaker offers a simple assertion—the main grammatical elements—and then goes on to tack on more and more and more, as in this passage:

> "Thish-yer Smiley had a mare—the boys called her the fifteen-
> minute nag, but that was only in fun, you know, because of course
> she was faster than that—and he used to win money on that horse,
> for all she was slow and always had the asthma, or the distemper, or
> the consumption, or something of that kind. They used to give her
> two or three hundred yards' start and then pass her under way, but
> always at the fag end of the race she'd get excited and desperate
> like, and come cavorting and straddling up and scattering her legs
> around limber, sometimes in the air and sometimes out to one side
> among the fences, and kicking up m-o-r-e dust and raising m-o-r-e
> racket with her coughing and sneezing and blowing her nose—and
> *always* fetch up at the stand just about a neck ahead, as near as you
> could cipher it."—Mark Twain, "The Notorious Jumping Frog of
> Calaveras County"

Loose sentences can be used in many ways. In Swift's *Gulliver's Travels* Gulliver describes the girl who takes care of him during his stay among the Brobdingnagians: "She was very good natured, and not above forty feet high, being little for her age." Everything is normal enough here until we get past the first comma, and then the sentence goes haywire, the comic effect of the last part of the sentence being all the greater for being put in contrast with the perfectly normal statement of the first, and major, part of the sentence.

You can withhold the key element until last

In a *periodic* sentence, the chief grammatical elements (subject-verb-complement) and the primary statement are withheld until the last part of the sentence; modifying statements and other subordinate elements open the sentence. While it is not a form that you would want to use all the time, or even very much, a periodic sentence offers a way of emphasizing a point—the end of a sentence often attracts more attention and stays longer in a reader's mind than any other part of a sentence—and it is also useful as a way of sustaining interest by withholding the key point until the end. In the sentence below, for example, the sense is not complete and our expectations are not satisfied until we get to the second verb, *drag*, and its complement, *the Atlantic Ocean*, at the end of the sentence:

> "When I'm playful I use the meridians of longitude and parallels of latitude for a seine and drag the Atlantic Ocean for whales."—Mark Twain, *Huckleberry Finn*

In the sentence below, notice the finality and assurance of the main assertion that closes the sentence:

> No matter how carelessly or how viciously man abuses the language he has inherited, he simply cannot live without it.—Melvin Maddocks, "The Limitations of Language"

The dependent construction that opens the following sentence ("From where the sun now stands") creates a sense of expectation that impels a reader toward the sad finality of the surrender that completes the sentence:

> From where the sun now stands, I will fight no more.—Chief Joseph of the Nez Percé

Because it is longer, if for no other reason, the periodic sentence below illustrates more dramatically the shape and appearance of this kind of sentence. The primary statement in the sentence begins with the subject, *a decent respect*, followed shortly by its verb, *requires*, and the noun clause that serves as the direct object. All that goes before *a decent respect* is preliminary, the preparation for the assertion that closes the sentence.

> When in the course of human events, it becomes necessary for one people to dissolve the political bands which have connected them with another, and to assume among the powers of the earth, the separate and equal station to which the Laws of Nature and of Nature's God entitle them, a decent respect to the opinions of mankind requires that they should declare the causes which impel them to the separation.—The Declaration of Independence

Exercises

1.   Combine the following groups of short sentences into loose sentences:

    a. The pianist practiced all day.
       She tirelessly practiced her scales.
       Her fingers were limber.
       They flickered over the keys.
       The sounds produced were melodic.
    b. The small tractor shoveled load after load out of the ground.
       Children from everywhere came to watch.
       The hole grew deeper and wider.
       The backyard was transformed into a huge crater.
    c. The driver of the car waited impatiently at the end of the line of cars.
       The day was hot.
       The cars were parked in front of the post office.
       It seemed like hours.
       Someone finally came out.
       The person got into his car.
       He just sat there.
       He licked stamps for all his monthly bills.

2.   Write five loose sentences of your own.

3.   Write five periodic sentences.

You can compress longer constructions into shorter ones or into single words

Entire sentences can be compressed into dependent clauses and embedded in other sentences (see the first section). Clauses can also be reduced to phrases, and phrases can sometimes be reduced to single words. Compression is a useful technique when you want your sentences to move along briskly, or when you want to break up a series of long sentences for the sake of variety. Compression is usually economical; reducing a clause to a phrase lets you say what you want with fewer words.

This sentence

Compression is a useful technique to use when you want your sentences to move along briskly, or when you want to break up a series of long sentences for the sake of variety.

can be reduced by compression to this:

Compression is a useful technique to make sentences brisk or to vary a series of long sentences.

The first sentence has 33 words, the second 17. Brevity is not a virtue in its own right, of course, but it is important when you need it.

This sentence

> *Anglo-Americans moved across the territory as far as the Fort Worth-Austin line as early as the 1830's, and they were still stalled there in the 1870's because they knew that out beyond that line the lonesome country was chancy and the Comanches were lords.*

can be reduced by compression to this:

> *Into the territory as far as the Fort Worth-Austin line as early as the 1830's, the Anglo-Americans were still stalled there in the 1870's, fearful of the chancy country and the lordly Comanches.*

The reduction here is from 45 words to 34 words. Some further reduction is possible:

> *As far west as the Fort Worth-Austin line by the 1830's, Anglo-Americans stalled there for forty years, fearful of the country and the Comanches.*

The sentence is now down to 25 words. That does not mean that the shortest sentence is the best sentence. All it means is that it is possible to shorten sentences by compressing. In your own writing, you have to determine whether longer or shorter sentences are better in a given situation by determining what's needed for the sake of precision and variety.

Exercise

Compress the following long sentences into as few words as possible. Remember this is just for practice. Short sentences are not necessarily the best.

1. The purge, the "expiation," after the fighting was over, was completed: the wounded were dispatched; in prisons, parks, streets and public squares, suspects were shot by rifle squads, except where there were too many, in which case the new machine guns were employed.— Joseph Barry, *Infamous Woman: The Life of George Sand*

2. A little while before sundown the men lounging about the gallery of the store saw, coming up the road from the south, a covered wagon drawn by mules and followed by a considerable string of obviously alive objects which in the levelling sun resembled vari-sized and -colored tatters torn at random from large billboards—circus posters, say—attached to the rear of the wagon and inherent with its own separate and collective motion, like the tail of a kite.—William Faulkner, *Spotted Horses*

3.   In the beginning he contented himself with circling timidly round the neighbouring square or, at most, going half way down one of the side streets: but when he had made a skeleton map of the city in his mind he followed boldly one of its central lines until he reached the custom house.—James Joyce, *A Portrait of the Artist as a Young Man*

You can develop longer constructions from single words or short constructions

Sometimes you may need to expand short sentences. Sometimes short sentences won't say all that you need to say, and sometimes you may need to break up a series of short sentences that, taken together, have begun to sound jerky and jumpy because of their brevity. Look at the first sentence above:

Sometimes you may need to expand short sentences.

If you want to, you can develop this in a number of ways. Suppose, for example, that it became important to show in the same sentence some of the occasions when longer sentences are useful. One way to do this would be to add modifying explanatory constructions:

Sometimes, when your sentences are all short or when the movement of your sentences is jumpy or when you want to create a slow and thoughtful tone, you may need to expand short sentences.

Or, instead of focusing only on occasions for longer sentences, it would be possible to change the sentence again by amplifying it to include in the sentence some of the consequences of changing the sentence:

Sometimes, when your sentences are all short or when the movement of your sentences is jumpy or when you want to create a slow and thoughtful tone, you may, for the sake of variety, rhythm, and interest, need to expand short sentences.

A simple way to amplify the sentence is to convert the single word *sometimes* into a dependent clause:

When you want to break up a passage of short, quick sentences, you may need to expand your sentences.

Or the sentence could be amplified by adding a phrase explaining *expand*:

Sometimes you may need to expand your sentences into more complex cumulative statements.

In the text of an advertisement given below, the sentences (or phrases punctuated as sentences) are characteristically short. Sometimes closely related items are separated from each other, presumably to break up what might otherwise be some relatively long sentences and to convert text into a visual design. I have numbered the sentences for reference later:

(1) The advent of quartz technology created a new method of precision timekeeping.
(2) Now, Omega has taken the next step.
(3) The quartz watches you see represent the beginning of a new generation of quartz watches.
(4) These new Omega quartz watches look and feel like fine jewelry on your wrist.
(5) They are thin, elegant, precision timepieces.
(6) Amazingly thin, when you consider that there are hundreds of transistors occupying a mere 5 square millimeters of space.
(7) Easy to set, because an exclusive mechanism in the crown allows you to make time zone adjustments without affecting the accuracy of the watch by a single second.
(8) Consistently precise, due to the quartz resonator which divides each second into precisely 32,768 equal parts. Creating a timepiece accurate to within one minute a year.
(9) Omega Quartz. . . . —Advertisement for Omega watches

As you'll see, sentences 4, 6, and 8 are closely related to sentence 5; each explains a quality only mentioned in sentence 5. In the advertisement text, the materials in 4, 6, and 8 are separated from 5, for purposes of emphasis, visual design, and ease in reading. In more conventional prose, however, sentence 5 could easily be amplified by including the materials of 4, 6, and 8 within it:

> *The new Omega quartz watches are amazingly thin, when you consider that there are hundreds of transistors in a mere five square millimeters; elegant, like fine jewelry on your wrist; and consistently precise because of the quartz resonator which divides each second into exactly 32,768 equal parts, making the watch accurate to within one minute a year.*

Most sentences can be reduced, and most can be amplified. You can decide how much you want them to hold.

Exercise

Combine the following groups of short sentences into single amplified sentences:

1.   When you visit Portugal, you'll smile on the outside because we make you feel good on the inside.

You'll smile at our sun. You'll smile at the beauty of our countryside; and at the warmth of our people.

You'll smile at the values you'll receive, and at our Portugal On A Silver Platter bonus plan.—Ad for Portugal

2.   Man, too, is a different expression of that natural force. He has fought his way from the sea's depths to Palomar Mountain. He has mastered the plague. Now, in some final Armageddon, he confronts himself.—Loren Eiseley, *The Invisible Pyramid*

3.   The laughter hung smokelike in the sudden stillness. I opened my eyes, puzzled. Sounds of displeasure filled the room. The M.C. rushed forward. They shouted hostile phrases at me. But I did not understand.—Ralph Ellison, *Invisible Man*

You can put equal items in similar or coordinate constructions

Your writing reflects your judgment, whether you intend it to or not. When you ask someone to read what you have written, you are asking him or her to understand your judgment, if only for a moment. There are some things you can do to *show* readers your judgment at work. If, for example, you think two things are about equal in value, meaning, or significance, you can put them in similar or coordinate constructions.

One clear signal to readers that you mean two elements of a sentence to be similar or coordinate occurs when you link the two elements with a *coordinate conjunction*:

and: signifies that you are adding two things that are similar or closely related: She likes natural foods *and* clean air.

or: signifies that you are putting two similar things together as alternatives: You may turn in the essay tomorrow in class *or* leave it in my mailbox.

nor: used with *neither*, signifies that you are putting two similar things together and excluding both: *Neither* Julia *nor* I was ready to go when they came.

but: signifies that of two similar things one contradicts the other: I will go to the party, *but* I won't like it.

yet: (not always used as a conjunction) signifies that one thing exists notwithstanding the other: I watch football games fairly often, *yet* I cannot believe in their educational value.

for: (not always used as a coordinate conjunction) signifies a cause-effect relationship between two things: He disciplines himself and works hard, *for* he expects to go on for graduate study in architecture.

Coordinate conjunctions are not the only signals of coordination. You can make two or more items coordinate by putting them in similar grammatical constructions. In the sentence below, there are three elements of approximately equal value; the first independent clause is separated from the second by a semicolon; the second is linked with the third by a conjunction:

Truth, beauty, and goodness (or "right choice") are relevant to study in every division within the university; the humanities, for example, have no corner on beauty or imagination or art, and the sciences have no corner on speculative truth.—Wayne C. Booth, "Is There Any Knowledge That a Man *Must* Have?"

Coordination is a sign of your judgment to your readers. In the sentence below *abilities* and *fortune* are to be taken as equal alternatives, and both *dead* and *living* languages are to be included in study, as are both *history* and *politics*:

The young people of superior abilities, or fortune, might now be taught, in another school, the dead and living languages, the elements of science, and continue the study of history and politics, on a more extensive scale, which would not exclude polite literature.—Mary Wollstonecraft, "Vindication of the Rights of Women"

In this sentence, the conjunction *and* indicates that *time* and *cost* are to be taken as equally important:

One has also to count the "dead time" absorbed in distant commuting and the cost of maintaining a vast web of public commuter transport.—Barbara Ward, "The City May Be as Lethal as the Bomb"

Three modifiers (*cutting, heightening, celebrating*) are coordinate in this sentence:

Therefore a good many city streets (not all) need visual interruptions, cutting off the indefinite view and at the same time visually heightening and celebrating intense street use by giving it a hint of enclosure and entity.—Jane Jacobs, *The Death and Life of Great American Cities*

Units of any size—words, phrases, or clauses—can be placed in coordination so that readers can see some equivalence. In this sentence, short phrases are coordinate, with *but* suggesting a contrast:

We observe today not a victory of party but a celebration of freedom.—John F. Kennedy, Inaugural Address

In the first of the two sentences below, two independent clauses are coordinate, but contrasting. In the second sentence, two independent clauses with no conjunction between them are coordinate, the first making a statement, the second amplifying and clarifying the statement:

Maybe—certainly—there was melancholy in it, but it was a good melancholy.

Sunshine and warm water seem to me to have full meaning only when they come after winter's bite; green is not so green if it doesn't follow the months of brown and gray.—John Graves, *Goodbye to a River*

You can put equivalent items
in identical or parallel grammatical constructions

Each of the two sentences just above contains two independent clauses, and the two independent clauses in each sentence are coordinate—that is, each is independent, each makes sense by itself, each could be punctuated as a sentence, each is as important as the other. You can make this equivalence more obvious to a reader by making coordinate items parallel, or identical in grammatical construction. In this sentence, you can see the parallel nature of the two dependent clauses when the sentence is rearranged slightly:

> The revolutionary advances of the past two centuries suggest that almost any problem of human welfare can be solved if it is properly formulated and if its solution is diligently pursued.—René Dubos, *Dreams of Reason*

> The revolutionary advances of the past two centuries suggest that almost any problem of human welfare can be solved
> > if it is properly formulated
> > and
> > if its solution is diligently pursued.

Consider the second of these sentences:

> Man, in this case the average American citizen, spends 76 per cent of his lifetime at home (males 69 per cent and females 83 per cent), and 24 per cent away from it. He spends 36 per cent sleeping, 20 per cent working, and 10 per cent eating, dressing, and bathing.—C. A. Doxiadis, "The Coming Era of Ecumenopolis"

When it is rearranged, the parallel construction is more obvious:

He spends
- 36 per cent sleeping,
- 20 per cent working, and
- 10 per cent
  - eating,
  - dressing,
  - and
  - bathing.

And look at this passage:

> Imagination is a contagious disease. It cannot be measured by the yard, or weighed by the pound, and then delivered to the students by members of the faculty.—Alfred North Whitehead, "Universities and Their Function"

Parallelism in the second sentence can be demonstrated in this way:

It cannot be
- measured by the yard
  - or
- weighed by the pound
  - and then
- delivered to the students
  - by members of the faculty.

As you may see from these examples, parallel constructions have particular effects. Sometimes they are appealing simply because of their rhythmic nature, an appeal that you can easily overdo, incidentally, if you depend on parallelisms too much. Sometimes parallel constructions, because they represent care and planning, or at least conscious thought about the sound of the language, seem more thorough than nonparallel statements, and have a sense of finality in them, as in this example:

> Without the assistance of that Divine Being who ever attended him, I cannot succeed. With that assistance, I cannot fail.—Abraham Lincoln, Farewell at Springfield

Exercises

1. Some writers write in such a highly coordinate way that their writing could be described as *conjunctional*, or joined with many connectives. Find and bring to class some examples of conjunctional writing.

2. Deliberately imitate the construction of the Booth sentence, page 214, the Graves sentence, page 214, the Dubos sentence, page 215, and the Lincoln sentence, page 216, with sentences of your own.

You can write balanced constructions to dramatize equivalence

Balanced constructions are parallel, but in addition to being similar in construction, they are identical in length. In the sentence on imagination above, the three phrases (*measured by the yard, weighed by the pound, delivered to the students*) are parallel and balanced. As you can see in the sentence below, balanced constructions have a sense of completeness—experience is thoroughly weighed, judged, and registered; the two clauses, identical in construction and length, but contrary in what they say, seem to be the thoughtful summation of experience:

> Fools act on imagination without knowledge; pedants act on knowledge without imagination.—A. N. Whitehead, "Universities and Their Function"

Balanced constructions may occur in any context where a writer wishes to show exact equivalence between similar things, or between dissimilar things:

> *The tackle blocked out the defensive end, and the tight end took out the middle linebacker.*

> *The tackle stopped the defensive end, but the tight end missed the middle linebacker.*

In the advertisement for quartz watches used above, the headline uses balanced sentences:

> *Quartz has set a new standard for accuracy. Omega has set a new standard for quartz.*

One effect of the balance here is to draw us into belief in the advertised product. The first statement speaks only of the accuracy of quartz; the second statement uses the same pattern, length, and rhythm to talk about a specific product. The first statement is probably not debatable, and the repetition of its form lends authority to the second statement.

Balanced constructions can be used, then, in many ways. Wherever they are used, however, they have the effect of summarizing a portion of experience. Whitehead's sentence above seems to summarize the diverse habits of fools and pedants. The two sentences about football catch an entire action. The sentences about quartz watches bring together the accuracy of quartz and the efficiency of the product.

Exercise

Many of our most memorable quotations use the effect of balanced construction:

> *And ye shall know the truth and the truth shall make you free.*
> —John 8:32

> *It is defeat that turns bone to flint; it is defeat that turns gristle to muscle; it is defeat that makes men invincible.*
> —Henry Ward Beecher, *Royal Truths*

Find five more examples of balanced construction or write five of your own.

You can arrange equal items in a series

When you want to show your readers that a group of ideas are equal in your mind, one way to do it is to arrange the ideas in a series. In a series, the elements are coordinate and ordinarily parallel:

> *His favorite foods are chocolate cake, baked beans, and sweet potatoes.*

In this sentence, the three elements are equal in importance, they are alike in form, and they are balanced, though elements in a series do not have to be identical in length as well as form. A series is still a series when modifiers are added:

> *His favorite foods are chocolate cake with thick icing, baked beans, and sweet potatoes with candied marshmallows.*

Single words can be arranged in a series:

> *She bought canvas, brushes, paint, and turpentine.*

Phrases can be arranged in a series:

> *The house has a large kitchen with new appliances, a huge living room with a working fireplace, a formal dining room with a graceful chandelier, and a small study with built-in book shelves.*

Clauses can be arranged in a series:

> *I am going to make some coffee, I am going to read the newspaper while I drink the coffee, and then I am going to loaf seriously.*

All forms of series have some things in common. In all series items are arranged one after the other, the items are coordinate, and they are often parallel. But not all forms of series have the same effect. For example, the series with two elements does not appear to have the same effect that a three-part series has, and neither seems to have the same effect as a series with more than three parts. When a series has only two parts, the effect seems to be clarity and certainty. The third sentence in the passage below includes a two-part series, and the sentence seems confident and unequivocal, as if the two items in the series exhausted all the alternatives and said all that needs to be said:

> There was a strange stillness. The birds, for example—where had they gone? Many people spoke of them, puzzled and disturbed. The feeding stations in the backyards were deserted.—Rachel Carson, *Silent Spring*

In the sentence below, the two-part series says all that can be said. When the memories are described as *vague* and *inarticulate*, no more is needed:

> Moreover, we remember the Great Depression, but these memories are vague and inarticulate.—Fred H. Schroeder, "And Now, a Word From the Silent Generation"

But a three-part series stretches out to be more inclusive; two items are not enough to account for any situation. The three-part series holds more and often seems more thoughtful and comprehensive. The three-part series of clauses below covers a whole year's climate:

> Winter brings blizzards, hot tornadic winds arise in the spring, and in summer the prairie is an anvil's edge.—N. Scott Momaday, *The Way to Rainy Mountain*

In the context in which the sentence below appears, the author is arguing that the deep-seated sources of people's thinking will have as much to do with the quality of their life as current trends and fashions will, and he uses a three-part series to try to name the sources of life's quality:

> Nevertheless, the quality of life in the year 2000 may depend as much upon such beliefs, attitudes, and faiths as it does upon the trends recognized by most of the prophets.—Joseph Wood Krutch, "What the Year 2000 Won't Be Like"

In the sentence below, the author uses a three-part series to make a thorough catalogue of the faults of his generation:

> The mental disease of the present generation is impatience of study, contempt of the great masters of ancient wisdom, and a disposition to rely wholly upon unassisted genius and natural sagacity.— Samuel Johnson, *Rambler* 154

But a series that has four or more parts has a different kind of effect. Such a series is stretched out still further; a series of four or more parts will often suggest abundance, unlimited plenty that can scarcely be caught in a series of words. In the sentence below, the four-part series (arranged in two paired units) tries to suggest the variety of animation among a group of Kiowa women at feast time:

> They made loud and elaborate talk among themselves, full of jest and gesture, fright and false alarm.—N. Scott Momaday, *The Way to Rainy Mountain*

In the sentence that follows the author suggests with a six-part series the abundance of bird life:

> On the mornings that had once throbbed with the dawn chorus of robins, catbirds, doves, jays, wrens, and scores of other bird voices there was now no sound; only silence lay over the fields and woods and marsh.—Rachel Carson, *Silent Spring*

The effect of a series is also partly determined by the connective words used. Probably the commonest form of series is a list with a connective, *and*, only before the last item, as in the bird series above. Notice what happens when the single connective is omitted:

> *On the mornings that had once throbbed with the dawn chorus of robins, catbirds, doves, jays, wrens, scores of other bird voices. . . .*

The series moves more quickly now, indeed has a staccato effect. At the other extreme, notice the effect when a connective is inserted after each name:

> *On the mornings that had once throbbed with the dawn chorus of robins and catbirds and doves and jays and wrens and scores. . . .*

Now the sentence moves more slowly and has a graver, more somber sound. Adding connectives will often create a statelier rhythm and a tone of gravity or finality. Deleting connectives in a series often tends to pick up the pace of the sentence and to create a perkier tone.

Exercises

1.   Describe the effect created by the series in each of the following passages:
   a.   Talk and talk and sit at cafés, and listen to everything, to Brahms, to Brubeck, to the Italian hour on the radio.—Ben Shahn, *The Shape of Content*
   b.   Think, if you will, of all the Indians who have emerged from fact, fancy, and fear to take their places in the pantheon of the American imagination: in history Squanto, who fed the Pilgrims; Pocahontas, who loved an Englishman; Chief Logan the eloquent; Sacajawea, the girl-mother who guided white men across the Continental Divide; Sequoia, who invented an Indian alphabet; Crazy Horse, who outfought Custer; and in fiction Hiawatha and the Last of the Mohicans. They are not many; and there is not one of them whose story haunts the imagination more than Ishi's.—Lewis Gannett, Foreword, *Ishi* by Theodora Kroeber
   c.   My dear brother, you know that I came to the South and threw myself into my work for a thousand reasons: wishing to see a different light, thinking that to look at nature under a bright sky might give us a better idea of the Japanese way of feeling and drawing, wishing also to see this stronger sun, because one feels that without knowing it one could not understand the pictures of Delacroix from the point of view of execution and technique, and that the colours of the prism are veiled in the mist of the North.—Vincent van Gogh, *Dear Theo*

2.   Make sentences that contain series that do the following:
   a.   give the impression of inclusiveness.
   b.   give the impression of forcefulness.
   c.   give the impression of a memory.

You can rank items and ideas by subordinating

Parallel constructions, balanced constructions, and the series are all forms of coordination. They are signals of equivalence, and they are convenient ways to show readers that elements in your sentences have similar value and importance.

You'll have more occasions, however, to show the *difference* between elements in your sentences, to show readers how you judge ideas, actions, objects, and people by differentiating among them, emphasizing one, minimizing the other, stressing the importance of one, reducing the importance of another. Subordination is a valuable way of showing this kind of judgment in your sentences. When you subordinate one thing to another, that means that you put it in a lower order, or make it secondary, or make it dependent upon the thing it is subordinate to.

Consider these simple statements:

I am going home.
I am going to bring in the paper.
I will make some coffee.
I will drink coffee and read the paper.
I will listen to some Mozart.
I will do some serious loafing.

These short sentences are all simple. As given above, each has about the same significance as the others—a series of events is listed, and no judgment has been exerted upon the events. Each is a complete independent statement. It's conceivable that a writer might want to use the sentences just as they are, perhaps to suggest a speaker who is tired, who doesn't want to think too much, who wants to get home and sit down. But it is also possible to stress some of the statements and to use the others as secondary material, as in this sentence:

When I get home and get the paper in and the coffee made, I'm going to drink coffee and read the paper; *then, when I've put some Mozart on,* I'm going to do some serious loafing.

Now there are only two complete independent statements, the two that are in roman type. Getting home, getting the paper in and the coffee made, and putting the Mozart records on have all been subordinated; these events are secondary to the two complete independent statements. The revised single sentence focuses a little more clearly on the notion of rest and leisure. But subordinating in another way can change the effect of the sentence:

When I get home and get the paper in and the coffee made and have had a chance to drink some coffee and read the paper, I am going to listen to some Mozart *while I'm loafing.*

Now there is only one complete independent statement, and the emphasis has shifted. The speaker in the sentence is no longer interested first in rest and leisure; the speaker is now chiefly interested in listening to some Mozart recordings. All the other materials are subordinate to this one statement. The way you subordinate depends upon what you want to say, what you want to stress, what you want to minimize. The first revised sentence above would fit well enough, for example, in an essay about the rigors of the rat race and the necessity for some rest and leisure. The second revised sentence above wouldn't fit well in that same essay. The speaker in the second revised sentence has some kind of interest in or commitment to music that gets the primary stress. Subordination will allow you to put stress where you want it in a sentence.

One problem that sometimes shows up in writing is "upside-down subordination," in which a key idea is made subordinate to a minor idea, as in this sentence:

> *I was shopping for shoes when I heard the explosion and saw fire shoot out of the store across the street.*

In almost any context the explosion and fire are more striking, more noticeable, and probably more important than shopping for shoes, as in this revision:

> *As I was shopping for shoes, I heard the explosion and saw fire shoot out of the store across the street.*

Subordination is a way of putting stress or emphasis in the right place. Subordination is also a way of making relationships between elements clear. The sentence above, for example, makes only a temporal connection between shopping and witnessing the explosion and fire. The explosion occurred *while* the speaker was shopping. A similar subordinating construction could suggest quite a different kind of relationship between the dependent element and the independent element:

> *Since I was shopping for shoes, I heard the explosion and saw fire shoot out of the store across the street.*

or

> *I heard the explosion and saw fire shoot out of the store because I happened to be shopping for shoes across the street.*

Subordination is central to good writing. Pertinent ideas need to get appropriate stress, and ideas need to be connected in useful, significant ways. All writing, in fact, is a kind of subordination: you select a subject, focus on that subject, stress that subject, and during the course of writing minimize everything else. Any essay, or short story, or book is an act of subordination since in each an author judges one thing to be worth primary attention and relegates other things to secondary attention, at least for the moment.

But subordination within sentences is at issue right now. The range of possible effects achieved by subordination is as great as the number of writers and their moods and intentions. Consider some examples:

I dug my cellar in the side of a hill sloping to the south, *where a woodchuck had formerly dug his burrow,* down through sumach and blackberry roots, and the lowest stain of vegetation, six feet square by seven deep, to a fine sand *where potatoes would not freeze in any winter.*—Henry David Thoreau, *Walden*

Given the context in which this sentence occurs, it is understandable that the focus in this sentence is on the speaker and his actions. This is a loose sentence (see above), and the primary sentence elements appear in the first four words. The two subordinate clauses italicized are important to the sentence; they give color and detail and specificity to the sentence, but they are not the central elements of the sentence.

It is inconceivable for our consciousness to imagine an actual ending of our own life here on earth, and *if this life of ours has to end,* the ending is always attributed to a malicious intervention from the outside by someone else.—Elisabeth Kubler-Ross, *On Death and Dying*

The form of subordination in this sentence exactly reflects the message of the sentence. The sentence focuses on how difficult it is for us to imagine our own death in the two independent elements that open and close the sentence. When the author concedes that death is possible, she does so in a conditional subordinate clause, italicized in the sentence. The reality of death is in a *minor* part of the sentence, which is exactly appropriate when we remember that the *main* parts of the sentence tell of our rejecting the idea of death.

At this second appearing to take the oath of the presidential office, there is less occasion for an extended address *than there was at the first.* Then a statement, somewhat in detail, of a course to be pursued, seemed fitting and proper. Now, at the expiration of four years, *during which public declarations have been constantly called forth on every point and phase of the great contest which still absorbs the attention, and engrosses the energies of the nation,* little *that is new* could be presented. The progress of our arms, *upon which all else chiefly depends,* is as well known to the public as to myself; and it is, I trust, reasonably satisfactory and encouraging to all. With high hope for the future, no prediction in regard to it is ventured.—Abraham Lincoln, Second Inaugural Address

Some of the subordinate elements in this passage have been italicized. Notice their effect. The subordinate clause in the first sentence is appropriately treated as minor because its only function is to make explicit a comparison that is already understood. A long subordinate construction occurs in the third sentence. The chief point of the sentence is that little can be added to what was said four years before. The long subordinate construction does not *add* to the main point, but provides evidence why it is so. A diagram of sorts may help:

> *Justification for brief address*:
> little can be added to the earlier message.

> *Secondary justification explains why it is so*:
> because frequent public communications
> have already informed everyone.

The subordinate construction in the fourth sentence is not crucial to the main meaning of the sentence, that the progress of arms is well known, but it does serve a useful secondary function, to remind the audience that everyone waits upon the successful pursuit of the war.

Look at one more example:

> When in the course of human events it becomes necessary for one people to dissolve the political bands which have connected them with another, and to assume among the powers of the earth, the separate and equal station to which the Laws of Nature and of Nature's God entitle them, a decent respect to the opinions of mankind requires that they should declare the causes which impel them to the separation.

> We hold these truths to be self-evident, that all men are created equal, that they are endowed by their Creator with certain unalienable Rights, that among these are Life, Liberty and the pursuit of Happiness.—The Declaration of Independence

The two sentences are mirror-images of each other. The first sentence (the entire first paragraph) withholds the key point until the end; the second sentence begins with the key point. The long subordinate construction that opens the first sentence provides a history and an occasion; the independent construction that ends the first sentence then speaks of the obligations of the present. Remember that the occasion for this document was revolution; history is important, but action in the present is what makes a primary claim on the attention. The first sentence ends by stressing the obligations of the present, to declare the causes. The second sentence, then, opens with a succinct, complete statement ("We hold these truths to be self-evident"). This independent construction is a natural response to the independent construction that closes the first sentence. The long subordinate construction that closes the second sentence, precious as it is to our history and identity, is there in a secondary function, to amplify and explain the *truths* that are self-evident.

Exercise

Write a paragraph that contains subordinated elements. After you finish, write a passage that explains your choice of elements to subordinate, that is, your rhetorical choices.

You can use sentence interrupters to modify the tone, pace, and rhythm of your sentences

When a word, a phrase, or a clause interrupts the conventional movements of a sentence, an obvious change occurs in the pace and rhythm of the sentence, and with it, often, a change in tone. Ordinarily, American sentences present a subject (S), a verb (V), and possible modifiers (M), or a subject (S), a verb (V), a complement (C), and possible modifiers (M). The introduction of an interruption (X) of some kind, clearly enough, changes the nature of the sentence:

$$S + V + M \neq S + X + V + M$$
$$S + V + C + M \neq S + V + X + C + M$$

There is no sure way of accounting for all the possible kinds of interruptions that can legitimately occur within sentences. They include, for example, parenthetical expressions, appositives, internal commentary on the material of the sentence, and other forms. Some samples may suggest the possibilities.

In the sentence below, the writer interrupts himself to provide illustrations for two general terms he has already used:

> So let us agree that the kind of painting and architecture which we find most representative of our times—say, the painting of Jackson Pollock and the architecture of the Lever building—is deeply different from the painting and architecture of the past, and is not a mere whim of fashion, but the result of a great change in our ways of thinking and feeling. —Kenneth Clark, "The Blot and the Diagram"

In this instance the interruption recaptures a conversational tone in a passage that might otherwise be fairly formal. The interruption is valuable, too, because it enables us to observe a man in the process of thinking: he knows the generalization he is working with, and we see him stop himself to supply the particulars that illustrate his meaning. A little later in the same essay this passage occurs:

> To find a form with the same vitality as a window molding of the Palazzo Farnese I must wait till I get back into an aeroplane, and look at the relation of the engine to the wing. That form is alive, not (as used to be said) because it is functional—many functional forms are entirely uninteresting—but because it is animated by the breath of modern science.

In the second sentence, two kinds of interruption occur. The first, in parentheses, adds information that is useful, though not vital to the sentence. The second, set off by dashes, adds a judgment that is also useful, though not vital to the sentence. In both instances, the author is willing to hesitate long enough to add flavor to the basic statement.

In the sentence below the interruption is used to provide illustrations for the term *new styles*:

> Having now convinced myself of all these things, I will crawl farther out on a limb and confess that I have often wondered if the new styles created by modern painters—pointillism, cubism, surrealism, and the mechanism of Leger (to say nothing of op and pop)—ought not to be regarded as gimmicks rather than actual styles.—Joseph Wood Krutch, "If You Don't Mind My Saying So"

In this passage, the interruption contained in parentheses is used to provide information secondary to the primary message of the sentence:

> Supposing that one thousand families in this city would be instant customers for infants' flesh, besides others might have it at merry meetings, particularly weddings and christenings, I compute that Dublin would take off annually about twenty thousand carcasses, and the rest of the kingdom (where probably they will be sold somewhat cheaper) the remaining eighty thousand.—Jonathan Swift, "A Modest Proposal"

In the essay from which this passage is taken the speaker is an economic planner who is proposing that Irish babies be used as food, thus providing income for poor parents and for the nation at large. He is interested in his economic plan, not in humanity. Even his parenthetical remarks focus on the economic plan; he appears to be unaware of the monstrous nature of the plan.

In this sentence, the author interrupts himself to define a term he has just used:

> Were they pressed hard enough, most men would probably confess that political freedom—that is to say, the right to speak freely and to act in opposition—is a noble ideal rather than a practical necessity.—Walter Lippman, "The Indispensable Opposition"

And in the passage below, the author stops to comment on the importance of what she is saying:

> When a patient is severely ill, he is often treated like a person with no right to an opinion. It is often someone else who makes the decision if and when and where a patient should be hospitalized. It would take so little to remember that the sick person too has feelings, has wishes and opinions, and has—most important of all—the right to be heard.—Elisabeth Kubler-Ross, *On Death and Dying*

Where interruptions occur in the passage below, as you'll see, they help to remind us that the author is talking easily and naturally about his home country and doesn't mind looking off in another direction for a moment:

Likely that bluff had a good name once before some dullard called it Inspiration Point. The nation's map is measled with names like that, pocks from the old nineteenth-century plague that made people build gazebos and well-tops of rough masonry with oaken buckets on ropes but no well beneath (unless it was a "wishing well"), and sing "Annie Laurie," and read Scott for his worst qualities, and long to own paintings by Bouguereau or Landseer or Alma-Tadema, and, disregarding the guts and soul in the old nomenclature of American places, rename them Inspiration Point and Lovers' Retreat (there's one of those up Eagle Creek) and Maiden's Leap. —John Graves, *Goodbye to a River*

Exercises

1. Write a sentence in which you accomplish an aside to the reader by means of interruption.

2. Write a sentence in which the interruption serves as an explanation.

3. Write a sentence in which an interruption establishes a conversational tone.

4. Explain the functions of the interruptions in the sentences below:
    a. The shield reminds me—just to linger a minute—the shield reminds me of the inverted shield spoken of in one of the books of the *Odyssey*, the book that tells about the longest swim on record. —Robert Frost, "Education by Poetry: A Meditative Monologue"
    b. But ideas—that is, opinions backed with genuine reasoning— are extremely difficult to develop. —Wayne Booth, "Boring from Within: The Art of the Freshman Essay"
    c. The Central School (naturally, the white school was Central) had already been granted improvements that would be in use in the fall. —Maya Angelou, *I Know Why the Caged Bird Sings*

You can use sentences of different grammatical types to achieve variety and emphasis

Sentences are classified by their grammatical structure as simple, compound, complex, or compound-complex. A simple sentence makes one primary statement:

He went to the grocery store.

The addition of words and phrases as modifiers doesn't change the sentence's classification:

After cashing a check, he went to the grocery store on the corner near his house.

A compound sentence makes two or more primary statements:

He went to the grocery store, and as usual he bought luxury items not on his shopping list.

A complex sentence makes one primary statement and one or more subordinate statements (dependent clauses):

After he had cashed a check, he went to the grocery store on the corner near his house.

A compound-complex sentence makes at least two primary statements and at least one subordinate statement:

After he had cashed a check, he went to the grocery store on the corner near his house, and as usual he bought more than he needed.

Each kind of sentence has its own special uses. A simple sentence provides a good way of calling attention to a single point. A compound sentence, with two primary statements, provides a good way of balancing or opposing or likening two points. A complex sentence is an especially useful way of showing your judgment since it focuses on one point but may use any number of corollary points. A compound-complex sentence may be a good way of presenting difficult ideas since the form allows considerable room for expansion and modification. Most writers use more simple and complex sentences than compound or compound-complex.

Probably the chief point to remember, however, is that ordinarily you shouldn't rely excessively on any single kind of sentence. Sooner or later a string of simple sentences will begin to sound jumpy and jerky. Or an unbroken string of complex sentences may begin to be tiresome to readers. (On some major freeways, designers placed lights, reflectors, and signs at irregular intervals after it was discovered that when they were regularly spaced, they had a deadening, dulling effect on drivers.) The different kinds of sentences make it possible for you to make easy changes in rhythm and to vary reading and breathing patterns. They also make it possible for you to emphasize points that deserve attention: for example, whenever you break a pattern of sentence types, the interruption is likely to call attention to itself, as when a short simple sentence appears among a series of longer complex and compound sentences.

Notice the variations in sentence type and length in the passage below (I have numbered the sentences for later reference):

(1) There is a book out called *Dog Training Made Easy* and it was sent to me the other day by the publisher, who rightly guessed that it would catch my eye. (2) I like to read books on dog training. (3) Being the owner of dachshunds, to me a book on dog discipline becomes a volume of inspired humor. (4) Every sentence is a riot. (5) Some day, if I ever get a chance, I shall write a book, or warning, on the character and temperament of the dachshund and why he can't be trained and shouldn't be. (6) I would rather train a striped zebra to balance an Indian club than induce a dachshund to heed my slightest command. (7) For a number of years past I have been agreeably encumbered by a very large and dissolute dachshund named Fred. (8) Of all the dogs whom I have served I've never known one who understood so much of what I say or held it in such deep contempt. (9) When I address Fred I never have to raise either my voice or my hopes. (10) He even disobeys me when I instruct him in something that he wants to do. (11) And when I answer his peremptory scratch at the door and hold the door open for him to walk through, he stops in the middle and lights a cigarette, just to hold me up. —E. B. White, "Dog Training"

Consider the types of sentence used and their length:

	Grammatical type	Length
(1)	compound-complex	31
(2)	simple	8
(3)	simple	18
(4)	simple	5
(5)	complex	32
(6)	simple	21
(7)	simple	20
(8)	complex	27
(9)	complex	14
(10)	complex	15
(11)	complex	34

Variations in type and length here create an easy flow from sentence to sentence. For example, when the somewhat longer simple third sentence ends with reference to "inspired humor," we are prepared for the very short and emphatic simple fourth sentence. In another example, the subordinate clause that opens the ninth sentence ("When I address Fred"), establishes immediate connection with the previous sentence's reference to "what I say." In one other example, the subordinate clause that opens the eleventh sentence, especially since it starts with *And*, connects easily with the tenth sentence, where a similar subordinate clause occurs.

Examine the sentence patterns in the poem below. Doing so may help you to see why there is such particular force in the final sentence:

When the jet sprang into the sky,
it was clear why the city
had developed the way it had,
seeing it scaled six inches to the mile.

There seemed an inevitability
about what on ground had looked haphazard,
unplanned and without style
when the jet sprang into the sky.

When the jet reached ten thousand feet,
it was clear why the country
had cities where rivers ran
and why the valleys were populated.
The logic of geography—
that land and water attracted man—
was clearly delineated
when the jet reached ten thousand feet.

When the jet rose six miles high,
it was clear that the earth was round
and that it had more sea than land.
But it was difficult to understand
that the men on the earth found
causes to hate each other, to build
walls across cities and to kill.
From that height, it was not clear why.

—Zulfikar Ghose, "Geography Lesson"

Exercise

Take a paragraph from one of your past papers and make a chart of the sentence types and lengths. If you discover a lack of variation, revise the paragraph for better variety.

Sometimes you can use fragments for particular effects

When words, phrases, or dependent (subordinate) clauses are punctuated as if they were complete sentences, the results are often called *fragments*. Since most of us ordinarily expect sentences to have all of the customary parts and to be grammatically independent, fragments don't occur very often in writing, and are clearly not thought of as conventional forms for frequent use. Indeed, in some composition classes, fragments are regarded, properly enough, as serious grammatical errors. (See page 466 for a discussion of inappropriate fragments.)

Even so, there are rare occasions when fragments can be used to good effect. In the passage below a single word is punctuated as a sentence. The fragment in this case is used to highlight a word in the previous sentence and to set the topic for ensuing sentences:

> I once asked a highly regarded music teacher what was the secret of his extraordinary success with students. He said, "First I teach them that it is better to do it well than to do it badly. Many have never been taught the pleasure and pride in setting standards and then living up to them."
>
> Standards! That is a word for every American to write on his bulletin board. . . . —John Gardner, *Excellence*

In this passage, three consecutive fragments are used simply to name examples of the term *memory stimuli*:

> Nor can I smell Henri Bendel jasmine soap without falling back into the past, or the particular mixtures of spices used for boiling crabs. There were barrels of crab boil in a Czech place in the 80's where I once stopped. Smells, of course, are notorious memory stimuli but there are other things which affect me the same way. Blue-and-white striped sheets. Vermouth cassis. Some faded nightgowns which were new in 1959 or 1960, and some chiffon scarves I bought about the same time.—Joan Didion, "Farewell to the Enchanted City"

In the following passage, the author has been describing a train station, especially a corner of it where old men sleep and pass their days. In the context, the single-word fragment stands as a kind of plea:

> Once in a while one of the sleepers will not awake. Like the brown wasps, he will have had his wish to die in the great droning center of the hive rather than in some lonely room. It is not so bad here with the shuffle of footsteps and the knowledge that there are others who share the bad luck of the world. There are also the whistles and sounds of everyone, everyone in the world, starting on journeys. Amidst so many journeys somebody is bound to come out all right. Somebody.—Loren Eiseley, *Night Country*

And who is there who hasn't seen, in movie house or on television screen, a western movie in which hero and villain walk toward each other on a dusty street. At the right distance from each other they stop. Then one says, "Whenever you're ready." It's a fragment, a mere subordinate clause, but we know the message it conveys. Fragments do have certain uses, but you should handle them with care.

Exercises

1.   Find and bring to class some examples of particularly well-used fragments.

2.   Discuss the suitability of the fragment in each of the following examples:
   a. Contented. That's how she always felt after the dishes were cleared and the coffee was ready.
   b. While I'm home this summer, I'll get to work on my tennis game. Which is my favorite pastime.
   c. Knowing she was late for work, the commuter had to creep along in the pouring rain. The windshield wipers underscored her anxiety. Hur-ry. Hur-ry. Hur-ry.
   d. The room was overrun with plants. Marigolds on the window ledges. Ivy on the bookshelves. Spider plants suspended in the corners. Piggybacks on the hearth. Rubber trees on each side of the couch.
   e. No more beautiful moment exists than immediately following a rain. When a break appears in the clouds, and a ray of sunlight pushes through.

You can *play* with sentences

No catalogue of things you can do with sentences can ever be complete. In addition to suggesting particular sentence techniques for you to try, I wanted in these last several pages to keep reminding you of a central point about sentences: they can be manipulated; their parts can be moved around. You can play with sentences—toss them and turn them, set them upside down and hindside front—and create interesting and useful effects by arranging them in particular ways. For example (see the discussion of items in a series above), you can speed up a sentence a little by deleting connectives from a series—which, by the way, is called *asyndeton*—or you can slow a sentence down a little by adding connectives between all the items in the series—which is called *polysyndeton*. Consider a few more examples.

You can arrange items in a sentence so that they move toward a climax.   In this sentence, three clauses occur, and the third is a climax, set in opposition to the first two:

> I do not expect the Union to be dissolved—I do not expect the house to fall—but I do expect it will cease to be divided.— Abraham Lincoln, Speech at Springfield

A climactic development is more easily discernible in this passage:

We shall go on to the end, we shall fight in France, we shall fight on the seas and oceans, we shall fight with growing confidence and growing strength in the air, we shall defend our Island, whatever the cost may be, we shall fight on the beaches, we shall fight on the landing grounds, we shall fight in the fields and in the streets, we shall fight in the hills; we shall never surrender, and even if, which I do not for a moment believe, this Island or a large part of it were subjugated and starving, then our Empire beyond the seas, armed and guarded by the British Fleet, would carry on the struggle, until, in God's good time, the New World, with all its power and might, steps forth to the rescue and the liberation of the old.—Winston Churchill, Speech following Dunkirk

While this climactic development should probably be used only once in a while, it is a form that has some drama in it. Done well, it can pull a reader forward to an emphatic conclusion.

You can form a sentence to begin with a general statement followed immediately by a list of details.   When you do this, the first half of your sentence is a generalization, the second half a series of specifications, and the effect is to give the generalization immediacy and impact. This kind of sentence is called *prolepsis*. In the passage below, Ulysses, the speaker, immediately lists what he has "seen and known":

> I am become a name;
> For always roaming with a hungry heart
> Much have I seen and known: cities of men
> And manners, climates, councils, governments,
> Myself not least, but honored of them all;
> And drunk delight of battle with my peers,
> Far on the ringing plains of windy Troy.
> —Alfred, Lord Tennyson, "Ulysses"

And in this sentence, Whitehead immediately explains what he means by "the intellectual pioneers of our civilisation" by listing the particular examples:

> The universities have trained the intellectual pioneers of our civilisation—the priests, the lawyers, the statesmen, the doctors, the men of science, and the men of letters.—Alfred North Whitehead, "Universities and Their Function"

You can write sentences so that succeeding clauses or sentences start with the same word or phrase.   When you do this, you can sometimes achieve a kind of implacable and grave rhythm that forces a point home, as in the passage from Lincoln's speech below, or a kind of calm, devoted focus, as in the New Testament beatitudes or in the fragment from an Indian night chant below:

> But in a larger sense we cannot dedicate, we cannot consecrate, we cannot hallow this ground.—Abraham Lincoln, The Gettysburg Address

> In Kininaéki.
> In the house made of dawn.
> In the story made of dawn.
> On the trail of dawn.
> O, Talking God!
> His feet, my feet, restore.
> His limbs, my limbs, restore.
> His body, my body, restore.
> His mind, my mind, restore.
> His voice, my voice, restore.
> His plumes, my plumes, restore.
> With beauty before him, with beauty before me.
> With beauty behind him, with beauty behind me.
> With beauty above him, with beauty above me.
> With beauty below him, with beauty below me.
> With beauty around him, with beauty around me.
> With pollen beautiful in his voice, with pollen beautiful in my voice.
> It is finished in beauty.
> It is finished in beauty.
>
> —Southwest Indian Song

This kind of construction, where succeeding clauses or sentences start with the same word or phrase, is called *anaphora*.

You can make succeeding clauses or sentences end with the same word or phrase.   This kind of construction, called *epistrophe*, is often especially effective when you want to draw particular attention to a word, as in this sentence:

> Gentlemen may cry peace, peace—but there is no peace.—Patrick Henry, Speech in Virginia Convention

Or consider the dreadful, drumming force of the repetition below:

> Tell General Howard I know his heart. What he told me before, I have it in my heart. I am tired of fighting. Our chiefs are killed. Looking Glass is dead. Toohoolhoolzote is dead. The old men are all dead. . . . —Chief Joseph, on his surrender to General Howard

But *epistrophe* doesn't have to be used only in grave contexts; President Harry S Truman, for example, once said

> I never give them hell. I just tell the truth and they think it's hell.

And Gertrude Stein is supposed to have remarked once about a city that she didn't care for:

> When you get there, there isn't any there.

You can use the word or phrase that ends one clause to start the next. In the sentence below, the last word of the opening dependent clause is used as the subject of the following independent clause:

> If you take care of the inside, the inside will take care of the outside.—Advertisement for Kretschmer Wheat Germ

This sentence form, called *anadiplosis*, generally guarantees a sense of continuity from one section of the sentence to the next, or from one sentence to the next. Immediate repetition also emphasizes the word or words being repeated, as in this passage:

> How dull it is to pause, to make an end,
> To rust unburnished, not to shine in use!
> As though to breathe were life. Life piled on life
> Were all too little, and of one to me
> Little remains. . . .
> —Alfred, Lord Tennyson, "Ulysses"

Repetition emphasizes a brand name in this form of *anadiplosis:*

> The Seamaster Deville. The watch that made Omega, Omega now makes in quartz.—Advertisement for Omega

You can use the same word or words at the beginning and at the end of a sentence. A sentence that begins and ends with the same word or words can be an especially dramatic statement because its circular form makes it a self-contained unit. It's as if the sentence—coming back at the end to where it was at the beginning—has said all there is to be said on a given point. In the passage below, this kind of construction, known as *epanalepsis*, occurs in the third speech by Mephistophilis, though not in its purest form (one clause starts with the word *hell*, and the following clause ends with the same word). Notice, too, that Faustus' first speech illustrates *epistrophe* (see above):

> *Mephistophilis.*   Now, Faustus, ask what thou wilt.
> *Faustus.*   First will I question thee about hell.
>   Tell me where is the place that men call hell?
> *Mephistophilis.*   Under the heavens.
> *Faustus.*   Ay, but whereabouts?
> *Mephistophilis.*   Within the bowels of these elements,
>   Where we are tortured and remain forever;
>   Hell hath no limits, nor is circumscribed
>   In one self place, for where we are is hell,
>   And where hell is, there must we ever be. . . .
> —Christopher Marlowe, *The Tragical History of Doctor Faustus*

In its pure form, *epanalepsis* would look like this:

> *Violence breeds violence.*
> *Crime leads to more crime.*
> *Cramming for tests tends to make you sleepy, which makes you miss class, and you wind up having to do more cramming.*

Another variation occurs in the advertisement below:

> Quartz has set a new standard for accuracy. Omega has set a new standard for quartz. —Advertisement for Omega watches

You can reverse the order of words in succeeding clauses. This construction, called *antimetabole*, is an especially interesting way to show contrast, as in this advertisement:

> Vandermint isn't good because it's imported. It's imported because it's good. —Advertisement for Vandermint

A better known example of *antimetabole* occurred in President John F. Kennedy's Inaugural Address:

> And so, my fellow Americans, ask not what your country can do for you; ask what you can do for your country.

And if you're desperate, you can in special places make sentence puns. The word *pun* is a generic name for different kinds of word play, as in the repetition of a word in two different senses (Benjamin Franklin's "If we don't hang together, we'll hang separately"), or in the use of words that are alike in sound, but different in meaning. An advertisement for Waterford Crystal in the *New York Times Magazine* (October 16, 1977) uses this headline: "When it pours, it reigns." The headline inverts the old saying, "When it rains, it pours," and puns on *rains/reigns*.

Exercise

Find or write examples of the following:
a. a general statement followed by details
b. *anaphora*
c. *epistrophe*
d. *anadiplosis*
e. *epanalepsis*
f. *antimetabole*
g. a pun

INSIGHT

A note on sentence variations

In the pages since the beginning of this chapter, some twenty-two different ways of writing or rewriting sentences have been briefly described. Actually, more than that have been mentioned, since some of the types of sentence constructions can be varied in a number of ways. But no matter how large the number, it is not large enough. No list of possible techniques for use in making sentences can be complete, and you should be wary of anyone who tells you that there are a given, finite number of ways to write sentences. Remember: You are the sentence-maker. You have to decide whether you wish to write the most conventional, subject-verb-complement sentences, whether you want to experiment with some of the methods shown above, or whether you want to go your way in forms not yet described. Learn how others write sentences. Appropriate their methods when you find them useful. But make your own sentences.

DIFFERENT SENTENCES
IN DIFFERENT CONTEXTS

Different kinds of writing in different kinds of situations may lead you to write different kinds of sentences. There is no particular reason to assume that you must always write the same kind of sentence. There is nothing wrong with writing relatively short and simple sentences in one context and relatively long and complex sentences in another. The way you present yourself may vary from one kind of writing to another. The way you treat a subject may vary from one kind of writing to another. The way you approach a subject may vary from one kind of writing to another. (It might be useful here for you to look back to the discussion of writer-audience relationships in Chapters 4 and 5.) Other writers change their tone and manner from time to time. If you examine diverse kinds of writing, you're likely to find diverse kinds of sentences. Consider the examples below. All are about the same length.

(1) Prestige versus money. It's the age-old conflict in college football.

There it is, the Rose Bowl—snugged tight against the brown, treeless mountains of Southern California, the gem of Pasadena.

More than 106,000 frenzied collegiate fans will jam the long rows of benches which ring that storied turf in the Arroyo Seco on

Monday, Jan. 2, 1978, to watch the 64th Rose Bowl championship game.

They'll be there with the ghosts of Ernie Nevers and Fielding H. "Hurry Up" Yost; the memories of the wizardry of Tom Harmon and Orenthal James "O. J." Simpson.

A hundred college players, the cream of the crop from the Pacific Eight and Big Ten conferences, will bang and crash, tug and pull, grind and groan for 60 minutes.

Their reward? It could be gridiron immortality. It also could be a slim line in an obscure record book.

Now let's shift the scene a few hundred miles to the southeast and run the clock ahead five days.

It's January 7, 1978, and the site is the Senior Bowl Stadium in Mobile, Alabama. And what's this? Somebody's giving those college players *money* to play football?

You bet.—*Dodge Adventurer*, "Settle Back, Relax and Enjoy Dodge's Fall-Winter TV Sports Card"

(2)   Common sense tells us that the more people there are in a given area, and the closer together they are, the more likely they are to feel crowded. And, presumably, the more crowded they are, the less effective, productive, or happy they will be; the more anxious, irritable, and unfriendly will be their behavior. But is it so? Does social density actually make a significant difference in the way people behave—in their productivity, for example?

The research into social density unfortunately provides no clear-cut answer to this question. A study conducted by consulting psychologist Stephen Emiley in 1975 is typical. He assigned male students to experimental conditions of high or low social density and had them work for 140 minutes on the assembly of an Erector Set. When Emiley asked them afterward about their reactions, students who had worked in the high-density setting rated their working space as being less satisfactory and felt more crowded than did those who had been assigned to the low-density setting. There was no difference, however, between the two groups in their success at performing the assigned task, nor was there any difference in their enjoyment of the experience.—Paul M. Insel and Henry Clay Lindgren, "Too Close for Comfort: Why One Person's Company Is Another's Crowd"

(3)   People having trouble falling asleep shouldn't automatically reach for the bottle of sleeping pills. It can be dangerous and fatal, warns the director of the National Institute of Drug Abuse.

Sleeping pills contributed to the deaths of nearly 5,000 Americans last year, institute director Dr. Robert L. DuPont said Saturday.

"People don't have to turn right to the pill when they have trouble sleeping," DuPont said in an interview. "They ought to know that some sleeplessness is a part of living."

Ironically, some people have trouble sleeping because they worry about being able to get to sleep, DuPont said. Others suffer from poor sleeping patterns brought on by late working hours or unusual bedtimes.

"People should be a lot less anxious about a few hours of missed sleep," he said. "The body has a way for making up for it. There's no need to get upset."

DuPont said he is suggesting educational programs to better inform doctors and the public of the dangers of sleeping pills and alternative ways to fall asleep.—*Fort Worth Star Telegram*, "Tossing Shouldn't Mean Turn to Pill"

(4) "Cézanne: The Late Work," the major offering of the Museum of Modern Art this year, was well worth the years of preparation and vast sums required to assemble more than 100 paintings and watercolors executed by the master between 1895 and his death in 1906. Drawn from collections throughout the world, many of the works have never before been exhibited publicly. Grouped together according to subject, the variations on the themes that occupied Cézanne during the last decade of his life, when he lived virtually as a hermit in his native town of Aix-en-Provence, emerge as moving examples of the aging artist's grappling again and again with a limited series of subjects he knew intimately, as if to distill their very essence.

When seen juxtaposed—for the first time in such comprehensive depth—the alternate versions of Mont Ste. Victoire, Cézanne's most celebrated landscape view, and the nearby rock quarry of Bibémus and forest of Château Noir reveal to us the artist's painful process of revising his perception of a subject by painting it from different points of view. We cannot really speak of these variations on a given set of themes, which became increasingly circumscribed as Cézanne grew older and more fixed in his preoccupations, as works in series; however, the visible progression from more naturalistic to more abstract versions of a motif must be seen as a turning point for the entire history of modern art.

—Barbara Rose, "Cézanne: The Autumn Years"

These four selections are clearly different: they have different intentions, different audiences, different reasons for being. The first is a quickly moving, casual piece, plainly not intended for slow, meditative reading. It appeared in a small, glossy magazine that serves as publicity for a car manufacturer. The second moves a little more slowly; it appeared in *Psychology Today*, a general distribution magazine presumably intended for an educated audience interested in learning about a subject that might not be accessible to them unless it is presented in a somewhat simplified form for popular appeal. The third is the opening of a front-page newspaper article. The last is a review of a major art exhibit, appearing in a general circulation magazine that has for some years been widely read by educated audiences.

Even a simple examination of these selections will show some important differences in the nature of their sentences, as the chart will suggest:

	1	2	3	4
Total words	189	195	172	238
Number of sentences	14	9	11	5
Range of sentence lengths	2–34	4–39	6–26	16–61
Average sentence length	13.5	21.6	14.7	47.6
Grammatical types				
simple	10	5	4	3
compound	1	0	0	0
complex	1	4	7	1
compound-complex	0	0	0	1
fragment	2	0	0	0

Other obvious differences among the four selections occur (most noticeable, perhaps, are the variations in paragraph development and length); examination of a longer portion of each article represented would, in all likelihood, show more pronounced variations in sentences.

Another way to see how sentences change in different settings is to study several pieces of writing by the same writer. Here are the opening paragraphs of E. B. White's essay, "Salt Water Farm":

> A seacoast farm, such as this, extends far beyond the boundaries mentioned in the deed. My domain is arable many miles offshore, in the restless fields of protein. Cultivation begins close to the house with a rhubarb patch, but it ends down the bay beyond the outer islands, hand-lining for cod and haddock, with gulls like gnats round your ears, and the threat of fog always in the pit of your stomach.
>
> I think it is the expansiveness of coastal farming that makes it so engrossing: the knowledge that your fence, on one side at least,

shuts out no neighbor—you may climb it and keep going if you have a boat and the strength to raise a sail. The presence in the offing of the sea's fickle yield, those self-sown crops given up grudgingly to the patient and the brave, is an attraction few men are proof against. Beyond one blue acre is another, each one a little farther from the house than the last. On a summer's day I may start out down the lane with a pail to pick a few berries for my wife's piemaking, but there is always the likelihood that I will turn up hours later with two small flounders and a look of profound accomplishment. A man who has spent much time and money in dreary restaurants moodily chewing filet of sole on the special luncheon is bound to become unmanageable when he discovers that he can produce the main fish course directly, at the edge of his own pasture, by a bit of trickery on a fine morning.—E. B. White, "Salt Water Farm"

To use a simple set of measures again, the sentences in this passage range in length from 13 words to 54 words; the average length is about 33 words. Three of the eight sentences are simple, one is compound, two are complex, and two are compound-complex. Here is another passage by E. B. White:

The barn was very large. It was very old. It smelled of hay and it smelled of manure. It smelled of the perspiration of tired horses and the wonderful sweet breath of patient cows. It often had a sort of peaceful smell—as though nothing bad could happen ever again in the world. It smelled of grain and of harness dressing and of axle grease and of rubber boots and of new rope. And whenever the cat was given a fish-head to eat, the barn would smell of fish. But mostly it smelled of hay, for there was always hay in the great loft up overhead. And there was always hay being pitched down to the cows and the horses and the sheep.

The barn was pleasantly warm in winter when the animals spent most of their time indoors, and it was pleasantly cool in summer when the big doors stood wide open to the breeze. The barn had stalls on the main floor for the work horses, tie-ups on the main floor for the cows, a sheepfold down below for the sheep, a pigpen down below for Wilbur, and it was full of all sorts of things that you find in barns: ladders, grindstones, pitch forks, monkey wrenches, scythes, lawn mowers, snow shovels, ax handles, milk pails, water buckets, empty grain sacks, and rusty rat traps. It was the kind of barn that swallows like to build their nests in. It was the kind of barn that children like to play in. And the whole thing was owned by Fern's uncle, Mr. Homer L. Zuckerman.—E. B. White, *Charlotte's Web*

The two passages have almost exactly the same number of words, but the first passage has eight sentences while the second has fourteen. Where the average length of sentences in the first passage is about 33 words, the average sentence length in the second is only about 19 words (even though one sentence in the second passage has over 70 words). Other differences occur: notice, for example, that while the sentences in the first passage are varied in their openings, 12 of the 14 sentences in the second passage begin either with *the barn* or with a pronoun standing for *barn*; and while there are four sentences in the first passage with over 40 words, the only two long sentences in the second passage are the sentences that include simple lists of things.

The point is that different audiences and different intentions may require different styles, including different kinds of sentences. And remember that you are at liberty to speak in different ways, at different times, in different places.

CONNECTIONS BETWEEN SENTENCES

Regardless of what kind of sentences you write, readers need to be able to get from one to the next without losing the trail. Ordinarily the shift from one sentence to the next should be as easy as possible for your readers, unless you specifically want some kind of dramatic break. At the very least, if you value your ideas and want them to be heard, you should try not to set hindrances in the path of your readers so that they have to guess or leap or puzzle to follow you from one sentence to the next.

But the ease and convenience of readers are not the only things at stake here—and may not even be the most important. Writing is by its nature a *sequence*; everything about writing is sequential. You write *after* you have a need to write. You write *when* you know what to write. When you write, one word *follows* another, and one sentence comes *after* the sentence before. You understand writing by *going through* it, that is, by reading it. If writing is a sequence, then it seems to follow that the more coherent and clear the sequence is, the better the writing will be. In other words, the ease and convenience of readers are not the only things at stake; your writing ought to be coherent for its own sake. Whatever is not *coherent* (that is, whatever does not stick or hold together) is likely to be *incoherent* (that is, to fall apart, to become discontinuous).

There is no system that will guarantee continuity between sentences. Repetition of key words sometimes helps, but is also sometimes tedious and dull. The use of a pronoun in one sentence that refers to a noun in the preceding sentence creates a connection, but not the kind you can count on in every pair of sentences. Often, if you are following a particular line of thought (a comparison, for example, or a definition), the line of thought will provide continuity for your sentences (see the discussion of methods of development in Chapter 7). The best way to learn about connections between sentences is to notice what other writers do. Consider this passage, for example (the sentences are numbered for reference):

> (1) That whole arc of country below the Point is ghost-laden. (2) Violent, obscure history piles in on you as you look off over the lowlands. (3) They were richer than the mountain country; therefore more people wanted them and came there. (4) People make trouble; trouble makes history, or anyhow tales, since not much of the history is reliable. (5) After the trouble, little of weight happened in that piece of country—no oil booms, no industry to speak of until the Fort Worth factories began to suck the people away—so that for a long time remembrance of the frontier was strong on the slowly eroding farms and the ranches, and in the little bypassed towns. (6) It sat on the land. (7) It still does, a little, if the land means anything to you.—John Graves, *Goodbye to a River*

The sentences in this paragraph are closely and plainly connected by various means so that the paragraph is tight and coherent. Sentence 2 is an amplification of the last word in Sentence 1: the country is "ghost-laden" because "Violent, obscure history piles in on you" there. Sentence 3 opens with the pronoun *they*, which directs us back to its antecedent at the end of the previous sentence, *lowlands*. Sentence 3 refers to the people who wanted the lowlands, and Sentence 4 opens with *people*. Sentence 4 twice mentions *trouble*, and Sentence 5 opens with "After the trouble." Sentence 6 opens with the pronoun *it*, which refers us to the antecedent *remembrance* in the preceding sentence, and Sentence 7 opens with the same pronoun having the same antecedent.

Continuity takes many forms, of course. In the stanza below, from Edwin Arlington Robinson's poem, "Mr. Flood's Party," coherence and continuity are generated, among other ways, by *sound*, the recurring *o* sounds keeping persistently before us the melancholy mood of the poem:

> Alone, as if enduring to the end
> A valiant armor of scarred hopes outworn,
> He stood there in the middle of the road
> Like Roland's ghost winding a silent horn.
> Below him, in the town among the trees,
> Where friends of other days had honored him,
> A phantom salutation of the dead
> Rang thinly till old Eben's eyes were dim.

Look at another example:

The word *home* is an obsession of the American language, not of the English. In four years of living in England, I never heard an Englishman use the word hometown, for instance. They have the parent word, of course, and most of its offspring—there is even a Home Office in their government (concerned, significantly, with internal affairs of the entire country)—but if home ever bore the meaning it has for Americans, the meaning has faded. In fact, the dense ganglion of emotion that Americans keep round it only began to settle on the English word in the fifteenth century.

The *Oxford English Dictionary* has citations from about A.D. 900; but they all define a tangible place, a particular village or house that "one regards as one's proper abode." The *OED* cannot find the word used in our sense (as "the place of one's dwelling or nurturing, with the conditions, circumstances, and feelings which naturally and properly attach to it") before about 1460. That first citation is suggestive. In the Towneley Mysteries a character says, "In euery place he shall haue hame": and home springs finally to life—for a people who had wandered restlessly—as the symbol of safe, warm rest, however brief. The

root of the (word) had similar force for our
Indo-European and Saxon linguistic ancestors, but many other European languages have no precisely equivalent current
(word.) Modern French, Italian, and Spanish
are content with their (word) for *house*. They
have approximations, all connoting
hearth—*foyer, focolare, hogar*—but like
the British, they show little need for a word
most Americans need many times a day—
*home, hometown, homemaker, home-
breaker, beautiful-brand-new-homes-for-
sale, homesick, homemade, homeward
bound*. Why do we?—Reynolds Price,
"Home: An American Obsession"

The section on continuity in Chapter 6 (pp. 118-122) may be helpful to
you as you think about how sentences connect with each other.

SOME LAST REMINDERS ABOUT SENTENCES

*When you write, you make a point, not by subtracting as
though you sharpened a pencil, but by adding. When
you put one word after another, your statement should
be more precise the more you add. If the result is
otherwise, you have added the wrong thing, or you have
added more than was needed.*—John Erskine, "The
Craft of Writing"

You don't have to leave your sentences as you found them. They may be
fine in the form you first give them on paper, or they may not be.
Remember that you can rework and rewrite your sentences; they don't
have to be finished when they first appear on paper. Here are some useful
points to keep in mind as you edit your sentences:

**1.   Unless there is some specific reason for them to be otherwise,
your sentences should be grammatically conventional and conform
to customary usage.**   That is to say, for example, the initial letter of

the first word should be a capital letter, the appropriate end punctuation should follow the last word, all of the customary grammatical parts of a sentence should be there, unless you are intentionally using a single word or a phrase to be punctuated as a sentence. The appendix on grammar, punctuation, and usage at the end of the book may be helpful to you in editing.

2. Your sentences should be economical.   Economy in a sentence means that you use exactly the number of words it takes to say exactly what you mean. Economy in a sentence does not mean that you should pare your sentences so that they are sparse and short. If it takes seventy-two words to say exactly what you mean, then the use of seventy-two words is economical—but the use of seventy-one is not, nor is the use of seventy-three.

3. A little variety helps in your sentences, but an excess of variety is distracting.   It's probably not best if all of your sentences are about the same length, or if all of them are of the same grammatical type. On the other hand, if you work too hard for variety and set out to dress up every sentence in different finery, the result will probably distract readers.

4. Some of Mark Twain's rules are worth remembering.   In his essay "Fenimore Cooper's Literary Offenses," Twain speaks of some "large rules" and then goes on to speak of "some little rules." It is these "little rules" that I am recommending here:

> These require that the author shall
> *Say* what he is proposing to say, not merely come near it.
> Use the right word, not its second cousin.
> Eschew surplusage.
> Not omit necessary details.
> Avoid slovenliness of form.
> Use good grammar.

5. And that's about all.   Except this: remember that a sentence is more than a grammarian's toy; a sentence is your way of taking hold of experience, experience inside you and experience outside you, and naming it so that you can understand it, use it, enjoy it, and remember it.

Exercises

1.   Write an essay in which you analyze the sentence style in a piece of writing you particularly like. Talk about any characteristic type of sentence used. Analyze length, transitions, and so on.

2.   Bring to class and analyze the sentence types used in several advertisements.

3.   Write a paper in which you analyze your own sentence style in two or three of the essays you have already written. Close with a summary, suggestions for improvement, and things you particularly want to work on.   Or, exchange several essays with someone else in your class, and do the same kind of analysis of each other's papers.

4.   Characterize the sentences in the following passages and discuss the rhetorical choices made by the writer:

   a. For their surface area, insects weigh very little. A beetle, falling from a high altitude, quickly achieves terminal velocity: air resistance prevents it from falling very fast, and, after alighting on the ground, it will walk away, apparently none the worse for the experience. The same is true of small mammals—squirrels, say. A mouse can be dropped down a thousand-foot mine shaft and, if the ground is soft, will arrive dazed but essentially unhurt. In contrast, human beings are characteristically maimed or killed by any fall of more than a few dozen feet: because of our size, we weigh too much for our surface area. Therefore our arboreal ancestors had to pay attention. Any error in brachiating from branch to branch could be fatal. Every leap was an opportunity for evolution. Powerful selective forces were at work to evolve organisms with grace and agility, accurate binocular vision, versatile manipulative abilities, superb eye-hand coordination, and an intuitive grasp of Newtonian gravitation. But each of these skills required significant advances in the evolution of the brains and particularly the neocortices of our ancestors. Human intelligence is fundamentally indebted to the millions of years our ancestors spent aloft in the trees.—Carl Sagan, *The Dragons of Eden*

   b. The kings of England formerly had their forests "to hold the king's game," for sport or food, sometimes destroying villages to create or extend them; and I think that they were impelled by a true instinct. Why should not we, who have renounced the king's authority, have our national preserves, where no villages need be destroyed, in which the bear and panther, and some even of the hunter race, may still exist, and not be "civilized off the face of the earth,"—our forests, not to hold the king's game merely, but to hold and preserve the king himself also, the lord of creation,—not for idle sport or food, but for inspiration and our own true recreation? or shall we, like villains, grub them all up, poaching on our own national domains?—Henry David Thoreau, *The Maine Woods*

   c. Water—the ace of elements. Water dives from the clouds without parachute, wings or safety net. Water runs over the steepest precipice and blinks not a lash. Water is buried and rises again;

water walks on fire and fire gets the blisters. Stylishly composed in any situation—solid, gas or liquid—speaking in penetrating dialects understood by all things—animal, vegetable or mineral—water travels intrepidly through four dimensions, *sustaining* (Kick a lettuce in the field and it will yell "Water!"), *destroying* (The Dutch boy's finger remembered the view of Ararat) and *creating* (It has even been said that human beings were invented by water as a device for transporting itself from one place to another, but that's another story). Always in motion, ever-flowing (whether at steam rate or glacier speed), rhythmic, dynamic, ubiquitous, changing and working its changes, a mathematics turned wrong side out, a philosophy in reverse, the ongoing odyssey of water is virtually irresistible. And wherever water goes, amoebae go along for the ride.— Tom Robbins, *Even Cowgirls Get the Blues*

Many paragraphs do not conclude much of anything.
But we want them to.

Virginia M. Burke, "The Paragraph:
Dancer in Chains"

. . . the paragraph is a flexible, expressive rhetorical instrument.

Arthur A. Stern, "When Is a Paragraph?"

10

Shaping Paragraphs

Following some opening notes about paragraphs, this chapter
includes

1. some suggestions about topic sentences and conventional
   methods of developing paragraphs (p. 250);

2. an account of paragraphs as marks of personal punctuation
   (p. 262);

3. some suggestions about paragraphing and continuity (p.
   268); and

4. notes on some special kinds of paragraphs, including opening, closing, and transitional paragraphs (p. 274).

Everyone knows what a paragraph is. A paragraph is a grouping of prose that has space around it. It may be almost any length, but it is separated from the grouping that goes before it and the grouping that comes after it by the space, for example, of a skipped line before and after, or by the indentation of its first line. Sometimes, instead of being indented, the first line begins with a □, or with a ●, or with a number, or with some other kind of typographical signal indicating that the author is shifting gear, or catching a breath, or turning to a new idea, or modifying a mood, or turning somehow in a new direction.

Everyone knows what a paragraph is.

But not really. No one knows ahead of time just *exactly* how long a paragraph ought to be, though many may be able to tell when a paragraph is too long or too short. No one knows ahead of time *exactly* all that ought to go into a paragraph, though many may be able to tell when something has been omitted, or when something unnecessary has been included. No one knows *exactly* why authors pace their paragraphs as they do. It's entirely likely, indeed, that many writers, including professionals, do not construct their paragraphs consciously or deliberately.

That doesn't mean, however, that there is nothing to observe or to know about paragraphs. It is always possible to learn something for your own writing by examining the paragraphs of other writers. You can in particular learn about and practice *some* kinds of paragraphs, and you can note how other writers use special kinds of paragraphs, or use paragraphs for special purposes.

It does mean, however, that there is no particular set of patterns for you to follow in making paragraphs. It means that, beyond particular patterns of paragraph development that are useful on many occasions, *you* are responsible for the length, content, and structure of your paragraphs. They take their shape and character from your personality, your way of taking your subject, and your response to possible readers.

SOME PARAGRAPH PATTERNS

Some identifiable patterns of paragraphing exist. They can sometimes be used in any kind of writing, and they can often be used in particular kinds of writing. They may be especially helpful when you are stuck—when you are blocked in your writing and can't see how to proceed, it's often possible to get started again by deliberately adopting a method or pattern other writers have worked out and frequently used.

Development from a topic sentence

One such method is the development of a paragraph from a *topic sentence*. When a sentence serves as a *topic sentence* for a paragraph, it sets a theme for the entire paragraph: every other sentence in the paragraph is related in some specific way to the topic sentence; it is the fixed post to which all the other sentences are tied. In a paragraph built from a topic sentence, the other sentences serve to illustrate what the topic sentence says, or to explain it, or to amplify it, or to modify it; or they are in some way extensions of the topic sentence. Look at some examples.

The first example below opens with a primary assertion, the generalization that serves as a topic sentence. The rest of the paragraph is devoted to one specific episode that dramatizes the truth of the primary assertion, or topic sentence:

A great thirst is a great joy when assuaged in time. On my first walk down Havasu Canyon, which is a small hidden branch of the Grand Canyon, never mind exactly where, I took with me only a one-quart canteen, thinking that would be enough water for a fourteen-mile downhill hike on a warm day in August. On the rim of the canyon the temperature was a tolerable ninety-six degrees, but it rose about one degree for each mile down and forward. Like a fool I rationed my water, drank sparingly, and could have died of sunstroke. When late in the afternoon I finally stumbled—sun-dazed, blear-eyed, parched as an old bacon rind—upon that blue stream which flows like a miraculous mirage across the canyon floor I was too exhausted to pause and drink soberly from the bank. Dreamily, deliriously, I slogged into the waist-deep water and fell on my face. Like a sponge I soaked up moisture through every pore, letting the current bear me along beneath a canopy of willow trees. I had no fear of drowning in the water—I intended to drink it all.—Edward Abbey, *Desert Solitaire*

The second example works in a different way. It is the second paragraph in an article about new architecture in Columbus, Indiana. The last part of the preceding paragraph is included so as to make the context clearer:

. . . it has become a bustling, vital community, a showcase of contemporary architecture—and the envy of urban developers everywhere.

There are no fewer than 41 modern buildings, all designed by nationally and internationally famed architects. On Sundays, the citizens of Columbus worship in churches designed by Eero and Eliel Saarinen. They borrow books at a library built from the innovative plans of I. M. Pei and embellished with a bronze arch sculpted by Henry Moore. They shop in a glass-enclosed piazza designed by Cesar Pelli, and send their children to schools conceived by architects Harry Weese, Eliot Noyes and John Warnecke. Along with distinctive new structures, the spirit and pride of Columbus have risen as well. All over town, old commercial buildings and residences are being fully restored. As Mayor Max Andress

puts it, "A sense of quality has rubbed off all over Columbus."—
Time, "Showplace on the Prairie"

The first sentence, or topic sentence, makes the primary declaration: "There are no fewer than 41 modern buildings, all designed by nationally and internationally famed architects." The next three sentences are clearly an extension of this topic, listing specific architects and buildings. But at the fifth sentence something new, though related, occurs. The first part of the sentence, "Along with distinctive new structures. . . ," connects this sentence with the original topic sentence. But the remainder of the fifth sentence, " . . . the spirit and pride of Columbus have risen as well," adds a new element to the paragraph, amplifying the topic sentence. The last two sentences are, then, more clearly related to the fifth sentence than they are to the original topic sentence.

In the example below, the topic sentence, which is first, barely suggests a theme that is then played out in the rest of the paragraph:

> This autumnal mellowness usually lasts until the end of November. Then come days of quite another kind. The winter clouds grow, and bloom, and shed their starry crystals on every leaf and rock, and all the colors vanish like a sunset. The deer gather and hasten down their well-known trails, fearful of being snowbound. Storm succeeds storm, heaping snow on the cliffs and meadows, and bending the slender pines to the ground in wide arches, one over the other, clustering and interlacing like lodged wheat. Avalanches rush and boom from the shelving heights, piling immense heaps upon the frozen lake, and all the summer glory is buried and lost. Yet in the midst of this hearty winter the sun shines warm at times, calling the Douglas squirrel to frisk in the snowy pines and seek out his hidden stores; and the weather is never so severe as to drive away the grouse and little nut-hatches and chickadees.—John Muir, "Shadow Lake"

The first sentence, or topic sentence, makes a suggestion of the coming of winter. The remaining sentences then show how the events around the author bring the "hearty winter."

The paragraph below develops from a topic sentence in another way:

> The well's importance goes far beyond that. Its discovery indicates that a major new gas-exploration effort in the Tuscaloosa Sand geological formation of southern Louisiana is hitting pay zones. That promises new production not only for Louisiana but for an energy-hungry nation that counts natural gas as both its cleanest-burning and most critically scarce fuel. Last week the Louisiana Office of Conservation estimated that gas reserves in the Tuscaloosa Sand may reach 3 trillion cu. ft. That would be equal to 86% of last year's production in Louisiana, which leads the nation in gas output, and 18% of annual consumption in the whole

> country. To its discoverers that much gas would be worth $5.5 billion at existing wellhead prices on Louisiana's intrastate free market. —*Time*, "Giant Gas Gusher in Louisiana"

The topic sentence simply announces that the discovery of a new gas well has far-reaching significance. The rest of the paragraph then spells out the well's importance. Notice that the sentences form a kind of chain reaction to show quite literally how the importance of the gas well "goes far beyond that." In the second sentence, we learn that new explorations are "hitting pay zones," and that means, in the third sentence, new production for the nation, and that means, in the fourth sentence, a potential reserve of 3 trillion cubic feet, and that means, in the fifth sentence, a bountiful new supply, and that means, in the sixth sentence, a bountiful new income. Each sentence literally goes beyond the preceding sentence, just as the topic sentence predicts.

Paragraphs that are built upon topic sentences have diverse uses. In a piece of writing built upon some logical sequence, for example, topic-sentence paragraphs provide a neat, clear, and orderly method. Suppose, for example, you are explaining some process in which the stages must be made clear and in which each stage requires some additional explanation. In such an account a series of topic-sentence paragraphs may be especially useful: each paragraph might deal with a stage in the process, announced in a topic sentence at or near the first of the paragraph, with the particular stage being explained in the course of the paragraph. Certain kinds of emotional exhortation may be handled in topic-sentence paragraphs—each paragraph opens with a declaration in its topic sentence, for example, and the rest of the paragraph provides room to explore the strength and appeal of the declaration in particular circumstances.

Remember, too, that topic-sentence paragraphs are practical in a pinch. If inspiration doesn't come and all else fails, a declarative sentence and a series of quick illustrations (as in the Muir paragraph above) or a declarative sentence and one fully developed illustration (as in the Abbey paragraph above) will make a paragraph. Three or four declarative sentences (provided they are related in some way) and a double handful of vivid examples will make a short essay, such as you might write in an examination. No one can guarantee that such paragraphs or such an essay will be excellent, but sometimes when you are stuck, simple competence looks attractive.

Don't imagine, however, that topic-sentence paragraphs are just simple gimmicks. Development of a paragraph from a topic sentence is a method that may be useful to you any time you wish to be sure that a reader can follow with ease the sequence of your thinking. If, for example, the stages of your thinking on a given subject occur as topic sentences at the beginning of your paragraphs, then readers should have little difficulty tracking you. (You may find it useful to review the section titled "Thesis and organization" in Chapter 6, particularly the discussion of how a thesis sentence may be used to form topics for the sections or paragraphs of your work.) Notice how the topic sentences in the passage below do three things: they establish a theme for their paragraph, they connect with each other, and they conduct you through the author's sequence of thought:

Pulling Up Roots

Before 18, the motto is loud and clear: "I have to get away from my parents." But the words are seldom connected to action. Generally still safely part of our families, even if away at school, we feel our autonomy to be subject to erosion from moment to moment.

After 18, we begin Pulling Up Roots in earnest. College, military service, and short-term travels are all customary vehicles our society provides for the first round trips between family and a base of one's own. In the attempt to separate our view of the world from our family's view, despite vigorous protestations to the contrary—"I know exactly what I want!"—we cast about for any beliefs we can call our own. And in the process of testing those beliefs we are often drawn to fads, preferably those most mysterious and inaccessible to our parents.

Whatever tentative memberships we try out in the world, the fear haunts us that we are really kids who cannot take care of ourselves. We cover that fear with acts of defiance and mimicked confidence. For allies to replace our parents, we turn to our contemporaries. They become conspirators. So long as their perspective meshes with our own, they are able to substitute for the sanctuary of the family. But that doesn't last very long. And the instant they diverge from the shaky ideals of "our group," they are seen as betrayers. Rebounds to the family are common between the ages of 18 and 22.

The tasks of this passage are to locate ourselves in a peer group role, a sex role, an anticipated occupation, an ideology or world view. As a result, we gather the impetus to leave home physically and the identity to *begin* leaving home emotionally.

Even as one part of us seeks to be an individual, another part longs to restore the safety and comfort of merging with another. Thus one of the most popular myths of this passage is: We can piggyback our development by attaching to a Stronger One. But people who marry during this time often prolong financial and emotional ties to the family and relatives that impede them from becoming self-sufficient.

A stormy passage through the Pulling Up Roots years will probably facilitate the normal progression of the adult life cycle. If one doesn't have an identity crisis at this point, it will erupt during a later transition, when the penalties may be harder to bear.—Gail Sheehy, *Passages*

Paragraphs developed from topic sentences have many uses, but notice that they don't all look alike and that not all paragraphs have clearly defined topic sentences.

Paragraphs with topic sentences (that is, sentences that identify the central theme of the paragraphs) come in different forms, as the examples shown a little earlier may suggest. Topic sentences themselves come in different forms. The kind of topic sentence I have been talking about (a single sentence establishing a subject or a theme for a paragraph) is a simple, more or less noticeable form.

Sometimes, however, it takes two sentences to establish a theme for a paragraph, and sometimes a topic or theme can only be discovered by assembling it from several sentences within a paragraph. In other words, you shouldn't expect all the paragraphs you read to have a clearly defined single topic sentence; neither should you suppose that all of your own paragraphs ought to have such a topic sentence. A recent study of paragraph form shows that somewhat fewer than half of the paragraphs examined had a single, plainly recognizable topic sentence. In the same sampling, only about 13% of the paragraphs began with the topic sentence. The same study shows, incidentally, that sometimes a topic sentence governs a series of paragraphs. Remember, however, that paragraphs developed from topic sentences are useful, and it's entirely likely and appropriate that you may be asked to write paragraphs with clear topic sentences and whole papers in which each paragraph has a clear topic sentence.

Other ways of developing paragraphs

Other conventional and recognizable patterns for developing paragraphs may be useful to you. Some have already been described in different contexts in earlier chapters. Chapter 7 describes twelve possible ways of developing material; the chapter recommends these twelve methods as possible ways of turning bare ideas or bare outlines into full essays. These are the twelve methods:

Definition, p. 131
Illustration, p. 135
Detail, p. 137
Comparison or contrast, p. 139
Analogy, p. 143
Classification and division, p. 145
Analysis, p. 148
Cause and effect, p. 150
Process, p. 153
Clarification and restatement, p. 156
Spatial order, p. 158
Chronological order, p. 160

These twelve methods of development will also serve as *twelve ways of shaping a paragraph*. If you'll go back to Chapter 7, you'll see that many of the passages used to illustrate these methods are single paragraphs. Even in the instances where the illustrative passages include several paragraphs, the design and use of individual paragraphs will be clear enough. The useful thing about these methods is that each of them will provide a design for making paragraphs. Single paragraphs can also be made by combining some of these methods. Since you have already seen each of these methods illustrated, consider now only one example using a single method, and one in which the methods are mixed.

The first paragraph below is a definition. The term to be defined, *game*, is put in a class with other terms; it belongs to the class *recurring transactions*, and the rest of the paragraph serves to distinguish *games* from other recurring transactions:

> A game is an ongoing series of complementary ulterior trans-actions progressing to a well-defined, predictable outcome. De-scriptively it is a recurring set of transactions, often repetitious, superficially plausible, with a concealed motivation; or, more col-loquially, a series of moves with a snare, or "gimmick." Games are clearly differentiated from procedures, rituals, and pastimes by two chief characteristics: (1) their ulterior quality and (2) the payoff. Procedures may be successful, rituals effective, and pastimes prof-itable, but all of them are by definition candid; they may involve contest, but not conflict, and the ending may be sensational, but it is not dramatic. Every game, on the other hand, is basically dishon-est, and the outcome has a dramatic, as distinct from merely exciting, quality.—Eric Berne, *Games People Play*

The paragraph below mixes cause-effect relationships with an account of a process. You'll note as the paragraph ends, incidentally, that the author is preparing to develop his ideas by illustration:

> Now it is clear that the decline of a language must ultimately have political and economic causes: it is not due simply to the bad influence of this or that individual writer. But an effect can become a cause, reinforcing the original cause and producing the same effect in an intensified form, and so on indefinitely. A man may take to drink because he feels himself to be a failure, and then fail all the more completely because he drinks. It is rather the same thing that is happening to the English language. It becomes ugly and inaccu-rate because our thoughts are foolish, but the slovenliness of our language makes it easier for us to have foolish thoughts. The point is that the process is reversible. Modern English, especially written English, is full of bad habits which spread by imitation and which can be avoided if one is willing to take the necessary trouble. If one gets rid of these habits one can think more clearly, and to think clearly is a necessary first step towards political regeneration: so

that the fight against bad English is not frivolous and is not the exclusive concern of professional writers. I will come back to this presently, and I hope that by that time the meaning of what I have said here will have become clearer. Meanwhile here are five specimens of the English language as it is now habitually written.—George Orwell, "Politics and the English Language"

INSIGHT

A note on mixed patterns of paragraph development

In the preceding pages, I have discussed paragraphs developed from topic sentences and paragraphs developed by one or more of twelve designs. Notice that a paragraph can be built from a topic sentence and still use one or more of the twelve patterns mentioned. These patterns of paragraph development don't exclude each other; they may mix and mingle. In the paragraph below, for example, the first sentence may be taken as a topic sentence; it sets a theme for the paragraph. But the paragraph also uses an *analogy* with warfare and gives a brief account of the *process* by which temptation comes:

Enemy-occupied territory—that's what this world is. Christianity is the story of how the rightful king has landed, you might say landed in disguise, and is calling us all to take part in a great campaign of sabotage. When you go to church you're really listening in to the secret wireless from your friends: that's why the enemy is so anxious to prevent us going. He does it by playing on our conceit and laziness and intellectual snobbery. I know someone will ask me, "Do you really mean, at this time of day, to reintroduce our old friend the devil—hoofs and horns and all?" Well, what the time of day has to do with it I don't know. And I'm not particular about the hoofs and horns. But, in other respects my answer is, "Yes, I do." I don't claim to know anything about his personal appearance. If anybody really wants to know him better I'd say to that person, "Don't worry. If you really want to, you will. Whether you'll like it when you do is another question."—C. S. Lewis, "What Christians Believe"

Building paragraphs by coordination, subordination, and completion

Other patterns of paragraph development are recognizable and may be useful to you: paragraphs may be built by *coordination*, by *subordination*, and by *completion*.

Coordination. In a paragraph developed by *coordination*, the sentences are likely to be similar to each other, and they may restate the same idea in different ways, approaching it from different directions, looking at it from different angles. The sentences are coordinate—that is, they are alike and have much the same value. One kind of coordinate paragraph, for example, would occur when all of the succeeding sentences rephrase the same idea expressed in the topic sentence. In the second paragraph of the passage below, the first sentence serves to enlarge the suggestion of charm as something "in the air" that ends the first paragraph:

> Charm is the ultimate weapon, the supreme seduction, against which there are few defences. If you've got it, you need almost nothing else, neither money, looks, nor pedigree. It's a gift, only given to give away, and the more used the more there is. It is also a climate of behaviour set for perpetual summer and thermostatically controlled by taste and tact.
>
> True charm is an aura, an invisible musk in the air; if you see it working, the spell is broken. At its worst, it is the charm of the charity duchess, like being struck in the face with a bunch of tulips; at its best, it is a smooth and painless injection which raises the blood to a genial fever. Most powerful of all, it is obsessive, direct, person-to-person, forsaking all others. Never attempt to ask for whom the charm-bells ring; if they toll for anyone, they must toll for you.—Laurie Lee, "Charm"

In the paragraph below, each sentence is in some way a restatement of the idea contained in the first sentence:

> I heartily accept the motto,—"That government is best which governs least"; and I should like to see it acted up to more rapidly and systematically. Carried out, it finally amounts to this, which also I believe,—"That government is best which governs not at all"; and when men are prepared for it, that will be the kind of government which they will have. Government is at best but an expedient; but most governments are usually, and all governments are sometimes, inexpedient. The objections which have been brought against a standing army, and they are many and weighty, and deserve to prevail, may also at last be brought against a standing government. The standing army is only an arm of the standing government. The government itself, which is only the mode the people have chosen to execute their will, is equally liable to be abused and perverted before the people can act through it. Witness the present Mexican war, the work of a comparatively few individuals using the standing government as their tool; for, in the outset, the people would not have consented to this measure.—Henry David Thoreau, "Civil Disobedience"

Often, in other words, paragraphs made by *coordination* are occasions for repetition and amplification of a point. But in other kinds of coordinate paragraphs, such as that shown below, each sentence is a separate statement and the paragraph serves to pile up a group of similar experiences and statements:

> I can remember the bare wooden stairway in my uncle's house and the turn to the left above the landing, and the rafters and the slanting roof over my bed, and the squares of moonlight on the floor and the white cold world of snow outside, seen through the curtainless windows. I can remember the howling of the wind and the quaking of the house on stormy nights, and how snug and cozy one felt under the blankets, listening; and how the powdery snow used to sift in around the sashes and lie in little ridges on the floor, and make the place look chilly in the morning and curb the wild desire to get up—in case there was any. I can remember how very dark that room was in the dark of the moon, and how packed it was with ghostly stillness when one woke up by accident away in the night, and forgotten sins came flocking out of the secret chambers of the memory and wanted a hearing; and how ill-chosen the time seemed for this kind of business and how dismal was the hoo-hooing of the owl and the wailing of the wolf, sent mourning by on the night wind.—Mark Twain, *Autobiography*

Subordination.   In the paragraph above, every sentence is equal to every other sentence. In a paragraph built by *subordination*, however, ordinarily there is a key statement, or topic sentence, and all of the remaining sentences depend upon that key or topic. Look again at the first paragraph of this chapter:

> *Everyone knows what a paragraph is. A paragraph is a grouping of prose that has space around it. It may be almost any length, but it is separated from the grouping that goes before it and the grouping that comes after it by the space, for example, of a skipped line before and after, or by the indentation of its first line. Sometimes, instead of being indented, the first line begins with a □, or with a ●, or with a number, or with some other kind of typographical signal indicating that the author is shifting gear, or catching a breath, or turning to a new idea, or modifying a mood, or turning somehow in a new direction.*

The second sentence depends upon the first for its subject, and begins where the first sentence leaves off. The third sentence depends upon the second sentence for its reference; the subject *It* in the third sentence refers to *paragraph* in the second sentence. The fourth sentence takes up with indentation, where the third sentence stops.

In the paragraph below, notice especially that from the fourth sentence on, each sentence depends for its meaning on the first three sentences of the paragraph:

> A writer of bad prose, to become a writer of good prose, must alter his character. He does not have to become good in terms of conventional morality, but he must become honest in the expression of himself, which means that he must know himself. There must be no gap between expression and meaning, between real and declared aims. For some people, some of the time, this simply means *not* telling deliberate lies. For most people, it means learning when they are lying and when they are not. It means learning the real names of their feelings. It means not saying "luncheon" or "home" for the purpose of appearing upper-class or well-educated. It means not using the passive mood to attribute to no one in particular opinions that one is unwilling to call one's own. It means not disguising banal thinking by polysyllabic writing or the lack of feeling by clichés that purport to display feeling.—Donald Hall, Introduction to *The Modern Stylists*

Completion.   Sometimes a writer needs all of the sentences in a paragraph in order to say completely the intended theme of the paragraph. In the paragraph below, for example, the second and third sentences complete the meaning that is only announced in the first sentence:

> Vigorous writing is concise. A sentence should contain no unnecessary words, a paragraph no unnecessary sentences, for the same reason that a drawing should have no unnecessary lines and a machine no unnecessary parts. This requires not that the writer make all his sentences short, or that he avoid all detail and treat his subject only in outline, but that *every* word tell.—William B. Strunk and E. B. White, *The Elements of Style*

In the paragraph below, the meaning is not at all complete until the end; indeed, the author uses the paragraph to show in the last sentence that what he had said in the first sentence is inadequate:

> Toward the end of the last century people began to speak of languages as being "born," producing "daughter" languages, and eventually "dying"—undoubtedly because the metaphor of a living organism came naturally to a generation that had recently learned about Darwinian evolution. Some languages were also thought to "give birth" to weak mutations, in which case euthanasia could always be practiced upon them by the eternally vigilant guardians of correct usage. The metaphor of language as a living organism persists to this day, but it is inherently false. A language does not live or die. And unless it is to be considered

merely a code to be broken (like Egyptian or Mayan hieroglyphics) or an intellectual pastime (like speaking Latin), a language has no life apart from the lives of the people who speak it. —Peter Farb, *Word Play*

As you can see, paragraphs made by *coordination* or by *subordination* or by *completion* are not entirely different from paragraphs made by other methods. The methods often mix. A paragraph of *definition* is likely to be a paragraph of *completion*, for example. A paragraph of *comparison* may also be a paragraph of *coordination*. A *topic-sentence* paragraph is likely to be a paragraph of *subordination*. But while the methods do mingle with each other, it's still worthwhile to know the names of the various methods suggested above and to know the conventional patterns associated with each name. The names do provide a convenient way of remembering that there are, in fact, many ways to make a paragraph.

General statements, supporting statements, and details

You can also see, if you have read the sample paragraphs along the way, that no matter what pattern is employed, paragraphs are made by using *general statements*, *supporting statements*, and *details*. Some paragraphs hold only general statements. Some contain only supporting statements that, for example, amplify or explain a general statement in an earlier paragraph. Some paragraphs contain only details. Many contain a mixture of general statements, supporting statements, and details. The sample paragraph by Edward Abbey above, for example, begins with the general observation that "A great thirst is a great joy when assuaged in time," and continues with sentences that detail what that means in particular experience. The sample paragraph from *Time* on the "Giant Gas Gusher" combines a general statement, the first sentence, with a series of sentences providing details. The paragraph by Mark Twain, however, consists entirely of details from the writer's memory.

Exercises

1. Find or write an example of a paragraph that
   a. has two or more sentences that make up the topic.
   b. has a topic sentence in the middle or at the end.
   c. has an implied, rather than a carefully stated topic.

2. Write five topic sentences for paragraphs. Exchange with a classmate and have him or her jot down his or her expectations for the paragraph created by the topic sentence. Choose the one that interests you the most and write the paragraph, fulfilling your classmate's expectations.

3.   Write a paragraph of repetition in which you amplify or restate your topic sentence.

4.   Write a paragraph in which you specify your topic sentence by example, illustration, or support.

PARAGRAPHS AS SIGNALS OF PERSONAL PUNCTUATION

Everyone knows what a paragraph is, but no one can tell you exactly how to make a paragraph at a given moment for a given context. You'll have to determine for yourself what pattern or patterns you'll work from. The patterns described above are useful, and they do occur in all kinds of published writing. They are usually helpful when you're stumped and can't get started with your writing, or when your writing has come to a stop and you can't get started again.

But it is also useful to think of paragraphs as signals to your reader, as marks of personal punctuation. Your paragraphs don't all have to be alike, and they don't have to be exactly like those that someone else writes. There is no measuring cup that tells you when you have written a paragraph. If you'll read as much as you can—and read a variety of things—and if you'll watch what other writers do with their paragraphs, you'll see that writers do indeed use paragraphs as a form of punctuation. They are used to signal a pause, a rest for the writer so that he or she can take stock; they give the writer a breathing space, and they give the reader time to think. A bit of white space and a new paragraph may be a writer's jumping-off place for a new treatment of the subject or for investigation of a new feature of the subject. A paragraph may be used simply as a bridge, to get from one section of a study to another, or as a summary, to bring freshly to mind what has been said before so that the writer can go on to new things. A paragraph may be simply a place to stop for remembering what has already taken place.

The best guide you can find for using paragraphs as a form of punctuation is what you'll learn by reading and watching what different writers do with paragraphs. Some writers will make paragraphs too short and jumpy for your taste, and some will make them long and cumbersome. Others will break up into several paragraphs material that you think should be put together as one unit. Usually, if you study the paragraphs that other writers make, you'll find some kind of order and purpose in their paragraphing—though what you find may not be to your liking. Consider some examples.

The first example below is taken from the opening page of this chapter. Remember that the point now is to watch what other writers do with paragraphs; the examples that follow are for study—they are not presented as ideals.

Everyone knows what a paragraph is. A paragraph is a grouping of prose that has space around it. It may be almost any length, but it is separated from the grouping that goes before it and the grouping that comes after it by the space, for example, of a skipped line before and after, or by the indentation of its first line. Sometimes, instead of being indented, the first line begins with a □, or with a ●, or with a number, or with some other kind of typographical signal indicating that the author is shifting gear, or catching a breath, or turning to a new idea, or modifying a mood, or turning somehow in a new direction.

Everyone knows what a paragraph is.

But not really. No one knows ahead of time just exactly how long a paragraph ought to be, though many may be able to tell when a paragraph is too long or too short. No one knows ahead of time exactly all that ought to go into a paragraph, though many may be able to tell when something has been omitted, or when something unnecessary has been included. No one knows exactly why authors pace their paragraphs as they do. It's entirely likely, indeed, that many writers, including professionals, do not construct their paragraphs consciously or deliberately.

The only thing particularly notable about this set of paragraphs is that a single short sentence serves by itself as the second paragraph. The first paragraph presents some of the obvious physical features of a paragraph as a way of completing what is proposed in the first sentence, that "Everyone knows what a paragraph is." The second paragraph, then, serves several purposes. It summarizes the first paragraph by repeating the opening sentence. Standing by itself as it does, it calls attention to the fact that some simple features of the paragraph are so obvious that everyone knows about them. It gives a clear point of contrast for the author to work against in the third paragraph, which begins to explore some of the things that we do not, after all, know about paragraphs.

The example below is from a newspaper. It appears on a page with the heading "In Brief." This page typically includes a number of short items of interest. In all likelihood, no one expects readers to linger over these short pieces (the example below is the entire story). They are meant for quick reading, which probably accounts for the quick, short paragraphs:

An Indian group in Michigan has accused some Oakland University anthropologists of desecrating an ancient Indian burial ground and demanded that the remains be returned.

The Indians also placed a curse on the persons who handled remains from the burial ground.

The anthropologists removed about 18 skeletons that had been unearthed in the burial ground by house builders. The skeletons were estimated to be between 700 and 1,000 years old.

The university is expected to return some of the remains soon. However, anthropologists want to study other parts of the remains for at least six months before returning them.

The Indians are unhappy with the timetable but have agreed to wait. They plan to re-bury the remains on Indian land near Mt. Pleasant, Mich.—*Chronicle of Higher Education*, "Indians Place Curse on Anthropologists"

In the context in which these paragraphs appear, no one expects full and detailed development. It's easy to imagine what might have been added to the first paragraph alone—the name and location of the Indian group, the identity and purpose of the anthropologists, the exact location of the burial ground, the exact nature of the remains. But since this is a quick news brief, each paragraph serves a quick, brief purpose: the first paragraph identifies the first action by the Indians; the second paragraph isolates their second action—it is particularly interesting and provides the headline; the third paragraph provides a little background; the fourth presents the response to the Indians' action; the fifth returns to the Indians, where the story began. Taken together, the five paragraphs sketch out a quick narrative of recent events.

The next example is taken from a magazine advertisement, and includes the first four paragraphs of the advertisement's text. In large letters at the top of the page, this sentence appears: "Our soft sides are made of something new and revolutionary." Just below that is a picture of five pieces of luggage. Below the picture, still in large letters, this sentence appears: "It's called thinking." Then these four paragraphs follow:

We know you.

You're a thinker. You like to think things out, get the most from every experience.

Well, we think out our soft-sided luggage, too. So that you can get the most from Ventura. The most efficiency when you travel on business. The most enjoyment when you travel for pleasure.

And you're sure to enjoy the way we keep your clothing in shape. That's because we've made Ventura soft where it has to be soft, hard where it must be hard—the best of all structural worlds. And we've made it elegant all over . . . because we've also thought quite a bit about you and style and we realize there can't be one without the other.—Advertisement for Ventura Luggage

Have you ever said to a friend, "I know you"? If you have, you know that the three-word sentence carries considerable meaning. It's meant to call to mind the experiences you've shared, the intimate confidences you've shared, the history you share, the knowledge of each other that you have. Apparently the three-word paragraph that opens this passage is supposed to resonate with the same meanings and suggest that the company has worked to understand you, to know your history, your taste, your preferences. The paragraph suggests that this is not a casual relationship, nor merely a commercial relationship, but one based on study and care. The second paragraph then shifts to focus on the reader, but the focus can't remain on the reader for long because the subject in question is the luggage being advertised. The third paragraph links the reader with the luggage, and the fourth paragraph begins to focus more nearly on the luggage alone.

The next example is from a popular magazine:

> Do very young children learn "good" messages as well as "bad" messages from watching television?
>
> Not long ago, two prominent psychologists from the State University of New York at Stonybrook contrived an elaborate experiment to explore this question. Dr. Robert M. Liebert, co-author of "The Early Window: Effects of Television on Children and Youth," and Dr. Eli A. Rubinstein, vice chairman and research director of the 1972 Surgeon General's Scientific Advisory Committee on Television and Social Behavior, assembled 30 first-grade boys and girls and told them they were going to play a game.
>
> One by one the children were brought into a room, seated at a table and told to push a button to score points. The more the child pressed, the higher the point score, and the higher the score, the more valuable the child's prize.
>
> While waiting his turn to play, each child was "allowed" to watch television. Ten children watched a *Lassie* episode specially selected because it carried a theme of helping others. Lassie tried to hide her runt puppy so it wouldn't be given away, but accidentally dropped it down an old mineshaft. Jeff, her owner, heard the puppy's whimpers and risked his life to rescue the little dog.
>
> Ten other children, also picked at random, watched a different episode of *Lassie*. The 10 "controls" watched *The Brady Bunch*. —*TV Guide*, "Here's What TV Is Doing to Us"

These are the first five paragraphs in an article. The paragraphs are a little longer here, but they are still not detailed in their development. The first paragraph, a single question, appears to be isolated as a paragraph in order to catch attention. After that, it is more difficult to account for the paragraphing in this passage. The opening sentence of the second paragraph introduces "an elaborate experiment," but a good part of the rest of the paragraph is devoted to establishing the authority for the experiment (the two psychologists). This same sentence controls (or serves as a topic for) the next three paragraphs, and in fact, for two further paragraphs not included here. There is no compelling reason why paragraphs three, four, and five are separated from each other; each of them is a part of the account of the "elaborate experiment." We can perhaps understand the paragraphing in this way: paragraph two introduces the game; paragraph three describes it generally; paragraph four details what one group does; and paragraph five quickly tells what the other two groups of ten each are doing.

But short paragraphs don't occur only in popular magazines, newspapers, and advertisements (or in textbook chapters about paragraphing). The passage below occurs in a speech made at a momentous occasion early in the Civil Rights Movement of the 1960's:

> Go back to Mississippi, go back to Alabama, go back to South Carolina, go back to Georgia, go back to Louisiana, go back to the slums and ghettos of our northern cities, knowing that somehow this situation can and will be changed. Let us not wallow in the valley of despair.
>
> I say to you today, my friends, so even though we face the difficulties of today and tomorrow, I still have a dream. It is a dream deeply rooted in the American dream.
>
> I have a dream that one day this nation will rise up and live out the true meaning of its creed: "We hold these truths to be self-evident, that all men are created equal."
>
> I have a dream that one day on the red hills of Georgia the sons of former slaves and the sons of former slaveowners will be aable to sit down together at the table of brotherhood; I have a dream—
>
> That one day even the state of Mississippi, a state sweltering with the heat of injustice, sweltering with the heat of oppression, will be transformed into an oasis of freedom and justice; I have a dream—
>
> That my four little children will one day live in a nation where they will not be judged by the color of their skin but by the content of their character; I have a dream today.—Martin Luther King, Jr., "I Have a Dream"

The paragraphs here are not intended to be full developments, but rather rhythmic exhortations. The material here is separated into paragraphs to make a kind of liturgical chant based on the refrain, "I have a dream."

The next example is the opening three paragraphs of the introduction to a book about Kiowa legends and their significance to the author:

> A single knoll rises out of the plain in Oklahoma, north and west of the Wichita Range. For my people, the Kiowas, it is an old landmark, and they gave it the name Rainy Mountain. The hardest weather in the world is there. Winter brings blizzards, hot tornadic winds arise in the spring, and in summer the prairie is an anvil's edge. The grass turns brittle and brown, and it cracks beneath your feet. There are green belts along the rivers and creeks, linear groves of hickory and pecan, willow and witch hazel. At a distance in July or August the steaming foliage seems almost to writhe in fire. Great green and yellow grasshoppers are everywhere in the tall grass, popping up like corn to sting the flesh, and tortoises crawl about on the red earth, going nowhere in the plenty of time. Loneliness is an

aspect of the land. All things in the plain are isolate; there is no confusion of objects in the eye, but *one* hill or *one* tree or *one* man. To look upon that landscape in the early morning, with the sun at your back, is to lose the sense of proportion. Your imagination comes to life, and this, you think, is where Creation was begun.

I returned to Rainy Mountain in July. My grandmother had died in the spring, and I wanted to be at her grave. She had lived to be very old and at last infirm. Her only living daughter was with her when she died, and I was told that in death her face was that of a child.

I like to think of her as a child. When she was born, the Kiowas were living the last great moment of their history. For more than a hundred years they had controlled the open range from the Smoky Hill River to the Red, from the headwaters of the Canadian to the fork of the Arkansas and Cimarron. In alliance with the Comanches, they had ruled the whole of the southern Plains. War was their sacred business, and they were among the finest horsemen the world has ever known. But warfare for the Kiowas was preeminently a matter of disposition rather than of survival, and they never understood the grim, unrelenting advance of the U. S. Cavalry. When at last, divided and ill-provisioned, they were driven onto the Staked Plains in the cold rains of autumn, they fell into panic. In Palo Duro Canyon they abandoned their crucial stores to pillage and had nothing then but their lives. In order to save themselves, they surrendered to the soldiers at Fort Sill and were imprisoned in the old stone corral that now stands as a military museum. My grandmother was spared the humiliation of those high gray walls by eight or ten years, but she must have known from birth the affliction of defeat, the dark brooding of old warriors.—N. Scott Momaday, *The Way to Rainy Mountain*

Perhaps the most obvious questions in this passage are about the short second paragraph: Why is it short? Why is it cut off from the third paragraph, which begins with similar phrasing? I'll come back to these questions in a moment. First, remember that these paragraphs have a dual function. They are the opening paragraphs in an introductory essay to a book, but they are also the opening paragraphs for the entire book. The long first paragraeph forgets time, except for seasonal change, to set the scene for the book, Rainy Mountain and its environs, the landscape "where Creation was begun." The paragrraph establishes the setting for the book, the land of the Kiowas, and it also sets a context for the author in his introductory essay, which tells of his efforts to recaPture his sense of the place and to retrace the path the Kiowas took through history on their way to Rainy Mountain. That helps to account for the relative brevity of the second paragraph. It brings the author into the scene he has set at a specific time and for a specific purpose. But once that is done, it is time to return to his subject. He abandons the contemporary scene and his return to visit his grandmother's grave, remembering "I was told that in death her face was that of a child." That returns him to the past, and he opens a new paragraph with "I like to think of her as a child," which leaves him free to move back into Kiowa history.

A last reminder or two about paragraphs as a form of punctuation may be in order. Read. Watch what writers do with paragraphs. Watch what happens to paragraphs in different kinds of writing. Notice how long or how short paragraphs are likely to be in various kinds of publications. Notice how full of details they are, or how spare and lean. Notice how quickly writers move from one paragraph to another, or how slowly and thoughtfully a writer lingers over a single paragraph. Scrutinize the paragraphs in your reading to learn why they change when they do. If you pay attention, you can usually see some kind of order in the paragraphs you read, some way of accounting for their length, movement, content, and development. It may not be an order you would choose. It may not even be a particularly interesting or effective order, or pattern of development. It may not be entirely justifiable. But an order of some kind usually emerges. Look for it. It may be the signal of a person thinking.

Exercises

1.   Bring to class some interesting examples of unusual paragraphing and discuss their effectiveness.

2.   Write a short paper in which you describe, justify, or talk about the effectiveness of the paragraphs in a piece of writing.

3.   Write an essay in which the choice of where to begin new paragraphs is deliberately affected by, or appropriate to, the subject matter.

PARAGRAPH CONTINUITY

One has to recognize the shifting direction of movement. . . .—Francis Christensen, Notes Toward a New Rhetoric

Remember to leave a trail so that your readers can follow you if they wish to. Let them know where you are in your thinking, and whenever possible, let them know how you arrived there. Provide directions so that it's possible for them to stay with you in the progress of your thinking and writing.

Paragraphs usually interlock with and relate to material in other paragraphs. Sometimes, however, the same thing that makes paragraphs recognizable to readers creates some difficulty for them in following you.

There is space between paragraphs, but where there is space, there has to be some way of getting across it. Since you have probably been thinking about your subject before you began to write about it, you've begun to be familiar with it and understand its parts, and their connection with each other. A reader is not in your mind, however, and may not make connections as you have. It's up to you to provide some signals for a reader to see the relationship between one paragraph and the next, so that he or she can understand the continuity of your work.

Continuity is not particularly difficult to achieve in a paragraph that is well developed, unified, and orderly. If everything in a paragraph follows from or relates to a topic sentence (see above), then readers can usually follow what you've said. If you have consistently followed one of the methods of development listed on p. 255 and discussed in greater detail in Chapter 7, Developing Your Material, then your paragraphs are probably unified and orderly—that is, every sentence in a given paragraph belongs to that paragraph and occurs in the right place. If you have built paragraphs by coordination, subordination, or completion (see above), then readers can probably follow what you have done. If all of the supporting statements and details are relevant to the general statements, then your paragraphs are probably unified, and if they are unified, then readers can probably follow your thinking easily enough, since no extraneous material occurs.

No formula exists for revealing continuity in your work. You'll notice as you read some simple methods—repetition of key words from one paragraph to the next, use of a pronoun to refer to an antecedent—but simple methods won't always work. Notice what other writers do as in the examples below.

In the first example, a fairly simple method of establishing continuity is used. The authors announce at the outset that there are four ways to say "no," and then open each of the paragraphs with "first," "second," and so on:

Four Ways to Say "No"

First of all, one of the most difficult hurdles to overcome is in assessing whether or not the other person's request of you is reasonable or unreasonable. This can be tricky. We as women must stop looking to the other person to find out if the request is reasonable. The mere fact that the request was made means that the person has decided that she/he wants something from you regardless of its reasonableness. Therefore, the assertive woman looks inside herself to find the answer to whether or not this is a reasonable request. If you find yourself hesitating or hedging, this may be a clue that you want to refuse. If you feel cornered, or trapped, or you notice a tightness or nervous reaction in your body, this may also mean that someone is requesting something unreasonable of you. You feel "uptight." Sometimes you may be genuinely confused or unsure because you just do not have enough information to go on in order to know whether something unreasonable is being asked of you.

Second, you need to assert your right to ask for more information and clarification. Women have often been conditioned to make judgments based on whatever is presented to us. Many of us grew up under the influence of such dicta as "Children should be seen and not heard," or under religious demands that we accept what we have heard as the truth, that to doubt or question is sinful, or that to be submissive and unquestioning was "ladylike." Nevertheless, the first step in asserting yourself when a request is made of you is to make sure you have all the facts. April does not commit herself to a yes or no until she fully understands what is being asked of her.

Third, practice saying "no." Once you understand the request and decide you do not want to do it or buy it, say no firmly and calmly. It is crucial that you give a simple "no" rather than a long-winded statement filled with excuses, justifications, and rationalizations about why you are saying "no." It is enough that you do not want to do this, simply because you do not want to do it. You can accompany your refusal with a simple, straight-forward explanation of what you are feeling. A direct explanation is assertive, while many indirect and misleading excuses are non-assertive and can get you into a lot of trouble by leaving you open for debate.

Fourth, learn to say "no" without saying "I'm sorry, but...." Saying "I'm sorry" frequently weakens your stand and the other person, especially Iris, may be tempted to play on your guilt feelings. When the assertive woman evaluates a situation carefully and decides the best thing for her is to say no, then she has nothing to be sorry about. In fact, April feels strong and happy with her decisions to say no.—Stanlee Phelps and Nancy Austin, *The Assertive Woman*

In the example below, logical relationships show us the connection of the paragraphs with each other. The second paragraph opens with what looks like a turn-about, as the author defines what he is talking about in the first paragraph by declaring what he is *not* talking about. The paragraph proposes certain causes, the results of which are then explored in the third paragraph:

I went on the "Today" show one morning to say that I was tired of ethnic jokes and would like to hear no more of them. I mentioned Polish jokes, among others. Letters came in praising me for "sticking up for the Poles," and I was asked to go on again to tell about the record of Polish Americans in Pennsylvania in volunteering for military service in the Second World War. Since I had said that all that Polish jokes amounted to was that Poles were stupid, I was also accused of saying that Poles were stupid. So much for the influence of the electronic medium in shaping the nation's dialogue.

I am not suggesting that American humor be denatured, that the vigor and bite be taken out of it. I know that much of the humor in this country, for as long as anyone now alive can remember, has been ethnic. That was logical and unavoidable: the unintentional misuse of English by immigrants who understood it imperfectly often had amusing results. The difficulty that many of the newcomers had in adapting to the customs of the United States also gave rise to amusing situations, though these often had overtones of sadness as well.

The result was a robust kind of humor, sometimes endearing, sometimes cruel, but one that many people could recognize as having some application to themselves. Even today, some ethnic content in American humor is still inevitable. . . .—Edwin Newman, *Strictly Speaking*

A different kind of continuity is established in the passage below. The second paragraph opens with the same words that the first does, and in the first sentence of the second paragraph, *this* refers to the entire quotation given in the first paragraph. There appears at first to be a kind of jump from the second paragraph to the third, but then we realize that it establishes an attitude in contrast with that pessimistically predicted in the first two paragraphs. The third paragraph ends with a reference to high standards, and the fourth takes up from there by opening with the single-word exclamation, "Standards!"

William James said, "Democracy is on trial, and no one knows how it will stand the ordeal. . . . What its critics now affirm is that its preferences are inveterately for the inferior. So it was in the beginning, they say, and so it will be world without end. Vulgarity enthroned and institutionalized, elbowing everything superior from the highway, this, they tell us, is our irremediable destiny. . . ."

William James himself did not believe this was our destiny. Nor do I. But the danger is real and not imagined. Democracy as we know it has proved its vitality and its durability. We may be proud of its accomplishments. But let us not deceive ourselves. The specter that William James raised still haunts us.

I once asked a highly regarded music teacher what was the secret of his extraordinary success with students. He said, "First I teach them that it is better to do it well than to do it badly. Many have never been taught the pleasure and pride in setting standards and then living up to them."

Standards! That is a word for *every* American to write on his bulletin board. . . .—John Gardner, *The Pursuit of Excellence*

A variety of connections occur in the passage below. The author's concern with a diet runs throughout the passage, clearly enough, so that we do not lose sight of his subject. The opening of the second paragraph does not immediately establish any direct connection with the first paragraph, but when we get to the third sentence of the second paragraph (where the author says that diets "sounded so simple when I was full"), we're reminded of the final sentence of the first paragraph, "Simple things must be the hardest to do." A reference to diet books early in the third paragraph picks up the discussion of diet books in the second paragraph. The third paragraph closes with the author suggesting that readers can pick and choose among different diets; the fourth paragraph opens with the indication that the author did just this: "Somewhere along the line, I'd read. . . ." The reference to breakfast, lunch, and dinner in the opening of the fourth paragraph then provides the transition for the remaining two paragraphs, the fifth commencing with lunch, the sixth with dinner:

> When I made that decision to diet, I had made a total commitment—a total dedication to a new lifestyle. I used to dream that Ronald Colman would come down and spirit me away to a slim Shangri-La where they grew nonfattening banana splits and flaky apple turnovers. But way down deep I knew there would never be any magic formula. I figured that I was alone in this diet—just me and that food in a *High Noon* showdown. If I was going to lose weight, I had to stop eating. Boy, does that sound simple. Simple things must be the hardest to do.
>
> Diet books have always been like hot buttered popcorn to me. I've leafed through almost every one published in the last twenty-five years. They all sounded so simple when I was full, but when I was hungry, my good intentions vanished like lemon meringue pie and I'd almost eat the book.
>
> Each of us is an individual with different tastes, appetites and lifestyles. Therefore any diet you pick must fit into your personal life plan. You can read a book, join a diet workshop or a fat farm or enroll in any number of diet courses and find a particular system that works for you. Or you can pick and choose from each of them and then—after clearing it first with your doctor—develop your own diet as I did.
>
> Somewhere along the line, I'd read the proper way to eat was to breakfast like a king, lunch like a prince and dine like a pauper. I've used that system for years and it works. I always ate two eggs every morning (don't remind me about the cholesterol), toast and coffee. Sometimes I'd throw in a little bacon or sausage. And I'd usually make sure to drink a glass of skimmed milk to get me rolling.
>
> Lunch was a sandwich and more skimmed milk. I always

took the top piece of bread off and put the two halves together. That way I saved the calories in an extra slice of bread.

Dinner was meat of some kind, chicken or turkey with cottage cheese or tomato.—Larry Goldberg, "How to Diet . . . and Still Keep Your Sense of Humor"

Consider a last example, and notice the way the author manages the transition from one paragraph to the next. The first paragraph ends with a question, which almost automatically connects this paragraph with those that follow. Unless we're warned otherwise, when we see a question put this way, we expect that what follows will be in some way an answer. So it is here: the following paragraphs form an answer to the question posed at the end of the first paragraph. Then notice the final sentence of the second paragraph: "Because some of these theories occasionally reappear today in new guises, let me mention several of them as a guide to the waery." When we read that, we know what to expect; each of the next three paragraphs will take up one of "these theories" that "occasionally reappear today in new guises":

The study of animal communication reveals that human language is not simply a more complex example of a capacity that exists elsewhere in the living world. One animal or another may share a few features with human language, but it is clear that language is based on different principles altogether. So far as is known, people can speak because of their particular kind of vocal apparatus and their specific type of mental organization, not simply because of their higher degree of intelligence. No prototype for language has been found in the apes and monkeys, and no parrot or mynah bird has ever recombined the words it learned into novel utterances. In contrast, every human community in the world possesses a complete language system. Obviously, something happened in evolution to create Man the Talker. But what was it?

Since sentences do not leave anything equivalent to the fossils and pottery shards that allow anthropologists to trace the prehistory of man, linguists can only speculate about the origins of language. Theories have been advanced, have won adherents for a while, then later were shown to be fanciful—and given derisive baby-talk names. Because some of these theories occasionally reappear today in new guises, let me mention several of them as a guide to the wary.

The Bow-Wow Theory states that language arose when man imitated the sounds of nature by the use of onomatopoeic words like *cock-a-doodle-do*, *cuckoo*, *sneeze*, *splash*, and *mumble*. This theory has been thoroughly discredited. It is now known that many onomatopoeic words are of recent, not ancient, origin and that some of them were not derived from natural sounds at all. But the most telling argument against the Bow-Wow Theory is that onomatopoeic words vary from language to language. If the human species had truly based its words on the sounds of nature, these words should be the same in all languages because of the obvious fact that a dog's bark is the same throughout the world. Yet the *bow-wow* heard by speakers of English sounds like *gua-gua* to Spaniards, *af-af* to Russians, and *wan-wan* to Japanese.

The Ding-Dong Theory dates back to Pythagoras and Plato and was long honored, but nowadays it has no support whatsoever. This theory claims a relationship between a word and its sense because everything in nature is supposed to give off a harmonic "ring," which man supposedly detected when he named objects. But the Ding-Dong Theory cannot explain what resonance a small four-footed animal gave off to make Englishmen call it a *dog* rather than any other arbitrary collection of vowels and consonants—and what different resonance it communicated to Frenchmen to make them call it a *chien* or to Japanese to make them call it an *inu*.

Still other explanations for the origin of language are. . . .—Peter Farb, *Word Play*

Exercise

In a group with your classmates, analyze the transition from paragraph to paragraph in an entire professional essay. After you have finished, see if you can arrive at some categories of transitions.

SPECIAL PURPOSE PARAGRAPHS

Not all paragraphs have as their main purpose moving the development of a subject forward. Some have special purposes, and three are worth particular attention—*opening* paragraphs, *transitional* paragraphs, and *closing* paragraphs. There is no reason for them to do all that other paragraphs do.

Opening paragraphs

Opening paragraphs have a special burden. If what you have written is good, it may be good in vain if no one reads it—and whether or not someone reads your work may depend to a considerable extent upon your first paragraph. Unfortunately, there is no recipe for making a fine first paragraph. It is useful if the opening attracts the attention of readers in some honest and legitimate way—not by ballyhoo or sensationalism, but, for example, by showing some particularly interesting or arresting feature of the subject. But the opening paragraph shouldn't serve merely to attract attention; it should also get the treatment of the subject under way. It should ordinarily, in other words, be a real beginning, not just an attractive preface. Where possible, it should both draw readers in and establish the subject. Many opening paragraphs lead to the thesis statement, which is a good way to establish your subject. (See the discussion of thesis sentences and of beginning with a thesis sentence in Chapter 6, Designing Your Work.) Watch what other writers do at the first of their work, and consider the examples that follow.

The first example is the opening paragraph of an excerpt from a book published in a popular magazine. As you will see, it arrests attention in an interesting way:

> I was quite happy that morning a couple of years ago, my knife poised over a swollen ear. Tristan, one elbow leaning wearily on the table, was holding an anesthetic mask over the nose of the sleeping dog when Siegfried came into the room.—James Herriot, *All Things Wise and Wonderful*

The opening sentence starts off innocuously enough with the initial main clause, but then something startling happens almost as an afterthought in the closing dependent phrase: the swollen ear is an attention-getter, but the rest of the paragraph goes on to set the scene.

The second example proceeds in a different way:

> Like a sad-faced clown, Eric was a wise-cracking, under-achieving contradiction; beneath the painted-on bravado of the class cutup, there was a lonely, forlorn boy who wanted more than anything to be "just another kid." His intelligence tested above average, but he consistently scored far below grade level in school. On the surface he talked and looked like other children his age, but something, some nameless affliction, kept him from learning.—Gerri Hirshey, "Family Circle Guide to Learning Disabilities"

The article in which this paragraph appears is about learning difficulties among children, but the author chose in the opening to picture the single individual rather than confronting the general problem. Many readers may be pulled more easily into the article by an account of the specific boy than by an account of an overwhelming but generalized problem.

The next example follows a similar pattern. Instead of addressing the general subject of the farmers' movement for improved farm incomes, the author opens with a dramatized account of a single moment in the movement:

> Belching diesel exhaust, 6,500 tractors lumbered along a Georgia interstate last weekend, bound for Atlanta. Meanwhile, eight "tractorcades" rumbled into Topeka, Kans., and similar demonstrations occurred in a dozen more Midwestern capitals. In Washington, D.C., 600 tractors and other farm vehicles gathered near the Washington Monument. Across the country, farmers were

rallying to show that they were ready to strike in order to force prices higher. Their motto: "No more producing, no more selling and no more buying."—*Time*, "Furious Farmers"

Several things work for the author in the next example. The passage quoted from the song serves part of the function of an opening paragraph—it says something about trucks and truckdrivers, and it attracts attention because it is set off from the text and looks different from the rest of the print. The actual first paragraph sets some of the tone for the article and announces a troublesome contradiction: "Americans are strangely sentimental about the heavy, long-distance truck," but the trucks "are nonetheless one of the great abominations of the Asphalt Age."

> *I got 10 forward gears and a Georgia overdrive*
> *I'm takin' little white pills and my eyes are open wide*
> *I just passed a Jimmy and a White*
> *I been passin' everything in sight*
> *Six days on the road, and I'm gonna make it home tonight.*

> —Earl Green and Carl Montgomery, "Six Days on the Road"
>   Copyright © 1963 Newkeys Music Inc.

> Americans are strangely sentimental about the heavy long-distance truck—the tractor-trailer outfit with a dozen or so gears and a dozen or so tires that washes the highways with waves of terrible noise and vibrations and towering arrogance. Trucks now carry about one-third of the nation's merchandise, and we probably could not do without them, but they are nonetheless one of the great abominations of the Asphalt Age.—Robert Sherrill, "Raising Hell on the Highways"

The example below, on the other hand, is a straightforward announcement of the subject, together with a brief account of the plan of the first part of the essay:

> Let us begin with the academy itself, and then consider the nature of the freedom which it enjoys. What is a university, and what are its functions?—Henry Steele Commager, "The Nature of Academic Freedom"

The last example works in still another way. The tone of the opening is anticipatory, and the paragraph raises enough questions to pull readers into the essay that follows in search of answers. The birds were "singing good-bye to the day, and their merged song seemed to soak the strange air in an additional strangeness." We have to wonder why the usually roundish spots of sunlight were all shaped like feathers, crescent, and why the baby's skin was awash with the same crescents:

I went out into the backyard and the usually roundish spots of dappled sunlight underneath the trees were all shaped like feathers, crescent in the same direction, from left to right. Though it was five o'clock on a summer afternoon, the birds were singing goodbye to the day, and their merged song seemed to soak the strange air in an additional strangeness. A kind of silence prevailed. Few cars were moving on the streets of the town. Of my children only the baby dared come into the yard with me. She wore only underpants, and as she stood beneath a tree, bulging her belly toward me in the mood of jolly flirtation she has grown into at the age of two, her bare skin was awash with pale crescents. It crossed my mind that she might be harmed, but I couldn't think how. *Cancer?*— John Updike, "Eclipse"

Transitional paragraphs

Transitional paragraphs are bridges between one segment of a discussion and another. Usually not designed to develop an idea or to illustrate a point on their own, they serve to close out one stage in a discussion and to initiate another, or to summarize past discussion as a way of introducing new discussion, or to establish relationships of some kind between parts of a discussion. Some examples may suggest the variety of forms transitional paragraphs may take.

In the first example below, a one-word question stands alone as a paragraph. It comes between the description of a problem and an account of the origins of the problem:

The Soviet-American negotiations for a new agreement— SALT II—that were resumed last spring have been making headway, but accord is still blocked by a number of technically complex issues. President Carter, Secretary of State Cyrus Vance, Secretary of Defense Harold Brown and Arms Control Director Paul Warnke have all shown a clear understanding of the dire potential consequences of the arms race, and have given arms control new priority on their agenda. Yet, despite the urgency of the situation, the Administration's policy, and the narrowness of the gap that separates the parties to the talks, there is real danger that no agreement will be reached—or, if reached, that it will not be ratified by the Senate.

Why?

Part of the answer has to do with the technicalities of missile performance, and with differences between the strategic doctrines and negotiating tactics of the two sides. But another, and perhaps the major, reason, is to be found in the domestic politics of arms control.—G. B. Kistiakowsky, "The Arms Race: Is Paranoia Necessary for Security?"

In the second paragraph of the passage below, the author takes up a question he asks in the first paragraph, and uses it to forecast what he is going to talk about next:

> On a thickly forested hill, not far from the sea at Carnac in Brittany, there rises an impressive grassy mound, with a rough slab of stone placed upright on its summit. A short distance away on the ground is another upright monolith, standing opposite an entrance façade leading into the middle of the mound. At the end of a short, dark passageway is a square chamber built from huge slabs of stone, roofed over by flat blocks supported at about ten feet from the chamber floor. In prehistoric times this structure was probably used as a tomb by successive generations for collective interment, and it has been dated by the radiocarbon method as far back as 5700 BC. It seems to be the earliest European example of constructions using large stones, known as 'megalithic' tombs. What the builders of the Kercado tomb believed in will never be known, but the passage and chamber layout (especially at other sites where the chamber was roofed over by the corbelling technique, creating a kind of dome) has suggested a womb-like place for the rebirth of the dead laid to rest inside. Another possibility is that the stone tombs imitated the forms of wooden houses, so that these constructions were 'houses for the dead.' Why was this idea of the megalithic tomb to have such a strong hold on the minds of simple farmers throughout Brittany?
>
> The question poses itself more insistently when we appreciate exactly how elaborate and ambitious some of these monuments were. A little to the east of Kercado, the inland sea of the Gulf of Morbihan flows between dozens of small islands. This area, stretching westwards to the curving promontory of Quiberon with its soaring cliffs, was one of the major centres of prehistoric culture in Europe for many thousands of years. It seems likely that some special sanctity was attached to the region.
>
> In the middle of the Gulf of Morbihan there rises a small island. . . .—Evan Hadingham, *Circles and Standing Stones*

In the example below, the author clearly signals a break in the text with a Roman numeral (Roman numeral one comes at the first of the essay), but the one-sentence paragraph that opens the second section of the essay is also transitional, picking up the term "weasel words" from the preceding paragraphs and introducing the discussion of common sources for weasel words:

> Before passing on into the area of true weasel words, where the desire to create a given effect is evident, a few more coinages bear mention. *Folknik* and *smutnik* have been added to the ever-growing family of *-niks*; *zodiatronics* has been formed to indicate

casting of a horoscope by computer; *satisficer* has been built out of *satisfy* and *suffice*.

All ingenious creations are by no means American. Professor Edward Misken, of the London School of Economics, is given credit for the following: *growthmen, illfare, uglifying, Newfanglia,* and even *bads*, the opposite of *goods*.

Among expressions that seem to display weasely intentions are the scientific *demute* (to turn up the sound volume); the medical *pregnancy interruption* for abortion; the labor *job action* to betoken a work slowdown, like the one carried on by the New York City police (wouldn't *job inaction* be more appropriate?); the educational *no-time syndrome* (where the professor can't take time to explain); *interpersonal relationships* (redefined as "kid fights"); *ancillary civic agencies for the support of discipline* (which really means to call in the cops to restore order); and columnist John Roche's *ivory foxholes*, to describe what the professors retreat into when the storm breaks over the university.

II

The four prime areas for weasel words are, as usual, the military, government, politics, and commercial advertising.

In the lower army ranks. . . .—Mario Pei, "The American Language in the Early '70s"

In the passage below, the first paragraph introduces the current "biological revolution" and a simultaneous "crisis in values," and then closes by introducing the religious outlook, which is the topic for the second paragraph. The third paragraph is a transitional paragraph. It looks both ways. It refers to the second paragraph in its first sentence: "For those who accept the revealed truth of a given religion, none of this presents a problem." The antecedent for *this* is the entire preceding paragraph. But the last sentence of the third paragraph anticipates what is to come in the fourth paragraph—an account of a contrary view, the scientific outlook:

The current "biological revolution," as it has rightly been called, happens to come along at the same moment we are all caught up in what has also rightly been called a "crisis in values." The two are curiously related. The biological revolution, on the one hand, contributes to the crisis but, on the other, might also help relieve it—though ethical and moral values usually fall within other provinces, notably that of religion.

Religion deals with human beings and human values—or, one might say, with divine or universal values as they apply to human behavior. A religious outlook does not necessarily (though it does customarily) incorporate a dogmatic theology. It is usually related to people's beliefs about their nature and origins; to the reasons for man's existence; to questions of life, death, and immortality; to man's relationship with his fellow beings; to codes of ethics by which man might guide his everyday conduct; to a sense of the sacred in nature and in life; to man's relationship with the Godhead in all its multifarious characterizations, whether personalized or diffuse.

For those who accept the revealed truth of a given religion, none of this presents a problem. All the answers are in. But for those who cannot so devoutly and explicitly accept revelation with any sense of intellectual or emotional comfort, the search continues.

Those who look to the sciences for answers will be disappointed—that is, if they believe that the sciences alone can provide the values we all seek to guide us through this time of troubles. But it would be a mistake to underrate the contribution the sciences— particularly the biological sciences—can make in this direction. "A coherent credo," wrote Theodosius Dobzhansky, "can neither be derived from science nor arrived at without science."—Albert Rosenfeld, "When Man Becomes as God"

Closing paragraphs

When readers read a final paragraph, they ought to be able to sense that the piece of writing is indeed finished. There are many ways to create this sense of an ending but no one can say exactly what goes into a closing paragraph. Some writers depend on a summary, recalling the major points they have made. Others sometimes use the last paragraph for a restatement of their chief point. Where the subject calls for it, writers sometimes use the final paragraph for a call to action. Others use the closing of a piece of writing for a last dramatized episode or example that illustrates or enlivens what they have been discussing. Consider some examples.

In the sample below, the author uses an emphatic statement as a closing paragraph. The essay is the last lecture given to an English class, in which the author talks about the failure of a new method of teaching and then about what he sees as the failure of the class to explore and exchange ideas, to grow, to become responsible. The final paragraph, then, is a fitting end:

Well, it's time, I suppose, to bring this to a halt, and let you go over to the Commons or wherever. As to the next-to-last comment, I invite you to listen to the lyrics of the Beatles' "Nowhere Man" and, if it fits, take it to heart.

Last, I will bid a good-bye (until the final) and say that if at any time some sly hint, or clue, or (God forbid) a half-truth slipped out of my unconscious and out of the corner of my mouth and (pardon the expression) "turned one of you on," then we have not failed, you and I.

And to all of you this: I love you for what you might be; I'm deeply disturbed by what you are.—Henry F. Ottinger, "A Few Parting Words"

In the example below, the last paragraph in an essay in which the author has been discussing the problems and perils of modern cities, the author summarizes all of the problems she has been discussing in one dramatic and memorable short paragraph:

Resources are not the problem. It is the shaping imagination, the liberating idea. With it, man's abundance can be used to make his urban life worth living. Without it, the city may be, in its slower way, as lethal as the bomb.—Barbara Ward, "The City May Be as Lethal as the Bomb"

The closing paragraph of Abraham Lincoln's second inaugural address is a rhythmic exhortation to duty, charity, and love:

With malice toward none; with charity for all; with firmness in the right, as God gives us to see the right, let us strive on to finish the work we are in; to bind up the nation's wounds; to care for him who shall have borne the battle, and for his widow, and his orphan—to do all which may achieve and cherish a just, and a lasting peace, among ourselves, and with all nations.

Earlier in this chapter, in a discussion of *opening* paragraphs, I cited the opening paragraph of John Updike's "Eclipse" for its anticipatory tone. In that essay, Updike tells of a neighbor's superstitions about eclipses and his own irrational feelings during the experience. The essay closes with the paragraph below, which gives a feeling of finality:

Superstition, I thought, walking back through my yard, clutching my child's hand as tightly as a goodluck token. There was no question in her touch. Day, night, twilight, noon were all wonders to her, unscheduled, free from all bondage of prediction. The sun was being restored to itself and soon would radiate influence as brazenly as ever—and in this sense my daughter's blind trust was vindicated. Nevertheless, I was glad that the eclipse had passed, as it were, over her head; for in my own life I felt a certain assurance evaporate forever under the reality of the sun's disgrace.

The example below is the final paragraph of an essay mentioned earlier, the introduction to a retelling of Kiowa legends. In the introductory essay, the author tells of returning to his ancestral home in Oklahoma to see his grandmother's burial place, and of the family and tribal history the visit evokes in his mind. The essay ends with this paragraph:

The next morning I awoke at dawn and went out on the dirt road to Rainy Mountain. It was already hot, and the grasshoppers began to fill the air. Still, it was early in the morning, and the birds sang out of the shadows. The long yellow grass on the mountain shone in the bright light, and a scissortail hied above the land. There, where it ought to be, at the end of a long and legendary way, was my grandmother's grave. Here and there on the dark stones were ancestral names. Looking back once, I saw the mountain and came away.—N. Scott Momaday, *The Way to Rainy Mountain*

Exercises

1.   Begin a list in your journal of some of your favorite openings and closings of essays, articles, ads, and other types of writing that you encounter.

2.   Advertisements rely heavily on catching the reader's attention with their opening statements (for example, "Read this and cry!"). Make a collection of these openings and see if you can make some generalizations about the types of opening statements that are most used.

3.   In articles in *Time* and *Newsweek*, it is particularly easy to pick out openers, transition paragraphs, and conclusions. Analyze several articles for these elements.

4.   Write some effective opening paragraphs for the following subjects. Then choose one that you were most successful with and write the essay.
    a. Exam Pressures
    b. A Forgotten Promise
    c. Solar Energy
    d. Increased Responsibility
    e. Job Scarcity
    f. Unfair Advertising

5.   Individually, or in a group with your classmates, analyze and evaluate the following elements in a professional essay:
    a. opener
    b. transitions and transition paragraphs
    c. topic sentences
    d. paragraph development (definition, process, cause-effect, coordination, subordination, etc.)
    e. conclusion

Use the same list to check one of your own essays for possible needed revisions.

6.   Analyze the patterns of development in the following paragraphs:
    a. When I began teaching I felt isolated in a hostile environment. The structure of authority in my school was clear: the principal was at the top and the students were at the bottom. Somewhere in the middle was the teacher, whose role it was to impose orders from textbooks or supervisors upon the students. The teacher's only protection was that if students failed to obey

instructions they could legitimately be punished or, if they were defiant, suspended or kicked out of school. There was no way for students to question the teachers' decisions or for teachers to question the decisions of their supervisors or authors of textbooks and teachers' manuals.—Herbert Kohl, *The Open Classroom*

b.   It is curious—the misassociation of certain words. For instance, the word Repentance. Through want of reflection we associate it exclusively with Sin. We get the notion early, and keep it always, that we repent of bad deeds only; whereas we do a formidably large business in repenting of good deeds which we have done. Often when we repent of a sin, we do it perfunctorily, from principle, coldly and from the head; but when we repent of a good deed the repentance comes hot and bitter and straight from the heart. Often when we repent of a sin, we can forgive ourselves and drop the matter out of mind; but when we repent of a good deed, we seldom get peace—we go on repenting to the end. And the repentance is so perennially young and strong and vivid and vigorous! A great benefaction conferred with your whole heart upon an ungrateful man— with what immortal persistence and never-cooling energy do you repent of that! Repentance of a sin is a pale, poor, perishable thing compared with it.—Mark Twain, *Something About Repentance*

c.   Reading readiness includes several different kinds of preparation for learning to read. Physical readiness involves a minimum level of visual perception such that the child can take in and remember an entire word and the letters that combine to form it. Language readiness involves the ability to speak clearly and to use several sentences in correct order. Personal readiness involves the ability to work with other children, to sustain attention, to follow directions, and the like.—Mortimer J. Adler and Charles Van Doren, *How to Read a Book*

d.   When applied to a place or a person, the word "nature" is as vague but also as rich in complex connotations as genius or spirit. According to dictionaries, one of the meanings of nature is "the essential character or constitution of something" or "the intrinsic characteristics and qualities of a person or thing." The word nature so defined provides a factual explanation for what the ancients called genius or spirit. It denotes not only the geographic, social, or human appearances but also, and especially, all the forces hidden beneath the surface of reality. For the people of the Greco-Roman classical age, no account of a place or of man's role in it was complete without the evocation of mysteries in which heroes and gods were the chief actors.—René Dubos, *A God Within*

. . . style is the proof of a human being's individuality.
. . . style is a gesture of freedom against inflexible
states of mind. . . .

Winston Weathers, "Teaching
Style: A Possible Anatomy"

11

What is style? It is many things, and it is sometimes hard to describe.
So after some introductory notes, this chapter includes

1. an account of definitions and confusions in the study of style
    (p. 286);

2. an account of the relationship between this chapter and those
    before and after (p. 289);

3. a discussion of the elements of style and an illustration of how
    style can change (p. 290); and

4. a collection of essays that is a sampling of styles (p. 294).

Even though you may not be able to define precisely what you mean by style, you can distinguish among different styles by various writers. You may not be able to distinguish the style of one news story from that of another in the same newspaper. You may not be able to tell the difference between the style of one "think piece" in a magazine and that of another "think piece" in the same magazine or in a similar magazine. And you may not be able right at the moment to distinguish among the advertising styles of various automobile companies. But your own observation and experience have taught you to recognize a good many things about different styles.

You probably know very well, for example, that teachers respond differently to various styles of speaking. In one class you may feel free to speak casually; in another you may not. If you are a reader of comic strips, you could probably, without seeing the pictures, distinguish the text of "Tank McNamara" from that of "The Wizard of Id." If you watch news programs on television, you probably watch one newscaster, as much for the way he or she presents the news as for any other reason. If you are a fan of sports programs on television, you probably prefer the manner of some sports commentators to that of others. You may not be able to distinguish between the styles of two news writers, but you can probably distinguish between the styles of some sports writers on the one hand and the styles of some news writers on the other.

An astounding array of different styles surrounds you all the time—in clothing, in food, in movies, in politics, in buildings, in writing, in television, in teaching, in studying, in everything—and you already make choices based on your reaction to style.

One easy way to remember that different styles do indeed occur and that you can make some distinctions among them (even if you feel that you can't talk about style) is to browse back through the *examples* used in this book, especially those that are at least a paragraph long, to note the variety, and to begin sorting out your responses to them. Look back at the sad, meditative, conversational passage from James Baldwin's *The Fire Next Time* (p. 35), at the colloquial patterns in the passage from Shirley Jackson's "The Lottery" (p. 42), both in Chapter 2. Look back at the plain, direct passage by Jane Van Lawick-Goodall (p. 55) and the breezy passage by Vine Deloria (p. 55) in Chapter 3. Remember the image-rich passage from N. Scott Momaday's *The Way to Rainy Mountain* (p. 72), and the elegiac speech of Chief Joseph (p. 88). Look again at the rather formal, exploratory passage by Kenneth Clark (p. 134), the plain, informative manner of George R. Stewart (p. 146), and the easy, forthright passage by Barbara Yuncker (p. 149). Turn back to the plain economy of Orwell's "Politics and the English Language" (p. 256) and the incantatory reminiscences in Twain's *Autobiography* (p. 259). Then look at your other textbooks, the magazines you read, and the billboards you pass, and listen to the records you own, and watch your favorite television programs. An astounding variety of styles whirls around you all of the time. You probably speak a surprising variety of styles yourself.

Exercises

1.   Keeping in mind that we all have many different styles, and that your style probably varies moment to moment, day to day, try to make some general descriptive remarks about your style of living as you see it at this moment.

2.   Describe a typical day in your life and talk about how your style varies from situation to situation.

CONFUSIONS AND DEFINITIONS

All of us can speak—and sometimes write—in different styles. We can usually react and respond to different styles, but we can't always name, describe, and remember them. The truth is, it is difficult even for people who specialize in the study of style to agree on just how best to name, describe, and remember different styles. It is difficult, indeed, for many to agree on just what a style is.

In other words, style gets discussed in many ways. Sometimes people use the word *style* to mean classiness or grace or beauty or modishness; we hear people say, for example, "Now *that* car has style," or "He has real style." Unfortunately, style is often discussed as if it were merely ornamentation, a kind of embroidery or decoration added to a message after it has already been completed. Style used in this sense— and this may be the most common understanding of the word—seems to suggest that writers can put down on paper all that they mean to say, and then go back and dress it all up prettily. Of course it's possible to do just that, though it's not clear why anyone would want to.

Some would agree with a definition of style set out some years ago by John Middleton Murry in his book *The Problem of Style*: style "is that personal idiosyncrasy of expression by which we recognize a writer." That's interesting, but perhaps not too helpful, unless we can figure out what "personal idiosyncrasy of expression" can mean. When other people talk of style, they seem to be thinking particularly of the sequence or general design of a writer's or a speaker's work. Sometimes, people assume that style means the particular way in which an author uses words; at other times, style is taken to mean both the language an author uses and the patterns in which words are arranged.

Perhaps it will help in your thinking about style if, from the beginning, you remember that the word *style* can quite properly be used in different senses. *At least two different uses of the word seem important.*

Style, in the first sense, is something very much like your identity. It is your way of being in the world, the way you move among your experiences, lingering over some, evading others, running headfirst and headlong into still others. It is your way of picking and choosing, your way of speaking or not speaking. Your style, in this sense, may be a manner that you have shaped and defined with great thought and deliberation, or it may have developed in a helter-skelter kind of way, partly by accident, partly by design, or it may be mostly a reflection of what other people are like and the way other people speak. Most of us, after all, act and talk in similar ways at least part of the time, and the style of any single person may develop as he or she simply accepts the prevailing manners and words of the day. When the word is used in this sense, every person has a style. It is the way we make ourselves known to each other.

But notice this: *style* understood only in this sense could be a prison. If I always live in one small province (and it's possible to do that in a large and cosmopolitan community), if I read no books at all, or always the same kind of books, if I restrict my view to what I already know, if my imagination won't let me see through another's eyes sometimes, if I always talk the way I first learned to talk, if I always accept the common language or popular jargon of friends, newspapers, radio, and television as the most accurate language there is, then I am in prison. I am already saying all I will ever be able to say. If I don't know any alternatives, then I can only talk in one way. And the prison may be even more constrictive. If the way I talk is just like the way everyone else talks, then I can't identify or express any unique qualities I might have. If the way I talk is totally unlike the way other people talk, then I probably won't be able to get them to listen to me. *Style* in this first sense, though it may be the mark of our identity, may also be a prison.

Fortunately, there is that other important sense in which *style* can be taken. All around us all of the time are enabling capacities—ways of doing things, techniques, methods, strategies, grammars, procedures that we may acquire. All of these are *styles*, or enabling capacities, that we may take as our own. *Style* taken in this second sense is liberating: we may learn new ways of seeing and speaking, new ways of making ourselves known, new ways of reaching an audience. The styles or methods that others have used in the past and those that others use in the present are available to us as inventive resources.

Style, of course, is often thought of as an end point in writing. It is that, to be sure. When you write something, it appears as a vocabulary and a set of structures—that is, as a style. What you search out and think through emerges as a style, and so style is an end point. But a style that you use in writing today is also a starting place to work from when you write tomorrow, and the styles developed by other people, past and present, are resources you can call on, starting places. *Style* in this second sense is an enabling capacity, or a set of enabling capacities, that will let you do what you had not been able to do before. In this sense, many things can be considered *styles*: methods of designing paragraphs, sentence patterns, new vocabulary possibilities, structures and styles that you can borrow from other writers and adapt for your own uses, methods of exploring a subject—in short, any skill or art or strategy that will enable you to do what you had not been able to do before. In this sense, knowing how to use a library and bring what you find there to the aid of your own thinking and writing is an enabling *style*, and knowing how to document your research in footnotes is an enabling *style*. When you know how to write a definition or a description or a comparison when you have to or want to, then you own these enabling *styles*.

The relationships between the two senses of style are interesting and important. You already have a *style* (personal identity) when you begin to acquire the *styles* associated with writing. As you acquire more enabling *styles*, your *style* (or identity) becomes more commodious. When you have capacities, skills, arts, then you are free to do what you will or must. We all prize our freedom of speech, but we have to learn how to speak before we are free to speak.

It is possible, however, for a person to take on a style dishonestly. Most affectations, for example, occur when someone adopts a style (of clothing, manner, speaking, or whatever) that does not fit his or her identity and circumstances. In many kinds of propaganda (including some advertising) a speaker adopts a style to use in addressing us that is calculated *not* to reveal true motives.

You have to take the responsibility of bringing the *styles* you acquire into some kind of harmony with your own character. There are teachers and editors and others who may help, but in the long run, you have to decide how you can be yourself, and you have to decide which styles and possibilities can work honestly for you.

Exercises

1. You already know much more than you perhaps think you know about analyzing writing styles. For example, you are bringing to this chapter knowledge about simple sentences, compound sentences, periodic sentences, loose sentences, similes, metaphors, sentence types, adjectives, and adverbs. Use your available knowledge to describe and characterize several pieces of writing that you have already done in this class. Choose several things written for different purposes, and see if your style has varied according to the purpose.

2. There are many ways to categorize style. Some that have been used in the past are *high*, *middle*, and *low*; *formal*, *informal*, and *colloquial*; *tough*, *sweet*, and *stuffy*; *plain* and *literary*. As a group with your classmates, arrive at some categories that seem useful and identify their characteristics.

Now write a common sentence; for example, "It's a hot day." Write down all the ways you can think of to say the same thing. Place the various ways that you have written the sentence into one of your categories.

3. Write a paragraph and identify the style you have written it in. Transform the paragraph into another style: elegant to plain, colloquial to formal, and so on. Do not change the essential content.

4. Write a series of letters to a variety of people: the President, the head of a company, your college president, your roommate, your girlfriend or boyfriend, your parents, your grandmother. Vary your style to fit the receiver of the letter.

WHY THIS CHAPTER IS ONLY AN INTERLUDE

At the beginning of the preceding section, I mentioned the difficulty of naming, describing, and remembering different styles. Yet it is important to keep trying to understand different styles, because you can't use various styles unless you know them, understand their particular features, and can call them to mind when you need them. If you are in a situation in which you want to write a curt, brisk, fast-moving piece, the stylistic practices that other people have used for such effects may help you—but only if you know them and can call them to mind. If you need or want to write a sober, detached piece, it helps to know how other people have achieved such effects—what they have done in their writing and what they have not done.

It's important, then, to know and to remember both what you have done before and what other writers have done to achieve particular qualities. But there is no chapter on style that can tell you all of the stylistic possibilities that are available to you. No single chapter can deal adequately with style because style cannot be separated from all other features of writing. Everything that happens in the process of writing helps to make your style, and your style, in turn, helps to determine everything that happens in the process of writing. This chapter, then, can only be an interlude. If a book on writing such as this one can say anything about style, to do so requires *all* of the chapters.

Everything you do in the course of writing something reveals your style—the way you think about subjects, the way you link things with each other, or choose not to link them, the kinds of problems and conflicts you look for, the way you look at things, the resources you call on, whether internal or external. The way you choose to organize and arrange your writing reveals your style. The ways you choose to develop, amplify or explore ideas and materials shows something about your style. The nature and extent of the vocabulary you use—how concrete, how abstract, how vague, how accurate—reveals your style. The kinds of sentences you write—whether long or short, simple or complicated, plain or artfully composed—reveal what your style is. The kinds of paragraphs you write, their length, their structure, and their purpose give evidence of your style. And while each of the chapters following this one is about some particular writing task, all of the remaining chapters are at the same time about style. It is a matter of style, after all, how you go about writing letters, reports, arguments, and critical essays. Everything in this book before this chapter is about style, and everything in this book after this chapter is about style. That is why this chapter is only an interlude.

Exercises

1.   To provide yourself with a set of questions that could be used to examine the style of a writer, make a list of questions either individually or in a group with your classmates that could be asked concerning style in each of the following categories:

    a. questions about the writer's inventive processes
    b. questions about the organization the writer chose
    c. questions about the paragraphs of the writing
    d. questions about the sentences
    e. questions about the writer's choice of words

2.   Test the questions that you have written for their effectiveness in analyzing a professional essay. Try the questions on an essay of your own.

MANAGING STYLES

You don't *have* to write in the same way all of the time. You can modify the character of your writing. Just as you don't have to sing the same note all the time, you can change your writing voice and slip or leap from one way of writing to another, and it's not dishonest to do so. Sometimes we suppose that moving from one style to another is deceitful, the sort of thing that's done by writers who want out of self-interest to manipulate the responses of their audience. Stylistic manipulations *are* deceitful, of course, if they are practiced for the purposes of deceit. But it's not dishonest or hypocritical to modify your style: after all, even birds change their tunes for various settings and purposes, and musicians regularly create new arrangements of songs, changing the style of the songs in the process. There is no overwhelmingly good reason to imagine that the words and sentences that come out of us first or most easily are therefore the one "right" style for us, the one true way to be ourselves. Surely we all hope to be able to say more things tomorrow than we did today, and to say them more accurately, more fruitfully. We can all manage to grunt and point pretty easily, but if we wish to be more precise and more compelling than that will permit, we have to acquire other styles.

One good way to gain new styles for yourself is by careful and consistent *revision* of your own work. Revision can be tedious, of course, if you think of it as merely a search for different words or for new places to put commas. It doesn't have to be drudgery—revision can, in fact, be play, if you think of it as a way of seeing what you can make words and sentences and paragraphs do. The character of a style can be changed in many ways through revision.

The short piece below was written by a student in a first-year writing class:

Down with Critics!

One thing that all musicians learn, sooner or later, is to ignore critics. Some of them are good and often have worthwhile things to say, but many more have no business putting pen to paper, at least on the subject of music. When a critic writes "last night Mr. Z. flailed away helplessly at the keyboard without the slightest understanding of what Schumann is about," what good is he doing? Suppose he is right. Mr. Z. knows that he doesn't understand Schumann and doesn't need to be told, or he will come to realize it in time on his own, or failing that, he will soon fade from the musical scene. Suppose the critic is wrong, and suppose Mr. Z. reads the review. At worst, he will doubt his own ability and cease to play Schumann, or at best, he will become livid and his blood pressure will go up.

A problem with critics, even those with courage enough to write what they believe and not what fashion dictates, is that they feel they're not worth their salt unless they denounce almost every artist they hear, reserving their praise for only a select few. This has several harmful consequences. The artists to whom it offers discouragement are often the youngest, who are the most vulnerable to it, and in the same way it withholds recognition from those who need it most. Furthermore, it makes the public think that music is more esoteric than it really is, when it tells them that a performance they may have enjoyed and thought was well done really wasn't.

I question the need for critics at all. Even if a performance is not "definitive" or "sublime" it has some musical value, since most standard repertory music has the strength to come through even a poor performance. If it doesn't, then most audiences have the discernment to see it for themselves. And if they don't, why spoil their enjoyment? Oh, I know critics will be around for a long time to come, for there are always people who want to be told what is good and what is bad. But as the Finnish Composer Jean Sibelius once said, "No one ever built a monument to a critic."

You can usually modify the style of your work by *compressing* sentences, paragraphs, or longer passages. Here, for example, is a second version of the second paragraph, in which some reduction has been made:

> *Even critics with courage enough to write what they believe and not what fashion dictates feel inadequate unless they disapprove of most artists they hear, praising only a select few. This has unfortunate consequences. They often discourage young, susceptible artists, withholding recognition from those who need it most, and they make the public think that music is more esoteric than it is when they disapprove of a performance that the public enjoyed.*

The paragraph has been reduced from 115 words to 72 words. The change in style is not a major shift. The original paragraph is somewhat more informal and conversational in manner; the revised version is somewhat more formal. The original version is appropriate to a personal essay; the revised version is more suitable for a study of music criticism.

Or consider what can happen to the style of a piece of writing when a passage is *expanded*:

> *A problem with critics—and it is a problem out of many they have—a problem even among those critics with courage enough to write what they believe and not what fashion dictates, is that they apparently feel that they are violating their own standards of taste and failing to support the principles of music criticism unless they disapprove of almost every artist they hear, reserving their praise for only a select few. This attitude has several unfortunate consequences. Behaving as they do, they offer discouragement to the youngest, most vulnerable and susceptible artists, withholding recognition from the very people who may need it most. And what is more, they tend to make the public think that music is more esoteric than it really is, when from their special point of view, often using a specialized language, they disapprove of performances that an audience may have enjoyed.*

The word count now has gone back up to 147, and the style has shifted a little again. The style now is still a little more formal than in the original version. Except for one, the sentences are appreciably longer. Grammatical constructions within the sentences are a little more complex. The revised version has more modifying constructions. And the tone has changed a little, too: the revised version is a little more clearly on the attack than is either of the other versions.

Shifting the tone is another way to revise and realize a new style. Here is another version of the same paragraph:

> *Most critics can't make up their own mind. They write whatever they think fashion dictates. Perhaps a few have courage*

enough to write what they believe. But all of them seem to think that they must save their praise for a select few. Attack and disapproval are their customs. They write as if they thought they would have to turn in their critics' badges unless they disapproved of almost every artist they hear. This attitude causes them to be harmful and contrary. They offer discouragement often to the youngest artists, hurting those who are most vulnerable and susceptible. Their contrary views often misguide the public; they make the public think that music is more esoteric than it really is when from their disdainful viewpoint they disapprove of a performance that audiences may have enjoyed.

This version is plainly on the attack. The style is angrier than in any of the other versions. The writer is not *studying* critics now; he is *attacking* them.

As you are revising, you may from time to time see the need for *structural shifts*, that is, for rearrangements in your writing, including everything from relatively simple rearrangement of sentences in a short passage to major organizational changes. Structural shifts will often create a change in the style of what you are writing. Go back to the original complete student essay, for example, and notice what would happen if the first and second paragraphs were reversed (it could be done with scarcely any change in wording). In the original version, the second paragraph is more clearly than the first an expression of disapproval. When it comes to an end, the third paragraph begins with "I question the need for critics at all." If the author reversed the first and second paragraphs, then the attacking paragraph would come first, but the more easygoing, underplayed paragraph (paragraph 1) would come just before the assertion, "I question the need for critics at all." If the paragraphs were reversed, in other words, the attack would be moderated considerably by the quieter paragraph that follows.

Other kinds of structural shifts are possible. Notice what would happen to the original essay, for example, if major *new* material were inserted (in this case, of course, a structural shift would also be an expansion of the original). With a little research, it would be possible to add to the first paragraph a series of anecdotes telling how famous musicians had schooled themselves to ignore music critics. If this were done, then the portion of the essay that is more easygoing would predominate, and the quiet, underplayed style would dominate the more disapproving tone of the second paragraph. On the other hand, a little research might make it possible to add to the second paragraph a review of several months' work by a single critic illustrating the author's point that critics praise few and attack many. Examination of all the music reviews available in a given week might provide the same kind of illustration. Were this done, then the attacking attitude would predominate in the essay.

Compression or reduction, expansion or amplification, tone shift and structural shift are forms of revision that usually will enable you to modify your style. These, of course, are not the only methods you can use. Any number of other kinds of revision may work. The point to remember is that you don't have to be trapped by your first version. You can revise your writing and by doing so change your style.

SOME STYLES FOR STUDY

A group of selections follows, illustrating stylistic variety. The questions below, dealing with such matters as word choice, sentence length, organization, and tone, are concerned with all the elements that generally characterize style. If you ask these questions about the passages you read, you should be able to make some distinctions and observations about style.

1. Can you characterize the vocabulary?   Is it simple? Conversational? Slangy? Specialized? Ornate? Formal? Difficult? Which words would you cite to illustrate the character of the vocabulary?

2. Is the language figurative?   Is it direct? Colorful? Trite? Fresh? Straightforward and ordinary? Which words or phrases would you single out for illustrations?

3. How would you describe the sentences?   Are they short or long, loose or periodic? What grammatical types occur? Does one grammatical type predominate? Would you describe the sentences as tightly constructed, or as loose and conversational? Which sentences would you pick to serve as illustrations of sentence style?

4. What can you say about the paragraphs?   Are they long or short? Are they brief and fast-moving, or long and packed? Can you follow the line of thought in the paragraphs? Are there discernible patterns of development in the paragraphs? Does the author depend on some patterns more than on others? Is it easy to follow the author from paragraph to paragraph? Which paragraphs would be useful examples to describe the style?

5. How would you describe the organization of the selection?   Is it clear, step-by-step, logical development? Is it impressionistic, moving from episode to episode or scene to scene by emotional associations or by some other kind of connection? Is there some presiding pattern of organization, such as comparison or definition? Can you single out key sentences and passages that reveal how the work is organized?

6. Can you characterize the tone or attitude at work in the selection?   What words would you use to describe the tone? What passages would you pick out to illustrate the tone or attitude?

Your Education

There is a world of difference between the modern home environment of integrated electric information and the classroom. Today's television child is attuned to up-to-the-minute "adult" news—inflation, rioting, war, taxes, crime, bathing beauties—and is bewildered when he enters the nineteenth-century environment that still characterizes the educational establishment where information is scarce but ordered and structured by fragmented, classified patterns, subjects, and schedules. It is naturally an environment much like any factory set-up with its inventories and assembly lines.

The "child" was an invention of the seventeenth century; he did not exist in, say, Shakespeare's day. He had, up until that time, been merged in the adult world and there was nothing that could be called childhood in our sense.

Today's child is growing up absurd, because he lives in two worlds, and neither of them inclines him to grow up. Growing up—that is our new work, and it is *total*. Mere instruction will not suffice.—Marshall McLuhan and Quentin Fiore, *The Medium Is the Massage*

From a Letter to a Friend

So while I do not pray for anybody or any party to commit outrages, still I do pray, and that earnestly and constantly, for some terrific shock to startle the women of this nation into a self-respect which will compel them to see the abject degradation of their present position; which will force them to break their yoke of bondage, and give them faith in themselves; which will make them proclaim their allegiance to woman first; which will enable them to see that man can no more feel, speak or act for woman than could the old slaveholder for his slave. The fact is, women are in chains, and their servitude is all the more debasing because they do not realize it. O, to compel them to see and feel, and to give them the courage and conscience to speak and act for their own freedom, though they face the scorn and contempt of all the world for doing it!—Susan B. Anthony

Red Raspberries

The raspberry is a child's fruit. It is candy on a tree, at his height, and filling up on it is nearly impossible. He goes deeper and deeper into the bramble, less and less conscious of the thorns, attracted by yet another cluster of berries only a step beyond his reach, and eventually surrounded by the bushes and lost in the forest.

Each raspberry is a discovery. The fattest and the sweetest hide under leaves, the choicest is the hardest to find. And no matter how thorough the search may be, a few berries are always left on the branches for the next hunter.

It is food fit for fairies and elves yet the mighty bear loves it, thrives on it. How can a fruit so small and ethereal satisfy an appetite so gross?

Raspberries do not travel well. Buying them in a little basket at the store always brings disappointment: the freshness is lost, and at the bottom are berries crushed or moldy. It is best to eat them off the branch, gently pulling them loose from the stem.

There is a right moment for picking. Many people like a raspberry when its flesh is firm, its color the red of red flags. Others wait until it is soft and a bit overripe, with just a suggestion of decay and the red on the eve of turning a royal scarlet.

Unless raspberry bushes are pruned and the suckers cut off, they conquer the earth. Their lateral roots are strong and spread far, and new shoots come up at the first sign of spring. It takes character to resist raspberry imperialism. But to let all branches bloom and to give all runners the right to grow means disorder, chaos—and a smaller fruit.

When compared with the essential apple, the richness of grape or the magnitude of watermelon, the raspberry is a footnote to Creation, an item unlisted in the GNP—a frill as useless as an idle thought.

The raspberry is a promise of sweet roundness, an invitation. It delivers an elusive aroma, a fleeting softness on the palate. It is a pretend fruit, with no more than a lacy whisper of a taste—an illusion.

The raspberry is a light kiss—not the passionate embrace of the juicy peach or the perfumed honeymoon of the mango, but a hint of affection, the beginning of a romance, a secret message.

A raspberry patch is the stuff memories are made of. It can be that enchanted garden of serenity that some of us try to find—to recapture another self, to savor once more the incomparable taste of an innocence that can never come again.—Charles Fenyvesi

Hell's Angels

O how faithfully our native intelligentsia has tried to . . . *do it right!* The model has not always been England. Not at all. Just as frequently it has been Germany or France or Italy or even (on the religious fringe) the Orient. In the old days—seventy-five-or-so years ago—the well-brought-up young intellectual was likely to be treated to a tour of Europe . . . we find Jane Addams recuperating from her malaise in London and Dresden . . . Lincoln Steffens going to college in Heidelberg and Munich . . . Mabel Dodge setting up house in Florence . . . Randolph Bourne discovering Germany's "charming villages" and returning to Bloomfield, New Jersey—*Bloomfield, New Jersey?*—which now "seemed almost too grotesquely squalid and frowsy to be true." The business of being an intellectual and the urge to set oneself apart from provincial life began to be indistinguishable. In July 1921 Harold Stearns completed his anthology called *Civilization in the United States*—a contradiction in terms, he hastened to note—and set sail for Europe. The "Lost Generation" adventure began. But what was the Lost Generation really? It was a post-Great War discount tour in which middle-class Americans, too, not just Bournes and Steffenses, could learn how to become European intellectuals; preferably French.

The European intellectual! What a marvelous figure! A brilliant cynic, dazzling, in fact, set like one of those Gustave Miklos Art Deco sculptures of polished bronze and gold against the smoking rubble of Europe after the Great War. The American intellectual did the best he could. He could position himself against a backdrop of . . . well, not exactly rubble . . . but of the booboisie, the Herd State, the United States of Puritanism, Philistinism, Boosterism, Greed and the great Hog Wallow. It was certainly a *psychological* wasteland. For the next fifty years, from that time to this, with ever-increasing skill, the American intellectual would perform this difficult feat, which might be described as the Adjectival Catch Up. The European intellectuals have a real wasteland? Well, we have a psychological wasteland. They have real fascism? Well, we have social fascism (a favorite phrase of the 1930s, amended to "liberal fascism" in the 1960s). They have real poverty? Well, we have relative poverty (Michael Harrington's great Adjectival Catch Up of 1963). They have real genocide? Well, we have cultural genocide (i.e., what universities were guilty of in the late 1960s if they didn't have open-admissions policies for minority groups).

Well—all right! They were difficult, these one-and-a-half gainers in logic. But they were worth it. What had become important above all was to be that polished figure amid the rubble, a vision of sweetness and light in the smoking tar pit of Hell. The intellectual had become not so much an occupational type as a status type. He was like the Medieval cleric, most of whose energies were devoted to separating himself from the mob—which in modern times, in Revel's phrase, goes under the name of the middle class.

Did he want to analyze the world systematically? Did he want to add to the store of human knowledge? He not only didn't want to, he belittled the notion, quoting Rosa Luxemburg's statement that the "pot-bellied academics" and their interminable monographs and lectures, their intellectual nerve gas, were sophisticated extensions of police repression. Did he even want to change the world? Not particularly; it was much more elegant to back exotic, impossible causes such as the Black Panthers'. Moral indignation was the main thing; that, and a certain pattern of consumption. In fact, by the 1960s it was no longer necessary to produce literature, scholarship, or art—or even to be involved in such matters, except as a consumer—in order to qualify as an intellectual. It was only necessary to live *la vie intellectuelle*. A little brown bread in the bread box, a lapsed pledge card to CORE, a stereo and a record rack full of Coltrane and all the Beatles albums from *Revolver* on, white walls, a huge *Dracaena marginata* plant, which is there because all the furniture is so clean-lined and spare that without this piece of frondose tropical Victoriana the room looks empty, a stack of unread *New York Review of Books* rising up in a surly mound of subscription guilt, the conviction that America is materialistic, repressive, bloated, and deadened by its Silent Majority, which resides in the heartland, three grocery boxes full of pop bottles wedged in behind the refrigerator and destined (one of these days) for the Recycling Center, a small, uncomfortable European car—that pretty well got the job done.

By the late 1960s, it seemed as if American intellectuals had at last ... Caught Up. There were riots on the campuses and in the slums. The war in Vietnam had developed into a full-sized Hell. War! Revolution! Imperialism! Poverty! I can still remember the ghastly delight with which literary people in New York embraced the Four Horsemen. The dark night was about to descend. All agreed on that; but there were certain ugly, troublesome facts that the native intellectuals, unlike their European mentors, had a hard time ignoring.

By 1967 Lyndon Johnson may have been the very generalissimo of American imperialism in Southeast Asia—but back here in the U.S. the citizens were enjoying freedom of expression and freedom of dissent to a rather astonishing degree. For example, the only major Western country that allowed public showings of *MacBird*—a play that had Lyndon Johnson murdering John F. Kennedy in order to become President—was the United States (Lyndon Johnson, President). The citizens of this fascist bastion, the United States, unaccountably had, and exercised, the most extraordinary political freedom and civil rights in all history. In fact, the government, under the same Johnson, had begun the novel experiment of sending organizers into the slums—in the Community Action phase of the poverty program—to mobilize minority groups to rise up against the government and demand a bigger slice of the pie. (They obliged.) Colored peoples were much farther along the road to equality—whether in the area of rights, jobs, income, or social acceptance—in the United States than were the North Africans, Portuguese, Senegalese, Pakistani, and Jamaicans of Europe. In 1966 England congratulated herself over the appointment of her first colored policeman (a Pakistani in Coventry). Meanwhile, young people in the U.S.—in the form of the Psychedelic or Flower Generation—were helping themselves to wild times that were the envy of children all over the world.

In short, freedom was in the air like a flock of birds. Just how fascist could it be? This problem led to perhaps the greatest Adjectival Catch Up of all times: Herbert Marcuse's doctrine of "repressive tolerance." Other countries had real repression? Well, we had the obverse, repressive tolerance. This was an insidious system through which the government granted meaningless personal freedoms in order to narcotize the pain of class repression, which only socialism could cure. Beautiful! Well-nigh flawless!

Yet even at the moment of such exquisite refinements—things have a way of going wrong. Another troublesome fact has cropped up, gravely complicating the longtime dream of socialism. That troublesome fact may be best summed up in a name: Solzhenitsyn.—Tom Wolfe, "The Intelligent Co-ed's Guide to America"

Phrasal Verbs to Trip Out On

Eat up all the chicken soup. Drink up. Live it up. Tear up. Give up. Situation normal, all fouled up, to bowdlerize the old army phrase.

Those *ups* in most cases have nothing to do with *up* in its most literal—or "how high is up?"—sense. In fact, in its most literal sense, *up* really means "out," as I believe Buckminster Fuller has noted. Since *up* indicates opposite directions on antipodal parts of the globe, we really should say "go outstairs" instead of "go upstairs"—*out* being away from the earth. I think we'd play hob with the language if we insisted on superimposing such a global point of view on our everyday modes of thinking though, and communication would get *fubar*, or fouled up beyond all repair, to bowdlerize still another old army phrase.

Drink up. Drink down. Put up with. Put on (in at least two senses, to don and to rib—she put on a stern expression, but she was just putting him on).

According to Fowler's *Modern English Usage*, these expressions are called "phrasal verbs. The name was given by Henry Bradley to those fixed combinations of verb and adverbial particle from which (to quote Pearsall Smith) 'we derive thousands of vivid colloquialisms and idiomatic phrases by means of which we describe the greatest variety of human actions and relations'—the combinations for instance of such verbs as *get, put, take,* and *set* with such adverbs as *in, out, to, from, up,* and *down* to create nuances of meaning."

I looked up Henry Bradley in my encyclopedia. He was one of the major guiding geniuses involved in the compilation of the *Oxford English Dictionary*. I also looked up Pearsall Smith. That was less easy not only because there are so many Smiths but because his full name was Logan Pearsall Smith. He was a Philadelphian who lived in England from 1888 until his death, in 1946. Among his writings are *The English Language* and *Words and Idioms*.

I'm grateful for the phrase *adverbial particle*. If you'd asked me a few weeks ago what that was, I'd probably have said that an adverbial particle was part of an adverb, like *-ly*, thus confusing the adverbial particle with the adverbial suffix.

These thoughts have been inspired by a couple of things. The first is that for several years I've been getting letters from people asking me to do a column on the gratuitous use of *up* after certain verbs. The second is that it has occurred to me that *out* has replaced *up* as the most common adverbial particle (now that I know what to call them). *Flake out. Flip out.*

Spaced out. Freaked out. Recently our niece, Candis, told us about a party where the food and drink were so plentiful and irresistible that she had "really pigged out."

Then last week, my wife's young cousin, Fran, dropped in for a brief visit. She's living in Ojai, a gentle town tucked away in one of the most scenic corners of the paradisiacal Ojai Valley, east of Santa Barbara. "Up in Ojai," Fran said, "almost everybody's really blissed out." That did it.

If it hadn't been for *pigged out* and *blissed out*, it might have been years before I found out about *phrasal verb* and *adverbial particle*.

All of which recalls a conversation I had with a young English teacher a few weeks ago. She said she thought that it was important to teach grammar to her pupils but that she didn't believe in labeling. What did she mean by "labeling"? "You know," she said. "Prepositions, adjectives, that sort of thing."

She was obviously intelligent, and she teaches English, whereas I don't, so maybe she knows a lot more about the language than I do. But I still have the strong opinion that knowing the difference between a preposition and an adjective is important and, in fact, that using a dictionary is easier if one knows that difference. I think, furthermore, that good writing is easier to master if one knows some of the labels. At least one should have a pretty good idea of what constitutes a sentence and of what subjects and predicates are.

Obviously, I'm the sort of queer duck that likes to discover even such obscure labels as *phrasal verb* and *adverbial particle*, so maybe I'm just prejudiced. Maybe all the while that I'm arguing the advantages of knowing the names of our linguistic tools, the fact is that labeling really blisses me out. —Thomas H. Middleton

Conventional Wisdoms

On dealing with the horrors of this world: I talk about them and try to work them into some kind of beauty. It is better not to ignore them, but make them less horrible by work, sweat, and blood, write them out like the few true stories that we made end well, and give the wisdom to another.

Sharks While Swimming

There is nothing innately frightening about sharks unless you are in the water with one.

"A Battle with the Horror of Life"

On December 20, 1967, Mr. and Mrs. Frank Boyd and Mr. and Mrs. James Williamson went swimming at the beach near Sarasota, Florida. It was eleven thirty-five P.M. There was a three-quarter moon. Mr. Williamson describes what happened:

Frank and Nora and I were treading water talking about the party, Bea had drifted off a little way. She was shy and hadn't wanted to come in. I heard her gasp and turned around to see her surface in a pool of phosphorescence. Nora said we should go to shore. I swam to Bea but she kept slipping out of my arms, yanked underwater by something stronger than us. She would come up again whining, thrashing, until I grabbed her arm and started to pull her toward shore. I felt something brush my leg and it began to sting. The only other thing I remember was the peculiar taste in the water. I carried her out onto the beach and gave her mouth-to-mouth resuscitation. The flesh was stripped from her leg. Frank ran up to the house to call an ambulance and find us all something to put on. Later a marine biologist came by the hospital and said he could tell from the positioning of the teeth marks that it was a tiger shark.

Whale and basking sharks are thirty or forty feet long and eat plankton. The others will eat almost anything, but they have different sized mouths. There are mako, mackerels, man-eaters, tigers, lemons, duskies, nurses, and others.

Each type of shark has its peculiarities of shape and size and behavioral pattern. The positive identification of a shark is best made after a close inspection of the teeth. The man-eater's teeth, for example, have serrated edges; the mako has a little cusp near the base of the denture, and the porbeagle has none—just its row of canines. The shark's teeth are so sharp that men bitten say they did not feel the first bite. The size of a shark bite depends on the size of the shark's mouth. A thirty-foot shark can take half a man.

Biologically, sharks are something between fish and mammal. Young sharks are born alive and immediately start operating like miniature reproductions of their parents. The mother offers no food or protection and, if hungry, may eat her young.

Anatomically, a shark has no swim bladder. This flotation device allows other fish to remain motionless in any space of water, but the shark must keep swimming or he will sink. So from birth until death he swims, dozing as he moves through protective waters, a fugitive from his own death.

Sharks are unpredictable. You can drag bait within inches of a shark's nose and he may ignore it. But if there is the slightest trickle of blood from the bait the shark will attack senselessly. On the open sea you can watch a shark intersect a blood trail. He can follow the trail to its inception, turn 180 degrees and come back the other way. Or he may come directly to your bait.

Torpedoed men sat in the water waiting for rescue while sharks ate them at leisure. In open seas it is suggested that you form groups with others in your own position, preferably excluding wounded or bleeding men, in hopes that, together, the shark will think you a larger animal than he. Men in such clusters have beat the water with their arms and legs and scared sharks off. Others have beat the water with their arms and legs and have been eaten. Once, a man scared away a shark by hitting him on the nose with an underwater camera. You can try to poke out the shark's eyes or dig your nails into his throat, but there is no reason to think this will do any good. You can pray.

According to a booklet issued PT-boat personnel, a man who finds himself in the water with a shark should grab the shark by the dorsal fin and ram a knife up under into the shark's stomach, drawing it backward to eviscerate. Now it is true that if you can slit a shark's stomach from end to end, its guts will fall out. But a blue shark has been observed calmly eating its own entrails. Shark hides were used by cabinet makers before sandpaper, and it is extremely hard to slit a shark's stomach even in a fish factory. In the water, as soon as a shark feels the knife tickle his stomach, he takes off like a shot to return from a different angle. It is better not to try to kill a shark if you are both in the water. The scent of blood, including his own, seems to increase his anger. It is best to have nothing to do with him. (Footnote: Shark Repellent: like a gas mask, something neither you nor I is likely to have if we need.)

There are deep-sea fishermen who cut bait if they get a shark on the line. Others deal with sharks in the following manner: bring the shark alongside, slip a knife into its gills and slice outward so the shark eventually bleeds to death (this method may attract other sharks like a multiplication of sins). Or slip a rope around the shark's tail and hoist him aloft so the stomach presses down on the shark's brain and frequently out of his mouth (this method may result in considerable damage to boat and onlookers, since it is dangerous to lift anything that large by the tail). Or put a good hook in the shark's mouth and hoist him aloft, strapping him around the middle to the mast.

Out of water it may take a shark six or seven hours to die. Man-eaters last longest. Some people shoot sharks, but it is an uncertain sport furthered by those who have lost parts of themselves or close relatives to the sharks of this world. A hit in the brain is the only sure kill, and the brain is exceedingly small, shaped rather like a wishbone. A three-inch naval gun will do the job if a direct hit is scored. One can wrap a hand grenade in beef with the fishline attached to the pull pin. But then the shark may swim toward you.

The truth of the matter is that, except for the occasional shark landed on a fishing boat or jostled by a depth charge, sharks are practically indestructible. Always moving, always hunting, like evil they assure the randomness and uncontrollability of life itself.

Afterthoughts: much of our horror of sharks comes from no shark at all but a dying cod flashed out of some fisherman's net. We fear the shark in ourselves, having gutted a friend, or slashed the innocence of young love, torn apart some opponent, or bite by bite teased our parents into skeletons. It is the quick gunmetal turn and darting of our own minds that rises up toward us in those night waters and threatens to discover our blood.

A friend says that most people in power are sharks. They play amid a school of dolphins.

A sand road runs outside my house back into the dunes, and footprints are soon blown over. There are primrose on either side, blueberry bushes, and on the field in back of the house there is a fishnet that fishermen left to dry years ago. Now the grass and blueberry bushes grow up through it, Queen Anne's lace, little snow flowers. A few buttercups lie amid the long grass. I don't pick them. They shine up from the green like bits of the sun. And the earth keeps pushing up her free treasure.—John Bart Gerald

A Day in Samoa

The life of the day begins at dawn, or if the moon has shown until daylight, the shouts of the young men may be heard before dawn from the hillside. Uneasy in the night, populous with ghosts, they shout lustily to one another as they hasten with their work. As the dawn begins to fall among the soft brown roofs and the slender palm trees stand out against a colourless, gleaming sea, lovers slip home from trysts beneath the palm trees or in the shadow of beached canoes, that the light may find each sleeper in his appointed place. Cocks crow, negligently, and a shrill-voiced bird cries from the breadfruit trees. The insistent roar of the reef seems muted to an undertone for the sounds of a waking village. Babies cry, a few short wails before sleepy mothers give them the breast. Restless little children roll out of their sheets and wander drowsily down to the beach to freshen their faces in the sea. Boys, bent upon an early fishing, start collecting their tackle and go to rouse their more laggard companions. Fires are lit, here and there, the white smoke hardly visible against the paleness of the dawn. The whole village, sheeted and frowsy, stirs, rubs its eyes, and stumbles towards the beach. "Talofa!" "Talofa!" "Will the journey start to-day?" "Is it bonito fishing your lordship is going?" Girls stop to giggle over some young ne'er-do-well who escaped during the night from an angry father's pursuit and to venture a shrewd guess that the daughter knew more about his presence than she told. The boy who is taunted by another, who has succeeded him in his sweetheart's favour, grapples with his rival, his foot slipping in the wet sand. From the other end of the village comes a long drawn-out, piercing wail. A messenger has just brought word of the death of some relative in another village. Half-clad, unhurried women, with babies at their breasts, or astride their hips, pause in their tale of Losa's outraged departure from her father's house to the greater kindness in the home of her uncle, to wonder who is dead. Poor relatives whisper their requests to rich relatives, men make plans to set a fish trap together, a woman begs a bit of yellow dye from a kinswoman, and through the village sounds the rhythmic tattoo which calls the young men together. They gather from all parts of the village, digging sticks in hand, ready to start inland to the plantation. The older men set off upon their more lonely occupations, and each household, reassembled under its peaked roof, settles down to the routine of the morning. Little children, too hungry to wait for the late breakfast, beg lumps of cold taro which they munch greedily. Women carry piles of washing to the sea or to the spring at the far end of the village, or set off inland after weaving materials. The older girls go fishing on the reef, or perhaps set themselves to weaving a new set of Venetian blinds.

In the houses, where the pebbly floors have been swept bare with a stiff long-handled broom, the women great with child and the nursing mothers, sit and gossip with one another. Old men sit apart, unceasingly twisting palm husk on their bare thighs and muttering old tales under their breath. The carpenters begin work on the new house, while the owner bustles about trying to keep them in a good humour. Families who will cook to-day are hard at work; the taro, yams and bananas have already been brought from inland; the children are scuttling back and forth, fetching sea water, or leaves to stuff the pig. As the sun rises higher in the sky, the shadows deepen under the thatched roofs, the sand is burning to the touch, the hibiscus flowers wilt on the hedges, and little children bid the smaller ones, "Come out of the sun." Those whose excursions have been short return to the village, the women with strings of crimson jelly fish, or baskets of shell fish, the men with cocoanuts, carried in baskets slung on a shoulder pole. The women and children eat their breakfasts, just hot from the oven, if this is cook day, and the young men work swiftly in the midday heat, preparing the noon feast for their elders.

It is high noon. The sand burns the feet of the little children, who leave their palm leaf balls and their pin-wheels of frangipani blossoms to wither in the sun, as they creep into the shade of the houses. The women who must go abroad carry great banana leaves as sun-shades or wind wet cloths about their heads. Lowering a few blinds against the slanting sun, all who are left in the village wrap their heads in sheets and go to sleep. Only a few adventurous children may slip away for a swim in the shadow of a high rock, some industrious woman continues with her weaving, or a close little group of women bend anxiously over a woman in labour. The village is dazzling and dead; any sound seems oddly loud and out of place. Words have to cut through the solid heat slowly. And then the sun gradually sinks over the sea. —Margaret Mead

No, It's Not Athlete's Foot

Everyone at some point in his life has felt a sinking feeling in the pit of his stomach. A sunny day turned dark, and he wished that the earth would swallow him. His eyes rolled towards the heavens, as he wondered why he had to go on living. This is not an illness from the medical journals. Nor is it a psychosis treated on the psychiatrist's couch. This strange ailment has afflicted man since he could open his mouth . . . and put his foot in it.

The symptoms described above refer to the sensation one gets after uttering the classic dumb remark. By this I mean the unintelligent response to an intelligent question, the overheard insult, et cetera. Since my mouth has more than one footprint in it, perhaps I should relate several examples of times I have wished I had never learned to talk.

When I was at camp one summer, my unit nominated me to try out for the camp advisory board. The senior members of the board interviewed me. I answered all their questions quite well—except the last one. They asked me what I thought could be done to improve the camp. My brilliant response was, "I can't think of anything now, but I'm sure I can think of something later." Immediately after I said it, I wished that I could take back the words, but it was too late. Needless to say, I was not selected for the advisory board.

The camp example only happened once, but the next incident has occurred on several occasions. Every time I am talking about someone behind his back, I find he is right behind me. At work I would say that one of the other employees was extremely slow, only to realize that she was standing beside me. Of course then I would pretend I knew she was there and make a big joke out of the situation.

My last example embarrassed me more than the other two combined. I was coming out of the drugstore one day when a girl passing by said, "Hi, [   ]."

I turned around, looked right at her, and said, "Hi, Diane."

With an odd look on her face, she said, "My name is Eileen!"

I had known her for over a year. I still do not know why I thought she was another girl I knew, but I cannot remember being more embarrassed. I made some polite conversation and, as quickly as I could, made my way to my car. When I got in, I just slumped down in the seat, put my head in my hands, and thought, "Why me? Why me?"

Other dumb actions cause the same sick feeling I had that day. Sleeping through an eight o'clock class or getting caught speeding gives one the same sensation. These feelings should be outlawed, as memories of them and their causes are painful and often darken brighter moments.

After many years, eighteen to be exact, of studying this problem, I have found one way to eliminate the illness: eliminate the cause. I do this by adhering to an old saying with a new twist. My motto is, "A closed mouth gathers no feet."—A student essay

Simplified Spelling

The first time I was in Egypt a Simplified Spelling epidemic had broken out and the atmosphere was electrical with feeling engendered by the subject. This was four or five thousand years ago—I do not remember just how many thousand it was, for my memory for minor details has suffered some decay in the lapse of years. I am speaking of a former state of existence of mine, perhaps my earliest reincarnation; indeed I think it was the earliest. I had been an angel previously, and I am expecting to be one again—but at the time I speak of I was different.

The Simplifiers had risen in revolt against the hieroglyphics. An uncle of Cadmus who was out of a job had come to Egypt and was trying to introduce the Phoenician alphabet and get it adopted in place of the hieroglyphics. He was challenged to show cause, and he did it to the best of his ability. The exhibition and discussion took place in the Temple of Astarte, and I was present. So also was the Simplified Committee, with Croesus as foreman of the Revolt—not a large man physically, but a simplified speller of acknowledged ability. The Simplifiers were few; the Opposition were multitudinous. The Khedive was the main backer of the Revolt, and this magnified its strength and saved it from being insignificant. Among the Simplifiers were many men of learning and distinction, mainly literary men and members of college faculties; but all ranks and conditions of men and all grades of intellect, erudition, and ignorance were represented in the Opposition.

As a rule the speeches on both sides were temperate and courteous, but now and then a speaker weakened his argument with personalities, the Revolters referring to the Opposition as fossils, and the Opposition referring to the Revolters as "those cads," a smart epithet coined out of the name of Uncle Cadmus.

Uncle Cadmus began with an object lesson, with chalk, on a couple of blackboards. On one of them he drew in outline a slender Egyptian in a short skirt, with slim legs and an eagle's head in place of a proper head, and he was carrying a couple of dinner pails, one in each hand. In front of this figure he drew a toothed line like an excerpt from a saw; in front of this he drew three skeleton birds of doubtful ornithological origin; in front of these he drew a partly constructed house, with lean Egyptians fetching materials in wheelbarrows to finish it with; next he put in some more unclassified birds; then a large king, with carpenter's shavings for whiskers and hair; next he put in another king jabbing a mongrel lion with a javelin; he followed this with a picture of a tower, with armed Egyptians projecting out of the top of it and as crowded for room as the cork in a bottle; he drew the opposing army below, fierce of aspect but much out of drawing as regards perspective. They were shooting arrows at the men in the tower, which was poor military judgment because they could have reached up and pulled them out by the scruff of the neck. He followed these pictures with line after line of birds and beasts and scraps of saw-teeth and bunches of men in the customary short frock, some of them doing things, the others waiting for the umpire to call game; and finally his great blackboard was full from top to bottom. Everybody recognized the invocation set forth by the symbols: it was the Lord's Prayer.

It had taken him forty-five minutes to set it down. Then he stepped to the other blackboard and dashed off "Our Father which art in heaven," and the rest of it, in graceful Italian script, spelling the words the best he knew how in those days, and finished it up in four minutes and a half.

It was rather impressive.

He made no comment at the time, but went to a fresh blackboard and wrote upon it in hieroglyphics:

"At this time the King possessed of cavalry 214,580 men and 222,631 horses for their use; of infantry 16,341 squadrons together with an emergency reserve of all arms, consisting of 84,946 men, 321 elephants, 37,264 transportation carts, and 28,954 camels and dromedaries."

It filled the board and cost him twenty-six minutes of time and labor. Then he repeated it on another blackboard in Italian script and Arabic numerals and did it in two minutes and a quarter. Then he said:

"My argument is before you. One of the objections to the hieroglyphics is that it takes the brightest pupil nine years to get the forms and their meanings by heart; it takes the average pupil sixteen years; it takes the rest of the nation all their days to accomplish it—it is a life sentence. This cost of time is much too expensive. It could be employed more usefully in other industries, and with better results.

"If you will renounce the hieroglyphics and adopt written words instead, an advantage will be gained. By you? No, not by you. You have spent your lives in mastering the hieroglyphics, and to you they are simple, and the effect pleasant to the eye, and even beautiful. You are well along in life; it would not be worth your while to acquire the new learning; the aspect of it would be unpleasant to you; you will naturally cling with affection to the pictured records which have become beautiful to you through habit and use, and which are associated in your mind with the moving legends and tales of our venerable past and the great deeds of our fathers, which they have placed before you indestructibly engraved upon stone. But I appeal to you in behalf of the generations which are to follow you, century after century, age after age, cycle after cycle. I pray you consider them and be generous. Lift this heavy burden from their backs. Do not send them toiling and moiling down to the twentieth century still bearing it, still oppressed by it. Let your sons and daughters adopt the words and the alphabet, and go free. To the youngest of them the hieroglyphics have no hallowed associations; the words and the alphabet will not offend their eyes; custom will quickly reconcile them to it, and then they will prefer it—if for no other reason, for the simple reason that they will have had no experience of any method of communication considered by others comelier or better. I pray you let the hieroglyphics go, and thus save millions of years of useless time and labor to fifty generations of posterity that are to follow you.

"Do I claim that the substitute which I am proposing is without defect? No. It has a serious defect. My fellow Revolters are struggling for one thing, and for one thing only—the shortening and simplifying of the spelling. That is to say, they have not gone to the root of the matter—and in my opinion the reform which they are urging is hardly worthwhile. The trouble is not with the spelling; it goes deeper than that; it is with the *alphabet*. There is but one way to scientifically and adequately reform the orthography, and that is by reforming the alphabet; then the orthography will reform itself. What is needed is that each letter of the alphabet shall have a perfectly definite sound, and that this sound shall never be changed or modified without the addition of an accent, or other visible sign, to indicate precisely and exactly the nature of the modification. The Germans have this kind of an alphabet. Every letter of it has a perfectly definite sound, and when that sound is modified an *umlaut* or other sign is added to indicate the precise shade of the modification. The several values of the German letters can be learned by the ordinary child in a few days, and after that, for ninety years, that child can always correctly spell any German word it hears, without ever having been taught to do it by another person, or being obliged to apply to a spelling book for help.

"But the English alphabet is a pure insanity. It can hardly spell any word in the language with any large degree of certainty. When you see the word *chaldron* in an English book no foreigner can guess how to pronounce it; neither can any native. The reader knows that it is pronounced *chaldron*—or *kaldron*, or *kawldron*—but neither he nor his grandmother can tell which is the right way without looking in the dictionary; and when he looks in the dictionary the chances are a hundred to one that the dictionary itself doesn't know which is the right way, but will furnish him all three and let him take his choice. When you find the word *bow* in an English book, standing by itself and without any informing text built around it, there is no American or Englishman alive, nor any dictionary, that can tell you how to pronounce that word. It may mean a gesture of salutation and rhyme with cow; and it may also mean an obsolete military weapon and rhyme with blow. But let us not enlarge upon this. The sillinesses of the English alphabet are quite beyond enumeration. That alphabet consists of nothing whatever except sillinesses. I venture to repeat that whereas the English orthography needs reforming and simplifying, the English alphabet needs it two or three million times more."

Uncle Cadmus sat down, and the Opposition rose and combated his reasonings in the usual way. Those people said that they had always been used to the hieroglyphics; that the hieroglyphics had dear and sacred associations for them; that they loved to sit on a barrel under an umbrella in the brilliant sun of Egypt and spell out the owls and eagles and alligators and saw-teeth, and take an hour and a half to the Lord's Prayer, and weep with romantic emotion at the thought that they had, at most, but eight or ten years between themselves and the grave for the enjoyment of this ecstasy; and that then possibly these Revolters would shove the ancient signs and symbols from the main track and equip the people with a lightning-express reformed alphabet that would leave the hieroglyphic wheelbarrow a hundred thousand miles behind and have not a damned association which could compel a tear, even if tears and diamonds stood at the same price in the market.—Mark Twain

On Gusto

Gusto in art is power or passion defining any object. It is not so difficult to explain this term in what relates to expression (of which it may be said to be the highest degree) as in what relates to things without expression, to the natural appearances of objects, as mere colour or form. In one sense, however, there is hardly any object entirely devoid of expression, without some character of power belonging to it, some precise association with pleasure or pain: and it is in giving this truth of character from the truth of feeling, whether in the highest or the lowest degree, but always in the highest degree of which the subject is capable, that gusto consists.

There is a gusto in the colouring of Titian. Not only do his heads seem to think—his bodies seem to feel. This is what the Italians mean by the *morbidezza* of his flesh-colour. It seems sensitive and alive all over; not merely to have the look and texture of flesh, but the feeling in itself. For example, the limbs of his female figures have a luxurious softness and delicacy, which appears conscious of the pleasure of the beholder. As the objects themselves in nature would produce an impression on the sense, distinct from every other object, and having something divine in it, which the heart owns and the imagination consecrates, the objects in the picture preserve the same impression, absolute, unimpaired, stamped with all the truth of passion, the pride of the eye, and the charm of beauty. Rubens makes his flesh-colour like flowers; Albano's is like ivory; Titian's is like flesh, and like nothing else. It is as different from that of other painters, as the skin is from a piece of white or red drapery thrown over it. The blood circulates here and there, the blue veins just appear, the rest is distinguished throughout only by that sort of tingling sensation to the eye, which the body feels within itself. This is gusto. Vandyke's flesh-colour, though it has great truth and purity, wants gusto. It has not the internal character, the living principle in it. It is a smooth surface, not a warm, moving mass. It is painted without passion, with indifference. The hand only has been concerned. The impression slides off from the eye, and does not, like the tones of Titian's pencil, leave a sting behind it in the mind of the spectator. The eye does not acquire a taste or appetite for what it sees. In a word, gusto in painting is where the impression made on one sense excites by affinity those of another.

Michael Angelo's forms are full of gusto. They everywhere obtrude the sense of power upon the eye. His limbs convey an idea of muscular strength, of moral grandeur, and even of intellectual dignity: they are firm, commanding, broad, and massy, capable of executing with ease the determined purposes of the will. His faces have no other expression than his figures, conscious power and capacity. They appear only to think what they shall do, and to know that they can do it. This is what is meant by saying that his style is hard and masculine. It is the reverse of Correggio's, which is effeminate. That is, the gusto of Michael Angelo consists in expressing energy of will without proportionable sensibility, Correggio's in expressing exquisite sensibility without energy of will. In Correggio's faces as well as figures we see neither bones nor muscles, but then what a soul is there, full of sweetness and of grace—pure, playful, soft, angelical! There is sentiment enough in a hand painted by Correggio to set up a school of history painters. Whenever we look at the hands of Correggio's women or of Raphael's, we always wish to touch them.

Again, Titian's landscapes have a prodigious gusto, both in the colouring and forms. We shall never forget one that we saw many years ago in the Orleans Gallery of Acteon hunting. It had a brown, mellow, autumnal look. The sky was of the colour of stone. The winds seemed to sing through the rustling branches of the trees, and already you might hear the twanging of bows resound through the tangled mazes of the wood. Mr West, we understand, has this landscape. He will know if this description of it is just. The landscape back-ground of the St Peter Martyr is another well known instance of the power of this great painter to give a romantic interest and an appropriate character to the objects of his pencil, where every circumstance adds to the effect of the scene,—the bold trunks of the tall forest trees, the trailing ground plants, with that tall convent spire rising in the distance, amidst the blue sapphire mountains and the golden sky.

Rubens has a great deal of gusto in his Fauns and Satyrs, and in all that expresses motion, but in nothing else. Rembrandt has it in everything; everything in his pictures has a tangible character. If he puts a diamond in the ear of a burgomaster's wife, it is of the first water; and his furs and stuffs are proof against a Russian winter. Raphael's gusto was only in expression; he had no idea of the character of anything but the human form. The dryness and poverty of his style in other respects is a phenomenon in the art. His trees are like sprigs of grass stuck in a book of botanical specimens. Was it that Raphael never had time to go beyond the walls of Rome? That he was always in the streets, at church, or in the bath? He was not one of the Society of Arcadians.*

Claude's landscapes, perfect as they are, want gusto. This is not

---

* Raphael not only could not paint a landscape; he could not paint people in a landscape. He could not have painted the heads or the figures, or even the dresses, of the St Peter Martyr. His figures have always an *in-door* look, that is, a set, determined, voluntary, dramatic character, arising from their own expression, which is connected with the accidents of nature and the changes of the elements. He has nothing *romantic* about him.

easy to explain. They are perfect abstractions of the visible images of things; they speak the visible language of nature truly. They resemble a mirror or a microscope. To the eye only they are more perfect than any other landscapes that ever were or will be painted; they give more of nature, as cognisable by one sense alone; but they lay an equal stress on all visible impressions. They do not interpret one sense by another; they do not distinguish the character of different objects as we are taught, and can only be taught, to distinguish them by their effect on the different senses. That is, his eye wanted imagination: it did not strongly sympathise with his other faculties. He saw the atmosphere, but he did not feel it. He painted the trunk of a tree or a rock in the foreground as smooth—with as complete an abstraction of the gross, tangible impression, as any other part of the picture. His trees are perfectly beautiful, but quite immovable; they have a look of enchantment. In short, his landscapes are unequalled imitations of nature, released from its subjection to the elements, as if all objects were become a delightful fairy vision, and the eye had rarefied and refined away the other senses.

The gusto in the Greek statues is of a very singular kind. The sense of perfect form nearly occupies the whole mind, and hardly suffers it to dwell on any other feeling. It seems enough for them *to be*, without acting or suffering. Their forms are ideal, spiritual. Their beauty is power. By their beauty they are raised above the frailties of pain or passion; by their beauty they are deified.

The infinite quantity of dramatic invention in Shakespear takes from his gusto. The power he delights to show is not intense, but discursive. He never insists on anything as much as he might, except a quibble. Milton has great gusto. He repeats his blows twice; grapples with and exhausts his subject. His imagination has a double relish of its objects, an inveterate attachment to the things he describes, and to the words describing them.

> – '*Or where Chineses drive*
> *With sails and wind their* cany *waggons* light.'
> . . . .
> '*Wild above rule or art,* enormous *bliss.*'

There is a gusto in Pope's compliments, in Dryden's satires, and Prior's tales; and among prose writers Boccaccio and Rabelais had the most of it. We will only mention one other work which appears to us to be full of gusto, and that is the *Beggar's Opera*. If it is not, we are altogether mistaken in our notions on this delicate subject.—William Hazlitt

Death in the Afternoon

From observation I would say that people may possibly be divided into two general groups; those who, to use one of the terms of the jargon of psychology, identify themselves with, that is, place themselves in the position of, animals, and those who identify themselves with human beings. I believe, after experience and observation, that those people who identify themselves with animals, that is, the almost professional lovers of dogs, and other beasts, are capable of greater cruelty to human beings than those who do not identify themselves readily with animals. It seems as though there were a fundamental cleavage between people on this basis although people who do not identify themselves with animals may, while not loving animals in general, be capable of great affection for an individual animal, a dog, a cat, or a horse for instance. But they will base this affection on some quality of, or some association with, this individual animal rather than on the fact that it is an animal and hence worthy of love. For myself, I have felt profound affection for three different cats, four dogs, that I remember, and only two horses; that is horses that I have owned, ridden or driven. As for horses that I have followed, watched race and bet on I have had profound admiration and, when I had bet money on them, almost affection for a number of these animals; the ones that I remember best being Man of War, Exterminator, I believe I honestly had affection for him, Epinard, Kzar, Heros XII, Master Bob, and a half-bred horse, a steeplechaser like the last two, named Uncas. I had great, great admiration for all of those animals, but how much of my affection was due to the sums staked I do not know. Uncas, when he won a classic steeplechase race at Auteuil at odds of better than ten to one, carrying my money on him, I felt profound affection for. But if you should ask me what eventually happened to this animal that I was so fond of that Evan Shipman and I were nearly moved to tears when speaking of the noble beast, I would have to answer that I do not know. I do know that I do not love dogs as dogs, horses as horses, or cats as cats.—Ernest Hemingway

Judo Is a Sport

Judo was not intended to be self-defense. The originator of judo, Dr. Jigaro Kano, was a college professor interested in physical education; he conceived of sport judo as the perfect physical development activity. Dr. Kano's own writing on the subject of judo indicates clearly that this is so.

Throwing techniques of judo are very inefficient for street defense; unless they are preceded by weakening and distracting techniques, they are much too difficult to apply. As shown in photo 2, the defender must come into fist range of his adversary to attempt his throw. Present day proponents of judo for self-defense, who insist that a highly skilled, very quick, judo-trained person can apply a throw before getting punched, are making a claim which flatly contradicts Dr. Kano's concepts.

Moreover, in basic self-defense we cannot expect to reach the high level of proficiency which is suggested as a requirement for using throws; if it could be reached, that high level of skill could not be *maintained* without constant practice.

Sport judo is a wonderful sport; there are easier, effective techniques for self-defense.

The traditional forms of fighting bear little relationship to actual situations with which you might be confronted on the street. Neither judo training nor traditional karate would prepare you for back attacks, gang attacks, weapon attacks, or many other common attacks.

The situations shown in photos 3 and 4 simply do not occur in contest. Students who train in tournament-oriented forms of judo and karate may study for many months without ever being taught defenses against common street attacks.—Bruce Tegner, *Self-Defense for Boys and Men*

An Era of Mousing Intrigue

An Easy Chair, and especially an old Easy Chair, may indulge its harmless fancies and dream dreams at its pleasure. And in that mood this Easy Chair often thinks of the amazement with which some of the simpler earlier fathers of the republic would look upon spectacles which have become so familiar to us that they are either unnoted or regarded as natural and necessary political phenomena. The republic that our fathers established was a rural republic, with the simple virtues of a simple people. Among the simple beliefs of the fathers was the conviction that if the community wished the services of any citizen, it would ask him to serve them. But that a man should propose himself as the man that the community wanted was not the practice. Political ambition was not unknown, for the race was English. But that George Washington ever offered himself as a proper person to fill any position; that he besought people to vote for him; that he sent for them, or went to them, and argued, cajoled, and implored them to give him an office; that he opened headquarters at a tavern, and established literary bureaus to praise him, and hired agents to urge his candidacy by writing and appealing and proclaiming—all this is not recorded.

John Jay was the second Governor of New York. His political friends earnestly and skillfully did all that they could to secure his election. They appealed to every motive which influences voters under such circumstances. Some votes even may have been bought for him with money, although there is no record of any such transaction, nor is such bribery any worse than bribery by the offer of place, which in this instance, and so far as Mr. Jay was concerned, was out of the question. But if Mr. Jay had busied himself to elect himself, if he had "buttonholed" and whispered and flattered, if he had done anything but pursue steadily the regular order of his life, willing to serve the people as Governor if the majority desired it, and not otherwise, he would not have been the John Jay whom Daniel Webster praised more than he praised any other man. If John Jay had undertaken in any other way than by frank and able discussion of public questions, and by plain declarations of his opinions, to persuade a majority to vote for him, he would have lost his self-respect and the reverence in which his memory is held.

Is it possible to suppose Washington and Jay—had they been Senators of the United States—when their terms were about expiring, leaving their seats in the Senate, hastening back to the capitals of their States, where the Legislature was to choose their successors, opening headquarters at a hotel, holding a kind of court in it, condescending to low arts, drawing a voter, who was to be propitiated, away from a chamber-maid's slop closet, lest some eavesdropper should be hidden in it to hear what he could—an incident in such a contest which the Easy Chair knew—and recommending themselves to voters by methods which as gentlemen they must have scorned? Such conduct in Washington and Jay is inconceivable. Such a spectacle at the beginning of the government of the United States under the Constitution would have been regarded as evidence that the system was rotten before it was ripe. Perhaps Washington and Jay were altogether too good for this world. But if a republic has no place for such men, what is it good for?

Times and methods have changed. The office of Governor sought John Jay, as that of President sought George Washington. In our time, however, the man seeks the office. At this point let not the incautious reader suppose that the Easy Chair is becoming querulous and ideally exigent, or that it secretly pines for an Oriental despotism. Do we denounce a lofty and patriotic political ambition? Do we demand an austere and impossible virtue? Do we mean to say that a man with the instinct and power of leadership shall not aspire to lead? Do we hint that in a self-governing state the desire to mould its decrees or to direct their execution is an unworthy and mean desire?

Far from it. Nothing is more natural, nothing more admirable, than the aspiration of good and capable men to lead men and to govern great states. But honorable objects must be honorably sought. A man with a true political ambition, with the instinct of leadership, advocates wise measures, and, by the power which belongs to the instinct, impresses his views upon the minds of others. He leads by natural ascendency, and they naturally and gladly follow. So Washington led. So Jay was a leader. But the modern system of a "still hunt," of private, illicit influence upon those whose votes elect to high place, of mousing intrigue, of bargain and barter and corruption, is not only dishonorable, but it is destructive of the essential principle of the government. The majority must rule. But only an honest majority can rule justly. To open headquarters at a capital in order to procure votes not by personal preference founded upon knowledge of character and of a career, but by private solicitation and representation and trade, and so to secure a majority, is to cheat the people and to caricature the popular principle. A majority so obtained is not a moral majority. It is not only not binding, it is to be repudiated as a crime against the people.

What was good enough for Jay and Washington, ought to be good enough for us.—*Harper's*, "Editor's Easy Chair" February 1882

Borstal Boy

The bed was wooden bench with a pillow of the same material, but I had three blankets.

I lay down, wrapped myself in the blankets, but the pillow was too much for me. I reversed, putting my feet on the pillow, with my head resting on my jacket. The pillow was too hard for my feet, and it strained my ankles, keeping them there. Then I wanted to use the lavatory. It was in a corner from the door. I stood over it, my bare toes on the cold concrete floor. As I stood, waiting over the lavatory, I heard a church bell peal in the frosty night, in some other part of the city. Cold and lonely it sounded, like the dreariest noise that ever defiled the ear of man. If you could call it a noise. It made misery mark time.

I got back on my bench, coiled myself up, so that my feet avoided the wooden pillow, in some comfort, and realized my doom. Even if I got away with a few years only, on account of my age, it was for ever. It wasn't even possible that Monday should come, when at least I'd get a walk up the stairs. The clock was not made that would pass the time between now and Monday morning. It was like what we were told about the last day, "Time is, time was, time is no more." And Jesus Christ, even now, I was only locked up ten minutes.

I put my mind on other things. It was at least and at last permissible to a man in my position.

Then I settled myself more comfortably and wondered if anyone else had done it in the same position. I didn't like to mention them by name, even in my mind. Some of them had left the cell for the rope or the firing squad. More pleasantly tired, from the exercise, I fell asleep.

Waking, I felt the hardness of my resting-place. I didn't wonder where I was. I knew that all right. I looked up at the grey light, through the barred windows, and remembered it better. A blunt and numbing pain it is, to wake up in a cell for the first time. I consoled myself, comparing it to the greater horror, surprise and indignation of a condemned man waking up the morning of his execution.

I lay for a while, and wondered if they would take me to court this morning. Maybe I'd be shifted to prison in the afternoon.

There were noises of key-jangling and door-banging. I hoped they would open my door. Even if they were distributing nothing better than kicks or thumps, I'd prefer not to be left out, in my cold shroud of solitude. Fighting is better than loneliness.—Brendan Behan

Music Lovers' Field Companion

I have come to the conclusion that much can be learned about music by devoting oneself to the mushroom. For this purpose I have recently moved to the country. Much of my time is spent poring over "field companions" on fungi. These I obtain at half price in second-hand bookshops, which latter are in some rare cases next door to shops selling dog-eared sheets of music, such an occurrence being greeted by me as irrefutable evidence that I am on the right track.

The winter for mushrooms, as for music, is a most sorry season. Only in caves and houses where matters of temperature and humidity, and in concert halls where matters of trusteeship and box office are under constant surveillance, do the vulgar and accepted forms thrive. American commercialism has brought about a grand deterioration of the *Psalliota campestris*, affecting through exports even the European market. As a demanding gourmet sees but does not purchase the marketed mushroom, so a lively musician reads from time to time the announcements of concerts and stays quietly at home. If, energetically, *Collybia velutipes* should fruit in January, it is a rare event, and happening on it while stalking in a forest is almost beyond one's dearest expectations, just as it is exciting in New York to note that the number of people attending a winter concert requiring the use of one's faculties is on the upswing (1954: 129 out of 12,000,000; 1955: 136 out of 12,000,000).

In the summer, matters are different. Some three thousand different mushrooms are thriving in abundance, and right and left there are Festivals of Contemporary Music. It is to be regretted, however, that the consolidation of the acquisitions of Schoenberg and Stravinsky, currently in vogue, has not produced a single new mushroom. Mycologists are aware that in the present fungous abundance, such as it is, the dangerous *Amanitas* play an extraordinarily large part. Should not program chairmen, and music-lovers in general, come the warm months, display some prudence?

I was delighted last fall (for the effects of summer linger on, viz. Donaueschingen, C. D. M. I., etc.) not only to revisit in Paris my friend the composer Pierre Boulez, rue Beautreillis, but also to attend the Exposition du Champignon, rue de Buffon. A week later in Cologne, from my vantage point in a glass-encased control booth, I noticed an audience dozing off, throwing, as it were, caution to the winds, though present at a loud-speaker-emitted program of *Elektronische Musik*. I could not help recalling the riveted attention accorded another loud-speaker, rue de Buffon, which delivered on the hour a lecture describing mortally poisonous mushrooms and means for their identification.

But enough of the contemporary musical scene; it is well known. More important is to determine what are the problems confronting the contemporary mushroom. To begin with, I propose that it should be determined which sounds further the growth of which mushrooms; whether these latter, indeed, make sounds of their own; whether the gills of certain mushrooms are employed by appropriately small-winged insects for the production of *pizzicati* and the tubes of the *Boleti* by minute burrowing ones as wind instruments; whether the spores, which in size and shape are extraordinarily various, and in number countless, do not on dropping to the earth produce gamelan-like sonorities; and finally, whether all this enterprising activity which I suspect delicately exists, could not, through technological means, be brought, amplified and magnified, into our theatres with the net result of making our entertainments more interesting.

What a boon it would be for the recording industry (now part of America's sixth largest) if it could be shown that the performance, while at table, of an LP of Beethoven's *Quartet Opus Such-and-Such* so alters the chemical nature of *Amanita muscaria* as to render it both digestible and delicious!

Lest I be found frivolous and light-headed and, worse, an "impurist" for having brought about the marriage of the agaric with Euterpe, observe that composers are continually mixing up music with something else. Karlheinz Stockhausen is clearly interested in music and juggling, constructing as he does "global structures," which can be of service only when tossed in the air; while my friend Pierre Boulez, as he revealed in a recent article (*Nouvelle Revue Française*, November 1954), is interested in music and parentheses and *italics*! This combination of interests seems to me excessive in number. I prefer my own choice of the mushroom. Furthermore it is avant-garde.

I have spent many pleasant hours in the woods conducting performances of my silent piece, transcriptions, that is, for an audience of myself, since they were much longer than the popular length which I have had published. At one performance, I passed the first movement by attempting the identification of a mushroom which remained successfully unidentified. The second movement was extremely dramatic, beginning with the sounds of a buck and a doe leaping up to within ten feet of my rocky podium. The expressivity of this movement was not only dramatic but unusually sad from my point of view, for the animals were frightened simply because I was a human being. However, they left hesitatingly and fittingly within the structure of the work. The third movement was a return to the theme of the first, but with all those profound, so-well-known alterations of world feeling associated by German tradition with the A-B-A.

In the space that remains, I would like to emphasize that I am not interested in the relationships between sounds and mushrooms any more than I am in those between sounds and other sounds. These would involve an introduction of logic that is not only out of place in the world, but time-consuming. We exist in a situation demanding greater earnestness, as I can testify, since recently I was hospitalized after having cooked and eaten experimentally some *Spathyema foetida*, commonly known as skunk cabbage. My blood pressure went down to fifty, stomach was pumped, etc. It behooves us therefore to see each thing directly as it is, be it the sound of a tin whistle or the elegant *Lepiota procera*.—John Cage

Occasions and Choices

Letters

Reports

Arguments

Critical Writing

Part Two

Occasions for Writing

12

Occasions and Choices

What are the occasions for writing? They are, of course, as various as we are, but often the occasion governs what we can do. This chapter says some general things about occasions, and then talks about

1. writing for a particular occasion, how the author makes turns and decisions (p. 322);

2. some of the categories and occasions you are likely to encounter, and how writing varies because of the occasion (p. 326); and

3. how you can use patterns other writers have used, for both similar and different occasions (p. 338).

The chapters before this one are grouped, you will recall, under the heading "The Process of Writing." As it is described in those first eleven chapters, this process is not a neat and systematic series of steps. It is, instead, a meditative, perpetually recycling, self-nurturing process. All its parts and stages feed and foster each other. When you are willing to invent, to explore thoroughly and thoughtfully, then you begin to know more structures and styles to work with, and when you learn more structures and styles, then the range of your inventive explorations stretches farther. Sometimes the process works swiftly. Sometimes it is slow and halting. Sometimes it comes to a complete stop. Sometimes it seems impossible to get started. Relatively few writers, indeed, ever declare that they are perfectly comfortable and content while they are writing.

The trouble is that sometimes you may have to write when there is little or no time available for reflection and trial efforts. The obligations and opportunities of work in college and in business may call for you to produce particular forms of writing—letters, budget justifications, reports on work in progress, critical studies, research reports, or others.

When this happens, the process of writing, as it is described in the first eleven chapters, may in some ways be modified. The process described in the earlier chapters calls for very nearly continual choice—*you* determine what is to be said, and *you* determine how to say it. Even in writing where you are completely free to do what you wish, however, choices begin to be limited as you begin to decide what and how to write. Ordinarily, for example, when you decide to write an essay, then you no longer have the opportunity to write a lyric poem. Any decision you make about your writing influences and customarily limits the choices that can be made thereafter. When you write *The* to start a sentence, you still have all kinds of choices open to you, but when you add the next word, let's say *car* for example, you eliminate some possibilities. If you have a sentence that begins with *The car*, you probably can't expect to use a verb such as *walked* or *read*.

When you have a particular assignment, that means that some choice has already been made (by an instructor, for example, or by requirements of work). From even before the start, this kind of writing has an end in view. Suppose, for example, that you work for a company that manufactures ball-point pens, and that you are responsible for developing a new retracting mechanism to fit a revolutionary new ink capsule and point for these pens. Company officials want to start making the new ink capsule and point soon, so they ask you for a *progress report* on the development of the retracting mechanism. The nature of this writing assignment restricts the choices you have open to you; certain expectations already exist about what you will write. If you are going to give what is asked for, for example, your report will have to include, at a minimum, an account of the work that has already been done, an explanation of what work is yet to be done, a proposed plan for getting the work done, and a forecast of the completion date. And other expectations already exist: the officials who asked for the report probably expect that it will be succinct, forthright, and prompt.

The process described in the first eleven chapters still operates, however, even in this kind of relatively restricted writing assignment. You still have to discover what needs to be said (Chapters 1 – 5), arrange and develop the material (Chapters 6 – 7), and say it in the most appropriate way (Chapters 8 – 10). The process is modified only in the sense that you probably don't have as many choices open to you at each stage as you would, for example, if you were writing something for your own pleasure.

On particular occasions, in other words, you are asked to accept choices that have already been made, and to develop your writing within the dimensions set by the prior choices. If you are asked to write a critical essay, for example, you still have considerable liberty, but if you wish to respond to that prior choice—that this piece of writing will be a critical essay—then you probably have to give up any wild impulse to write a sonnet. You're still at liberty, of course, to write the sonnet, but you should know that it may be rejected because it is not a critical essay.

The chapters following this one are about forms of writing done to satisfy the requirements and expectations of particular occasions and assignments. In most cases, somebody (you, or a teacher, or a work supervisor) or something (course or work requirements, for example) has made a prior choice. When you know what the prior choice is, when you know what end is in view, then you begin to know what kinds of choices to make in order to satisfy the requirements and to fulfill the opportunities of the occasion.

No text, of course, can provide guides for all the possible kinds of writing that you may need or wish to do. In the remainder of this chapter, you'll find (1) a short account of a particular writing assignment and the choices, possibilities, and limitations it presented for the writer; (2) a display of some categories of writing that may help you to anticipate and differentiate among occasions for writing; and (3) some suggestions for using patterns in writing that other people have used successfully. In the remaining chapters of this section, you'll find suggested plans and possibilities for doing some particular kinds of writing—letters, reports, research writing, arguments, and critical essays.

WRITING FOR A PARTICULAR OCCASION

Any piece of writing gives you some freedom of choice as you write, even if it is done to meet a specified assignment. If you don't have freedom in choosing a subject, for example, then you have freedom in the ways you think about the subject. If you don't have complete freedom in the ways you can think about the subject, then you have freedom in the way you organize what you're saying. If you don't have complete freedom in the way you can organize your thoughts on paper (if, for example, you are writing a particular kind of report with designated sections), then you have freedom to shape the sentences and to choose the words. No one wants you to abandon your own personality and convictions in order to write a particular assignment or to fulfill a job requirement.

Still, it's worth remembering that jobs do have to get done and on particular occasions specific requirements have to be satisfied. These requirements may mean that you will need to investigate carefully to determine what should be done, what can be done, what must be done, and to learn what is expected of the writing you will do.

It may be helpful to you to consider a specific case in which a writing assignment was given. In this case, the writer had to meet certain conditions in the assignment, and the occasion for which the writing was done made certain demands.

In most businesses, it is customary to honor in some way employees about to retire. High-school and college graduating classes often honor a class sponsor or special advisor. At such occasions a special citation for the honored person is read, and perhaps a gift is presented. In fact, the popular "roasts" of entertainment celebrities and politicians include humorous "citations" of the same sort. The specific assignment in this instance, then, is a retirement citation for an employee of a university library, and the specific occasion is that the citation will be read and presented at a retirement dinner.

The nature of the assignment and of the occasion established limits to what the writer could do. Certain conditions had to be met in the assignment, and the occasion made certain demands. Consider some of them.

1.   The citation had to be of such length, no more than 250 words, that it could be engraved on a certificate.

2.   Though no one expected the writer to lie, it was expected that the citation would praise the retiring person; if praise did not seem to be in order, then it was expected that the citation would register the University's gratitude for service rendered.

3.   The citation was to be read aloud at the dinner; then the certificate on which it was printed was to be given to the retiring person.

4.   If the citation was to mean anything at all, it had to contain more than some general statement of gratitude; it had to express gratitude in a particular way appropriate to the work the retiring person had done—the message had to be personally appropriate, but suitable to be read aloud at a formal dinner.

All of these conditions and demands existed before the writer ever began work, and each of them created other needs.

The length limit, for example, required that the writer exclude most details of the retiring person's life and focus instead on a few qualities and characteristics. The piece couldn't be long, not over 250 words, but it couldn't be much shorter than that, either, lest the citation be thought skimpy. The occasion—a dinner at which the citation was read aloud to a fairly large group—required that the passage be readable, that is, that its sentences not be too gnarled and knotty and hard for a reader to read or for an audience to follow. Other conditions and limits no doubt existed at the outset.

At any rate, the piece below was one of the citations produced for the occasion. The sentences are numbered for later reference.

Melinda Green

(1) A library cataloger always works away from public view. (2) The circumstances of a cataloger's daily work are, therefore, best known only by near colleagues. (3) Those who worked with Melinda Green, who saw every day the form and quality of her work, prize her for her deep loyalty to the University, for her commitment to her profession, for the exemplary character of her librarianship: the initials MG on a catalog card, her colleagues knew, meant that excellence and accuracy of the highest order had been at work.

(4) But if a library cataloger's work is shut away from public view, its results are not. (5) They rest exposed to public view, every day for generations; and it is just here that the University community owes its particular respect to Melinda Green. (6) We forget at times that the library cataloger, too, is at the center of the educational process. (7) A resource that is not available is not a resource; a book that cannot be reached offers no learning. (8) For twenty-two years Melinda Green has served us all: She has helped to make learning public; she has put books in our hands. (9) We are grateful to her for her care.

All of the limitations and conditions mentioned above were *antecedent* and *exterior* to the writing. That is, the subject, the occasion, the audience, the length, and some of the character of the writing were already determined ahead of time, and were not in question. But as the writer began work on this particular piece, certain *interior* problems and limitations also presented themselves.

In the first place, the writer did not know the retiring person well, and so had to rely upon what could be learned from personnel files and from talking with her friends and colleagues. One of them said, midway in a conversation, almost exactly what appears as the final part of the third sentence in the citation, indicating that her initials on a card were enough to assure everyone of accuracy. That struck the writer as a signal of both high-level professionalism and colleague respect.

That's where the *interior* problems and limitations began to occur. The writer felt, reasonably enough, that he couldn't open the citation by talking about the initials on a card. He wanted to make that point, but he felt that in order to say that, he first had to create a context in which it could appear. Sentence 1 and sentence 2, then, seemed necessary to establish Melinda Green's working context. What the writer wanted to say later, in other words, set demands upon him in what he could say earlier.

Then another demand occurred. The relatively restrained praise of the third sentence was just and accurate, but it did not seem sufficient because it only expressed the praise of close colleagues—it did not connect Green and her work with the rest of the university community. It seemed important to say how her work mattered to others and not just to immediate co-workers. The writer, accordingly, shifted direction slightly in sentence 4 to introduce what there was in her work that reached others, though she herself remained hidden. Once that was done, sentence 4 allowed the writer to go on with the rest of the citation.

Please remember that I am not trying to make any claim for the worth of this short piece, but only to show how a writer sometimes has to work under both exterior and interior limitations and expectations. Some settings and some work requirements will have formal patterns you must follow and expectations you must fulfill in your writing. There is no discredit in conforming your work to reasonable, established requirements.

Exercises

1.   Your campus newspaper, say, has decided it focuses too much on the "celebrities" on campus and wants to try to remedy that by doing a series of sketches about the people who make up the majority of the university or college—those who contribute to campus life but are never "featured." The editors of the paper have called upon your composition class, because you are exemplary writers, to provide these sketches. Here are the instructions:
   a.   The sketch must be no more than 200 words.
   b.   The writer should briefly introduce the person and then focus on the unique way the person contributes to the college.
   c.   The information should be appropriate for publication.
       Write one of these sketches.

2.   A friend of yours who is applying for resident advisor of his or her dormitory asks you to write a letter of recommendation for him or her and gives the required form to you. After checking the appropriate box behind a series of items, you encounter these directions:
       "Below in the space provided write a concise summary of the applicant's particular qualifications to be a resident advisor."
       The space provided gives you room for about one hundred words. Write the summary.

SOME CATEGORIES AND OCCASIONS

No one can anticipate all the kinds of writing you may do, or all the possible occasions on which you'll do it. It may be helpful, however, to consider some simple ways of differentiating among kinds of writing. It will be useful, at least, if it helps you to remember that different kinds of writing have different purposes, they have different possibilities, and they serve on different occasions.

You may remember some simple distinctions from earlier portions of this book—from the discussion of purpose in Chapter 3, from the discussion of audience in Chapters 4 and 5, and from the discussion of methods of development in Chapter 7. These are the kinds of writing that recur in all different occasions:

Personal writing: writing in which the author expresses himself or herself, as in diaries, letters, some poems, with no other end in view and perhaps with no audience in mind

Referential writing: writing that refers to or is about something other than the author, as in many reports and other forms of explanatory writing

Active writing: writing that wants to do something, to move or change or persuade an audience

Narrative writing: writing that records a sequence of events

Descriptive writing: writing that wants to enable readers to see something as the author has seen it

Expository writing: writing that sets out to explain something

Argumentative writing: see *active writing* above, writing that presents a belief for acceptance, or repudiates other beliefs, or examines various positions in order to present the most preferable

By looking at these in some other ways, you can get an interesting sense of various types of writing and of various occasions on which you do different kinds of writing. But remember that the categories of writing and occasions for writing suggested in the chart on the next page are not terribly important in their own right; they are useful if they help you see needs and possibilities in what you write.

The chart is not in any way a complete representation of occasions and types of writing. There are far more categories than shown in this configuration, and within each category there are far more specific kinds of writing. Obviously there are many kinds of writing other than those listed here.

Just as obviously, the system of classification used in the chart does not always work neatly. For example, the chart does not indicate that

	Narrative	Descriptive	Expository	Argumentative

Personal writing	autobiography
	family history
	diaries
	letters
	personal
	  reminiscence
	tall tales
	anecdotes
	letters to editors
	regional history
	travel writing
		autobiography
		reminiscence
		travel writing
		family, regional
		  history
		diaries
		familiar essays
			social commentary
			family, regional
			  history
			political speech
			letters to
			  editors
			letters of
			  application,
			  acceptance,
			  refusal
			literary
			  criticism
				political discussions
				social commentary
				cultural criticism
				literary criticism
				sermons
				position papers
				letters to editors

Referential writing	historical writing
	letters of
	  information
	background
	  studies
	critiques
	social, cultural
	  commentary
	process
	  explanations
	instructions
	progress reports
	biography
		progress reports
		lab reports
		biography
		letters of
		  recommendation
		introductions
		designs, plans
		briefings
			literary
			  criticism
			social, cultural
			  commentary
			historical
			  writing
			legal writing
			briefings
			critiques
				literary criticism
				social, cultural
				  commentary
				political discourse
				historical writing
				sermons
				proposals

Active writing	committee reports
	historical writing
	legal writing
	political writing
		committee reports
		proposals,
		  campaigns
		letters of
		  recommendation
			progress reports
			committee
			  reports
			briefings
				position papers
				sermons
				political discourse
				social criticism

different works may have different time orientations, and sometimes the time orientation shifts within a single piece of writing. In a single (referential) progress report, for instance, you may have to explain what has already been done on a given project (expository past), describe the current state of the project (descriptive present), and tell what is going to happen in the future (narrative future). Or you may be required to explain what has already taken place (referential past), tell what is going on at the moment (narrative present), and justify what you think ought to happen next (active future).

Still, while the system of classification used in the chart is not tidy and final, seeing the categories may help you remember variations in writing assignments, their possibilities, and the expectations you may need to meet.

Any shift in focus may present new possibilities. When the focus of the writing is *personal*, you probably have a considerable liberty to explore, to speculate, to muse. Authentic observation and good, honest reporting of first-hand experience are important. In personal writing, you may be trying, more than anything else, to come to terms with your own experience. In *referential* writing, on the other hand, your first concern is with something outside yourself, and you may need to concentrate on making a clear, accessible, intelligent message that readers can follow easily. And when you turn to *active* writing, there may be other concerns not so common in the other types: you turn to look at an audience, to consider their possible reactions, to consider whether anything you say can make a difference.

And of course there are other ways of seeing the different occasions that make different choices possible in your writing. Leo Rockas, in *Modes of Rhetoric*, classified forms of writing according to the dominant means of procedure:

> *Static*: In description and definition, for example, change and passing time are relatively unimportant. Static forms focus on something as it is at a given time, frozen and fixed. That makes it possible for the writer to linger over details, images, and clarifications.

> *Temporal*: In narration and process, for example, change and passing time are particularly important. Temporal forms focus on something happening in time, going through a sequence. That allows the writer to concentrate on pacing, tempo, and change.

> *Mimetic*: These forms exist by imitating the actions and words of people. In drama and dialogue, for example, the focus is on the sound and interaction of human voices and on the sequence of human actions.

> *Mental*: In revery and persuasion, for example, the focus is on clarification of the writer's own state of mind and on expression of the writer's own view.

In *The Attitudes of Rhetoric*, Winston Weathers and Otis Winchester classified forms of writing according to writers' attitudes towards their subjects and audiences. They concluded that attitude influences the choices of strategies that carry a message to an audience, and proposed nine different kinds of writing classified according to attitude:

> Confident writing
> Judicious writing
> Quiet writing
> Imperative writing
> Impassioned writing
> Compassionate writing
> Critical writing
> Angry writing
> Absurd writing

James Moffett, in *Teaching the Universe of Discourse*, classified forms of writing according to the distance in time and space between the speaker and the listener:

> *Reflection*: Intrapersonal communication between two parts of one nervous system (as in a journal or an interior monologue, where, as in a novel, we hear what is in a speaker's mind)
>
> *Conversation*: Interpersonal communication between two people in vocal range
>
> *Correspondence*: Interpersonal communication between remote individuals or small groups with some personal knowledge of each other
>
> *Publication*: Impersonal communication to a large anonymous group extended over space and/or time

Exercise

The passages below were all written to satisfy different requirements. Examine them to distinguish variations in occasion, purpose, direction, and focus, and to see how these variations are accompanied by changes in the character of the writing.

After discussing the occasion, purpose, and audience of the passages with your classmates, choose two of the passages and write a paper comparing their purposes and styles.

The American Woman in Sport

The emergent pattern of women's sport went through three distinct periods. The first, or early period is basically a nineteenth century phenomenon. The second period came to fruition in the "golden decade" of 1925–1935. The third period is the contemporary era, now flourishing in the 1970s.

Essentially, sport for women in nineteenth century America can be characterized as follows. Initially the acceptable activities were relatively few in number. Croquet, archery, bowling, tennis and golf were the primary sports, though a few women played baseball, rowed, and participated in track and field competitively. Vigorous activities were not developed for women, nor for most men. The clothing did not permit much movement and those who engaged in sport were typically gentlemen and gentlewomen who had no taste for hard effort and were content to engage in that which was readily available to them. Sports were chosen which could be performed without acquiring an indelicate sweat.

The primary purpose of sport or early physical recreation seemed to be the opportunity for a respectable social encounter. In an age of Puritanical sexual morality, it gave men and women something to do together. Therefore physical activities, including competitive sports, were most often conducted in a coeducational setting. Since the skill level and effort was not high for either sex, it was feasible for men and women to compete with one another individually or in couples.

The activities were chiefly of an outdoor nature, indoor facilities not having been constructed on any large scale. This of course placed further restrictions on the development of new activities and also affected the participation levels. Sport was essentially an activity of the upper classes, those who had leisure and the finances to belong to clubs which had facilities for playing. Municipal and federal governments had not yet developed facilities for the common people, though croquet and bicycling were two physical activities in which the masses could and did participate.

Activities were almost always of the individual sport type. Only when the colleges began to develop programs of physical activity for women did the team sports develop. However, that phenomenon did not occur until close to the end of the century. Prior to that time sports in the colleges were similar to those in the larger social environment. The colleges were also responsible for influencing a change from coeducational sport to separate sport for men and women. Probably this was due—at least in part—to the advent of physical education programs, which required dress and activities that the women teachers thought were best performed in female seclusion.

By the late twenties the nature of women's sport had undergone considerable change. The number of available activities had increased greatly. In addition to the earlier activities, large numbers of women played basketball, volleyball, and softball. Field hockey, lacrosse, polo, speedboat and sailboat racing, squash, badminton, fencing, swimming, diving, skiing, figure skating, speed skating, bobsledding, and aviation all had their adherents, though in limited numbers. The activities were far more vigorous than heretofore and sometimes dangerous.

Participants were no longer drawn primarily from the upper class, but a distinction still prevailed which saw the upper class taking part in the more expensive activities that required special facilities and the working class enjoying the basketball, bowling, and baseball sponsored by industries and municipal recreation departments and agencies. It is possible that the latter group made up the bulk of the competitors. Industries, municipalities, agencies such as the YMCA and YWCA, and educational institutions built large gymnasiums and pools to accommodate sports participants. In this era, the most popular activities, such as basketball and bowling, were indoor sports.

The growth of organized competition was the most prominent feature of the decade with national and international tournaments promoted for most sports. Related to the increased opportunities for high level competition was the growth of women's sport organizations. These were either separately established or formed as special women's committees within previously established groups.

One of the most far-reaching occurrences of this time period was the division that took place between sport in the larger social environment and sport in the schools and colleges. Precisely at the time when sport in society was extending in the ways just described, sport in the colleges was being circumscribed. The available activities were limited and the level of competition was lowered to the point of disappearing altogether.

Very little sport was coeducational by this time. The level of skill had grown too high to permit realistic competition between the sexes and there were other opportunities for social encounters in the jazz age.

By the contemporary era sport for women again had undergone several changes. Bowling, softball, tennis, and golf still seem to have the greatest number of adult players. A few activities such as polo virtually disappeared for women. In their place are a number of new activities such as motorcycle racing, the martial arts, parachuting, non-tackle football, kayaking, cross-country running and skiing, marathon running, surfing, and water skiing. Most of the new activities are not only vigorous but are eustressing, that is, involve pleasurable stress that comes from controlling the danger involved. Several of the sports in which women now compete demand great endurance, a quality in sport not pursued by many women until the contemporary era.

The growth of organized competition continues to expand at a rapid rate with state, regional, national, and international competition available in an even greater variety of sports. Even women's collegiate teams are now taking part in competition through to the international level (e.g., the World University Games).

The division between college sport and sport in the larger social milieu is disappearing. A renewed emphasis on the club system in colleges has brought men and women together in activities which were previously not available on a college campus. Thus the return to more coed sport is taking place—and ways are being found for men and women to compete against each other in mixed teams such as are common in coed volleyball. Almost all national sport organizations now admit and encourage women members.

Though a class distinction still remains in sport, the generally greater funds available for leisure have helped to minimize this feature. Activities like water skiing which were once beyond the reach of most people are now more available.

One radical change in sport for women has been the growth of opportunities for professional play. Both the number of sports and the amounts of the purses are growing speedily.

A new interest in outdoor activities is evident, though the currently popular ones such as skiing, kayaking, cross-country running, sky diving, soaring, and mountain climbing are far more rugged than the croquet, archery, and tennis of the nineteenth century. Furthermore, they are of the natural sport variety in which elements of nature play a crucial role.

With all the changes, the biggest one is the growth of sport for women in comparison to men. Certainly, comparatively more women now take part in organized sport competition than at any other time in history.—Ellen W. Gerber, Jan Felshin, Pearl Berlin, Waneen Wyrick

The Weaker Sex? Hah!

Women playing lacrosse? Hockey? Women tackling each other in rugby and mixing it up in the scrum? Women running marathons? Small wonder that fathers, husbands and friends worry about the physical strains that the supposedly weaker sex is undergoing these days. Relax, fellas: there is little to be concerned about. Women are well suited to take part in rugged athletics. Indeed, women hold many long-distance swimming records for both sexes and have run men into the ground during ultra-marathon races 50 miles long. Says Dr. Joan Ullyot, a physiologist at San Francisco's Institute of Health Research and a world-class marathoner herself: "The evidence suggests that women are tougher than men."

Nature certainly designed women better than men for sport in one basic way. "A man's scrotum is much more vulnerable than a woman's ovaries," says Dr. John Marshall, director of sports medicine at Manhattan's Hospital for Special Surgery and the trainer for Billie Jean King. "A woman's ovaries sit inside a great big sac of fluid—beautifully protected." A woman's breasts are also not easily damaged. Scotching an old myth, Marshall says: "There's no evidence that trauma to the breasts is a precursor of cancer."

Such injuries as girls and women do suffer can often be blamed on improper condition or coaching. Girls are more loose-jointed than boys, making them somewhat more susceptible to injuries like dislocated shoulders. Women can also have problems with what is known as the "overload phenomenon"—putting too much force on a muscle, tendon or ligament. But that can be avoided with proper training. Says Dr. C. Harmon Brown, director of Student Health Services at California State University in Hayward: "Four years ago it was not O.K. for girls to participate in sports, and they were forced to be sedentary. Now it's suddenly O.K., but teachers are not equipped to show girls how to gradually improve their physical fitness and cut down on injuries."

A girl's training need not be less vigorous than a boy's. Dr. Barbara Drinkwater, a research physiologist at the University of California's Institute of Environmental Stress, found that prepubertal girls are precisely the same as boys in cardio-respiratory (heart-lung) endurance capacity. Parents who worry about their young daughters overtaxing tender hearts while turning a fast 440 should realize that the human machine is designed to shut down—through leg cramps, side stitches, and dizziness—if the strain is too severe.

Then there is the canard that a woman's menstrual cycle inhibits peak performance. World and Olympic records, however, have been set by women who were having their periods. Nor does exertion disrupt the cycle for most women athletes. Says one world-class runner: "I'm so regular, it's ridiculous." However, some women undergoing hard training do stop menstruating for months at a time. This cessation of the cycle, called amenorrhea, occurs in about 45% of women who run over 65 miles a week—as well as in dancers, ice skaters and gymnasts. Many experts link amenorrhea directly to loss of body fat, a result of exercise. A cutback in training, with subsequent weight gain, generally restores the normal cycle.

Even pregnancy should not automatically deter the athletic woman. Most obstetricians advocate exercise, at least during the first and second trimesters. Dr. Marshall calmly watched his wife enter her first ski race when she was eight months pregnant. Says he: "I didn't mind seeing my wife even take a fall because the baby is very well protected." Last month, Wendy Boglioli, 23, a former Olympic champion, competed in the national A.A.U. 100-yd. freestyle competition while five months pregnant. She failed to place and felt unusually tired, but suffered no damage.

Many women claim that athletics increases their sex drive. "Exercise puts sparkle in a woman's eyes, pink in her cheeks and creates a physical vitality that almost bursts out," says Dr. Ullyot. "She becomes body centered and very sensual."

A serious woman athlete—even one who trains with weights— hardly faces the specter of turning into a Tarzan. The female body composition is only 23% muscle, in contrast to 40% for men. Dr. Jack Wilmore, president of the American College of Sports Medicine, has found that women, because they have low levels of the androgenic hormones that enlarge muscles, can increase their strength 50% to 75% with no increase in muscle bulk. Witness Virginia Wade, sleek and slender, who can serve a tennis ball at 92 m.p.h.

A top woman athlete has legs just as strong as those of a man her size in the same condition, but the man's arms would be twice as strong. Women have trouble throwing a ball as far as a man not only because of weaker muscles, but because their arms are relatively shorter and their shoulders not as broad. The result is less leverage and power.

One thing is certain: women have only just begun to achieve their athletic potential. Since women started to play the game later than men, they have some catching up to do—and they are. Men now run the 800 and 1,500 meters only about 10% faster than women; in the middle-distance swimming events, the difference is about 7%. Top women marathoners now finish about 30 minutes behind the male winners, and their times are improving every year. Yet the International Olympic Committee recently refused to allow women to run more than 1,500 meters in the 1980 Olympics. Ridiculous, says Dr. Wilmore. "You can train women as hard as you can train men, and the records will fall by the wayside."—*Time* Magazine

Comes the Revolution

Steve Sweeney paces the sideline, shoulders hunched against the elements. A steady downpour has turned an Atlanta soccer field into a grassy bog. A few yards away, his team of eight- and nine-year-olds, sporting regulation shirts and shorts, churns after the skittering ball. One minute, all is professional intensity as the players struggle to start a play. The next, there is childhood glee in splashing through a huge puddle that has formed in front of one goal. Sweeney squints at his charges and shouts, "Girls, you gotta pass! *Come on, Heather!*"

At eight, Kim Edwards is in the incubator of the national pastime—tee-ball. There are no pitchers in this pre—Little League league. The ball is placed on a waist-high, adjustable tee, and for five innings the kids whack away. Kim is one of the hottest tee-ball players in Dayton and a fanatical follower of the Cincinnati Reds. Her position is second base. She pulls a Reds cap down over her hair, punches her glove, drops her red-jacketed arms down to rest on red pants, and waits for the action. Kim has but a single ambition: to play for her beloved Reds. When a male onlooker points out that no woman has ever played big league baseball, Kim's face, a mass of strawberry freckles, is a study in defiant dismissal: "So?"

The raw wind of a late-spring chill bites through Philadelphia's Franklin Field, but it cannot dull the excitement of the moment. For the first time in the 84-year history of the Penn Relays, the world's largest and oldest meet of its kind, an afternoon of women's track and field competition is scheduled. The infield shimmers with color, a kaleidoscope of uniforms and warmup suits. One thousand college and high school athletes jog slowly back and forth, stretch and massage tight muscles, crouch in imaginary starting blocks, huddle with coaches for last-minute strategy sessions, or loll on the synthetic green turf, sipping cocoa and waiting. Susan White, a 19-year-old hurdler from the University of Maryland, surveys the scene. There is a trace of awe in her voice: "When I was in high school, I never dreamed of competing in a national meet. People are finally accepting us as athletes."

Golfer Carol Mann is chatting with friends outside the clubhouse when a twelve-year-old girl walks up, politely clears her throat and asks for an autograph. Mann bends down—it's a long way from 6-ft. 3-in. Mann to fan—and talks softly as she writes. After several moments, the girl returns, wide-eyed, to waiting parents. Mann straightens and smiles.

"Five years ago, little girls never walked up to tell me that they wanted to be a professional golfer. Now it happens all the time. Things are changing, things are changing."

They are indeed. On athletic fields and playgrounds and in parks and gymnasiums across the country, a new player has joined the grand game that is sporting competition, and she's a girl. As the long summer begins, not only is she learning to hit a two-fisted backhand like Chris Evert's and turn a back flip like Olga Korbut's, she is also learning to jam a hitter with a fastball. Season by season, whether aged six, 60 or beyond, she is running, jumping, hitting and throwing as U.S. women have never done before. She is trying everything from jogging to ice hockey, lacrosse and rugby, and in the process acquiring a new sense of self, and of self-confidence in her physical abilities and her potential. She is leading a revolution that is one of the most exciting and one of the most important in the history of sport. Says Joan Warrington, executive secretary of the Association for Intercollegiate Athletics for Women: "Women no longer feel that taking part in athletics is a privilege. They believe it is a right."

Spurred by the fitness craze, fired up by the feminist movement and buttressed by court rulings and legislative mandates, women have been moving from miniskirted cheerleading on the sidelines for the boys to playing, and playing hard, for themselves. Says Liz Murphey, coordinator of women's athletics at the University of Georgia: "The stigma is nearly erased. Sweating girls are becoming socially acceptable."—*Time* Magazine

Sports

It is, the old wisdom suggests, on the playing fields of America where young boys are made into men. It never happens that way, of course, but it is supposed to. But since athletic competition serves as a masculinity rite, it is not surprising that women who participate in competitive sports are faced with a degree of discrimination and oppression that at least equals that which women encounter in any other area of American society. The woman athlete, no matter how high her level of athletic skill may be, is never fully accepted in this milieu with all its male mythology. Nothing could be more devastating for a male athlete than to be defeated by a woman; and at the same time, the qualities of aggressivity and muscularity required for athletic success result in women athletes often being ostracized by other women. Because she is perceived as a threat by both men and women, the woman athlete is often a lonely, marginal person, never fully accepted by either group.

Marie Hart, a prominent woman physical educator, succinctly describes this dilemma: "American society cuts the penis off the male who enters dance and places it on the woman who participates in competitive athletics." Mildred "Babe" Didrikson Zaharias, described by Paul Gallico, one of America's most distinguished sports writers, as "probably the most talented athlete, male or female, ever developed in our country" encountered the difficulties suggested by Dr. Hart on an almost daily basis throughout her athletic career that lasted from the early 1930s to shortly before her death from cancer in 1955. Mrs. Zaharias won national and international titles in nearly every sport open to women during her 25-year career as a competitive athlete. Before turning to golf during the later years of her career, where she won every amateur and professional title available to a woman, she was a star in track and field at the 1932 Olympic Games and was a perennial All-American in basketball. Though she stood only 5 feet, 6 and one-half inches and weighed no more than 125 pounds, she was constantly portrayed by the male sportswriters of the time as having a boyish appearance. She wore her hair short for convenience but she was an extremely attractive woman. Despite this, she was always referred to as a tomboy, and according to Gallico, one of the favorite jokes of the male sportswriters was that athletic promoters never knew whether to assign her to the men's or women's locker room when she showed up for a competition.

It is of course true that there are some women athletes whose size and appearance qualify them as being "unfeminine" according to traditional Western standards, but, as was the case with Mrs. Zaharias, most women athletes are treated the same regardless of their actual physical appearance or behavior. (The exceptions to this occur in sports that are characterized by graceful movements and little physical exertion, such as ice skating, diving, gymnastics, skiing and similar activities, where a woman can participate without being typed as "masculine.")

Not surprisingly, most women who participate in competitive athletics are extremely conscious about looking "feminine." Vicki Foltz, a 27-year-old married woman who is probably America's finest woman long distance runner, was asked in a recent interview whether she had any "feminine hangups about running." She responded, "Yes, I have lots of hangups. You wouldn't believe it. I always worry about looking nice in a race. I worry about my calf muscles getting big. But mostly I worry about my hair. The morning before my last big race it was hailing and blowing, but there I was in the hotel with rollers in my hair. I knew the rain would ruin my hairdo, but I fixed it anyway. I suppose it's because so many people have said women athletes look masculine. So a lot of us try, subconsciously maybe, to look as feminine as possible in a race. There's always lots of hair ribbons in the races!"

If an attractive, mature married woman with children like Vicki Foltz feels this pressure, one can only imagine what it must be like for younger women athletes such as the female swimmers who often participate in the Olympics while still in their early teens. Marion Lay, for instance, participated in the Tokyo Olympic Games when she was only 14 years old. By 1967 she had developed into one of the finest female swimmers in the world, and she won four silver medals at the Pan

American Games that year. She won a medal at the 1968 Olympic Games and also served as captain of the Canadian Olympic women's swimming team despite being only 18. But in many ways, her career was frustrated. The only coaches available to her were men, since in swimming, as in nearly all other sports, it is next to impossible for a woman to advance in the coaching profession. Marion found that nearly all the male coaches and officials she met refused to accept the fact that she was as dedicated to swimming as any of the male athletes. The attitude of male coaches and officials seems to be that women are somehow incapable of being as dedicated to sports as men, whereas in reality the opposite is often true. Being a marginal person, as I pointed out earlier, the female athlete often dedicates herself to sport with a fervor unmatched by male athletes since athletic success is one of the few satisfactions available to her. Unlike the case for male athletes, athletic prowess does not assure a woman of social status. The final step in the Catch-22 of women's sports is that those women athletes who do totally dedicate themselves to sport are invariably labeled as being masculine by the male-controlled sports establishment.

All the desirable qualities athletes must possess if they want to achieve a high level of success have been made synonymous with our cardboard concept of masculinity. This point was brought home to me when in a recent *Sports Illustrated* article the male diving coach of Micki King, America's, and perhaps the world's, finest woman diver, attempted to compliment Miss King by saying he knew early in her career that she was going to be great because, "She dives like a man." My immediate reaction on reading that statement was that she sure as hell doesn't dive like me or any other man I ever met. In fact, she doesn't dive like 99 percent of the men in America. What she obviously does do is dive *correctly*.

Another myth that the male-dominated athletic world works to perpetuate about women, especially the female teenage swimming sensations who began their careers at the age of 12 or so, is that they invariably retire when they get to be about 17 because they become interested in boys and no longer have time for competitive athletics. Conveniently ignored is the fact that most male athletes are not known for their sexual abstinence. If male athletes have time for girl friends, there is obviously no reason why female athletes could not also continue to participate in sports while dating. The shortness of their careers is due to other circumstances: the tremendous social pressures I've mentioned, and also the fact that only a handful of colleges in the entire United States gives even partial athletic scholarships to women. Compared to men, the opportunities for women to be supported while competing in athletics after high school are almost non-existent. Additionally, most women college physical educators attempt to steer women students away from highly competitive athletics.

If a woman does survive all this, she faces a double standard even after achieving a sufficient skill level to participate in national or international level competition. This past track season the AAU barred one of our most prominent female track stars from international competition because of "unladylike" behavior on a foreign tour the previous summer. Her "unladylike" behavior involved a member of the US men's international team that was touring along with the women's team, but this individual was not even reprimanded.

The frustration of the woman athlete is further compounded by her inability, because of basic differences in speed and strength, to ever achieve success according to male standards. Hopefully, our society will come to the point where women will not only be given equal opportunity to participate in sport, but will not be made to feel that they are somehow inferior athletes because they run 100 yards in 10.5 rather than 9.5. Simone de Beauvoir best sums it up in *The Second Sex* where she writes, " . . . In sports the end in view is not success independent of physical equipment; it is rather the attainment of perfection within the limitations of each physical type: the featherweight boxing champion is as much of a champion as is the heavyweight; the woman skiing champion is not the inferior of the faster male champion; they belong to two different classes."—Jack Scott

USING PATTERNS THAT OTHERS HAVE USED

The chapters that follow this one will discuss some particular types of writing, and will from time to time recommend set forms you may follow when you have particular kinds of writing to do. The chapters before this one have frequently stressed the great freedom of choice you have as a writer. Through eleven chapters the book appears to prize freedom; now it recommends that you follow certain models to satisfy the expectations of certain kinds of writing occasions and assignments. That appears to be contradictory, but it needn't be.

The world is full of various needs. The world always needs more direct, lucid communication than it has; it always needs thoughtful explorations of complex situations; it always needs writers to mediate between specialists and lay people who need to use their special knowledge. Some of the occasions on which you write will call for particular forms. Take these forms and use them to your own purposes.

Samuel Johnson remarks in his *Rambler* 154 that "it is far easier to learn than to invent." Remember that you don't have to create a brand-new system of organization every time you write something. It is often possible and entirely proper to use a design or form that other writers have used. There is nothing dishonest about such a practice. Every one of us belongs to some community of writers. Every novel owes something to the novels that defined the art of the novel, to the innovative novels of the past. Every tragedy owes something to other tragedies. Use other writers. Adapt their schemes of organization to suit your own purposes, or use them as they are. Lecturing young painters, Sir Joshua Reynolds told them, "Study therefore the great works of the great masters, for ever. . . . consider them as models which you are to emulate, and at the same time as rivals with whom you are to contend." Read as much as you can, and don't hesitate to borrow as your own the structure another writer has developed.

And don't be surprised if you find help even for practical writing chores in surprising places. Shakespeare's Sonnet 73, shown below, may suggest to you a usable pattern for a report. In the first twelve lines the poet examines a situation in three different ways, each given four lines, and then in the final two lines he announces a concluding observation. The pattern of the poem has something in common with a report in which you investigate a problem from three different points of view, giving each equal time, and then arrive at a conclusion.

> That time of year thou mayst in me behold
> When yellow leaves, or none, or few, do hang
> Upon those boughs which shake against the cold,
> Bare ruined choirs where late the sweet birds sang.
> In me thou see'st the twilight of such day
> As after sunset fadeth in the west,
> Which by-and-by black night doth take away,
> Death's second self that seals up all in rest.
> In me thou see'st the glowing of such fire
> That on the ashes of his youth doth lie,
> As the deathbed whereon it must expire,
> Consumed with that which it was nourished by.
>> This thou perceiv'st, which makes thy love more strong,
>> To love that well which thou must leave ere long.

Remember that you can sometimes successfully use plans that others have used and that you can sometimes find help for even practical chores in surprising places. Nor does borrowing a plan of organization from another writer mean that you have to give up your own ideas or original notions.

In the longer example that follows the writer has taken over for his own use in recording his thoughts a framework that he found in William Humphrey's novel *The Ordways.* (Although *The Ordways* is a novel, the passage reprinted here seems like autobiography: another possible example of using other forms for one's own purposes.) Here is the original passage from Humphrey's novel:

> To grow up a boy in Clarksville in my time was to be a double dreamer. For there where the woods joined the prairie was the frontier where two legends met. At one's back one heard the music

of a banjo and the strains of "Dixie," the tramp of marching men, the roll of drums and bugle calls, the rattle of musketry, the thunder of cannonades. A boy gazing in that direction saw proud, tattered ensigns streaming above the haze of battle; saw burst from the clouds of gunsmoke gray-uniformed figures waving sabers and long horsepistols, shouting the rebel yell, grinning at death, glory-bent and beckoning him to follow. Those wooded hills rang all the way back with the names of Jeb Stuart and Stonewall Jackson and Texas's own Albert Sidney Johnston and the hapless but coura-geous John Bell Hood, and the sonorous Miltonic roll of place names where battles were fought: First Manassas, Antietam, The Wilderness, Chickamauga, Chattanooga, Shiloh.

In the other direction stretched Blossom Prairie, the vastness alone of which would have drawn out the soul in vague yearnings, even if beyond it had not lain a place already fabled as a land of romance and the home of heroes. What the ocean is in that once-famous picture of the boy Raleigh shown sitting on the shore with his knees drawn up to his chin and his eyes fixed on strange distant lands below the horizon, my prairie was to me. Except that I knew what lay beyond my ken. Just beyond the range of my vision the prairie became the plains, and there another world com-menced. It was a new world, and in it a new man had come into being, the most picturesque the world has ever produced: the cowboy. There was no place there for old men or for women. Life was spiced with danger there. A man wore his law strapped round his waist out there. Strong, fearless, taciturn, the cowboy was a natural aristocrat, chivalrous towards women, loyal to his friends unto death, reserved towards strangers, relentless towards his enemies, a man who lived by a code as rigid and elaborate as a medieval knight's. The cowboy was a man whose daily occupation was an adventure, whose work clothes a sultan might have envied. A man lifted above the plodding pedestrian world: a horseman— just the best ever known. On that wind which blew in my face off Blossom Prairie I seemed to catch the lowing of vast herds of cattle and the strumming of a guitar to the tune of "The Old Chisholm Trail," and along that flat rim where the earth met the sky there would sometimes appear in silhouette a lone rider sitting tall in the saddle, wearing a broad-brimmed sombrero and chaps, a bandana knotted round his throat, the sunlight glinting on the pearl handle of the pistol slung low on his thigh.

Lee surrendered to Grant on April 9, 1865. The news was two months reaching Texas. I did not hear about it until 1931. I learned by reading on to the end of my school history book. Before that time I had sensed that we were in for a long struggle, but I had no idea that things were going that bad. We had suffered set-backs—that was war; but we had given as good as we had gotten, and, no one having told me any different, I supposed that the fighting was still going on. Suddenly at the age of ten I not only had snatched away from me any chance ever to avenge my great-grandfather and redeem our losses and cover myself with glory on my country's battlefields, I had to swallow down my pride and learn to live with the chronic dyspepsia of defeat.

Nothing had prepared me for this. My knowledge of American history up to that point had conditioned me to the habit of success and leadership. I had theretofore identified myself with my country's eminence and expansion, and as a Southerner I had belonged to the dominant party. The founding fathers, the early generals, the great presidents, were Southerners. In the War, as presented to me, we had fought the better fight. At the point at which the account of it had always previously left off, we were winning. Now all of a sudden it was over, and we had lost. For me, a Texan (which is just another word for "proud"), this was even harder to accept than for most Southerners.

I say that, yet is it true? The moment when he discovers that the Civil War is lost comes to every Southern boy, and proud Texan though I was, it was perhaps less shattering for me than for most. I had, right on my doorstep, another myth to turn to. When the last bugle call went echoing off into eternity and the muskets were stacked and the banners lowered and that star-crossed flag hauled down—in short, when Appomattox came to me and I was demobilized and disarmed and returned home, filled with wounded pride and impatient with peacetime life—like many another veteran—I began to face about and look the other way, towards Blossom Prairie, where the range was open and the fancy free to roam. In my fashion I was repeating not only the history of my family, but of the country. For the West provided America with an escape from the memory of the Civil War.—William Humphrey, *The Ordways*

And here is the short essay based on the general plan of the passage above:

Sometimes I Can't See the Forest for the Trees, and Sometimes It's the Other Way Around

At certain seasons of the year, often in November, often in late March or early April, sometimes at inner seasons cycled by some whimsy, I'm unable to decide what to do about trees. Sometimes I want to learn their names, to follow their horticultural histories, and to watch understandingly their transformations, giving to each stage and feature its own right name. Names have a power, I think, and if I know their names I can carry trees with me, have them when I wish, recalling them to my mind and eye by saying their names. And if I know their histories, too, then I think others will be able to see the trees I name, their histories giving them a shape in the mind.

At other times I want only to be in their presence, to look closely at their shapes and colors and textures, and to sense what's learnable if I watch well. Then I think it enough just to stand and watch, learning if I can how volunteer trees know what distance to put between themselves, how when two or more varieties come together they negotiate which shall grow tall and which shall be stunted, how a blossom grows through a bud, how a tree accepts the wind.

From where I sit in my office I can see a magnolia, some red oaks, and a sycamore. Of the magnolia I've learned little. A genus including some fifty species, of which the commonest in this area are *magnolia grandiflora*, *magnolia acuminata*, *magnolia liliflora*, and *magnolia soulangeana*, it has its name from one Pierre Magnol, a French botanist who died in 1715. What we call *sycamore* is not the scriptural sycamore that the prophet Amos tended. Ours—elsewhere better known as the plane tree, a species of which is the most widely planted street tree in London and Paris, successful because it resists abuse, smoke, and dirt—is *platanus occidentalis*, probably the largest deciduous tree in our environs. Genus *quercus*, to which the red oaks belong, includes over 200 species. Such things come invariably as a surprise to me, since my experience numbers only red oak, live oak, pin oak, white oak, holm oak, and scrub oak. The red oak, *quercus rubra*, is characteristically a relatively fast growing and tall tree, whence I am familiar with its top from my third-story window. Were my window larger, or located elsewhere, I could see nearby laurel and hawthorne, Spanish oak, honey locust, hackberry, live oak, and, tucked away near the chapel, two trees of such wood as arks are made of. At the moment, I can't see them, and it's just as well, for my learning fails.

And I'm undisturbed, at any rate, for other questions pester at my mind, questions unconnected with the names of things. From my window I can see two red oaks. They are near-twins in size, but not in other ways. For some years now, looking out this window, I've been trying to puzzle out why, when they seem so alike and are so near each other, they do not go to color at the same time or in the same way. The one nearest goes first and to a deeper, richer red. I'd not be thought vain: it's not the oaks in my window alone that reveal this anomaly; other trees outside my view at the moment behave so. I've inquired why this variation in coloring should occur. Some say the rate of coloring depends on when rain came before the first frost. Some say the variation depends upon the tree's exposure to the north wind. Some say the variation depends upon how water reservoirs in the ground below each tree. Some say this, and some say that. I believe them all. Yet I still did not understand, until just now, why these two trees should be so different in color when they are so near, so like, so similarly situated to wind, sun, and water. But just now I think I came to understand—I'm forever being startled into learning, and now I've been lessoned by the trees. The truth is, they go to color at a different rate and are different in color because they are different. They're different because they're different. The mistake was mine: I thought that because they were both red oaks, they must behave in similar ways. I was prepared to grant them different sizes, but otherwise I expect I thought they must be alike, act alike, look alike. Now I know better. They are of the same genus. They are of the same species. But one is twenty yards south of the other, and one is twenty yards north of the other. One is a red oak, and the other is a red oak; genus and species notwithstanding, each can be itself, and I am lessoned thereby.

In this piece, as in the passage by Humphrey, paragraphs 1, 3, and 4 look one way, and paragraphs 2 and 5 look the other. The first paragraph in each pair raises possibilities which are then explored or modified in the second paragraph of each pair. In the selection by Humphrey, the first two sentences of the first paragraph tell us clearly that a two-part discussion is going to follow. We know that he lived "where two legends met." Then the third sentence of the first paragraph introduces the first of these two legends, the dream of a romanticized South. The rest of the first paragraph pictures that dream, detailing the images that fill it. Notice that the first paragraph focuses on specific images ("tattered ensigns," "gray-uniformed figures waving sabers and long horsepistols") and specific names of people and places. The second paragraph looks "in the other direction," to the dream of the West, and the paragraph, again, presents a rich array of images associated with the cowboy. Paragraph 3 returns to the South, but does so in order to show what became of that special dream, and paragraph 4 depicts the desolation that follows the ending of one dream. Paragraph 5 turns back to the West and provides the consolation of knowing that the speaker "was repeating not only the history of my family, but of the country. For the West provided America with an escape from the memory of the Civil War."

The second essay, done on the same general plan as the Humphrey selection, simplifies the scheme a little. It has four paragraphs, and is evenly split, two moving in one direction, two in the other. The first paragraph opens in much the same way as the Humphrey selection: we know from the first sentence that the speaker has at least more than one alternative before him. The second sentence introduces the hope for specific, careful knowledge, and the rest of the paragraph explores the power of that kind of knowledge. The second paragraph, then, turns in another direction, just as the Humphrey passage does, and introduces the other hope, of a kind of emotional sympathy and understanding instead of the specific knowledge presented in the first paragraph. The third paragraph tentatively explores the author's particular knowledge of trees, but concludes "my learning fails." The final paragraph, then, turns to the consolation of that other alternative, a sort of peaceful sympathy.

The chapters that follow—on letters, reports, arguments, and critical essays—will suggest some of the ways that other people have found to do these particular kinds of writing. You'll find there some account of how particular occasions raise opportunities, expectations, and needs and make different choices possible in your writing. You'll find there, too, some patterns you can follow if you need to.

Exercise

Using one of the samples given on the previous pages or another sample of your own choosing as a pattern, do one of the following:
a. Write a critique of a meeting you have recently attended or of a particularly interesting class period in one of your courses.
b. Write a letter to a prospective employer applying for a summer job.
c. Pretend that your school advisor has announced that he or she is looking for an assistant to help advise students, or that your favorite professor is looking for a research assistant, and write a letter applying for the opening.
d. If you have already decided on a career, write a possible statement of your career objectives.

13

Letters, of course, provide a particular occasion for writing, yet letters vary considerably in content and purpose. In this chapter you'll see some of that variety, as well as some of the conventional forms of letters. The chapter includes

1. a sampling of letters, showing their variety and personal voice (p. 347); and

2. a discussion of public letters, including some criteria of language (p. 353), conventional form of public letters (p. 360), and some typical content of public letters (p. 362).

Some say that letters are obsolete. They say that letters are no longer a particularly efficient means of communication. Given the extraordinary and increasing masses of mail that it distributes each year, the United States Postal Service would probably not agree that written, long-distance communication belongs to the past. Still, it is obvious that other kinds of remote communication, as they have come to be used more widely and more readily, have in some ways diminished the need for letters.

For example, the average number of calls made on single telephones has more than quadrupled in the last twenty years, and the possibilities of electronic remote communication grow almost every day. Several people in different places can hold a conference by telephone. Telephones can communicate with typewriters so that information can be stored for later retrieval—indeed, systems already exist that do not require a human mediator; a computer system at one end talks to a telephone, which in turn talks to a telephone in another location, which in turn stores information in a second computer system. A person in one city can sit down at a console and ask a computer in another location for a photocopy of material stored earlier.

But it's unlikely that machines will entirely replace letters. Letters still afford some qualities that we prize. For one thing, it's probably still possible for us to be more precise in written communication than in communication by tape or telephone or other electronic means. For another, it's easier for us to read into a letter, pause, reflect, and read again than it is for us to pause and reflect in the midst of electronic communication. And there is a third advantage in letters. We can send letters a long way. We can keep letters a long time. We can carry letters with us anywhere and read them when we choose. We can do all of that without instrumentation, and still find in letters the echo of a human voice, still speaking. In his book *Goodbye to a River*, John Graves tells of his farewell canoe trip down a river he knew well to see it a last time before it was dammed and changed. At one point, he stops to wander above the river bank, and comes upon a long-deserted house. He tells of poking and puttering through the house:

> The other rooms, accessible through doors that opened to latchstrings, were much like that one. In the lean-to kitchen, where mouse-gnawed stains of grease outlined the stove's square absence, a dome-topped rotten trunk had been dumped on its side, and letters flowed from it onto the floor. I looked at one. It was dated April 17, 1899, and was from someone named Elnora in Hood's Cove, Kentucky, to someone named Addie. It said that crops were what you might expect, but that Alfred had never given up his hanker to move southwest, what did Addie think? It said that Bella's baby had died of colic at six months of age, which only left her two,

and the new preacher had "gotten Alfred's *Irish* up" with what he said about Negroes, and it ended:

> *. . . I do not know where Time goes and when he said the other Day that it was* Twenny Five Years *since You All went out to Texas and I begann to cry, Dear Sister, because I do not believe that we are Like to see Each Other any more. . . .*

—John Graves, Goodbye to a River

The uses of letters are as various as the letter writers. It may be helpful to distinguish *private* letters from *public* letters.

Private letters are not at issue here. Private letters are a form of private conversation; ordinarily exchanged with friends and family, they are your concern, not the concern of other people, though the *published* private letters of notable people are a legitimate resource for historical, critical, and other kinds of study. In private letters, you do whatever you please, and you use whatever structure and style serve you. Private letters serve as quick news notes; they sometimes serve as long newspapers, where, for example, one member of a family brings other members of a family up to date on a whole series of events. They serve as sermons, as arguments, as emotional outlets. They serve for self-examination. Some private letters are well-crafted familiar essays; others could serve as formal position papers. Private letters are endlessly varied, as varied as we are. William James remarked once that "As long as there are postmen, life will have zest."

Your private letters can also help you develop your writing skill, both for public letters and for other kinds of writing. Your letters to your friends, your parents, your spouse, and others close to you probably speak with your personal voice. The fluidity with which you write these letters and the personality that is in them can serve as a model for the fluidity and voice in your other writing.

A private letter may also be one of the best devices for reminding you of the role of your reader or audience when you write, because you are almost assuredly, even though unconsciously, always considering your reader as you write a personal letter. That's good practice for keeping your reader, no matter how much of a stranger to you, in mind as you write a public or business letter.

VARIETY AND VOICE IN LETTERS

A variety of personal and public letters is reprinted below. Notice variations in tone and style, and think about whether the letters seem carefully designed, hurried, casual, formal, intimate, aloof, or something else entirely.

In the first letter, Samuel Johnson rejects the help offered by Lord Chesterfield:

February 7, 1755

My Lord,

I have been lately informed, by the proprietor of the World, that two papers, in which my Dictionary is recommended to the publick, were written by your Lordship. To be so distinguished, is an honour, which, being very little accustomed to favours from the great, I know not well how to receive, or in what terms to acknowledge.

When, upon some slight encouragement, I first visited your Lordship, I was overpowered, like the rest of mankind, by the enchantment of your address; and could not forbear to wish that I might boast myself *Le vainqueur du vainqueur de la terre*;—that I might obtain that regard for which I saw the world contending; but I found my attendance so little encouraged, that neither pride nor modesty would suffer me to continue it. When I had once addressed your Lordship in publick, I had exhausted all the art of pleasing which a retired and uncourtly scholar can possess. I had done all that I could; and no man is well pleased to have his all neglected, be it ever so little.

Seven years, my Lord, have now past, since I waited in your outward rooms, or was repulsed from your door; during which time I have been pushing on my work through difficulties, of which it is useless to complain, and have brought it, at last, to the verge of publication, without one act of assistance, one word of encouragement, or one smile of favour. Such treatment I did not expect, for I never had a Patron before.

The shepherd in Virgil grew at last acquainted with Love, and found him a native of the rocks.

Is not a Patron, my Lord, one who looks with unconcern on a man struggling for life in the water, and, when he has reached ground, encumbers him with help? The notice which you have been pleased to take of my labours, had it been early, had been kind; but it has been delayed till I am indifferent, and cannot enjoy it; till I am solitary, and cannot impart it; till I am known, and do not want it. I hope it is no very cynical asperity not to confess obligations where no benefit has been received, or to be unwilling that the Publick should consider me as owing that to a Patron, which Providence has enabled me to do for myself.

Having carried on my work thus far with so little obligation to any favourer of learning, I shall not be disappointed though I should conclude it, if less be possible, with less; for I have been long wakened from that dream of hope, in which I once boasted myself with so much exultation,

My Lord,
Your Lordship's most humble,
Most obedient servant,
Sam. Johnson

Do you think that Samuel Johnson meant this letter to be forever private and personal, or did he plan for its publication even as he wrote it?

Ralph Waldo Emerson, in the letter below, writes to greet Walt Whitman "at the beginning of a great career":

> Concord 21 July
> Mass^tts 1855
>
> Dear Sir,
>
> I am not blind to the worth of the wonderful gift of "Leaves of Grass." I find it the most extraordinary piece of wit & wisdom that America has yet contributed. I am very happy in reading it, as great power makes us happy. It meets the demand I am always making of what seems the sterile and stingy Nature, as if too much handiwork or too much lymph in the temperament were making our Western wits fat and mean. I give you joy of your free & brave thought. I have great joy in it. I find incomparable things said incomparably well, as they must be. I find the courage of *treatment*, which so delights us, & which large perception only can inspire.
>
> I greet you at the beginning of a great career, which must yet have had a long foreground somewhere, for such a start. I rubbed my eyes a little to see if this sunbeam were no illusion; but the solid sense of the book is a sober certainty. It has the best merits, namely, of fortifying & encouraging.
>
> I did not know until I, last night, saw the book advertised in a newspaper, that I could trust the name as real & available for a post-office.
>
> I wish to see my benefactor, & have felt much like striking my tasks, & visiting New York to pay you my respects.
>
> R. W. Emerson
> [To] Mr Walter Whitman

In the following letter, humorist Bill Nye writes to General Frank Hatton accepting appointment as postmaster of Laramie, Wyoming. Usually a public letter written in the line of professional duty will be more formal; Nye in fact parodies the stiffness of many such letters in his third paragraph:

> Office of *Daily Boomerang*, Laramie City, Wy.,
> August 9, 1882.
>
> My Dear General:
>
> I have received by telegraph the news of my nomination by the President and my confirmation by the Senate, as postmaster at Laramie, and wish to extend my thanks for the same.
>
> I have ordered an entirely new set of boxes and post office outfit, including new corrugated cuspidors for the lady clerks.
>
> I look upon the appointment, myself, as a great triumph of eternal truth over error and wrong. It is one of the epochs, I may

say, in the Nation's onward march toward political purity and perfection. I do not know when I have noticed any stride in the affairs of state which so thoroughly impressed me with its wisdom.

Now that we are co-workers in the same department, I trust that you will not feel shy or backward in consulting me at any time relative to matters concerning post office affairs. Be perfectly frank with me, and feel perfectly free to just bring anything of that kind right to me. Do not feel reluctant because I may at times appear haughty and indifferent, cold or reserved. Perhaps you do not think I know the difference between a general delivery window and a three-m quad, but that is a mistake. My general information is far beyond my years.

With profoundest regard, and a hearty endorsement of the policy of the President and the Senate, whatever it may be,

I remain, sincerely yours,

Bill Nye, P.M.

Gen. Frank Hatton, Washington, D.C.

The next letter was written as a message to the public by Captain Robert Falcon Scott. Together with his official record and other letters, it was found with the bodies of Scott and two companions where they had died on their return across Antarctica from the South Pole:

The causes of the disaster are due not to faulty organisation, but to the misfortune in all risks which had to be undertaken.

1. The loss of pony transport in March 1911 obliged me to start later than I had intended, and obliged the limits of stuff transported to be narrowed.

2. The weather throughout the outward journey, and especially the long gale in 83° S., stopped us.

3. The soft snow in lower reaches of glacier again reduced pace.

We fought these untoward events with a will and conquered, but it cut into our provision reserve.

Every detail of our food supplies, clothing and depôts made on the interior ice-sheet and over that long stretch of 700 miles to the Pole and back, worked out to perfection. The advance party would have returned to the glacier in fine form and with surplus of food, but for the astonishing failure of the man whom we had least expected to fail. Edgar Evans was thought the strongest man of the party.

The Beardmore Glacier is not difficult in fine weather, but on our return we did not get a single completely fine day; this with a sick companion enormously increased our anxieties.

As I have said elsewhere we got into frightfully rough ice and Edgar Evans received a concussion of the brain—he died a natural death, but left us a shaken party with the season unduly advanced.

But all the facts above enumerated were as nothing to the surprise which awaited us on the Barrier. I maintain that our arrangements for returning were quite adequate, and that no one in the world would have expected the temperatures and surfaces which we encountered at this time of the year. On the summit in lat. 85° 86° we had −20°, −30°. On the Barrier in lat. 80°, 10,000 feet lower, we had −30° in the day, −47° at night pretty regularly, with continuous head wind during our day marches. It is clear that these circumstances come on very suddenly, and our wreck is certainly due to this sudden advent of severe weather, which does not seem to have any satisfactory cause. I do not think human beings ever came through such a month as we have come through, and we should have got through in spite of the weather but for the sickening of a second companion, Captain Oates, and a shortage of fuel in our depôts for which I cannot account, and finally, but for the storm which has fallen on us within 11 miles of the depôt at which we hoped to secure our final supplies.

Surely misfortune could scarcely have exceeded this last blow. We arrived within 11 miles of our old One Ton Camp with fuel for one last meal and food for two days.

For four days we have been unable to leave the tent—the gale howling about us. We are weak, writing is difficult, but for my own sake I do not regret this journey, which has shown that Englishmen can endure hardships, help one another, and meet death with as great a fortitude as ever in the past. We took risks, we knew we took them; things have come out against us, and therefore we have no cause for complaint, but bow to the will of Providence, determined still to do our best to the last. But if we have been willing to give our lives to this enterprise, which is for the honour of our country, I appeal to our countrymen to see that those who depend upon us are properly cared for.

Had we lived, I should have had a tale to tell of the hardihood, endurance, and courage of my companions which would have stirred the heart of every Englishman. These rough notes and our dead bodies must tell the tale, but surely, surely, a great rich country like ours will see that those who are dependent on us are properly provided for.

R. Scott

The following letter from E. B. White to Donald A. Nizen of *The New York Times* shows how a personal voice can be heard even in typical business correspondence.

[North Brooklin, Me.]
October 24, 1975

Dear Mr. Nizen:
Thanks for your letter of October 16 about the Great White

Mixup. The *Times* is arriving every day now. For a while we were receiving *two* copies, and this proved oppressive.

You say in your letter that the *New Yorker* magazine owes us a refund. They owe us a refund provided the *Times* has refunded some money to the magazine. Has it?

As nearly as I can reconstruct the events, this is what happened:

1. The newspaper stopped coming, without warning.

2. A form letter from Mr. Innelli arrived, saying that a computer was taking over.

3. My wife, disturbed at receiving no newspaper, phoned the New Yorker and asked them to renew the *Times* for us and to pay the bill.

4. Our secretary at the magazine, Mrs. Walden, shot off a letter to the *Times*, dated September 10, enclosing a check for $114 made out to the *Times* by the magazine's accounting department.

5. Not knowing that my wife had done this, I sent the *Times* a check for $114, with instructions to renew our subscription.

6. When I learned that my wife had been busy, and that the magazine had sent you $114, I sent off a check to the New Yorker to reimburse them. That means, of course, that the *Times* got paid twice—you got a check from me, and you got a check from the New Yorker.

7. Two papers began arriving in every mail.

8. I wrote Ms. Zenette Pomykalo, telling her what had happened, and explaining that we were getting two copies of the *Times* and that two payments had been made. I suggested that she cancel one subscription and refund the money. The subscription that apparently got cancelled was the one in the name of Mrs. K. S. White, so I presume that the *Times* refunded some money to the New Yorker. If this has happened, then the New Yorker owes us the refund.

It all goes to show that a husband and wife should check on each other's actions from minute to minute, not just from day to day. Katharine and I ought to know this by now—we will have been married forty-six years come November 13.

> Sincerely,
> E. B. White

P.S. Today's mail has just arrived, and there are two communications from the *Times*. One is from Mr. Innelli, saying that "only one payment was received," and that "we cancelled the duplicate order which was registered to terminate on September 28, 1976." What Mr. Innelli and the computer can't seem to get through their heads is that one of the two payments arrived at the *Times* in a letter from the New Yorker and that the check enclosed was made out *by* the New Yorker. If we could just convince Innelli of this, we would be making progress. Mr. Innelli also suggests that I forward copies of the cancelled checks. Well, I did that quite a while ago, and you very kindly returned them. Of course, maybe the *Times* will have to see the cancelled check that the New Yorker sent. I'm not sure it will be a simple matter to get my hands on this crucial document, but I'll give it a try if the *Times* insists. I have it on the word of Mrs. Harriet Walden, who is utterly reliable, that a check *was* sent, in a letter dated September 10.

The other item in the mail is addressed to Mrs. E. B. White and is a subscription invoice. It says "Pay this amount—$114." The chances of our sending the *Times* still a third payment of $114 are so slight as to be negligible.

Carry on.

Exercise

In your journal write one or two private letters of the kind we all intend to write but never seem to get around to: to your parents, to a relative, to a friend, to a favorite teacher, to someone you know who does his or her job well day after day but never receives recognition, etc. The letters may be the kind you never intend to mail, or you just might decide to mail one of them.

PUBLIC LETTERS

Private letters are likely to be extended, long-distance forms of private conversation, though some may in the course of time come to have public uses and be publicly displayed. *Public* letters are a part of public discourse; they are typically not written forms of private or intimate conversation. They are written, usually, where there is work to be done, where public decisions are to be made and registered, where records must be kept.

But that doesn't mean that public letters must, as a consequence, be impersonal, cold, or nonhuman; certainly the letter from E. B. White to Donald Nizen shows how business can be transacted between human beings.

Many public letters—letters of recommendation, job applications, information letters, and others—are stylized, ritualized performances. Their authors sometimes fall into the habit of using a stiff, impersonal style that is remote and official-sounding, or they lapse into the jargon of a particular trade or profession, or they fall into the strange world where bureaucratic dialects are accepted as good English, where simple things become complex and complex things become impossible.

It's not uncommon, for example, to find business, professional, technical, and semi-technical letters depending excessively on current fad words—*parameter*, for example, and *viable* and *dialogue* and *charisma* and *prioritize*. It's easy enough to fall into the habit of over-using some words and phrases, such as these:

After a dialogue with for *after talking with*
Implementing a decision for *deciding*
Making a survey in depth for *studying*
Causative factor for *cause*
Optimum for *most* or *best*
Answer in the affirmative for *yes*
In accordance with your request for *as you asked*
Pursuant to our agreement for *as we agreed*
Basic fundamentals for *fundamentals*
Consensus of opinion for *consensus*

The list might go on and on. You may find it useful to look again at the section of Chapter 8 entitled "Languages That Tyrannize," page 193.

There are at least three reasons why we all sometimes use such stylized, pompous, trite, or unnecessary words and phrases. In the first place, we see enough of such language—in income tax instructions, federal prose, legal documents, sales agreements, and elsewhere—that it's natural for us to conclude that there is an "official" kind of language. If we have to write something "official" ourselves, then we want it to sound "official." What's needed, however, is not an "official" language, but a clear and direct language.

In the second place, many people who write business, professional, and technical letters have to write *many* such letters. If a person has to write, let's say, thirty or forty letters in a single day, it's certainly understandable if he or she relies on certain phrasings and words, repeating them again and again, using them over and over in different letters. It's understandable, but it's not desirable: when a writer depends upon certain habits of phrasing, then those habits of language become binding, and govern what a writer can say.

Third, we often depend upon standardized forms when we write public letters. If you have to write twelve letters in one afternoon requesting payment for a bill, then it's entirely likely that you will use the same or nearly the same form in each letter. Many companies, in fact, have some standardized forms that can be used in writing the various company letters that go out from the company. Some companies have a *style book* or a *style guide* or a *manual for written forms* (the names vary with the companies) to provide standardized letter forms. If we often depend upon standardized forms, then it's understandable if we often depend also upon standardized, "official-sounding" language.

Exercises

1.   Find and bring to class some examples of business letters that are particularly offensive in the use of "official" language.

2.   Try to find an example of a "human" business letter. Don't be surprised if this is the hardest assignment in this textbook!

Some criteria for public letters

The language and style of public letters do not have to be standardized or "official." That's one reason for lingering over and remembering private and public letters in the opening pages of this chapter. Even where you need to use a standardized letter form, you can still speak in your own voice and be yourself.

The first criterion for public letters is a natural, unstilted style.   A public letter—for example, a letter intent upon the conduct of some business—does not have to be written in an "official" language. Even when you are writing as a representative of a company, you can still be human and sound like a particular human being, yourself. That doesn't mean that you should write public letters that are cute or highly personal or full of folksy, back-slapping chatter.

The E. B. White letter to Donald Nizen is a good example, but consider a more typical business letter. The letter below was written in response to a customer's letter detailing specific complaints about gas mileage in a new car recently purchased from an automobile manufacturer's sales dealer. The customer's letter was mailed directly to the manufacturer's public representative in Detroit. The public representative in Detroit apparently then sent the letter back to a company agent in the area where the customer lived. The letter is the local agent's reply to the customer's original letter (the names have been changed to protect the innocent and the guilty):

Mr. Patrick C. Wayne
7313 Arena Drive
Madrigal, Missouri

Dear Mr. Wayne:

This will acknowledge your letter to Detroit which has been referred to this office for handling.

We have been unable to contact you by phone during normal working hours; however, we have reviewed your gas consumption problem with the Service Manager at Westside Reo Motor Company, Mr. Ted Warsaw. We suggest you call him for an appointment that can be arranged when our Service Development Manager will be at the dealership in order that he may assist in checking out your vehicle.

We do thank you for writing.

Very truly yours,

B. M. Bell
Customer Relations Manager

Now this is not a "bad" letter. It gets a certain job done. But it was written by a human being to be read by a human being, and such a letter might as well *sound* human. A letter is no less truthful or businesslike because it has a real person in it speaking. The first sentence, for example, might just as easily read as follows:

> *I have the letter you sent to our Detroit office.*
> or
> *Our Detroit office has sent me your letter.*

In the original opening sentence, there is no human speaker; the customer has been turned over to "this office" for "handling," which sounds altogether impersonal, nonhuman, and generally unattractive. And notice an oddity in the original letter: nowhere does it acknowledge that the customer is a thinking person who *might* be right in his complaints about the car. A new second sentence or an addition to the first might be helpful:

> *I have the letter you sent to our Detroit office, and I am sorry to learn of the problems you have had with your new Reo.*
> or
> *Our Detroit office has sent me your letter. I hope we can work out the problems you have had with your new Reo.*

Once the author of the original letter gets to the second paragraph, things go better. There is, however, no good reason for the writer to use *we; I* would do as well, and is probably more accurate. *Vehicle* in the last sentence of the second paragraph is not particularly useful. *Car* is a little more specific and might be comforting to the customer—if the customer saw the word *car*, he might believe that the author of the letter actually knew which kind of vehicle was under discussion.

A human being ought to show up even in most public letters, and the human being can write in a natural, even personal style. Impersonal language is not more accurate or official than natural, human language.

A second standard for public letters, no less important than the first, is that they be accurate.   Information should be complete and correct. Judgments should be stated clearly as judgments so that readers can tell when you are expressing an evaluation. Opinions and interpretations should be clearly identified as what they are. Consider some simple examples, all public letters to the editor from *Time* Magazine (June 27, 1977). The first three were all written in response to an earlier article on jogging.

> I am happy to see that the American people are finally awakening to the benefits and joys of running. I am a long-distance runner, and I intend to run forever.

This is a complete letter, containing only the three short, relatively simple assertions. The first is clearly a statement of attitude, the second is a simple statement of fact not easily open to question, and the third is another statement of attitude. We know where the author stands, and we know that he is making no demands on our credibility. The letter is accurate in the sense suggested above.

The second letter is also short:

> Joggers make me sick. There are plenty of them around here. They run past me with supercilious smirks on their red faces. What are they trying to prove? I hope they all drown in their own sweat.
>
> I'm 100 lbs. overweight and love it. I eat and drink what I please. To hell with the physical-fitness fanatics.

This letter is also accurate in the sense suggested above. We know what we are reading, clearly enough an expression of opinion, and we can assume it is reliable, though we don't have to like it. We do know that we are not being asked to accept opinions as facts. The third letter is similar:

> I see that jogging is now a full-blown fad. Good! If we are to judge from other fads, that means it will blow over in a few months, or at most a year or so. Like, for instance, Hula Hoops.
>
> As an old Army man, I can tell you what jogging really is. Jogging is double time. And I say, the hell with it!

We get reliable signals from this letter, too. The first sentence is clearly a report on the author's perception ("I see . . ."), and we can accept it for what it is. The second statement is a single word, and the exclamation point following the single word testifies that this is the author's enthusiastic judgment. In the third sentence, the author avoids making a dogmatic and unsupportable statement by acknowledging the conditions ("If we are to judge from other fads, . . ."). The author's use of hula hoops as an example in the fourth statement seems accurate enough; it can easily enough be tested by our own knowledge or quick research.

The three letters above are accurate. They make no false claims. They do not pretend to be other than what they are. We are not asked to accept questionable data.

The fourth letter is different. It was written in response to an earlier article in *Time* about the nation's defense:

I want to commend you for your in-depth cover story analyzing the state of the nation's defenses.

One small part of the article is of deep concern to me, however. It perpetuates the myth about the cost of the volunteer force. In fact, the active-duty military personnel share of the Defense Department budget has gone down from 31% to 27% since the end of the draft. Retirement, civilian personnel costs and other nonvolunteer force-related costs have gone up, but these increases are not tied to the end of the draft.

At one point, we can't be quite sure of this letter's accuracy. The author wants to oppose "the myth about the cost of the volunteer force," and to that end cites the budget reduction from 31 percent to 27 percent. Information at this spot in the letter is, if not inaccurate, at least not full enough to be significant to us. Since we're not told how much money is actually involved, the percentage figures don't mean very much: 31 percent of ten billion dollars is less than 27 percent of twenty billion dollars. The volunteer force may very well be costing substantially more than it did when the draft ended.

Public letters need to be accurate (and that entails providing full and open information) for at least three reasons. In the first place, accuracy is or should be both a goal and an obligation for anyone, and the point is not just to *seem* accurate and therefore trustworthy, but to *be* accurate. In the second place, in many of the public transactions that are conducted through letters, your reader will not know as much as you will know, which makes it particularly important that you share as fully and accurately as you can. Finally, even when your reader knows most or all of what you know, it is still important that you record fully and accurately the information you are using. As often as not, it is important and valuable for readers to know how you use information, how you organize data, how you call on what you know in order to make decisions and to render judgments.

A third standard for public letters is that they should provide a track for readers to follow.   Readers must be able to understand the context in which a letter is written. They should be able to understand why a letter is written, what its origins are, or what occasion the letter is responding to. They need to be able to see your connections and follow the sequence of your thoughts. If they can't, then your letter is likely to seem either abrupt and rude, dismissing readers without giving them adequate opportunity for understanding, or tyrannical, expecting readers to agree with your assertions simply because they are your assertions.

Consider a typical good example. This letter is from a college student to an attorney; the writer is asking the reader to participate in a survey:

Dear Mr. Abernathy:

You and several other prominent local lawyers were recently quoted in *The Daily News* in a discussion of current problems in education, especially problems in language use. The discussion and your comments so interested me that I decided to write my term paper in Political Science 1053 on "The Legal Profession's View of Today's Pre-law Education."

I hope you will be willing to complete the enclosed questionnaire. All you will need to do is to check *yes* or *no* in response to each of the questions. Your answers will be kept confidential. If you wish, I will send you a summary of the results based on my survey of fifty lawyers in this area.

Your answers, of course, will be useful to me in writing my paper. More than that, I believe they will be useful in discussions of changes in education. I hope you will check the answers and return the questionnaire in the enclosed, self-addressed envelope.

Sincerely yours,

The letter provides the information necessary to let the reader understand the occasion and the context. The first sentence explains how the writer, a stranger, came to be writing, and the second sentence establishes the particular occasion. The second paragraph makes a specific request and explains the terms the writer offers. The last paragraph explains the potential uses of the information that the writer is seeking. Throughout the letter the writer has undertaken to explain his mission clearly, and has tried to make it possible for the receiver of the letter to respond easily and conveniently.

Whether you are writing to an institution or to a person, to a stranger or to an acquaintance, be sure that you provide a context for the letter, that you explain the occasion, and that you tell readers enough for them to follow the sequence of your thoughts. It is not necessary, however, to go back over the context during an exchange of letters. For example, Mr. Abernathy wouldn't have responded to the letter above in this way:

Here is my completed questionnaire in response to your letter asking me to give you some opinions about pre-law education. . . .

The letter writer knows why he or she wrote to Mr. Abernathy, and the completed questionnaire is response enough.

The sample letters at the end of this chapter should serve as guides for the kind of information needed to set a letter in its context.

Exercises

1.   Rewrite a form letter written in official language that you or someone else has received. Use natural, human language.

2.   Find and bring to class examples of "letters to the editor" that contain inaccurate or unsupported information.

3.   Find examples of "letters to the editor" that seem abrupt or rude and analyze why they seem so.

4.   Rewrite one of the letters that you found in exercise three correcting the parts that seem abrupt, misleading, or difficult to follow.

Form in public letters

If you work for a company or institution that does a lot of public correspondence, the chances are that the company or institution will have a standard letter form for customary use. Such a guide to letter form will not tell you what goes in a letter, but it should show you how a letter ought to look on a sheet of paper (and for that matter, you can usually get some guidance about the contents of letters by looking at similar letters in company files).

If you don't have some kind of standard letter form available, the sample letter shown on page 361 may help you arrange your letter suitably on the page.

(1)   The inside address of the writer is against the right-hand margin (about one and a half inches from the edge of the paper). No punctuation marks occur at the ends of the lines. Use a comma to separate the name of the city from the name of the state and to separate the date of the month from the year.

(2)   Note that throughout the rest of the letter, everything is against the left-hand margin. It has become customary in recent years not to indent the first line of a paragraph, though you may, of course, if you wish.

(3)   The inside address should be complete, including any titles, departmental names, or other information that will make it easier for the letter to reach its proper destination.

(4)   A colon is customary after the greeting. If you do not know the name of a particular person to send your letter to, it's still acceptable to say *Dear Sir:* or *Dear Madam:*, but if you do not wish to assume that you know the gender of the person receiving your letter, it's acceptable to use the name of a company or department in your greeting:

Dear Ajax Tire Company:

Dear Sales Department:

(5)   Be sure to put a comma after the complimentary close. It's also acceptable to align the complimentary close and signature with your inside address, but the block style is currently more widely used.

(1) 856 East Oceanside Drive
Los Angeles, California 90016
October 5, 1978

(2)

(3) Dr. Robert Gruen
Director of Research
Bloch-Peterson Foundation
780 West Augusta Boulevard
Los Angeles, California 90004

(4) Dear Dr. Gruen:

I understand from the classified notice in the current Journal
of Pathology that you are looking for a bacteriologist for
your staff. Because of my academic training and professional
experience, I believe that I am qualified to fill the position.

For the past five years, I have been working within the field
of pathology--specifically in bacteriology. As a laboratory
assistant, I learned how to prepare, analyze, and compile
research information. My work with Dr. Roth at the Froude
Institute trained me to organize statistical tables, and my
present position with Dr. Lucille Lesiack has instructed me in
the type of research that Bloch-Peterson specializes in.

My academic background includes a Master of Science in
Bacteriology from the University of Southern California and a
Bachelor of Science in Biology from Midwestern University.
Details about my education and professional work can be found
on the enclosed resume.

I am most interested in the available position and would like
to arrange for an interview at your convenience. I can be
reached at (213) 689-4486 or at the address shown above.

(5) Sincerely,

Joanne Trestrail

Joanne Trestrail

Content in public letters

If your college or professional work requires you to write public letters regularly, you may want to acquire one of many good books devoted entirely to business letter writing. A good reference work will show you some of the standard forms for various kinds of letters, and it may help you to know what kinds of things you should say in different kinds of letters. One standard book on business writing, for example, includes a chapter on letter writing, which discusses and provides examples of letters of inquiry, order letters, letters answering inquiries, claim and adjustment letters, credit letters, collection letters, sales letters, and letters of application. Another standard reference book on letters includes discussion and examples of letters that correct errors, letters asking for information, letters giving instructions, letters asking for favors, help, contributions, reconsideration, or more time, letters suggesting change, letters seeking or giving advice, letters of acceptance or refusal, letters conveying compliments, commendations, or reprimands, letters concerning credit, advertising and sales letters, announcement letters, letters expressing thanks, and letters conveying congratulations, sympathy, or condolence.

No one, however, can tell you exactly what should go in a public letter that you are writing. Some standard advice usually given, however, is to think of the feelings of the reader, even if your letter is a complaint or refusal of some kind (advice not too different from always considering your audience, in whatever kind of writing). Good business letters are also tactful, seldom blunt. Even the letters bearing the most unpleasant news or request (as for an unpaid bill) usually open with a positive statement, followed by the bad news, courteously put, and also offer a possible course of action or an alternative solution to the problem.

The sample letters that follow may serve to show you what other people characteristically do when they write certain kinds of letters; both the content and the tone may help you in your own letter writing.

Letter of complaint

Director of Customer Complaints
Bolton's Stores Inc.
107 Townley Blvd.
Chicago, Illinois 60690

Dear

I want to compliment you on your prompt service in delivering the FX-31 pocket calculator that I ordered through your 24-hour phone service. I was pleased to find that you carried the specific model that I needed.

However, I'm sorry to say that the calculator has not produced the results that were advertised. Instead of showing eight digits, this machine has five. The independent memory bank also does not record more than one entry.

I am sure that this particular instrument is not representative of your products and that you will see that the enclosed FX-31 is properly repaired or replaced.

As a regular customer of Bolton's, I am generally pleased with your merchandise and hope to continue shopping at your store.

Sincerely,

John Neal

Letter suggesting change

Trustees of the Board
Town Hall
River Shores, Michigan 49019

Dear Sirs:

Last week I celebrated the anniversary of my move to River Shores. That was fifteen years ago. Since then, I have been fortunate to watch my children grow up in the friendly and charming atmosphere of River Shores. Unlike the majority of suburbs, River Shores has kept its character without succumbing to the influence of modern developers.

As residents of River Shores, you can probably imagine the horror I felt when I read about the proposal to build a Hot Dog Hut on the site of the old post office. Not only would it or any other fast food service destroy the picturesque quality of the town, but it would set a precedent for future changes of the same kind.

I am not suggesting that River Shores should never change; however, I am concerned that the changes match the nature of the town. River Shores is unique and should remain so. Wouldn't something like a small cafe with a terrace better capture the feeling of the town?

I am confident that as long-term residents of River Shores, your sentiments are not foreign to mine, and as trustees of the town you will strive to protect its character.

Sincerely yours,

Mary Lutz

Letter of refusal

Ms. Ellen Blake
1147 Harris Ave.
Weldon, Virginia 21389

Dear Ms. Blake:

You were more than kind to submit the manuscript SHADOWS which we have now had a chance to read. I regret that my colleagues and I do not feel it possible to send it on to the judges for further consideration. You may be sure it was read with due care and with an attempt to discern what you were trying to do. You will understand, I trust, that because of the large number of manuscripts received we are unable, when returning manuscripts, to give an analytic account of our reasons for doing so. Your manuscript is being returned to you under separate cover.

When you have another manuscript of an appropriate length, I hope you will want to submit it to the Gothic Novel Program.

With every good wish,

Cordially yours,

Robert Jackson
General Editor

Letter of recommendation

Teacher Placement Bureau
Homer Hall, 108
Central University
Central, Alabama

To whom it may concern:

I am writing at the request of Mr. Bob Boyd so that this letter may be added to the dossier which you are compiling.

Mr. Boyd and I first became acquainted in 1970 when he was enrolled in my freshman design class. He was an alert and able student, and during the several years of his stay here, and his subsequent careers at Western University and Northern State University, my opinion of him as a student and friend continued to strengthen even more. He belongs to that small group of former students that all of us know, whom we can recommend to any possible employer without reservation.

Yours truly,

Rachel Wade
Associate Professor of Art

Exercises

1.   To practice the form for a business letter given on page 361, write an imaginary letter of application, letter to a company, letter to someone in your college or university, and so on. Better still, find a real occasion for one of these letters.

2.   Start your own file of collectible letters, that is, letters that are admirably written which you may want to use later for reference.

14

Reports are among the most widely written kinds of writing, both in college and at work. This chapter, besides reprinting some examples of different kinds of reports, discusses

1. some of the qualities shared by reports and all kinds of writing (p. 367);

2. some of the qualities that are distinctive of reports, including research-based reports (p. 372); and

3. some methods of writing reports (p. 386).

If you're not accustomed to writing them, reports can seem formidable. A *report* somehow seems to be terribly official; we're likely to assume that a report is supposed to be thorough, untainted by personal judgment, and correct, carrying more verifiable and objective information than a human soul can manage. On the other hand, if the prospect isn't a little scary, then it's likely to be merely dreary. There's nothing particularly exciting about the sound of the thing, and we're inclined to assume that a report is supposed to be colorless, but proper. The truth is, there's no reason to be either scared or bored.

Reports are usually defined as objective discussions of some particular subject: news stories are typical reports, but so are many student research papers, scientific articles on research, annual business reports to stockholders; in other words, almost any essay based on and giving an account of some outside information is a report.

The word *report* comes from the Latin *reportare*, which was made from the prefix *re-*, meaning "back," and the word *portare*, meaning "carry." Used as a verb, report means to take back to another, as in bearing information to someone else, to make or give an account of something, to state the result of consideration or investigation; it also means to act as a reporter, or to present oneself. Used as a noun, which is the way it is used in this chapter, *report* means something like an announcement, or a statement, or an account, or the formal statement of the result of an investigation. When you write a report, you are taking (or sending) what you know in your present circumstances back to another person who is not in your present circumstances.

If you'll think about reports in that way, remembering where the word comes from and what it means, perhaps they won't seem formidable. Certainly they won't seem much different from other kinds of writing you have done. A report isn't something strange and different, official and ominous, after all. Everything you have written and most of what you have said is a report of some kind. When you write a letter, you are reporting on yourself in your present circumstances, telling what you know, what you have done, what you propose to do next. When you write an essay examination, you are reporting to a teacher on the present state of your knowledge about a given subject. When you make a telephone call home, you are reporting—even if you are just reporting that you need money. When you write any term paper, you are bearing to your instructor the results of your thinking and investigation.

QUALITIES SHARED BY REPORTS
AND OTHER KINDS OF WRITING

A report is not something set totally apart from other kinds of good writing. If you think of a report as something entirely different from other forms, something special and official, then it's easy to conclude that a report requires some kind of special language, a particular jargon, an "objective" style (*see* Chapter 8). But a report, while it may have to use some special terms, does not require a special, differentiated language. *Indeed, the first requirement in a report is that its language be lucid, direct, and economical.* Reports share this need with all other forms of good writing.

There are other features that good reports share with the various kinds of good writing. In any kind of writing, the writer is the gathering intelligence responsible for the writing. In reports, you may need to be scrupulously fair and accurate, and you may need to be as objective as possible, putting yourself in the background so that the subject gets the primary attention (*see* below), but *you are still the central intelligence responsible for the work.* While reports may need to be objective, they don't have to be impersonal or lifeless. It's even permissible to use first-person pronouns (I, me, my, mine, we, us, our, ours). A piece of writing doesn't become subjective and prejudiced just because you use *I* or *we.* The passage below is a short report on the character of an environmental sciences program, written as part of a larger college report.

Environmental Sciences Program

The Environmental Sciences Program is an interdepartmental, interdisciplinary program sponsored by the Departments of Biology and Geology. The program is designed to develop the knowledge and skills needed to maintain and improve the quality of our natural environment. To accomplish this goal, the program was founded with a strong base in the natural sciences, principally biology, geology, and chemistry with augmentation from mathematics and physics. As such, Balfour University's program holds a unique and advantageous position since most environmental science programs are oriented toward the engineering or social sciences. This is not to say that the program overlooks these disciplines, but only that they are generally taken as electives.

Another unique feature of the Environmental Sciences Program is its encouragement of undergraduates to do research. This approach allows the student to participate in research seminars and discussions, operate intricate scientific equipment, and acquire an understanding of how problems are solved. This research is supervised by the interdisciplinary faculty of the program and results in the production of scholarly scientific papers co-authored with the undergraduates. It is felt that by providing a strong background in science and then encouraging the student to apply this knowledge to solve "real-life" problems, he receives an education in environmental sciences that he could acquire at very few other institutions in the nation.

Notice that with a few revisions (substitution of active voice for passive voice, introduction of first person in some places, other slight changes), the language becomes a little more direct, and we become a little more aware that real people designed this program and that real people are speaking in the report:

Environmental Sciences Program

The Environmental Sciences Program is an interdepartmental, interdisciplinary program sponsored by the Departments of Biology and Geology. The program develops the knowledge and skills needed to maintain and improve the quality of our natural environment. We designed the program with a strong base in the natural sciences, principally biology, geology, and chemistry, augmented by mathematics and physics. For this reason, we believe that Balfour University's program is unique and advantageous since most environmental science programs rely chiefly on the engineering or social sciences. Our program does not overlook these disciplines; our students generally study them as electives.

Another unique feature of the Environmental Sciences Program is that we encourage undergraduates to do research. Students participate in research seminars and discussions, operate intricate scientific equipment, and acquire an understanding of how problems are solved. The interdisciplinary faculty members of the program supervise this research and co-author the scholarly papers produced as a result. We believe that by providing a strong background in science and then by encouraging students to apply this knowledge to solve actual problems, we can help students to receive a distinctive and useful education in environmental science.

Good reports share a third quality with other forms of good writing. *In any good writing, a writer has to share history with readers*. That means that a writer has to provide enough background and context so that readers may know why the subject at hand matters, why the subject came up at the time it did, the background it came from, and the setting in which it can be seen and understood. Readers need to be able to connect what they read with other things in their lives; they need to be able to hook new information onto old information that they already possess. If the brief report above, for example, did not include its first sentence, many readers would not be able to understand what an Environmental Science Program is, even with the explanation that follows. With the first sentence, readers know that this program grew out of departments they are already familiar with.

The report below is a student essay about genealogical research done into her family background. The first paragraph provides some basic history—why certain people began to emigrate. Then the writer narrows the focus to her own family, and traces its history on both her father's and her mother's side. But even though the material is objective, except for the last sentence, the writing is lively, clear, and interesting.

Presbyterian, Family-Oriented, Individualistic

McLean

The stubborn Irish, British subjects for hundreds of years, still refused to become docile. In the 1590's, Queen Elizabeth's forces defeated the Irish earls and confiscated their lands. Bitter demoralization ensued and the Irish only became more obstinat. Later, James I, in an effort to subdue the "natives," invited the Scots to settle in Ulster, North Ireland, offering more productive farmlands, or, perhaps, an escape from debts. Thousands of Scots came, mostly from the Lowlands, and were, as one historian said, "poor, Presbyterian and pertinacious." Life was better, the experiment successful, and by 1717 the Scotch-Irish outnumbered the Irish in Ulster five to three.

One Scotch-Irishman, John McLean, and his wife, descendants of those early migrants, reared their family of four children in Ulster. The second child, Ephraim, when he was about twenty, joined the tide of Scotch-Irish emigrants to America, probably during the 1754–55 wave, and settled in North Carolina. Definitely Presbyterian, Ephraim might have been a minister, as were many of his descendants, or, perhaps, he was a poor farmer seeking better opportunities, as had his ancestors. In 1761 he married Elizabeth Davidson in North Carolina, and one year later the first of their eleven children was born.

Wouldn't it be fascinating to step back into the revolutionary period and view North Carolina from the eyes of these Presbyterian, Scotch-Irish immigrants! Having been in the colonies only twenty to twenty-five years, would Ephraim have joined the Patriots? Horace Walpole told Parliament that "there is no use crying about it. Cousin America has run off with a Presbyterian parson, and that is the end of it." Perhaps Ephraim McLean participated in the 1780 annihilation of Ferguson's command at King's Mountain, delaying the British advance into North Carolina; maybe he was one Patriot who bravely battled Cornwallis at Guilford Court House in March, 1791. And the children—imagine their terror when awakened by the cracks of gunfire!

One of those children, James Davidson McLean, grew to adulthood and married a young woman, Mary, whose last name is unknown. Speculation suggests Mary might have been kin to James McGready, Scotch-Irish frontier evangelist known primarily for his hell-fire brand of Presbyterianism. Support of this theory rests on several factors: (1) James and Mary McLean's first son, born in 1821, was named James McGready. (2) The McGready and McLean families resided in North Carolina at the same time. (3) Both families were staunch Presbyterians of Scotch-Irish descent. (4) James McGready is a name handed down through the McLean family to even the present generation. James McGready McLean became a minister, and for the next two generations several McLean men answered the Calvinistic call to preach. By the early twentieth century, most of the descendants of James McGready had migrated to Texas. One grandson, Samuel Cater McLean, came with his family to Fort Worth about 1910 where he married Margaret Ethel Bound, a women's-libber before her time. But more about that later.

Bound

John Bound, a cobbler, married Ann Bowern of Wimburn, Dorcet-shire, England, in 1845, and lived in Christ's Church on the English Channel. England was enjoying rapid growth in the area of science, the industrial revolution had been accelerated by the invention of the steam engine, and the mood was one of boundless optimism. But in 1853, John and his wife packed some possessions and their six children and emi-grated to America where they settled in Cleveland, Ohio. One wonders why. Perhaps because of the industrialization in England, John's trade there as a cobbler was no longer a profitable business; maybe America offered more options. Whatever the reasons, John and his family arrived in August, 1853. Four more children were born in Cleveland before the family moved in the late 1860's to Texas, finally settling in Fort Worth in 1876.

One child, also named John, at the age of twenty-two left home to "seek his fortune," not to be heard from again for forty-three years. In 1921 he was located through the Associated Charities of Cleveland at the County Farm in Los Angeles. Destitute and suffering from tuberculosis and heart trouble, John died one month later, but not until communica-tion had finally been re-established with the family. He spent his last days in the care of a cousin living in the Los Angeles area.

Another son, George, grew to manhood and on March 23, 1892, married Mary Belle Spaulding, a young telegrapher from Weatherford, Texas. Telegrams written in flourishing longhand offered greetings such as "It is my wish / Sincere and profound / That you will be happy / in being 'Bound' to 'Bound' " and "May your future be / An unbroken circuit of bliss / Full of earth's happiness / Crowned with heaven's kiss / Well balanced at all times / Clear of all grounds / Strewn with blessings / 'Bountiful' from becoming Bound." George and Mary Belle made their home in Fort Worth where he established the Bound Electric Company. One early advertisement, a flyer, inquired, "Have you ever thought of the advantages of electric lights? No greasy lamps to fill, no wicks to trim, no odor, no oil to spill, no lamp chimneys to clean, no lamps that can blow out, flicker or possibly explode or catch on fire and perhaps catch the house on fire. . . . When your house is wired for lights, you can also have an electric iron and in summer an electric fan and don't need to go to Galveston to get a Gulf breeze but can make it at home for yourself, on the hottest summer nights for ⅓ of a cent an hour."

From this marriage, five children were born, including a set of twins, Margaret Ethel and Earl. Earl died from food poisoning when he was eight. Ethel grew up in her father's business where she kept books and repaired fans. As a young woman, Ethel played the piano at College Avenue Presbyterian Church and actively participated in charity work. She also has the distinction of being the first woman in Fort Worth to drive a car. When twenty-five, Ethel married Samuel Cater McLean, owner of a small hardware business. The depression came, though, and they went broke. Thereafter Sam worked for others in the hardware business, and together Sam and Ethel provided a secure home for their five children.

Presbyterian, family-oriented, individualistic—these were traditions Ethel Bound and Sam McLean brought to their marriage and to my family. As their granddaughter, I am proud of the separate ancestries of each, and cherish my heritage.

Good reports, then, share some qualities with all kinds of good writing. The language is clear, direct, and economical. The author is present as a central focusing intelligence, even in objective writing. The background and context necessary to make the subject relevant to readers are provided in reports. But reports aren't like other kinds of good writing in *every* respect. Most of the reports you have read are not like personal essays, nor are they like arguments or directives. Reports share some qualities with other kinds of writing, but they are also different in some ways from other kinds of writing.

Exercises

1.   Find a longer news item in your local paper or in a weekly magazine like *Time* or *Newsweek* that should be of interest to college students, and using the principal information, rewrite the story in a shorter version that might appear in your school newspaper. Concentrate on clear, direct language, keeping yourself present in the writing, and making the subject relevant to other college students.

2.   Write a report about one of your classes that might appear in a student publication to help students choose classes and teachers. Be sure to be economical (no more than 200 words) and to provide adequate *objective* information, keeping in mind that you are reporting so that others can make a choice.

DISTINCTIVE QUALITIES IN REPORTS

Three particular qualities of reports are worth special notice. You may remember discussions in various places throughout this book about some basic differences among kinds of writing (see Chapter 5, for example). Some kinds of writing are personal or expressive; they grow out of personal experience, meditation, revery, or private conviction, and they give authors the opportunity to express themselves, to make themselves known. Some kinds of writing are active or persuasive; they want to have an effect on readers and cause things to happen. Some kinds of writing are referential; they refer to something other than the author; they explain or account for things without necessarily attempting to persuade readers to new thoughts or new actions.

Most reports are referential.   In a report, the author may be closely involved with the subject, deeply committed to it, and the author is surely the responsible, organizing agent for the report. For that reason, an author may appear in a report as a spokesperson or as an investigator (even recording first-person observations and opinions), but the author is not part of the subject.

Some subject other than the author is examined.   A report is not meant, usually, as an occasion for self-expression. Neither is a report usually meant to be persuasive, though some reports end with recommendations proposing a decision or a line of action. More often than not, a report examines or discusses a subject for its own sake; decision or action wait upon the readers and their use of the report material.

For example, in a business, one department—say market research—may report to another—product development—on the habits and preferences of a certain segment of the market, but the report won't recommend how a certain kind of product be developed; that's up to product development. A research report that you are likely to write in college may suggest various courses of action to resolve an issue, and what you think the results of the various actions might be, but you wouldn't necessarily have to recommend that one solution be implemented above the others.

In the report below, notice that the author seems to be chiefly concerned with conveying information. Paragraph 2 provides some immediate background—figures on women's employment during the past ten years. The third paragraph connects the report with other contemporary issues, including traditional conceptions of sex roles and arguments associated with women's liberation. Paragraph 5 provides further background, an account of the traditional reasons cited for employment of women. But by paragraph 6, the writer is dealing with the new features of women's employment, seen against the quick background he has sketched.

Money Need, Social Change
Combine to Cut Apron Strings

(1)   Sometime this year, probably within the next month or so, the percentage of American women who hold or are looking for work is expected to reach 50. According to figures released last week, in April,

49.7 percent of all women—a new high—were in the labor force, an increase from March's 49.3 percent and a signal of a continuing upward swing.

(2)   In the last decade, the Labor Department says, 14 million new jobs have been filled in this country and women have filled 10 million of them. Last year, in large part because of the rapid entry of women into the labor market, the number of jobseekers grew just about as rapidly as the number of jobs. That is one reason why the unemployment rate stayed so high last year—the average, 7 percent, give or take a tenth of a point—despite the fact that employment rose at a record rate, by 4.1 million jobs.

(3)   Some economists and politicians discuss the phenomenon in a faintly accusatory manner. Though the suggestion is never directly put, it is there: If only women would stay in their traditional homemaker's role, instead of seeking liberation through a different lifestyle, the nation's unemployment troubles would be solved. Or, such commentators recommend, unemployment should be redefined, so that "nontraditional" workers such as women be properly weighted. But such scapegoat thinking, other experts contend, only obscures fundamental economic reasons for the trend.

(4)   Undoubtedly, social factors play a role in the growing flood of women into the work force. "But the fact is more and more women are working out of necessity," says Alexis M. Herman, director of the Women's Bureau of the Labor Department. "Women don't have the option of working inside the home or outside the home any more," she adds. "Economic needs require that they go out and find a job."

(5)   Miss Herman has estimated that 60 to 65 percent of women who hold jobs do so for purely economic reasons. Many of them must work because they are the only source of economic support for themselves and their families. A Women's Bureau study published in mid-1976 showed that over 23 percent of working women have never been married. Another 19 percent of women workers were widowed, divorced or separated from their husbands, and because of social and cultural trends, the number of women living without husbands is increasing. In 1960, for example, 28 percent of women aged 22 to 24 were single; by 1976 the number had risen to 46 percent. For most of them, there is little alternative to work other than welfare or unemployment compensation. As Geraldine Coleman, a 27-year-old mother of three who works as an auto mechanic for Sears Roebuck and Co., puts it, a job is not simply a matter of lifestyle: "I work because it is a matter of survival. A single parent like me needs a job and needs one at a male salary."

(6)   More than half of all working women, however, are married, some of them to men who are unable to work, and still more have husbands who are unemployed for one reason or another. These women, too, must work as the sole support of their families and themselves. Of working women with working husbands, close to half had husbands who earned $10,000 a year or less when the data for the 1976 women's bureau study

was collected. "Often," Miss Herman explains, "a second income means the difference between poverty and an adequate standard of living."

(7)   But it is not just the wives of low-wage earners who are taking jobs to supplement their husband's income, and help keep the family budget solvent in the face of inflation. Women in middle-income families are taking jobs in response to the economic squeeze. In part, such women are going to work to maintain the standard of living to which they have become accustomed. But increasingly, a second income is being sought to achieve traditional goals, such as college education for their children or for a one-family home.

(8)   Sandra Hall, whose husband is a Secret Service agent, recently went to work as a computer repair specialist. "I work first of all for the money," she said. "One income wasn't sufficient. We want to maintain a middle-class lifestyle—meaning for us a townhouse in Reston [Va.] and braces on the boy's teeth. Also they are continually raising utility rates and other things are going up all the time. Of course I've always wanted to work anyway. I've been working all my adult life."

(9)   "I'm working at this job for one reason—to make enough money to put my kids through college," said a woman with a civil service job in Washington whose $26,000 a year salary is only marginally below her husband's. When both children are in college at the same time all of her after-tax salary, working costs deducted, would go for tuition and school expenses.

(10)   The cost of that other American dream, the suburban home, is also rising so fast that it is fading beyond the reach of many one-income families that could, in past generations, have afforded one. In fact, the cherished notion of the American family, in which the father goes out to earn daily bread and the mother stays at home in a cottage, with or without a rose garden, to take care of the children, is now more myth than reality.

(11)   Two years ago, the Urban Institute extrapolated from Bureau of Labor Statistics data that only 19 percent of all Americans were members of families in which the father worked and the mother stayed at home, with one or more children. Ralph Smith, an economist with the institute, said that the number of these supposedly archetypical family groups will continue to shrink.

(12)   Changes in the structure of the economy have also contributed to the rapid growth of the percentage of women in the labor force, says Julius Shiskin, director of the Bureau of Labor Statistics. While employment has been declining or stagnant in manufacturing and construction industries, which are dominated by men, it has been rising fairly rapidly in clerical and service industries. Few working women now have jobs such as Mrs. Coleman's: Being an auto mechanic is generally considered man's work. Women are concentrated chiefly into 20 of the 480 job categories listed by the Labor Department, most of them clerical, such as secretarial or bookkeeping, or service, such as sales clerks, nurses aides

and waitresses. But with women pouring into the workplace at an accelerated rate, most economists predict that more of them will be moving away from such traditional women's work.—Philip Shabecoff

Reports are often based on research.   Reports are *referential*; they are about something other than the author. They exist to *convey* information and opinion. These two qualities help account for a third distinctive quality of reports: *they are characteristically based on investigation,* not meditation or personal opinion. The previous report was based on research.

Investigation may take many forms. Sometimes it occurs as members of a committee split to track down sources of a particular problem in an institution. Sometimes it occurs as a single person interviews people to determine opinion. Sometimes it occurs when a group or a person sets out to track information through reading and study. Since reports are usually based on investigation, they may have to be documented—that is, you may need to show the sources of your information through footnotes and attach a list of references.

INSIGHT

Reports and research papers

Many of the research papers that you are asked to do for college classes are reports. Sometimes, of course, your research papers may be simple descriptions or narratives; sometimes you may use research as a basis for making an argument (see Chapter 15). But probably more often than not, college research papers are reports—that is, they are systematic gatherings of information and insight, or systematic investigations of some particular problem. In general, they are often objective discussions of some particular subject, ordinarily based on outside information. So this seems a fitting time to stop and discuss some of the suggestions that are available in this book for research papers.

1.   At the end of the book, in Chapter 17, is a guide to research writing, including some basic sources, suggestions for gathering information, and some standard forms for footnotes and bibliographic entries.

2.   You will want to consider your subject carefully, both in terms of its focus and of its interest to you. The early chapters on finding and exploring subjects may give you some ideas for approaching broad subject areas.

3.   Since research papers, especially those that are reports, are likely to be longer than other kinds of writing you do in college and are likely to take more of your time (often a whole term), it is often

important to pay particular attention to each step in the process, organizing your work carefully and keeping careful account of all that you do. Chapter 6, Designing Your Work—particularly the section on outlining—may be helpful in this connection. The suggestions on evaluating resources and taking notes in Chapter 17 may also be useful.

4. The discussion that follows in this chapter, Some Methods of Writing Reports, also applies to writing research papers.

Some general suggestions about research reports also merit some attention. Remember, first, that in a report, the writing is referential—that is, you are usually going to be writing about something outside yourself, and you are usually going to be expected to distance yourself from your subject enough to be objective. Remember, too, that however you finally organize your research report, your readers will probably expect you to present three essential accounts:

—What did you investigate and why did you investigate it?

—What were the results of your investigation?

—What summary, synthesis, or suggestions can you offer from your study?

Exercises

1. If you have chosen your major, or if you are considering a particular field, do a research report from library sources about how another field relates to the field of your choice. Consider as your audience others who might have the same major field.

2. Choose a topic that you are interested in, or a subject that increasing your knowledge about might help in one of your other courses, and make a list of all of the sources about the subject available in your library. Compile a bibliography from these sources. Be sure that your subject is limited enough for you to locate all of the possible resources and that the subject can be handled comprehensively in a report of reasonable length.

3. Take notes from the sources you found in exercise two and write a documented report on the subject you chose. You should discuss your topic with your teacher to be sure that you can handle it.

The paper that follows is a sample student report. It may be helpful for you to study it for its style and content and for the way the notes and bibliography were handled.

JANE ADDAMS AND HULL HOUSE

Jane Addams was a remarkably progressive woman. Born in the Victorian Age, Addams fought against traditional concepts about class distinction and worked to lessen the educational and cultural gap between classes. Although she initiated many social reform programs and headed several philanthropic institutes, her most famous contribution was the founding of Hull House--a settlement designed to improve the welfare of Chicago's poorer neighborhoods.

The roots of Addams' decision to establish Hull House began in her childhood. At an early age, Addams was serious, conscientious, and anxious to make an important contribution to society. Her father, John H. Addams, encouraged her humane views by exposing her to the oppressive conditions of the poor. These experiences made lasting impressions. Addams recalls from her first introduction to urban slums that she "felt the curious distinction between the ruddy poverty of the country and [the squalor] which even a small city presents . . . ."[1] A family legend celebrates a statement that Addams made at age seven as a forecast of her decision to found Hull House. After visiting the slums of Freeport, Illinois, Addams vowed to live in a large house like her father's, "but it would not be built among the other large houses, but right in the midst of horrid little houses like these."[2] Eventually, Addams did live in Hull House, a mansion amid slums.

Next to her father's teachings and her childhood exper-

2

iences, Addams' years at Rockford Seminary were crucial to
the development of her social awareness. During the first
year, she became friends with an ambitious and intellectual
group of women. They petitioned for and finally succeeded
in receiving the first B.A.'s awarded by Rockford Seminary.
Because they were the first generation of women to earn a
college degree, they felt obliged, if not inspired, to use
their knowledge to its fullest.[3] Many of the women became
missionaries. Others taught the handicapped. But Addams was
different. She rejected missionary work; for although she
was religious, she had never joined a church. The other
alternatives--teaching or marriage--were equally unacceptable.
Teaching would not be challenging enough, and marriage would
interfere with a career. Her childhood memories of the
worker's poverty suggested that she do something to benefit
the poor. Believing that medicine would be a good means,
Addams enrolled in the Women's Medical College in Philadelphia
However, her poor health forced her to leave school.[4] She
never resumed her medical study because she "discovered that
there were other genuine reasons for living among the poor
than that of practicing medicine upon them. . . ."[5]

During the following six years, Addams began a search
for those other genuine reasons that ended with the founding
of Hull House. She discovered her goal while traveling in
Europe with Ellen Starr, a friend from Rockford. After witnessing the filth and poverty of the London slums, Addams
wanted to become a social worker. She hoped to "aid in the

3

solution of the social and industrial problems which are
engendered by the modern conditions of life in a great city."[6]
Including Starr in her plans, Addams prepared to work on opening the lines of communication between social classes and
between nationalities by providing a common urban center with
cultural and educational activities for all.

In January 1889, the two women returned to Chicago to
launch their project. After soliciting aid from some of the
city's established residents, Addams and Starr rented an old
mansion in the slums on South Halsted Street. It was a "large
house" in the middle of other "horrid little houses." Named
after its original owner, Charles J. Hull, Hull House became
the center of cultural and political events for the surrounding vicinity.

The scope and focus of Hull House activities grew and
changed with the needs of the neighborhood. Addams' ability
to speak several European languages helped to bring together
the different immigrant and ethnic groups that lived in the
area. Clubs, lectures, and classes soon replaced the informal
nightly gatherings at Hull House. Addams aimed "to preserve
and keep whatever of value [the immigrants'] past life contained and to bring them in contact with a better type of
American."[7] Music, art, and craft lessons along with college
level courses attracted both the wealthy and the poor. Soon
boarders began to fill the empty mansion rooms keeping Hull
House open twenty-four hours a day.

Because of its success, Hull House soon needed more space.

4

Helen Culver, the owner of Hull House, provided a lease that
allowed for new construction while gifts and donations from
wealthy Chicagoans financed four additions. The Butler Art
Gallery, built in 1891, housed a branch of the public library
and provided room to exhibit the works of local artists and
artisans. Two years later a coffee house with a second floor
gymnasium provided greater recreational space. By 1895 a
residence hall for men and the "Jane Club," a cooperative
dormitory for women who could not afford to pay rent, joined
the original structures.[8]

In addition to providing cultural education, Hull House
promoted political and social change. Under Addams' guidance,
settlement residents pioneered in better housing, parks, and
playgrounds. They petitioned for better child labor laws, an
eight-hour workday for women, workman's compensation, and the
first juvenile court laws. One committee, headed by Florence
Kelly, investigated child labor in Chicago. The result led
to the first factory law of Illinois regulating sanitary
conditions and setting a minimum working age of fourteen.[9]
Addams personally oversaw the sanitation project in the neighborhood. Her improvements, which included organizing garbage
collectors and sewer maintenance crews, won her the title of
garbage inspector and the only salary of her career.[10]

From 1895 until 1914, Hull House flourished. The political campaigns made it nationally famous and its cultural-
events program became a model for future settlements. Many
social workers came to Hull House to study its progressive

5

educational methods and to learn the reasons for its success.
Donations continued to support the settlement while volunteers
and residents helped to run it.

The outbreak of World War I brought a close to these
productive years. Conservatives distrusted the socially
minded Hull House leaders. Because many Hull House residents
were German immigrants, rumors circulated that Hull House was
sympathetic to the Germans. Criticism increased when Addams
began a crusade for world peace in 1915. Her message was to
end the war through mediation, but most people interpreted it
as pro-German propaganda. When Addams founded the American
Women's Peace Party, donations from former supporters ceased
altogether.[11]

Hull House failed to regain its former stature after the
war. The excitement of social causes and reforms died as the
lighthearted Twenties began. Though Hull House programs
managed to survive, the once dynamic level of activity was
fading. Fewer people attended the lectures and classes. Even
Addams spent less time at Hull House. Her new work as President of the Women's International League for Peace and Freedom
demanded much attention, though her devotion to Hull House
remained constant. The Depression dealt a major blow to the
settlement. It forced the suspension of all activities,
drained the house funds, and sent the residents to work in
bread lines. The New Deal brought hope and some financial
aid, but not enough to stabilize the settlement.

The most serious crisis for Hull House was Addams' death

6

on May 21, 1935. Not only was she the founder of Hull House, but she was the President, Head Resident, and real strength behind it. Her death left the residents grieved and the institution floundering. Lack of unity, purpose, and leadership plagued Hull House for eight years. Finally, Louise deKoven Bowen, a close friend of Addams, managed to salvage it. She established the Jane Addams Memorial Fund to resolve financial debts and appointed Adena Miller Rich to fill the position as Head Resident.[12]

Hull House began a slow recovery. However, in 1960, trouble returned. The University of Illinois planned to extend its campus and wanted the Harrison-Halsted area with Hull House at the center to be its new site. The Hull House Association brought the matter to court. The Illinois Supreme Court decided in favor of the University. After nearly seventy years, the activities of Hull House were without a home. But six new locations throughout Chicago were found. As a memorial to Addams, the city restored the original Hull mansion and the Residents' Dining Hall, making them a historic site on June 14, 1967.[13]

Though their social pioneering days are over, the Hull House Centers of today still provide many of the activities that Addams began. Her vision, courage, and sense of social justice not only originated America's most famous settlement, but also established a continuing means for improving the welfare of Chicago's poorer districts.

7

Notes

[1] Jane Addams, "First Impressions," in <u>When I Was a Child</u>, ed. Edward Wagenknecht (New York: E. P. Dutton, 1946), p. 138.

[2] Jane Addams, <u>Twenty Years at Hull House</u> (New York: Macmillan, 1934), pp. 4-5.

[3] Henry and Dana Lee Thomas, "Jane Addams," in <u>Living Biographies of Famous Women</u> (Garden City, New York: Blue Ribbon Books, 1946), pp. 264-65.

[4] Esse V. Hathaway, <u>Partners in Progress</u> (New York: McGraw-Hill Book Co., 1935), p. 255.

[5] "Jane Addams," in <u>Readings in Biography</u> (New York: Macmillan, 1931), p. 278.

[6] "Jane Addams," <u>Encyclopedia Americana</u>, 1978 ed.

[7] "Jane Addams," (Chicago: University of Chicago Press, 1967), p. 3.

[8] Thomas and Thomas, p. 267.

[9] Allen Davis, <u>Eighty Years at Hull House</u> (Chicago: Quadrangle Books, 1969), p. 22.

[10] Addams, <u>Twenty Years</u>, pp. 200-201.

[11] Thomas and Thomas, p. 272.

[12] "Jane Addams," (Chicago: University of Chicago Press, 1967), p. 17.

[13] Davis, p. 142.

8

List of Works Consulted

Addams, Jane. "First Impressions." In When I Was a Child.
Ed. Edward Wagenknecht. New York: E. P. Dutton, 1946,
pp. 136-48.

Addams, Jane. Twenty Years at Hull House. New York: Macmillan, 1934.

Davis, Allen. Eighty Years at Hull House. Chicago: Quadrangle
Books, 1969.

Hathaway, Esse V. Partners in Progress. New York: McGraw-
Hill Book Co., 1935.

"Jane Addams." Chicago: University of Chicago Press, 1967.

"Jane Addams." Encyclopedia Americana. 1978 ed.

"Jane Addams." Encyclopaedia Britannica: Macropaedia.
1974 ed.

"Jane Addams." In Readings in Biography. Ed. Clara L. Myers.
New York: Macmillan, 1931, pp. 277-92.

Linn, James Weber, Jane Addams. New York: Appleton-Century
Co., 1938.

Thomas, Henry, and Dana Lee Thomas. "Jane Addams." In
Living Biographies of Famous Women. Garden City, New
York: Blue Ribbon Books, 1946, pp. 261-73.

SOME METHODS OF WRITING REPORTS

Remember that you needn't reinvent the wheel every time you write something new; that is, remember that other writers have probably used forms and organizational structures similar to those you will need, and that you should make use of these models whenever you can.

If you must write reports for your work, remember that your company may have a guide of its own for report writing—many companies do. If there is no such printed guide, remember that others have written reports before you, and their work is probably available in company files. If your college course work requires you to write reports, your instructors may suggest particular plans or formats for the work, or show you examples of other reports. In either instance—at work or at college—remember that almost any library, regardless of size, will have books on business and professional writing that will usually include guides to report writing. Other people have written reports; you don't have to start from nothing.

It's important that you remember and use available resources—company guide books, files, instructors' examples, books on business and professional writing. The occasions in which reports must be written are so diverse and the kinds of reports that may be called for are so many that no single guide, including this book, can show you how to write every conceivable kind of report.

However, there is a basic organizational pattern common to many reports:

Introduction:
> a statement of the problem
> the occasion or need for exploring the problem
> anticipated or proposed method for exploring the problem

Middle:
> an account of the procedure followed in exploring the problem
> an account of the information resulting from the investigation—tests, samplings, interviews, questionnaires, statistical investigations, library research of any kind

End:
> a presentation of the final findings, last suggestions, or proposals; a display of results, conclusions, and sometimes recommendations

Not all reports, of course, will have all of these parts, and not all reports will follow this order specifically. Many reports do follow a pattern much like this, but some have special requirements:

A *memorandum*, for example, may present only the *end* of a chain of thought or an investigation. In all likelihood, no one writes a memorandum without privately going through many of the steps suggested above, but often only the conclusion is presented. A company leader, for instance, having faced a company problem (introduction) and explored it tentatively (middle), may write down only his or her proposal, that a major investigation be undertaken to explore the problem thoroughly.

A *progress report* has mostly to do with the *middle* steps suggested above. What is called for in a progress report is an account of what has been done so far in a given investigation or a given procedure.

A *briefing report* is meant, usually, to anticipate what is going to happen, to anticipate what should be known or done first, last, and in between, to anticipate problems. A *briefing* is intended to prepare someone or some group for work that is to come.

A *critique*, or *evaluation*, on the other hand, looks at an enterprise or a piece of work after it is over. The pattern sketched above can be useful: one way to write a *critique* is to look back at the beginning to see if the work was begun at the best place, to look back at the middle to see if everything was done that should be done, in order to look at the conclusion to see if it can be validated.

A *committee report* or other kinds of *formal reports* may very well follow the general plan sketched above. Such reports may need to provide full accounts of the starting place and occasion, full accounts of the procedures followed and of the information gained, and full justifications of results, conclusions, and recommendations.

If you'll look back at the samples throughout the chapter, you may notice that while none of them has three parts clearly labeled *Introduction, Middle, End*, the parts are nevertheless there. The brief report on the environmental sciences program starts with its beginnings in Biology and Geology (Introduction), tells how it was designed and why (Middle), and concludes with an account of the expected consequence of the program (End). The little report on women in the work force begins with background about the changes that have already occurred in the number of women working outside the home; the middle of the report gives reasons why women work; and the end makes some predictions about the jobs women will hold in the future. Each of the samples develops all or some of the three key parts of a report shown above.

Whatever form you follow, remember that within your writing you can call upon most of the methods used in other kinds of writing. Reports depend upon description, narration, exposition, and argumentation, and each of the other chapters of this book is relevant to report writing.

You may want to review especially Chapter 7 and the account there of various methods for developing and exploring material—definition, illustration, comparison, contrast, classification, cause-and-effect analysis, and the others.

Finally, as you prepare your own reports or as you study the reports of others, keep these questions in mind:

Is the language clear and direct, free of jargon?

How does the author show up in the work?

How is a context established for the work?

In what sense is the work referential? Does the subject dominate the work, or do other factors interfere?

Is the subject clearly examined? Are questions left unasked and unanswered?

What kind of investigation supports the work?

How is the work organized?

What methods of development are used?

Exercises

1.   Write a report about a little-known feature of your campus. It might be a special counseling service provided for students, a special collection in the library, a source of financial aid, etc. As you prepare your report, make use of resource persons, available brochures, and other information. Consider sending the report to your school or local newspaper.

2.   Write a report on an event in your community or on your campus. Try to report not only what happened, but also the circumstances surrounding the event.

3.   Research and write a documented report about something that directly affects the lives of college students; for example, the availability of jobs in a particular field, alcoholism on campus, etc. Try to use all kinds of available resources: newspapers, books, films, interviews, pamphlets. Be sure you choose a specific topic so that you can make a full and complete report.

4.   Find a situation on your campus or in your community that you feel needs remedying, and write a fact-finding report that could bring the situation to the attention of a dean, a city council member, or other person who might have some power in correcting it.

15

After some introductory remarks to differentiate argument from other kinds of writing, the chapter attempts some answers to these questions about argument:

1. what are the occasions for argument and the goals of persuasion (p. 391)?

2. what can be learned about persuasion and how to argue fairly and effectively (p. 393)?

3. what are different kinds of arguments and how can they be classified (p. 404)? and

4. what are the special responsibilities involved in persuasive writing (p. 412)?

A private letter or a familiar essay can afford to be purely personal, expressing the author's own convictions, attitudes, prejudices, and feelings. A diary or a lyric poem doesn't have to do anything but express the author's own thoughts or recount an author's experiences or catch an author's feelings of the moment—for that matter, a diary or a lyric poem doesn't have to do anything except what pleases the author. These are *expressive* forms, or *personal* forms (see Chapter 5). *Referential* forms, as you know, do a different kind of work, and we can legitimately expect different kinds of things from them. A report, for example, is normally supposed to tell about something outside the author, that the author has investigated in some way. Each kind of writing carries its own responsibilities. Of *personal* writing, we can at the very least expect honesty. Of *referential* writing, we can at the least expect accuracy. But neither has overt designs on readers. Either may amuse or inform readers, show them things they had not known or seen, or enable them to think in new ways, but neither is especially intent on changing readers.

Argumentative or *persuasive* writing has much in common with personal and especially with referential writing; they are all based on facts or impressions, but argumentative writing, rather than intending to inform or divert, *uses* the information to support or test a belief. And in supporting a specific point of view, persuasive writing may be intended and designed to change the way readers believe, think, or behave. A politician's campaign speech or position statement, for example, plainly wants to influence the way people vote. The text of an advertisement is intended to influence readers' actions (by getting them to buy a product or use a service), and may try to persuade readers directly and obviously or more subtly and indirectly. A minister's sermon may work with calm, thoughtful confidence or with fire and brimstone to influence a congregation.

Some key words come into play in most discussions of arguments; they, too, can help provide a starting place in thinking about argument. The word *argument* comes originally from a Latin word, *arguere*, which in the beginning appears to have meant *to make clear*. The word *argument* now appears to be used chiefly to mean *a reason or reasons given in proof*. The word *argumentation*, then, means to most of us something like *the process of forming reasons and drawing conclusions*. Incidentally, the root word *arguere* was also used at times in its history to signify *prating*, or *empty talk*, or *noise*. The word *persuade* comes originally from the Latin *persuadēre*, which in turn was made from *per-*, meaning thoroughly, and *suadēre*, meaning *advise* or *urge*. Now, when we use the word *persuasion*, we usually mean something like *the process of moving by argument or entreaty to a belief, position, or course of action*.

That doesn't mean that persuasive writing is an arm-twisting enterprise. It is sometimes, to be sure, but it doesn't have to be. A writer undertaking to persuade may of course want very plainly to influence or to change readers, and may work on them quite obviously. But a writer

INSIGHT

All writing can be persuasive

In a sense, anything you write may be taken as persuasive writing. If you write a description of something and show your writing to someone else, presumably you want the reader to see the thing as you do, to believe and accept your way of seeing. If you define something in writing, presumably you want a reader to believe that your definition is accurate. If you look at matters in this way, any piece of writing may be considered an effort to persuade readers. It may be more useful, however, to make some distinctions among pieces of writing. Some, expressive forms, are more concerned with revealing or explaining or presenting their authors. Some, referential forms, are more concerned with displaying their subjects accurately. And some, persuasive forms, are more concerned with influencing readers' ideas and actions.

may want only to present quietly and usefully something that readers will find believable, something they can accept and appropriate for their own uses; a writer may want only to advocate certain beliefs that readers can share so that writer and readers can identify with each other and find some sense of community.

But whether it is obvious or quiet, open or indirect, persuasive writing does want to reach readers, to enter their lives, to change them. For this reason persuasive writing entails special responsibilities. If you are going to try to change others, a decent respect for them requires that you meet some special responsibilities that are not so apparent in other forms of writing.

OCCASIONS FOR ARGUMENT

The world is full of arguments and of arguable matters, and if there aren't space, time, and reasons for arguments, we'll make do and argue anyway. So we don't have to look far to find occasions both for arguing and for studying argument. Argument (or persuasive writing) has immediate and practical significance in our lives. We harangue each other. We assert things to each other, or at each other. We beguile each other, or try to. We assume certain things are true that other people think ought to be established as true. We oversimplify some things, claiming to others that some complex things are really quite simple if they'll just learn to see and do things our way (as when a writer proclaims that he or she has found THE FOUR BASIC STEPS TO SUCCESS, or THE ONE PATH

TO TRUE SERENITY THROUGH MEDITATION AND ALIMENTARY CONDITIONING). We overcomplicate things for each other, claiming that there are some things others can't possibly understand unless they have our special language, our special procedure, our special professional expertise (as when a management expert, for example, argues that we can scarcely hope to change fruitfully unless we have planned for change in his or her way, with a dramatic flowchart to map the whole procedure).

We spend a lot of time arguing about things we probably shouldn't argue about. There is no reason to argue about matters of taste or preference. If one person likes pineapple pie and Bach, then another person who prefers chocolate pie and the Rolling Stones probably ought to leave him or her alone in the pleasure of pineapple pie and Bach, and not try to argue that chocolate and Mick Jagger are preferable, better, more relevant, or more significant. There is no good reason, either, to argue about simple matters of information that can be checked. You can find out what Jack Nicklaus did on a given hole in the U.S. Open in a given year—there's little point in arguing about the matter. You can find out with a little checking when Amelia Earhart flew around the world—there's little point in arguing about it. But there is point in arguing about matters of judgment, where available evidence and thoughtful reasoning can sometimes show one view or judgment to be wiser than another.

The frequency of disputes, our sometime unwillingness to pay much attention, and all the questions and possibilities that are raised by disputes are surely reason enough to study and understand and practice arguments. Argument has immediate and practical significance for writing and speaking. The study of argument is also a whetstone for sharpening our critical senses: we need always to be learning how to search out the issues at stake in discussions and arguments; we need always to be learning how to discover basic assumptions in discussions and arguments; we need always to be learning how to catch prejudices wherever they may stalk; we need always to be learning how to sense and understand threats and hostilities. Argument is around us, and in us. Occasions are everywhere.

Exercises

1.   For a day keep a list of all of the occasions in which you are either involved in or witness to arguments. (Your roommate tries to convince you to go get a pizza, your professor urges your class to read their assignments, and so on.)

2.   Find three recent written examples of short arguments. For each of these, write answers to the following questions:
   a.   What is the occasion for the argument?
   b.   What are the major steps with which the argument proceeds?

3. Jot down the content of a discussion which you overhear between two people in which one is trying to persuade the other to do something. When you have finished writing the dialogue, write an analysis of what you observed about the approaches the persuader used, his or her attitude toward the other person, and the possible reasons for his or her success or failure.

The goals of argument

Arguments, the mixed, varied forms that argumentation and persuasion take, are aimed at some kind of change. They occur where there is some kind of conflict or controversy, as for example in the recent and continuing discussions and debates about the Equal Rights Amendment, where views are clearly divided and often opposed to each other. Or a piece of argumentative writing can sometimes *create* a conflict or controversy. For example, during the years from about 1960 to about 1970, several pieces of writing—Rachel Carson's book *Silent Spring* is an example—examined an area in which controversy had been minimal, quiet, or nonexistent, that is, the ecological condition of the earth; by their examination of waste disposal, pesticide and herbicide use, and energy usurpation the writers were able to awaken large numbers of people to new issues and questions.

Arguing, of course, involves *revelation*, as in personal or expressive writing; when you argue, you have to know yourself to some extent at least, to know your own views, to weigh the strength of your own convictions. Arguing also involves *display*, as in referential writing; when you argue, you presumably know something about the subject at hand and can show its features to an audience. Sometimes, to be sure, arguers get wrapped up in themselves and the beauty or virtue of their arguments, and sometimes they forget their audience in the interest of exploring the issues and problems in the subject before them. But ordinarily, arguing involves turning toward an audience and moving near it, engaging an audience so as to generate *change* among its members.

DEVELOPING ARGUMENTS

But what do you do when you want to argue? You can yell, of course, and if you yell loudest and last, perhaps you can win. You can simply assert what you believe people ought to think or do, and if what you say happens to suit them, perhaps they'll agree. You can gather the evidence in accord with your views, and if nobody notices the discordant evidence you've omitted, perhaps others will assent to your views. You can marshal evidence thoroughly, examine it thoughtfully, draw conclusions from it properly, and present it all engagingly, and others may listen and agree. And they may not. Don't expect a guarantee that a good argument will win agreement and achieve harmony, and don't forget that a free-thinking citizen may well be obliged to argue nevertheless.

But how do you make a good argument? The world is full of arguments and arguers. Occasions and needs and personalities vary. Your own interests will shift and shift again. It's clear, as this book has repeatedly said, that there is no perfect pattern for a particular kind of writing. There are, however, some cautions and some recommendations that can help us argue effectively and fairly.

Using resources and evidence

When we state our opinions in informal situations, we often give little or no evidence to support them: "John is a reckless driver"; "The cost of living is going up every day"; "Divorce is the main cause of juvenile delinquency." This does not mean that we have no good reasons for believing as we do, but simply that our reasons are usually known and accepted by our listeners. On occasions when our opinions are questioned, we may attempt to support them with facts drawn from our experience and reading: "John had two accidents last month, and he always drives too fast." "Steak is up sixty cents a pound, and a refrigerator costs almost twice as much today as it did six years ago." "Psychologists say that emotional stability depends on a secure family life." Such evidence is considered acceptable or even convincing in informal situations, usually because the listener's personal regard for the speaker lends some weight to the evidence.

In writing, however, the relationship with your audience is far more impersonal; authority must rest much more on the facts themselves. Readers who know neither John nor you will want to know what kind of accidents John had and who was at fault; they will wonder whether "too fast" means in excess of speed limits; they may suspect that "always" is an exaggeration. Before accepting your opinion in regard to the relation between divorce and delinquency, they may want to hear what psychologists say in their own words, to be sure you are not misinterpreting their remarks or ignoring opposed opinions.

The more facts supporting your opinion that you can gather from experience or from the written statement of others, the more reason you can give your readers to accept that opinion. You will probably not be able to present absolute *proof*, but the greater the weight of your evidence, the more probable it will seem to them that your belief is the best one.

Modes of argument

There are also some ways of thinking about kinds of argument that may provide both guidance and some flexibility and adaptability for you when you are developing arguments; they may help you see what to do in your own arguments and judge what others have done in theirs.

First, it is helpful to think about different *modes* of argument. *Mode*, in the sense used here, means something like the prevailing attitude in an argument. A set of terms that you may find useful is a classification of arguments by *mode*:

Logical argument

Emotional argument

Ethical argument

Any kind of argument can be done in any *mode* of argument. An attacking argument may be logical, or emotional, or ethical, or it may be all three.

Logical argument is what we like to think we always practice when we argue. A logical argument characteristically rests either upon a sure, clear, and appropriate sequence of thought or upon a mass of evidence and a following conclusion. The discussion in Chapter 7, "Developing Your Material," may help you to see ways of building logical sequences in your arguments.

INSIGHT

A dozen dependable aids to logic

A few special reminders may help you form logical arguments:

1.   Any evidence you use should be as specific and detailed as possible. Let readers know exactly what your evidence is, where it came from, and how you got it. (For documenting evidence, see the section on notes and bibliographies in Chapter 17.)

2.   If you go looking for particular pieces of evidence, take pains to look at enough samples and at a fair representation of samples. If you're going to attack television, you can ill afford to study only the programs you particularly dislike.

3.   In your study and research, try to be sure that the information you get is reliable information. A single newspaper report about a political movement may not tell you all you need to know.

4.   Be cautious in reaching conclusions about a whole group on the basis of observing some of the members of the group. Knowing your sisters, your mother, five aunts, and forty women school teachers is not a sufficient basis, usually, for reaching conclusions about women. Drawing conclusions about a group from observation of part of the group is sometimes called *stereotyping*.

5.   Avoid any easy conclusion that because one thing happens first and another thing happens second, the first caused the second. In one early society, it was concluded that body lice brought good health. What seemed to happen was this: a person got sick and ran a fever; because of the fever, the lice left the body; when the fever went down, the lice returned; the fever having abated, health returned; therefore lice bring health. This kind of fallacious reasoning is referred to by some as *post hoc ergo propter hoc* ("after this, therefore because of this").

6.   Try to be sure that any conclusion you draw really does follow in a reasonable way from the evidence. If you argue that because a man doesn't drink, spit, smoke, chew, or fornicate unwisely, he is therefore a good politician, you are guilty of the fallacy in reasoning called *non sequitur* ("it does not follow").

7.   Don't beg the question. That means assuming something is true that needs to be proved. If you start an argument with the primary assumption that "abortion is murder," you are begging the question.

8.   Where conflicts and various possibilities exist, be cautious in reducing your alternatives to two, either this or that.

9.   If you disagree with somebody on a particular issue or problem, deal with the problem or issue in your argument, not the person. Attacking the person instead of the issue is sometimes called the *ad hominem* ("to the man") fallacy.

10.   Be slow to argue for something because everybody else does it. It might be right for them, but not for you. And they may be wrong. An argument *ad populum* is an argument that uses the prejudices and interests of the people in an audience.

11.   Calling people names and generally vilifying them may sometimes seem gratifying, but it doesn't do much toward helping with a sequential argument that faces particular issues and problems.

12.   If you depend a lot on glittering generalities ("the American sense of fair play," "Up with people"), you may appeal to those who like your glittering generalities, but you probably won't get much else done.

Exercises

1.   Look for a fallacy in each of the following advertisements:
   a.   Our attitude puts us ahead. We'll do anything for our customers and our city.—Ad for a car dealer
   b.   The spirit of the Czar lives on.—A vodka ad

   c. This car makes the neighborhood service station a nice place to visit.—An automobile ad

   d. Get rich and famous.—A candy bar ad in a comic book

   e. Pour it with arrogance.—A bourbon ad

   f. Why people who love the outdoors also love trucks.—A truck ad

2. Find some examples of advertising that contain fallacies and describe the fallacy you see there.

3. Describe what is wrong with the following thesis statements:

   a. The very fact that through all of these centuries only a few women have ever risen to positions of power in government or business proves that women are less capable than men in these areas.

   b. Prejudice just does not exist anymore. In my high school everyone was treated equally.

   c. Politicians are all alike—lining their pockets at the expense of the taxpayers who elected them.

   d. School teachers only work from eight to three; they don't deserve to make high salaries.

   e. If inflation continues at the present rate, another depression is inevitable.

Emotional argument works by evoking emotional responses in the audience. It's fairly common to find people assuming that there is something inherently wrong with emotional argument. There is, if you depend upon arousing emotional sympathy in place of offering evidence and sequential thought. *Slanted writing* (see Chapter 8, Saying the Words) is a form of emotional argument in which an author tilts an argument to one side by presenting his or her views in positive, emotionally gratifying language and an opponent's views in unfavorable language ("I am firm in my views; you are pig-headed"). But there is nothing basically wrong with emotional argument if you use it fairly and use it as a supplement to evidence. In the Gettysburg Address, for example, one of the effects of that marvelous opening is to remind us of our emotional commitment to the origins of this country.

Ethical argument is more difficult to explain. Sometimes we believe an author because he or she is believable. We respond to the author's honesty in disclosing his or her own interests, or we see the author using evidence fairly, or we find the author admitting opposing views into his or her mind, or something happens that enables us to see the author as a trustable person. Sometimes, of course, we trust the wrong person, perhaps because he or she is calculatedly seeking our trust. Ethical argument is argument that rests at last not solely upon evidence, reasoning, or emotional sympathy, but upon the character of the arguer. The catch is, no one can tell you how to be deemed trustable. Perhaps you'll find some help in the last portion of this chapter, Special Responsibilities in Argument.

These three terms, *logical argument, emotional argument,* and *ethical argument,* won't solve all your problems as you shape your own arguments, but they do represent discernible modes in arguments. As often as not you'll find them mixed in a single argument—examine the Declaration of Independence, for example, to determine when it is logical, when emotional, when ethical. The terms can be useful if they help you to know what you're doing in an argument and why you're doing it.

Parts of argument

In Chapter 6 a set of terms devised by early rhetoricians to name different parts of a discourse was introduced:

Exordium, or beginning, in which an author seeks to gain attention and perhaps to establish his or her own identity, station, or credentials.

Narratio, or background, in which an author provides the necessary context or background for the discussion at hand.

Propositio, or proposition or thesis, in which the author states his or her chief theme or proposition.

Partitio, or partition, in which the author forecasts the parts or steps of his or her discussion.

Confirmatio, or confirmation, or proof, in which the author offers his or her evidence in support of the proposition.

Confutatio, or refutation, in which the author shows the inadequacies of opposing views and propositions.

Digressio, or digression, not to be taken as a literal digression, but an occasion for the author to present related items or analogous arguments.

Peroratio, or conclusion, in which an author summarizes key points, dramatizes a main point, calls for action.

This set of terms may be useful to you in the context of argument in two different ways. First, taken just as they are, they provide an outline for an argument, and if you'll watch in your reading, you'll find many arguments following a pattern generally suggested by these terms. And of course you can rearrange the terms and create different organizational patterns. For example, it might sometimes be useful to begin with the fifth step proposed above, attacking contrary views first, both as a way of attracting attention and as a way of preparing for your own argument. You can make a design for an argument simply by following the first, fifth, and eighth steps proposed. Proportions may vary widely. Normally, you might expect the *confirmatio*, or proof, to take up most of the space of an argument, but sometimes it may be necessary to provide a carefully detailed background.

Second, the terms may be useful to you as a critical tool. Don't try to force everything you read to fit the eight terms, but don't hesitate to try the terms out, using them in your reading to determine when an author is doing what and inquiring why he or she does things in the sequence given. You'll find strange anomalies: for example, a speaker lingering over the *exordium*, establishing his or her own identity, when he or she ought to be getting to some evidence, or a writer getting so wrapped up in righteously repudiating other arguments that he or she forgets to develop a proposition, which is left to be assumed.

The best source of guidance is not in someone's precept or rule, however, but in the practice of other writers, whether good or bad. Study all of the examples used throughout this chapter—look to see what kind of evidence is used and how it is documented, follow the reasoning if you can and test it for foolishness, determine what kind of appeal is being made to you, whether essentially logical, emotional, or ethical, and examine the organization of the arguments. The following argument is developed according to the classical pattern. Can you tell what *kind* of appeal is being made in various parts?

Exordium   Lately we have been blessed or afflicted, deceived or enlightened, by a new category of television purporting to educate us in the facts and events of history. The new category has also provided us with a new word: "docudrama."

Narratio   These docudramas have been carrying us back into history, recent or distant, and into engagements with the lives of people famous or infamous. We have flown with Joseph Kennedy Jr. to heroic death in World War II; we ran with Wilma Rudolph in the 1960 Olympics; we die with Caryl Chessman in the gas chamber at San Quentin prison in the same year—and with Mary White, sweet 16, girl on horseback, in Emporia, Kan., 1921.

Why, we even go where history itself has never been: into the trial of General Custer who, though he died at Little Bighorn in 1876, was resurrected by docudrama for trial in New York on grounds of his having been careless of other men's lives; into the trial of Lee Harvey Oswald, shot to death at Dallas on November 24, 1963, also resurrected by the magic of docudrama for yet another inquiry into the assassination of John F. Kennedy.

These docudramas, in their choices of subjects, seem often to be at the verge of raising questions that ought to be raised, of focusing our attention upon moments of the past that ought not to be lost. Cherish the memory of spirited Mary White! Cherish the stamina and discipline of Wilma Rudolph! Was Custer mad? Was Oswald guilty? Was Chessman guilty? What might we learn about crime and punishment from Chessman's long, legal struggle to save himself?

Propositio

However, we seem to be heading somewhere else. The docudrama neither dramatizes nor documents history. We are not seeing the world out there. We are seeing ourselves, watching our own fantasies of life in high places. We are not being illuminated. Rather, we are being, in the simplest sense, entertained, immersed in a psychological bath that is painless, soothing fun. The docudrama is routine television dressed up to look serious—soap opera, situation comedy, cop shows, Westerns and old-fashioned success stories, rags to riches. We are tantalized by medical crises, suffering and succumbing in a pattern made familiar to us by docudramas adapted from the lives of Babe Didrikson, Lou Gehrig, Brian Piccolo and Karen Ann Quinlan.

In one way or another we are always pleased to identify with the central characters of these docudramas. We are General Custer, perhaps a patriot, perhaps a mad killer, tried at law, ambiguously acquitted. The pattern of the docudramas is to allow full play for all our ambivalences, permitting us to be lawbreakers, outlaws in our fantasies, but restoring us to our own proper self-respecting reality by the end of the television hour.

We are Lee Harvey Oswald, lone killer perhaps, conspirator perhaps, or perhaps the portrait of pure innocence. In ABC's "The Trial of Lee Harvey Oswald," he appears to be an impish cross between Mickey Rooney and Mickey Mantle, and we can hardly help but love him. At one point in that docudrama the prosecutor comes to his senses, perhaps as the writers for a moment came to theirs. "What the hell is happening to this country?" the prosecutor cries out. "A little creep kills the President and a lot of other deranged creeps try making him a folk hero."

We are Chessman, outwitting authority upon occasion after occasion, adored through his prison bars by his beautiful attorney, Rosalie Asher. But after we have had our fun he is punished, according to all the rules of classical popular storytelling, and now we can have another kind of fun: watching Chessman die, writhing, gasping, a morbidly realistic climax toward which the film was heading all along, for it was the only scene elaborately and painstakingly achieved.

Confirmatio

We think we are seeing the insides of things—Washington behind closed doors. We are taken to the bosom of the Kennedy family in "Young Joe, the Forgotten Kennedy." Joe's father is grooming him for President, but they bluntly agree that one can hardly be President without first having been a war hero. We have sailed small boats, played touch football with all our brothers and sisters on the lawn, we attend Harvard, now off we go into Naval aviation.

After our tour of duty on antisubmarine patrol we are eligible to go home, but we decline, for we have yet to become a hero. (Brother Jack has been a hero. In one of the most unlikely lines of dialogue ever written, Joe said to Jack beforehand, "PT boats are dangerous, Jack.") We volunteer for a dangerous mission. We will fly a slow airplane loaded every square inch with one dozen tons of Torpex—an explosive twice as powerful as TNT. The odds are against us. We know that we will probably die.

At this point we cease to be Joe Kennedy and become again a commonplace fellow like ourselves, one "Mike Krasna," a creation of docudrama. "I'm glad I'm not going on the mission with you, Joe," Mike Krasna says. He charges Joe with playing "Jack Armstrong, the All-American Boy." Like us, Krasna is at first suspicious of Joe Kennedy's wealth, speech and aristocratic bearing, and he raises the sore question of Ambassador Kennedy's early opposition to the war.

Confutatio

But in docudrama, hard and troublesome questions are raised only to be dismissed: one good fist fight and Mike and Joe are friends forever. Another chorus figure says to Joe not long afterward, "I think, Lieutenant, that if I was the son of an ambassador I'd get my tail out of here." This is a speech laundered in its transit from Hank Searls' fine book "The Lost Prince" to the docudrama, with which it has little in common. The Joseph Kennedy of Searls' book is a whole man, troubled and conflicted, by no means the fun-loving Rover boy of ABC's film, playing tricks on brother Jack, stealing Jack's girl, plunging mindlessly toward death.

Docudrama also satisfies our psychological desire for chaos and subversion. Its pattern is to implant in our minds the idea that social process never really functions, that most institutions such as law and the courts don't really work, that democracy doesn't really work, that we are victims of the whims of a few powerful persons. After we have been bathed in these options, we are carried at the end of each program back to our law-abiding selves.

Courageous now with all the courage of hindsight, docu-dramas freely cast suspicion over persons and agencies they formerly respected obsequiously. In "The Trial of Lee Harvey Oswald" the assassination or its cover-up is variously attributed as a possibility to the FBI ("I don't care if he was J. Edgar Hoover's boy friend," exclaims our brave prosecutor), the CIA, "Bobby," President Johnson (who is not named but whose accent is imitated), the Secret Service, the Mafia, Cuba and the Cubans. The prosecutor vows to continue "no matter how many Presidents call from Washington telling me to stop digging." But no docudrama feels itself forced to the necessity of substantiating anything. Thus where "docu" fails, "drama" may become a most distorted and dangerous instrument of innuendo.

. The new word "docudrama," which has not yet appeared, as far as I know, in any dictionary, is made of course from the words "documentary" and "drama."

Documentary: "a television or motion picture presentation of factual, political, social or historical events or circumstances, often consisting of actual news films accompanied by narration."

Drama: "a composition in prose or verse portraying life or characters by means of dialogue and action and designed for theatrical performance; a play; a series of real events having dramatic unity and interest."

In practice, the docudrama is a synthetic product having neither the "factual . . . actual" air of a documentary film nor the "unity and interest" of drama. It usually inflates a key incident to the length of an hour or more ("Mary White" or "Young Joe"), hoping to engage our interest because of the fame of the families involved; or it is based upon no documentation whatever ("Custer" or "Lee Harvey Oswald"). At the end of "The Court-Martial of George Armstrong Custer," NBC carries the disclaimer, flashing by with the credits, "This has been a work of fiction." And yet, how many people must now believe that such a trial actually occurred with results approximately as the docudrama describes? For the Chessman film, "Kill Me If You Can," NBC prepared the announcement that "although some of the characters and incidents are fictional, the story is based on fact." But this impression is nowhere nearly as powerful as our final vision of an unattended telephone perhaps ringing in a new stay of his execution. In fact, no such news was on the way.

Every story is in some way "based" on "fact." In the docudrama of Chessman's prison years, certain headline facts are sufficiently accurate, but, as soon as gross facts shade off into the minute data necessary to furnish drama, the portrait of Chessman bubbles away into soap opera. This is all the more regrettable since the resourcefulness of Chessman made him a truly inspiring example of the possibility of rehabilitation of even (if he was) the most wanton thief and rapist. Instead, he comes to us as a fine-featured hero; and the noble Rosalie Asher, who devoted years to his defense, is reduced to a pretty face.

Docudrama, such as it is, may be most promising when it breaks from its obsession with violence and male heroics. "Mary White" seemed to begin with good intentions. Its basic document was the eloquent editorial her father wrote for his Emporia Gazette on the day after Mary's funeral. But the docudrama strayed from its base of reality into those violations of data and spirit that characterize the genre.

"Mary White" implies that had Mary survived she would have been the Jane Addams of her generation. We are asked to be beguiled by her in the way we were asked to be beguiled by Joseph Kennedy Jr.—not for what they were but for what they might have become. We are present at a supposed meeting in Emporia between Mary White and Jane Addams. It is unlikely that the two women ever met. When Addams visited the Whites in Kansas in 1908, Mary was a 3-year-old baby, not yet enunciating the liberalism the docudrama puts into her mouth. Her liberalism, moreover, like her father's, was the liberalism of Kansas Republicans of the 1920s, not the liberalism of Southern California in 1977. It is certainly true that William Allen White hated and fought the Ku Klux Klan, but it is a pipe dream that he and Mary laughed it out of existence at a street rally in Emporia: according to White himself, "the Ku Klux Klan had captured the City Building at the spring elections" of 1923—less than two years after Mary's death.

Scene after scene of "Mary White" is gratuitous invention— her love affair, her journey to New York, her schoolroom encounters and her exchanges with her parents and her brother. When I became curious whether *any* of this ever happened, I asked John DeWitt McKee, authority on William Allen White, at the New Mexico Institute of Mining & Technology. Said Prof. McKee, "I sat there looking at things I never heard of."

Wilma Rudolph, like Mary White and Joe Kennedy, is purified beyond belief. Born "small and sickly," she grows in an atmosphere of amiability, suspiciously suggesting one of the practical problems of docudrama: when you are dealing with living people you'd better make them nice. Wilma's tender father, her ever-loving family, her all-wise coaches are all so *appealing* that I began to yearn for a little natural human irritation.

Why do the proprietors of television make docudramas this way? Basically, a docudrama is cheaper to make than a reliable documentary report. It requires only the most superficial research, and often no research at all. Most docudramas are made in a hurry, scenes thrown together like the script itself with little regard for overall coherence, logic, connection or integration. The docudrama is a way to do things without having to do the work that ought to go into them, and yet, however badly done, a docudrama will attract an audience on the grounds of its being "true."

It is one thing to be innovative, but it is another for television to defy the very history it pretends to respect. Document is one thing. Drama is another. The reason these ancient forms assumed clear distinctions in the minds of mankind is precisely that we may all be as certain as possible where fiction ends and fact begins. And *vice versa*. Without that confidence in our reporters, human affairs cannot proceed. Minglings or combinations of these forms raise the deepest questions of motive.

Oddly, while docudramas so often express patriotic attitudes toward such subjects as war and soldiery, the act of scrambling history is not itself patriotic. The patriotic act lies in probing useful knowledge the hard way, if necessary, whether in documentary or drama, not in serving up the merely marketable.

The problem is not the form but the execution. Docudrama is an ancient means of imparting history. Shakespeare's "Henry V" is a docudrama, and so is "Jesus Christ Superstar."

Peroratio   But current television docudrama hopes to achieve its objective without having done the work. Perhaps all this is what we want. It is certainly what we are getting. But will we be satisfied with history as it is seen, interpreted, reduced, and oversimplified and falsified by docudrama?—Mark Harris, "Docudramas Unmasked"

CLASSIFICATION OF ARGUMENTS

Not all arguments aim at the same kind of change, and not all aim at change in the same way. Arguments take many forms, and each may be aimed at different accomplishments.

Full-dress argument.   Sometimes writers undertake a thorough review of an area of conflict so that their arguments present a background against which we can view their convictions. There is no clear and fixed pattern by which this can be done, but it's likely to include gathering and presenting evidence, arriving at a proposition, affirming the proposition by showing its evolution from the evidence, surveying and where necessary repudiating opposing views, and calling for decision, action, new policy, or new thought (some suggestions for handling this kind of argument appear in the section above entitled Parts of Arguments). The Declaration of Independence is an argument of this type; its authors present their proposition against a full background that includes an account of the causes for their decisions and some brief account of opposing views. The piece that follows is another example. It begins with a statement of the author's position as a researcher, summarizes earlier studies in paragraphs two and three, rejects previous approaches in paragraphs four, five, and six, proposes the main point in paragraph seven, and thereafter calls for new and better research, policy, and action.

My point of view is that of a cancer researcher who has been working for the last 20 years with RNA viruses that cause cancer in chickens.

Since the early years of this century, it has been known that viruses cause cancer in chickens. In more recent years viruses have been shown to cause cancer not only in chickens, but also in mice, cats, and even in some primates. Therefore, it was a reasonable

INSIGHT

Classifying arguments

Arguments, of course, can be classified in any number of ways. Above, for example, in the section Developing Arguments, I have already suggested one system of classification by indicating that arguments may be logical, emotional, or ethical. In the discussion that follows, another system for classifying at least some arguments may help you to think about your own.

These traditional kinds of argument may suggest certain ways of thinking about your material that will lead you to the evidence you need. One is the *argument from nature.* Not long ago on a college campus a young man who wished to call attention to inadequacies in the campus guidebook petitioned to have his name placed on the ballot in an election for homecoming queen. He maintained that he was eligible on the grounds that the guidebook stipulated only that candidates should be students under twenty-one; sex was not mentioned in the body of the rules. The young man's petition was denied through an argument from nature. Pointing out that the rules came under the heading "Eligibility requirements for homecoming queen," his opposition seized on the meaning of the word *queen*—by nature a female—to deny his eligibility. An argument from nature may be developed by a number of techniques: by defining the nature of a thing; by studying the meanings attached to the key words in a proposition; by classifying the subject in order to establish a frame of reference in terms of which it can be discussed.

People cannot always agree on the nature of things, of course, and for that reason they have often turned to other kinds of argument. The *argument from analogy* brings a subject and argument into a reader's knowledge by suggesting its similarity to something better known, as in the fairly common—but often ineffective—analogy of government and business. The evidence you bring to this kind of argument must show that the comparison is both significant and accurate.

The *argument from consequence* enforces a proposition by examining cause and effect, antecedent and consequence. This is a useful kind of argument, but it is limited by the fact that human affairs are not ordered by certain laws of causality. Poverty *sometimes* breeds crime; prolonged tyranny *frequently* leads to revolution; honesty is *occasionally* rewarded. Before expressing an opinion about the outcome of some course of action, or about the cause of some event, make sure that the weight of evidence lends probability to your statement.

The *argument from authority* depends upon the testimony of respected persons, the authority of institutions, the weight of important documents. This is probably the least popular of the traditional kinds of argument, for most audiences prefer to feel that the truth is *discovered* in the course of an argument, rather than that it has been *pronounced* by authority.

hypothesis that viruses might cause cancer in humans and that, if a human cancer virus existed, it could be prevented by a vaccine as so many other virus diseases have been prevented.

Experiments performed in recent years have led to an understanding of much of the genetic basis of how viruses cause cancer in animals, namely, by adding their genetic information to the DNA, that is, the genetic material, of the cell. With this understanding and the tools of molecular biology, it has been possible to look for viruses potentially preventable by vaccines that might cause human cancer. Unfortunately, I think we can now conclude that most human cancer is not caused by such viruses.

Scientifically this conclusion is an advance, for science progresses by disproving hypotheses. But, in terms of preventive medicine, I believe this conclusion ends the hope for a vaccine that would prevent cancer caused by viruses.

Must we, therefore, give up hope of preventing cancer?

No. For in recent years, the hypothesis that chemicals and radiation probably cause cancer by mutation of the cell genome has been strongly supported. Furthermore, epidemiological evidence has shown that the incidence of human cancer is not the same in all parts of the world and in all population groups, but that the incidence of human cancer varies from country to country, region to region, and population group to population group depending on the nature of the environment. Therefore, there must be environmental features that play a determining role in the formation of human cancer. One of the most clearly established of these environmental features is smoking, especially cigaret smoking. Cigaret smokers not only have a much greater probability of developing lung cancer than do otherwise similar nonsmokers, but the smokers have a greater probability of dying from a number of other diseases. Therefore, our best present hope of preventing cancer does not appear to lie in a vaccine against viruses, but in removing or reducing the levels of chemical carcinogens from the environment.

The single most important source of these carcinogens and the one which should be most easily removable is tobacco, probably especially the tars from tobacco. The American Cancer Society estimates that the life expectancy of a man of 25 who continually smokes 2 packs of cigarets a day is 8 years less than that of a 25-year-old nonsmoker. Stopping cigaret smoking would have the greatest effect on increasing life expectancy, but, if that is not possible, reducing the level of tar from tobacco would at least serve to reduce the cancer risk of smokers. Therefore, if a tax based on the level of tar and nicotine in cigarets decreased the amount of exposure to tar, it would help to prevent some of the cancers which otherwise would be caused by smoking.

However, further research is still needed on cancer and other diseases both to help prevent those diseases that are not caused by smoking and to help cure those diseases that cannot be prevented. For example, we need to develop better therapies for cancer based upon an understanding of the differences in biochemistry and control of cell multiplication between cancer cells and normal cells. Comparison of virus-transformed cells and normal cells is one of the best systems to find such differences.

However, we must try even harder to prevent cancer before it starts, since so far it has been difficult to find many biochemical differences between cancer cells and normal cells that can be exploited in therapy. For prevention, we must devise better methods of testing for factors in the environment, including chemicals from industrial processes and possibly food additives, that can cause cancer, and after we find these factors we must try to remove them. In addition, we must try to understand more of the mechanisms by which chemicals and radiation cause cancer in the hope that such knowledge will make it easier for us to recognize these carcinogens and perhaps to devise means to prevent their action. However, when, as in the case of smoking, we find that a carcinogen exists, we must act to prevent it from entering the environment.

From the point of view of a scientist engaged in cancer research, it is paradoxical that the U.S. people, through Congress, spend hundreds of millions of dollars a year for research to prevent and cure human cancer. But when we can say how to prevent much human cancer, namely, stop cigaret smoking, little or nothing is done to prevent this cancer. In fact, I believe the U.S. government even subsidizes the growing of tobacco. As I said at the Nobel festival banquet in Stockholm, I am outraged that this one major method available to prevent much human cancer, namely the cessation of cigaret smoking, is not more widely adopted.

I should also like to comment on a possible large increase in funding for biomedical and other health-related research. At present the U.S. system of support of biomedical research and the results of this biomedical research are the best in the world. Therefore, we must be careful before undertaking drastic changes in the way we fund biomedical research, and we should especially be careful to ensure that quality is stressed in all biomedical research. An excellent way to insure this quality is the system of peer review of grants used at NIH. Furthermore, although at a particular time we might wish to work on a particular problem in biomedical research or solve some health-related problems, if techniques and theoretical knowledge are not advanced enough to supply a proper foundation for the research, it may not be possible to approach such problems. Nature yields her secrets slowly, and only when a proper foundation of previous knowledge exists. Therefore, I wonder about the advisability of trying to spend rapidly much larger sums of money in this area. I suggest that a large and rapid increase in money is not warranted. More important is a mechanism for assurance of continuing support of good basic biomedical research and a good peer review system.

In conclusion, I feel that the support previously extended to cancer research by the U.S. people through the Congress indicates a concern with preventing this disease. Research indicates that the best present method available to prevent much cancer is to decrease smoking. I, therefore, support Congressional action to decrease smoking.—Howard Temin, "A Warning to Smokers"

Exercises

1.   In discussion, identify the methods of development (definition, comparison, analogy, etc.) that Temin uses in "A Warning to Smokers" above.

2.   Choose one of your strongest opinions to defend and make an outline for a full-dress argument.

3.   Collect all of the evidence (authority, statistics, etc.) that will support the opinion you chose in exercise two, and write the argument.

Attack.   The argument above *promotes* particular convictions against a surveyed background that includes opposition. Other kinds of arguments are interested not so much in promoting a particular proposition or view as in repudiating some proposition, some view, policy, action, or way of thinking that already exists. They may promote some view indirectly, of course; presumably if one attacks a given practice, one does so in the conviction that there can be a better practice. But such arguments are more intent upon attacking than upon promoting. The argument that appears on page 399, "Docudramas Unmasked," is intent upon demonstrating error in a contemporary form of television programming, not in advocating a different specific kind of programming.

Exercise

Find a letter to the editor, an editorial, or some other expression of opinion with which you disagree, and write an answer in which you simply demonstrate the error in the opinion.

Satire.   Some kinds of arguments work in indirect, sometimes strange, often even funny ways. Satire is a form of argument. We recognize it chiefly as a form of attack; we expect satire to ridicule the follies of people, practices, and institutions. If we look closely enough, however, we can usually find in satire some values that are being promoted indirectly. They are often unexpressed. They may exist only as a kind of unsaid opposite to the practices that are being ridiculed or laughed at or gently mocked.

Satire, like other forms of attack, can occur in many moods. Sometimes it is relatively genial: we can watch the creator of "Doonesbury" poke fun at current practices, deflate egos, and demonstrate our general folly, and still know that beyond these habits that mostly deserve laughter there lie possibilities for virtue and strength. Sometimes satire is bitter and strong. The following satire is an example. It attacks the economic system and social consciences that the writer sees as both causing unemployment and being unconcerned about the welfare of the unemployed. It is, by the way, closely modeled on Jonathan Swift's "A Modest Proposal" (easily found in anthologies), one of the most famous and scathing satires of all time.

> I must confess that I have been much disturbed of late by the murmurings of ill-informed malcontents among the unemployed. True, there are certain inconveniences that the unemployed must bear during the current recession, but do these inconveniences justify selfish (if not subversive) attacks on the capitalist system? Is it true that the millions of unemployed symbolize the failure of capitalism? I submit that the case is quite the contrary. Clearly, the unemployed are evidence that the capitalist system is working as well as it has ever worked, and my feeling is that if the unemployed can be brought to see the truth of this claim, they will be encouraged to develop a new sense of pride in their condition. In what follows, therefore, I respectfully beg the reader's patience while I outline what the unemployed are now contributing to society, and then proceed to a modest proposal which, I trust, will inspire them to jointly make a yet greater contribution to the capitalist cause.
>
> First, the unemployed remind us of the cyclical nature of capitalism. Capitalism cannot have employment and prosperity today without economic crisis, stagnation, and unemployment tomorrow. This is not mere theory. From all I can gather, it is an iron law, which neither planning nor genius can hope to change.
>
> Second, I suggest that the unemployed are in the vanguard of the fight against inflation. Whether on welfare or on unemployment insurance, they can buy only the minimum means of subsistence. Spending frugally, they do not bid up the price of anything. They create less demand for less goods, thus causing the lowering of prices. As the wise Washington economists declare, the unemployed should be grateful and proud that they can serve their country as a cheap and handy weapon against inflation. It is, perhaps, not too much to assert that without their assistance the

entire capitalist structure would be inflated like a heated balloon, the bursting of which would be catastrophic.

Third, I would suggest that the unemployed have the mysterious power to reinvigorate those sound and pious capitalists who well know that because of Adam's Fall the economic marketplace is divided into the elect and the damned—the elect being the rich and the employed, the damned being the poor and the unemployed. Though this situation seems to annoy blasphemous malcontents, I point to it as a most fortunate one. It brings into relief an involuntary religious function by the unemployed.

Fourth, by proving that the capitalist damned exist by the will of God, the unemployed accomplish wonders, in general, for the morale of the rich and the employed. With fresh assurance that they are not only among the elect, but also among the fittest in the Darwinian struggle for existence, these predestined fortunates are stimulated to buckle down to their jobs and to improve their investments. In consequence, they are able again to flood the economy with surplus value. What is the result of this surplus value? The result is that, as if by magic, a new prosperity appears, confirming those cyclical revolutions of classical capitalism to which I have alluded. The system revives and blossoms; unemployment withers and disappears.

Surely these few examples of how the unemployed figure in the capitalist system are sufficient to earn them the national gratitude and to fill them with capitalist pride. There is yet another way, however, for them to serve the system. I refer to my modest proposal.

In these distressing times, the Malthusians have not been given their fair due. On every side, sophistical babblers imply that the Malthusian theory does not work. Yet the unemployed are clear evidence that it does. They show that capitalism cannot support everyone who wishes to venture into this wonderful world. In the natural course of things, the unemployed would efficiently starve to death and make room for the younger generation to participate fully in the next cycle of prosperity.

But what is happening in the unnatural, inefficient, modern world? The unemployed are kept alive by welfare and unemployment benefits, for which the rich and the employed are tyrannically taxed to the extent of billions of dollars, no matter how strenuously they may object.

No one will claim that this unnatural situation is or has been due to proper, laissez-faire capitalism. No, the situation has been and is due to socialism. It is socialism that has been flouting the iron laws of biology and religion based on the Darwinian struggle for survival and the Fall of Man. If these laws were permitted to prevail, the unemployed would be free to find dignity in death, knowing that they were tokens and mementos of the Malthusian theory.

Now, assuming—and I am willing to assume—that the unemployed, for the most part, are loyal to the classical truths of the American capitalist system and wish to see them preserved, I propose that they immediately declare through their established unions that they will no longer cooperate with the impious socialist plot to keep them alive against nature, God, and Malthus. I hereby suggest that they petition for the right to prove the soundness of the Malthusian theory. Like men of noble mold, they should insist upon their God-given right to perish with Malthusian dignity.

I know that my elect brethren will agree that a gesture of this magnitude by the damned unemployed would be sublime. Not only would it solve the unemployment problem; it would restore society to the true principles of biology, religion, and capitalist economics. It would set up a firm precedent for handling the future unemployed. It would reduce taxes. It would dispense with the bureaucracies of welfare and unemployment insurance. It would please God.

Summing up: the unemployed, rightly viewed, are capitalist blessings in disguise. They confirm the truths of the system. They inspire the economic elect with a sense of their own election. In addition, they have the opportunity to eliminate themselves as a capitalist embarrassment and to spare themselves the personal awkwardness of having to await the next upturn in the economy. Having faith in the rationality of America's unemployed, I for one believe that they will, indeed, respond favorably to this modest proposal, especially when they realize that it is offered free of charge, without any strings, in the best tradition of philanthropic capitalism. Having been blessed by the wisdom granted to the elect, I feel that I can do no less, being fully cognizant that in such distressing times as these, God, nature, and capitalism shall not forgive those who fail to do their duty.—Allen B. Borden, "A Satire for the Unemployed—And Ayn Rand"

Exercises

1.   Write down some possibilities for ways of handling in satire the following subjects from any point of view you wish to take:
   a. Property tax reform
   b. Gun control
   c. Marijuana
   d. Government funding of the arts, environmental projects, space exploration, etc.
   e. ERA

2.   Most of the subjects in exercise one would probably be too broad to be written about well unless you have quite a bit of information at hand. Find a subject that is closer to your own life such as a situation on your

campus or in your community, or a situation in which you were directly involved with one of the subjects in exercise one, and write a satirical argument attacking what is wrong.

SPECIAL RESPONSIBILITIES IN ARGUMENT

Any piece of writing that you give to someone else to read makes some kind of claim on him or her. But arguments make special claims, and so demand special responsibilities. Arguments want change, or at least acknowledgment, from an audience. If you ask for that, there's much you are obliged to give.

Some think that persuasion is a form of power, an exertion of control. We have to grant that it is sometimes. But we don't have to use persuasion that way. We can refuse to concede that persuasion can only take place if we offer an audience some kind of gratification. We can refuse to concede that persuasion is after all a form of power, a controlling manipulation of the minds of other people. We are various, and because we are, our virtues and our follies mixed and interesting, we can learn better than that.

One way to begin to see a better way of understanding persuasion and its special responsibilities is to turn the world upside down. Put yourself at the other end of an argument. Imagine something that you don't want to be told—say, for example, that there will be a huge tuition increase beginning next semester, or that there will be an extraordinary tax increase next year. Then ask yourself, "Under what circumstances could I tolerate that or agree to it?" When you make an argument, you can't always be conciliatory. Sometimes an issue is too profound and dear for you to alter your views in any way. Sometimes it becomes necessary to declare independence without compromise or conciliation. Sometimes it becomes necessary to declare that we will not kill, maim, defame, or repudiate other humans without compromise or conciliation. But most human enterprises will allow community exploration, community examination, some conciliation. When you argue, your audience is made of other humans. They should not—except possibly under the rarest of circumstances—be moved by power or manipulation. If when you argue you will keep asking yourself what it is like at the other end of your argument, if you will ask, "Under what circumstances could I tolerate an alien, perhaps threatening proposal, or even agree to it?" that may help you to know when you have the right to try to persuade others and when you may expect to persuade them.

You have the right to try to persuade others any time you please, of course. There are, to be sure, some arguments you shouldn't make, and that others shouldn't listen to. Some arguments are intolerable ("Let us ignore the hungry"; "Let us ignore whole populations and take their country"; "Let us kill six million Jews"), but you have the right, even, to propose intolerable arguments. You shouldn't, however, expect to be welcomed with your arguments or respected for your arguments. You owe much to yourself, but you also owe something to the person reading your argument. If you believe something and want to proclaim it, want to share it, and if you don't want persuasion to occur only through manipulation, control, force, or promised gratification, you need to remember some special responsibilities.

You are, at the least, obliged not to be ignorant, not to be dogmatic, not to be arrogant. You owe that to yourself and to the person reading your argument. That means you owe full explanations, meticulous evidence, scrupulous reasoning. That means that you owe full disavowal of coercion, of manipulation, of image-making, where you *seem* to be something whether you are or not. That means that you owe welcomes, not threats, disclosure, not deceit, generosity, not hostility. That means that you owe the making of a common world, with room in it for yourself and a reader.

Exercises

1.   Describe a situation which you have witnessed or experienced in which a person seemed to be using the wrong kind of appeal; for example, an emotional appeal when a logical appeal would have worked better.

2.   Hold a discussion with your class concerning some controversial issue in which each person must carefully restate the point made by the last person to speak before he or she can add his or her remarks.

3.   Locate an argument in which you believe the author establishes strong ethical appeal. Write a paper describing specifically how you believe the author establishes that ethical quality.

4.   The Intensify/Downplay pattern for analyzing communication, persuasion, and propaganda was developed by Hugh Rank and endorsed by the Committee on Public Doublespeak of the National Council of Teachers of English. Essentially the pattern shows that all people *intensify* some things and *downplay* others as they communicate, but that the average citizen should observe how "professional persuaders" intensify and downplay in order to cope with organized persuasion. Examine some advertisements to determine what has been intensified and what has been downplayed. For example, a cigarette advertisement might intensify the pleasures of smoking while downplaying the hazards.

5.   Choose a proposition that you feel is arguable and important to you, and write a complete argument. Use all possible resources available to you. Keep in mind as you write the principal divisions of classical argument and the types of appeal. When you have finished, you may wish to use the parts of the classical argument as a checking device to see if you have presented an adequate argument.

16

This chapter discusses the need for making critical judgments about many things, but emphasizes

1. the conditions a writer must meet to make responsible critical judgments (p. 415), and

2. some of the approaches to writing criticism about literature (p. 425).

The term *critical writing* doesn't refer to some single kind of writing, and it doesn't refer to writing that has a fixed subject matter. From your high-school English classes, or from other connections with English and English teachers, you may have come to think of critical writing as something that you do only in English classes and only when you are studying and writing about literature. To be sure, it is a common practice to write critical essays about literary selections, but that is not the only occasion for critical writing.

Some definitions may help you to remember all that is possible in critical writing. The Greek word *krinein*, meaning *to decide*, appears to be the source for a related Greek term, *krites*, meaning *judge*. From these words come two related English words, *criterion*, a standard or rule by which something is judged, and *critic*, one who judges. The verb form, *to criticize*, in ordinary conversation often means to judge severely, but the verb also more generally means to pass judgment on the qualities of something. The adjective form, *critical*, gets used in several ways. We use the word sometimes to refer to someone who is given to faultfinding, but we also use it in a more general sense to refer to someone or to some thing (such as a piece of writing) that exhibits careful, precise judgments and evaluations. Most of these definitions are worth remembering. *Critical writing* is writing that is associated with *deciding, judging,* and *evaluating*. Critical writing records judgments, decisions, and evaluations.

If we understand critical writing in that way, then it is easy to see that there are many occasions for the kinds of critical thinking that lead to critical writing. Most reasonable shoppers, for example, though they may not write down the results, judge and evaluate various objects and then decide among them. Before you register for classes at school, you have usually done some judging, evaluating, and deciding, as you have when you decide among competing television programs. Possible subjects for critical writing are, indeed, everywhere—the paperback books at your local newsstand may require some critical judgment, if not writing, and so may school systems, churches, governmental systems, paintings, buildings, motion pictures, television, newspapers, and politicians.

CONDITIONS FOR CRITICAL WRITING

Plenty of occasions exist for critical writing, then, and moreover there is ample *need* for critical writing. The world is full of wondrous things and foolish things, wicked things and splendid things. We need to stop and notice and decide what makes one thing wondrous, another foolish, one thing wicked, another splendid, and we need to test and temper our judgments against those of others. How shall we learn, otherwise?

That is why critical writing is so valuable a form of writing. It calls on us to stop, to take notice, to judge, and to test our judgment. If you're to evaluate a building or a painting or a group of musicians or yourself or a curriculum, you're going to have to stop long enough to study your subject and to explore it until you know what you think about it and what justifies your judgment. That suggests some basic conditions for critical writing.

You are the critic, or judge. *Here is the first condition, then: if you are going to do critical writing, you'll have to trust yourself as an evaluator, a judge, a critic.* That doesn't mean that you should simply be content with the ideas and judgments that you already have or that you should simply announce your prejudices and expect everyone else to accept them. It does mean that you can look at evidence (a story, a picture, a movie, a TV program, or whatever your subject is), ask good questions, and come to a conclusion about the subject before you. It also means that when you take a position or make a judgment, it counts for something. You can just accept the judgments that others make from now on, if you'd rather, and it is always possible to learn from the judgments of others, but you're also entitled to be your own judge. Your own critical evaluations count. They count for you, and they may count for others.

A second condition is suggested in the paragraphs above: you're going to have to stop and take time to notice. *Responsible critical writing requires a meditative pause, however brief.* In order to make a reasonable judgment about a poem, for example, you have to stop, not just to read it, but to re-read it, to look again at particular lines, to study particular images, to examine the poem closely. In order to make a reasonable judgment about a building, you have to stop and look at it, then move to another side and look again, then move inside and look again. If you're judging a piece of music, you have to listen and listen again until you can begin to know it. Of course you can't pause while you're watching a movie or a TV program, but you can get some of the same effect by calling particular moments back to your memory time and again. It's scarcely possible, indeed, to imagine critical writing without a prior pause for meditation and exploration. It's that pause that makes it possible for you to ask interesting and useful questions about your subject—How does it work? Why is it put together as it is? What goes wrong just here and what works well just there? How do the parts relate to each other? What effect does it have and what gives it that effect? If it works well, why does it do so? If it works poorly, what has gone wrong? And the questions go on and on.

Critical writing calls for you to make a judgment or take a position. *A third condition necessary in this kind of writing is that you justify your judgment.* You cannot guarantee that readers will agree with all that you say, but you can show them why you say what you say. When you're writing about a poem, you can quote the lines that illustrate your point or the lines that lead you to think as you do. When you're talking about a movie or a TV program, you can describe the scenes or episodes that lead you to a judgment. The form of a critical essay, in fact, is often determined by your use of evidence. One kind of critical essay, for example, can be depicted in this way:

I believe X is true. You can see X illustrated in A, B, C, and D.

In a critical essay that follows this form, the writer has studied a subject and come to a conclusion about it ("I believe X is true"). Having come to this conclusion, the writer then goes back to the text, the movie, the music, or whatever, to cite particular passages or features that illustrate or account for the conclusion. Other critical essays reverse this procedure:

I note that A has particular characteristics.
I note that B has particular characteristics.
I note that C has particular characteristics.
I note that D has particular characteristics.
As a result, I believe X is true.

In this form the writer observes particular details and uses them to form a conclusion. Whatever form you use, and of course there are many, critical writing calls for you to provide specific evidence for your judgments, specific illustrations of the points you wish to make, specific accountings for the positions you take. When you show readers the particulars, they can at least track you in your thinking; they can see where you have been and how you got to where you are. Without the particulars, your judgments and evaluations are only bald assertions.

In the pages that follow, you'll find several samples of critical writing—a book review, a television review, a movie review, a very brief review of an art exhibit, and a music review. But a few examples can't begin to suggest the range and variety that are possible in critical writing. Subjects can be found in any category of human experience, and the forms and styles found in critical writing can vary widely.

The following questions are useful to keep in mind as you read any piece of critical writing. Try to answer them as you read each of the selections that follow.

1. How and where does the author express his or her primary judgments or evaluation? How is the first condition of critical writing discussed above satisfied?

2. What kinds of questions does the author ask and answer? What does he or she take time to notice? How does the author reveal his or her knowledge of the subject? How is the second condition met?

3. How and when does the author provide illustrations or cite particular evidence? How is the third condition of critical writing satisfied?

Injury Time *By Beryl Bainbridge*

At the wine-and-cheese party where she and Edward meet, Binny likens middle age, on which they are both well launched, to the last half of a football match: the weary players toil on, waiting for the final whistle. "Suddenly depressed, he longed to go home and watch television." But Edward goes home with Binny instead.

The football simile recurs often to Edward in subsequent months: his liaison is an exhausting enterprise. Binny's latest idea, for instance, is that Edward should invite some of his friends to her house for dinner. Why should she be hidden away in shadowy bars? A prosperous accountant who likes to putter about in the garden, Edward is terrified that his wife will find out about Binny, who is hardly presentable, being a total slattern, much given to verbal abuse. So he drags along Simpson and Muriel, whom he barely knows. The four have an opportunity to get to know one another better soon enough, after their dinner party has been invaded by bank robbers who hold them hostage for several days. The event seems to Binny like something she'd seen on television, and during the entire course of it Edward wonders how he is ever going to explain his lateness to his wife, should the final whistle fail to rescue him.

Plot synopses only hint at the flavor of Beryl Bainbridge's novels, black comedies of Britain's postwar disarray. Her characters grub for certainties in the ruins of a civilization they barely understand and which is plainly too much for them: the menace of the commonplace overwhelms them. At her best, Mrs. Bainbridge infuses the flotsam of modern industrialism with an almost talismanic power. Binny's house has the ominous logic of a house in a dream: eggshells in the hedge, vacuum cleaner at the bottom of the garden steps, baked apples stowed behind the refrigerator, and in the dark hallway a bicycle that malevolently gouges the ankles of male visitors.

Such a vision works best when left a bit dreamlike, and Mrs. Bainbridge's earlier books have a marvelously disturbing, oneiric resonance. In "Injury Time," though, she tells exactly what troubles her characters, and it's just the familiar Op-Ed page catalogue of late 20th-century ills: television, teen-agers, family breakdown, all that. Now, no sociological explanation can really account for dislocation on the epic scale of Binny and her friends: they are simply too out of it. Burdened by social comment, they lose their fictional force—like explicated jokes or analyzed dreams—and seem merely contrived. When Binny is raped by one of the kidnappers and feels no emotion, we know she is merely a stick figure being used to illustrate certain ideas about modern life, and we want to say: Listen! No one is *that* alienated because of watching too much television.

Although it has moments of comic vigor, much of "Injury Time" reads like a trivializing of Mrs. Bainbridge's best work, almost like self-parody. In a single chapter, Binny and her friend Alma are accosted by a drunken shopping-bag lady on their way to have coffee at a fast-food restaurant, where a hostile waitress serves them cups of "pale yellow liquid"; Alma tells Binny the circumstances under which her son called her a "toe-rag," and Binny notes that the ketchup bottle has "a crust like blood," and she adds darkly: "Anywhere you can possibly go, it's waiting around the corner. Faces with scabs . . . hit-and-run drivers"; and then: "I keep thinking I'm watching television. There doesn't seem to be much difference." When the bill comes, she is shocked by the high service charge and muses, "I wonder if we should hit the children more." Finally, things take a turn for the better: shopping done, Binny "was able to smile quite charitably, after she had leapt to safety, at a youth who failed to run her down on the zebra crossing."

Such foreboding, indiscriminately lavished on everything from random violence to dirty restaurants, is bound to make the real world look like a pretty cheerful place after all.—Katha Pollitt

The Muppet Show

Like some people I know, the Muppets always seem better than whatever they're doing.

They used to do *Sesame Street*, a terrible show that became wonderful whenever the Muppets appeared, with their ugly, fuzzy, plaintive little faces and goofy physiques, their personalities earnestly silly and sweet—even the pompous ones.

Sesame Street was born of the idea that disadvantaged preschoolers could get a head start by learning numbers and letters earlier. The neighborhood kids and I would suffer through all those heavy-handed cartoon sequences in which squads of little voices would pointlessly yammer the numbers 1 through 10 or bellow out 20 words beginning with B. We endured all this because we got to see Bert and Ernie, Oscar the Grouch (who lived in a garbage can and liked dirt), Kermit the Frog and the Cookie Monster.

I always had my doubts about the head-start concept, but in this case it didn't matter. The Muppets had made *Sesame Street* a success as pure entertainment.

In the present Muppet series, again, there's more fun in watching Muppets move than in hearing them exchange queasy jokes with Milton Berle. The Muppets make you smile even when the scriptwriters don't. A Muppet, when you get down to it, is somebody's arm in a piece of cloth. But Jim Henson and his puppeteers invest their little characters with love, which is the same as making them live.

Too much of the current series depends on the guest of the week. That can mean a wonderful show when the guest is someone like Peter Sellers, who can enter the Muppet world with his own luminous fancies—as a mad German chiropractor who ties a pig into knots, or a mellifluous ham reciting "Richard III" while squeezing a clucking chicken under each arm.

But most humans just don't mix with Muppets. Elton John didn't know what to do except play one song after another, though it was a nice bit of lunacy when his "Crocodile Rock" was accompanied by three crocodiles singing "la la la."

The Muppets are fun just to look at, but they're at their best in characteristic set-pieces—as when the monster eats the talking computer, or Kermit sings of the mixed blessings of being green. The more the show falls back on standard variety-show moves, the more it loses the Muppet magic.

I think maybe there are too darned many Muppets in the present series, and I don't care for the two old gaffers in the balcony who make awful jokes about the show; they seem anti-Muppet somehow. But I like some of the new characters: Gonzo, the scrawny little critter with the turnip beak; Sam, the stuffy American Eagle who is incensed at the suggestion that Mozart wore high heels and silk stockings. And I'm still fond of Kermit, a small-town frog who is still a bit dazzled to be in show business.

At their very best, the Muppets give me delight. That's rarer than laughter, and maybe better.—Robert MacKenzie

American Graffiti

Small towns and the fifties had this in common: many people wanted to get out of both. Then, at a safe distance of miles and years, a certain nostalgia began inching its way into memory like a balm. In recent years several entertainments have distilled that nostalgia—*The Last Picture Show*, for example, and the Broadway musical *Grease*. But none has had the vigor and precision of *American Graffiti*. This superb and singular film catches not only the charm and tribal energy of the teenage fifties but also the listlessness and the resignation that underscored it all like an incessant bass line in an old rock-'n'-roll song.

The movie is cast in the mold of one of those teenage escapade flicks which American International Pictures used to stock the drive-ins with during the late fifties and the sixties. This allows director George Lucas to mock, carefully and compassionately, the conventions and stereotypes of a genre as well as a generation. All the details are here, from the do-whop music and lovingly customized cars to the slang, which hovered between Ivy League and street gang, and the clothes, which seemed, like the time, both shapeless and confining. Even the jokes come straight from AIP: "How'd you like a knuckle sandwich?" inquires a hood of a nervous, bespectacled sad sack outside the local hamburger drive-in. "No, thanks," says the sad sack. "I'm waiting for a double Chubby Chuck."

Graffiti was shot in Techniscope, a wide-screen process that yields the authentic sandpaper grain of the AIP pictures, implying low budgets and quick takes. The vital difference is that *Graffiti* was photographed by Haskell Wexler, that most subtle and agile of cameramen. Most of the action takes place at night under harsh light and neon, a landscape that Wexler turns into extravagantly impressionistic honky-tonk images of glaring, insistent beauty.

Set in a small California town in 1962—the proper, if not the chronological, end of the fifties—*Graffiti* provides a series of vignettes of the last night of summer. On the following day two of the local boys (Richard Dreyfuss and Ronny Howard) are set to leave for college. Howard and his girl (Cindy Williams) are surrogates of AIP's Frankie Avalon and Annette Funicello, the straight-arrow guy and his girl, the latter a believer in early marriage and eternal obligation. Comic relief is provided by Charlie Martin Smith as the sad sack, and a glimpse into the classic cruising style by Paul Le Mat, who slides down the street in an unbeatable car, his hair in an unruffled d.a., his pack of Camels rolled in the sleeve of his T shirt. The greaser villains, led by Bo Hopkins, have the traditional approach to any problem in interpersonal relations: "Tie him to a car and drag him." The scenes between these young people and the girls they fall in with or fall for (notably Candy Clark and Mackenzie Phillips) are mostly funny, but they leave a lingering melancholy.

The characters seem locked in—to careers, to whole lives. The only one who will break out is Dreyfuss, smarter and more sensitive than the others but careful not to show it. His high school teacher tells him of the time he left town to go to college but came back after only a semester ("I wasn't the competitive type"); the scene captures the slightly anxious self-deceptions that Dreyfuss's contemporaries will soon be using. Dreyfuss climbs aboard his plane for college still carrying a radio tuned to the favorite local station. The radio plays until he is in the air and finally out of range, and the crackle of static is his first intimation—though he does not know it—of freedom.

Lucas is a young filmmaker whose only other feature was *THX-1138*, a cool, cautionary science-fiction tale released in 1970. It established him as a director of great technical range and resource. *Graffiti* reveals a new and welcome depth of feeling. Few films have shown quite so well the eagerness, the sadness, the ambitions and small defeats of a generation of young Americans. Bitchin', as they said back then. Superfine.—Jay Cocks

The Late Cézanne: A Symposium

I love Cézanne; some of my favorite works were in "Cézanne: The Late Work," yet I hated the show and thought the pictures looked sadly diminished by it. What was wrong?

The arts of displaying art and of studying it are in a state of confusion. Publishers often try to cram exhibitions between covers, museums to hang books on the walls. The hybrid results, in my opinion, do not allow art, scholarship and display to play appropriate roles. Scholarship is an end in itself; it uses pictures as evidence and illustration. It has its own forms and methods, and these do their job best in books, catalogues and lectures. Display is a feeling for the life of pictures; it does not use them or control their life: it releases it, and its form is the exhibition. In these terms, "Cézanne: The Late Work" was not an exhibition. It borrowed its form from scholarship; it was a three-dimensional checklist.

Pictures for exhibition should be chosen and hung so they are free to be themselves. This means: they should not tire (c.f. the Turners at the Tate), and they should not make a point. Twenty-four mountains all in a row did both. They made Cézanne into a serialist, or a groper. But Cézanne did not paint those pictures for the sake of the interest created between them, nor was he groping after something he did not attain. On the contrary, when I see a fine Cézanne hanging in a museum, I see this: Cézanne was certain about his uncertainty; by embracing it he was able to make something stable and grand out of it, and that's the paradox I love in Cézanne.

I think Cézanne, of all artists, is encumbered by his reputation; so much, from the problematic to the portentous, has been tagged onto his pictures. A great Cézanne show, to me, would consist of the 40 finest available works, without theme, raison d'être or fanfare; then we could take a clean look.—Rackstraw Downes

In Rock, the Music Must Sustain the Message

When we look back on the musical 1960's, much of what we recall had a strongly political cast—folksingers and rockers using music to galvanize the political passions of the day. Bob Dylan and Joan Baez spring to mind immediately. But rock bands playing at political benefits, rallies and marches were a common occurrence, and political themes often formed the subject of songs. The 60's were hardly all political, to be sure—there was too much psychedelia and sensualism to make that generalization stick. But in comparison to our mostly "mellow" and conservative 70's, 60's music seems to have been positively charged with politics.

But recently in New York a number of artists have come up with overtly political songs, and the unfamiliar frequency of such music has set this observer to rethinking the whole question of when and how a political song can be successful.

First we had Bonnie Raitt's benefit concert a few weeks ago at the Paladium in support of the anti-nuclear power drive—a concert that included James Taylor and Carly Simon and that ended with a sing-along on a song by John Hall called "Power." Mr. Hall had included that same song in his own set at the Bottom Line a few days before. It consists of a straightforward denunciation of nuclear "poison" coupled with the fervent hope that mankind will turn to such "natural" energy sources as the sun, wind and water.

Since then we had Thom Bishop, a folk-singer from California by way of Chicago who is now based here and who was singing at the Other End. Mr. Bishop has a song in his repertory called "Neutron Blues," which suggests in no uncertain terms that the neutron bomb is a bad thing.

Around the same time the Tom Robinson Band was at the Bottom Line, and his debut concert there—his first in New York—was broadcast live on WNEW-FM. Mr. Robinson is best known for the frank espousal of his own homosexuality, and has a catchy anthem to that effect called "Glad to Be Gay." Or perhaps more precisely the tune of the chorus is catchy, but the verses describe with a good deal of bitterness the lot of the British homosexual, set upon by louts, beaten and otherwise made to feel a pariah.

Mr. Robinson's politics hardly stop there. He has a few non-political songs—above all his biggest hit so far, a song about cars and the pleasures to be derived from driving them entitled "2-4-6-8 Motorway." But most of his numbers concern themselves explicitly with what Mr. Robinson perceives to be the rise of Fascism and a polarized left-right split in Britain, hypocrisy and an implacable class society and pacifism. And he backs up his song subjects with frequent appearances at benefits in Britain.

Finally we had Bob Marley's concert at Madison Square Garden, which offered the unlikely sight of some 20,000 people swaying ecstatically to songs about the divinity of Haile Selassie (one of the encores even incorporated a whole chunk of a speech by the late Ethiopian emperor), marijuana as a sacrament, the necessity for justice and the betterment of social conditions on earth and the need to fight for one's rights.

One thing that can affect the potency of overtly political music is the context in which it's created and perceived. The music of Mr. Robinson and such other strongly political British new-wave rock bands as the Clash comes from a social and political situation that seems far more tense and polarized than does our relatively placid country. Similarly Mr. Marley is the leading exponent of reggae music and of the Rastafarian religious-political sect, both of which might seem rooted in Jamaica and the Third World.

Yet Mr. Robinson's music has enjoyed surprising acceptance in sophisticated American cities, by the press and on FM radio (even though his Bottom Line concert was something of a disappointment after his recorded work). And while there were admittedly a good many West Indians in Mr. Marley's audience at the Garden, there were at least as many middle-class whites, and *everybody* seemed caught up in the rapture by the end. So there must be more than context to have us determine the varying degrees of effectiveness that political songs enjoy.

One non-musical explanation has to do with political affinities. Perhaps Americans—even American leftists—aren't themselves directly concerned with Fascism in Britain or the plight of Kingston's Trenchtown black district. But there is something broader in any local assumption of such a stance that will awaken empathy on the part of people throughout the world who share the same basic political opinion. One responds to Mr. Robinson fighting his fight in London or Mr. Marley fighting his in Kingston because the mere vision of a battle taken up provides an emotional release that can translate into esthetic response.

But there is another, more intrinsically esthetic argument. Music has generally been exalted (or damned) by philosophers as the deepest, most profoundly emotional of the arts. But it gains this profundity in part by its very lack of specificity. Inherently abstract (unlike words or representational visual arts), it makes its most powerful impact by bypassing the concrete and evoking archetypal resonances within each of us.

The trouble with some political songs is that by confining music's strengths to a specific, worldly issue, the music is trivialized instead of the issue being elevated. Mr. Hall's "Power" and Mr. Bishop's "Neutron Blues" seem superficial next to both the intensity of their political concerns and music itself.

But that's not the whole of it. Mr. Marley's lyrics are often extremely explicit, as are Mr. Robinson's. Yet they succeed and (relatively speaking) fail in live performance because of the nature of the two men's performing and because of their music, considered abstractly.

Mr. Robinson's personality is a strange one, for an American in general and for an American used to the rude irreverence of the typical lower-class British rock performer in particular. He's upper-middle-class (even if he sings some songs in lower-class accents) and conveys a demeanor that is alternately warm, patronizing and smug.

Mr. Marley, on the other hand, projects a bizarre abandon onstage that is almost shamanistic in its intensity. By this time it's quite clear that at least some of his strangeness—the ropey Rastafarian "dreadlocks" falling about his head, the oddly hopping dance steps, the vacantly visionary stare—is in part a carefully assumed theatrical stance, but no less powerful for that. Through the compelling mysticism of his personality, he lists his politics from parochialism to universality.

But ultimately the real key to the success of any song, political or otherwise, lies in the music. If the words are too silly or flatly specific, they may hinder the effect of the music, but finally it's the music that will determine the song's impact. Not all of Mr. Robinson's songs reach his own best level. But the finest—"Glad to Be Gay," "Martin," "Motorway" and a screaming, passionately political effort called "Up Against the Wall"—strike home through the very strength of their music.

Similarly, for all the sometimes stirring, sometimes oddly provincial words and the lurching-dervish stage antics, it is Mr. Marley's music that turns large arenas into celebrations. The steadily rocking, off-beat accents of his Wailers band, the softly insinuating Jamaican *patois* and the directly communicative phrasing of his singing rate very high on a strictly musical scale, and they sustain his political message.

The moral? That songwriters will do well to avoid clumsily topical lyrics, if they don't wish to limit their potential depth and breadth of appeal. But great music will redeem almost anything. If political sentiments are borne aloft by memorable music, then that music will invest the words with universality all by itself.—John Rockwell

Exercises

1. Choose one of the samples of critical writing from the preceding pages and write a short paper discussing the style of the writer using as criteria the questions you learned to formulate in judging a writer's style in Chapter 11, An Interlude on Style.

2. Find a movie or book that has been often reviewed and compare two of the reviews using the questions on page 417 to guide you.

3. Write a short review of a movie, book, art exhibit, television show, musical event, or record album that has not been reviewed often.

WRITING LITERARY CRITICISM

Even though the range of critical writing is vast, it is possible to suggest some subjects to consider and some possible approaches to take in critical writing *about literature*. Critical papers about other arts may also consider some of the same features as literary criticism, and more: staged drama has all the components of printed drama, plus actors' and directors' interpretations, staging, and the like. Films can be approached in ways similar to literature and drama, with the additional considerations of cinematic techniques.

Painting and sculpture generally require different knowledge: about spatial relationships and the properties of the medium used, for example. Music and dance also require more specialized background knowledge, but that shouldn't stop you from seeing, and listening, and learning, and making judgments.

More often than not, however, if you are asked to write a critical piece in your college work, it will be an assignment that calls for you to evaluate a *text* of some kind, usually a literary text. For that reason, it seems fitting to suggest some ways to start and some possibilities to consider.

First, some general reminders. Remember that in a piece of critical writing *you* are the judge. Readers may be interested in what others say, in the opinions of scholars whose work you quote, but you are the judge, and it is your judgments that should be at the center of your work. Remember that the text you are writing about deserves careful study. Stop to know what you are writing about. Remember to show readers what accounts for your thinking; point to the specific lines, passages, and features of the text that have led you to think as you do.

And remember that you are not alone. A library can provide good company. You may find help or suggestions in any number of places, and you may get ideas about how to proceed with your own writing from any number of sources: from critical books about various authors or groups of authors, from critical essays and articles in various periodicals, from general studies of literature. You are the critic or judge, but a critic is responsible for knowing what he or she is talking about, and that may require consulting what others have written. (As a specific example of the use of other sources to support and guide a writer, you should know that several books provided ideas for the pages that follow: B. Bernard Cohen, *Writing About Literature*; Wilfred L. Guerin, et al., *A Handbook of Critical Approaches to Literature*; and Edgar V. Roberts, *Writing Themes About Literature*.)

INSIGHT

A note about documentation

Since it is sometimes necessary to consult the work of others and since in critical writing you frequently must quote from the text you are discussing, you'll often need to document your critical papers—that is, provide appropriate footnotes and bibliographical references. Please see Chapter 17 for a discussion of note and bibliographical form.

Some possible approaches to critical writing

The most obvious—and probably the best—place to start is with something in the text that arrests your interest. When a question occurs in your mind about something in the text, or when a puzzle develops for you, or when something troubles you in the text—then you have a beginning place: to answer the question, to solve the puzzle, to work out what is troubling you. Any number of things may catch your attention—an interesting pattern that you see in the writing, a startling idea that is explored in several ways by several characters in a novel, a striking mood that is established by images and sounds. If you're caught up by something in the text, explore it, follow where it leads, and let it be your subject.

But if no single thing arrests your interest, and if you are in some doubt about where to start and what to do, you may find that one of the possible approaches listed below will give you the suggestion you need to get started.

Critical report.   Critical writing doesn't have to be complicated. Sometimes, in the assignments they give, instructors are only interested in finding out whether you have in fact read the texts that they assigned. If it is clear that a rather simple report is all that is called for, then you can rest when you have (1) provided evidence *that you have read* the text, for example by giving a concise summary; (2) indicated *that you understand* the text by giving brief commentary on key points or key episodes, or by discussing the significance of key passages; and (3) shown *that you are ready to respond* by presenting, for example, brief evaluations of the text or of some portions of it.

Character analysis.   Some texts lend themselves well to study of the characters that appear in the texts. If you are working with fiction, for example, or drama, where a number of different characters speak and act and influence the behavior of other characters, then one good way to write a critical essay is to focus on character development in the text. You can focus on a single character in a single text, on similar characters in several texts, on a group of related characters, or on two characters in some special, close relationship; no doubt there are other groupings you can devise. If you set out to examine character in a text, you'll face such questions as these: How are characters created? How do you learn about the characters in the text? Are they realistically presented? If so, how is the realistic presentation achieved? If not, is there some reason why they are not realistically presented? Why do they behave as they do? How do they influence the actions and beliefs of other characters? Answering any one or all of these questions—and you'll find other questions to ask— may be the basis of a critical essay.

A related point: while the created characters in a novel, short story, or play may seem to be more obvious objects of study, the same examination can be applied to the speaker in a poem and the speaker in an essay. It may be important to the analysis of the poem or essay to learn about these characters and their contribution to the piece.

Study of point of view.   Often it becomes important to understand the point of view in a novel, short story, play, poem, or essay. A speaker—whether it's the author or some character in the text—is always standing somewhere when he or she speaks, seeing some things but not seeing others, knowing some things but not able to know other things. Knowing where speakers stand and how they look at the events, people, and ideas around them helps readers to understand more fully the significance of what they are saying. Some speakers are more reliable than others. Some writers use several viewpoints, shifting from one speaker to another in a novel, for example, or sometimes speaking in their own voice. It's always important to know who is speaking, why that person is speaking, and what is gained or lost for us by the speaker's point of view.

Study of setting.   The place in which a text occurs is important. "Place" can mean anywhere from the geographical locale to a specific spot in a room, as well as the time in which something occurs. Mars in 2001 would be one setting; a bench in Arden Forest in 1605 another. In fiction, drama, and some poetry, especially, the setting may establish the atmosphere, the mood, the tone that influence and sometimes even govern the acts, words, and thoughts of the character. If the setting seems to deserve attention, then you'll need to consider at least two questions: How important is the setting to the text you're studying? How is the setting presented?

Examination of ideas in the text.   Sometimes, instead of studying features of the writing—character development, setting, and so on—it is more important to study the ideas presented in a text, what they are, the value apparently assigned to them, and the way they are presented. Ideas can emerge in a text in any number of ways. Sometimes the author directly expresses ideas. Sometimes ideas are revealed indirectly by the language and imagery the author uses, as for example when a writer uses images of darkness and a series of long vowel sounds to create a sense of brooding, mournful despair. Sometimes an author states ideas through a character. But you need to be watchful when this occurs. When an author creates a *persona*, a character whose point of view he uses throughout a text, the ideas expressed by the *persona* will sometimes be those of the author, but not always. In *Gulliver's Travels*, Lemuel Gulliver no doubt sometimes says things for Jonathan Swift, but sometimes he is his own zany self.

Ideas are expressed in other ways too: characters in a text may state ideas or put ideas in conflict; sometimes characters stand for ideas. Often, however, when ideas are expressed, they are expressed in a number of ways, not in some one single way.

Close reading of a single passage.   This kind of critical essay, often called an *explication*, consists of a word-by-word, phrase-by-phrase, or line-by-line reading or interpretation of a passage from a text. Most of the time, this critical approach is used with poetry, but it can be used with fiction or drama. Usually, all the elements discussed above—characters, point of view, setting, and ideas, as well as devices of language, meter, and symbolism—are all taken into account.

There is no way to suggest a pattern to follow in a close reading or explication; what you do in this kind of critical writing depends entirely on the passage in question. Sometimes explications serve to show a pattern of development in a passage, or to comment on a series of images, or to show how an idea is being developed, but in the end there is no way to predict what an explication ought to do, except to say that it ought to respond carefully to the details of a textual passage. The following explication of a short poem by Robert Frost is a good example of how various elements can be discussed. Explication can be used, too, as part of a critical discussion that ultimately has a different purpose.

Dust of Snow

The way a crow
Shook down on me
The dust of snow
From a hemlock tree

Has given my heart
A change of mood
And saved some part
Of a day I had rued.

—Robert Frost

Frost's "Dust of Snow"

In Robert Frost's short poem "Dust of Snow" the speaker has known sorrow so pervasive that only a part of his day was brightened by the crow's unintended joke. We infer that he enjoys a closeness to nature because he was out-of-doors on a winter day and because he names the species of bird and the type of tree. Another characteristic of the speaker is his sense of humor: he can recognize a joke and "take it," even during a period of sadness.

The structure of the poem is that of a simple sentence; the first stanza is its subject and the second stanza is its predicate. This sentence portrays the event in chronological order, although its final clause, "of a day I had rued," directs our attention beyond the incident, in both directions, establishing the context of an entire day. In matters of mood, the structure is balanced in the sense that the poet treats the crow's joke in the first stanza and his day of sadness in the second.

Weighing the poem's suggestive power, we observe that the imagery is tightly related to the structure of the poem, which is essentially a play of contrasting elements. Just as the moods contrast from light to dark, the cold snow descends upon the warm neck of the speaker. We may appreciate, as well, the black-white contrast of "crow" on "snow." There is an avalanche of concrete details in the first stanza, while the second stanza is the speaker's interpretation of the event.

Rhythmically, the poem races to the "day" of the last line, and then the importance of the final three words, without intervening unstressed syllables, slows the pace of the poem to a solemn conclusion.

The poet's diction, furthermore, turns the crow's practical joke into a play of finer humor. Besides the particularity of the images of the first stanza, the associations which they trigger have a curious unity. First of all, the bird is a *crow*, a member of the raven family, a bird of prey. The only striking metaphor of the poem compares snow to *dust*. This metaphor works nicely on the level of sheer imagery; nonetheless, we may legitimately hear an echo of the phrase "dust to dust." And, finally, the tree which was the crow's perch was the *hemlock* (from which a deadly poison comes). When these three symbols of death converge upon the speaker on a day of bitter sadness, it's as though nature said, "If you think you have troubles now, friend—" We get the impression, too, that the speaker would not take the joke from any other source.

The further humorous turn to the poem is that the crow's message brightens his day. Frost caps this turn with his extraordinary selection of the word "saved" (line 7)—in complete contradiction to the pronouncement of doom. And so the feelings which the poem weaves are a fabric of sadness, delight, and wisdom. And on the level of wordless experience the poem speaks to us of life and death, as well as of mortal man's use of nature and his use of imagination.—Edgar H. Knapp

Comparison.   Comparisons may provide you any number of possibilities for critical writing, whatever your subject, whether fiction, drama, poetry, nonfiction, television, movies, or something else. Examining how one thing stacks up against something else may give you a way of judging the failures and successes of either one of the items compared, or of both. Comparing the way one character speaks with the way another character in the same story speaks, for example, may tell you something about both characters, about the author's style, or about other features of the story. Possible comparisons are many: you may compare different works by the same author, different features of the same work by an author, works by different authors; you may compare styles, forms of organization, settings, ideas, points of view, or any features or elements of writing; you may compare the work of an author in one era with the work of an author in another era, or the works of authors living at the same time. The possibilities for comparison are numerous; the point of comparison in critical writing is to evaluate one or the other or all of the works or features being compared.

Speaker (writer)-audience relationships.   It is sometimes useful to explore how audiences have reacted to a given piece of writing. This kind of information, of course, is not always available (and seldom available without research) for either current writers or for writers of former times, but it may help you judge a piece of writing if you know something about how it has been received. Remember, too, that there are speakers and audiences *inside* many works, especially in fiction and drama, and sometimes in poetry. That is, there are characters who speak and other characters who listen, and you may learn a great deal about the merits of a piece of writing by exploring the relationship between speakers and audiences within the work.

Structural or organizational studies.   It is almost always useful to explore how a piece of writing is put together, to identify its parts, to see what connects them, to see what shape can be discerned in the work you are studying. You may find a number of different types of structures at work in different pieces of writing, and you may find more than one kind of structure developed in a single work. For example, the progression of a piece of writing presumably has some kind of *logical* base; its parts respond to each other in some way. There may also be a *chronological* structure and a structure based on *conflict* (developed as oppositions within a work continue in various forms until some kind of resolution is reached). You may find *emotional* structures, built upon varying emotional responses that are elicited at different times in a piece of writing. It may also be useful to you in your evaluation to examine how the structure of a given work relates to the structures of similar works (if you are studying a short story, how does its design compare to other short stories? if you are studying a tragedy, how does its structure relate to the structures of other tragedies?).

Stylistic studies.   If you set out to study the style of a text, you may need to explore any number of its features, or you may discover that any one feature of a writer's style will give you a standard to judge by. You may need to examine the vocabulary (whether complex, simple, specialized), the frequency and type of figurative language, the kinds of sentences used (whether long, short, or middling, whether simple, compound, complex, or compound-complex, whether loose or periodic, whether conventional and direct or characterized by unusual constructions), the tone (whether formal, loose, colloquial, breezy, conversational), the length and function of the paragraphs, and other features of the writing. In stylistic studies of some writing, especially of poetry, you may need to examine the *imagery*—the words, figures of speech, and descriptions that capture and express sense experience and the associations that it suggests. Images may be embodied in single words (the word *nightingale* by itself tends to suggest a romantic setting and a romantic mood), in extended descriptions, in figurative language (see Chapter 8 on words), in symbols. In stylistic studies of poetry you may need to examine *prosody*, the rhythm and rhyme patterns, the line characteristics, and the verse forms of poetry.

Stylistic criticism can be complex and demanding. Remember,

however, that it can start from fairly simple questions: How does a writer get the effect or tone that he or she achieves in a text? Why does an author do what he or she does in a text? How is one writer different from another writer?

Psychological criticism.   The psychological approach provides another perspective for interpretation and judgment of a text. It is a form of criticism that can be easily abused (as when a critic sets out determinedly to find a deep or deeper meaning in every single act or speech from a text or when a critic tries to psychoanalyze every character in a text), and it's difficult to find any clear-cut guide to psychological criticism. Perhaps it's enough for now to suggest that psychological criticism may focus on two primary questions. The first is, "Why do things happen as they do in a text?" Trying to answer that question will lead you to explore the origins of what is said and done in a text, the psychological roots from which words and deeds spring, and the relationships that exist within a text among the characters or between the speaker and the subject or between the speaker and an audience either within the text or outside the text. The second question is, "What consequences do acts and words in the text have for those who do or say them, for those who hear or participate, and for those who only watch?" Trying to answer that question will lead you to explore the effects of what is said and done in a text, the psychological results of words and deeds.

Archetypal criticism.   In his book *Metaphor and Reality*, Philip Wheelright discusses "archetypes," or universal symbols, which are, he says,

> *those which carry the same or very similar meanings for a large portion, if not all, of mankind. It is a discoverable fact that certain symbols, such as the sky father and earth mother, light, blood, up-down, the axis of a wheel, and others, recur again and again in cultures so remote from one another in space and time that there is no likelihood of any historical influence and causal connection among them. (p. 111)*

Archetypal criticism explores the occurrence of such symbols, images, and patterns in literary texts, and attempts to determine the significance of the various versions of these archetypes. It may help you see some of the possibilities in this kind of critical writing if you see some of the images and patterns that critics have discussed as archetypes. The list below only suggests the nature of archetypal occurrences:

Water   tends to suggest creation, birth, purification, growth, sometimes death, and sometimes resurrection
Sun   often suggests energy, wisdom, spiritual vision
Black   often used to suggest mystery, the unknown, death, evil

Circle	often suggests wholeness, unity, God
Wind	suggests inspiration, soul, spirit
Ship	may suggest any voyage through time and space
Garden	often suggests innocence, fertility, unspoiled beauty or innocence
Desert	may suggest death, spiritual despair

Sequences of events, archetypal motifs or patterns, occur in the literature of many countries and many ages. Almost every mythology, for example, is based on some Creation motif, and many texts re-enact the creation sequence. A dream of immortality occurs time and again in texts of all eras and languages, and it recurs in literature as a hope for a return to paradise, an escape from time. Certain kinds of heroes and heroic actions occur again and again:

The Quest: The Hero undertakes a long journey during which he must overcome great obstacles to save himself, a kingdom, or something precious; the quest may be physical or spiritual or psychological, actual or figurative.

The Initiation: The Hero goes through a process of education, passing from ignorance and immaturity to spiritual maturity.

The Scapegoat: The Hero must bear the burden of his people's sins and atone for them.

As you can see, archetypal images and patterns, only briefly suggested here, occur again and again and take many forms. One goal of criticism is to identify them and search out the significance of their appearances and transformations in various texts.

Research-related criticism. Any of the critical approaches suggested above may require research. You may need to consult reference works (for example, to study prosody before examining the rhyme and rhythm patterns of a poem), or other critical studies of the text you are examining. Some kinds of criticism will almost certainly require research:

1. It is sometimes useful to study the relationship between one work by an author and another work by the same author—so that, for example, you may study the author's development or trace a theme or technique in the author's work.

2. Sometimes you may need to study an author's life in order to determine whether details of his or her life will illuminate or explain features of the text you are studying.

3. Sometimes an author's letters, journals, conversations, and revisions of his or her work will enable you to learn about the creative process that resulted in the text before you.

4. You may wish at times to study literary theory so that you may judge the text against the literary beliefs and conceptions of the time in which it was produced.

5. You may need to learn about the author's effect upon the time in which he or she lived, or about the effect of the time upon the author, including the influences of other writers upon the author.

6. You may wish to explore the relationship between the text you are studying and some subject-matter field such as folklore, religion, philosophy, political science, or others.

There are many possible approaches to critical writing. You may not be able to stop with just one method of study and evaluation; you may need to come at the text you are studying from many angles with the advantage of many different perspectives. Remember that a text is not an object to be adored or ignored; a text is part of a conversation, the rest of which you are at liberty to provide. You can begin to make a text your own—that is, understand it so that you can use it, share its insight, and grow with the added perspective—by responding to it, judging it, and working out your evaluation for yourself and an audience.

The following student essay was written in response to an assignment, so the writer assumes that the audience is familiar with the four novels under discussion. This paper combines some of the elements for critical analysis listed above: it is a paper showing the similarities of one aspect of cowboys' characters, their use of language, in different books of the same genre; thus, it combines elements of comparison, character analysis, and study of ideas. Note, by the way, the form of documentation: the first reference to each novel is listed in an endnote; further citations are handled in the text.

How It Must Be: The Cowboy's Silence

"I am goin' my own course. . . . Can't yu see how it must be about a man?"

In a scene familiar to us all, a dusty western town with its main street nearly deserted, two men walk down the street, approaching each other. The two men, who will let cold, ugly guns settle their argument, take their revenge, or answer another's challenge, stop at a proper distance. They draw and fire, and when the shooting is over, one man lies dead. A violent act has been done, and not one word has been spoken.

The scene is familiar, for we have encountered it many times in our literature, films, and television. The western hero is an integral and intimate part of us. If we look, we recognize ourselves in him. He is an inarticulate man, like ourselves. His life is filled with action, but because he is uncomfortable with accepted modes of expression, perhaps because he is incapable of using them, the action in his life often takes violent forms. We envisage our western hero as a cowboy, and we bestow on him remarkable skills for physical action, yet we deny him full powers of speech. The cowboy, who spends long hours on a lonely range, is a man who lacks a vocabulary and a grammar. As a result his means of expression and communication are limited, and the outcome of this limitation is often tragic.

It is not unusual for the description of the cowboy to include his physical appearance, but a man's character holds more than can be described about his person. So writers generally include an account of a man's attitude, his bearing, and his manner of speech. In his initial encounter with the Virginian, the narrator of Wister's novel sees a man who had "been sent to look after me, he would do so, would even carry my valise; but I could not be jocular with him." [1] It is only after years of acquaintance that these two converse with any degree of freedom.

Harry Destry is another whose personal speech is recognizably limited. Upon his return from six years in jail, he "spoke little and generally preluded every remark with an apology." [2] This posturing is of course a sham, but even when it is seen that "a devil that's ten times worse" (*Destry*, p. 39) has returned, this particular hero is still laconic. During the encounter with the Ogdens at a bar, Harry "spoke not a word, invited no comment, asked for no opinion. . . . There was no conversation at all." (*Destry*, p. 36) When Harry is finished with the Ogden brothers, one is dead; the other is crippled for life.

The Ox-Bow Incident is more violent yet, for the violence committed wrongs everyone concerned. Certainly not enough is spoken to avert the lynching. Almost every member of the mob is distinguished by his speech traits, and they are all remarkably taciturn. When Art and Gil are first introduced, Art admits that "We didn't dare talk much, and we wanted to feel easy together again." [3] Acknowledging their uneasiness with each other, Gil faults Art: "Well, he wouldn't talk . . . and somebody had to." (*Ox-Bow*, p. 9) Kincaid, the man whom everyone believes to have been murdered, was a man who "never offered to say anything, but only made short answers when he had to, and then you had to be close to hear him." (*Ox-Bow*, p. 29) When Ma Grier rides up to join the mob, she is readily accepted, for as Art observes, "she had . . . a way of talking to us in our own language so we'd laugh and still listen." (*Ox-Bow*, p. 76)

As for the "criminals" of *The Ox-Bow Incident*, nothing they say is satisfactory. The members of the mob are disgusted with Martin, for at first "he wouldn't talk, and now he talks too much." (*Ox-Bow*, p. 160) When it is discovered that the Mexican does speak English, he readily admits to speaking "ten other languages . . . but I don't tell anything I don't want to in any of them." (*Ox-Bow*, p. 175) Throughout the story, there is a striking paucity of words spoken effectively by any man.

From Shane's first appearance at the Starrett ranch, the young boy, Bob, perceives that his idol has a striking manner of speech: "his voice was so gentle," [4] but he was "so silent and stern." (*Shane*, p. 54) Marian Starrett also senses this outstanding feature after her first meeting with Shane: "'Wasn't it peculiar,' I heard mother say, 'how he wouldn't talk about himself?'" (*Shane*, p. 8)

Shane differs from the other cowboys who have been described, for he is a gunfighter who willingly associates with the ranchers. He talks more, but mostly to a young boy, and Bob believes that "he could talk to me because I was only a kid." (*Shane*, p. 99) Still, Shane distinguishes himself through his talking, and Bob is the beneficiary, for "Shane was speaking to me the way I liked, as if maybe I was a man and could understand all he said." (*Shane*, p. 82)

Although the cowboy is inarticulate for the most part, he can recognize what he considers "good" English and even use it on appropriate occasions. When the Virginian is forced to put up a visiting minister for the night, he pretends to feel the devil threatening him; so he and the minister spend the night wrestling for his soul. "'I spoke awful good English to him most of the time,' said he. 'I can, yu' know, when I cinch my attention tight on to it.'" (*Virginian*, p. 177) The Virginian knew the right time and place for good grammar. Marian Starrett was another who "always knew when to talk and when not to talk." (*Shane*, p. 78)

"Good grammar" is recognized, appreciated, even desired. Chastising Molly for her lack of response to the Virginian's courtship, Mrs. Taylor says, "Since the roughness looks bigger to you than the diamond, you had better go back to Vermont. I expect you'll find better grammar there, deary." (*Virginian*, p. 233) In *Destry Rides Again*, Mr. Dangerfield criticizes his daughter on similar grounds:

> "If you aint gunna get yourself a husband," said he, "you might get yourself some grammar; which a man would think that you never been to school, to listen at you talk!"
>
> "I only dress up my talk once a week," said she, "and the rest of the time I'd rather go around comfortable and let the pronunciation take care of itself. What difference does it make to an adjective if it's used for an adverb? It don't give the word no pain; it's easier for me; the niggers understand me better, and everybody's happy all around." (*Destry*, p. 42)

Harry Destry is also appreciative of Charley's skill: "How you talk up right out of a school book, when you ain't thinkin'!" (*Destry*, p. 50) References to good grammar are generally found in contexts where women appear. Perhaps women, as gentle creatures of the wild west, can be left to their own quiet, gentle word games, where "good grammar" is valued.

The cowboy hero seems to have a keen sense of the appropriateness of words. He knows that there is a fine distinction between a time for talk and a time for silence, silence which is "clean and wholesome." (*Shane*, p. 26) So the narrator of *The Virginian* realizes that "for an hour we had been shirking real talk." (*Virginian*, p. 282) It was a time for silence, as a lynching was in progress. Steve feels the necessity for silence as he is about to be hanged. The Virginian mourns his friend: "Steve never said a word to me all through. He shunned it. . . ." (*Virginian*, p. 285) Yet he comes to appreciate Steve's sensitivity in his posthumous message: "Good-by, Jeff . . . I could not have spoke to you without playing the baby." (*Virginian*, p. 303) Silence is also appropriate in places other than conversation. The Virginian objects to a book lent to him by Molly because it "talks too much." (*Virginian*, p. 100) This desire to refrain from talking is justified to the cowboy. To him, it is too easy to "hate a man you've talked too much to. He's like a man who's seen you show yellow." (*Ox-Bow*, p. 200)

Just as there is a time for quiet thought, there is a time to speak out. Art and Gil worry over Davies, who was "just sipping his drink, and being too quiet." (*Ox-Bow*, p. 39) At the close of the book, after the lynching, Davies attempts to purge himself through speech: " 'I've got to talk,' he protested. 'I've got to talk so I can get some sleep.' " (*Ox-Bow*, p. 198) In the great episode in *Shane*, when Joe and Shane conquer the ironwood stump, young Bob feels that "they should at least say something to each other." (*Shane*, p. 27) Bob is young and does not understand the nuances of speech and silence.

The realization that there is a very proper time and place for speech shows the attitude that the cowboy has towards language. "A man can't live on bread alone. He's gotta have words, too," claims Harry Destry. (*Destry*, p. 57) Words are given a great deal of importance. When Molly exclaims, "It's murder!" the Virginian answers almost angrily, "Don't call it that name." (*Virginian*, p. 342) If words expressing his reluctance to face Trampas were spread around to his friends, "there'd be nothing to explain. There'd just be the fact." (*Virginian*, p. 343) Shane makes a curt reply to a derogatory remark, and lets "the words lie there, plain and short and ugly." (*Shane*, p. 89) He knows the power that words can have. It is for this reason that Bob sees, when neighbors come to visit, that Shane "would share little in their talk. With us he spoke freely enough. We were, in some subtle way, his folks." (*Shane*, p. 36) Words with the Starretts mean a great deal to Shane.

Although the cowboy's regard for the spoken word recurs throughout literature, at the last the cowboy will always rely on action—violent action—rather than words. This is inevitable, for the thoughts of the cowboy are not expressed verbally: "When Gil gets low in spirit, or confused in his mind, he doesn't feel right again until he's had a fight." (*Ox-Bow*, p. 15) The final choice lies between more words and action, and the cowboy usually makes the choice that requires more of him in a loud, physical, heroic way—because he must.

Until the final moment, though, the choice is still there. Problems can be solved; they can be worked out with words or with action, but only with one. Words and deeds do not coincide. Art is incredulous when he hears of Gerald Tetley's suicide: "He couldn't have. He talked too much." (*Ox-Bow*, p. 204) Gerald had disgusted Art earlier with a spate of self-indulgent comments. He had been unsuccessful at two suicide attempts. Only when he can no longer fall back on words, when there is no one, not even his father, to talk with, does he achieve his own violent death.

When Shane and Joe Starrett get fully involved in the battle against the ironwood stump, the silence is almost complete:

> . . . . Their eyes met over the top of the stump and held and neither one of them said a word. Then they swung up their axes and both of them said plenty to that old stump. . . .
>
> . . . . "Must be a taproot," he said. That was the one time either of them had spoken to the other, as far as I knew, the whole afternoon through. Father did not say anything more. And Shane said nothing. (*Shane*, pp. 19, 24)

In one long afternoon of grueling physical action, few words are spoken between the two men. At the end, words won't work in place of their decisions to act. Joe tells Shane to stay out of town and out of his business. Shane responds to him, "There's no man living can tell me what I can't do. Not even you, Joe. You forget there is still a way," (*Shane*, p. 103) and knocks him unconscious with the barrel of his gun. He has made the final decision for the violence that follows.

When Gil is accused of cowardice, he is instantly ready for action: "'Mister, take it easy with that talk,' Gil said, swinging out of line and hitching a thumb over his gunbelt." (*Ox-Bow*, p. 157) For most men, talk goes a very short way. The decision for violence is reached as easily as a holster.

Admiration for an inarticulate man seems at first glance to be undeserved. What is admirable about a man who resorts to violence instead of reasoned speech? Perhaps one justification is found in Bob Starrett's last observation of Shane: "He was riding away and I knew that no word or thought could hold him." (*Shane*, p. 113) The cowboy hero has freed himself from the courteous niceties of speech. Words for him are equipment as practical as chaps and bandannas, but they are not essential. Envied by the average person, the cowboy can ride away, and not be held back by any word. Given the limitless setting of the western, the cowboy has set boundaries of his own design, and not those imposed by the conventions of speech. He is outside our grammar. He is free, always, to act.

Notes

[1] Owen Wister, *The Virginian* (New York: Pocket Books, 1956), p. 8. Further references to this book will be identified in the text.

[2] Max Brand, *Destry Rides Again* (New York: Pocket Books, 1944), p. 25. Further references to this book will be identified in the text.

[3] Walter van Tilburg Clark, *The Ox-Bow Incident* (New York: New American Library, 1940), p. 6. Further references to this book will be identified in the text.

[4] Jack Schaefer, *Shane* (New York: Bantam Pathfinder Editions, 1963), p. 3. Further references to this book will be identified in the text.

Exercises

1.   Familiarize yourself with the PMLA Bibliography in your library. After that, consult with your reference librarian concerning other resources available in your library for doing critical writing about literature.

2.   Explicate a short poem or several lines from a poem. Be sure you check with your teacher to see if the work you have chosen can be successfully handled with the resources available to you. You should first read and re-read the poem to determine your own interpretation, and *then* research what others have said about the poem.

3.   Just as a few examples can't begin to suggest the range and variety that are possible in critical writing, so also a few exercises can't begin to suggest the range of possible kinds of critical writing that you will be asked to do without its becoming busywork. Your teacher, however, may wish to assign a critical paper for this class to give you the kind of experience you need. If so, start by reading, re-reading, reflecting, and meditating before you go to your resources. Also, be sure to explore all of the possible approaches made available to you in this chapter to choose the approach that seems most fruitful and appropriate for the text you are considering.

Forms and Procedures in Research Writing

A Brief Guide to Grammar, Punctuation, and Usage

Part Three

Reference Materials
for Writing

17

Forms and Procedures in Research Writing

After a short summary of the other sections in this book that are applicable to research writing, this chapter discusses the ways that you can

1. take advantage of available resources (p. 443);

2. keep a systematic account of your resources (p. 447);

3. take useful and complete notes (p. 449);

4. plan your paper before you write (p. 450);

5. give appropriate credit for the work and words of others (p. 451);

6. use a consistent form in acknowledging the work of others (p. 454);

7. submit a complete paper (p. 460).

Most of the chapters in this book will have some uses in the preparation of research papers. The same problems that face writers with any kind of paper face writers of research papers: finding a subject and its proper focus, and organizing and developing the paper. Because of the often formal organization features of research papers, Chapter 6, Designing Your Work, and Chapter 7, Developing Your Material, might be especially helpful. Chapter 14, Reports, has a brief discussion of the aims and content of research reports, as well as an example of a research paper. For more specific help with research procedures and forms of documentation, the suggestions below may be fruitful.

TAKE ADVANTAGE OF AVAILABLE RESOURCES

The library card catalog

The card catalog is an alphabetical card index of the items in the library. Most card catalogs, in addition to listing all books in the library, give the titles of periodicals (and indicate what copies the library has), encyclopedias, government publications, and other works.

Almost all books are listed alphabetically in three places in the card catalog of most libraries: by author, by subject, and by title. The cards issued by the Library of Congress are almost universally used for cataloging.

You can save yourself many hours of thumbing through books that are not relevant to your subject by learning to interpret and evaluate the information given in the card catalog. The subject card includes the following information:

1. Subject. The subject heading on the catalog card tells in general what the book is about. Also listed on the card are the other subject headings under which the book is cataloged.

2. Call number. The call number in the upper left-hand corner tells where the book is located in the library.

3. Author's name. If you are already familiar with the subject you are investigating, the author's name may tell you whether the book is likely to be authoritative.

4. Title and facts of publication. The date of publication is sometimes an important clue to the usefulness of a book.

5. Number of pages, illustrations, height. The number of pages in the book suggests how extensive its coverage is.

6. Special information. The catalog card indicates if a book has a bibliography, illustrations, or other helpful material.

7.   *Other subject headings.*   The list of other subject headings under which the book is cataloged may give you ideas of other subject areas to look under for more material on your topic, as well as provide a further clue to the contents of the book listed.

Trade bibliographies

The bibliographies published for booksellers and librarians should be consulted to locate books that are not listed in the card catalog of your library or to learn if a book is still in print. The most important trade bibliographies are these:

Books in Print. A listing by author and by title of books included in *Publishers' Trade List Annual,* which lists—by publisher—all books currently in print.

Cumulative Book Index. Gives complete publication data on all books published in the English language, listing them by author and by title. Published monthly, with cumulative volumes issued periodically.

Paperbound Books in Print. Especially useful since some important books are available *only* in paperback. Published monthly, with cumulative volumes issued three times a year.

Subject Guide to Books in Print. An invaluable index to the titles listed in *Books in Print.*

Periodical indexes

A great deal of essential material, particularly on current topics, is available only in periodicals, which may range from popular magazines and newspapers to technical journals and learned publications. This material is cataloged in various guides and indexes, some of them published monthly, others annually. Knowing how to use periodical indexes will not only simplify the task of research but will also enable you to make your reference paper more authoritative and up-to-date. Most libraries have lists of the periodicals they have which tell also where the periodicals are indexed.

Readers' Guide.   The most generally useful of all periodical guides is the *Readers' Guide to Periodical Literature,* which indexes the articles in more than 120 magazines of general interest. It is published monthly in paperbound volumes which are afterwards gathered in large cumulative volumes covering a year or more.

The entries in the *Readers' Guide* are listed alphabetically both by subject and by author. The abbreviations used in the listings—for the titles of periodicals, the month of publication, and various facts about the article itself—are explained on the first page of each volume.

Other periodical indexes. In locating sources for a reference paper you may find it useful to refer to one of the specialized periodical indexes listed below. Most of them appear annually; the year after the title shows when publication began. The indexes are listed alphabetically.

Applied Science and Technology Index (1913). Subject index to periodicals on science, technology, and related subjects.

Art Index (1929). Author and subject index for fine-arts periodicals and museum bulletins.

Bibliographic Index: A Cumulative Bibliography of Bibliographies (1938).

Biography Index: A Cumulative Index to Biographical Material in Books and Magazines (1946/47).

Book Review Digest (1905). Author, subject, and title index to published book reviews; gives extracts and exact references to sources.

Business Periodicals Index (1958). Subject index to periodicals on all phases of business, including particular industries and trades.

Catholic Periodical Index: A Guide to Catholic Magazines (1930).

Dramatic Index (1909–1949). Index to articles and illustrations concerning the American and English theater.

The Education Index (1929–1964). Author and subject index for educational periodicals, books, and pamphlets.

Humanities Index (1974). Author and subject index to periodicals from various countries; devoted to articles in the humanities; valuable supplement to the *Readers' Guide.*

Poole's Index to Periodical Literature (1802–1881). Subject index to American and English periodicals, many of which are no longer published but are still important; precedes coverage of *Readers' Guide.*

Public Affairs Information Service (1915). Subject index to books, periodicals, pamphlets, and other material on economics, government, and other public affairs.

Social Sciences and Humanities Index (1907–1974). Author and subject index to periodicals from various countries; devoted chiefly to the humanities and social sciences; formerly titled *International Index to Periodicals;* now superseded by two separate indexes.

Social Sciences Index (1974). Author and subject index to periodicals focusing on the social sciences; supplements *Readers' Guide.*

United States Government Publications Monthly Catalog (1895). Lists various publications of the government in all fields.

Special indexes

The New York Times Index. Monthly index to articles appearing in *The New York Times,* with annual volumes. Since it gives the dates of events, speeches, and important documents, this index is helpful for finding articles of general interest in local papers as well.

Ulrich's International Periodical Directory. Classifies American and foreign periodicals by subject area and tells which periodical index covers them.

Vertical File Index: A Subject and Title Index to Selected Pamphlet Material. Describes each pamphlet listed, tells how to purchase it, and lists the price.

Encyclopedias

The following general encyclopedias are authoritative and include many bibliographies and cross-references. All are regularly revised; several are supplemented annually with yearbooks.

Chamber's Encyclopaedia
Collier's Encyclopedia
Columbia Encyclopedia
Encyclopaedia Britannica
Encyclopedia Americana

Many subject areas, from art to science, are covered by reference works that go into more detail than general encyclopedias, and their coverage is more specialized. You should be able to find most of these by browsing in the reference room of your library. The librarian will also be able to tell you what reference works exist for your area of interest.

Yearbooks and annuals

The following annuals provide up-to-date facts and figures on a wide variety of subjects, particularly those of current interest.

Information Please Almanac.

Social Work Year Book. Social work and related fields.

The Statesman's Year-Book: Statistical and Historical Annual of the States of the World, 1864 –. Historical and statistical events throughout the world.

The World Almanac and Book of Facts. This is one general reference that any student can afford to own, and one that anyone with a serious interest in current affairs can hardly afford to be without. The index is in the front of each volume.

Yearbook of the United Nations. Activities of the United Nations.

Guides to reference materials

Many other specialized reference works can be found by consulting the following guides:

Barton, Mary N., comp. *Reference Books: A Brief Guide for Students and Other Users of the Library.*

Murphey, Robert W. *How and Where to Look It Up.*

The Reader's Adviser: A Layman's Guide to Literature.

Shores, Louis. *Basic Reference Sources: An Introduction to Materials and Methods.*

Walford, Arthur J., ed. *Guide to Reference Material.*

Winchell, Constance M. *Guide to Reference Books.*

KEEP A SYSTEMATIC ACCOUNT OF YOUR RESOURCES

A working bibliography is a list of the books, magazine articles, and other resources that you intend to consult when you are gathering material for your paper. It is a *working* list, not a *finished;* there may be entries there that you won't use, and you may need to keep adding items as you work.

Some instructors will want you to use 3-by-5 inch or 4-by-6 inch note cards to maintain a working bibliography. The cards are handy. If you put a single reference only on each card, it's easy to keep the pile in some kind of order. (You may want to use 3-by-5 cards for the bibliography, and 4-by-6 cards for the notes you take.) If you don't use note cards, devise some system that is really a system, that will let you keep track of all possible resources. As you are gathering resources, you should systematically keep the information that will let you (1) find the resource again when you need it, and (2) make a final bibliographical entry for your finished paper. The necessary information is shown below, together with two sample bibliography cards. For other bibliographic forms, see page 457.

1. *Author's name,* with the last name first, followed by a period. If the book is edited, use the editor's name, followed by a comma, followed by *ed.* If the article or pamphlet is unsigned, write the title first on the card.

2. *Title of the book,* underlined and followed by a period, or title of the article, in quotation marks and followed by a period.

3. *Facts of publication:*
   a) For a book: the city of publication, followed by a colon; the name of the publisher, followed by a comma; and the date, followed by a period. Former practice often left out the pub-

lisher's name, and usage is still divided. However, unless you are told otherwise, it's always safe to include it.

b) *For a magazine article:* the name of the magazine, underlined and followed by a comma; the date of the issue, followed by a comma; and the pages covered by the article, preceded by *pp.* and followed by a period.

c) *For a journal article:* the name of the journal, underlined and followed by a comma; the volume number in Arabic numbers; the date, in parentheses, followed by a comma; the page numbers, without *p.* or *pp.*, followed by a period.

d) *For a newspaper article:* the name of the newspaper, underlined and followed by a period; the date, followed by a comma; the section number, followed by a comma; the page on which the story appeared, followed by a period. The column number may be added after the page number, separated from it by a comma.

4.   *Library call number,*   or the location of a reference work in the library. This information, placed in the upper left-hand corner, should be written just as it appears in the card catalog, so that you can relocate the reference if the need arises.

5.   *Index number,*   a number or code that you assign to the work, should be placed in the upper right-hand corner of the card. This same number should be used on any note cards you make that refer to this source.

For a book by one author

E
155
58
1958
Stewart, George R.
Names on the Land: A
Historical Account of
Place-Naming in the
United States. Boston:
Houghton-Mifflin, 1958.   ①

For a magazine article

Periodical
Desk
Sutton, Horace. "America
Falls in Love with Its
Cities-Again." Satur-
day Review, August
1978, pp. 16-21.   ⑤

TAKE USEFUL AND COMPLETE NOTES

Accurate and full notes are essential for writing a good reference paper. You can save time when taking notes if you approach the problem efficiently. Don't try to take down everything you read; instead, spend a little time looking over the book, the article, or the pamphlet to see if it contains the information you want. If you have given enough thought to formulating and narrowing your topic, you will have a pretty clear idea of what you are looking for.

When examining a book, look first at the index and the table of contents to see in what sections your subject is treated. See also if there are any tables, graphs, bibliographies, or further references that might be useful. Skim each chapter or article to find out what it covers. Then go over it again carefully, taking down the notes you will need.

Notes should be taken on either 3-by-5 inch or 4-by-6 inch cards so that you can later arrange the material according to the plan of your paper. It is usually a waste of effort to try to take notes in numbered outline form since you probably won't know the final plan of your paper until you have finished your research. What is important is to make each note card accurate, clearly written, and clearly labeled. Each note card should contain these essential parts:

1. The *heading* at the top of the card, showing what material it contains.

2. The *index number* to identify the source and *page number*, accurately noted.

3. The *content*, facts or opinions (summarized in your own words or directly quoted) accurately recorded.

Notes that cannot be readily interpreted a week or a month after they have been written are obviously of little use; so too are incomplete or carelessly written notes. You can avoid a good deal of tedious, unnecessary work, including rereading and rechecking, by following these simple rules:

1. Use *one side* of each card only. Your material will then be easier to classify and arrange, and you won't run the risk of overlooking a statement on the back of a card.

2. Include only *one major point* or a few closely related facts from the same source on a single card. If the information is too extensive to write on one side of a card, use two or three cards and number them in sequence.

3. Get all the information accurately the first time you consult a source so that you won't have to make extra trips to the library.

4. Put all *direct quotations* in quotation marks. This includes all statements, single sentences, and phrases that you copy word for word from any source. If you omit a word or words in a direct quotation use ellipsis periods (. . .) to indicate the omission. If you are paraphrasing the source, state the idea in your own language.

5. Write your notes in ink (penciled notes may become blurred with frequent handling) so that you won't have to recopy them. When you use abbreviations, be sure that you will know later on what they mean.

It isn't necessary to write out all your notes in complete sentences; practical shortcuts such as the omission of *a*, *the*, *was*, and other such words are good for summarizing material. If the method you use for taking notes in lecture courses or on your textbooks has proved successful, use it also for your reference paper.

Accurate notes are one of the chief tools of scholarship. Early and careful practice in taking them is excellent training that may be useful in later work.

PLAN YOUR PAPER BEFORE YOU WRITE

The central or controlling purpose of a research paper should be clear in your mind long before you have finished investigating all your resources. You know, for instance, whether you are trying to reach a conclusion about two opposing viewpoints or whether you are trying to explain an event or situation. When you have gathered a sufficient amount of material to put your topic in focus, it is time to formulate a thesis sentence that will state your controlling purpose and to outline the order in which you will develop your material.

Examining and arranging your notes

First read through all your notes to refresh your memory and determine the general order in which you will arrange your material. Then arrange the notes in piles, grouping together all the notes on a particular aspect of your subject. The headings at the top of each card will be useful in helping you sort and arrange your material. At this stage you should note any gaps in your material that will have to be filled in with further reading before you start your first draft.

If any of the notes you have taken no longer seem relevant to your purpose in writing, put them aside in a tentative discard pile. Almost anyone engaged in research finds that a good deal of carefully recorded material has to be discarded. Don't succumb to the temptation to include material that has no bearing on your thesis simply because it is interesting or because you worked hard to find it.

Making a preliminary outline

When you have arranged your note cards to your satisfaction, state the central idea of your paper in a thesis sentence (not in two or more sentences nor in the form of a question). Then make a rough outline showing the order in which you intend to present your material. Each point in the outline should contribute in some way to the development of your central idea or thesis. Often your instructor will want to see your working outline before you go much further with the work. To crystallize your plan and to make it possible for your instructor to examine it and make suggestions, you should follow standard outline form. At this stage a topic outline is generally sufficient; if necessary, you can later expand the entries into complete sentences.

Neither your preliminary outline nor your thesis sentence needs to be considered as final. It is better, in fact, to make a reasonably flexible outline so that you can make whatever changes seem desirable as you write and revise your first draft.

GIVE APPROPRIATE CREDIT
FOR THE WORK AND WORDS OF OTHERS

Any time you use the work of others, you should acknowledge each and every source from which an idea or a statement is taken. In a research paper, these acknowledgments are made in footnotes or endnotes—notes at the bottom of the page or at the end of the paper numbered to correspond to the references in your text. These notes should show exactly where you obtained the passage you quote or the ideas and information that you use. Footnotes or endnotes are essential in two situations:

1. *After direct quotations.* Each statement taken word for word from a printed source should have a reference number at the end of the quotation and be properly identified in a note. The only exceptions to this rule are well-known expressions, such as familiar Biblical quotations ("Blessed are the poor"), famous lines from literature ("Something is rotten in the state of Denmark"), and proverbs ("A bird in the hand is worth two in the bush").

2. *After all important statements of fact or opinion taken from written sources and expressed in your own words.* Facts include figures, dates, scientific data, and descriptions of events and situations about which you have no firsthand knowledge, such as what happened at a session of the United Nations, how coffee is cultivated in Brazil, or the role of Madagascar in World War II. Opinions and interpretations that are not actually your own would include statements such as one writer's reasons for the popularity of baseball in the United States, or an opinion on foreign policy from a newspaper editorial.

In some publications, notes are also used for comments or additional information that the writer does not wish to include in the text. In most research papers, however, this practice should be kept to a minimum; if a statement is worth making, it usually belongs in the text.

Notes are *not* needed for statements that would pass without question. These include obvious facts ("Certain chemicals cannot be used in the preservation of foods in the United States"), matters of common knowledge ("Hiroshima was devastated by an atomic bomb in August 1945"), general statements and expressions of the writer's own opinion ("The medical and biological sciences have made unbelievable progress in the last twenty years").

If you have a full page in your draft without any references, you should probably check it again to see if any documentation is needed. A great many notes on a single page may indicate that some of the material could better be combined or rephrased to eliminate unnecessary references.

The following sections discuss some things to consider in integrating noted material into the text of your paper.

Using direct quotations

In incorporating material from sources into your research paper, you will often have to decide whether to quote directly or to restate the material in your own words. In general, direct quotations are preferable only in these situations:

1.   *Important statements of information, opinion, or policy.*
Whenever the *exact* wording of a statement is crucial in its interpretation, it should be quoted in full:

> *President Kennedy told Khrushchev that Russia could not expect to spread Communism abroad without opposition: "What your government believes is its own business; what it does in the world is the world's business."* [2]

2.   *Interpretations of literary works.*   When a statement or opinion in your paper is based on a passage in a poem, essay, short story, novel, or play, quote from the passage so that the reader can see the basis for your interpretation:

> *The closing passages of* Moby Dick *also suggest that the whale represents some omnipotent force hostile to man. Ishmael says that Moby Dick rushed at the ship with a "predestinating head," and that "retribution, swift vengeance, external malice were in his aspect . . . in spite of all mortal man could do."* [1]

When you are writing a paper that requires frequent references to a literary work, however, you need to note the edition of the text you are using only once, the first time you use a quotation. Thereafter, you may identify quotations by giving (immediately after the quotation, in parentheses) the page numbers for fiction; the line numbers for poetry; the act and scene for drama (followed by the line numbers if the play is in verse):

> *Man, who once stood at the center of the universe, confident that he was the end of Creation and could claim kinship with the angels, is now—to use the playwright's favorite figure—shrouded in a "mist" that isolates him from God and shuts off all his questioning about the problems of ultimate order. As Webster says of the Cardinal in* The Duchess of Malfi, *Man,*
> > *which stood'st like a huge pyramid*
> > *Begun upon a large and ample base,*
> > *Shalt end in a little point, a kind of nothing. (V.v.96 – 98)*

3. Distinctive phrasing. If your source states some idea or opinion in a particularly forceful or original way that would be weakened by paraphrasing, quote the exact words:

> *Russell does not believe that our age lacks great ideas because religion has declined: "We are suffering not from the decay of theological beliefs but from the loss of solitude."* [13]

A quotation should be smoothly integrated into the text of your paper. Even though its source is given in an endnote, it should be preceded by some brief introductory remark like "one leading educator recently said that . . ."; "as Edmund Wilson points out . . ."; "an editorial in the *New York Times* argued that. . . . " The best way to learn about integrating quotations in your own work is to observe how professional writers use quotations.

Paraphrasing

Although a reference paper relies heavily on the writings of others, it should not consist simply of a long string of word-for-word quotations from sources. Like any other paper, it should represent your own style. Except in the situations described in the preceding section, information from a source should ordinarily be *paraphrased*—restated or summarized in your own words. Otherwise your paper will have a jumbled, patchwork effect that may distract or confuse the reader. Compare the two following passages for effectiveness:

> *Too Many Direct Quotations:* Authorities disagree about the dating of these pyramids. Professor Sheldon Muncie says, "The preponderance of evidence collected by investigators in recent years

points to a date no earlier than 1300 A.D. for the construction of the lowest level."[1] Professor William Price basically agrees with him: "Bricks of this type were not used in the surrounding areas until the late fourteenth century."[2] But Robert McCall found that "The radiocarbon readings are completely out of line with the standard textbook dates; the original substructure is at least 700 years older than Muncie's earliest estimate."[3]

Paraphrase: Authorities disagree about the dating of the pyramids. Professors Sheldon Muncie and William Price concluded, on the basis of the type of brick used and other evidence, that they were begun no earlier than the fourteenth century.[1] But Robert McCall's radiocarbon readings indicate a date earlier than 600 A.D.[2]

The best way to write a smooth paraphrase is to absorb the content of the source passage and then, without looking at it, to write its information down in your own words. When you have finished, you should check it for accuracy and any unconscious borrowing of phrases and sentences. Remember that even though the words are your own, the information or ideas are not; you will still have to use a note to identify the source.

Plagiarism

Most writers know that copying another's work word for word without giving the author credit is considered plagiarism. But they often assume that this practice is frowned on only when long passages are involved—whole pages or paragraphs. Consequently, they feel free to copy phrases and sentences without using quotation marks and notes. Actually, any uncredited use of another's information, ideas, or wording is plagiarism. Under the mistaken notion that they are paraphrasing, students often reproduce sources almost exactly, changing only a word here and there. An honest paraphrase, however, is one in which the *ideas* of the source are stated in the writer's *own words*.

USE A CONSISTENT FORM IN ACKNOWLEDGING THE WORK OF OTHERS

Practices in note form vary, though the purpose remains essentially the same in all forms, to identify exactly the sources you use. This section follows the form recommended by the *MLA Handbook for Writers of Research Papers, Theses, and Dissertations.* Alternative forms are frequently used in different fields, and if your instructor doesn't specify a form of documentation to use, it's a good idea to inquire which he or she prefers. Recently, some writers have begun to recommend a much simplified system for noting (one suggests, for example, that you simply list at the end all references you have used and that for notes you provide only a last name and a page number). Whatever system you use, it ought to be consistent, and it ought to suit the needs of the audience you are writing for.

Numbering and spacing of endnotes

In the text of the paper, the endnote number is placed *at the end of the quotation or statement* for which the source is being given; it is never placed before the borrowed material. The number is raised slightly above the line and is placed outside the end punctuation of the statement to which it refers: " . . . nearly 400,000 in 1953." [13]

Endnotes are numbered consecutively throughout the paper in Arabic numerals beginning with 1. If the last note on the first page is numbered 3, the first note on the second page will be numbered 4, and so on.

In typed manuscript, endnotes begin on a new page, headed "Notes," at the conclusion of your paper. They are double-spaced, and the first line of each is indented five spaces, as for a paragraph. One letterspace appears between the raised number and the first word of the note.

Endnotes for books

First reference. Study the sample notes below, noting the order of the information and the punctuation used between each element. The first time you refer to a source in an endnote, include as much of the information as is relevant in each case. However, if the author's full name has been given in a text, it need not be repeated in the note. This is sometimes called a *split note.*

A book with one author:

[1] Walter Gellhorn, American Rights: The Constitution in Action (New York: Macmillan, 1960), p. 178.

Two or three authors:

[2] Giles W. Gray and Claude M. Wise, The Bases of Speech, 3rd ed. (New York: Harper & Row, 1959), p. 322.

More than three authors:

[3] Walter Blair and others, The Literature of the United States, 3rd ed. (Glenview, Ill.: Scott, Foresman, 1966), I, 80.

[The Latin abbreviation *et al.* may be used instead of *and others.*]

An edited book:

[4] Letters of Noah Webster, ed. Harry R. Warfel (New York: Library Publishers, 1954), p. 352.

[If the editor's name is more relevant to the citation than the author's, put that name at the beginning of the note: Harry R. Warfel, ed., *Letters of Noah Webster*.]

An article in an edited book of selections written by various authors:

[5] Harry Levin, "Literature as an Institution," in Literary Opinion in America, ed. Morton Dauwen Zabel (New York: Harper & Row, 1951), pp. 658-59.

A translated book:

[6] Paul Valéry, Monsieur Teste, trans. Jackson Mathews (New York: Alfred A. Knopf, 1947), p. 47.

A book for which no author is given:

[7] A Manual of Style, 12th ed. (Chicago: Univ. of Chicago Press, 1969), p. 27.

A revised edition:

[8] James C. Coleman, Abnormal Psychology and Modern Life, 5th ed. (Glenview, Ill.: Scott, Foresman, 1976), pp. 254-55.

A multi-volume work, all volumes published in the same year:

[9] Walter Blair and others, The Literature of the United States, 3rd ed. (Glenview, Ill.: Scott, Foresman, 1966), I, 80.

[Note that if the note includes a volume number, the abbreviation *p.* or *pp.* is omitted.]

A multi-volume work, the volumes published in different years:

[10] Harold Child, "Jane Austen," in The Cambridge History of English Literature, ed. A. W. Ward and A. T. Waller, XII (London: Cambridge Univ. Press, 1914), 231–33.

[The volume number in this instance precedes the facts of publication.]

A book that is part of a series:

[11] David Fowler, Piers the Plowman, Univ. of Washington Publications in Lang. and Lit., No. 16 (Seattle: Univ. of Washington Press, 1961), p. 23.

Subsequent references.   For subsequent references to the same work, a short form should be used: the author's last name only, if not more than one work by the same author is being cited, and the page number (*ibid.* is no longer widely used):

[12] Gellhorn, p. 150.

If two sources by the same author have been previously cited, the short form must also include the title, to make clear which work the note refers to. A shortened form of the title may be used:

[13] Gellhorn, American Rights, p. 150.

If the book has no author, the title should be used:

[14] A Manual of Style, p. 92.

Notes for magazine, journal, and newspaper articles

Endnotes for magazine and newspaper articles are handled in much the same way. However, the volume number is usually used in noting an article from a scholarly journal, but not for a weekly or monthly magazine or a newspaper.

Signed article in a magazine:

[15] Reed Whittemore, "The Newspeak Generation," Harper's, Feb. 1977, p. 20.

Unsigned article in a magazine:

[16] "How to Save Energy," Newsweek, 18 April 1977, p. 72.

Article in a scholarly journal with continuous pagination throughout the annual volume:

[17] Steward Justman, "Mass Communication and Tautology," College English, 38 (1977), 635.

[The abbreviation *p.* or *pp.* is omitted if the volume number is given.]

Article in a scholarly journal with the pages in each issue numbered separately:

[18] Elizabeth E. McMahan, "The Big Nurse as Ratchet: Sexism in Kesey's Cuckoo's Nest," The CEA Critic, 37, No. 4 (1975), 25.

Signed article in a newspaper:

[19] Edward Cowan, "Mapping Out a National Energy Policy," New York Times, 10 April 1977, Sec. 3, p. 1, col. 4.

Unsigned articles and subsequent endnotes to the same article are handled in the same way as unsigned articles in magazines. Subsequent references to articles in periodicals may be shortened in the same way as those for books.

Notes for other sources

Generally, using common sense and the formats given above as a guide will lead to the proper form for endnotes for sources such as encyclopedia articles, pamphlets and bulletins, unpublished works, interviews, and recordings. If you consult a large number of unusual sources in your research, look at one of the many complete guides to writing research papers for forms of documentation.

The final bibliography

The finished research paper concludes with a bibliography of the sources used in the paper. If the list includes only those books, articles, and other sources that have been documented in the endnotes, the bibliography is titled "List of Works Cited." If the list also includes references that you have explored in depth but have not cited directly, the bibliography should be labeled "List of Works Consulted." Your instructor will tell you which form you should use.

The form for a bibliography differs somewhat from endnote form:

Endnote entry:

¹ Walter Gellhorn, American Rights: The Constitution in Action (New York: Macmillan, 1960), p. 128.

Bibliography entry:

Gellhorn, Walter. American Rights: The Constitution in Action. New York: Macmillan, 1960.

Follow these general guidelines and the examples that follow for an acceptable bibliography form:

1.   List all entries in alphabetical order, by the author's last name, or, if the author is unknown, by the first significant word of the title (disregard A or The). When two or more works by the same author are listed, use a line of ten dashes, followed by a period, for all but the first work.

2.   Do not give the page numbers for books, but do list the inclusive pages for articles in periodicals and newspapers.

3.   Do not separate the list according to kinds of publications. Since the bibliography for most student papers is short, all sources should appear in the same list.

4.   Do not number the entries.

Punctuation varies in different bibliographic styles, mainly in the use of commas, colons, and parentheses. The form shown in the examples illustrates one widely used style, but be sure to note carefully any different practices your instructor may want you to follow.

Bibliography form for books

One author:

Coleman, James C. Abnormal Psychology and Modern Life. 5th ed. Glenview, Ill.: Scott, Foresman, 1976.

Two or three authors:

Gray, Giles W., and Claude M. Wise. The Bases of Speech. 3rd ed. New York: Harper & Row, 1959.

[Notice that only the first author's name is listed last name first.]

More than three authors:

Blair, Walter, and others. The Literature of the United States. 3rd ed. 3 vols. Glenview, Ill.: Scott, Foresman, 1969.

Two books by the same author:

Rush, Myron. <u>How Communist States Change Their Rulers</u>. Ithaca, N.Y.: Cornell University Press, 1974.

----------. <u>Political Succession in the U.S.S.R.</u> New York: Columbia University Press, 1965.

[Notice that these are arranged alphabetically by title.]

An edited book, especially one of another writer's work:

Shakespeare, William. <u>The Complete Works of Shakespeare</u>. Rev. ed. Hardin Craig and David Bevington, eds. Glenview, Ill.: Scott, Foresman, 1973.

An edited collection; date of publication unknown:

Reed, William L. and Eric Smith, eds. <u>Treasury of Vocal Music</u>. 6 vols. Boston: Branden Press, n.d.

A translation:

Pasternak, Boris. <u>My Sister, Life</u>. Trans. Olga A. Carlisle. New York: Harcourt Brace Jovanovich, 1976.

An encyclopedia article:

McG[uire], W[illiam] J. "Persuasion." <u>Encyclopaedia Britannica: Macropedia</u>. 1974 ed.

Reprint:

Dexter, Walter. <u>The London of Dickens</u>. 1923; rpt. Philadelphia: Richard West, 1973.

Bibliography form for periodicals

Signed article in a magazine:

Whittemore, Reed. "The Newspeak Generation." <u>Harper's</u>, February 1977, pp. 17-21.

Unsigned article in a magazine:

"How to Save Energy." <u>Newsweek</u>, 18 April 1977, pp. 70-80.

Article in a scholarly journal:

Tinder, Glenn. "Community: The Tragic Ideal." <u>The Yale Review</u>, 65 (1976), 550-64.

Newspaper article:

Cowan, Edward, "Mapping Out a National Energy Policy." <u>New York Times</u>, 10 April 1977, sec. 3, p. 1.

Unpublished dissertation:

Smith, Wallace Joseph. "The Fur Trade in Colonial Pennsylvania." Diss. Univ. of Washington, 1950.

SUBMIT A COMPLETE PAPER

The research paper, usually submitted in a manila folder, should contain all the parts in the order your instructor has assigned. Typically, the completed paper has the following units. Make sure that you include any other material (such as your first outline or first draft) that your instructor asks for.

1. Title page.   The title of the paper should be centered; your name, the date, the course number, and any other information your instructor requests should be put in the lower right-hand corner, unless your instructor gives you different instructions.

2. Outline.   Some instructors will expect you to turn in your final outline (topic or sentence outline) and the thesis sentence. The revised outline should correspond to the organization of the final paper.

3. Text of the paper.   The final copy of the paper, complete with charts and diagrams wherever needed. The numbering of the text usually begins on the second page, with Arabic numerals centered at the top or at the top right-hand corner.

4. Notes.   The notes should begin on a new page.

5. Bibliography.   The final bibliography should follow the last page of the notes, starting on a separate page.

This extended explanation may suggest to you that writing a research paper is an impossible task to accomplish in a mere five or six weeks of work. It isn't. Done carefully, with due attention to each of the stages outlined in this section, it may be accomplished with no more effort than you would use for your other courses. And if your research paper represents your best work, you will find the assignment a satisfying one and good training for later work.

18

A Brief Guide to Grammar, Punctuation, and Usage

This handbook section is intended mainly to refresh your memory about conventional points of grammar or usage; the main points covered include

1. sentence grammar (p. 462);

2. sentence errors (p. 466);

3. punctuation (p. 477); and

4. mechanics and conventions (p. 484).

This brief guide is intended to sketch in some of the main features of grammar, punctuation, and usage, focusing especially on those areas where problems and errors are most likely to occur. It is not meant to be complete: it does not survey grammar thoroughly, nor does it examine all the possibilities of punctuation, nor does it investigate all the major or minor problems of usage. However, it may help answer many of the questions that arise in those areas; if not, further investigation can be made in a more complete handbook.

SENTENCE GRAMMAR

Sentence elements are classified by words (parts of speech), by their function (subject, predicate, and so on), and by their structure (phrases and clauses). Since some of the definitions and classifications are interrelated, a brief review of these elements might be helpful. It's also helpful to know these elements so that you can use them correctly and so that you can alter or rearrange them for stylistic qualities that you want to create.

Parts of speech

A *noun* designates a person, place, thing, quality, action, or idea: *plumber, France, piano, anger, studying, truth.* Nouns function in sentences chiefly as subjects, objects, complements, and appositives.

A *pronoun* functions as a noun but does not name a specific person, place, thing, or idea: *I, you, it, who, which, himself, this, everyone.* A pronoun usually serves as a substitute for a previously stated noun.

A *verb* indicates action, condition, or process: *walk, is, become.* When forms of verbs are used in sentences as nouns or modifiers rather than as verbs, these verb forms are called *verbals.* Verbals are classified by form and function as *infinitives* (*to talk, to think*), which function either as nouns or modifiers; as *participles* (*talking, talked, thinking, thought*) which function as adjectives; and as *gerunds* (*talking, thinking*) which function as nouns.

A verbal phrase consists of a participle, gerund, or infinitive plus its object or complement and modifiers. A participle phrase functions as an adjective; a gerund phrase as a noun; and an infinitive phrase as either a noun, an adjective, or an adverb.

Sentences *containing several unrelated ideas* [participle phrase modifying *Sentences*] are seldom effective.

Containing the enemy [gerund phrase used as subject] was their first objective.

The easiest way *to understand grammatical construction* [infinitive phrase modifying *way*] is *to analyze your own sentences* [infinitive phrase used as complement].

Modifiers are usually *adjectives* or *adverbs,* or serve those functions. An adjective modifies a noun or noun equivalent: *blue, glamorous, older.* An adverb modifies a verb, an adjective, another adverb, or a whole statement: *soon, quietly, especially, incidentally.*

A *preposition* shows the relationship between a noun or noun equivalent and some other word in the sentence: *in, at, of, before.* The preposition introduces the prepositional phrase, which consists of the preposition followed by a noun, plus any modifiers of the noun: *in the tree, at me, of great importance, before dinner.* Prepositional phrases usually function as modifiers, either adjectival or adverbial, depending on the element modified: He lives *in a small cottage* (modifies the verb *lives*) *by the lake* (modifies the noun *cottage*).

A *conjunction* links together words, phrases, or clauses: *and, but, since, because.*

An *interjection* is an expression of emotion that either stands alone or is inserted into a sentence without being grammatically related to it: *oh, wow, help, no.*

Main sentence elements classified by function

A *subject* is a noun or noun equivalent that performs an action or is in a particular state of being; it usually appears before the verb and determines the number (singular or plural) of the verb.

A *verb* signifies the action or state of being of the subject. The *predicate* is the verb and all words related to it.

The noun or noun equivalent that answers the question asked by adding *what?* or *whom?* to the verb is the *direct object.* The *indirect object* is the noun that names the receiver of some action, answering the question *to whom or what?* or *for whom or what?* added to the verb. It comes before the direct object.

A *complement* is a noun or adjective in the predicate, following a *linking verb*; it refers to the subject rather than the verb, because a linking verb expresses a condition rather than direct action.

Examples:

          S   V   DO
Careless drivers may injure pedestrians.

      S   V   IO   DO
Charity may give the needy financial aid.

          S   LV   C
Some drivers are often careless.

        S LV   C
Charity is often the last resort of the needy.

English sentences are constructed of *words, phrases,* and *clauses.* Words and phrases have been discussed above. Clauses contain both a subject and a verb, and can be classified as follows:

A *main* (or independent) *clause* contains a subject and predicate and is the grammatical core of a sentence. In the three sentences below, the main clauses are in boldface. Each is a complete expression and could stand alone as a sentence:

<pre>S   V</pre>
I laughed because I couldn't help myself.

<pre>S   V   O   S   V   O</pre>
She hated English, but **she needed one more course to graduate.**

<pre>   S   V   O</pre>
If I were you, **I would find a new job.**

A *subordinate* (or dependent) *clause* also has a subject and a predicate, but it functions as *part* of a sentence. It is related to the main clause by a connecting word that shows its subordinate relationship, either a relative pronoun (*who, which, that*) or a subordinating conjunction (*because, although, since, after, if, when,* etc.):

I laughed **because I couldn't help myself.**

Subordinate clauses are used like nouns (as subjects, objects, or complements), like adjectives (modifying nouns or pronouns), or like adverbs (expressing relationships of time, cause, result, degree, contrast, and so forth). The subordinate clauses are emphasized in the following examples:

He confessed **that he loved me.** [noun clause, object of *confessed*]

Many of the criminals **whose cases crowded the docket each year** were third- or fourth-time offenders. [adjective clause modifying *criminals*]

After you plant the seeds, you should water the garden right away. [adverb clause of time]

The peas in his garden were stunted **because he did not water soon enough.** [adverb clause of cause]

Sentence structures

You can make sentences of different grammatical structures. They vary according to the number and kind of clauses they contain.

Simple sentences.   A simple sentence contains one independent clause and no subordinate (dependent) clauses:

The man went across the street.

Although simple sentences contain only one clause, they need not be limited to a small, simple idea. They may contain any number of modifiers, and either the subject or the predicate (or both) may be compound:

For the first time in four billion years a living creature had contemplated himself and heard with a sudden, unaccountable loneliness, the whisper of the wind in the night reeds. [compound predicate]— Loren Eiseley, *The Immense Journey*

Journalism professors, books, editors and reporters often explain news in terms of characteristics or values. [compound subject]—Ivan and Carol Doig, *News: A Consumer's Guide*

Colleges and universities do not exist to impose duties but to reveal choices. [compound subject, compound object]—Archibald Mac-Leish, "Why Do We Teach Poetry"

Compound sentences.   Compound sentences contain two or more main clauses and no subordinate clauses:

> The nations of Asia and Africa are moving with jet-like speed toward gaining political independence [first main clause], but we still creep at horse-and-buggy pace toward gaining a cup of coffee at a lunch counter.—Martin Luther King, Jr., "Letter from Birmingham Jail"

Each clause in a compound sentence is independent and is *coordinate* (of equal rank) with the other clauses. The clauses may be joined (or separated) with coordinating conjunctions (*and, but, or, nor, for, yet* or the correlatives *either . . . or, neither . . . nor, both . . . and, not only . . . but also*), separated by semicolons, or joined with conjunctive adverbs (*accordingly, also, consequently, however, nevertheless, therefore, then*). However, the connective function of adverbs is weak, and a semicolon should be used before them:

> The urban renewal program has many outspoken opponents; nevertheless, some land has already been cleared.

Complex sentences.   A complex sentence consists of one main clause and one or more subordinate clauses:

> As far as I could determine [subordinate clause], Paris hadn't changed at all [main clause] since I last visited it ten years before [second subordinate clause].

In published writing today, complex sentences are used far more frequently than the other three types are. Complex sentences offer more variety than simple sentences do; it is often possible, for example, to shift subordinate clauses around in the sentence in order to get different emphases or different rhythms. And complex sentences are often more precise than compound sentences are: a compound sentence treats two ideas equally, while a complex sentence establishes a more exact relationship.

Compound-complex sentences.   A compound-complex sentence contains two or more main clauses and one or more subordinate clauses:

> When two men fight a duel [first subordinate clause], the matter is trivial [first main clause], but when 200 million people fight 200

million people [second subordinate clause], the matter is serious
[second main clause].—Bertrand Russell, *The Impact of Science
on Society*

Compound-complex sentences occur very seldom in English because
they are likely to sound awkward.

SENTENCE ERRORS

Some errors in sentence construction are both more serious and
more common than others. Watch especially for *fragments, comma
faults, fused sentences, mixed constructions, errors in subject and verb
agreement, errors in pronoun and antecedent agreement, faulty subordination,* and *misrelated and dangling modifiers.*

Fragmentary sentences

A *fragmentary sentence* is an incomplete statement—a phrase or a
subordinate clause—punctuated as a complete sentence. Fragmentary
sentences occur frequently in speech, but in writing a fragment is likely to
be a fragmentary idea that needs to be finished or added to another idea.

A sentence fragment can be corrected in various ways:

1. By joining it to another sentence:

> *Sentence fragment*: The next afternoon we made our way through
> the harbor of Okinawa. **That island, which had made history
> during World War II.**
>
> *Revised*: The next afternoon we made our way through the harbor
> of Okinawa, the island which had made history during World
> War II.

> *Fragment*: I cite these examples to show you how interesting
> accounting can be. **And to give you an idea of the kind of
> problems an accountant has to solve.** [The fragment has no
> main subject and verb. It is an infinitive phrase; *to give* belongs in
> the first sentence parallel with *to show*.]
>
> *Revised*: I cite these examples to show you how interesting ac-
> counting can be and to give you an idea of the kind of problems
> an accountant has to solve.

> *Fragment*: Professor Brown suddenly glanced up from his notes.
> **His eyes twinkling with suppressed laughter.** [*Twinkling* is a
> participle, not a full verb.]
>
> *Revised*: Professor Brown suddenly glanced up from his notes, his
> eyes twinkling with suppressed laughter.

Fragment: At the time, my old rowboat with its three-horsepower motor seemed a high-speed job to me. **Although it only attained a speed of about twelve miles an hour.** [This is an adverb clause, beginning with *Although*.]

Revised: At the time, my old rowboat with its three-horsepower motor seemed a high-speed job to me, although it only attained a speed of about twelve miles an hour.

2. By supplying a subject, a predicate, or both:

Fragment: He talked for fifty minutes without taking his eyes off his notes. **Apparently not noticing that half the class was asleep.** [*Noticing* is a participle, not a verb.]

Revised: He talked for fifty minutes without taking his eyes off his notes. Apparently he did not notice that half the class was asleep. [The subject is *he*; the predicate is the verb *did notice* plus the words related to it.]

3. By rewriting the passage in which it occurs:

Fragment: The people who only said, "Oh, too bad," on seeing the lifeless puppy, the small boy who removed the dead puppy from the gutter, and the middle-aged man who kept saying that people were making a greater fuss about this incident than had been made over his own accident at this same corner a year ago, when he was almost run over by a taxi.

Revised: When the small boy removed the dead puppy from the gutter, some people only said, "Oh, too bad." But the middle-aged man kept saying that people were making a greater fuss about this incident than they had made over his own accident at this same corner a year ago, when he was almost run over by a taxi.

Comma faults

A comma fault (sometimes called a *comma splice*) is two or more independent clauses not joined by a coordinating conjunction and written with only a comma between them. The result is that one clause is simply backed up against the other:

The card catalog is the key to the books in the library, many large libraries have separate catalogs for certain collections of books.

A comma fault can be corrected in various ways:

1. By using a period instead of the comma, making two full sentences:

Comma fault: He took a couple of steps, stopped, reached out, and turned a valve, as he did so he told us the valves had to be checked daily.

> *Repunctuated*: He took a couple of steps, stopped, reached out, and turned a valve. As he did so, he told us the valves had to be checked daily.

2. By substituting a semicolon for the comma. This is appropriate when the ideas expressed in the two clauses are closely related:

> *Comma fault*: Charley then crossed the room and threw a switch which started the motor, returning, he wiped the sweat from his forehead with the back of his hand.
>
> *Repunctuated*: Charley then crossed the room and threw a switch which started the motor; returning, he wiped the sweat from his forehead with the back of his hand.

> *Comma fault*: The person with a college education has training far beyond that which can be obtained solely from books, therefore his or her chances for success may be greater than are those of a person without this education.
>
> *Repunctuated*: The person with a college education has training far beyond that which can be obtained solely from books; therefore, his or her chances for success may be greater than are those of a person without this education.

3. By revising the sentence, using a connective that will show the relation between the statements.

> *Comma fault*: It is a personal matter, everyone has to cope with it sooner or later.
>
> *Revised*: It is a personal matter **that** everyone has to cope with sooner or later.

> *Comma fault*: I enjoy being in the midst of a party, particularly if I feel some responsibility for its success, conversation is a stimulant more powerful than drugs.
>
> *Revised*: I enjoy being in the midst of a party, particularly if I feel some responsibility for its success, **because** conversation is a stimulant more powerful than drugs.

Fused sentences

A fused sentence is the same kind of error as a comma fault, except that no punctuation at all appears between the main clauses. It should be corrected in the same way as a comma fault:

1. Make two sentences of the fused sentence;

2. Use a semicolon to separate the two main clauses;

3. Rewrite the passage.

Fused sentence: Two volumes of this work are now completed the first will be published next year.
Possible revisions: Two volumes of this work are now completed. The first will be published next year.
Two volumes of this work are now completed, the first of which will be published next year.

Mixed constructions

When several sentence faults are combined or when a construction is not one of the standard sentence types, the result is sometimes called a mixed construction. Repunctuating cannot correct errors of this kind; the whole passage must be rewritten into acceptable sentence units.

Mixed construction: I had always admired his novels, and when I had a chance to meet him, a real delight. [independent and subordinate clauses improperly joined by *and*]
Possible revision: I had always admired his novels and was delighted when I had a chance to meet him.

Mixed construction: Charles was a hard worker, but I wondered how was he going to get everything finished on time? [shift from statement to question]
Possible revision: Although Charles was a hard worker, I wondered how he was going to finish everything on time.

Lack of subject-verb agreement

In English, parts of speech that change form to show number, gender, or person should agree or correspond when they are related to each other. Pronouns agree with their antecedents and verbs with their subjects. Agreement or correspondence means, for example, that if a subject is plural, then its verb ought to be plural as well.

Agreement between subject and verb is not always a problem in general English because our verbs don't change form much. Except for the verb *be*, verbs have only two forms in the present tense: *I swim, you swim, he swims, she swims, it swims*. In the past tense, the same form is used for all.

Questions about agreement of subject and verb are most likely to arise when verbs have compound subjects or when the number of the subject (whether it is singular or plural) is blurred by other words between the subject and verb.

Verbs with compound subjects. A compound subject is made up of two or more words, phrases, or clauses joined by *and, or, nor*. The number of the verb depends on which conjunction is used and on the meaning of the subject. Subjects joined by *and* usually take a plural verb:

> **Bob, Ted,** and **Sandra swim** with the varsity team.

> The first **draft** of your paper and the **version** finally turned in **differ** in several ways.

Exception: When the words of a compound subject refer to the same person or are considered together as a unit, the verb is usually singular:

> **Law and order means** different things to people with different political opinions.

Compound subjects joined by *or, nor, either . . . or, neither . . . nor* sometimes take singular verbs and sometimes plural.

1.   When both subjects are singular, the verb ordinarily is singular:

> **One** or the **other is** certainly to blame.

> Neither **Senator Jackson** nor **Senator Kennedy has been invited** to debate the health-care bill.

Exceptions: In questions, where the verb precedes the subject, general usage tends to use a plural verb:

> **Are** [formal: *Is*] either **Stevenson** or **Percy** supporting the bill?

2.   When both subjects are plural, the verb is plural:

> No artificial **colorings** or **preservatives are used.**

3.   When one subject is singular and the other plural, usage varies. In formal writing the verb usually agrees with the nearer subject:

> One major **accident** or several minor **ones seem** to occur at this corner *every* weekend.

> Neither the **revolutionists** nor their **leader was** to blame.

In general usage a plural verb is often used even if the nearer subject is singular:

> Neither the **revolutionists** nor their **leader were** to blame.

4.   When the subjects are pronouns in different persons, formal usage requires that the verb agree in person and number with the nearer subject. In general usage (and even in formal usage if the alternative is awkward) the verb is usually plural:

> *Formal*: Either **you** or **she is** likely to be elected.
> *General*: Either **you** or **she are** likely to be elected.
> *Formal and general*: Neither **you** nor **I are** trained for that job. [*Am* would sound unnatural.]

Such problems of agreement can usually be avoided by substituting a different, more natural construction:

> **One** of you **is** likely to be elected.
> **Neither** of us **is** trained for that job.

In formal usage a singular subject followed by a phrase introduced by *as well as, together with, along with, in addition to* ordinarily takes a singular verb:

> **The treasurer as well as the president was held** responsible for the mismanagement of the company.

Blind agreement.   "Blind agreement" occurs when a writer makes a verb agree with a nearby expression rather than with its actual subject. The error usually occurs in the following situations:

1.   When a plural noun occurs between subject and verb. A singular subject followed by a phrase or clause containing plural nouns is still singular:

> Here and there a **man** [subject] such as Columbus, Galileo, and others **has** [not *have*] ventured into the unknown physical and intellectual worlds.

2.   When a sentence begins with the introductory (or "dummy") word *there* (sometimes referred to as an "anticipating subject"). The number of the verb is determined by the subject which follows:

> There **are** conflicting **opinions** [subject] about smoking in the classrooms.
>
> There **is** great narrative and dramatic **power** [subject] in the first part of this novel.

3.   When subject and complement differ in number. A verb agrees with its subject and not with its complement or its object:

> Our chief **trouble** [subject] **was** [not *were*] the black flies that swarmed about us on the trip.
>
> The **black flies** [subject] that swarmed about us on our trip **were** [not *was*] our chief trouble.
>
> The **material** [subject] that was most interesting to me when I worked on my reference paper **was** [not *were*] the books that stated the facts forcefully.

When subject and complement differ in number, the sentence usually sounds less awkward if the subject and verb are plural, as in the second example above.

4.   When the word order is inverted. When the verb appears before the subject, care must be taken to make the verb agree with its subject and not with some other word:

> Throughout the story **appear** thinly disguised **references** [subject] to the author's own boyhood.

> **Is** any **one** [subject] of these pictures for sale?

5.   When subjects like *series*, *portion*, *part*, or *type* are used. These subjects take singular verbs even when modified by a phrase with a plural noun:

> A **series** of panel discussions **is** scheduled for the convention.

> Λ substantial **portion** of the reports **is** missing.

Faulty agreement of pronoun and antecedent

To be clear in meaning, a pronoun must agree in number with its antecedent—the particular noun to which it refers. When a pronoun serves as subject, the number of the verb is determined by the pronoun's antecedent.

Personal pronouns.   Personal pronouns, like nouns, have both singular and plural forms. A personal pronoun referring to a singular antecedent should be singular; one referring to a plural antecedent should be plural. Errors in agreement are most likely to occur when a pronoun is separated from its antecedent by some intervening element:

> *Inaccurate*: After reading his **arguments** in favor of abolishing property, I found that I was not convinced by **it.** [*Arguments* is plural; *it* is singular.]
>
> *Accurate*: After reading his **arguments** in favor of abolishing property, I found that I was not convinced by **them.** [Both *arguments* and *them* are plural.]

A pronoun referring to coordinate nouns joined by *and* is ordinarily plural:

> When **Linda and Gail** returned, **they** found the house empty.

A singular pronoun is used to refer to nouns joined by *or* or *nor*:

> **Dick or Stan** will lend you **his** car.

In general, the principles governing agreement between a pronoun and coordinate nouns are the same as those governing agreement between a compound subject and verb.

Relative pronouns.   When a relative pronoun is used as the subject of a dependent clause, the antecedent of the pronoun determines the number of the verb and of all reference words:

> George is one of those people who **have** trouble making up **their minds.** [The antecedent of *who* is the plural *people*, which requires the plural verb, *have*; *who* also requires the plural reference *their* for the same reason.]

> George is a person who **has** trouble making up **his mind.** [The antecedent of *who* is *person*.]

Indefinite pronouns.   A number of words of greater or lesser indefiniteness often function as pronouns: *some, all, none, everybody, somebody, anybody, anyone.* Some of these words are considered singular; others may be singular or plural, depending on the meaning of the statement. In revising your papers be sure that verbs and reference words agree in number with indefinite pronouns.

Everyone, everybody, anyone, anybody, someone, somebody, no one, nobody are singular forms and are used with singular verbs (Everyone *has* left; Somebody *was* here; Nobody ever *calls*).

Spoken usage and written usage, however, often differ in the form of the pronouns used with these words. In writing, a singular reference word is standard (Everyone brought *his* book); in speaking, a plural reference word is often used.

> *Written*: Not **everyone** is as prompt in paying **his** bills as you are.
> *Spoken*: Not **everyone** is as prompt in paying **their** bills as you are.

But more writers are using either the nonsexist *his or her* or accepting the plural reference that occurs often in speech. And in some statements a singular reference word would be puzzling or nonsensical with the indefinite pronoun:

> When I finally managed to get to my feet, everybody was laughing at me, and I couldn't blame **them** [*him* would be impossible] because I was a funny sight.

All, any, some, most, more are either singular or plural, depending upon the meaning of the statement:

> All of the turkey **has** been eaten.
> All of these questions **were** answered.
> Some of the dialog **is** witty.
> Some of the farmers **have** opposed price supports.

None may be either singular or plural, depending upon the context. In current usage it is commonly used with a plural verb, but formal usage still prefers a singular verb unless the meaning is clearly plural.

None of our national parks **is** more scenic than Glacier.

None of the charges **has** been proved.

None of the new homes **are** as well constructed as the homes built twenty-five years ago. [The sentence clearly refers to all new homes.]

The emphatic *no one* is always singular:

I looked at a dozen books on the subject, but no one **was** of any use to me.

Each is a singular pronoun and usually takes a singular verb and singular reference words:

Each of the players on the football team **has his** own idea about physical training.

Faulty subordination

Faulty subordination usually results from a careless stringing together of ideas as they happen to come into the writer's mind. Consider, for example, the haphazard use of dependent constructions in the following sentence:

Because her mother died when Barbara was five years old, and since her father lived a solitary life, Barbara had a very unhappy childhood, having no family to confide in.

The elements in this cluttered statement might be rearranged to establish a better sense of order and proportion:

Barbara had a very unhappy childhood. She was five years old when her mother died, and since her father led a solitary life, she had no family to confide in.

When you go over the first draft of your papers, revise any subordinate elements that weaken your sentences or obscure their meaning.

Tandem subordination.   It is usually best to avoid statements in which a series of dependent clauses are strung together, one after another. Too many clauses beginning with similar connectives (*who, which, that; when, since, because*), each built upon the preceding one, are called tandem subordination, or "house-that-Jack-built" constructions:

Tandem subordination: He had carefully selected teachers **who** taught classes **that** had a slant **that** was specifically directed toward students **who** intended to go into business.

Revised: He had carefully selected teachers who specifically slanted their courses toward students intending to go into business.

Sentences that begin and end with the same kind of subordinate clauses are awkward because of their seesaw effect:

When he came home from work, Dad would always complain **when** the children weren't there to meet him.

Such constructions can be improved by changing one of the connectives. Usually it is possible to choose a connective that is more exact:

When he came home from work, Dad would always complain **if** the children weren't there to meet him.

Inverted subordination.   Putting the main idea of a sentence in a subordinate clause or phrase ("inverting" the proper relationship between statements) may result in an awkward or incongruous statement:

Inverted: She was eighteen when her hands were severely burned, which meant that she had to give up her goal of becoming a concert pianist.

More accurate: When she was eighteen, [main clause:] **her hands were severely burned.** As a result, [main clause:] **she had to give up her goal of becoming a concert pianist.**

Inverted or "upside-down" subordination frequently occurs in sentences that trail off into weak participle phrases:

The road was blocked, **causing us to make a twenty-mile detour.**

Such sentences can be improved by putting the less important statement in an adverb clause:

We had to make a twenty-mile detour **because the road was blocked.**

Misrelated modifiers

Verbals, either as single words or in phrases, are most often used as modifiers of individual words:

I first noticed him **sitting alone in a corner.** [present participle, modifying *him*]

The town hall, **completely renovated four years ago,** always impresses visitors. [past participle, modifying *town hall*]

> He still had three years **to serve in prison** before he would be eligible for parole. [infinitive, modifying *years*]

Like other modifiers, verbal modifiers should be clearly related to the words that they modify. When a verbal construction seems from its position to refer to a word that it cannot sensibly modify, it is said to be *misrelated*. Participle phrases usually give writers the most trouble:

> *Misrelated*: On the other side of the valley, **grazing peacefully like cattle,** we saw a herd of buffalo. [the participle phrase seems to refer to *we*]
> *Revised*: On the other side of the valley **we** saw a herd of buffalo, **grazing peacefully like cattle.** [the phrase clearly refers to *buffalo*]

Misrelated modifiers may be momentarily confusing to the reader (or unintentionally humorous) and should therefore be avoided. Sometimes the correction can be made by putting the modifier immediately before or after the word it is meant to modify, as in the example above, but often it is better to rewrite the sentence completely:

> *Misrelated*: One early-day western senator is said to have passed out campaign cards to the voters **pinned together with five-dollar bills.** [the participle phrase seems to refer to *voters*]
> *Revised*: One early-day western senator is said to have pinned five-dollar bills to the campaign cards he passed out to voters.

Occasionally modifiers are placed so that they seem to refer to either of two elements in the sentence. These constructions (sometimes called *squinting modifiers*) can be avoided by changing the position of the modifier or by otherwise revising the sentence:

> *Squinting*: The woman who was standing in the doorway **to attract attention** dropped her purse.
> *Revised*: The woman who was standing in the doorway dropped her purse **to attract attention.**
> *Or*: The woman, standing in the doorway **to attract attention,** dropped her purse.

Dangling modifiers

Dangling modifiers refer to a word that is implied rather than actually stated in the sentence. Like misrelated modifiers, they can make a sentence confusing or ludicrous:

> **Having moved at fifteen,** his home town no longer seemed familiar.

This error often occurs when passive rather than active verbs are used:

Dangling: **In painting four of these pictures,** his wife was used as his model.

Revised: **In painting four of these pictures,** he used his wife as his model.

Dangling: **To find the needed information,** the whole book had to be read.

Revised: **To find the needed information,** I had to read the whole book.

Usually the easiest way to correct a dangling modifier is to name the agent or "doer" of the action immediately after the phrase, as in the revisions shown above. It is often better, however, to revise the sentence entirely, making the relationships more accurate by using other constructions. Changing the verbal phrase to a subordinate clause often improves the sentence:

Dangling: **Having been delayed by a train accident,** the leading role was played by a local actress.

Revised: **Because the leading lady was delayed by a train accident,** her role was played by a local actress.

PUNCTUATION

Punctuation is a guide to the reader and a device that makes your meaning clear. Even though careful, accurate use of punctuation won't be noticed, careless or unconventional use can change your meaning, confuse your reader, and leave a poor impression.

End punctuation

Periods are the most common end stops; they mark the end of all sentences that are not direct questions or exclamations. An indirect question is really a statement about a question, and is never followed by a question mark. A "courtesy question," a polite request phrased as a question, is also followed by a period:

He asked us where we got the money. (A direct question would be *Where did you get the money?*)

May we hear from you at your earliest convenience.

Question marks are used after a sentence expressing a direct question:

What can we do?

When a sentence begins with a statement but ends with a question, the ending determines the punctuation:

Perhaps this explanation is poor, but is there a better one?

A question mark stands immediately after a question that is included within a sentence:

> Someone once remarked (wasn't it Mark Twain?) that old second-hand diamonds are better than no diamonds at all.

> "Are you engaged?" he blurted.

When a question mark and quotation marks occur together, the question mark goes inside the quotation marks if the quotation is a question. The question mark goes outside the quotation marks if the whole sentence is a question:

> He asked himself, "Is this the best of all possible worlds?"

> Do you agree that this is "the best of all possible worlds"?

A question mark is used, with or without parentheses, to show that a statement is approximate or questionable:

> Geoffrey Chaucer, 1340(?) – 1400

> Geoffrey Chaucer, 1340? – 1400

An *exclamation mark* is used after an emphatic interjection (Oh! Ouch! Fire! Help! No, no, no!) and after statements that are genuinely exclamatory only:

> The building had disappeared overnight!

> What torments they have endured!

Commas

Commas are troublesome and necessary. They are essential at times to signal direction to your reader, to mark grammatical units, and to help determine the tempo of your writing by introducing mild breaks or brief pauses. Ordinarily, you should use commas in the places shown below.

1.   Between coordinate clauses when they are joined by *and, or, nor,* if the clauses are long or not closely related; when they are joined by *but* or *yet;* and when they are joined by *for:*

> The woods were full of mysterious sounds, and I felt myself wishing I were home in my own bed.

> This town does not actually exist, but it has come to seem real to thousands of movie goers.

> He was an easy target, for he was so naive he would believe anything.

2.   After long introductory elements, such as a long adverb clause preceding the main clause or a long modifying phrase preceding the main

clause. (The comma is optional if the clause or phrase is short and closely related to the main clause.)

> When she said that we would be expected to write a theme every day, I nearly collapsed.

> Leaning far out over the balcony, he could see the beach from his hotel room.

3. With nonrestrictive modifiers, to set off subordinate clauses and phrases that do not limit or restrict the meaning of the term they modify, and to set off appositives:

> Last night's audience, which contained a large number of college students, applauded each number enthusiastically.

> Thomas Malthus, author of the first serious study of population growth, foresaw one of our greatest modern problems.

4. To set off interrupting and parenthetical elements:

> A home, after all, is not just a collection of furniture.

5. To separate coordinate words, phrases, or clauses in a series not connected with conjunctions, and to separate a series of adjectives, all modifying the same noun:

> We were taught how to turn sharply, how to stop suddenly, and how to climb back up the hill.

> He spoke of the violent, exciting, challenging era that followed the civil war.

6. To prevent misreading, as in the following constructions:
    a. when the subject of a clause may be mistaken for the object of a verb or preposition that precedes it:

> As far as I can see, the results have not been promising.

    b. when a word has two possible functions, to guide the reader in interpreting it properly. Words like *for*, *but*, and *however*, for example, may be used in several ways:

> However, I interpreted his remarks liberally and went on with my work.

> However I interpreted his remarks, they made no sense.

    c. when one expression might be taken for another:

> After he broke his hand, writing was very difficult for him.

    d. when the same word occurs consecutively, a comma may help the reading:

> What is, is right.

Too many commas are as bad as too few. There are certain situations in which commas should ordinarily not be used; you should not use commas in the places described below (there should be no commas where the brackets stand in the examples):

7.   There should be no commas between main sentence elements that naturally go together: subject and verb, verb and object or complement, preposition and object:

> Many prominent psychologists and other researchers [] have often pointed out [] that a person's physical characteristics may influence personality.

8.   Use no comma between two words or phrases joined by *and*:

> Primitive agricultural tools [] and bits of pottery were found.

9.   Use no comma between main clauses without a connective; this will result in a comma fault (see p. 467).

10.   Use no comma with restrictive modifiers, that is, those that are essential to the sentence's meaning:

> The cabbage moth is an insect [] whose larva can destroy cabbages almost overnight.

11.   Use no comma after the last item in series:

> He imagined himself as a rich, handsome, successful [] man of the world.

Semicolons and colons

Semicolons and colons make sharper breaks than commas in your sentences, and they are used for rather specific purposes.

Semicolons.   As a mark of separation, the semicolon is much stronger than a comma and almost as definite as a period. The few constructions in which a semicolon is required are listed below. Notice that in all its uses the semicolon marks a separation between *coordinate* elements—expressions of equal rank.

1.   Use a semicolon to separate main clauses that are not joined by one of the coordinating conjunctions (*and, but, for, or, nor, yet*):

> The penalty for not turning work in on time is a lowered grade; the penalty for not turning it in at all is failure.

2.   Use a semicolon before conjunctive adverbs like *however, therefore, consequently,* and *nevertheless* when they occur between clauses:

On your income tax return you can deduct the cost of meals and lodging for business trips; **however,** you cannot deduct the cost of meals if you were not away overnight.

3.   Use a semicolon between main clauses connected by coordinating conjunctions if:
    a. the clauses are unusually long,
    b. the clauses are not closely related,
    c. one or more of the clauses contain commas, or
    d. the writer wishes to show an emphatic contrast between statements:

> I have known many black men and women and black boys and girls who really believed that it was better to be white than black, whose lives were ruined or ended by this belief; **and** I myself carried the seeds of this destruction within me for a long time.—James Baldwin, "Unnameable Objects, Unspeakable Crimes"

4.   Semicolons are often used in lists and series to separate elements that contain commas or other marks. In the following sentence, for example, the semicolons are necessary for clarity:

> In response to a request for information from columnists Helen and Sue Bottel, the following changes were volunteered by young readers: "groovy" to "gravy baby"; "right on" to "right there" or "left arm"; "out of sight" to "out of state"; "scram" to "make like a banana and split."—Mario Pei, "The Language of the Election and Watergate Years"

Colons.   A colon is a mark of anticipation, directing attention to what follows. Writers sometimes confuse colons and semicolons, but their functions are entirely different. The distinction is simple: a colon introduces or indicates what is to follow; a semicolon separates coordinate elements. (That sentence illustrates the correct use of both marks.) Use a colon in the following places:

1.   To indicate that a list, an illustration, or a summation is to follow:

Be sure when you are packing for camp you have everything you need: tent, stove, sleeping bag, cooler, and fishing pole.

The colon is used as an anticipatory mark only after grammatically complete expressions. Do not use a colon between verbs and their objects or complements, or between prepositions and their objects:

Colon: He visited the following cities: Boston, Dallas, Chicago, Miami, and Seattle.

No colon: He visited [ ] Boston, Dallas, Chicago, Miami, and
Seattle.

2.   Between two main clauses when the second clause is an illustration, a restatement, or an amplification of the first:

I was impractical: I wanted to marry a poet.—Lillian Hellman,
Pentimento

3.   Between an introductory statement and a grammatically complete
quotation, especially if the quotation is more than one sentence:

Here is a well-known verse from *Ecclesiastes:* "I returned and saw
under the sun, that the race is not to the swift, nor the battle to the
strong, neither yet bread to the wise, nor yet riches to men of
understanding, nor yet favour to men of skill; but time and chance
happeneth to them all."

When a short quotation is built closely into a sentence, it may be
preceded either by a comma or by a colon, depending on how it is
introduced:

As Alexander Pope said, "A little learning is a dangerous thing."

She reminded him of the words of Pope: "A little learning is a
dangerous thing."

4.   A colon is customary in the following places:
a.   after an expression introducing examples or a large body of
material (as after *places* in the preceding sentence).
b.   between hours and minutes expressed in figures (11:30 A.M.).
c.   between chapter and verse of the Bible (Matthew 4:6) and
between the title and subtitle of a book (*China: A Modern
Enigma*).
d.   after the formal salutation in a letter (Dear Sir:).

Other punctuation marks

Dashes.   Dashes are used to set off parenthetical expressions and
abrupt interruptions in thought. The dash is a useful mark of separation,
but since it is a more emphatic way of setting off elements than either
commas or parentheses, it should not be used to excess or in places
where another mark (or none) would be more appropriate. On the
typewriter a dash is made with two unspaced hyphens; there should
likewise be no space on either side of the dash, between it and the words
it separates.

Dashes are customarily used in the situations shown below.

1.   To set off parenthetical expressions and abrupt interruptions:

In reality, the whole idea of a specifically feminine—or, for the matter of that, masculine—contribution to culture is a contradiction of culture.—Brigid Brophy, "Women Are Prisoners of Their Sex"

2.   To mark sharp turns in thought:

He praised Ann's intelligence, her efficiency, her good taste—and then proposed to her sister.

3.   To enclose parenthetical elements (usually to give greater emphasis to elements that could also be set off with commas):

Still we do condemn—we must condemn—the cruelties of slavery, fanaticism, and witch-burning.—Herbert Muller, *The Uses of the Past*

For clarity, dashes are sometimes used instead of commas to set off parenthetical elements that have internal punctuation. Note that *two* dashes are necessary to enclose a parenthetical element that falls in the middle of a sentence.

4.   To set off an expression that summarizes or illustrates the preceding statement:

He founded a university, and devoted one side of his complex genius to placing that university amid every circumstance which could stimulate the imagination—beauty of buildings, of situation, and every other stimulation of equipment and organisation.— Alfred North Whitehead, "The Idea of a University"

Parentheses and brackets.   *Parentheses* are curved marks used chiefly to enclose incidental or explanatory remarks as shown below.

1.   To enclose incidental remarks:

He was adored (I have spent some time looking for the right verb, and that's it) by the members of the *Journal* staff, who greeted him each afternoon, in a sudden silence of typewriters, as if they hadn't seen him for a long time.—James Thurber, "Franklin Avenue, U.S.A."

2.   To enclose details and examples:

For seven long years (1945 – 1952) austerity was the key word in British economic life.

3.   To enclose figures or letters used to enumerate points:

> The main questions asked about our way of life concern (1) the strength of our democracy, (2) our radical practices, (3) our concept of modern economy, and (4) the degree of materialism in our culture.—Vera Dean and J. B. Brebner, *How to Make Friends for the U.S.*

No punctuation marks are used before a parenthetical statement that occurs within a sentence. If a comma or period is needed after the parenthetical material, it is placed *outside* of the *closing* marks:

> There is talk with music (tapes and records), talk with film and tape (movies and television), talk with live public performance (demonstrations and "confrontation").—William Jovanovich, "A Tumult of Talk"

When the parenthetical statement comes between sentences, the appropriate end punctuation is placed *inside* the closing mark:

> Fearing federal intervention, Vincent Columbraro, the Buttered Toast King, called for a truce. (Columbraro has such tight control over all buttered toast moving in and out of New Jersey that one word from him could ruin breakfast for two-thirds of the state.)—Woody Allen, *Getting Even*

Brackets are used to insert brief editorial comments and explanations in material quoted from other writers, to show that the speaker or writer didn't actually use the enclosed words. The latin word *sic* is sometimes inserted in brackets to indicate that a reprinted error appeared in the original. This practice has declined, however.

MECHANICS AND CONVENTIONAL USAGE

Quotation marks

Quotation marks are necessary to set off direct speech and material quoted from other sources. They are also used around some titles and around words used in special ways.

Usage varies, but double quotations (" ") are the usual marks in American publications. Follow this convention, using single marks (' ')—made on the typewriter with apostrophes—only for a quotation within a quotation. Whether double or single, quotation marks are always used in *pairs*, before and after the quoted material.

Use quotation marks in the following situations:

1.   Enclose statements representing actual speech or conversation by quotation marks. In dialog the words of each speaker are usually indented like paragraphs, but when short speeches or statements are quoted to illustrate a point in exposition, they are usually included in the paragraph where they are relevant, rather than set off:

The health-care bill is currently being debated in the Senate, but Senator Pearson had no comment for the press: "At the present time," the Senator said, "I haven't made up my mind about the bill."

Note that only direct discouse, which represents the actual quote, and not indirect discourse, is enclosed in quotes:

Direct discourse: The coach said, "Get in there and fight."
Indirect discourse: The coach told us to get in there and fight.

2.   Words taken directly from another writer or speaker must be clearly set apart, either by quotation marks or by some other conventional typographic device such as setting them in reduced type. Whether you are quoting a phrase or several paragraphs, make sure that you follow the exact wording and punctuation of your source.

a.   Use quotation marks around quoted phrases and statements included within the body of a paragraph. The quoted material may be worked into the structure of a sentence or may stand by itself:

Another immortal pun is Eugene Field's comment on the actor Creston Clarke that "he played the king as though he were in constant fear that somebody else was going to play the ace."—Max Eastman, *The Enjoyment of Laughter*

While Iago, for example, is gulling Roderigo, he scoffs at him with superb disdain: "I have rubb'd this young quat almost to the sense/And he grows angry" (*Othello*, 5.1.11 – 12).—Maurice Charney, *How to Read Shakespeare*

b.   When quoted material is relatively long—more than one full sentence from the original source or more than four lines in your paper—it is usually indented and single spaced but not enclosed in quotation marks:

A British member of Parliament, A. P. Herbert, also exasperated with bureaucratic jargon, translated Nelson's immortal phrase, "England expects every man to do his duty":

England anticipates that, as regards the current emergency, personnel will face up to the issues, and exercise appropriately the functions allocated to their respective occupational groups.
                        —Stuart Chase, *The Power of Words*

c.   Use single quotation marks around quoted material that appears within a quotation which is itself enclosed in double marks:

> If they depended solely on economic theory to guide them, they would be in the position of the man John Williams mentions: "About the practical usefulness of the theory, I have often·felt like the man who stammered and finally learned to say, 'Peter Piper picked a peck of pickled peppers,' but found it hard to work into conversation."—C. Hartley Grattan, "New Books"

3.   Use quotation marks to set off the titles of short written words such as single poems, essays, short stories, and magazine articles. The titles of books and the names of newspapers and magazines are italicized:

> *The Oxford Book of English Verse* includes only two poems by Oliver Goldsmith: "Women" and "Memory."

A few titles are neither set off by quotation marks nor underlined for italics: the Bible, Old Testament, the Constitution of the United States, Lincoln's Gettysburg Address, Montgomery Ward Catalog, the Denver Telephone Directory (or any other catalog or directory).

4.   Words used in some special way within a sentence are often set apart by quotation marks or by italics (underlining).
   a.   A word used as a word or as an example rather than for its meaning in a passage is either italicized or enclosed by quotation marks. Use one or the other consistently:

> People often confuse the meanings of words that sound alike, such as "allusion" and "illusion."

> I have trouble typing *artificial* and *expectation*.

   b.   In serious writing, an expression associated with unedited or colloquial forms of English is sometimes put in quotation marks to show that the writer knows it is not considered appropriate in formal usage:

> The disheartening outcome of recent international conferences has convinced some of our statesmen that certain nations consider us as little more than "fall guys."

The trouble with apologetic quotes is that they focus the reader's attention on the expression and make him wonder why the writer chose to use it. If you think a word or phrase is right for what you are saying, it's best to use it without apology.

5.   The following conventions govern the use of other punctuation with quotation marks:
   a.   Commas and periods are always placed *inside* the closing quotation mark:

> "Yes," Roger agreed, "it's too late to worry about that now."

Her watch case was described as "waterproof," but "moisture-resistant" would have been more accurate.

b. Semicolons and colons are placed *outside* the closing quotation mark:

This critic's attitude seems to be "I don't like any movie"; on a few occasions, though, he has said kind words for a travelog or a documentary film.

Fully a third of the railroad passengers were what trainmen call "deadheads": people who ride on passes and never tip.

c. Question marks, exclamation points, and dashes are placed inside *or* outside the final quotation mark, depending upon the situation. They come *inside* when they apply to the quotation only:

Mother looked at me and asked, "Why do you say that?"

They are placed *outside* the final quotation mark when they apply to the entire statement:

Who was it who said that "good guys finish last"?

End punctuation marks are never doubled. If a quotation ends your sentence, the end punctuation within quotation marks also indicates the end of the sentence.

Ellipses

A punctuation mark of three spaced periods, called an ellipsis (plural: *ellipses*), indicates that one or more words have been omitted from quoted material. If an ellipsis comes at the end of a sentence, the sentence period (or other end punctuation) is retained, and the three periods of the elipsis follow it. There is no space between the last word and the end punctuation:

Does this sound harsh today? . . . Yes, but I cannot sell my liberty and my power, to save their sensibility.—Ralph Waldo Emerson, "Self-Reliance"

To indicate that an entire paragraph or more or an entire line or more of poetry has been omitted, a full line of ellipses is used:

That's my last Duchess painted on the wall.
Looking as if she were alive. . . . [two words are omitted here]
. . . . [two lines omitted]
Will't please you sit and look at her?
      —Robert Browning, "My Last Duchess"

Ellipses are sometimes used, especially in narrative, to indicate interruptions in thought, incompleted statements, or hesitation in speech, but this is a convention that should not be overused.

Italics

Words are set off or emphasized in most published works by printing them in slanting type called *italics*. In handwritten or typed papers, such words are underlined. Italics are used in the following places:

1.   The names of newspapers and magazines and the titles of books, plays, films, and other complete works published separately are conventionally italicized (or underlined):

> *Newsweek*
> *The Great Gatsby*
> *The Chicago Tribune* (or: the Chicago *Tribune*)

Titles of articles, short stories, poems, and other short pieces of writing that are part of a larger work are usually enclosed in quotation marks:

> "The Easy Chair" was a regular feature in *Harper's Magazine*.

2.   Words used as words or as examples rather than as parts of a sentence should be italicized or set off by quotation marks. (See Quotation Marks above.)

3.   Words from foreign languages that have not been absorbed into English should be italicized, not set off by quotation marks:

> Sometime soon after he arrives in Hawaii, a sweet lassitude creeps over the *malihini* (newcomer).—*Time* Magazine

Scientific names for plants, insects, and so forth are also italicized:

> The mistletoe (*Phoradendron flavescens*) is the state flower of Oklahoma.

Dictionaries usually designate words that are now part of the English language and those that are not; if you are certain that an expression marked "foreign" is familiar to your readers, you need not underline it.

Abbreviations of the less common Latin words and phrases used mainly in reference works are sometimes italicized, but Latin abbreviations in general use are not:

> cf.   e.g.   et al.   etc.   ibid.   i.e.   vs.   viz.

4.   Italics are used in printed material to indicate an emphatic word or stressed statement, but they should be used sparingly. When used excessively or with words that do not deserve stress, this device may strike a reader as affected.

Apostrophes

An apostrophe (') is used in contractions, to mark the plural form of some expressions, and to indicate the possessive case of nouns. Although it is a minor mark that seldom affects the reader's interpretation of a statement, its omission or misuse is noticeable.

1.   When a contraction is appropriate in writing, use an apostrophe to indicate the omission of one or more letters:

can't	I'll	it's (it is)	we're
don't	I'm	o'clock	won't
haven't	isn't	shouldn't	

Notice that *till* (as in "from morning till midnight") is *not* a shortened form of *until* and no apostrophe is used with it.

2.   Use an apostrophe with the singular and plural forms of nouns and indefinite pronouns to mark the possessive case:

John's car	children's games
New York's parks	your parents' permission

An apostrophe is *not* used with the possessive forms of the personal pronouns *his, hers, its, ours, yours, theirs.*

3.   Use an apostrophe before an *s* to form the plurals of figures, letters of the alphabet, and words considered as words:

the early 1900's [*or* 1900s]
There are four *s*'s, four *i*'s, and two *p*'s in *Mississippi.*

Hyphens

Hyphens are used to connect two or more words used as a single expression (*heavy-hearted, will-o'-the-wisp*) and to keep parts of other words distinct (*anti-inflation*).

Hyphens are needed in some instances to prevent misreading (*un-ionized*) or to differentiate between the same words used in different ways (a *drive in* the evening, a *drive-in* theater). But generally they are used as a matter of convention (*brother-in-law, hocus-pocus*).

Since practice is likely to vary with many of these forms, you often have the option of using or not using a hyphen. Where no confusion of terms is apt to arise, most writers would omit the hyphen. If you are in doubt whether a hyphen is necessary, consult a good, recent dictionary.

Sometimes hyphens are used for clarity, as shown below:

1.   When two or more words act as a closely linked modifier immediately before another word:

gray-green eyes	a nineteenth-century poet
a well-kept lawn	an all-out effort

2.   To prevent a possible misreading:

a slow-motion picture   a pitch-dark room
a navy-blue uniform   some reclaimed-rubber plants

3.   When present or past participles form compound modifiers preceding a noun:

a good-looking man   a well-planned attack

Such phrases are not usually hyphenated in other positions:

Her father was good looking.   The attack was well planned.

4.   Between certain prefixes and the root word either as a matter of convention or to prevent ambiguity.
    a. between a prefix and a proper name:

    pre-Renaissance   un-American   ex-President Truman

    b. between some prefixes that end with a vowel and a root word beginning with a vowel:

    re-elected   semi-independent   re-ink

    but: cooperation   coordinate   preexistent

    c. to prevent possible confusion with a similar term or when the prefix is stressed:

        to **re-cover** a sofa (to *recover* from an illness)
        a **run-in** with the police (a *run in* her stocking)

Abbreviations

Dictionaries list most current abbreviations, either as regular entries or in a separate section, but they don't indicate when these forms should be used. The following sections list abbreviations that are appropriate in most writing as well as some forms that should not be used. If you are in doubt whether a particular abbreviation is appropriate, you will usually do better to avoid it.

1.   Abbreviations for titles, degrees, and given names. Courtesy titles such as *Dr.*, *Mr.*, *Mrs.*, and *Messrs.* are always abbreviated when used with proper names as are *Jr.* and *Sr.* Academic degrees are also generally abbreviated: *M.A.*, *Ph.D.*, *LL.D.*, *M.D.*, *D.D.S.* If a degree or honorary title is added after a name, it is the only title used:

William Carey, M.D., *or* Dr. William Carey [not *Dr.* William Carey, *M.D.*]

Titles like *Reverend, Professor, President, Senator, Admiral* are usually written out in full, but they may be abbreviated *if* the first name or initials of the person are used:

Professor John Moore	*not*	Prof. Moore
Professor Moore		John Moore is an English Prof.
Prof. John R. Moore		

Spell out given names (sometimes called Christian names) or use initials. Avoid such abbreviations as *Geo., Thos., Chas., Wm.*

Saint is almost always abbreviated when it is used with a name: St. Francis, Ste. Catherine.

2.   Abbreviations for agencies and organizations. If a government agency or other organization is known primarily by its initials (or by some other shortened name), use the familiar abbreviation rather than the full name:

FBI   TVA   AFL-CIO   NBC Network   UNESCO

3.   Abbreviations for place names and dates. The names of countries, states, months, and days are usually written out except in journalistic writing and reference works:

United States	Ghent, Belgium	Wednesday, November 3
South America	Portland, Oregon	Christmas [not *Xmas*]

Write out words like *Street* and *Avenue* in general writing.

4.   Abbreviations for units of measurement. Most expressions for time, weight, and size are usually written out:

in a minute	*rather than*	in a min.
several pounds		several lbs.
a half inch		½ in. or ½″
sixty centimeters		60 cm.

These units are abbreviated in directions, recipes, references, and technical writing when they are used with figures: ¼ lb. butter.

5.   Abbreviations for scientific and technical terms. Some scientific words, trade names, and other expressions are referred to by their abbreviations when they are familiar to readers and would be needlessly long if written out:

DDT   Rh factor   DNA   FM radio

If an abbreviation is to be used repeatedly and may not be familiar to every reader, explain it the first time it is introduced:

The International Phonetic Alphabet, commonly known as the IPA, provides a more precise method of recording speech than does our conventional alphabet.

Measurements expressed in technical terms are abbreviated when they are used with figures, but spelled out when used without figures:

Tests show the car's highest speeds to be 34 **mph** in low gear, 58.7 **mph** in second, and 93.5 **mph** in third.

The speed of a ship is usually given in knots rather than in **miles per hour.**

6.   Other standard abbreviations. There are a few standard abbreviations that are used in all types of writing:

a. *a.m., p.m.* are always abbreviated: 6:00 a.m., 12:24 p.m. Current usage prefers small letters for these abbreviations, but they may be capitalized. They are used only in referring to a specific time:

Standard: He had an appointment at 3:00 p.m.
Not: He had an appointment in the p.m.

b. *B.C., A.D.* are always abbreviated. B.C. means "before Christ," and follows the date; A.D. stands for *anno Domini,* "in the year of our Lord," and *precedes* the date.

836 B.C.   A.D. 76   A.D. 1984

Periods with abbreviations.   A period should be put after the abbreviation of a single word and usually between the letters of abbreviations for longer terms:

p.   doz.   N.Y.   c.o.d.   Nov.   A.T.&T.

Usage is divided about the punctuation of abbreviated names made of two or more letters written as a unit. The solid form (without periods—*PTA, BBC*) is now used frequently, especially when the abbreviation is regularly used instead of the full name. Some dictionaries list optional forms. It doesn't make much difference which form you use as long as you are consistent throughout your paper.

When an abbreviation falls at the end of a sentence, only one period is used: He owned a hundred shares of A.T.&T.

Numbers

There are few firm rules about using figures or words for numbers occurring in most writing. In general, write out all simple one- and two-digit numbers and round numbers that can easily be read (sixteen, thirty thousand); use figures for numbers that cannot be written in two words and for series of numbers that are to be compared:

He shot three quail and one rabbit.

The next ship unloaded 3500 pounds of king salmon, 947 pounds of chinook salmon, and 200 pounds of crab.

Whichever form you use, be consistent. Don't change needlessly from words to figures in the same piece of writing.

Here are the few special situations in which figures are customary:

1. Dates are always written in figures except in formal social correspondence, such as wedding invitations. The forms *1st, 2nd, 3rd,* and so on are sometimes used in dates, but only when the year is omitted:

10 October 1976   Oct. 10, 1976   October 10   October 10th

2. Hours are written in figures before *a.m.* or *p.m.*; they are spelled out before *o'clock*:

7 a.m.	1800 hours (military usage)	twelve noon
11:35 p.m.	one o'clock	twelve midnight

3. Mathematical and technical numbers, including percentages:

3.14159	longitude 74°02′E.
99.8 percent, 99.8%	.410 gauge shotgun

Except in dates and street numbers, a comma is used to separate thousands, millions, etc., although it may be omitted in four-digit figures:

1,365 (or 1365) pounds   8,393,624   17,016

4. Page numbers and similar references:

pp. 183–86	page 12
chapter iv	Genesis 39:12
Ch. 19	Act III, scene iv, line 28 (III, iv, 28)

5. Sums of money, except sums in round numbers or sums that can be written in two or three words:

$4.98   two thousand a year   a dollar a pound

6. Street numbers (with no commas between thousands):

2027 Fairview North   Apartment 3C, 1788 Grand North

7. Statistics and series of more than two numbers, especially when the numbers are to be compared:

The survey showed that the class contained 24 Democrats, 18 Republicans, and 3 Socialists.

8. Plurals of figures are written either with *'s* or *s*:

Six nines: six 9's, six 9s

Index

Acknowledgments continued

From *Ranald S. Mackenzie on the Texas Frontier* by Ernest Wallace, pp. 138–139. Copyright © 1965 by West Texas Museum Association. Reprinted by permission.

From "More Major Minor Inventions" by Stacy V. Jones. *New York Times Magazine,* May 23, 1976. Copyright © 1976 The New York Times Company. Reprinted by permission.

From "Grandchildless" by Russell Baker. *New York Times Magazine,* July 25, 1976. Copyright © 1976 The New York Times Company. Reprinted by permission.

From an advertisement for Carlyle Custom Convertibles. Reprinted by permission.

From "Who Needs the B-1?" by John W. Finney. *New York Times Magazine,* July 25, 1976. Copyright © 1976 The New York Times Company. Reprinted by permission.

From "The Case Against Regular Physicals" by Richard Spark. *New York Times Magazine,* July 25, 1976. Copyright © 1976 by The New York Times Company. Reprinted by permission.

From advertisement for The Barclay. Reprinted by permission.

"God Don't Never Change" by Geneva Smitherman, from *College English,* March, 1973. Copyright © 1973 by the National Council of Teachers of English. Reprinted by permission of the publisher and the author.

From "Vicissitudes of Language" (Putting Down Words) by Monroe C. Beardsley, from *College English,* April, 1974. Copyright © 1974 by the National Council of Teachers of English. Reprinted by permission of the publisher and the author.

From "Language Teaching: Naming" by Jenny Joseph in *Rose in the Afternoon and Other Poems,* J. M. Dent & Sons, Ltd., 1974. Reprinted by permission of John Johnson.

From *Goodbye to a River* by John Graves. Copyright © 1959 by Curtis Publishing Company. Reprinted by permission of Alfred A. Knopf, Inc.

From *Leaving the Surface* by Sydney J. Harris. Copyright © 1968 by Sydney J. Harris. Reprinted by permission of Houghton Mifflin Company.

From *Prejudices: Fifth Series* by H. L. Mencken. Copyright 1926 by Alfred A. Knopf, Inc. and renewed 1954 by H. L. Mencken. Reprinted by permission of Alfred A. Knopf, Inc.

From Whirlpool advertisement. Reprinted by permission of Whirlpool Corporation, Benton Harbor, Michigan.

From advertisement for "Nuance" by Coty. Reprinted by permission of Coty Inc.

From "Mr. Flood's Party" by Edwin Arlington Robinson. Copyright 1921 by Edwin Arlington Robinson, renewed 1949 by Ruth Nivison. Reprinted with permission of Macmillan Publishing Co., Inc.

Advertisement for Wild Meadow fragrances of Shulton, Inc. Reprinted by permission.

"A Family Turn" from *Stories That Could Be True* by William Stafford. Copyright © 1966 by William E. Stafford. Reprinted by permission of Harper & Row, Publishers, Inc.

From advertisement for Parker Pens. Reprinted by permission.

From "Introduction: An Ethic of Clarity" by Donald Hall in *The Modern Stylists* edited by Donald Hall. Copyright © 1968 by Donald Hall. Reprinted with permission of Macmillan Publishing Co., Inc.

From an Omega Watch advertisement. Reprinted by permission of the Omega Watch Company.

Reprinted by permission of Centro de Turismo de Portugal, New York.

From "Standard Dialects and Substandard Worlds" by San-Su C. Lin, *English Education,* Spring 1970. Copyright © 1970 by the National Council of Teachers of English. Reprinted by permission of the publisher and the author.

From "The City May Be as Lethal as the Bomb" by Barbara Ward. *New York Times Magazine,* April 19, 1964. Copyright © 1964 by The New York Times Company. Reprinted by permission.

From the Foreword by Lewis Gannett to *Ishi* by Theodora Kroeber. Copyright © 1961 by the Regents of the University of California. Reprinted by permission.

From "The Blot and the Diagram" by Kenneth Clark, *Encounter,* January 1963. Reprinted by permission.

Reprinted from Joseph Wood Krutch, *If You Don't Mind My Saying So* (New York, William Sloane Associates, 1964), by the permission of the Trustees of Columbia University in the City of New York as copyright owner.

From *One Man's Meat* by E. B. White: From p. 198 "Dog Training"–November 1940. Copyright, 1940 by E. B. White. Reprinted by permission of Harper & Row, Publishers, Inc.

"Geography Lesson" from *Jets From Orange* by Zulfikar Ghose. Copyright © 1967 by Zulfikar Ghose. Reprinted by permission of Harold Matson Co., Inc.

From advertisement for Kretschmer Wheat Germ Products. Reprinted by permission of International Multifoods Corporation.

From advertisement for Vandermint®. Reprinted by permission of General Wine and Spirits Company.

From "Settle Back, Relax and Enjoy Dodge's Fall-Winter, TV Sports Card" from *Dodge Adventurer Magazine,* November/December, 1977. Copyright © 1977 Chrysler Corporation. Reprinted by permission.

Paul M. Insel, Henry Clay Lindgren, *Too Close for Comfort: The Psychology of Crowding,* © 1978. Reprinted by permission of Prentice-Hall, Inc., Englewood Cliffs, New Jersey.

From The Associated Press, November 28, 1977. Copyright 1977 The Associated Press. Reprinted by permission of The Associated Press.

From "Cézanne: The Autumn Years" by Barbara Rose, *Saturday Review,* November 26, 1977. Reprinted by permission.

From *One Man's Meat* by E. B. White: From p. 37 "Salt Water Farm"–January 1939. Copyright, 1939 by E. B. White. Reprinted by permission of Harper & Row, Publishers, Inc.

Excerpt from *Charlotte's Web* by E. B. White. Copyright, 1952, by E. B. White. By permission of Harper & Row, Publishers, Inc.

From "Home: An American Obsession" by Reynolds Price, *Saturday Review,* November 26, 1977. Reprinted by permission.

From "Showplace on the Prairie," *Time,* December 5, 1977. Reprinted by permission from TIME, The Weekly Newsmagazine; Copyright Time Inc. 1977.

"Shadow Lake" by John Muir from *The Mountains of California.* Copyright © 1971 by Ten Speed Press. Reprinted by permission.

From "Giant Gas Gusher in Louisiana," *Time,* December 5, 1977. Reprinted by permission from TIME, The Weekly Newsmagazine; Copyright Time Inc. 1977.

From "Politics and the English Language" by George Orwell in *Shooting an Elephant and Other Essays.* Copyright 1945, 1946, 1950 by Sonia Brownell; renewed 1973, 1974 by Sonia Orwell. Reprinted by permission of Harcourt Brace Jovanovich, Inc., Mrs. Sonia Brownell Orwell and Martin Secker & Warburg.

From "What Christians Believe" in *The Case for Christianity* by C. S. Lewis. Published in the United States, 1943. Reprinted by permission of Macmillan Publishing Co., Inc. and William Collins Sons & Co., Ltd.

From *Word Play: What Happens When People Talk* by Peter Farb. Copyright © 1973 by Peter Farb. Reprinted by permission of Alfred A. Knopf, Inc.

Acknowledgments continued

From an advertisement for Ventura Luggage. Reprinted by permission of Ventura Travelware, Inc.

From "Here's What TV Is Doing To Us" from *TV Guide*, December 17, 1977. Reprinted by permission.

From "I Have a Dream" by Martin Luther King, Jr. Reprinted by permission of Joan Daves. Copyright © 1963 by Martin Luther King, Jr.

From Phelps, Stanlee and Austin, Nancy, *The Assertive Woman*. Copyright © 1975, Impact Publishers, Inc., San Luis Obispo, California. Reprinted by permission of the publisher.

From *Goldberg's Diet Catalog*. Copyright © 1977 by Larry Goldberg. Reprinted by permission of Macmillan Publishing Co., Inc.

From "Furious Farmers," *Time*, December 19, 1977. Reprinted by permission from TIME, The Weekly Newsmagazine; Copyright Time Inc. 1977.

From *Six Days on the Road* by Earl Green and Carl Montgomery. Copyright © 1963 by Newkeys Music, Inc. Reprinted by permission.

From "Raising Hell on the Highways" by Robert Sherrill. *New York Times Magazine*, November 27, 1977. Copyright © 1977 The New York Times Company. Reprinted by permission.

Copyright © 1963 by John Updike. Reprinted from *Assorted Prose* by John Updike, by permission of Alfred A. Knopf, Inc.

From "The Arms Race: Is Paranoia Necessary for Security?" by G. B. Kistiakowsky. *New York Times Magazine*, November 27, 1977. Copyright © 1977 by The New York Times Company. Reprinted by permission.

From "The American Language in the Early '70's" by Mario Pei, *Modern Age*, Fall 1971. Copyright © Intercollegiate Studies Institute, Inc. Reprinted by permission.

From "When Man Becomes as God" by Albert Rosenfeld, *Saturday Review*, December 10, 1977. Reprinted by permission.

From "A Few Parting Words" by Henry F. Ottinger. *New York Times*, July 22, 1971. Copyright © 1971 The New York Times Company. Reprinted by permission.

"Your Education" from *The Medium Is the Massage* by Marshall McLuhan and Quentin Fiore. Copyright © 1967 by Bantam Books, Inc. Reprinted by permission of Bantam Books, Inc.

"Red Raspberries" by Charles Fenyvesi, *The New Republic*, August 20 & 27, 1977. Copyright © 1977 by The New Republic, Inc. Reprinted by permission.

From "The Intelligent Co-Ed's Guide to America" by Tom Wolfe, from *Harper's Magazine*, July, 1976. Copyright © July 1976 by Harper's Magazine Company. Reprinted by permission of A. D. Peters & Co. Ltd.

From "Light Refractions" by Thomas H. Middleton, *Saturday Review*, July 8, 1978. Reprinted by permission.

A selection from *Conventional Wisdoms* by John Bart Gerald. Copyright © 1970, 1971, 1972 by John Bart Gerald. Reprinted with the permission of Farrar, Straus & Giroux, Inc.

Excerpt from pp. 14–17 "A Day in Samoa" in *Coming of Age in Samoa* by Margaret Mead. Copyright © 1928, 1955, 1961 by Margaret Mead. By permission of William Morrow & Company.

From "Judo Is a Sport" in *Self Defense for Boys and Men* by Bruce Tegner, pp. 15–16. Copyright © 1968 Bruce Tegner and Alice McGrath. Reprinted by permission of Thor Publishing Co., Ventura, California 93001.

"An Era of Mousing Intrigue" from Editor's Easy Chair, *Harper's Magazine*, February 1882 and July 1976. Reprinted by permission.

From *Borstal Boy* by Brendan Behan. Copyright © 1958, 1959 by Brendan Behan. Reprinted by permission of Alfred A. Knopf, Inc. and Hutchinson Publishing Group Limited.

"Music Lover's Field Companion" by John Cage. Copyright © 1954 by John Cage. Reprinted from *Silence* by permission of Wesleyan University Press.

Gerber/Felshin/Berlin/Wyrick, *The American Woman in Sport*, © 1974, Addison-Wesley, Reading, Massachusetts. pp. 4, 6, & 8. Reprinted with permission.

"The Weaker Sex? Hah!" from *Time*, June 26, 1978. Reprinted by permission from TIME, The Weekly Newsmagazine; Copyright Time Inc. 1978.

From "Comes the Revolution" from *Time*, June 26, 1978. Reprinted by permission from TIME, The Weekly Newsmagazine; Copyright Time Inc. 1978.

"Sports" by Jack Scott, from *Ramparts*, February, 1972. Copyright 1972 by Noah's Ark, Inc. (for Ramparts Magazine), reprinted by permission.

From *The Ordways* by William Humphrey. Copyright © 1964 by William Humphrey. Reprinted by permission of Alfred A. Knopf, Inc.

Letter to Donald A. Nizen (pp. 655–657) from *Letters of E. B. White*. Copyright © 1976 by E. B. White. Reprinted by permission of Harper & Row, Publishers, Inc.

Letters to the editor of *Time*, June 27, 1977. Reprinted by permission from TIME, The Weekly Newsmagazine; Copyright Time Inc. 1977.

From "Money Need, Social Change Combine to Cut Apron Strings" by Philip Shabecoff. *New York Times*, May 7, 1978. Copyright © 1978 The New York Times Company. Reprinted by permission.

"Docudramas Unmasked" by Mark Harris, *TV Guide*, March 4, 1978. Reprinted with permission from TV GUIDE® Magazine. Copyright © 1978 by Triangle Publications, Inc. Radnor, Pennsylvania and The Fox Chase Agency, Inc.

Dr. Howard Temin's address to the U.S. Congress on the effects of smoking as it appeared in "Editor's Notebook," *Wisconsin State Journal*, March 3, 1976. Reprinted by permission of the author.

"A Satire for the Unemployed-and for Ayn Rand," by Allen B. Borden, *Harper's Magazine* (July, 1975). Copyright © 1975 by *Harper's Magazine*. Reprinted by permission of *Harper's Magazine*.

Book Review of "Injury Time" by Katha Pollitt, *New York Times*, February 26, 1978. Copyright © 1978 by The New York Times Company. Reprinted by permission.

From "The Muppet Show" by Robert MacKenzie. *TV Guide*, March 4, 1978. Reprinted with permission from TV GUIDE® Magazine. Copyright © 1978 by Triangle Publications, Inc. Radnor, Pennsylvania.

From review of *American Graffiti* by Jay Cocks, *Time*, August 20, 1973. Reprinted by permission from TIME, The Weekly Newsmagazine; Copyright Time Inc. 1973.

From "The Late Cézanne: A Symposium" by Rackstraw Downes, *Art in America*, March/April 1978. Copyright © 1978 by Art in America. Reprinted by permission.

From "In Rock, the Music Must Sustain the Message" by John Rockwell. *New York Times*, July 2, 1978. Copyright © 1978 The New York Times Company. Reprinted by permission.

From "Frost's 'Dust of Snow'" by Edgar H. Knapp, *The Explicator*, September 1969, Vol. XXVII, No. 1. Reprinted by permission of Heldref Publications.

From *Handbook of Current English*, 5th Edition, by Jim W. Corder. Copyright © 1978, 1975, 1968 Scott, Foresman and Company.